COMPUTER ARCHITECTURE

The Oxford Series in Electrical and Computer Engineering

Adel S. Sedra, Series Editor

COMPUTER ARCHITECTURE

FROM MICROPROCESSORS TO SUPERCOMPUTERS

Behrooz Parhami

University of California, Santa Barbara

New York   Oxford

OXFORD UNIVERSITY PRESS

2005

Oxford University Press

Oxford   New York
Auckland   Bangkok   Buenos Aires   Cape Town   Chennai
Dar es Salaam   Delhi   Hong Kong   Istanbul   Karachi   Kolkata
Kuala Lumpur   Madrid   Melbourne   Mexico City   Mumbai   Nairobi
São Paulo   Shanghai   Taipei   Tokyo   Toronto

Published by Oxford University Press, Inc.
198 Madison Avenue, New York, New York 10016
www.oup.com

Oxford is a registered trademark of Oxford University Press

Library of Congress Cataloging-in-Publication Data

Parhami, Behrooz.
   Computer architecture : from microprocessors to supercomputers / Behrooz Parhami.
      p. cm.—(Oxford series in electrical and computer engineering)
   Includes bibliographical references and index.
   ISBN-13: 978–0–19–515455–9
   ISBN 0–19–515455–X
   1. Computer architecture. I. Title. II. Series.

   QA76.9.A73P375 2005
   004.2'2–dc22   2004052063

Printing number: 9 8 7 6 5 4 3 2 1

Printed in the United States of America
on acid-free paper

To four women who helped shape my world
from childhood to early adulthood;
my mother Kowkab, the architect,
and my sisters Behnaz, Mahnaz, and Farnaz,
exemplifying resilience, precision, and speed.

STRUCTURE AT A GLANCE

	Parts	Chapters
	1. Background and Motivation	1. Combinational Digital Circuits 2. Digital Circuits with Memory 3. Computer System Technology 4. Computer Performance
	2. Instruction-Set Architecture	5. Instructions and Addressing 6. Procedures and Data 7. Assembly Language Programs 8. Instruction-Set Variations
C	3. The Arithmetic/Logic Unit	9. Number Representation 10. Adders and Simple ALUs 11. Multipliers and Dividers 12. Floating-Point Arithmetic
P U	4. Data Path and Control	13. Instruction Execution Steps 14. Control Unit Synthesis 15. Pipelined Data Paths 16. Pipeline Performance Limits
	5. Memory System Design	17. Main Memory Concepts 18. Cache Memory Organization 19. Mass Memory Concepts 20. Virtual Memory and Paging
	6. Input/Output and Interfacing	21. Input/Output Devices 22. Input/Output Programming 23. Buses, Links, and Interfacing 24. Context Switching and Interrupts
	7. Advanced Architectures	25. Road to Higher Performance 26. Vector and Array Processing 27. Shared-Memory Multiprocessing 28. Distributed Multicomputing

CONTENTS

PREFACE

*" . . . there is a tendency when you really begin to learn something about a thing
not to want to write about it but rather to keep on learning about it . . . unless
you are very egotistical, which, of course, accounts for many books."*

—*Ernest Hemingway, Death in the Afternoon*

■ The Context of Computer Architecture

Computer architecture is an area of study dealing with digital computers at the interface between hardware and software. It is more hardware-oriented than "computer systems," an area typically covered in courses by the same name in computer science or engineering, and more concerned with software than the fields known as "computer design" and "computer organization." The subject matter, nevertheless, is quite fluid and varies greatly from one textbook or course to another in its orientation and coverage. This explains, in part, why there are so many different textbooks on computer architecture and why yet another textbook on the subject might serve a useful purpose.

Computer architecture encompasses a set of core ideas that are applicable to the design or understanding of virtually any computer, from the tiniest embedded microprocessors that control our appliances, cameras, and numerous other devices through personal, server, and mainframe machines to the most powerful supercomputers found only in (and affordable only by) large data centers or major scientific laboratories. It also branches into more advanced subfields, each with its own community of researchers, periodicals, symposia, and, of course, technical jargon. Computer designers must no doubt be familiar with the entire field to be able to use the range of available methods in designing fast, efficient, and robust systems. Less obvious is the fact that even simple computer users can benefit from a firm grasp of the core ideas and from an awareness of the more advanced concepts in computer architecture.

A common theme in computer architecture is coping with complexity. Much of this complexity arises from our desire to make everything as fast as possible. Some of the resulting techniques, such as predictive and speculative execution, are at odds with other goals of system design that include low cost, compactness, energy economy, short time to market, and testability. It is the constant push and pull of such conflicting requirements that makes computer architecture a thriving and exciting field of study. Adding to the excitement are the opposing forces of innovation and compatibility with existing investments in skills, systems, and applications.

■ Scope and Features

This textbook, an outgrowth of lecture notes that the author has developed and refined over many years, covers the core ideas of computer architecture in some depth and provides an overview of many advanced concepts that may be pursued in higher-level courses such as those on supercomputing, parallel processing, and distributed systems.

Six key features set this book apart from competing introductory textbooks on computer architecture:

   a. *Division of material into lecture-size chapters:* In the author's approach to teaching, a lecture is a more or less self-contained module with links to past lectures and pointers to what will transpire in future. Each lecture, lasting one to two hours, has a theme or title and proceeds from motivation to details to conclusion.

   b. *A large number of meaningful problems:* At least 16 problems have been provided at the end of each of the 28 chapters. These are well-thought-out problems, many of them class-tested, that clarify the chapter material, offer new viewing angles, link the chapter material to topics in other chapters, or introduce more advanced concepts.

   c. *Emphasis on both the underlying theory and actual designs:* The ability to cope with complexity requires both a deep understanding of the theoretical underpinnings of computer architecture and examples of designs that help clarify the theory. Such designs also provide building blocks for synthesis and reference points for cost-performance comparisons.

   d. *Linking computer architecture to other subfields of computing:* Computer architecture is nourished by, and in turn feeds, other subfields of computer system design. Such links, from the obvious (instruction-set architecture vis-à-vis compiler design) to the subtle (interplay of architecture with reliability and security), are explained throughout the book.

   e. *Broad coverage of important topics:* The text covers virtually all the core topics in computer architecture, thus providing a balanced and complete view of the field. Examples of material not found in many other texts include detailed coverage of computer arithmetic (Chapters 9–12) and high-performance computing (Chapters 25–28).

   f. *Unified and consistent notation/terminology:* Every effort is made to use consistent notation/terminology throughout the text. For example, r always stands for the number representation radix, k for word width, and c for carry. Similarly, concepts and structures are consistently identified with unique, well-defined names.

■ Summary of Topics

The seven parts of this book, each composed of four chapters, have been written with the following goals:

Part 1 sets the stage, provides context, reviews some of the prerequisite topics, and gives a taste of what is to come in the rest of the book. Included are two refresher-type chapters on digital circuits and components, a discussion of computer system types, an overview of digital computer technology, and a detailed perspective on computer system performance.

Part 2 lays out the user's interface to computer hardware, also known as the instruction-set architecture (ISA). For concreteness, the instruction set of MiniMIPS (a simplified, yet very realistic, machine for which open reference material and simulation tools exist) is described. Included is a chapter on variations in ISA (e.g., RISC vs CISC) and associated cost-performance trade-offs.

The next two parts cover the central processing unit (CPU). Part 3 describes the structure of arithmetic/logic units (ALUs) in some detail. Included are discussions of fixed- and floating-point number representations, design of high-speed adders, shift and logical operations, and hardware multipliers/dividers. Implementation aspects and pitfalls of floating-point arithmetic are also discussed.

Part 4 is devoted to the data paths and control circuits comprising modern CPUs. Beginning with instruction execution steps, the needed components and control mechanisms are derived. This material is followed by an exposition of control design strategies, use of a pipelined data path for performance enhancement, and various limitations of pipelining due to data and control dependencies.

Part 5 is concerned with the memory system. The technologies in use for primary and secondary memories are described, along with their strengths and limitations. It is shown how the use of cache memories effectively bridges the speed gap between CPU and main memory. Similarly, the use of virtual memory to provide the illusion of a vast main memory is explained.

Part 6 deals with input/output and interfacing topics. A discussion of I/O device technologies is followed by methods of I/O programming and the roles of buses and links (including standards) in I/O communication and interfacing. Elements of processes and context switching, for exception handling or multithreaded computation, are also covered.

Part 7 introduces advanced architectures. An overview of performance enhancement strategies, beyond simple pipelining, is presented, and examples of applications requiring higher performance are cited. The book concludes with design strategies and example architectures based on vector or array processing, multiprocessing, and multicomputing.

■ Pointers on How to Use the Book

For classroom use, the topics in each chapter of this text can be covered in a lecture of duration 1–2 hours. In his own teaching, the author has used the chapters primarily for 1.5-hour lectures, twice a week, in a 10-week quarter, omitting or combining some chapters to fit the material into the 18–20 lectures that are available. But the modular structure of the text lends itself to other lecture formats, self-study, or review of the field by practitioners. In the latter two cases, the readers can view each chapter as a study unit (for one week, say) rather than as a lecture. Ideally, all topics in each chapter should be covered before moving to the next chapter. However, if fewer lecture hours are available, then some of the subsections located at the end of chapters can be omitted or introduced only in terms of motivations and key ideas.

Problems of varying complexities, from straightforward numerical examples or exercises to more demanding studies or miniprojects, have been supplied for each chapter. These problems form an integral part of the book and have not been added as afterthoughts to make the book more attractive for use as a text. A total of 491 problems are included. Assuming that two lectures are given per week, either weekly or biweekly homework can be assigned, with each assignment having the specific coverage of the respective half-part (two chapters) or part (four chapters) as its "title."

An instructor's manual, with problem solutions, is available and can be requested by qualified instructors from Oxford University Press in New York (www.oup.com/us/highered). Power-Point presentations, covering the seven parts, are available electronically through the author's Web page for the book at www.oup.com/us/PARHAMI. The book's Web page also includes a list of corrections and additional topics.

References to seminal papers in computer architecture, key design ideas, and important state-of-the-art research contributions are listed at the end of each chapter. These references provide good starting points for doing in-depth studies or for preparing term papers/projects. A large number of classical papers and important contributions in computer architecture have been reprinted in [Swar76], [Siew82], and [Sohi98]. New ideas in the field appear in papers presented at the annual International Symposium on Computer Architecture [ISCA]. Other technical meetings of interest include Symposium on High-Performance Computer Architecture [HPCA], International Parallel and Distributed Processing Symposium [IPDP], and International Conference on Parallel Processing [ICPP]. Relevant journals include *IEEE Transactions on Computers* [TrCo], *IEEE Transactions on Parallel and Distributed Systems* [TrPD], *Journal of Parallel and Distributed Computing* [JPDC], and *Communications of the ACM* [CACM]. Overview papers and topics of broad interest appear in *IEEE Computer* [Comp], *IEEE Micro* [Micr], and *ACM Computing Surveys* [CoSu].

▧ Acknowledgments

This text, *Computer Architecture: From Microprocessors to Supercomputers,* is an outgrowth of lecture notes the author has used for the upper-division undergraduate course ECE 154: Introduction to Computer Architecture at the University of California, Santa Barbara, and, in rudimentary forms, at several other institutions prior to 1988. The text has benefited greatly from keen observations, curiosity, and encouragement of my many students in these courses. A sincere thanks to all of them! Thanks are also due to engineering editors at Oxford University Press (Peter Gordon, who started the project, and Danielle Christensen, who guided it to completion) and to Karen Shapiro, who ably managed the production process. Finally, the granting of permission by Dr. James R. Larus, of Microsoft Research, for the use of his SPIM simulators is gratefully acknowledged.

▧ General References and Readings

The list that follows contains references of two types: (1) books that have greatly influenced the current text and (2) general reference sources for in-depth studies or research. Books and other resources that are relevant to specific chapters are listed in the end-of-chapter reference lists.

[Arch]   WWW Computer Architecture Page, a Web resource kept by the Computer Science Department, University of Wisconsin, Madison, has a wealth of information on architecture-related organizations, groups, projects, publications, events, and people: http://www.cs.wisc.edu/~arch/www/index.html

[CACM]   *Communications of the ACM,* journal published by the Association for Computing Machinery.

[Comp]   *IEEE Computer,* technical magazine published by the IEEE Computer Society.

[CoSu]   *Computing Surveys*, journal published by the Association for Computing Machinery.

[Henn03]   Hennessy, J. L., and D. A. Patterson, *Computer Architecture: A Quantitative Approach,* Morgan Kaufmann, 3rd ed., 2003.

[HPCA]   *Proceedings of the Symposium(s) on High-Performance Computer Architecture,* sponsored by IEEE. The 10th HPCA was held on February 14–18, 2004, in Madrid, Spain.

[ICPP]   *Proceedings of the International Conference(s) on Parallel Processing,* held annually since 1972. The 33rd ICPP was held on August 15–18, 2004, in Montreal, Canada.

[IPDP]   *Proceedings of the International Parallel and Distributed Processing Symposium(s)* formed in 1998 from merging IPPS (held annually beginning in 1987) and SPDP (held annually beginning in 1989). The latest IPDPS was held on April 26–30, 2004, in Santa Fe, New Mexico.

[ISCA]   *Proceedings of the International Symposium(s) on Computer Architecture,* held annually since 1973, usually in May or June. The 31st ISCA was held on June 19–23, 2004, in Munich, Germany.

[JPDC]   *Journal of Parallel and Distributed Computing,* published by Academic Press.

[Micr]   *IEEE Micro,* technical magazine published by the IEEE Computer Society.

[Muel00]   Mueller, S. M., and W. J. Paul, *Computer Architecture: Complexity and Correctness,* Springer, 2000.

[Patt98]   Patterson, D. A., and J. L. Hennessy, *Computer Organization and Design: The Hardware/Software Interface,* Morgan Kaufmann, 2nd ed., 1998.

[Rals93]   Ralston, A., and E. D. Reilly (eds.), *Encyclopedia of Computer Science,* Van Nostrand Reinhold, 3rd ed., 1993.

[Siew82]   Siewiorek, D. P., C. G. Bell, and A. Newell, *Computer Structures: Principles and Examples,* McGraw-Hill, 1982.

[Sohi98]   Sohi, G. (ed.), *25 Years of the International Symposia on Computer Architecture: Selected Papers,* ACM Press, 1998.

[Stal03]   Stallings, W., *Computer Organization and Architecture,* Prentice Hall, 6th ed., 2003.

[Swar76]   Swartzlander, E. E., Jr (ed.), *Computer Design Development: Principal Papers,* Hayden, 1976.

[TrCo]   *IEEE Trans. Computers,* journal published by the IEEE Computer Society.

[TrPD]   *IEEE Trans. Parallel and Distributed Systems,* journal published by the IEEE Computer Society.

[Wilk95]   Wilkes, M. V., *Computing Perspectives,* Morgan Kaufmann, 1995.

PART ONE

BACKGROUND AND MOTIVATION

"Architecture is the learned game, correct and magnificent, of forms assembled in the light."
—*Le Corbusier*

"I think that the future computer architect is a systems architect, not simply a processor architect; so one must bring together software technology, systems applications, arithmetic, all in a complex system which has a statistical behavior that is not immediately or simply analyzed. . . ."
—*Michael J. Flynn, looking forward, circa 1998*

TOPICS IN THIS PART

1. Combinational Digital Circuits
2. Digital Circuits with Memory
3. Computer System Technology
4. Computer Performance

Computer architecture encompasses a set of core ideas that are applicable to the design or understanding of virtually any digital computer, from the tiniest embedded systems to the largest supercomputers. Computer architecture isn't just for computer designers; even simple users benefit from a firm grasp of the core ideas and an awareness of the more advanced concepts in this field. Certain key realizations, such as the fact that a $2x$ GHz processor is not necessarily twice as fast as an x GHz model, require a basic training in computer architecture.

We begin this part by reviewing hardware components used in the design of digital circuits and subsystems. Combinational elements, including gates, multiplexers, demultiplexers, decoders, and encoders, are covered in Chapter 1, while sequential circuits, exemplified by register files and counters, constitute the topic of Chapter 2. In Chapter 3, we present an overview of developments in computer technology, and its current state. This is followed by a discussion of absolute and relative performance of computer systems in Chapter 4, perhaps the single most important chapter, setting the stage for performance enhancement methods that are presented throughout the rest of the book.

1

COMBINATIONAL DIGITAL CIRCUITS

"We used to think that if we know one, we knew two, because one and one are two. We are finding that we must learn a great deal more about 'and'."
—*Sir Arthur Eddington*

"This product contains minute electrically charged particles moving at velocities in excess of 500 million miles per hour. Handle with extreme care."
—*Proposed truth-in-product-labeling warning to be put on all digital systems (source unknown)*

Familiarity with digital design is required for studying computer architecture and is assumed of the reader of this book. The capsule review presented in this and the following chapter is intended to refresh the reader's memory and to provide a basis for understanding the terminology and designs in the rest of the book. In this chapter, we review some of the key concepts of combinational (memoryless) digital circuits and introduce a number of very useful components that are found in many diagrams in this book. Examples include tristate buffers (regular or inverting), multiplexers, decoders, and encoders. This review is continued in Chapter 2, which deals with sequential digital circuits (with memory). Readers who have trouble understanding the material in these two chapters should consult any of the logic design textbooks listed at the end of the chapter.

■ 1.1 Signals, Logic Operators, and Gates

All information elements in digital computers, including instructions, numbers, and symbols, are encoded as electronic signals that are almost always *two-valued*. Even though *multivalued signals* and associated logic circuits are feasible and occasionally used, modern digital

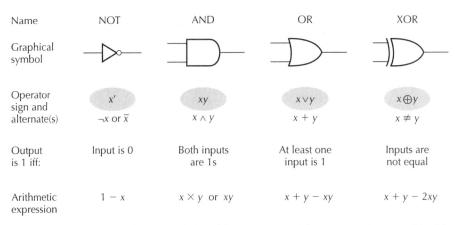

Name	NOT	AND	OR	XOR
Graphical symbol				
Operator sign and alternate(s)	x' $\neg x$ or $\bar{x}$	xy $x \wedge y$	$x \vee y$ $x + y$	$x \oplus y$ $x \not\equiv y$
Output is 1 iff:	Input is 0	Both inputs are 1s	At least one input is 1	Inputs are not equal
Arithmetic expression	$1 - x$	$x \times y$ or xy	$x + y - xy$	$x + y - 2xy$

Figure 1.1 Some basic elements of digital logic circuits, with operator signs used in this book highlighted.

computers are predominantly binary. *Binary signals* can be represented by the presence or absence of some electrical property such as voltage, current, field, or charge. We refer to the two values of a binary signal as "0" and "1." These values can represent the digits of a radix-2 number in the natural way or be used to denote states (off/on), conditions (false/true), options (path A/path B), and the like. The assignment of 0 and 1 to binary states or conditions is arbitrary, but having 0 represent "off" or "false" and 1 correspond to "on" or "true" is more common. When binary signals are represented by high/low voltage, assigning high voltage to 1 leads to *positive logic* and the opposite is considered to be *negative logic*.

Logic operators are abstractions for specifying transformations of binary signals. There are $2^2 = 4$ possible single-input operators, because the truth table of such an operator has two entries (corresponding to the input being 0 or 1) and each entry can be filled with 0 or 1. A two-input operator with binary inputs can be defined in $2^4 = 16$ different ways, depending on whether it produces a 0 or 1 output for each of the four possible combinations of input values. Figure 1.1 depicts the single-input operator known as NOT (*complementer* or *inverter*) and three of the most commonly used two-input operators: AND, OR, and XOR (exclusive OR). For each of these operators, the sign used in logical expressions, and alternate form favored in books on logic design, are given. The operator signs used in this books are highlighted in Figure 1.1. In particular, we use "$\vee$" instead of the more common "+" for OR because we also talk a great deal about addition and in fact on occasion addition and OR are used in the same paragraph or diagram. For AND, on the other hand, simply juxtaposing the operands does not give rise to any problem because AND is identical to multiplication for binary signals.

Figure 1.1 also relates logic operators to arithmetic operators. For example, complementing or inverting a signal x yields $1 - x$. Because both AND and OR are *associative,* meaning that $(xy)z = x(yz)$ and $(x \vee y) \vee z = x \vee (y \vee z)$, these operators can be defined with more than two inputs, without causing any ambiguity about their outputs. Also, given that the graphical symbol for NOT consists of a triangle that represents the identity operation (or no operation at all) and a small "bubble" that signifies inversion, logic diagrams can be made simpler and less cluttered by allowing inversion bubbles on inputs or outputs of logic gates. For example, an AND gate and an inverter connected to its output can be merged into a single NAND gate, drawn as an AND gate with a bubble placed on its output line. Similarly, NOR

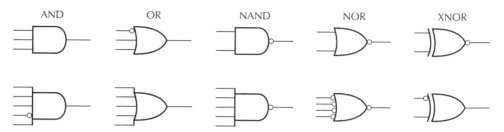

Figure 1.2 Gates with more than two inputs and/or with inverted signals at input or output.

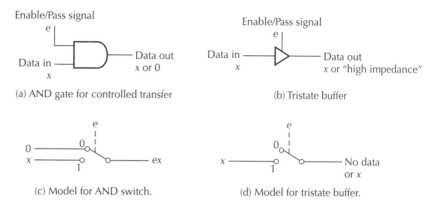

(a) AND gate for controlled transfer

(b) Tristate buffer

(c) Model for AND switch.

(d) Model for tristate buffer.

Figure 1.3 An AND gate and a tristate buffer can act as controlled switches or valves. An inverting buffer is logically the same as a NOT gate.

and XNOR gates can be defined (Figure 1.2). Bubbles can also be placed on a gate's inputs, leading to the graphical representation of operations such as $x' \vee y \vee z$ with one gate symbol.

Much as variables in a program are named, the name of a logic signal must be chosen with care to convey useful information about the signal's role. Names that are very short or very long must be avoided if possible. A control signal whose value is 1 is referred to as "asserted," while a 0 signal is deasserted. Asserting a control signal is a common way of causing an action or event to occur. If signal names are chosen carefully, a signal named "*sub*" will likely cause a subtraction operation to be performed when asserted, while a 3-bit signal bundle "*oper*" may encode one of eight possible operations to be performed by some unit. When it is the deassertion of a signal that triggers an event, the signal name should appear in complemented form for clarity; for example, the signal add', when deasserted, may cause addition to be performed. It is also possible to apply a name such as $add'sub$ to a signal that causes two different actions depending on its value.

If one input of a two-input AND gate is viewed as a control signal and the other as a data signal, one can say that assertion of the control signal allows the data signal to propagate to the output, whereas deassertion of the control signal forces the output to 0, independently of the input data (Figure 1.3). Thus, an AND gate can act as a switch or data valve that is controlled by an *enable* or *pass* signal. An alternate mechanism for this purpose, also shown in Figure 1.3, is a *tristate buffer* whose output is equal to the data input x when the control signal e is asserted and assumes an indeterminate value (high impedance in electrical terms) when e is deasserted. A tristate buffer effectively isolates the output from the input whenever

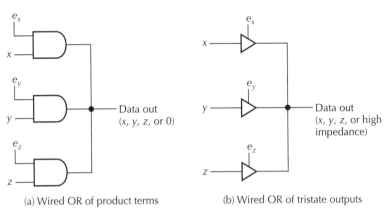

(a) Wired OR of product terms   (b) Wired OR of tristate outputs

Figure 1.4 Wired OR allows tying together of several controlled signals.

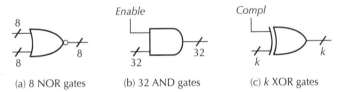

(a) 8 NOR gates   (b) 32 AND gates   (c) k XOR gates

Figure 1.5 Arrays of logic gates represented by a single gate symbol.

the control signal is deasserted. An XOR gate with one control and one data signal can be viewed as a *controlled inverter* that inverts the data if its control is asserted and lets it through unchanged, otherwise.

Outputs of several AND switches, tristate buffers, or inverting buffers can be connected to each other for an implicit or wired OR function. In fact, a primary application of tristate buffers is to connect a possibly large number of data sources (such as memory cells) to a common data line through which data travels to a receiver. In Figure 1.4, when only one of the enable signals is asserted, the corresponding data passes through and prevails at the output side. When no enable signal is asserted, then the output will be 0 (for AND gates) or high impedance (for tristate buffers). When more than one enable signal is asserted, the logical OR of the associated data inputs prevails at the output side, although this situation is often avoided.

We frequently use an array of identical gates to combine bundles of signals. In depicting such an arrangement, we draw just one gate and indicate, by using a tick mark and an integer next to it, how many signals or gates are involved. For example, Figure 1.5a shows bitwise NOR operation performed on two 8-bit bundles. If the input bundles are x and y and the output bundle z, then this is equivalent to setting $z_i = (x_i \vee y_i)'$ for each i. Similarly, we can have an array of 32 AND switches, all tied to the same *Enable* signal, to control the flow of a 32-bit data word from the input side to the output side (Figure 1.5b). As a final example, an array of k XOR gates can be used to invert all bits in a k-bit bundle whenever *Compl* is asserted (Figure 1.5c).

1.2 Boolean Functions and Expressions

A signal that can be either 0 or 1 is a *Boolean variable*. An *n*-variable *Boolean function* depends on *n* Boolean variables and produces a result in $\{0, 1\}$. Boolean functions are of interest to us because a network of logic gates with *n* inputs and one output implements an *n*-variable Boolean function. There are various ways for specifying Boolean functions.

a. A *truth table* is a listing of the function results for all combinations of input values. The truth table for an *n*-variable Boolean function has *n* input columns, an output column, and 2^n rows. A truth table with *m* output columns might be used to specify *m* Boolean functions of the same variables at once (see, e.g., Table 1.1). A *don't-care* entry "x" in an output column means that the function result is of no interest in that row, perhaps because that combination of input values is not expected to ever arise. An "x" in an input column means that the function result does not depend on the value of the particular variable involved.

b. A *logic expression* is made of Boolean variables, logic operators, and parentheses. In the absence of parentheses, NOT takes precedence over AND, which takes precedence over OR/XOR. For a given assignment of values to variables, a logic expression can be evaluated to yield a Boolean result. Logic expressions can be manipulated using laws of Boolean algebra (Table 1.2). Usually, the goal of this process is to obtain an *equivalent* logic expression that is in some way simpler or more suitable for hardware realization.

■ **TABLE 1.1** Three 7-variable Boolean functions specified in a compact truth table with don't-care entries in both input and output columns.

Line #	Seven inputs							Three outputs		
	s_{lever}	c_{25}	c_{10}	a_{gum}	a_{bar}	p_{gum}	p_{bar}	r_{coins}	r_{gum}	r_{bar}
1	0	x	x	x	x	x	x	0	0	0
2	1	0	0	x	x	x	x	x	0	0
3	1	0	1	x	x	x	x	1	0	0
4	1	1	0	x	x	x	x	1	0	0
5	1	1	1	x	x	0	0	1	0	0
6	1	1	1	x	x	1	1	1	0	0
7	1	1	1	x	0	0	1	1	0	x
8	1	1	1	x	1	0	1	0	0	1
9	1	1	1	0	x	1	0	1	x	0
10	1	1	1	1	x	1	0	0	1	0

■ **TABLE 1.2** Laws (basic identities) of Boolean algebra.

Name of law	OR version	AND version
Identity	$x \vee 0 = x$	$x 1 = x$
One/Zero	$x \vee 1 = 1$	$x 0 = 0$
Idempotent	$x \vee x = x$	$xx = x$
Inverse	$x \vee x' = 1$	$xx' = 0$
Commutative	$x \vee y = y \vee x$	$xy = yx$
Associative	$(x \vee y) \vee z = x \vee (y \vee z)$	$(xy)z = x(yz)$
Distributive	$x \vee (yz) = (x \vee y)(x \vee z)$	$x(y \vee z) = (xy) \vee (xz)$
DeMorgan's	$(x \vee y)' = x'y'$	$(xy)' = x' \vee y'$

A logic expression formed by ORing several AND terms is in (*logical-*)*sum-of-products* form, for example, $xy \lor yz \lor zx$ or $w \lor x'yz$. Similarly, ANDing of several OR terms leads to a *product-of-*(*logical-*)*sums* expression, for example, $(x \lor y)(y \lor z)(z \lor x)$ or $w'(x \lor y \lor z)$.

c. A *word statement* can describe a simple logic function of a few Boolean variables. For example, a statement such as "The alarm will sound if the door is opened while the security system is engaged or when the smoke detector is triggered" corresponds to the Boolean function $e_{\text{alarm}} = (s_{\text{door}}s_{\text{security}}) \lor d_{\text{smoke}}$, which relates an enable signal to a pair of status signals and a detector signal.

d. A *logic diagram* is a graphical representation of a Boolean function that also carries information about its hardware realization. Deriving a logic diagram from any of the specification types just named is the *logic circuit synthesis* process. Going backward from a logic diagram to another form of specification is known as *logic circuit analysis*. In addition to gates and other elementary components, a logic diagram may include boxes of various shapes that represent standard building blocks or previously designed subcircuits.

We often use a combination of the preceding four methods, in a hierarchical scheme, to represent computer hardware. For example, a high-level logic diagram, composed of subcircuits and standard blocks, may provide the big picture. Each of the nonstandard elements, which is not simple enough to be described by a truth table, logic expression, or word statement, may in turn be specified through another diagram, and so on.

Example 1.1: Proving equivalence of logic expressions   Prove that the following pairs of logic expressions are equivalent.

    a. Distributive law, AND version: $x(y \lor z) \equiv (xy) \lor (xz)$
    b. DeMorgan's law, OR version: $(x \lor y)' \equiv x'y'$
    c. $xy \lor x'z \lor yz \equiv xy \lor x'z$
    d. $xy \lor yz \lor zx \equiv (x \lor y)(y \lor z)(z \lor x)$

Solution: We prove each part by a different method to illustrate the range of possibilities.

    a. Use the truth table method: form an 8-row truth table corresponding to all possible combinations of values for the three variables x, y, and z. Observe that the two expressions lead to the same value in each row. For example, $1(0 \lor 1) = (1\ 0) \lor (1\ 1) = 1$.

    b. Use the arithmetic substitutions shown in Figure 1.1 to convert this logic equality problem into the easily proven algebraic equality $1 - (x + y - xy) = (1 - x)(1 - y)$.

    c. Use case analysis: for example, derive simplified forms of the equality for $x = 0$ (prove $z \lor yz = z$) and $x = 1$ (prove $y \lor yz = y$). You may have to divide a more complex problem further.

    d. Use logic manipulation to convert one expression into the other: $(x \lor y)(y \lor z)(z \lor x) = (xy \lor xz \lor yy \lor yz)(z \lor x) = (xz \lor y)(z \lor x) = xzz \lor xzx \lor yz \lor yx = xz \lor yz \lor yx$.

1.3 Designing Gate Networks

Any logic expression composed of NOT, AND, OR, XOR, and other types of gates is a specification for a gate network. For example, the logic expression $xy \lor yz \lor zx$ specifies the gate network of Figure 1.6a. This is a two-level AND-OR logic circuit with AND gates in level 1

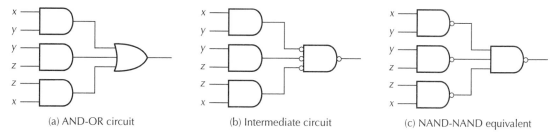

(a) AND-OR circuit   (b) Intermediate circuit   (c) NAND-NAND equivalent

Figure 1.6 A two-level AND-OR circuit and two equivalent circuits.

and an OR gate in level 2. Because according to DeMorgan's law (Table 1.2, last row, middle column), an OR gate can be replaced by a NAND gates with complemented inputs, Figure 1.6b is readily seen to be equivalent to Figure 1.6a. Now, by moving the inversion bubbles at the inputs of the level-2 NAND gate in Figure 1.6b to the outputs of the AND gates in level 1, we derive the two-level NAND-NAND circuit of Figure 1.6c that realizes the same function. A similar process converts any two-level OR-AND circuit to an equivalent NOR-NOR circuit. In both cases, any signal that is input directly to a level-2 gate must be inverted (because the bubble remains).

Whereas the process of converting a logic expression to a logic diagram, and thus an associated hardware realization, is trivial, obtaining a logic expression that leads to the best possible hardware circuit is not. For one thing, the definition of "best" changes depending on the technology and implementation scheme being used (e.g., custom VLSI, programmable logic, discrete gates) and on the design goals (e.g., high speed, power economy, low cost). For another, the simplification process, if not done via automatic design tools, is not only cumbersome but also imperfect; for example, it might be based on minimizing the number of gates employed, without taking into account the speed and cost implications of wires that connect the gates together. In this book, we do not concern ourselves with the simplification process for logic expressions. This is because every logic function that we will encounter, when suitably divided into parts, is simple enough to allow the required parts to be realized by means of efficient logic circuits in a straightforward manner. We illustrate the process through two examples.

Example 1.2: BCD-to-seven-segment decoder   Figure 1.7 shows how the decimal digits 0–9 might appear on a seven-segment display device. Design logic circuits to generate the enable signals that cause the segments to be lit or darkened, given a 4-bit binary representation of the decimal digit (binary-coded decimal or BCD code) to be displayed as input.

Figure 1.7 Seven-segment display of decimal digits. The three open segments may be optionally used. The digit 1 can be displayed in two ways, with the more common right-side version shown.

Solution: Figure 1.7 is a graphical representation of rows 0-9 of a 16-row truth table, where each of the rows 10–15 constitutes a don't-care condition. There are four input columns

x_3, x_2, x_1, x_0 and seven output columns e_0–e_6. Figure 1.8 shows the numbering of segments and the logic circuit that produces the enable signal for segment number 3. The truth table output column associated with e_3 contains the entries 1, 0, 1, 1, 0, 1, 1, 0, 1, 0, x, x, x, x, x, x (9 displayed without segment 3). This is easily translated to the logic expression $e_3 = x_1 x_0' \vee x_2' x_0' \vee x_2' x_1 \vee x_2 x_1' x_0$. Note that e_3 is independent of x_3. Deriving the logic circuits for the remaining six segments is done similarly.

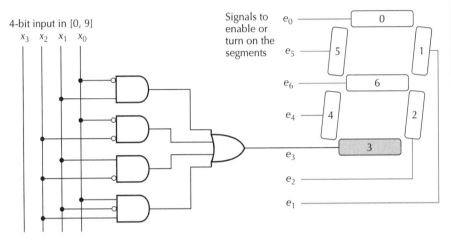

Figure 1.8 The logic circuit that generates the enable signal for the lowermost segment (number 3) in a seven-segment display unit.

Example 1.3: Simple vending machine actuator   A small vending machine can dispense a pack of gum or a candy bar, each costing 35 cents. The customer must deposit exact change consisting of a quarter and a dime, indicate preference for one of the two items by pressing the corresponding pushbutton, and pull a lever to release the desired item into a bin. The actuator is a combinational circuit with three outputs: $r_{gum}(r_{bar})$, when asserted, causes a pack of gum (candy bar) to be released; assertion of r_{coins} causes the deposited coins to be returned when, for any reason, a sale cannot be completed. Inputs to the actuator are the following signals:

   a. s_{lever} indicating the state of the lever (1 means that the lever has been pulled)
   b. c_{25} and c_{10}, for quarter and dime, supplied by a coin detection module
   c. a_{gum} and a_{bar} supplied by devices that sense the availability of the two items
   d. p_{gum} and p_{bar} coming from two pushbuttons holding the customer's preference

Solution: Refer again to Table 1.1, which is the truth table for the vending machine actuator. When the lever has not been pulled, all outputs must be 0, regardless of the values of other inputs (line 1). The rest of the cases that follow correspond to $s_{lever} = 1$. When no coin has been deposited, neither item should be released; the value of r_{coins} is immaterial in this case, since there is no coin to be returned (line 2). When only one coin has been deposited, no item should be released and the coin must be returned to the customer (lines 3–4). The rest of the cases correspond to 35 cents having been deposited and the lever pulled. If the customer has made no selection, or has selected both items, the coins must be returned and no item released (lines 5–6). If a candy bar has been selected, a candy bar is released or the coins are returned, depending on a_{bar} (lines 7–8). The case for the selection of a pack of gum is similar (lines 9–10). The following logic expressions for the three outputs are readily obtained by inspection:

$$r_{gum} = s_{lever}c_{25}c_{10}p_{gum}, \quad r_{bar} = s_{lever}c_{25}c_{10}p_{bar}, \quad r_{coins} = s_{lever}(c'_{25} \vee c'_{10} \vee p'_{gum}p'_{bar} \vee p_{gum}p_{bar} \vee$$
$$a'_{gum}p_{gum} \vee a'_{bar}p_{bar}).$$

1.4 Useful Combinational Parts

Certain combinational parts can be used in the synthesis of digital circuits, much as one utilizes prefabricated closets or bathroom fixtures in constructing a house. Such standard building blocks are numerous and include several arithmetic circuits to be discussed in Part III of the book. In this section, we review the design of three types of combinational components used primarily for control purposes: multiplexers, decoders, and encoders.

A 2^a-to-1 multiplexer, mux for short, has 2^a data inputs $x_0, x_1, x_2, \ldots$, a single output z, and a selection or address signals $y_{a-1}, \ldots, y_1, y_0$. The output z is equal to the input x_i whose index i has the binary representation $(y_{a-1} \ldots y_1y_0)_{two}$. Examples include 2-to-1 (two-way) and 4-to-1 (four-way) multiplexers, depicted in Figure 1.9, which have one and two address inputs, respectively. Like arrays of gates, several muxes controlled by the same address lines can be used to select one bundle of signals over another (Figure 1.9d). An n-to-1 mux, where n is not a power of 2, can be built by simply pruning the unneeded parts of a larger mux with 2^a inputs, where $2^{a-1} < n < 2^a$. For example, the design in Figure 1.9f can be converted to a 3-input mux by simply removing the mux with inputs x_2 and x_3, and then connecting x_2 directly to the second-level mux. At any given time, the output z of a mux is equal to one of its

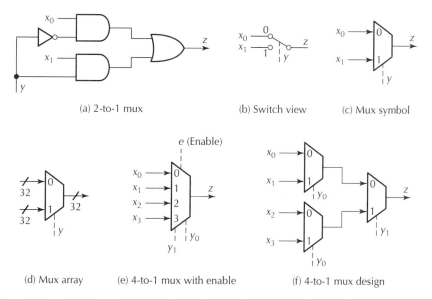

(a) 2-to-1 mux   (b) Switch view   (c) Mux symbol

(d) Mux array   (e) 4-to-1 mux with enable   (f) 4-to-1 mux design

Figure 1.9 A multiplexer (mux), or selector, allows one of several inputs to be selected and routed to output depending on the binary value of a set of selection or address signals provided to it.

inputs. By providing a multiplexer with an enable signal e, which is supplied as an extra input to each of the AND gates in Figure 1.9a, we get the option of forcing the output to 0 independently of data and address inputs. This is essentially equivalent to none of the inputs being selected (Figure 1.9e).

Multiplexers are versatile building blocks. Any a-variable Boolean function can be implemented by means of a 2^a-to-1 mux, where the variables are connected to the address inputs and each of the 2^a data inputs carries a constant value 0 or 1 according to the function's truth table value for that particular row. In fact, if the complement of one of the variables is available at input, then a smaller 2^{a-1}-to-1 mux suffices. As a concrete example, to implement the function e_3 defined in Example 1.2, one can use an 8-to-1 mux with address inputs connected to x_2, x_1, x_0 and data input carrying 1, 0, 1, 1, 0, 1, 1, 0, from top to bottom. Alternatively, one can use a 4-to-1 mux, with address lines connected to x_1 and x_0 and the data lines carrying x_2', x_2, 1, and x_2', again from top to bottom. The latter four terms are easily derived from the expression for e_3 by successively fixing the value of $x_1 x_0$ at 00, 01, 10, and 11.

An a-to-2^a (a-input) decoder asserts one and only one of its 2^a output lines. The output x_i that is asserted has an index i whose binary representation matches the value on the a address lines. The logic diagram for a 2-to-4 decoder is shown in Figure 1.10a, with its shorthand symbol given in Figure 1.10b. If outputs of such a decoder are used as enable signals for four different elements or units, then the decoder allows us to choose which one of the four unit is enabled at any given time. If we want to have the option of not enabling any of the four units, then a decoder with an enable input (Figure 1.10c), also known as a *demultiplexer* or *demux*, might be used, where the enable input e is supplied as an additional input to each of the four AND gates in Figure 1.10a (more generally 2^a AND gates). The name demultiplexer indicates that this circuit performs the opposite function of a mux: whereas a mux selects one of its inputs and routes it to the output, a demux receives an input e and routes it to a selected output.

The function of an *encoder* is exactly the opposite of a decoder. When one, and only one, input of a 2^a-input (2^a-to-a) encoder is asserted, its a-bit output supplies the index of the

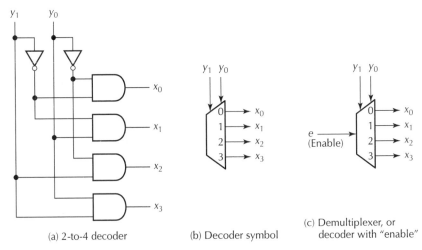

(a) 2-to-4 decoder   (b) Decoder symbol   (c) Demultiplexer, or decoder with "enable"

Figure 1.10 A decoder allows the selection of one of 2^a options using an a-bit address as input. A demultiplexer (demux) is a decoder that only selects an output if its enable signal is asserted.

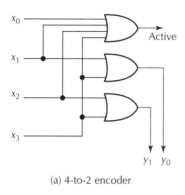
(a) 4-to-2 encoder

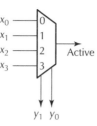
(b) Encoder symbol

Figure 1.11 A 2^a-to-a encoder outputs an a-bit binary number equal to the index of the single 1 among its 2^a inputs.

asserted input in the form of a binary number. The logic diagram for a 4-to-2 encoder is shown in Figure 1.11a, with its shorthand symbol given in Figure 1.11b. More generally, the number n of inputs need not be a power of 2. In this case, the $\lceil \log_2 n \rceil$-bit encoder output is the binary representation of the index for the single asserted input, that is, a number between 0 and $n - 1$. If a decoder is designed as a collection of OR gates, as in Figure 1.11a, it produces the all-0s output when no input is asserted or when input 0 is asserted. These two cases are thus indistinguishable at the encoder's output. If we lift the restriction that at most one input of the encoder can be asserted and design the circuit to output the index of the asserted input with the lowest index, a *priority encoder* results. For example, assuming that inputs x_1 and x_2 are asserted, the encoder of Figure 1.11a produces the output 11 (index $= 3$, which does not correspond to any asserted input), whereas a priority encoder would output 01 (index $= 1$, the smallest of the indices for asserted inputs). The "Active" signal allows us to differentiate between the cases of none of the inputs being asserted and x_0 being asserted.

Both decoders and encoders are special cases of *code converters*. A decoder converts an a-bit binary code into a 1-out-of-2^a code, a code with 2^a codewords each of which is composed of a single 1 and all other bits set to 0. An encoder converts a 1-out-of-2^a code to a binary code. In Example 1.2, we designed a BCD-to-seven-segment code converter.

■ 1.5 Programmable Combinational Parts

To avoid having to use a large number of small-scale integrated circuits for implementing a Boolean function of several variables, IC manufacturers offer large arrays of gates whose connections can be customized by the process known as programming. With respect to the programming mechanism, there are two types of such circuits. In one type, all connections of potential interest are already made but can be selectively removed. Such connections are made via *fuses* that can be blown open by passing a sufficiently large current through them. In another type of programmable circuit, *antifuse* elements are used to selectively establish connections where desired. In logic diagrams, the same convention is used for both types: a connection that is left in place, or is established, appears as a heavy dot on crossing lines, whereas for a connection that is blown open, or not established, there is no such dot. Figure 1.12a shows how the two functions $w \lor x \lor y$ and $x \lor z$ can be implemented by programmable OR gates. An array of such OR gates, connected to the outputs of an a-to-2^a decoder allows us to implement several functions of a input variables at once (Figure 1.12c). This arrangement is known as programmable read-only memory or PROM.

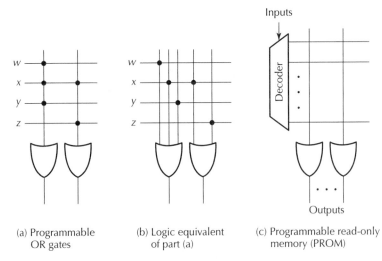

(a) Programmable
OR gates

(b) Logic equivalent
of part (a)

(c) Programmable read-only
memory (PROM)

Figure 1.12 Programmable connections and their use in a PROM.

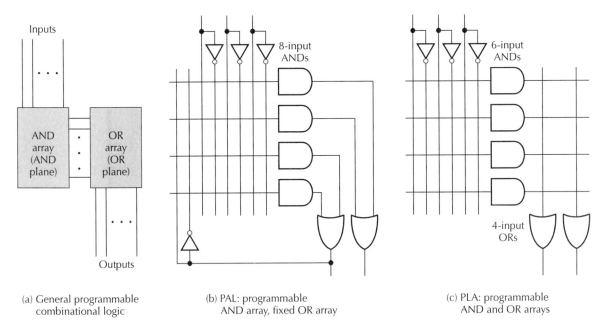

(a) General programmable
combinational logic

(b) PAL: programmable
AND array, fixed OR array

(c) PLA: programmable
AND and OR arrays

Figure 1.13 Programmable combinational logic: general structure and two classes known as PAL and PLA devices. Not shown is PROM with fixed AND array (a decoder) and programmable OR array.

Figure 1.13a shows a more general structure for programmable combinational logic circuits in which the decoder of Figure 1.12c has been replaced by an array of AND gates. The n inputs, and their complements formed internally, are provided to the AND array, which generates a number of product terms involving input variables and their complements. These product terms are input to an OR array that combines the appropriate product terms for each of up to m functions of interest to be output. PROM is a special case of this structure where the AND array is a fixed decoder and the OR array can be arbitrarily programmed. When the OR array has fixed connections but the inputs to the AND gates can be programmed, the result is a programmable array logic or PAL device (Figure 1.13b). When both the AND and OR arrays can be programmed, the resulting circuit is known as programmable logic array or PLA (Figure 1.13c). PAL devices and PLAs are more efficient than PROMs because they generate far fewer product terms. PAL devices are more efficient, but less flexible, than PLAs.

In commercial PAL parts, because of the limited number of product terms that can be combined to form each output, a feedback mechanism is often provided that makes some of the outputs selectable as inputs to AND gates. In Figure 1.13b the left output is fed back to the AND array, where it can be used as an input into the AND gates contributing to the formation of the right output. Alternatively, such fed-back outputs can be used as primary inputs if additional inputs are needed. A commonly used PAL product is the PAL16L8 device. The numbers 16 and 8 in the device's name refer to input and output lines, respectively; the package has 20 pins for 10 inputs, 2 outputs, 6 bidirectional I/O lines, power, and ground. The programmable AND array of this device consists of 64 AND gates each with 32 inputs (all 16 inputs and their complements). The 64 AND gates are divided into eight groups of 8 gates. Within each group, 7 AND gates feed a 7-input OR gate producing one output, and the remaining AND gate generates an enable signal for an inverting tristate buffer.

PLAs are not used as commodity parts but as structures that allow regular and systematic implementation of logic functions on custom VLSI chips. For example, we will see later (in Chapter 13) that the instruction decoding logic of a processor is a natural candidate for PLA implementation.

■ 1.6 Timing and Circuit Considerations

When the input signals to a gate vary, any requisite output change does not occur immediately but rather takes effect with some delay. The gate delay varies with the underlying technology, gate type, number of inputs (gate *fan-in*), supply voltage, operating temperature, and so on. However, as a first-order approximation, all gate delays can be considered equal and denoted by δ. A two-level logic circuit can then be said to have a delay of 2δ. For the CMOS (complementary metal-oxide semiconductor) technology used in the great majority of modern digital circuits, the *gate delay* may be as little as a fraction of a nanosecond. Signal propagation on wires that connect gates also contributes some delay, but again in the context of an approximate analysis, such delays can be ignored to simplify analyses; as circuit dimensions are scaled down, however, such an omission is becoming more and more problematic. The only accurate way for estimating the delay of a logic circuit is to run the complete design, with full details of logic elements and wiring, through a design tool. Even then, safety margins must be included in the timing estimates to account for process irregularities and other variations.

When delays along various paths in a logic circuit are unequal, as they are bound to be owing to the unequal number of gates through which different signals pass and/or the aforementioned variations, a phenomenon known as *glitching* occurs. Suppose we were to implement the function $f = x \vee y \vee z$ using the circuit of Figure 1.13b. Because the OR gates in the target circuit have only two inputs, we must first generate $a = x \vee y$ on the left output and then use the result to form $f = a \vee z$ on the right output. Note that the signals x and y pass through four gate levels, whereas z passes through only two levels. This leads to the situation shown in the timing diagram of Figure 1.14 where $x = 0$ throughout, whereas y changes from

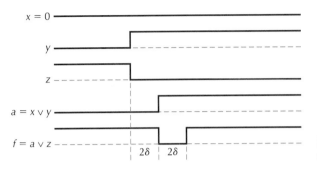

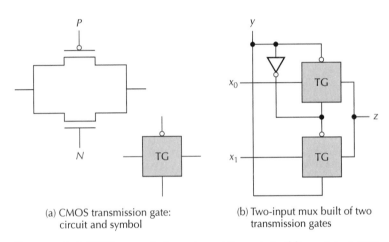

Figure 1.14 Timing diagram for a circuit that exhibits glitching.

(a) CMOS transmission gate: circuit and symbol

(b) Two-input mux built of two transmission gates

Figure 1.15 A CMOS transmission gate and its use in building a 2-to-1 mux.

0 to 1 at about the same time as z changing from 1 to 0. Theoretically, the output should be 1 at all times. However, because of unequal delays, the output assumes the value 0 for 2δ time units. This is one reason why we need accurate timing analyses and safety margins to ensure that adequate time is allowed for changes to fully propagate through the circuit, and for the outputs to assume their correct final values, before the generated results are used in other computations.

Even though in this book we deal exclusively with combinational logic circuits built of gates, we should mention for completeness that with CMOS technology, other circuit elements can be derived and used that do not directly correspond to a gate or gate network. Two examples are presented in Figure 1.15. The two-transistor circuit depicted in Figure 1.15a, alongside its symbolic representation, is known as a *transmission gate* (TG). It connects its two sides when the N control signal is asserted and disconnects them when P is asserted. If the signals N and P are complementary, the transmission gate behaves like a controlled switch. Two transmission gates and an inverter (another two-transistor CMOS circuit) can be used to form a 2-to-1 mux, as shown in Figure 1.15b. A 2^a-input mux can be built by using 2^a transmission gates and a decoder that converts the selection binary number $(y_{a-1} \cdots y_1 y_0)_{\text{two}}$ into a single asserted signal that feeds one of the transmission gates.

PROBLEMS

1.1 Universal logic elements

The three logic elements AND, OR, and NOT form a universal set because any logic function can be implemented by means of these elements, requiring nothing else.

a. Show that removing AND or OR from the set leaves the remaining set of two elements universal.
b. Show that the XOR forms a universal set with either AND or OR.
c. Show that the NAND gate is universal.
d. Show that the NOR gate is universal.
e. Show that the 2-to-1 multiplexer is universal.
f. Is there any other two-input element, besides NAND and NOR, that is universal? *Hint:* There are 10 functions of two variables that depend on both variables.

1.2 Vending machine actuator

Extend the vending machine actuator design of Example 1.3 in the following ways:

a. Each of the two items costs 65 cents.
b. There are four items to choose from.
c. Both changes of parts a and b.
d. Modify the design for part a to accept any amount up to one dollar (including a dollar bill) and to return change.

1.3 Realization of Boolean functions

Design a three-input, single-output logic circuit that implements any desired Boolean function of the three inputs based on a set of control inputs. *Hint:* There are 256 different three-variable Boolean functions, so the control input to the circuit (the opcode) must contain at least 8 bits. The truth table of a three-variable Boolean function has eight entries.

1.4 BCD-to-seven-segment decoder

Consider the BCD-to-seven-segment decoder partially designed in Example 1.2.

a. Complete the design, assuming that none of the three open segments in Figure 1.7 is included.
b. Redo the design using a 4-to-16 decoder and 7 OR gates.
c. Determine what will be displayed when the logic circuits derived in part a are fed with each of the 6 forbidden inputs 1010 through 1111.
d. Repeat part c for the design of part b.

1.5 BCD-to-seven-segment decoder

Design modified forms of the BCD-to-seven-segment decoder of Example 1.2 under each of the following sets of assumptions. In all case assume that "1" is represented by the two segments on the right edge of the panel.

a. Inputs are BCD digits; the digits 6, 7, and 9 are displayed with 6, 3, and 6 segments, respectively (see Figure 1.7).
b. Inputs are hexadecimal digits, with the added digits 10–15 represented as uppercase (A, C, E, F) or lowercase (b, d) letters. Use the assumptions of part a for 6, 7, and 9.
c. Inputs are BCD digits and the display shapes are chosen so that any single segment enable signal becoming permanently stuck on 0 does not lead to an undetectable display error.
d. Repeat part c for a single enable signal becoming permanently stuck on 1.

1.6 Parity generation and checking

An n-input *even-parity generator* produces a 1 output iff an odd number of its inputs are 1s. The circuit is so named because attaching the produced output to the n-bit input yields an even-parity $(n + 1)$-bit word. An n-input *even-parity checker* produces a 1 output (error signal) iff an odd number of its inputs are 1s.

a. Design an 8-input even-parity generator using only XOR gates.
b. Repeat part a for an odd-parity generator.
c. Design a 9-input even-parity checker using only XOR gates. How is your design related to those in parts a and b?
d. Repeat part c for an odd-parity checker.
e. Show that the fastest parity generator circuits can be built in a recursive manner, basing the design of

an n-input circuit on two $(n/2)$-input circuits of suitable types. What happens when n is odd?

1.7 Multiplicity of Boolean functions

There are four single-variable Boolean functions of which only two actually depend of the input variable x (x and x'). Similarly, there are 16 two-variable function of which only 10 depend on both variables (exclude x, x', y, y', 0, and 1).

a. How many three-variable Boolean functions are there, and how many of them actually depend on all three variables?

b. Generalize the result of part a for n-variable functions. *Hint:* You must subtract from the number of n-variable functions all the ones that depend on $n - 1$ or fewer variables.

1.8 Equivalent logic expressions

Prove each of the four equivalences in Example 1.1 using the other three methods listed in the example.

1.9 Equivalent logic expressions

Use the arithmetic substitution method to prove the following pairs of logic expressions equivalent.

a. $xy' \vee x'z' \vee y'z' \equiv xy' \vee x'z'$
b. $xyz \vee x' \vee y' \vee z' \equiv 1$
c. $x \oplus y \oplus z = xyz \vee xy'z' \vee x'yz' \vee x'y'z$
d. $xz \vee wy'z' \vee wxy' \vee w'xy \vee x'yz' \equiv$
   $xz \vee wy'z' \vee w'yz' \vee wx'z'$

1.10 Equivalent logic expressions

Prove that the following pairs of logic expressions are equivalent, first by the truth table method and then by means of symbolic manipulation (using the laws of Boolean algebra).

a. $xy' \vee x'z' \vee y'z' \equiv xy' \vee x'z'$
b. $xyz \vee x' \vee y' \vee z' \equiv 1$
c. $x \oplus y \oplus z \equiv xyz \vee xy'z' \vee x'yz' \vee x'y'z$
d. $xz \vee wy'z' \vee wxy' \vee w'xy \vee x'yz' \equiv$
   $xz \vee wy'z' \vee w'yz' \vee wx'z'$

1.11 Design of a 2 × 2 switch

Design a combinational circuit that acts as a 2 × 2 switch. The switch has data inputs a and b, one

"cross" control signal c, and data outputs x and y. When $c = 0$, a is connected to x and b to y. When $c = 1$, a is connected to y and b to x (i.e., the inputs are crossed).

1.12 Numerical comparison circuits

Assume $x = (x_2x_1x_0)_{two}$ and $y = (y_2y_1y_0)_{two}$ are 3-bit unsigned binary numbers. Write down a logic expression in terms of the six Boolean variables x_2, x_1, x_0, y_2, y_1, y_0 that assumes the value 1 iff:

a. $x = y$
b. $x < y$
c. $x \leq y$
d. $x - y \leq 1$
e. $x - y$ is even
f. $x + y$ is divisible by 3

1.13 Numerical comparison circuits

Repeat Problem 1.12 (all parts), but assume that the 3-bit inputs x and y are 2's-complement numbers in the range -4 to $+3$.

1.14 Sum of products and product of sums

Express each of the following logical expressions in sum-of-products and product-of-sums forms.

a. $(x \vee y')(y \vee wz)$
b. $(xy \vee z)(y \vee wz')$
c. $x(x \vee y')(y \vee z') \vee x'$
d. $x \oplus y \oplus z$

1.15 Hamming SEC/DED code

A particular type of Hamming code has 8-bit codewords $P_8 D_7 D_6 D_5 P_4 D_3 P_2 P_1$ that encode 16 different data values. The parity bits P_i are obtained from the data bits D_j according to the logic equations $P_1 = D_3 \oplus D_5 \oplus D_6$, $P_2 = D_3 \oplus D_5 \oplus D_7$, $P_4 = D_3 \oplus D_6 \oplus D_7$, $P_8 = D_5 \oplus D_6 \oplus D_7$.

a. Show that this code is capable of correcting any single-bit error and derive the correction rules. *Hint:* Think in terms of computing four parity check results, such as $C_1 = P_1 \oplus D_3 \oplus D_5 \oplus D_6$, all of which must yield 0 for an error-free codeword.

b. Show that the code detects all double-bit errors in addition to correcting single errors (thus it is a SEC/DED code).

c. Design the encoding circuit, using only 2-input NAND gates.
d. Design the decoding circuit that includes single-error correction and assertion of an error indicator signal in case of double errors.
e. Derive a PROM implementation of the decoding circuit of part d.

1.16 Mux-based implementation of logic functions

Show the inputs required to implement the following two logic functions using 4-to-1 multiplexers if only input x is available in complemented form.

a. $f(x, y, z) = y'z \vee x'y \vee xz'$
b. $g(w, x, y, z) = wx'z \vee w'yz \vee xz'$

1.17 Mux-based implementation of logic functions

a. Show that any three-variable logic function $f(x, y, z)$ can be realized using three 2-input multiplexers, assuming that x' is available as input.
b. Under what condition(s) can one realize a 3-variable function using three 2-input multiplexers, without requiring any complemented input?
c. Give an example of a three-variable function (truly depending on all three variables) that can be realized using only two 2-input multiplexers, with no complemented input available. Also show a diagram of the two-multiplexer realization of the function.
d. Can a three-variable function that is realizable with a single 2-input multiplexer truly depend on all three variables? Give an example or prove why such an arrangement is impossible.

1.18 Iterative number comparator

A iterative comparator for k-bit unsigned binary numbers consists of k cells arranged in a linear or cascade circuit. A cell receives one bit from each of the two operands x and y, and a pair of signals G_E ($x \geq y$ thus far) and L_E ($x \leq y$ thus far) from a neighboring cell, and produces G_E and L_E signals for the other neighbor. Note that $G_E = L_E = 1$ means that the two numbers are equal thus far.

a. Design the required cell assuming that G_E and L_E signals propagate from right to left.
b. Repeat part a for left-to-right signal propagation.
c. Show that the cells of part a or b can be connected into a tree structure, as opposed to linear array, to produce a faster comparator.

1.19 Arithmetic expressions for logic gates

The arithmetic expressions characterizing logic gates (Figure 1.1) can be extended to gates with more than two inputs. This is trivial for AND gates. Write the equivalent arithmetic expressions for 3- and 4-input OR gates. Generalize the expression to an h-input OR gate.

1.20 Programmable combinational parts

a. Show how to realize the logic function $f(x, y, z) = y'z \vee x'y \vee xz'$ on the PLA of Figure 1.13c.
b. Repeat part a on the PAL of Figure 1.13b.
c. Show that any function that can be realized by the PAL of Figure 1.13b is also realizable by the PLA of Figure 1.13c. Note that this is not a statement about PALs and PLAs in general but rather about the specific instances shown in Figure 1.13.

REFERENCES AND FURTHER READINGS

[Brow00]   Brown, S., and Z. Vranesic, *Fundamentals of Digital Logic with VHDL Design,* McGraw-Hill, 2000.

[Erce99]   Ercegovac, M. D., T. Lang, and J. H. Moreno, *Introduction to Digital Systems,* Wiley, 1999.

[Haye93]   Hayes, J. P., *Introduction to Digital Logic Design,* Addison-Wesley, 1993.

[Katz94]   Katz, R. H., *Contemporary Logic Design*, Benjamin/Cummings, 1994.

[Parh99]   Parhami, B., and D.-M. Kwai, "Combinational Circuits," in *Encyclopedia of Electrical and Electronics Engineering,* Wiley, Vol. 3 (Ca-Co), 1999, pp. 562–569.

[Wake01]   Wakerly, J. F., *Digital Design: Principles and Practices,* Prentice Hall, updated 3rd ed., 2001.

[WWW]   Web names of some manufacturers of PALs and PLAs: altera.com, atmel.com, cypress.com, latticesemi.com, philips.com, vantis.com.

2

DIGITAL CIRCUITS WITH MEMORY

"Microprocessors were not a product of the computer industry at all. They were the outcome of the desire—and the imperative need—of the young semiconductor industry to find a profitable application for early VLSI. . . . The Intel engineers knew little about computer architecture. Their immediate objective was to make programmable devices that would replace random logic."

—*Maurice Wilkes, Computing Perspectives*

"The days of the digital watch are numbered."

—*Tom Stoppard*

TOPICS IN THIS CHAPTER

2.1 Latches, Flip-Flops, and Registers

2.2 Finite-State Machines

2.3 Designing Sequential Circuits

2.4 Useful Sequential Parts

2.5 Programmable Sequential Parts

2.6 Clocks and Timing of Events

The behavior of a combinational (memoryless) circuit depends only on its current inputs, not on past history. A sequential digital circuit, on the other hand, has a finite amount of memory whose content, determined by past inputs, affects the current input/output behavior. In this chapter, we present a capsule review of methods for defining and realizing such sequential circuits by means of storage elements (latches, flip-flops, registers) and combinational logic. We also introduce a number of very useful components that are found in many diagrams in this book. Examples include register files, shift registers, and counters. As in Chapter 1, readers who have trouble understanding this material should consult any of the logic design textbooks listed at the end of the chapter.

■ 2.1 Latches, Flip-Flops, and Registers

The design of sequential circuits exhibiting memory requires the use of storage elements capable of holding information. The simplest storage element is capable of holding a single bit and can be *set* to 1 or *reset* to 0 at will. The SR latch, depicted in Figure 2.1a, is one such

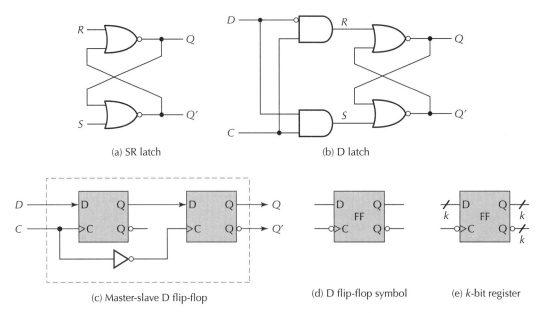

(a) SR latch   (b) D latch

(c) Master-slave D flip-flop   (d) D flip-flop symbol   (e) k-bit register

Figure 2.1 Latches, flip-flops, and registers.

element. When both R and S inputs are 0, the latch is in one of two stable states correspond-ing to $Q = 0$ ($Q' = 1$) or $Q = 1$ ($Q' = 0$). Asserting the R input resets the latch to $Q = 0$, while asserting S sets the latch to $Q = 1$. Either state then persists after the asserted input has been deasserted. Adding two AND gates to an SR latch, as in Figure 2.1b, produces a D latch with data (D) and clock (C) inputs. When C is asserted, the output Q of the SR latch follows D (the latch is set if $D = 1$ and reset if $D = 0$). We say that the latch is open or *transparent* for $C = 1$. Once C has been deasserted, the SR latch closes and maintains at its output the last value of D before deassertion of C.

Two D latches can be connected as in Figure 2.1c to form a master-slave D flip-flop. When C is asserted, the master latch is open and its output follows D, while the slave latch is closed, maintaining its state. Deassertion of C closes the master latch and causes its state to be copied into the slave latch. Figure 2.1d shows the shorthand notation for a D flip-flop. The bubble on the C input indicates that the new state of the flip-flop takes effect on the *neg-ative edge* of the clock input, that is, when the clock goes down from 1 to 0. Such a flip-flop is said to be *negative-edge-triggered*. We can build a *positive-edge-triggered* D flip-flop by inverting the C input in Figure 2.1c. An array of k flip-flops, all tied to the same clock input, forms a k-bit register (Figure 2.1e). Because a master-slave flip-flop maintains its content as it is being modified, it is ideal for use in building registers that are often read from and writ-ten into in the same machine cycle.

Figure 2.2 depicts how changes in the D and C inputs affect the Q output in a D latch and a negative-edge-triggered D flip-flop. In a D latch, the output Q follows D whenever C is as-serted and remains stable at its last value when C is deasserted. So, any change in Q coincides with a positive or negative edge of C or D; a small delay is involved owing to signal propaga-tion time through gates. Arrows in Figure 2.2 indicate cause-effect relationships. In a D flip-flop, changes in Q coincide with negative edges of C; again, a small delay is involved. To avoid metastability, which causes improper flip-flop operation (see Section 2.6), the value of

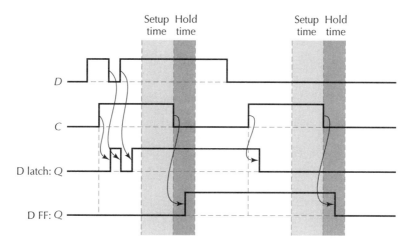

Figure 2.2 Operations of D latch and negative-edge-triggered D flip-flop.

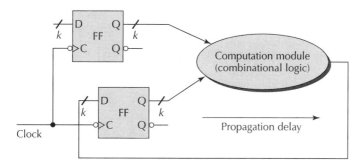

Figure 2.3 Register-to-register operation with edge-triggered flip-flops.

D should remain stable during a small window before and after a falling edge of *C*. The required stability time for *D* before the falling edge is known as *setup time,* while that after the falling edge is *hold time*.

Figure 2.3 shows a typical interconnection of registers and combinational components in synchronous sequential systems driven by a clock signal. One or more source registers provide the data used in a computation, and the result is stored in a destination register. Because of the master-slave register design leading to edge-triggered operation, the destination register may be the same as one of the source registers. As operand signals propagate through the computation module and begin to affect the input side of the destination register, the output of source registers remain stable, leading to the needed stability in the inputs of the destination register. As long as the clock period is greater than the sum of latch propagation delay, propagation delay through the combinational logic, and latch setup time, correct operation is ensured; as a rule, hold time can be ignored because it is usually smaller than latch propagation delay.

Because almost all the sequential circuits needed in this book use D flip-flops, while a few are based SR flip-flops that are easily derivable from the SR latch of Figure 2.1a, we do not cover other flip-flop types such as JK and T. Such flip-flops, described in virtually any textbook on logic design, lead to design simplifications in some cases; we avoid them, however, to keep the focus on notions in computer architecture rather than on details of logic circuit implementation.

■ 2.2 Finite-State Machines

Just as Boolean functions and truth tables are abstract characterizations of combinational digital circuits, *finite-state machines* (or simply *state machines*) and *state tables* are used to specify the sequential behavior of a digital circuit with memory. For simple sequential circuits, we prefer the graphical representation of state tables, known as *state diagrams*. More complex circuits are described in an algorithmic fashion, given that both the state table and state diagram representations grow exponentially with the number of state variables. A finite-state machine with *n* bits of storage can have up to 2^n states; therefore, even a digital circuit with a single 32-bit register as memory is already too large to be described in state table form. We illustrate the process of deriving simple state tables through an example.

Example 2.1: Coin reception state machine   A small vending machine can dispense items each costing 35 cents. Customers must use only quarters and dimes. The machine is not equipped to return change, but it is set to dispense the desired item when $0.35 or more has been deposited. Derive a state table for the coin reception unit of this vending machine, assuming that coins are deposited, and thus detected, one at a time.

Solution: Figure 2.4 depicts a possible state table and the associated state diagram. The starting state is S_{00}. As coins are deposited, the unit moves from one state to another to "remember" the amount of money paid thus far. For example, the first dime deposit takes the unit from S_{00} to S_{10}, where the state name S_{10} is chosen to convey the amount deposited. The state S_{35} corresponds to the deposited amount being enough for dispensing an item. Once in the "sale

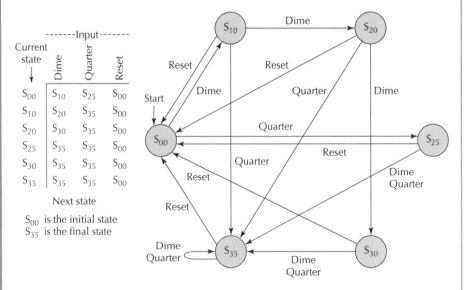

Current state →	Dime	Quarter	Reset
S_{00}	S_{10}	S_{25}	S_{00}
S_{10}	S_{20}	S_{35}	S_{00}
S_{20}	S_{30}	S_{35}	S_{00}
S_{25}	S_{35}	S_{35}	S_{00}
S_{30}	S_{35}	S_{35}	S_{00}
S_{35}	S_{35}	S_{35}	S_{00}

Next state

S_{00} is the initial state
S_{35} is the final state

Figure 2.4 State table and state diagram for a vending machine coin reception unit.

enabled" state S_{35}, the finite-state machine undergoes no state change due to additional coin deposits. The machine has three inputs, which correspond to three events: insertion of a dime, insertion of a quarter, and reset (due to the sale conditions not being met, causing coin return, or sale completion). Because states S_{25} and S_{30} are completely equivalent from the viewpoint of the coin reception process (both need an additional dime or quarter to allow transition to S_{35}), they can be merged to obtain a simpler five-state machine.

The finite-state machine represented in Figure 2.4 is known as a *Moore machine* because the machine's output is associated with its states. In state S_{35}, dispensing of the selected item is enabled, whereas in all other states, it is disabled. In a *Mealy machine,* on the other hand, outputs are associated with the transitions between states, and thus the output depends on both the present state and the current input received. Figure 2.5 shows how Moore and Mealy machines may be realized in hardware. The machine's state is held in an l-bit register that allows up to 2^l states. The next-state logic circuit produces the excitation signals required to effect a change of state based on n inputs and l state variables, while the output logic circuit produces the machine's m output signals. When the state register is composed of D flip-flops, the number of next-state excitation signals is the same as the number of state variables, because each D flip-flop needs one data input. Outputs are derived based on state variables only (Moore machine) or state variables and inputs (Mealy machine).

■ 2.3 Designing Sequential Circuits

Hardware realization of sequential circuits, according to the general structure in Figure 2.5, begins with the selection of memory elements to be used. Here, we deal exclusively with D flip-flops, so this step of the design process is predetermined. Next, the states must be encoded using l state variables for a suitable value of l. The choice of l obviously affects the cost of memory elements. However, this does not automatically mean that we always aim to minimize l; often a sparser encoding of states, using more state variables, leads to simpler combinational circuits for generating the excitation signals and the outputs. A detailed review of this *state assignment* process and associated trade-offs is beyond the scope of our discussion. We note only that the choices range from the densest possible encoding, where 2^l is strictly less than twice the number of states, to the sparsest, where l is equal to the number of states and

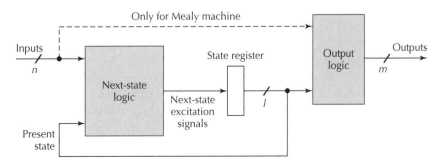

Figure 2.5 Hardware realization of Moore and Mealy sequential machines.

each state code is an *l*-bit string containing a single 1 (this is known as *one-hot encoding*). After state assignment, the truth tables for the two combinational blocks in Figure 2.5, and thus their circuit realizations, are easily derived. We illustrate the complete design process through two examples.

Example 2.2: Building a JK flip-flop   Design a JK flip-flop out of a single D flip-flop and combinational logic elements. A JK flip-flop, a memory element with two inputs (J and K) and two outputs (Q and Q'), holds its state when $J = K = 0$, is reset to 0 when $J = 0$ and $K = 1$, is set to 1 when $J = 1$ and $K = 0$, and inverts its state (changes from 0 to 1 or 1 to 0) when $J = K = 1$.

Solution: The problem statement defines the state table for JK flip-flop (Table 2.1) which is essentially the truth table for a function D of three variables (J, K, Q). The following excitation input for the D flip-flop is easily derived from Table 2.1: $D = JQ' \vee K'Q$. The resulting circuit is depicted in Figure 2.6. Because the D flip-flop used in the design is negative-edge-triggered, so is the resulting JK flip-flop.

■ **TABLE 2.1** State table for a JK flip-flop defined in Example 2.2.

Next state for → Current state ↓	$J = 0$ $K = 0$	$J = 0$ $K = 1$	$J = 1$ $K = 0$	$J = 1$ $K = 1$
0	0	0	1	1
1	1	0	1	0

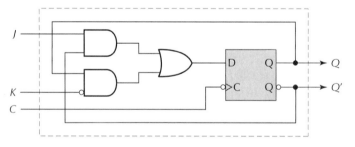

Figure 2.6 Hardware realization of a JK flip-flop (Example 2.2).

Example 2.3: Sequential circuit for a coin reception unit   Consider the state table and state diagram for the vending machine coin reception unit derived in Example 2.1. Assume that states S_{25} and S_{30} are merged into state $S_{25/30}$, as suggested at the end of the solution for Example 2.1. Design a sequential circuit to implement the resulting five-state machine using D flip-flops with separate asynchronous reset inputs.

Solution: There are five states, only one of which allows a sale to be completed. We need at least 3 bits to encode the five states. Because only the state S_{35} allows the sale to proceed, it seems natural to distinguish that state by encoding it as $Q_2 Q_1 Q_0 = 1xx$, making Q_2 the "enable sale" output. For the remaining states, the following assignments might be used: 000 for S_{00} (because it is the reset state), 001 for S_{10}, 010 for S_{20}, and 011 for $S_{25/30}$. Let q and d be the inputs which, when asserted for one clock cycle, indicate the detection of a quarter and a dime, respectively. Because coins are inserted and detected one at a time, $q = d = 1$ is a don't-care condition. These choices lead to an encoded state table (Table 2.2), which is essentially the truth table for three functions (D_2, D_1, D_0) of five variables (q, d, Q_2, Q_1, Q_0). The following excitation inputs for the D flip-flops are easily derived: $D_2 = Q_2 \vee q Q_0 \vee q Q_1 \vee d Q_1 Q_0$, $D_1 = q \vee Q_1 \vee d Q_0$, $D_0 = q \vee d' Q_0 \vee d Q_0'$. The resulting circuit is depicted in Figure 2.7.

■ **TABLE 2.2** State table for a coin reception unit after the state assignment chosen in Example 2.3.

Next state for → Current state ↓	$q = 0$ $d = 0$	$q = 0$ $d = 1$	$q = 1$ $d = 0$	$q = 1$ $d = 1$
$S_{00} = 000$	000	001	011	xxx
$S_{10} = 001$	001	010	1xx	xxx
$S_{20} = 010$	010	011	1xx	xxx
$S_{25/30} = 011$	011	1xx	1xx	xxx
$S_{35} = 1xx$	1xx	1xx	1xx	xxx

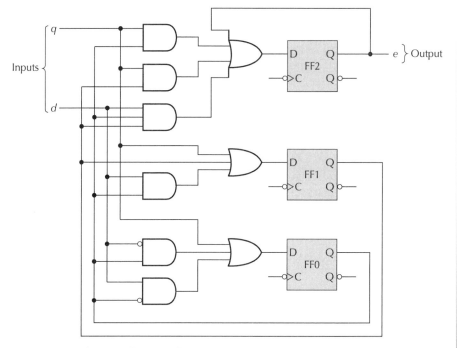

Figure 2.7 Hardware realization of a coin reception unit (Example 2.3).

■ 2.4 Useful Sequential Parts

A register is an array of flip-flops with individual data inputs and common control signals. Certain special types of register are commonly used in building digital systems. For example, a shift register can be loaded with new content or with its old content shifted to the right or left. Conceptually, a shift register can be built of an ordinary register connected to a multiplexer. A register capable of single-bit left shift is shown in Figure 2.8. When the register is clocked, a new data word or the left-shifted version of the word stored in the register replaces its old content. By using a larger multiplexer and appropriate control signals, other types of shift can be accommodated. Multibit shifts are accommodated either by doing several single-bit shifts over successive clock cycles (which is rather slow) or by using a special combinational circuit that can shift by various amounts. The design of such a *barrel shifter,* which is primarily used in the alignment and normalization of floating-point operands and results, will be discussed in Chapter 12.

Just as a register is an array of flip-flops (Figure 2.1e), a *register file* is an array of registers (Figure 2.9). The index or address of a register is used to read from it or to write into it. For a register file with 2^h registers, the register address is an h-bit binary number. Because many operations require more than one operand, register files are almost always *multiported,* meaning that they are capable of supplying the data words stored in multiple registers at once, while at the same time writing into one or more registers. Registers built of negative-edge-triggered master-slave flip-flops can be read out and modified in the same clock cycle, with changes in content taking effect in the next clock cycle. Thus, an operation such as $B \leftarrow A + B$, where A and B are stored in registers, can be executed in a single clock cycle, given that writing of the new value of B does not interfere with reading of its present value (see Figure 2.3).

A *FIFO* (pronounced fie-foe) is a special *first-in, first-out* register file whose elements are accessed in the same order that they were put in. Thus, a FIFO, does not need an address input; rather, it is equipped with one read port, one write port, and special indicator signals designating "FIFO empty" and "FIFO full." As shown in Figure 2.9c, the write enable and read enable signals for a FIFO are called "push" and "pop," respectively, indicating whether data is to be pushed into the FIFO or popped from it. A FIFO is basically a hardware-implemented *queue* with a fixed maximum size.

An SRAM (static random-access memory) device is much like a register file, except that it is usually single-ported and much larger in capacity. A $2^h \times g$ SRAM chip (Figure 2.10) receives an h-bit address as input and supplies g bits of data as output during a read operation. For a write operation, g bits of input data are written into the selected location. Input and output data usually share the same pins, given that they are never used at the same time. The write

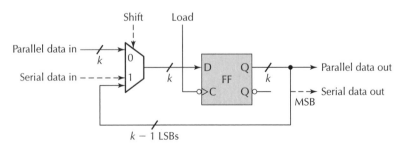

Figure 2.8 Register with single-bit left shift and parallel load capabilities. For logical left shift, the serial data in line is connected to 0.

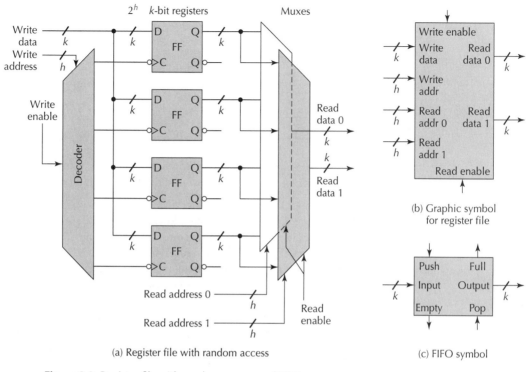

(a) Register file with random access

(b) Graphic symbol for register file

(c) FIFO symbol

Figure 2.9 Register file with random access and FIFO.

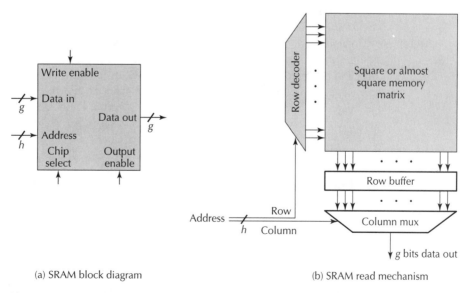

(a) SRAM block diagram

(b) SRAM read mechanism

Figure 2.10 SRAM memory is simply a large, single-port register file.

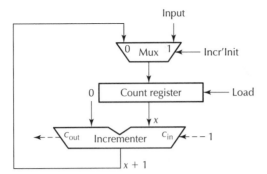

Figure 2.11 Synchronous binary counter with initialization capability.

enable signal has the same role here as in register files. The output enable signal controls a set of tristate buffers supplying the output data, thus allowing us to connect a number of such chips to a single set of output or bus lines. To form a memory with k-bit words, where $k > g$, we connect k/g such chips in parallel, with all of them receiving the same address and control signals and each supplying or receiving g bits of the k-bit data word (in the rare event that g does not divide k, we use $\lceil k/g \rceil$ chips). Similarly, to form a memory with 2^m locations, where $m > h$, we use 2^{m-h} rows of chips, each containing k/g chips, with an external $(m - h)$-to-2^{m-h} decoder used to select the row of chips that should have its chip select signal asserted.

SRAM technology is used to implement small fast memories located near the processor (often on the same chip). The larger main memory of a computer is implemented in DRAM or dynamic random-access memory technology, to be discussed in Chapter 17. Briefly, DRAM requires the use of one transistor to store one bit of data, whereas SRAM needs several transistors per bit. This difference makes DRAM denser and cheaper, but also slower, than SRAM. *Read-only memories* (ROMs) are also commonly used in the design of digital system. A $2^h \times g$ ROM can be used to realize g Boolean functions of h variables and can thus be viewed as a form of programmable logic. ROM contents can be loaded permanently at the time of manufacture or be "programmed" into the memory by means of special ROM programming devices. In the latter case, we have a *programmable ROM* (PROM) device. An *erasable PROM* (EPROM) can be programmed more than once.

An *up counter* is built of a register and an incrementer, as shown in Figure 2.11. Similarly, a *down counter* is composed of a register and a decrementer. In the absence of explicit qualification, the term "counter" is used for an up counter. An *up/down counter* can count either up or down under the control of a direction signal. The counter design shown in Figure 2.11 is adequate for most applications. It can be made faster by using a fast incrementer with carry-lookahead feature similar to that used in fast adders, to be discussed in Chapter 10. If still higher speed is required, the counter can be divided into blocks. A short initial block (say, 3 bits wide) can easily keep up with the fast incoming signals. Increasingly wider blocks to the left of the initial block need not be as fast because they are adjusted less and less frequently.

■ 2.5 Programmable Sequential Parts

Programmable sequential parts consist of programmable arrays of gates with strategically placed memory elements to hold data from one clock cycle to the next. For example, a commonly used form of PAL with memory elements has a structure similar to Figure 1.13b, but each OR gate output can be stored in a flip-flop and the device output is selectable from among

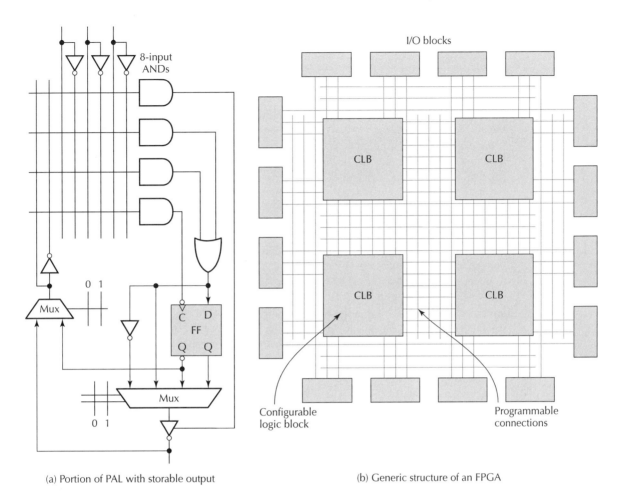

(a) Portion of PAL with storable output

(b) Generic structure of an FPGA

Figure 2.12 Examples of programmable sequential logic.

the OR gate output, its complement, and the flip-flop outputs (Figure 2.12a). Either the OR gate output or the flip-flop output can be fed back into the AND array through a 2-to-1 multiplexer. The three signals controlling the multiplexers in Figure 2.12a can be linked to logic 0 or 1 through programmable connections.

Programmable circuits similar to the one depicted in Figure 2.12a provide all the elements necessary for implementing a sequential machine (Figure 2.5) and can also be used as a combinational parts if desired. Such devices have two distinct parts. The *gate array,* which is essentially a PAL or PLA like the ones shown in Figure 1.13, is provided for its ability to realize desired logic functions. The *output macrocell,* containing one or more flip-flops, multiplexers, tristate buffers, and/or inverters, forms the required outputs based on values derived in the current cycle and those derived in earlier cycles and stored in the various memory elements.

The ultimate in flexibility is offered by *field-programmable gate arrays* (FPGAs), depicted in simplified form in Figure 2.12b, which are composed of a large number of configurable logic blocks (CLBs) in the center, surrounded by I/O blocks at the edges. Programmable connections fill the spaces between the blocks. Each CLB is capable of realizing one or two arbitrary logic functions of a small number of variables and also has one or more memory elements. Each I/O block is similar to the output macrocell in the lower half of Figure 2.12a. Groups of CLBs and I/O blocks can be linked together via programmable interconnections to form complex digital systems. The memory elements (typically SRAM) that hold the connectivity pattern between cells can be initialized from ROMs upon start-up to define the system's functionality. They might also be loaded with new values at any time to effect *run-time reconfiguration*. Special software packages, supplied by manufacturers of FPGAs and independent vendors, allow automatic mapping onto FPGAs of algorithmically specified hardware functionality. A more detailed discussion of FPGAs and other sequential programmable parts can be found in the end-of-chapter references.

■ 2.6 Clocks and Timing of Events

A clock is a circuit that produces a periodic signal, usually at a constant frequency or rate. The inverse of the clock rate is the clock period. For example, a one-gigahertz (GHz) clock has a frequency of 10^9 and a period of $1/10^9$ s $= 1$ ns. Typically, the clock signal is at 0 or 1 for about half the clock period (Figure 2.13). The operation of a synchronous sequential circuit is governed by a clock. With edge-triggered flip-flops (FFs), correct operation of the circuit shown in Figure 2.13 can be ensured by making the clock period long enough to accommodate the worst-case delay through the combinational logic, t_{comb}, while still leaving enough time for the setup time of FF2. Given that any change in FF1 is not instantaneous either but requires an amount of time known as *propagation time, t_{prop}*, we arrive at the following requirement:

$$\text{Clock period} \geq t_{prop} + t_{comb} + t_{setup} + t_{skew}$$

The extra term t_{skew}, for *clock skew*, accounts for the possibility that owing to signal propagation delays and certain anomalies, the clock signal controlling FF2 may arrive slightly ahead of that for FF1, thus effectively shortening the clock period. Note that the flip-flop hold time is absent from the foregoing inequality because it is almost always less than t_{prop} (i.e., during t_{prop}, a flip-flop's output remains at its previous value, thus satisfying the hold time requirement).

One way to allow higher clock rate, and thus greater computation throughput, is to use *pipelining*. In pipelined mode, the combinational logic of Figure 2.13 is divided into stages

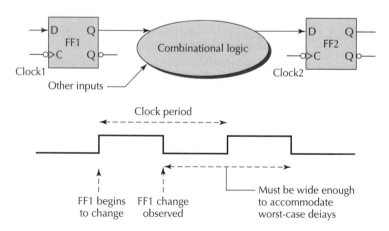

Figure 2.13 Determining the required length of the clock period.

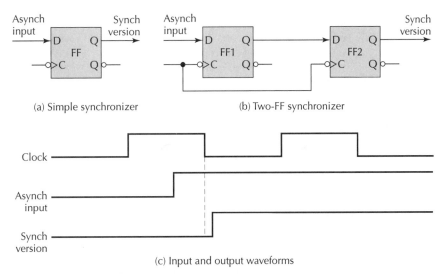

(a) Simple synchronizer

(b) Two-FF synchronizer

(c) Input and output waveforms

Figure 2.14 Synchronizers are used to prevent timing problems that might otherwise arise from untimely changes in asynchronous signals.

and storage elements inserted between stages to hold partial computation results. In this way, a new computation can begin as soon as results of the first stage are safely stored. However, this technique affects only the t_{comb} term in the preceding inequality. The clock period must still accommodate the other three terms. For this reason, there is a limit beyond which adding more pipeline stages will not be cost-effective.

Implicit in the foregoing inequality is the assumption that signals do not change within the clock period thus determined. In other words, if the constraint is barely satisfied, as is often the case when we try to use the fastest possible clock rate to maximize performance, then any change in signal values within the clock period could lead to a timing violation. Because many signals of interest may come from units that are not governed by the same clock (these are known as *asynchronous inputs*), their variations are beyond our control. For this reason, such signals are passed through special circuits known as *synchronizers* whose function is to ensure signal stability for the required duration of time. Figure 2.14a shows how a single flip-flop might be used to synchronize an asynchronous input. Any change in the asynchronous input can be observed only immediately after the next negative clock edge. There is a chance, however, that the change may occur too close to the next negative clock edge (Figure 2.14c), leading to a metastability condition where the observed signal is neither 0 nor 1; worse yet, the signal may appear as 0 to some units and as 1 to others. For this reason, two-FF synchronizers (Figure 2.14b) are preferred. While such synchronizers do not eliminate metastability altogether, they do make it so improbable that practical problems are avoided.

Somewhat faster operation results if we use latches and level-sensitive timing rather than edge-triggered flip-flops (to see this, compare the latch and flip-flop circuits in Figure 2.1). With level-sensitive operation, instead of abrupt changes that coincide with clock edges, a latch remains open for the entire time during which the clock signal is high. This can lead to problems if two successive latches are ever open at the same time. For this reason, level-sensitive timing is often used in conjunction with *two-phase clocking*. In this scheme, depicted in Figure 2.15, two nonoverlapping clock signals, ϕ_1 and ϕ_2 (for phase 1 and phase 2), are used to control successive latches in the computation path. This helps ensure that when a

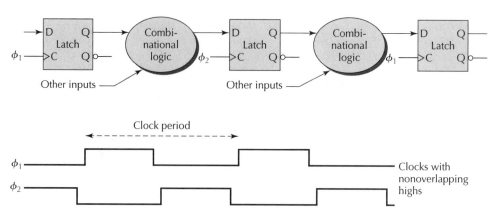

Figure 2.15 Two-phase clocking with nonoverlapping clock signals.

latch is open, the next latch downstream is always closed, and vice versa. As a result, signals propagate only from one latch to the next, as in the edge-triggered method. For simplicity, we always think of our circuits as having edge-triggered timing, knowing that we can convert any such design to level-sensitive operation through two-phase clocking.

PROBLEMS

2.1 Alternate forms of the D latch

a. By using the fact that an OR gate is replaceable by a NAND gate with inverted inputs, show that the D latch can be built of four NAND gates and an inverter.

b. Show that the inverter in the design of part a can be removed, leaving only four NAND gates, by feeding the output of one of the other gates to the gate that had the inverter on one input.

2.2 D latch vs D flip-flop

Characterize all input signal pairs, D and C, that when applied to a D latch and a D flip-flop lead to exactly the same observed output Q in terms of values and timing.

2.3 Other types of flip-flop

The negative-edge-triggered master-slave D flip-flop is but one of many types of flip-flop that can be built.

Each flip-flop can be described by a characteristic table that relates its change of state to changes on its input line(s). The JK flip-flop case was discussed in Example 2.2. Show how each of the following flip-flop types can be built from a D flip-flop and a minimal amount of combinational logic.

a. An SR (set/reset) flip-flop that holds its state for $S = R = 0$, is set to 1 for $S = 1$, is reset to 0 for $R = 1$, and behaves unpredictably for $S = R = 1$. You can use the latter combination of input values as a don't-care, assuming that it will never occur in operation.

b. A T (toggle) flip-flop, with one input T, that holds its state for $T = 0$ and inverts its state for $T = 1$.

c. A D flip-flop with separate preset and clear inputs that essentially have the same effects as the S and R inputs of an SR flip-flop defined in part a. When either S or R is asserted, the flip-flop behaves like an SR flip-flop; otherwise, it behaves like a D flip-flop. The case $S = R = 1$ is considered a don't-care condition.

2.4 Other types of flip-flop

Assume the availability of T flip-flops defined in part b of Problem 2.3. Show how each of the following flip-flop types can be built from a T flip-flop and a minimal amount of combinational logic.

a. An SR (set/reset) flip-flop that holds its state for $S = R = 0$, is set to 1 for $S = 1$, is reset to 0 for $R = 1$, and behaves unpredictably for $S = R = 1$. You can use the latter combination of input values as a don't-care, assuming that it will never occur in operation.
b. A JK flip-flop, as defined in Example 2.2.
c. A D flip-flop with separate preset and clear inputs that essentially have the same effects as the S and R inputs of an SR flip-flop defined in part a. When either S or R is asserted, the flip-flop behaves like an SR flip-flop; otherwise, it behaves like a D flip-flop. The case $S = R = 1$ is considered a don't-care condition.

2.5 Sequential circuits

Let the state of a sequential circuit built of h D flip-flops with outputs designated $Q_{h-1}, \ldots, Q_1, Q_0$ and inputs labeled with $D_{h-1}, \ldots, D_1, D_0$ be identified with the binary number $(Q_{h-1} \cdots Q_1 Q_0)_{two}$. For each of the following sequential circuits, defined by the logic equations for the D flip-flop inputs, draw a logic diagram, construct a state table, and derive a state diagram. In these equations, a and b are inputs and z is the output. In each case, specify whether the circuit represents a Mealy or Moore machine.

a. $D_1 = a(Q_1 \vee Q_0), D_0 = aQ_1', z = a'(Q_1 \vee Q_0)$
b. $D_1 = a'b \vee aQ_1, D_0 = a'Q_0 \vee aQ_1, z = Q_0$
c. $D_2 = a' \oplus Q_0 \oplus Q_1, D_1 = Q_2, D_0 = Q_1$

2.6 Design of a programmable 2 × 2 switch

Design a programmable 2 × 2 switch. The switch has data inputs a and b, a stored "cross" control signal c, and data outputs x and y. It has two modes, programming and normal operation, distinguished by the external *Prog* control signal. In programming mode, the data input a is stored in the control flip-flop, with b acting as a load enable signal. Normal

operation of the switch depends on the value of c. When $c = 0$, a is connected to x and b to y. When $c = 1$, a is connected to y and b to x (i.e., the inputs are crossed).

2.7 Design of a sorting 2 × 2 switch

A sorting 2 × 2 switch has numerical unsigned binary inputs a and b that enter bit-serially, beginning with the most significant bit (MSB), and data outputs x and y produced in the same manner one clock cycle after the arrival of inputs which is indicated by the control signal a_{MSB}. Output x is the smaller of the two inputs, while y is the larger of the two inputs. Thus the switch sorts its inputs in nondescending order.

a. Present the complete design of a sorting 2 × 2 switch. *Hint:* Use two muxes and two FFs that are initially reset; one FF is set when it has been established that $a < b$ and the other is set for $b < a$.
b. Show how three such switches can be interconnected to form a sorting 3 × 3 switch. What is the input-to-output latency of this switch?
c. Outline the changes that would be needed in the 2 × 2 switch if each numerical input were preceded by its sign bit (1 for negative, 0 for positive). There is no need to present a complete design.

2.8 Designing counters

Present the complete design of a 4-bit counter that can be initialized to its first state and counts cyclically:

a. According to the sequence 1000, 0100, 0010, 0001 (ring counter)
b. According to the sequence 0000, 1000, 1100, 1110, 1111, 0111, 0011, 0001 (Johnson counter)
c. From 0 to 9 (decade counter)
d. By threes, modulo 16; thus, the counter proceeds according to the sequence 0, 3, 6, 9, $\ldots$, wraps around to 2 after reaching 15, and proceeds to 1 after 14

2.9 Shift register with parallel load and reset

Using 4-to-1 multiplexers and D latches, design a shift register with a 2-bit control signal interpreted as follows: 00, hold data; 01, load input data in parallel; 10, left-shift the content, discarding the leftmost bit and setting the rightmost bit to the value supplied on a serial input; 11, reset all bits to 0s.

2.10 Extending the coin reception unit

Extend the coin reception unit of Example 2.3 so that nickels are also accepted. All other specifications of the vending machine and its coin reception unit remain the same.

2.11 Another vending machine

A vending machine sells three items costing 50 cents, 75 cents, and one dollar. It accepts only quarters or single dollar bills and returns up to two quarters in change when the amount inserted exceeds the cost of the selected item. Assume for simplicity that whenever change is to be returned, the required number of quarters is available in the machine. State all your assumptions.

2.12 Digital combination lock

A safe lock opens if the two pushbuttons A and B are pressed in the sequence AABABA (a real safe would have more pushbuttons and/or a longer code). Pressing B three times in a row resets the lock to its initial state. Pressing A when B should have been pressed sounds an alarm. Pressing any pushbutton after the lock has opened will reset the lock.

a. Construct the state diagram of the digital combination lock as a Mealy machine.
b. Implement the sequential machine defined in part a.
c. Construct the state diagram of the digital combination lock as a Moore machine.
d. Implement the sequential machine defined in part c.

2.13 Sequential machine implementation

When the behavior of a sequential machine is defined in terms of a short history of past inputs, it may be possible to design the machine directly with a shift register holding the short history (state). In some such cases, deriving a state table or state

diagram may be cumbersome in view of the large number of states.

a. Using this method, design a Mealy sequential machine with one binary input and one binary output. The output should be 1 whenever the last six input bits, when interpreted as a binary number with its least significant bit (LSB) arriving first, represent a prime number.
b. Repeat part a for a Moore sequential machine.

2.14 Sequential machine implementation

When the behavior of a sequential machine is defined in terms of the multiplicity of certain input values or events, it may be possible to design the machine directly with one or more counters holding the various counts of interest (state). In some such cases, deriving a state table or state diagram may be cumbersome in view of the large number of states.

a. Using this method, design a Mealy sequential machine with one binary input and one binary output. The output should be 1 whenever the number of 1s received thus far is $8m + 1$ for some integer m.
b. Repeat part a for a Moore sequential machine.

2.15 Building larger shift registers and counters

a. Explain how you would build a 32-bit shift register, given two 16-bit shift registers.
b. Repeat part a for a 32-bit up counter, given two 16-bit up counters.
c. Repeat part b for up/down counters.

2.16 Deriving state diagrams

A bit-serial binary adder receives two unsigned numbers beginning from their least significant bits and produces the sum in the same manner.

a. Viewing this adder as a Mealy machine, construct its state diagram (you need two states).
b. Implement the Mealy machine of part a with one D flip-flop.
c. Repeat part a for a Moore sequential machine (four states are required).
d. Implement the Moore machine of part c with two D flip-flops.

2.17 Simple traffic light controller

A traffic light at the intersection of north-south (NS) and east-west (EW) streets goes through the following cycle of states: both red (5 s), NS green (30 s), NS yellow (5 s), both red (5 s), EW green (30 s), EW yellow (5 s). A 0.2 Hz clock signal (one clock pulse every 5 s) is available for timing. Both streets are equipped with sensors that detect the presence of a car close to the intersection. Whenever there is a car close to the intersection on the street currently having its light red while there is no car approaching the intersection on the street with green light, the switchover is advanced and the green light immediately turns to yellow. Design a sequential circuit for this traffic light controller.

2.18 Bit-serial number comparator

A bit-serial comparator for unsigned binary numbers receives one data input bit from each of the two operands x and y, producing the output signals G ($x > y$ thus far) and E ($x = y$ thus far).

a. Design the comparator circuit assuming that data inputs arrive beginning with their most significant bits and that a reset signal is asserted in the clock cycle prior to data arrival.

b. Repeat part a for inputs supplied from the least significant end.

c. Briefly discuss how the design of part a or b can be modified to operate with 2's-complement inputs.

2.19 Register file

We have two register files, each containing 32 registers that are 32 bits wide.

a. Show how to use these two register files, and additional logic elements as needed, to form a register file with 64 registers of width 32 bits.

b. Repeat part a for a register file with 32 registers of width 64 bits.

c. Repeat part a for a register file with 128 registers of width 16 bits.

2.20 Bidirectional shift register

Augment the shift register of Figure 2.8 with additional logic elements as needed so that depending on the status of a control input, Left′Right, both single-bit left and right shifts can be performed.

REFERENCES AND FURTHER READINGS

[Brow00]   Brown, S., and Z. Vranesic, *Fundamentals of Digital Logic with VHDL Design,* McGraw-Hill, 2000.

[Erce99]   Ercegovac, M. D., T. Lang, and J. H. Moreno, *Introduction to Digital Systems,* Wiley, 1999.

[Haye93]   Hayes, J. P., *Introduction to Digital Logic Design,* Addison-Wesley, 1993.

[Katz94]   Katz, R. H., *Contemporary Logic Design,* Benjamin/Cummings, 1994.

[Tocc01]   Tocci, R. J., and N. S. Widmer, *Digital Systems: Principles and Applications,* 8th ed., Prentice Hall, 2001.

[Wake01]   Wakerly, J. F., *Digital Design: Principles and Practices,* Prentice Hall, updated 3rd ed., 2001.

[WWW]   Web names of some manufacturers of sequential programmable logic devices: actel.com, altera.com, atmel.com, cypress.com, latticesemi.com, lucent.com, philips.com, quicklogic.com, vantis.com, xilinx.com.

■ CHAPTER 3

COMPUTER SYSTEM TECHNOLOGY

"The one on the left will be obsolete in eight months, whereas for only $300 more, you can have the model on the right that won't be obsolete for a full year."
—*Salesperson's explanation to befuddled shopper trying to decide which of two computers to buy (caption of cartoon by unknown artist)*

"I have found that many people have taken credit for having predicted where we've come [in information technology]. They happen to be mostly people who write fiction for a living."
—*Nick Donofrio, 2001 Turing Memorial Lecture*

Computer architecture is driven by developments in computer technology and in turn motivates and influences such developments. This chapter provides some background on the past progress and current trends in computer technology to the extent needed for proper appreciation of the topics in the rest of the book. After tracing the development of computer systems through the ages, we briefly review the technology of digital integrated circuits. Among other things, we show how the experimentally derived Moore's law has accurately predicted performance and density improvements for integrated circuits over the past two decades and what this trend means for computer architecture. This presentation is followed by discussions of processor, memory, mass storage, input/output, and communication technologies. A look at software systems and applications concludes the chapter.

▪ 3.1 From Components to Applications

Artifacts of electronic, mechanical, and optical engineering are found throughout modern computer systems. Here, we are primarily interested in the electronic data manipulation and control aspects of computer design. We take the mechanical (e.g., keyboard, disk, printer) and optical (e.g., display) parts for granted, not because these are less important than electronic parts but because the focus of computer architecture is on the latter. The chain that links the capabilities of electronic components on one side of Figure 3.1 to application domains pursued by end users on the other side involves several subdisciplines of computer engineering and the associated specialties. In this chain, the computer designer or architect occupies a central position between hardware designers dealing with logic- and circuit-level notions and software designers occupied with system and application programming. Of course, this should not come as a surprise; had this been a book on flower arrangement, the florist would have been depicted as being at the center of the universe!

As we move from right to left in Figure 3.1, we encounter increasing levels of abstraction. The circuit designer has the lowest-level view and deals with the physical phenomena that make the computer hardware perform its tasks. The logic designer deals primarily with models such as gates or flip-flops discussed in Chapters 1 and 2, relying on design tools to accommodate any circuit considerations that may show through the imperfect abstraction. The computer architect needs to be knowledgeable about the logic-level view, although she deals primarily with higher-level digital logic primitives such as adders and register files. She must also be aware of issues in the area of system design whose aim is to provide a layer of software that facilitates the task of application design and development. In other words, the system designer envelopes the raw hardware with key software components that shield the user from the details of hardware operation, file storage formats, protection mechanisms, communication protocols, and so on, providing instead an easier-to-use interface to the machine. Finally, the application designer, who has the highest-level view, uses the facilities provided by the hardware and lower-level software to devise solutions to application problems that interest a particular user or a class of users.

Computer architecture, whose name is intended to reflect its similarity to building architecture (Figure 3.2), has been aptly described as being at the interface between hardware and software. Traditionally the software side is associated with "computer science" and the hardware

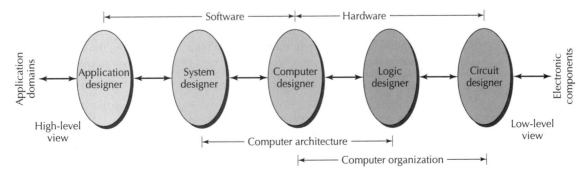

Figure 3.1 Subfields or views in computer system engineering.

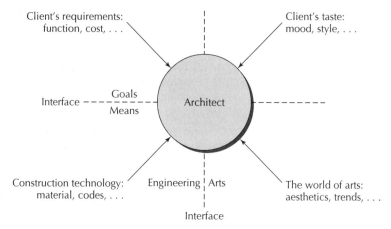

Figure 3.2 Like a building architect, whose place at the engineering/arts and goals/means interfaces occupies the center of this diagram, a computer architect reconciles many conflicting or competing demands.

side with "computer engineering." This dichotomy is somewhat misguided, since there are many scientific and engineering considerations on both sides. On the one hand, software development is an engineering activity; the process of designing a modern operating system or a database management system is only superficially different from that of designing an airplane or a suspension bridge. On the other hand, much of hardware designers' daily routines involves software and programming (as in programmable logic devices, hardware description languages, and circuit simulation tools). Meeting time, cost, and performance goals, which are required in both software and hardware projects, are hallmarks of engineering activities, as are adherence to standards for compatibility and interoperability of the resulting products.

Computer architecture isn't just for machine designers and builders; informed and effective users at every level benefit from a firm grasp of the core ideas and an awareness of the more advanced concepts in this field. Certain key realizations, such as the fact that a $2x$ GHz processor is not necessarily twice as fast as an x GHz model (see Chapter 4), require a basic training in computer architecture. In a way, using a computer is like driving a car. You can do a decent job by just learning about the driver interfaces in your car and the rules of the road. To be a really good driver, however, you must have some knowledge of what makes the car go and how the parameters affecting performance, comfort, and safety are interrelated.

Because in describing computer systems and their parts we encounter both extremely large and very small quantities (multigigabyte disks, subnanometer circuit elements, etc.), we include Table 3.1, which lists the prefixes prescribed by the metric system of units and clarifies our convention with regard to prefixes used to describe memory capacity (kilobytes, gigabits, etc.). We have included, for completeness, some very large multiples and extremely small fractions that have not yet been used in connection with computer technology. As you read the following sections on the pace of progress in this area, you will understand why these may become relevant in a not-so-distant future.

■ **TABLE 3.1** Symbols and prefixes for multiples and fractions of units.

Multiple	Symbol	Prefix	Multiple	Symbol*	Prefix*	Fraction	Symbol	Prefix
10^3	k	kilo	2^{10}	K or k_b	b-kilo	10^{-3}	m	milli
10^6	M	mega	2^{20}	M_b	b-mega	10^{-6}	μ or u	micro
10^9	G	giga	2^{30}	G_b	b-giga	10^{-9}	n	nano
10^{12}	T	tera	2^{40}	T_b	b-tera	10^{-12}	p	pico
10^{15}	P	peta	2^{50}	P_b	b-peta	10^{-15}	f	femto
10^{18}	E	exa	2^{60}	E_b	b-exa	10^{-18}	a	atto
10^{21}	Y	yotta	2^{70}	Y_b	b-yotta	10^{-21}	y	yocto

*Note: The symbol K is generally used to mean $2^{10} = 1024$. Because the same convention cannot be applied to other multiples whose symbols are already uppercase letters, we use a subscript b to denote comparable powers of 2. When specifying memory capacity, the subscript b is always understood and may be left out; that is, 32 MB and 32 M_bB represent the same amount of memory. The power-of-2 prefixes are read as binary-kilo, binary-mega, and so on.

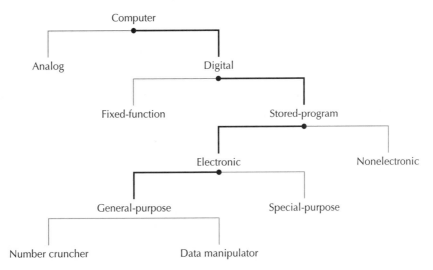

Figure 3.3 The space of computer systems: heavy lines point to what we normally mean by the word "computer."

■ 3.2 Computer Systems and Their Parts

Computers can be classified according to size, power, price, applications, technology, and other aspects of their implementation or purpose. When we talk of computers these days, we usually mean a type of computer whose full name is "general-purpose electronic stored-program digital computer" (Figure 3.3). Such computers used to be designed in versions optimized for number crunching, needed in numerically intensive computations, and data manipulation, typical of business applications. The differences between these two categories of machines have all but disappeared in recent years. Analog, fixed-function, nonelectronic, and special-purpose computers are also used in large numbers, but our focus in studying computer architecture is on the most common type of computer, which corresponds to the highlighted path in Figure 3.3.

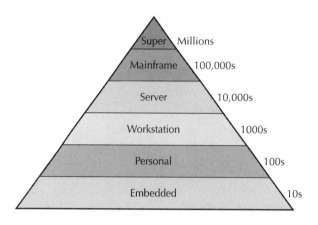

Figure 3.4 Classifying computers by computational power and price range (dollars).

A useful categorization of computers is based on their computational power or price range: from tiny *embedded microcontrollers* (basically, simple, low-cost microprocessors) at the bottom of the scale through *personal computers, workstations,* and *servers* at the middle to *mainframes* and *supercomputers* at the top. The pyramid shape of Figure 3.4 to implies that computers closer to the bottom are more numerous and also represent a greater investment in their aggregate cost. As computers have achieved better performance/cost ratios, user demand for computational power has grown at an even faster pace, so that a top-of-the-line supercomputer tends to cost between $10 million and $30 millions. Similarly, the cost of a personal computer of modest power tends to hover around $1000–$3000. These observations, along with the highly competitive nature of the computing market, imply that the cost of a computer system is a surprisingly accurate indicator of its capabilities and computational power, at least more accurate than any other single numerical indicator. Note, however, that the costs shown in Figure 3.4 are expressed in easy-to-remember round numbers.

Embedded computers are used in appliances, autos, phones, cameras, and entertainment systems, and in many modern gadgets. The type of computer used varies by the intended processing tasks. Appliances tend to contain very simple *microcontrollers* that are capable of monitoring status information from sensors, converting between analog and digital signals, measuring time intervals, and activating or disabling actuators through the assertion of enable and inhibit signals. Most current automotive applications are similar, except that they require microcontrollers of more resilient types. Increasingly, though, on-board computers in autos are expected to do more than simple control functions (Figure 3.5), given the trend toward greater use of information and entertainment facilities. Phones, digital cameras, and audio/video entertainment systems require many signal processing functions on multimedia data. For this reason, they tend to use a *digital signal processor* (DSP) chip instead of a microcontroller.

Personal computers are similarly varied in their computational power and intended use. They fall in two main categories: *portable* and *desktop*. Portable computers are known as *laptops* or *notebooks,* with *subnotebooks* and *pocket PCs* constituting smaller, more limited models. *Tablet* versions, intended to replace notepads and pens, are also available. A *desktop computer* may have its CPU and peripherals in a unit that doubles as the monitor stand or in a separate "tower" (Figure 3.6) that offers more room for expansion and can also be hidden out of view. Since flat displays are now quite affordable, desktops increasingly come with flat screens that offer the additional benefits of clearer image, lower power consumption,

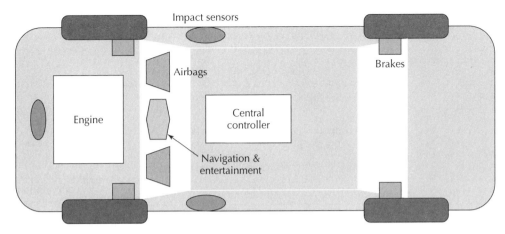

Figure 3.5 Embedded computers are ubiquitous, yet invisible. They are found in our automobiles, appliances, and many other places.

Figure 3.6 Notebooks, a common class of portable computers, are much smaller than desktops but offer substantially the same capabilities. What are the main reasons for the size difference?

and less heat dissipation (hence, lower air conditioning cost). A *workstation* is basically a high-end desktop computer, with more memory, greater I/O and communications capabilities, larger display screen, and perhaps more advanced system and application software.

Whereas a personal computer or workstation is generally associated with a single user, *servers* and *mainframes* are workgroup, or departmental, or enterprise computers. At the low end, a server is much like a workstation and is distinguished from the latter by more extensive software/support, larger main memory, bigger secondary storage, greater I/O capabilities, higher communication speed/capacity, and/or higher reliability. Robustness and reliability are particularly important factors, given the often severe technical and financial consequences of unscheduled downtime. It is common to use multiple servers to achieve the capacity, bandwidth, or availability requirements. At the extreme, this approach leads to the use of *server farms*. A high-end server is basically a smaller or less expensive version of a mainframe, what in previous decades would have been called a *minicomputer*. A mainframe computer, with all its peripheral devices and support equipment, might fill a room or perhaps a large hall.

Supercomputers are the glamour products of the computer industry. They account for a tiny fraction of the total dollar amount of products shipped and an even tinier fraction of the number of computer installations. Yet, these machines, and the grand-challenge computational problems that motivate their design and development, always make the headlines. Part of our fascination with supercomputers results from knowing that many of the advances introduced in such machines often find their way a few years down the road into our workstations and desktops; so, in a sense, they provide us with a window into the future. A supercomputer has been half-jokingly defined as "any machine still on the drawing board" and "any machine costing \$30M." The computational power of the largest available computers has gone from millions of instructions or floating-point operations per second (MIPS, FLOPS) circa 1970 through GIPS/GFLOPS in mid-1980s and TIPS/TFLOPS at the turn of the twenty-first century. Machines now on the drawing board are aiming for PIPS/PFLOPS. Besides numerically intensive computations that are always associated with supercomputers, such machines are increasingly being used for data warehousing and high-volume transaction processing.

Regardless of its size, price range, or application domain, a digital computer is composed of certain key parts depicted in Figure 3.7. This diagram is intended to reflect all the different views that have been advanced; from the three-part view (CPU, memory, I/O) through four (processor, memory, input, output) and five (data path, control, memory, input, output) parts that one sees in most textbooks to our preferred six-part view that includes an explicit mention of the link component. Note that any of these versions, including ours, represents a simplified view that lumps together functionalities that may in fact be distributed throughout the system. This is certainly true of control: memory often has a separate controller, as do the input/output subsystem, individual I/O devices, the network interface, and so on. Similarly, processing

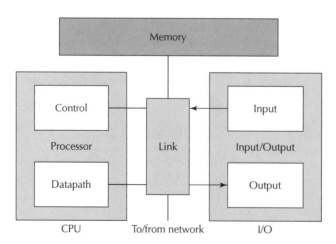

Figure 3.7 The (three, four, five, or) six main units of a digital computer. Usually, the link unit (a simple bus or a more elaborate network) is not explicitly included in such diagrams.

capabilities exist virtually everywhere: in the I/O subsystem, within various devices (e.g., printer), at the network interface, and so on. However, bear in mind that one does not try to learn about airplanes by using the Concorde or a sophisticated military jet as the starting point!

■ 3.3 Generations of Progress

Most chronologies of computer technology distinguish a number of *computer generations,* each beginning with a major breakthrough in component technology. Typically, four generations are specified that coincide with the use of vacuum tubes, transistors, small- to medium-scale integrated circuits (SSI/MSI ICs) and large- to very-large-scale integration (LSI/VLSI). To these we add all the prior history of computing as generation 0 and the dramatic advances of the late 1990s as generation 5 (Table 3.2). Note that the entries in Table 3.2 are somewhat oversimplified; the intention is to show a broad-brush picture of the advances and trends, rather than a cluttered table that lists all technological advances and innovations.

Concern with computation, and mechanical gadgets to facilitate it, began very early in the history of civilization. Introduction of the abacus by the Chinese is of course well known. The first sophisticated aids to computation appear to have been devised for astronomical calculations in ancient Greece. For practical purposes, the roots of modern digital computing can be traced back to the mechanical calculators designed and built by the seventeenth-century mathematicians Schickard, Pascal, and Leibniz, among others. By devising his difference engine for computing mathematical tables in the 1820s and the programmable analytical engine a decade or so later, Charles Babbage established himself as the father of digital computing as we know it today. Even though the technology of the nineteenth century did not allow full implementation of Babbage's ideas, historians agree that he had workable realizations of many key concepts in computing, including programming, instruction set, operation codes, and program loops. It was the arrival of reliable electromechanical relays in the 1940s that brought many of these ideas to fruition.

■ **TABLE 3.2** The five generations of digital computers, and their ancestors.

Generation (when begun)	Processor technology	Main memory innovations	I/O devices introduced	Dominant look and feel
0 (17th century)	(Electro-) Mechanical	Wheel, card	Lever, dial, punched card	Factory equipment
1 (1950s)	Vacuum tube	Magnetic drum	Paper tape, magnetic tape	Hall-size power cabinet
2 (1960s)	Transistor	Magnetic core	Drum, printer, text terminal	Room-size mainframe
3 (1970s)	SSI/MSI	RAM/ROM chip	Disk, keyboard, video monitor	Desk-size mini
4 (1980s)	LSI/VLSI	SRAM, DRAM	Network, CD, mouse, sound	Desktop/laptop micro
5 (1990s)	ULSI/GSI/WSI, system on chip	SDRAM, flash	Sensor, actuator, point/click, DVD	Invisible, embedded

The ENIAC, built in 1945 under the supervision of John Mauchly and J. Presper Eckert at the University of Pennsylvania, is often cited as the first electronic computer, although we now know of several other earlier or concurrent efforts, notably those by John Atanasoff at Iowa State University and Konrad Zuse in Germany. ENIAC weighed 30 tons, occupied about 1500 m^2 of floor space, used 18,000 vacuum tubes, and consumed 140 kW of power. Computationally, it could perform about 5000 additions per second. The notion of computing with a stored program was devised and perfected in groups headed by John von Neumann in the United States and Maurice Wilkes in England, leading to working machines in the late 1940s and commercial digital computers for scientific and business applications in the early 1950s. These first-generation, general-purpose, stored-program digital computers were customized for scientific or business applications, a distinction that has since largely disappeared. Example first-generation machines included the UNIVAC 1100 series and the IBM 700 series.

The onset of the second generation is generally associated with the changeover from vacuum tubes to much smaller, cheaper, and more reliable transistors. However, equally if not more important are developments in storage technology along with the introduction of high-level programming languages and system software. NCR and RCA pioneered second-generation computer products, but they were followed shortly by the 7000 series of machines from IBM and, later, by PDP-1 from Digital Equipment Corporation (DEC). These computers began to look more like office machines than factory equipment. This fact, along with the ease of use afforded by more sophisticated software, led to the proliferation of scientific computing and business data processing applications.

The capability to integrate several transistors and other elements, theretofore built as *discrete components,* into a single circuit solved several problems that were becoming quite serious as the complexity of computers grew to tens of thousands of transistors and beyond. *Integrated circuits* not only brought about the third generation of computers but also kicked off an all-encompassing *microelectronics revolution* that continues to shape our information-based society. Perhaps the most successful and influential third-generation computer product, which also helped put the focus on computer architecture as being distinct from particular machines or implementation technologies, is the IBM System 360 family of compatible machines. This series started from low-end, relatively inexpensive machines for small businesses and extended up to very large multimillion-dollar supercomputers that used the latest technological and algorithmic innovations to achieve the ultimate in performance, all based on the same overall architecture and instruction set. Another influential machine in this generation, DEC's PDP-11, brought with it the age of affordable minicomputers capable of operating at the corner of an office or lab, instead of needing a large air-conditioned computer room.

With integrated circuits getting larger and denser, it finally became possible in the early 1970s to put a complete processor, albeit a very simple one, on a single IC chip. This, along with phenomenal increases in memory density allowing the complete main memory to reside on a handful of chips, led to the popularization of low-cost microcomputers. Apple Computer Corporation was the undisputed leader in this area, but it wasn't until IBM introduced its PC with open architecture (meaning that components, peripherals, and software from different vendors could coexist in a single machine) that the PC revolution took off. To this date, the term PC is synonymous with IBM and IBM-compatible microcomputers. Larger computers also benefited from advances in IC technology; with fourth-generation desktops offering the capabilities of supercomputers from earlier generations, new higher-performance machines continued to push forward the frontiers of scientific computing and data-intensive commercial applications.

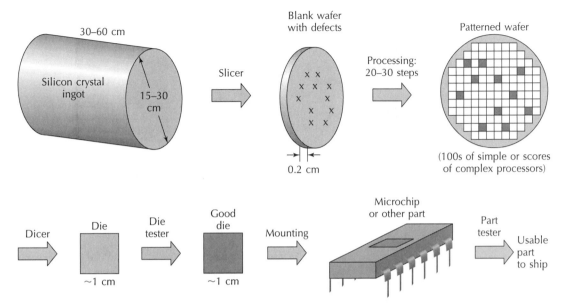

Figure 3.8 The manufacturing process for an integrated circuit part.

There is no general agreement about whether we have already moved past the fourth generation and, if so, when the transition to fifth generation occurred. In the 1990s, we witnessed dramatic improvements not only in IC technology but also in communications. If the advent of pocket PC, GFLOPS desktop, wireless Internet access, gigabit memory chips, and multi-gigabyte disks barely larger than a wristwatch are inadequate to signal the dawn of a new era, it is hard to imagine what would be. The IC part of these advances is variously described as ultralarge-scale, grand-scale, or wafer-scale integration. It is now possible to put a complete system on a single IC chip, leading to unprecedented speed, compactness, and power economy. Today, computers are viewed primarily as components within other systems rather than as expensive systems in their own right.

A brief look at the process of manufacturing integrated circuits (Figure 3.8) helps us understand some the current difficulties as well as challenges to be overcome for continued growth in computer capabilities in future generations. Integrated circuits are essentially imprinted on silicon dies using a complex, multistep chemical process of depositing layers (insulation, conductor, etc.), etching away the unneeded parts of each layer, and proceeding with the next layer. As many as hundreds of dies are formed on a single blank wafer that has been sliced from a crystal ingot. Because the ingot and the deposition process (involving minute features in extremely thin layers) are imperfect, some of the dies thus formed will not perform as expected and must thus be discarded. Other imperfections arise during the mounting process, leading to more discarded parts. The ratio of the usable parts obtained at the end of this process to the number of dies we started with is known as the *yield* of the manufacturing process.

Many factors affect the yield. One key factor is the complexity of the die in terms of the area it occupies and the intricacy of its design. Another is the defect density on the wafer. Figure 3.9 shows that a given distribution of 11 tiny defects on the surface of the wafer might lead to 11 defective dies among 120 (yield = 109/120 ≅ 91%), whereas the same defects would make 11 out of 26 larger dies unusable (yield = 15/26 ≅ 58%). This is only the

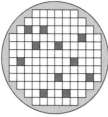
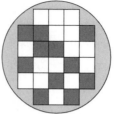

120 dies, 109 good   26 dies, 15 good

Figure 3.9 Visualizing the dramatic decrease in yield with larger dies.

contribution of the wafer defects; the situation will be made worse by defects arising from the more complex structure and interconnection patterns on the larger dies.

Beginning with the definition

Die yield = (Number of good dies)/(Total number of dies)

we arrive at the following for the cost of a die, exclusive of testing and packaging costs:

Die cost = (Cost of wafer)/(Total number of dies × Die yield)
         = (Cost of wafer) × (Die area/Wafer area)/(Die yield)

The only variables in the preceding equation are die area and yield. Because yield is a decreasing function of die area and defect density, the cost per die is a superlinear function of die area, meaning that doubling the die area to accommodate greater functionality on a chip will more than double the cost of the finished part. To be more concrete, we note that experimental studies have shown die yield to be

Die yield = Wafer yield × [1 + (Defect density × Die area)/a]$^{-a}$

where wafer yield accounts for wafers that are completely unusable and the parameter a is estimated to range from 3 to 4 for modern CMOS processes.

Example 3.1: Effect of die size on cost   Assume that the dies in Figure 3.9 are 1×1 and 2×2 cm^2 in size and ignore the defect pattern shown. Assuming a defect density of 0.8/cm^2, how much more expensive will the 2×2 die be than the 1×1 die?

Solution: Let the wafer yield be w. From the die yield formula, we obtain a yield of $0.492w$ and $0.113w$ for the 1×1 and 2×2 dies, respectively, assuming $a = 3$. Plugging these values into the formula for die cost, we find that the 2×2 die costs $(120/26) \times (0.492/0.113) = 20.1$ times as much as the 1×1 die; this represents a factor of $120/26 = 4.62$ greater cost attributable to the smaller number of dies on a wafer and a factor of $0.492/0.113 = 4.35$ due to the effect of yield. With $a = 4$, the ratio assumes the somewhat larger value $(120/26) \times (0.482/0.095) = 23.4$.

3.4 Processor and Memory Technologies

As a result of advances in electronics, processor and memory have improved at an astounding rate. The need for faster processors and larger memories has in turn fueled the phenomenal growth of the semiconductor industry. A key factor in these improvements has been the relentless increase in the number of devices that can be put on a single chip. Part of this growth has resulted from our ability to design and economically manufacture larger dies; but for the most part, increased density of devices (per unit of die area) has been the key factor. The exponential increase in the number of devices on a chip over the years has come to be known as *Moore's law,* which predicts an annual increase of 60% ($\times$ 1.6 per year $\cong$ $\times$ 2 every 18 months $\cong$ $\times$ 10 every 5 years). This prediction has proved so accurate that a long-term plan known as the semiconductor industry roadmap is based on it. For example, according to this roadmap, we know with reasonable certainty that in 2010, billion-transistor chips will become technically and economically feasible (memory chips of this size are already available).

Currently, the best-known processors are Intel's Pentium family of chips and compatible products offered by AMD and other manufacturers. The 32-bit Pentium processor has its roots in the 16-bit 8086 chip and its accompanying 8087 floating-point coprocessor introduced by Intel in the late 1970s. As the need was felt for 32-bit machines, which among other things can handle wider memory addresses, Intel introduced the 80386 and 80486 processors before moving on to Pentium and its improved models identified by the suffixes II, III, and IV (or 4). The most recent versions of these chips not only contain the floating-point unit on the same chip but also have on-chip cache memories. Each model in this sequence of products introduces improvements and extensions to the previous model, but the core instruction-set architecture is not altered. At this writing, the 64-bit Itanium architecture has been introduced to further increase the addressable space and computational power of the Pentium series. While Itanium is not a simple extension of the Pentium, it is designed to be able to run programs written for the latter. Power PC, made by IBM and Motorola, which derives its fame from incorporation in Apple computers, is an example of modern RISC processors (see Chapter 8). Other examples of this category include products from MIPS and the DEC/Compaq Alpha processor.

As a result of denser and thus faster electronic circuits, along with architectural enhancements, processor performance has been growing exponentially. Moore's law predicting a factor of 1.6 improvement in component density per year is also applicable to the trend in processor performance measured in executed instructions per second (IPS). Figure 3.10 shows this trend along with data points for some key processors (Intel Pentium and its 80x86 predecessors, Motorola 68000 series, and MIPS R10000). Moore's law, when applied to memory chips, predicts capacity improvement by a factor of 4 every 3 years (memory chip capacity is almost always an even power of 2; hence, the appropriateness of the factor-of-4 formulation). Figure 3.10 shows the memory chip trend since 1980 and its projection over the next few years. With the gigabit chip (128 MB), the memory needs of a typical PC fit on one or a handful of chips. The next short-term challenge is putting processor and memory on the same device, thus enabling a personal computer composed of a single chip.

Processor and memory chips must of course be connected to each other and to the other parts of the computer depicted in Figure 3.7. Various packaging schemes are used for this purpose, depending on the computer type and cost/performance targets. The most common form of packaging is depicted in Figure 3.11a. Memory chips are mounted on small printed-circuit (PC) boards known as *daughter cards.* One or more such cards, often with a single row of connecting pins (single in-line memory modules or SIMMs), are then mounted on the *motherboard* that holds the processor, the system bus, various interfaces, and a variety of connectors. All the circuitry for a small computer might fit on a single motherboard, whereas larger machines might require multiple such boards mounted in a *chassis* or *card cage* and interconnected through a *backplane.* The single motherboard, or chassis holding multiple boards, is then packaged with peripheral devices, power supply, cooling fan, and other required components in a box or cabinet, leaving sufficient space inside for future expansion.

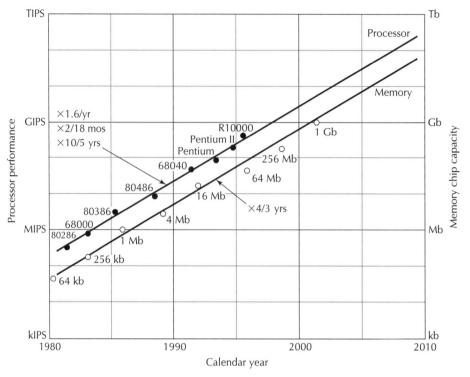

Figure 3.10 Trends in processor performance and DRAM memory chip capacity (Moore's law).

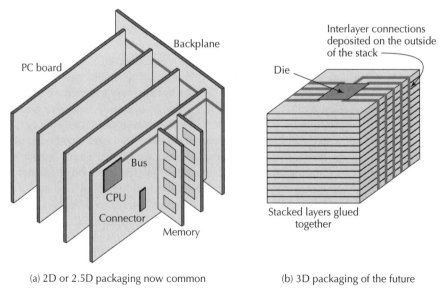

(a) 2D or 2.5D packaging now common   (b) 3D packaging of the future

Figure 3.11 Packaging of processor, memory, and other components.

Virtually all the 10^{18} or so transistors estimated to have been incorporated into integrated circuits to date have been built on "ground level," directly on the surface of silicon crystals. Just as one can increase population density in a city by resorting to multistory and high-rise buildings, it is possible to fit more transistors into a given volume by using 3D packaging [Lee02]. Research is continuing on 3D packaging technologies and products incorporating these technologies have begun to emerge. One promising scheme under consideration (Figure 3.11b) allows direct linking of components through connectors deposited on the exterior of a 3D cube formed by stacking 2D integrated circuits, thereby removing much of the bulk and cost of current methods.

The dramatic improvements in processor performance and memory chip capacity have been accompanied by equally significant cost reductions. Both the computing power and memory capacity per unit cost (MIPS/$ or MFLOPS/$, MB/$) have increased exponentially over the past two decades and are expected to continue on this course for the near future. Up to a decade or so ago, we used to proclaim, jokingly, that soon we will have zero- or negative-cost components. Little did we know that by the turn of the twenty-first century, computer hardware was in fact being given away in anticipation of profits to be made from services and software products.

To drive home the significance of the aforementioned improvements in computer performance and the accompanying cost reductions, an interesting comparison is sometimes used. It is postulated that if the aviation industry had advanced at the same rate as the computer industry, traveling from the United States to Europe would now take a few seconds and cost a few pennies. A similar analogy, applied to the auto industry, leads to the expectation of being able to buy a luxury car that travels as fast as a jetliner and runs forever on a single tank of gas for the same price as a cup of coffee. Unfortunately, the reliability of application and system software has not improved at the same rate, leading to the counterstatement that had the computer industry developed in the same way as the transportation industry, the Windows operating system would crash no more than once in a century!

3.5 Peripherals, I/O, and Communications

The present state of computing would not have been possible just with the improvements in processor performance and memory density discussed in Section 3.4. Phenomenal progress in input/output technologies, from printers and scanners to mass storage units and communication interfaces, has played an equally important role. Today's $100 hard disk that fits easily in the thinnest of notebook computers can store as much data as a roomful of cabinets packed with dozens of very expensive disks of the 1970s vintage. Input/output devices are discussed in greater detail in Chapter 21. Here, we present a brief overview of I/O device types and their capabilities with the aim of completing the broad-brush picture of modern computer technology. The main categories of I/O devices are listed in Table 3.3. Note that punched-card and paper-tape readers, printing terminals, magnetic drums, and other devices not in current use have not been listed.

Input devices can be categorized in various ways. Table 3.3 uses the type of input data as the main characteristic. Input data types include symbols from a finite alphabet, position information, identity checks, sensory information, audio signals, still images, and video. Within each class, prime examples and additional examples are provided, along with typical data rates and main application domains. Slow input devices are those that do not produce a lot of data and thus do not need a great deal of computing power to be serviced. For example, the peak

■ **TABLE 3.3** Some input, output, and two-way I/O devices.

Input type	Prime examples	Other examples	Data rate (b/s)	Main uses
Symbol	Keyboard, keypad	Music note, OCR	10s	Ubiquitous
Position	Mouse, touchpad	Stick, wheel, glove	100s	Ubiquitous
Identity	Barcode reader	Badge, fingerprint	100s	Sales, security
Sensory	Touch, motion, light	Scent, brain signal	100s	Control, security
Audio	Microphone	Phone, radio, tape	1000s	Ubiquitous
Image	Scanner, camera	Graphic tablet	1000s-millions	Photos, publishing
Video	Camcorder, DVD	VCR, TV cable	1000s-billions	Entertainment

Output type	Prime examples	Other examples	Data rate (b/s)	Main uses
Symbol	LCD line segments	LED, status light	10s	Ubiquitous
Position	Stepper motor	Robotic motion	100s	Ubiquitous
Warning	Buzzer, bell, siren	Flashing light	A few	Safety, security
Sensory	Braille text	Scent, brain stimulus	100s	Personal assistance
Audio	Speaker, audiotape	Voice synthesizer	1000s	Ubiquitous
Image	Monitor, printer	Plotter, microfilm	1000s	Ubiquitous
Video	Monitor, TV screen	Film/video recorder	1000s-billions	Entertainment

Two-way I/O	Prime examples	Other examples	Data rate (b/s)	Main uses
Mass storage	Hard/compact disk	Floppy, tape, archive	Millions	Ubiquitous
Network	Modem, fax, LAN	Cable, DSL, ATM	1000s-billions	Ubiquitous

input rate from a keyboard is limited by how fast humans can type. Assuming 100 words (500 bytes) per minute, a data rate of about 67 b/s is obtained. A modern processor could handle incoming data from millions of keyboards, if required. At the other extreme, high-quality video input may require the capture of millions of pixels per frame, each encoded in 24 bits (8 bits per primary color), say, at a rate of 100 frames per second. This translates to a data rate of billions of bits per second and challenges the power of the fastest computers available today.

Output devices have been similarly categorized in Table 3.3, with the category in the "identity" row replaced by "warning." Theoretically, activation of an alarm needs a single bit and thus represents the slowest possible I/O rate. Again, at the high end, real-time video output may require a data rate of billions of bits per second. A high-speed printer, printing dozens of color pages per minute, is somewhat less demanding. For both video and still images, the data rate can be reduced through image compression. However, compression affects only the data transmission and buffering rates between the computer and printer; at some point, on the computer side and/or within the print engine controller, the full data rate implied by the number of pixels to be transferred unto paper must be handled. Note that a single megapixel color image needs about 3 MB of storage. Many modern computers have a dedicated video memory of this size or larger. This allows for an entire screen image to be stored and data transfer from the CPU limited only to the elements that change from one image to the next. Most I/O devices listed in Table 3.3 are in common use today; a few are considered exotic or at an experimental stage (glove for 3D location/motion input, input or output of scents, detection or generation of brain signals). However, even these are expected to achieve mainstream status in the near future.

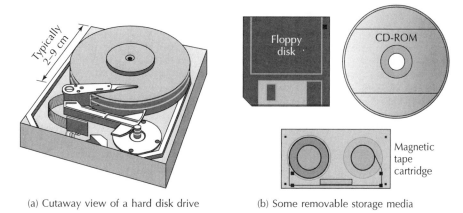

(a) Cutaway view of a hard disk drive   (b) Some removable storage media

Figure 3.12 Magnetic and optical memory units.

Certain two-way devices can be used for both input and output. Chief among these are mass storage units and network interfaces. Hard and floppy magnetic disks, as well as optical disks (CD-ROM, CD-RW, DVD), work more or less on the same principles. These devices (Figure 3.12) read or record data along densely packed concentric tracks on the surface of a rotating disk platter. On hard disks, a read/write mechanism, which can move radially on the disk surface, is aligned with the desired track and the data read out or recorded on the fly as the appropriate part of the track passes under the head. These simple principles have been in use for decades. What makes today's mass storage units marvels of modern technology is their ability to detect and correctly handle bits of data packed so tightly together that a single dust particle under the head might wipe out thousands of bits. Over the years, the diameter of magnetic disk memories has shrunk more than tenfold, from tens of centimeters to a few centimeters. Given this 100^+-fold shrinkage in recording area, increases in capacity from mere megabytes to many gigabytes are even more remarkable. Speed improvements have been less impressive and have been achieved through faster actuators for moving the heads (which now need to travel shorter distances) and greater rotation speeds. Floppy and other removable-type disks are similar except that due to the lesser precision (leading to lower recording density) and slower rotation, they are both slower and smaller in capacity.

Increasingly, our inputs arrive via communication lines, rather than from conventional input devices, and our outputs are written to data files that are accessed through a network. It is not uncommon for a printer located next to a computer in an office to be connected to it not directly by means of a printer cable, but rather via a local-area network. Through a computer network, machines can communicate with each other as well as with a variety of peripherals such as file servers, appliances, control devices, and entertainment equipment. Figure 3.13 shows the two key characteristics of bandwidth and latency for a variety of communication systems, from high-bandwidth buses that are less than 1-m long to wide-area networks that span the globe. Computers and other devices communicate through a network by means of network interface units. Special protocols are followed to ensure that diverse hardware devices can understand the data being transmitted correctly and consistently. Modems of various types (phone line, DSL, cable), network interface cards, switches, and routers take part in relaying the data from a source to the desired destination through connections of many different types (copper wires, optical fibers, wireless channels) and network gateways.

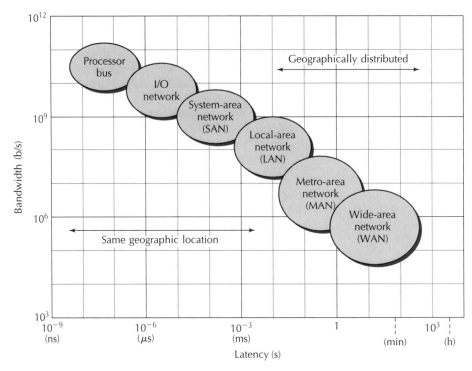

Figure 3.13 Latency and bandwidth characteristics of different classes of communication links.

■ 3.6 Software Systems and Applications

Instructions that are understood by computer hardware are encoded as strings of 0s and 1s and are thus indistinguishable from numbers on which they might operate. A set of such instructions constitute a *machine language program* that specifies a step-by-step computational process (Figure 3.14, right end). Early digital computers were programmed in machine language, a cumbersome process that was acceptable only because programs in those days were quite simple. Subsequent developments led to the invention of *assembly language,* which allows symbolic representation of machine language programs, and high-level procedural languages that resemble mathematical notation. These more abstract representations, along with translation software (*assemblers* and *compilers*) for automatic conversion of programs to machine language, significantly simplified program development and increased programmer productivity. Much of user-level computing nowadays is done through very-high-level notations that possess a great deal of expressive power for specific domains of interest. Examples include word processing, image editing, drawing logic diagrams, and producing graphs or charts. These abstraction levels in programming, and the process of going from each level to the next lower level, are depicted in Figure 3.14.

As shown in Figure 3.15, computer software can be divided into the classes of *application software* and *system software*. Application software encompasses word processors, spreadsheet programs, circuit simulators, and many other programs that are designed to tackle

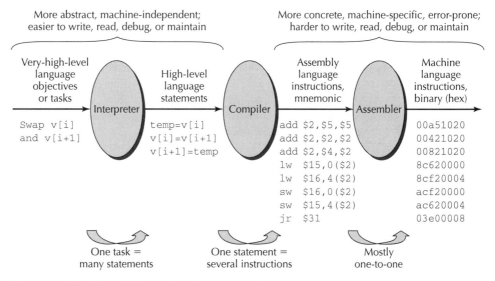

Figure 3.14 Models and abstractions in programming.

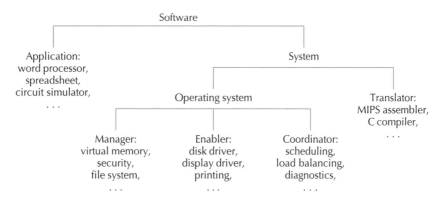

Figure 3.15 Categorization of software, with examples in each class.

specific tasks of interest to users. System software in turn is divided into programs that translate or interpret instructions written in various notational systems (such as MIPS assembly language, or C programming language) and those that provide managerial, enabling, or coordination functions for programs and system resources.

These are functionalities that are required by a great majority of computer users and are thus incorporated into the *operating system*. Details of operating system functions are found in many textbooks on the subject (see the references at the end of the chapter). We will discuss some of these topics briefly in subsequent chapters of this book: virtual memory and some aspects of security in Chapter 20, file systems and disk drivers in Chapter 19, I/O device drivers in Chapters 21 and 22, and certain aspects of coordination in Chapters 23 and 24.

PROBLEMS

3.1 Defining computer architecture

It is year 2010 and you have been asked to write a one-page article on computer architecture for a children's encyclopedia of science and technology. How would you describe computer architecture to grade-school children? You are allowed to use one diagram if necessary.

3.2 The role of an architect

Add one more word before each of the four ellipses in Figure 3.2.

3.3 The central place of computer architecture

In Figure 3.1, the computer designer, or architect, occupies a central position. This is no accident; we like to view ourselves or our professions as central. Witness the map of the world as drawn by Americans (North and South America at the center, flanked by Europe, Africa, and parts of Asia on the right, with the rest of Asia plus Oceania on the left) and by Europeans (the Americas on the left and all of Asia on the right).

a. Had this been a book on logic circuits, you might have seen the equivalent of Figure 3.1, with logic designer in the middle. Describe what we might then see in the two blobs on each side.
b. Repeat part a for a book on electronic circuits.

3.4 Complex man-made systems

Computer systems are certainly among the most complex man-made systems.

a. Name a few systems that you think are more complex than a modern digital computer. Elaborate on your complexity criteria.
b. Which of these systems, if any, has led to a separate field of study in science or engineering?

3.5 Multiples of units

Assuming that X is the symbol for an arbitrary power-of-10 multiple in Table 3.1, what is the maximum relative error if one mistakenly uses X_b instead of X, or vice versa?

3.6 Embedded computers

One function frequently needed in embedded control applications is analog-to-digital (A/D) conversion. Study this problem and prepare a two-page report on your findings. The report should include:

a. At least one way of performing the conversion, including a hardware diagram
b. Description of one application for which A/D conversion is needed
c. A discussion of the accuracy of the conversion process and its implications

3.7 Personal computers

List all the reason that you can imagine for a laptop or notebook computer being so much smaller than a desktop computer of comparable computational power.

3.8 Supercomputers

Find out as much information as you can about the most powerful supercomputer currently in existence and write a two-page report about it. Begin your study with [Top500] and include the following.

a. Criteria that led to ranking the supercomputer as the most powerful.
b. Company or organization that built the machine and its motivation/customer.
c. Identity and relative computational power of its closest competitor.

3.9 Parts of a computer

Name one or more human organs that have functions similar to those associated with each part in Figure 3.7.

3.10 History of digital computing

Charles Babbage, who lived some two centuries ago, is generally regarded as the (grand)father of digital computing. Yet, many believe that digital computing has much older roots.

a. Study the article [deSo84] and prepare a two-page essay on the topic.
b. Using a modern electronic calculator and a few of the machines described in [deSo84], plot the

trends in size, cost, and speed of calculating machines over the centuries.

3.11 The future of pocket/desk calculators

The abacus, though still in use in certain remote areas, has become a museum piece in much of the world. The slide rule became obsolete in much shorter time. What do you think will become of today's pocket and desk calculators? Do you think they will still be in use in the year 2020? Discuss.

3.12 Babbage's planned machine

Charles Babbage planned to build a machine that could multiply 50-digit numbers in less than one minute.

a. Compare the speed of Babbage's machine to that of a human calculator. Can you compare the two with regard to reliability?
b. Repeat the comparisons of part a with a modern digital computer.

3.13 Cost trends

Plotting the cost of a computer per unit of computational power, we get a sharply declining curve. Zero-cost computers are already here. Can you envisage negative-cost machines in future? Discuss.

3.14 Yield variation with die size

Figure 3.9 and Example 3.1 show the effect of increasing the die size from 1×1 cm^2 to 2×2 cm^2.

a. With the same assumptions as in Example 3.1, calculate the yield and relative die cost for 3×3 square dies.
b. Repeat part a for 2×4 rectangular dies.

3.15 Effects of yield on die cost

A wafer containing 100 copies of a complex processor die costs $900 to manufacture. The area occupied by each processor is 2 cm^2 and the defect

density is 2/cm^2. What is the manufacturing cost per die?

3.16 Number of dies on a wafer

Consider a circular wafer of diameter d. The number of square dies of side u on the wafer is upper-bounded by $\pi d^2/(4u^2)$. The actual number will be smaller because there are incomplete dies at the edge.

a. Argue that $\pi d^2/(4u^2) - \pi d/(1.414u)$ is a fairly accurate estimate for the number of dies.
b. Apply the formula of part a to the wafers shown in Figure 3.9 to obtain an estimate for the number of dies and determine the error in each case. The dies are 1×1 and 2×2 and $d = 14$.
c. Suggest and justify a formula that would work for nonsquare $u \times v$ dies (e.g., 1×2 cm^2).

3.17 Processor and memory technologies

Find performance and capacity data on the latest processor and DRAM memory chips. Mark the corresponding points in Figure 3.10. How good is the fit to the extrapolated lines? Do these new points indicate any slowdown in the rate of progress? Discuss.

3.18 Computer packaging

We plan to build a 4096-node parallel computer. The nodes are organized as a $16 \times 16 \times 16$ 3D mesh, with each node connected to six neighbors (two along each dimension). We can fit 8 nodes on a custom VLSI chip, and 16 chips can be placed on a printed-circuit board.

a. Devise a partitioning scheme for the parallel computer that will minimize the number of off-chip, off-board, and off-chassis links.
b. Considering the packaging scheme of Figure 3.11a and the partitioning suggested in part a, would we be able to accommodate 8-bit-wide channels between neighboring processors?
c. Does the 3D packaging scheme of Figure 3.11b offer any benefits for this design?

REFERENCES AND FURTHER READINGS

[Alla02]   Allan, A. et al., "2001 Technology Roadmap for Semiconductors," *IEEE Computer,* Vol. 35, No. 1, pp. 42–53, January 2002.

[deSo84]   de Solla Price, D., "A History of Calculating Machines," *IEEE Micro,* Vol. 4, No. 1, pp. 22–52, February 1984.

[Lee02]   Lee, T. H., "Vertical Leap for Microchips," *Scientific American,* Vol. 286, No. 1, pp. 52–59, January 2002.

[Raba96]   Rabaey, J. M., *Digital Integrated Circuits: A Design Perspective,* Prentice Hall, 1996.

[Rand82]   Randell, B. (ed.), *The Origins of Digital Computers: Selected Papers,* Springer-Verlag, 3rd ed., 1982.

[SIA00]   Semiconductor Industry Association, *International Technology Roadmap for Semiconductors,* San Jose, CA, 2000 update. http://public.itrs.net/

[Stal03]   Stallings, W., *Computer Organization and Architecture,* Prentice Hall, 6th ed., 2003.

[Tane01]   Tanenbaum, A., *Modern Operating Systems,* Prentice Hall, 2nd ed., 2001.

[Top500]   Top 500 Supercomputer Sites, a Web site maintained by University of Mannheim and University of Tennessee. http://www.top500.org/

[Wilk95]   Wilkes, M. V., *Computing Perspectives,* Morgan Kaufmann, 1995.

[Wu00]   Wu, L. et al., "The Advent of 3D Package Age," *Proceedings of the International Electronics Manufacturing Technology Symposium,* 2000, pp. 102–107.

CHAPTER 4

COMPUTER PERFORMANCE

"Peak performance: a level of performance that is guaranteed to be greater than the performance actually achieved."
—*From the Computing Folklore, source unknown*

"The Fast drives out the Slow even if the Fast is wrong."
—*William Kahan*

TOPICS IN THIS CHAPTER

4.1 Cost, Performance, and Cost/Performance

4.2 Defining Computer Performance

4.3 Performance Enhancement and Amdahl's Law

4.4 Performance Measurement vs Modeling

4.5 Reporting Computer Performance

4.6 The Quest for Higher Performance

In Chapters 1–3, we acquired the needed background to study computer architecture. The last item to consider before delving into details of our topic is computer performance. We tend to equate "performance" with "speed," but this is at best a simplistic view. There are many aspects to performance. Understanding all these aspects helps us make sense of the various design decisions encountered in the forthcoming chapters. For many years, performance has been the key driving force behind advances in computer architecture. It is still quite important, but given that modern processors have performance to spare for most run-of-the-mill applications, other parameters such as cost, compactness, and power economy are quickly gaining in significance.

■ 4.1 Cost, Performance, and Cost/Performance

A great deal of work in computer architecture deals with methods for improving machine performance. We will encounter examples of such methods in the forthcoming chapters. Virtually all design decisions in building computers, from the instruction-set design to the use of implementation techniques such as pipelining, branch prediction, cache memories, and parallelism, if not primarily motivated by performance enhancement, are at least made with an eye toward it. Given this focus, it is important for us to have a precise working definition for performance, know its relationships with other aspects of computer quality and usefulness, and learn how it can be quantified for comparison purposes and trade-off decisions.

A second key attribute of a computer system is its cost. In any given year, we can probably design and build a computer that is faster than the fastest commercially available computer. However, the cost might be so prohibitive that this ultimate machine either is never built or is built in very small numbers for agencies that are interested in advancing the state of the art and do not mind spending an exorbitant amount to achieve this goal. Thus, the highest-performance machine that is technologically feasible might never materialize because it is *cost-ineffective* (has an unacceptably high *cost/performance ratio*). It would be highly simplistic to equate the cost of a computer with its purchase price. One should instead try to evaluate its *life-cycle cost,* which includes upgrading, maintenance, usage, and other recurring costs. Note that a computer that we buy for $2000 has different costs depending on our point of view. It may have cost $1500 to the manufacturer (for hardware components, software licenses, labor, shipping, advertising), with the extra $500 covering sales commissions and profit. It may cost us $4000 over its lifetime once we add in service, insurance, additional software, hardware upgrades, and so on.

To appreciate that computer performance is multifaceted and any single indicator provides at best an approximate picture of it, we use an analogy with passenger planes. In Table 4.1, six commercial passenger aircraft are characterized by their passenger capacity, cruising range, cruising speed, and purchase price. Based on the data in Table 4.1, which of these aircraft would you say has the highest performance? You would be justified to answer this question by another one: Performance from whose viewpoint?

A passenger interested in minimizing her travel time might equate performance with cruising speed. The Concorde clearly wins in this regard (ignore the fact that the Concorde is no longer in service). Note that because of the time taken by aircraft preparation, taxiing, takeoff, and landing, the travel time advantage is lower than the ratio of speeds. Now suppose that a passenger's destination city is 8750 km away. Ignoring pre- and postflight delays for simplicity, we find that DC-8-50 would get there in 10 hours. Concorde's flight time would be only 4 hours, but some of its advantage disappears once the mandatory stop for refueling is factored in. For the same reason, the DC-8-50 is very likely better than the faster Boeing 747 or 777 for flights whose distances exceed the range of the latter.

And this was just the passenger's view. An airline might be more interested in *throughput,* defined as the product of passenger capacity and speed (we will deal with cost issues shortly).

■ **TABLE 4.1** Key characteristics of six passenger aircraft: all figures are approximate; some relate to a specific model/configuration of the aircraft or are averages of cited range of values.

Aircraft	Passengers	Range (km)	Speed (km/h)	Price* ($M)
Airbus A310	250	8,300	895	120
Boeing 747	470	6,700	980	200
Boeing 767	250	12,300	885	120
Boeing 777	375	7,450	980	180
Concorde	130	6,400	2200	350
DC-8-50	145	14,000	875	80

*Prices are derived through extrapolation and some guesswork. Passenger planes are often sold at deep discounts from list prices. Some models, like the now retired Concorde, are no longer in production or were never sold in the open market.

If airfare were proportional to the distance flown, which in the real world it is not, throughput would represent the airline's income from ticket sales. Our six planes have throughputs of 0.224, 0.461, 0.221, 0.368, 0.286, and 0.127 million passenger-kilometers per hour, respectively, with the Boeing 747 exhibiting the highest throughput. Finally, performance from the viewpoint of the Federal Aviation Administration is primarily related to a plane's safety record.

Of course performance is never viewed in isolation. Very few people considered the travel time advantage of the Concorde worth its much higher airfare. Similarly, very few airlines were willing to pay the Concorde's higher purchase price. For this reason, combined indicators of performance and cost are of interest. Suppose performance is specified by a numerical indicator so that higher values of this indicator are preferable (aircraft speed is an example). Then, *cost/performance,* defined as the cost of a unit of performance, or its inverse, the performance achieved per unit cost, can be used to compare the *cost-effectiveness* of various systems. So, equating performance with throughput and cost with the purchase price, the cost/performance figures of merit for the six aircraft in Table 4.1 are 536, 434, 543, 489, 1224, and 630, respectively, with smaller values deemed better.

The foregoing comparison is of course quite simplistic; the cost of an aircraft to an airline involves not just its purchase price but also fuel economy, parts availability/price, frequency/ease of maintenance, safety-related costs (e.g., insurance), and so on. For all practical purposes, the cost factor for a passenger is simply the airfare. Note that such a composite measure is even less precise than performance or cost alone because it incorporates two hard-to-quantify factors.

A final observation regarding our airplane analogy is in order. The higher performance of a system is of interest only if one can truly benefit from it. For example, if you were traveling from Boston to London and the Concorde flew out of New York only, then its higher speed might have had no significance to you for this particular trip. In computing terms, this is akin to a new 64-bit architecture offering no benefit when the bulk of your applications have been designed for older 32-bit machines. Similarly, if you want to go from Boston to New York, the flight time is such a small fraction of the total time spent that it won't make much difference whether your aircraft is a Boeing 777 or a DC-8-50. For the computing analog of this situation, consider that at times replacing a computer's processor with a faster one will not have a significant impact on performance because performance is limited by memory or I/O bandwidth.

Plotting performance against cost (Figure 4.1) reveals three types of trend. Superlinear growth of performance with cost indicates *economy of scale:* if you pay twice as much for

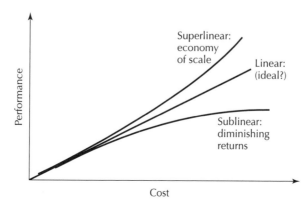

Figure 4.1 Performance improvement as a function of cost.

something, you get more than twice the performance. This was the case in the early days of digital computers when large supercomputers could perform significantly more computations per dollar spent than smaller machines. Today, however, we often observe a sublinear trend. As we add more and more hardware to a system, some of the theoretically possible performance is lost to management and coordination mechanisms needed to run the more complex system. Similarly, a leading-edge processor that costs twice as much as an older model may not offer twice as much performance. With this type of trend, we soon reach a point of *diminishing returns* beyond which further investment does not buy us much in performance. In this context, linear performance improvement with cost may be considered an ideal to strive for.

4.2 Defining Computer Performance

As users, we expect a higher-performing computer to run our application programs faster. In fact, the execution time of programs, whether long-running computations or simple commands to which the computer must react immediately, is a universally accepted indicator of performance. Because longer execution time implies lower performance, we might write:

Performance = 1/Execution time

So, a computer that executes a program in half the time taken by another machine has twice the performance. All other indicators are at best approximations to performance that are used because we cannot measure or predict the execution times for real programs. Possible reasons include lack of knowledge about exactly which programs will be run on the machine, cost of porting programs to a new system for the sole purpose of comparative evaluation, and need to assess a computer that has not yet been built or is otherwise unavailable for experimentation.

As with the airplane analogy in Section 4.1, there are other views of performance. For example, a computer center that sells machine time to a variety of users might consider *computational throughput,* the total amount of tasks performed per unit time, to be more relevant because it directly affects the center's revenues. In fact, the execution of certain programs may be purposely delayed if this leads to better overall throughput. The strategy of a shuttle bus whose driver chooses the passenger drop-off order to minimize the total service time is a good analogy for this situation. Practically speaking, execution time and throughput are not completely independent in that improving one usually (but not always) leads to an improvement in the other. For this reason, in the rest of our discussion, we focus on the user's perception of performance, which is the inverse of execution time.

In fact, a user might be concerned not with the program execution time per se but with the total *response time* or *turnaround time,* which includes additional latency attributable to scheduling decisions, work interruptions, I/O queuing delays, and so on. This is sometimes referred to as *wall clock time* because it can be measured by looking at a wall clock at the start and termination of a task. To filter out the effects of such highly variable and hard-to-quantify factors, we sometime use the *CPU execution time* to define user-perceived performance:

Performance = 1/CPU execution time

This renders our evaluation much more manageable in cases that entail analytic, rather than experimental, evaluation methods (see Section 4.4). Such a view does not lead to any inaccuracy for computation-intensive tasks that do not involve much I/O. For such *CPU-bound tasks,* processing power is the bottleneck. I/O-bound tasks, on the other hand, will be

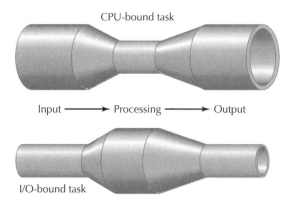

CPU-bound task

Input ⟶ Processing ⟶ Output

Figure 4.2 Pipeline analogy shows that imbalance between processing power and I/O capabilities leads to a performance bottleneck.

I/O-bound task

ill-served if only CPU execution time is taken into account (Figure 4.2). For a balanced system that has no bottleneck, we would not err too much if we considered only the CPU execution time in our evaluation of performance. Note that system balance is absolutely essential. If one replaces a machine's processor with a model having twice the performance, this will not double the overall system performance unless corresponding improvements are made to other parts of the system (memory, system bus, I/O, etc.). We mention in passing that doubling processor performance does not mean replacing an x GHz processor with a $2x$ GHz one; we will see shortly that the clock frequency is but one of several factors affecting performance.

When one is comparing two machines M_1 and M_2, the notion of relative performance comes into play.

(Performance of M_1)/(Performance of M_2)
= Speedup of M_1 over M_2
= (Execution time of M_2)/(Execution time M_1)

Note that performance and execution time vary in opposite directions. To improve execution time, we must lower it; improving performance is synonymous with raising it. We tend to favor the use of "improve" over other terms because it allows us to apply a common term for many different strategies that impact performance indicators, regardless of whether the indicator must go up or down for better performance.

The comparative performance measure just defined is a dimensionless ratio such as 1.5 or 0.8. It indicates that machine M_1 offers x times the performance, or is x times as fast, as another machine M_2. When $x > 1$, we can express the relative performance in one of two equivalent ways:

M_1 is x times as fast as M_2 (e.g., 1.5 times as fast).

M_1 is $100(x - 1)\%$ faster than M_2 (e.g., 50% faster).

Failing to differentiate these two presentation methods is a fairly common error. So, remember, a machine that is 200% faster is not twice as fast but three times as fast. More generally, $y\%$ faster means $1 + y/100$ times as fast.

Each time we run a given program, a number of machine instructions are executed. This number is often different from one run to another, but let us assume that we know the average number of instructions executed over many runs of the program. Note that this number may have little to do with the number of instructions in the program code. The latter is the *static instruction count,* whereas we are interested in the *dynamic instruction count,* which is usually much greater than the static count owing to loops and repeated calls to some procedures. The execution of each instruction takes a certain number of clock cycles. Again, the number is different for various instructions and may in fact depend not only on the instruction but also the context (instructions executed before and after a given instruction). Let's assume we have an average value for this parameter as well. Finally, each clock cycle represents a fixed time duration. For example, the cycle time of a 2 GHz clock is 0.5 ns. The product of these three factors yields an estimate of the CPU execution time for our program:

$$\text{CPU execution time} = \text{Instructions} \times (\text{Cycles per instruction}) \times (\text{Seconds per cycle})$$
$$= \text{Instructions} \times \text{CPI}/(\text{Clock rate})$$

where CPI stands for "cycles per instruction" and clock rate, expressed in cycles per second, is the inverse of "seconds per cycle."

The three parameters instruction count, CPI, and clock rate are not completely independent, so improving one by a given factor may not lead to an overall improvement in execution time by the same factor.

Instruction count depends on the instruction-set architecture (which instructions are available) and how effectively the programmer or compiler uses them. Instruction-set issues are discussed in Part II of the book.

CPI depends on the instruction-set architecture and hardware organization. Most organizational issues that directly influence CPI are introduced in Part IV of the book, with concepts covered in Part III also being relevant.

Clock rate depends on hardware organization and implementation technology. Some aspects of technology affecting the clock rate were covered in Chapters 1–3. Other issues will come up in Parts III and IV.

To give just one example of these interdependencies, consider the effect of rising clock rates on performance. If the clock rate of an Intel Pentium processor is improved by a factor of 2, the performance will likely improve but not necessarily by the same factor. Given that different models of the Pentium processor use substantially the same instruction set (with the occasional extensions introduced not a factor if we continue to run preexisting programs), performance would double only if CPI remains the same. Unfortunately, however, rising clock rates are often accompanied by an increase in CPI. We will learn the reasons for this increase in Part IV. Here, we just point out that one technique for accommodating higher clock rates is to divide the instruction execution process into a larger number of steps within a deeper pipeline. The penalty in clock cycles for stalling or flushing such a pipeline, which would be needed in cases of data and control dependencies or cache misses, is proportional to its depth. Hence, CPI is an increasing function of the pipeline depth.

The effect of clock rate on performance is even harder to judge when one is comparing machines with different instruction-set architectures. Figure 4.3 uses an analogy to convey this difficulty. Doubling of clock rate is the analog of one person taking steps twice as fast as another. However, if the faster-stepping person needs five times as many steps to go from point A to point B, his travel time will be 2.5 times as long. Based on this analogy, one should not be surprised if the vendor of an *x* GHz processor claims performance advantage over the 2*x* GHz processor of another company. Whether such a claim is accurate is another story; we will later see examples of how performance claims can be misleading or totally false.

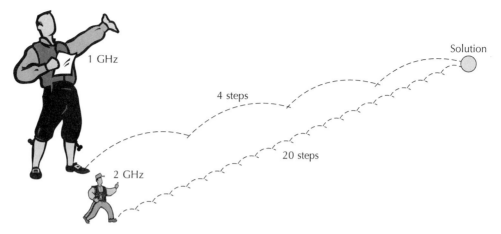

Figure 4.3 Faster steps do not necessarily mean shorter travel time.

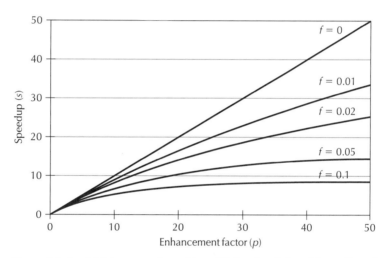

Figure 4.4 Amdahl's law: speedup achieved if a fraction f of a task is unaffected and the remaining $1 - f$ part runs p times as fast.

■ 4.3 Performance Enhancement and Amdahl's Law

Gene Amdahl, an architect of early IBM computers who later founded the company bearing his name, formulated his famous law (Figure 4.4) to point out some limitations of parallel processing. He asserted that programs contain certain computations that are inherently sequential and thus cannot be speeded up through parallel processing. If f represents the fraction of a program's running time due to such unparallelizable computations, even assuming that the remainder of the program enjoys the perfect speedup of p when run on p processors, the overall speedup would be:

$$s = \frac{1}{f + (1 - f)/p} \leq min\left(p, \frac{1}{f}\right) \qquad \text{[Amdahl's speedup formula]}$$

Here, the 1 in the numerator is the original running time of the program and $f + (1 - f)/p$ is the program's improved execution time with p processors. The latter is the sum of the running time for the unparallelizable fraction f and that of the remaining fraction $1 - f$, which now runs p times as fast. Note that the speedup s cannot exceed p (*linear speedup* achieved for $f = 0$) or $1/f$ (maximum speedup for $p = \infty$). Thus, for $f = 0.05$, one can never hope to achieve a speedup greater than 20, no matter how many processors are used.

Despite its original formulation in terms of the speedup that is possible with p processors, Amdahl's law is far more general and can be applied to any situation involving no change in the running time for a fraction f of a program and improvement by a factor p (not necessarily an integer) for the remaining part. This general interpretation suggests that if we leave a part of a program that accounts for a fraction f of its running time unchanged, no amount of improvement for the remaining $1 - f$ fraction will produce a speedup greater than $1/f$. For example, if floating-point arithmetic accounts for $1/3$ of a program's running time and we improve only the floating-point unit (i.e., $f = 2/3$), the overall speedup cannot exceed 1.5, no matter how much faster floating-point arithmetic becomes.

Example 4.1: Amdahl's law used in design   A processor chip is used for applications in which 30% of execution time is spent on floating-point addition, 25% on floating-point multiplication, and 10% on floating-point division. For the new model of the processor, the design team has come up with three possible enhancements, each costing roughly the same in design effort and manufacturing. Which one of these enhancements should be chosen?

 a. Redesign the floating-point adder to make it twice as fast.
 b. Redesign the floating-point multiplier to make it three times as fast.
 c. Redesign the floating-point divider to make it ten times as fast.

Solution: We can apply Amdahl's law to three options, using $f = 0.7$, $f = 0.75$, and $f = 0.9$, respectively, for the unmodified fraction in the three cases.

 a. Speedup for adder redesign $= 1/[0.7 + 0.3/2] = 1.18$
 b. Speedup for multiplier redesign $= 1/[0.75 + 0.25/3] = 1.20$
 c. Speedup for divider redesign $= 1/[0.9 + 0.1/10] = 1.10$

Thus, redesigning the floating-point multiplier offers the greatest performance advantage, although the difference with floating-point adder redesign is not great. One lesson we learn from this example is that the significant speedup of the divider is not worth the effort because of the relative rarity of floating-point divisions. In fact, even if we could make divisions infinitely fast, the speedup achieved would still be only 1.11.

Example 4.2: Amdahl's law used in management   Members of a university research group frequently go to the campus library to read or copy articles published in technical periodicals. Each trip to the library takes 20 minutes. An administrator orders subscriptions for a handful of periodicals that account for 90% of the trips to the library. For these periodicals, which now are kept in the group's private library, access time is reduced to 2 minutes on the average.

 a. What is the average speedup in accessing technical articles due to the subscriptions?
 b. If the group has 20 members, each making two weekly trips to the campus library on average, determine the annual expenditure that is financially justifiable for taking on the subscriptions. Assume 50 working weeks per year and an average worth of $25/h for a researcher's time.

Solution: We can apply Amdahl's law to this situation where 10% of the accesses are unchanged ($f = 0.1$) and the remaining 90% are speeded up by a factor of $p = 20/2 = 10$.

    a. Speedup in article access time $= 1/[0.1 + 0.9/10] = 5.26$

    b. The time saved by the subscriptions is $20 \times 2 \times 50 \times 0.9(20 - 2) = 32{,}400$ min $= 540$ h representing a cost recovery of $540 \times \$25 = \$13{,}500$; this is the amount that can be financially justified for the cost of subscriptions.

Note: This example is the analog of using a fast cache memory close to the processor with the goal of accessing frequently used data more quickly. Details will be covered in Chapter 18.

■ 4.4 Performance Measurement vs Modeling

The surest, most reliable method of performance evaluation is to run real programs of interest on candidate machines and measure the execution or CPU times. Figure 4.5 shows an example with three different machines being evaluated on six programs. Based on the evaluation data shown, machine 3 clearly comes out ahead because it has the shortest execution time for our six programs. Usually, however, the result is not so clear-cut, as is the case between machines 1 and 2 in Figure 4.5. Machine 1 is faster than machine 2 for two of the programs and slower for the other four. If we were to choose between machines 1 and 2 (say, because machine 3 is much more expensive or does not satisfy some other key requirement), we might attach weights to the programs and choose the machine for which the *weighted sum of execution times* is smaller. The weight for a program could be the number of times it is executed per month (based on collected data or a forecast). If, for example, all six programs are executed the same number of times, and are thus given equal weights, machine 2 will have a slight advantage over machine 1. If, on the other hand, program B or E constitutes the bulk of our *workload,* machine 1 will likely prevail. We will elaborate on methods for summarizing or reporting performance, and associated pitfalls, in Section 4.5.

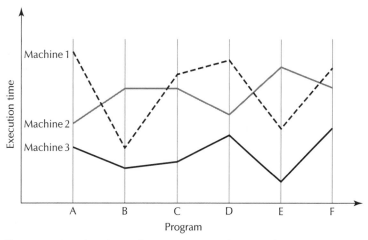

Figure 4.5 Running times of six programs on three machines.

Experimentation with real programs on real machines is not always feasible or economically viable. If you are planning to buy hardware, the candidate machines may not be accessible to you for extensive experimentation. Similarly, the programs you will be running may not be available or even known. You may have an idea that you will be running programs of certain types (company payroll, linear equation solver, graphic design, etc.); some of the required programs will have to be designed in-house and others will be outsourced. Remember that you should consider not only the current needs but also future ones. In such cases, evaluation might be based on *benchmarking* or *analytic modeling*.

Benchmarking

Benchmarks are real or synthetic programs that are selected or designed for comparative evaluation of machine performance. A *benchmark* suite is a collection of such programs intended to represent an entire class of applications and to foil any attempt to design hardware that would do well on a specific, more limited benchmark program (this is known as *designing to benchmarks*). Of course, benchmarking results are relevant to a user only if the programs in the suite closely resemble the programs that the user will run. Benchmarks facilitate comparison across different platforms and computer classes. They also make it possible for computer vendors and independent firms to evaluate many machines upon their entry into the market and to publish the benchmarking results for the benefit of users. In this way, the user may not need to perform any benchmarking at all.

Benchmarks are intended primarily for use when the hardware to be evaluated and the relevant compilers needed to run the programs in the suite are already available. Most compilers have optimization capabilities that can be turned on or off. Typically, to avoid tuning of the compiler differently for each program in the suite, it is required that the entire benchmark suite be run with a single setting of the optimization flags. It is also possible to use a benchmark suite, especially one with shorter programs, for evaluation of machines or compilers not yet available. For example, the programs in the suite might be hand-compiled and the results presented to a software simulator of the hardware being developed. Alternatively, instruction counts may be extracted from the hand-compiled code and used to evaluate performance in the manner outlined under analytic modeling that follows.

A fairly popular benchmark suite for evaluating workstations and servers includes integer and floating-point programs and is developed by the Standard Performance Evaluation Corporation (SPEC). The 2000 version of the SPEC CPU benchmark suite, known as SPECint2000 for the collection of 12 integer programs and SPECfp2000 for another set of 14 floating-point programs, is briefly characterized in Table 4.2. Instead of supplying absolute execution time data, it is common to report how much faster a machine ran the programs compared with some base machine; the larger this *SPEC ratio,* the greater the machine's performance. The ratio,

▇ **TABLE 4.2** Summary of SPEC CPU2000 benchmark suite characteristics.

Category	Program types	Program examples	Lines of code
SPECint2000	C programs (11) C++ program (1)	Data compression, C language compiler Computer visualization (ray tracing)	0.7k to 193k 34.2k
SPECfp2000	C programs (4) Fortran77 programs (6) Fortran90 programs (4)	3D graphics, computational chemistry Shallow water modeling, multigrid solver Image processing, finite-element method	1.2k to 81.8k 0.4k to 47.1k 2.4k to 59.8k

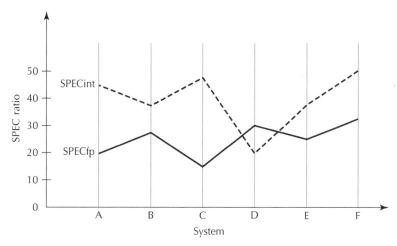

Figure 4.6 Example graphical depiction of SPEC benchmark results.

computed separately for SPECint and SPECfp, may then be plotted to visualize the differences between several machines, or for the same machine with different compilers or clock rates. Figure 4.6 shows example results for six different systems, where a system might be the combination of a processor with a given clock rate and cache/memory size, particular C and Fortran compilers with specific optimization setting, and known I/O capabilities.

Example 4.3: Performance benchmarks   You are an engineer at Outtel, a start-up company aspiring to compete with Intel via its new processor technology that outperforms the latest Intel processor by a factor of 2.5 on floating-point instructions. To achieve this level of floating-point performance, the design team had to make some compromises that led to a 20% average increase in execution times of all other instructions. You are in charge of choosing benchmarks that would showcase Outtel's performance edge.

    a. What is the minimum required fraction f of time spent on floating-point instructions in a program on the Intel processor to show a speedup of 2 or better for Outtel?

    b. If on the Intel processor, execution time of a floating-point instruction is on average three times as long as other instructions, what does the fraction in your answer to part a mean in terms of the instruction mix in the benchmark?

    c. What type of benchmark would Intel choose to counter your company's claims?

Solution: We use a generalized form of Amdahl's formula in which a fraction f is speeded up by a given factor and the rest is slowed down by another factor.

    a. Speedup factor $= 2.5$, slowdown factor $= 1.2 \Rightarrow 1/[1.2(1 - f) + f/2.5] \geq 2 \Rightarrow$ $f \geq 0.875$

    b. Let the instruction mix be x floating point and $1 - x$ other. Then, the total running time is proportional to $3x + (1 - x) = 2x + 1$. So, the fraction of running time due to floating-point operations is $3x/(2x + 1)$. Requiring that this fraction be greater than or equal to 0.875 leads to $x \geq 70\%$ (floating-point fraction in instruction mix).

    c. Intel would try to show a slowdown for Outtel: $1/[1.2(1 - f) + f/2.5] < 1 \Rightarrow f < 0.125$. In terms of the instruction mix, this means $3x/(2x + 1) < 0.125$ or $x < 4.5\%$.

Performance Estimation

It is possible to estimate machine performance without resorting to direct observation of the behavior of real programs or benchmarks executed on real hardware. Methods range from simplistic estimates to the use of very detailed models that capture the effects of design features in hardware and software. Performance models are of two main types. *Analytic models* use mathematical formulations to relate performance to some key, observable and quantifiable system or application parameters. *Simulation models* basically imitate the behavior of the system, often at a high level of abstraction to keep the model size and its processing time in check. The results obtained from any model are only as good as the faithfulness of the model in representing real-world capabilities, limitations, and interactions. It is a mistake to think that a more detailed model necessarily provides a more accurate estimate of performance. In fact, model complexity sometimes hinders understanding and thus leads to an inability to see how the effect of inaccuracy in estimating the model parameters might affect the final results.

The simplest performance estimation model is one that yields the system's *peak performance,* so named because it represents the absolute highest level of performance that one can ever hope to extract from the system. Peak performance of a computer is like a car's maximum speed and can be just as meaningless as a figure of merit for comparison purposes. Peak performance is often expressed in units of *instructions per second* or IPS, with MIPS and GIPS preferred to keep the numbers small. The advantage of peak performance is that it is easy to determine and report. For scientific and engineering applications that involve primarily floating-point calculations, *floating-point operations per second* (FLOPS) is used as the unit, again with megaflops (MFLOPS) and gigaflops (GFLOPS) preferred. A machine achieves its peak performance for an artificially constructed program that includes only instructions of the fastest kind. For example, on a machine that has instructions taking 1 and 2 clock cycles to execute, the peak performance is achieved if the program uses exclusively 1-cycle instructions, perhaps with a few 2-cycle instructions thrown in, if necessary, to form loops and other program constructs.

Somewhat more detailed, and also more realistic, is an analysis based on average CPIs (CPI was defined in Section 4.2). The average CPI can be calculated, given an instruction mix obtained from experimental studies. Such studies might examine a large number of typical programs to determine the proportion of various instruction classes, expressed as fractions that sum to 1. For example, Table 4.3 provides typical instruction mixes. If we choose instruction classes such that all instructions in the same class have the same CPI, we can compute the average CPI from the corresponding fractions:

$$\text{Average CPI} = \sum_{\text{All instruction classes}} (\text{Class-}i \text{ fraction}) \times (\text{Class-}i \text{ CPI})$$

■ **TABLE 4.3** Usage frequency, in percentage, for various instruction classes in four representative applications.

Application → Instruction class ↓	Data compression	C language compiler	Nuclear reactor simulation	Atomic motion modeling
A: Load/Store	25	37	32	37
B: Integer arithmetic	32	28	17	5
C: Shift/Logical	16	13	2	1
D: Floating-point	0	0	34	42
E: Branch	19	13	9	10
F: All others	8	9	6	4

Once the average CPI is known, we can pretend that all instructions have this common CPI and use the formula

CPU execution time = Instructions × (Average CPI)/(Clock rate)

derived in Section 4.2 for performance estimation.

Example 4.4: CPI and IPS calculations   Consider two different hardware implementations M_1 and M_2 of the same instruction set. There are three classes F, I, and N of instructions in the instruction set. M_1's clock rate is 600 MHz. M_2's clock cycle is 2 ns. The average CPI for the three instruction classes on M1 and M2 are as follows:

Class	CPI for M_1	CPI for M_2	Comments
F	5.0	4.0	Floating-point
I	2.0	3.8	Integer arithmetic
N	2.4	2.0	Nonarithmetic

a. What are the peak performances of M_1 and M_2 in MIPS?

b. If 50% of all instructions executed in a certain program are from class N, and the rest are divided equally among F and I, which machine is faster and by what factor?

c. Designers of M_1 plan to redesign the machine for better performance. With the assumptions of part b, which of the following redesign options has the greatest performance impact and why?

   1. Using a faster floating-point unit with double the speed (class-F CPI = 2.5).

   2. Adding a second integer ALU to reduce the integer CPI to 1.20.

   3. Using faster logic that allows a clock rate of 750 MHz with the same CPIs.

d. The CPIs given include the effect of instruction cache misses at an average rate of 5%. Each cache miss imposes a 10-cycle penalty (i.e., adds 10 to the effective CPI of the instruction causing the miss, or 0.5 cycle per instruction on the average). A fourth redesign option is to use a larger instruction cache that would reduce the miss rate from 5% to 3%. How does this compare to the three options in part c?

e. Characterize application programs that would run faster on M_1 than on M_2; that is, say as much as you can about the instruction mix in such applications. *Hint:* Let x, y, and $1 - x - y$ be the fraction of instructions belonging to classes F, I, and N, respectively.

Solution

a. Peak MIPS for M_1 = 600/2.0 = 300 (assume all class I)
   Peak MIPS for M_2 = 500/2.0 = 250 (assume all class N)

b. Average CPI for M_1 = 5.0/4 + 2.0/4 + 2.4/2 = 2.95
   Average CPI for M_2 = 4.0/4 + 3.8/4 + 2.0/2 = 2.95
   Average CPIs are the same, so M_1 is 1.2 times as fast as M_2 (ratio of clock rates).

c. 1. Average CPI = 2.5/4 + 2.0/4 + 2.4/2 = 2.325; MIPS for option 1 = 600/2.325 = 258
   2. Average CPI = 5.0/4 + 1.2/4 + 2.4/2 = 2.75; MIPS for option 2 = 600/2.75 = 218
   3. MIPS for option 3 = 750/2.95 = 254 ⇒ option 1 has the greatest impact.

d. With the larger cache, all CPIs are reduced by 0.2 owing to the lower cache miss rate.
   Average CPI = 4.8/4 + 1.8/4 + 2.2/2 = 2.75 ⇒ option 4 is comparable to option 2.

e. Average CPI for $M_1 = 5.0x + 2.0y + 2.4(1 - x - y) = 2.6x - 0.4y + 2.4$
Average CPI for $M_2 = 4.0x + 3.8y + 2.0(1 - x - y) = 2x + 1.8y + 2$
We are seeking conditions under which $600/(2.6x - 0.4y + 2.4) > 500/(2x + 1.8y + 2)$.
Thus, M_1 performs better than M_2 for $x/y < 12.8$. Roughly speaking, M_1 does better unless there is excessive floating-point arithmetic, for which M_1 is slightly slower, or too little integer arithmetic, for which M_2 is substantially slower (class-N instructions are immaterial because they execute at the same speed on both machines).

Example 4.5: MIPS rating can be misleading   Consider two compilers producing machine code for a given program to be run on the same machine. The machine's instructions are divided into class A ($CPI = 1$) and class B ($CPI = 2$). Machine language programs produced by the two compilers lead to the execution of the following number of instructions from each class:

Class	Instructions for compiler 1	Instructions for compiler 2	Comments
A	600M	400M	$CPI = 1$
B	400M	400M	$CPI = 2$

a. What are the execution times of the two programs, assuming a 1 GHz clock?
b. Which compiler produces faster code and by what factor?
c. Which compiler's machine language output runs at a higher MIPS rate?

Solution
a. Running time for the output of compiler 1 $= (600M \times 1 + 400M \times 2)/10^9 = 1.4$ s
   Running time for the output of compiler 2 $= (400M \times 1 + 400M \times 2)/10^9 = 1.2$ s
b. The code produced by compiler 2 is $1.4/1.2 = 1.17$ times as fast as that of compiler 1.
c. Average CPI for the output of compiler 1 $= (600M \times 1 + 400M \times 2)/1000M = 1.4$
   Average CPI for the output of compiler 2 $= (400M \times 1 + 400M \times 2)/800M = 1.5$
   So, the MIPS rating of compiler 1, which is $1000/1.4 = 714$, is somewhat higher than that for compiler 2, which is $1000/1.5 = 667$, even though according to our results in part a, the output of compiler 1 is decidedly inferior.

▨ 4.5 Reporting Computer Performance

Even with the best method chosen for performance measurement or modeling, care must be taken in the interpretation and reporting of the results. In this section, we review some of the difficulties in distilling performance data into a single numerical indicator.

Consider the execution times for three programs A, B, and C on two different machines X and Y, shown in Table 4.4. The data indicates that for program A, machine X is 10 times as fast as machine B, whereas for both B and C, the opposite is true. Our first attempt at summarizing this performance data might be to find the average of the three speedups and assert that machine Y is on average $(0.1 + 10 + 10)/3 = 6.7$ times as fast as machine X. This, however, is incorrect. The last row of Table 4.4 shows the total running times for the three programs and an overall speedup of 5.6, which would be the correct speedup to report if these programs are run the same number of times within our normal workload. If this last condition does not hold, then the

■ **TABLE 4.4** Measured or estimated execution times for three programs.

	Time on machine X	Time on machine Y	Speedup of Y over X
Program A	20	200	0.1
Program B	1000	100	10.0
Program C	1500	150	10.0
All three programs	2520	450	5.6

overall speedup must be computed by using weighted, rather than simple, sums. This example is quite similar to finding the average speed of a car that is driven to a city 100 km away at 100 km/h and on the return trip at 50 km/h; the average speed is not $(100 + 50)/2 = 75$ km/h but must be obtained from the fact that the car travels 200 km in 3 hours.

Because for SPEC benchmarks execution times are normalized to a reference machine rather than expressed in absolute terms, we should look at summarizing performance data in this case as well. For example, if in Table 4.4 we take X as the reference machine, then the normalized performance of Y is simply given by the speedup values in the rightmost column. We know from the preceding discussion that the average (arithmetic mean) of speedups (normalized execution times) is not the correct measure to use. We need a way of summarizing normalized execution times that is consistent and its outcome does not depend on the reference machine chosen. Arithmetic mean clearly lacks this property as well. Had we chosen Y as the reference machine, X would exhibit speedups of 10, 0.1, and 0.1 for programs A, B, and C, respectively. The average of these values is 3.4; not only did we not get the inverse of 6.7 (purported speedup of Y over X), but we arrived at the contradictory conclusion that each machine is faster than the other!

One solution to the aforementioned problem is to use the *geometric mean* instead of the arithmetic mean. The geometric mean of n values is the nth root of their product. Applying this method to the speedup values in Table 4.4, we get the single relative performance indicator of $(0.1 \times 10 \times 10)^{1/3} = 2.15$ for Y relative to X. Note that we do not call this the overall speedup of Y over X because it is not; it is simply an indicator that moves in the right direction in the sense that larger values correspond to higher performance. Had we used Y as the reference machine, the relative performance indicator for X would have become $(10 \times 0.1 \times 0.1)^{1/3} = 0.46$. This is now consistent, because 0.46 is the approximate inverse of 2.15. This consistency arises from the fact that the ratio of geometric means is the same as the geometric mean of ratios.

Using geometric mean solves the consistency problem but creates another problem: the numbers derived have no direct relationship to execution times and may in fact be quite misleading. Consider, for example, only programs A and B in Table 4.4. Based on these two programs, machines X and Y have the same performance, because $(0.1 \times 10)^{1/2} = 1$. Yet this is clearly not the case if programs A and B are executed the same number of times in our workload. The execution times on the two machines would be the same only if the fraction a of executions that correspond to program A (hence, $1 - a$ for program B) satisfied the following equality:

$$a \times 20 + (1 - a) \times 1000 = a \times 200 + (1 - a) \times 100$$

This requires $a = 5/6$ and $1 - a = 1/6$, implying that program A must be executed five times as often as program B; this may or may not be the case in our workload.

Example 4.6: Effect of instruction mix on performance   Consider the data compression and nuclear reactor simulation applications in Table 4.3 and assume that the average CPIs for instruction classes A–F on two machines M_1 and M_2 are as follows:

Class	Average CPI for M_1	Average CPI for M_2	Comments
A	4.0	3.8	Load/Store
B	1.5	2.5	Integer arithmetic
C	1.2	1.2	Shift/Logical
D	6.0	2.6	Floating-point
E	2.5	2.2	Branch
F	2.0	2.3	All others

a. Compute the effective CPI for these two applications on each machine (four results).
b. For each application, compute the speedup of M_2 over M_1, assuming that both machines have the same clock rate.
c. Using geometric mean, quantify the overall performance advantage of M_2 over M_1.

Solution
a. CPI for data compression application on $M_1 = 0.25 \times 4.0 + 0.32 \times 1.5 + 0.16 \times 1.2 + 0 \times 6.0 + 0.19 \times 2.5 + 0.08 \times 2.0 = 2.31$
CPI for data compression application on $M_2 = 2.54$
CPI for nuclear reactor simulation application on $M_1 = 3.94$
CPI for nuclear reactor simulation application on $M_2 = 2.89$
b. Because programs and clock rates are the same, speedup is given by the ratio of CPIs: $2.31/2.54 = 0.91$ for data compression (1.10 slowdown), $3.94/2.89 = 1.36$ for nuclear reactor simulation.
c. The overall performance advantage of M_2 over M_1 is $(0.91 \times 1.36)^{1/2} = 1.11$.

◼ 4.6 The Quest for Higher Performance

The state of available computing power at the turn of the twenty-first century can be summarized thus:

Gigaflops on the desktop
Teraflops in the supercomputer center
Petaflops on the drawing board

Given the exponential growth in computer performance, in 10–15 years we should witness a change from G, T, and P above to T, P, and E (see Table 3.1). Over the years, achieving performance milestones, such as teraflops and petaflops, has been one the major driving forces in computer architecture and technology.

Certain government agencies and other advanced users support research and development projects in supercomputing to help solve larger, or heretofore intractable, problems within their domains of interest. Over time, new methods of performance improvement that are introduced into high-end supercomputers find their way into smaller systems, eventually showing up in personal computers. For this reason, major computer companies are also active in designing and building ultrahigh-performance computer systems, even though the market for such

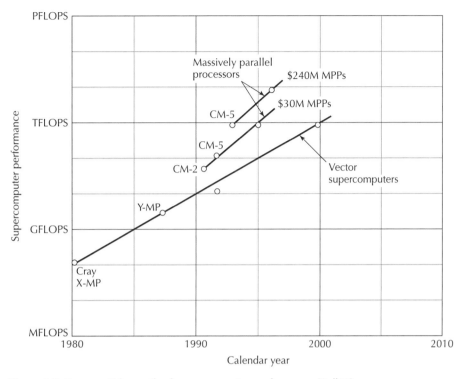

Figure 4.7 Exponential growth of supercomputer performance [Bell92].

expensive high-end machines is very limited (see Figure 3.4). As seen in Figure 4.7, super-computer performance has followed exponential growth. This trend applies to both vector supercomputers and massively parallel processors (MPPs).

To ensure that the progress in supercomputer performance is not slowed down by the high research and development cost for such machines, the U.S. Department of Energy has spon-sored the Accelerated Strategic Computing Initiative (ASCI) program, more recently described as the Advanced Simulation and Computing Initiative, which had as its goal the development of supercomputers with leading-edge performance—from 1 TFLOPS in 1997 to 100 TFLOPS in 2003 (Figure 4.8). Even though these numbers correspond to peak performance, there is hope that increases in peak computing power will translate to similarly impressive advances in sustained performance for real applications.

In the near future, both microprocessor and supercomputer performance are expected to grow at the current pace. So, interpolation of the trends seen in Figures 4.7 and 4.8 leads to ac-curate predictions of the level of performance that will be achieved in the next decade. Beyond that, however, the picture is much less clear. The problem is that we are approaching some fun-damental physical limits that might be difficult, or even impossible, to overcome. One concern is that the shrinking of feature size on integrated circuits, which is an important contributor to speed improvements, is bringing us ever closer to atomic dimensions. Another issue is that the speed of signal propagation on connectors between chip elements is inherently limited; it is cur-rently a fraction of the speed of light and can never exceed the latter (about 30 cm/ns). For example, if a memory chip is 3 cm away from the processor chip, we can never hope to send data from one to the other in a time shorter than 0.1 ns. Therefore, we need more work on architectural

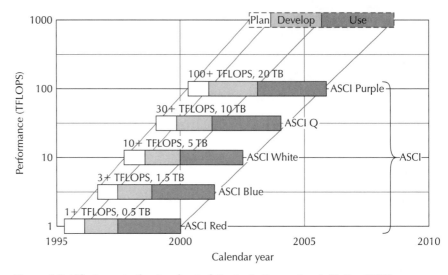

Figure 4.8 Milestones in the Accelerated Strategic Computing Initiative (ASCI) program, sponsored by the U.S. Department of Energy, with extrapolation up to the PFLOPS level.

techniques that obviate the need for frequent long-distance communication between circuit elements. Note that parallel processing by itself does not solve the "speed of light" dilemma; multiple processors still need to communicate with each other.

PROBLEMS

4.1 Amdahl's law

A program runs in a thousand seconds on a particular machine, with 75% of the time spent doing multiply/divide operations. We want to redesign the machine to provide it with faster multiply/divide hardware.

a. How much faster should the multiplier/divider become for the program to run three times as fast?
b. What if we want the program to run four times as fast?

4.2 Performance benchmarks

A benchmark suite B_1 consists of equal proportion of class-X and class-Y instructions. Machines M_1 and M_2, with identical 1 GHz clocks, have equal performance of 500 MIPS on B_1. If we replace half of class-X instructions in B_1 with class-Y instructions to derive another benchmark suite B_2, M_1's running time becomes 70% that of M_2. If we replace half of class-Y instruction with class-X

instructions to transform B_1 into B_3, M_2 becomes 1.5 times as fast as M_1.

a. What can you say about the average CPIs of M_1 and M_2 for the two instruction classes?
b. What is the IPS performance of M_1 on the new benchmark suites B_2 and B_3?
c. What is the maximum possible speedup of M_1 over M_2 and for what instruction mix is it achieved?
d. Repeat part c for the performance of M_2 relative to M_1.

4.3 Cycles per instruction

In all the examples in this chapter, supplied and computed CPIs are greater than or equal to 1. Can CPI be less than 1? Explain.

4.4 Clock frequency and speedup

A company sells two versions of its processors. The "pro" version runs at 1.5 times the clock frequency but has an average CPI of 1.50, vs 1.25 for the "deluxe" version. What speedup, relative to the deluxe version, would you expect when running a program on the pro version?

4.5 Performance comparison and speedup

Consider two different implementations M_1 and M_2 of the same instruction set. M_1 has a clock frequency of 500 MHz. M_2's clock cycle is 1.5 ns. There are three classes of instructions with the following CPIs:

Class	CPI for M_1	CPI for M_2
A	2	2
B	1	2
C	3	4

a. What are the peak performances of M_1 and M_2 expressed as MIPS?
b. If the number of instructions executed in a certain program is divided equally among the three classes, which machine is faster and by what factor?
c. We can redesign M_2 such that with negligible cost increase, the CPI for class-B instructions improves from 2 to 1 (class-A and class-C CPIs remain unchanged). This change, however, would increase the clock cycle from 1.5 ns to 2 ns. What should the minimum percentage of class-B instructions be in an instruction mix for this redesign to result in improved performance?

4.6 Amdahl's law

A program spends 60% of its execution time doing floating-point arithmetic. Of the floating-point operations in this program, 90% are executed in parallelizable loops.

a. Find the improvement in running time if the floating-point hardware is made twice as fast.
b. Find the improvement in running time if we use two processors to run the program's parallelizable loops twice as fast.
c. Find the improvement in running time resulting from both modifications a and b.

4.7 Instruction mix and performance

This problem is a continuation of Example 4.6. We can redesign machine M_1 so that its clock rate is 1.4 times the current rate (say, 1.4 GHz instead of 1 GHz).

Doing this will require other design changes that increase all the CPIs by 1. How does M_2 compare with the redesigned M_1 in terms of performance?

4.8 Instruction mix and performance

Redo Example 4.6, but instead of considering only data compression and nuclear reactor simulation, consider all four applications listed in Table 4.3.

a. Tabulate results for individual applications on each machine.
b. Find composite results for the two integer (data compression and C language compiler) and two floating-point (nuclear reactor simulation and atomic motion modeling) applications by averaging the instruction mixes.
c. Using geometric mean and the results of part b, quantify the overall performance advantage of M_2 over M_1.

4.9 Performance gain with vector processing

A vector supercomputer has special instructions that perform arithmetic operations on vectors. For example, vector-multiply on vectors A and B of length 64 is equivalent to 64 independent multiplications $A[i] \times B[i]$. Assume that the machine has a CPI of 2 on all scalar arithmetic instructions. Vector arithmetic on vectors of length m takes $8 + m$ cycles, where 8 is the start-up/wind-down overhead for the pipeline that allows one arithmetic operation to be initiated in every clock cycle; thus, vector-multiply takes 72 clock cycles for vectors of length 64. Consider a program with only arithmetic instructions (i.e., ignore all else), with half these instructions involving scalar and half involving vector operands.

a. What is the speedup achieved if the average vector length is 16?
b. What is the break-even vector length for this machine (average vector length to result in equal or greater performance due to vector processing)?
c. What is the required average vector length to achieve a speedup of 1.8?

4.10 Amdahl's law

A new version of machine M, called Mfp++, executes all floating-point instructions four times as fast as M.

a. Plot the speedup achieved by Mfp++ relative to M as a function of the fraction x of time that M spends on floating-point arithmetic.

b. Find the speedup of Mfp++ over M for each of the applications shown in Table 4.3, assuming that the average CPI for floating-point instructions on M is five times that of all other instructions.

4.11 MIPS rating

A machine used by your company has an average CPI of 4 for floating-point arithmetic instructions and 1 for all other instructions. Applications that you run spend half their time on floating-point arithmetic.

a. What is the instruction mix in your applications? That is, find the fraction x of executed instructions that perform floating-point arithmetic.

b. How much higher would the MIPS rating of the machine be if you used a compiler that simulated floating-point arithmetic by means of sequences of integer instructions instead of using the machine's floating-point instructions?

4.12 Performance comparison and speedup

Consider two different implementations M_1 (1 GHz) and M_2 (1.5 GHz) of the same instruction set. There are three classes of instructions with the following CPIs:

Class	CPI for M_1	CPI for M_2
A	2	2
B	1	2
C	3	5

a. What are the peak performances of M_1 and M_2 expressed as MIPS?

b. Show that if half the instructions executed in a certain program are from class A and the rest are divided equally among classes B and C, then M_2 is faster than M_1.

c. Show that the second assumption in part b is redundant. In other words, if half the instructions executed in a certain program are from class A, then M_2 will always be faster than M_1, regardless of the distribution of the remaining instructions among classes B and C.

4.13 Supercomputer performance trends

Data on the most powerful supercomputers currently in existence are regularly published [Top500].

Produce the following scatter plots based on data for the top five supercomputers in each of the last 10 years and discuss the observed trends:

a. Performance versus number of processors

b. Performance versus total amount of memory and per-processor memory (use two types of marker on the same scatter plot)

c. Number of processors versus year of introduction

4.14 Relative performance of machines

Referring to Figure 4.5, we note that the relative performance of machines 1 and 2 fluctuates widely for the six programs shown. For example, machine 1 is twice as fast for program B, whereas the opposite holds true for program A. Speculate about what differences in the two machines and the six programs might have contributed to the observed execution times. Then, compare machine 3 to each of the other two machines.

4.15 Amdahl's law

You live in an apartment from which you have a 7-minute drive for your twice-a-week shopping trips to a nearby supermarket and a 20-minute drive to a warehouse store where you shop once every 4 weeks. You are planning to move to a new apartment. Compare the following candidate locations with respect to the speedup they offer for your driving time during shopping trips:

a. An apartment that is 10 minutes away from both a supermarket and a warehouse store

b. An apartment that is 5 minutes away from a supermarket and 30 minutes from a warehouse store

4.16 Amdahl's law

Suppose that based on operation counts (not time spent on them), a numerical application uses 20% floating-point and 80% integer/control operations. The execution time of a floating-point operation is on average three times as long as other operations. A redesign of the floating-point unit is being considered to make it faster.

a. What speedup factor for the floating-point unit would lead to 25% overall improvement in speed?

b. What is the maximum possible speedup achievable by modifying only the floating-point unit?

4.17 Benchmark performance and MIPS

A particular benchmark is meant to be executed repeatedly, with the computer performance specified as the number of times the benchmark can be executed per second. So, a repetition rate of 100/s represents a higher performance than 80/s. Machines M_1 and M_2 exhibit a performance of R_1 and R_2 repetitions per second. During these executions, M_1 has a MIPS performance rating of P_1. Would it be correct to conclude that the MIPS rating of M_2 on this benchmark is $P_1 \times R_2/R_1$? Justify your answer fully.

4.18 Aircraft performance analogy

In Section 4.1 and Table 4.1, we compared several passenger aircraft with respect to their performance and noted that performance is judged differently depending on the evaluator's viewpoint. Information on U.S. military aircraft is available from the Web sites of Periscope (periscopeone.com), NASA, and American Institute of Aeronautics and Astronautics.

a. Construct a table similar to Table 4.1, listing relevant performance-related parameters of U.S. fighter jets (such as F-14, F-15/15E, F-16, and F/A-18) and discuss how the chosen planes compare from different viewpoints.
b. Repeat part a for bomber aircrafts of the U.S. military such as B52-H, B-1B, B-2, and F-117.
c. Repeat part a for unmanned aerial vehicles of the U.S. military such as Black Widow, Hunter, Predator, and Global Hawk.

4.19 Supercomputer trends

Science and Technology Review published a timeline of supercomputers at the Lawrence Livermore National Laboratory, from UNIVAC 1 in 1953 to the 10 tera-ops ASCII White in 2000 [Park02].

a. From this data, derive a growth rate figure for supercomputer performance over the last five decades of the twentieth century and compare it against the microprocessor performance growth in Figure 3.10.
b. Is the growth rate of part a consistent with Figure 4.7? Discuss.
c. Try to obtain data about the size of main memory on these computers. Derive growth rates for main memory size and compare it to the performance growth rate of part a.
d. Repeat part c for mass memory.

4.20 MIPS rating

A computer has two classes of instructions. Class-S instructions have a CPI of 1.5 and class-C instructions have a CPI of 5.0. The clock rate is 2 GHz. Let x be the fraction of instructions in a set of programs of interest that belong to class S.

a. Plot the variation in MIPS rating for the machine as x varies from 0 to 1.
b. Specify the range of x values for which a speed-up of 1.2 for class-S instructions leads to better performance than a speed-up of 2.5 for class-C instructions.
c. What would be a fair average MIPS rating for this machine if we know nothing about x? (That is, the value of x is uniformly distributed over [0, 1] for different applications of potential interest.)

REFERENCES AND FURTHER READINGS

[Bell92]   Bell, G., "Ultracomputers: A Teraflop Before Its Time," *Communications of the ACM,* Vol. 35, No. 8, pp. 27–47, August 1992.

[Crow94]   Crowl, L. A., "How to Measure, Present, and Compare Parallel Performance," *IEEE Parallel & Distributed Technology,* Vol. 2, No. 1, pp. 9–25, Spring 1994.

[Henn00]   Henning, J. L., "SPEC CPU2000: Measuring CPU Performance in the New Millennium," *IEEE Computer,* Vol. 33, No. 7, pp. 28–35, July 2000.

[Henn03]   Hennessy, J. L., and D. A. Patterson, *Computer Architecture: A Quantitative Approach,* Morgan Kaufmann, 3rd ed., 2003.

[Park02]   Parker, A., "From Kilobytes to Petabytes in 50 Years," *Science and Technology Review,* published by LLNL, pp. 20–26, March 2002. http://www.llnl.gov/str/

[Patt98]   Patterson, D. A., and J. L. Hennessy, *Computer Organization and Design: The Hardware/Software Interface,* Morgan Kaufmann, 2nd ed., 1998.

[Smit88]   Smith, J. E., "Characterizing Computer Performance with a Single Number," *Communications of the ACM,* Vol. 31, No. 10, pp. 1202–1206, October 1988.

[Top500]   Top 500 Supercomputer Sites, a Web site maintained by University of Mannheim and University of Tennessee: http://www.top500.org/

PART TWO

INSTRUCTION-SET ARCHITECTURE

"Instruction set anthropologists of the 21st century will peel off layer after layer from such [inelegant, haphazardly extended] machines until they uncover artifacts from the first microprocessor. Given such a find, how will they judge 20th-century computer architecture?"
—*David A. Patterson and John L. Hennessy, Computer Organization and Design, 1998*

"In all the mathematics that I did, the essential point was to find the right architecture. It's like building a bridge. Once the main lines of the structure are right, then the details miraculously fit."
—*Freeman Dyson, in a 1994 interview*

Instructions are words of the language understood by the machine, and instruction set is its vocabulary. A programmer writing programs for the machine, a rarity these days, or a compiler translating high-level language programs to the language of the machine, must understand this vocabulary and where each word might be properly used. The instruction-set architecture of a machine is its vocabulary together with parts of the machine and their functions that must be mastered by a user to produce correct, compact, and fast programs.

We introduce the core of a simple, yet realistic and useful, instruction-set architecture in Chapters 5 and 6; additional parts of the instruction set will be introduced later in the book, particularly in Part 4 dealing with the ALU. The structure of assembly language programs is discussed in Chapter 7. Throughout, the emphasis is not on mastering this particular instruction set or being able to effortlessly program in it; rather, we aim to learn enough about this instruction set to understand the rationales behind differences among machines and how various choices affect hardware cost and performance. The RISC/CISC dichotomy and other aspects of instruction-set design are covered in Chapter 8.

CHAPTER 5

INSTRUCTIONS AND ADDRESSING

"We still have judgment here, that we but teach bloody instructions, which, being taught, return to plague th' inventor."
—*William Shakespeare, Macbeth*

"The most important thing in the programming language is the name. A language will not succeed without a good name. I have recently invented a very good name and now I am looking for a suitable language."
—*Donald E. Knuth, 1967*

In this chapter, we begin our study of a simple instruction set that will help us understand the elements of a modern instruction-set architecture, the choices involved in its making, and aspects of its execution in hardware. The instruction set chosen is called MiniMIPS; it defines a hypothetical machine that is very close to the real MIPS processors, a family of processors offered by a company of the same name. This instruction set is nicely documented, has been used in several other textbooks, and has a free simulator that can be downloaded for practice and programming exercises. By the end of this chapter, we will be able to compose instruction sequences to perform nontrivial computational tasks.

■ 5.1 Abstract View of Hardware

To drive an automobile, you must become familiar with some key elements such as the gas and brake pedals, the steering wheel, and a number of dashboard instruments. Collectively, these devices allow you to control the automobile and its various parts and to observe the status of certain critical subsystems. The corresponding interface for computer hardware is its instruction-set architecture. You must learn this interface to be able to instruct the computer to perform computational tasks of interest. In the case of automobiles, the user interface is so standard that you can easily operate a rental car of a make you have never driven before. The same cannot be said about digital computers, although many common instruction-set features have developed over time. Once you become familiar with one machine's instruction set, others can be learned with little effort; the process is more like improving your vocabulary or studying a new dialect of English than learning a whole new language.

The MiniMIPS (minimal MIPS) instruction set is quite similar to what one finds on many modern processors. MiniMIPS is a load/store instruction set, meaning that data elements must be copied or "loaded" into registers before they can be processed; operation results also go into registers and must be explicitly copied back into memory through separate "store" operations. Thus to understand and be able to use MiniMIPS, we need to know about data storage schemes in memory, functions of load and store instructions, types of operation allowed on data elements kept in registers, and a number of other odds and ends that enable efficient programming.

To drive an automobile, you do not need to know where the engine is located or how it powers the wheels; yet, most instructors begin to teach driving by showing their students a diagram of an auto with its various parts. At this juncture, Figure 5.1 is presented in the same spirit, although in later parts of the book we will examine computer hardware in much greater detail. The assembly language programmer (compiler) is concerned with:

Registers

Memory locations where data might be stored

Machine instructions that operate on and store data in registers or memory

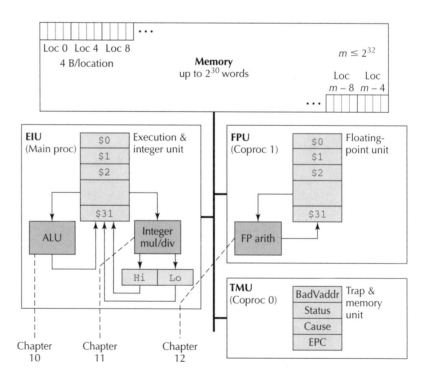

Figure 5.1 Memory and processing subsystems for MiniMIPS.

Figure 5.1 shows the MiniMIPS memory unit, with its up to 2^{30} words (2^{32} bytes), an execution and integer unit (EIU), a floating-point unit (FPU), and a trap and memory unit (TMU). FPU and TMU are shown for completeness; we will not examine the instructions that exercise these units in this part of the book. FPU-related instructions will be covered in Chapter 12, while Part VI reveals some of the uses of TMU. It is the EIU that interprets and executes the basic MiniMIPS instructions covered in this part of the book. The EIU has 32 general-purpose registers, each of which is 32 bits wide and can thus hold the content of one memory location. The arithmetic/logic unit (ALU) executes addition, subtraction, and logical instructions. A separate arithmetic unit is dedicated to multiplication and division instructions whose results are placed in two special registers, named "Hi" and "Lo," from where they can be moved into general-purpose registers.

A view of MiniMIPS registers and data sizes is presented in Figure 5.2. All registers except register 0 ($0), which permanently holds the constant 0, are general-purpose and can be used

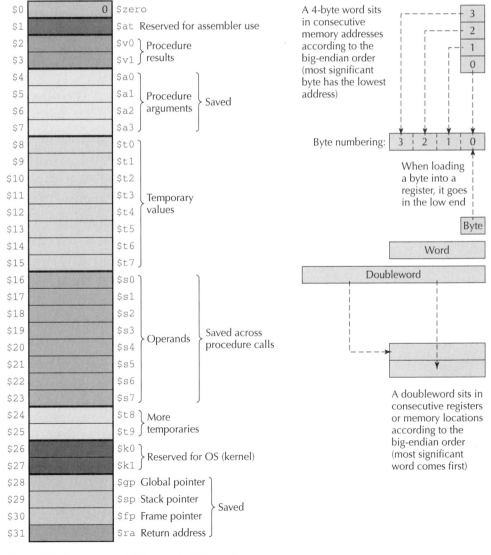

Figure 5.2 Registers and data sizes in MiniMIPS.

to store arbitrary data words. However, to facilitate efficient program development and compilation, certain restrictions on register usage are commonplace. A useful analogy for these restrictions is the way in which a person may decide to put change, keys, wallet, and so on in specific pockets to make it easier to remember where the items can be found. The restrictions used in this book are also shown in Figure 5.2. Most of these conventions do not make sense to you at this point. Thus, we will use only registers $8 through $25 (with symbolic names $s0-$s7 and $t0-$t9) in our examples until usage conventions for the other registers are discussed.

A 32-bit data element stored in a register or a memory location (with an address that is divisible by 4) is referred to as a "*word*." For now, we assume that a word holds an instruction or a signed integer, although later we will see that it can also hold an unsigned integer, a floating-point number, or a string of ASCII characters. Because MiniMIPS words are stored in a byte-addressable memory, we need a convention to establish which end of the word appears in the first byte (the one with the lowest memory address). Of the two possible conventions in this regard, MiniMIPS uses the "*big-endian*" scheme, where the most significant end appears first.

For certain values that do not need the full range of a 32-bit word, we might use 8-bit *bytes*. When a byte-size data element is put in a register, it appears at the register's right end (lowest byte). A *doubleword* occupies two consecutive registers or memory locations. Again, the convention about ordering of the two words is big-endian. When a pair of registers hold a doubleword, the smaller of the two registers always has an even index, which is used to refer to the doubleword location (e.g., we say "the doubleword is in register $16" to mean that the high end of it is in $16 and the low end in $17). So, only even-numbered registers can hold doublewords.

A final point to be made before embarking on a discussion of specific instructions for MiniMIPS is that even though a programmer (compiler) does not need to know more about hardware than is covered in this part of the book, the implementation details to be presented in the rest of the book are still quite important. With regard to our automobile analogy, you can drive legally with virtually no knowledge of how an automobile is built or how its engine operates. To extract maximum performance from the machine, or to be a very safe driver, however, you need to know a great deal more.

■ 5.2 Instruction Formats

A typical MiniMIPS machine instruction is add $t8, $s2, $s1, which causes the contents of registers $s2 and $s1 to be added, with the result stored in register $t8. This might correspond to the compiled form of the high-level language statement a = b + c and is in turn represented in a machine word using 0s and 1s to encode the operation and register specifications involved (Figure 5.3).

As in the case of high-level language programs, sequences of machine or assembly language instructions are executed from top to bottom unless a different order of execution is explicitly specified via jump or branch instructions. Some such instructions will be covered in Section 5.5. For now, we focus on the meaning of simple instructions by themselves or in short sequences corresponding to compound operation. For example, the following sequence of assembly instructions performs the computation g = (b + c) - (e + f) as a sequence of single-operation instructions, written one per line. The portion of each line that follows the "#" symbol is a comment inserted to help the reader of the instruction sequence and is ignored during machine execution.

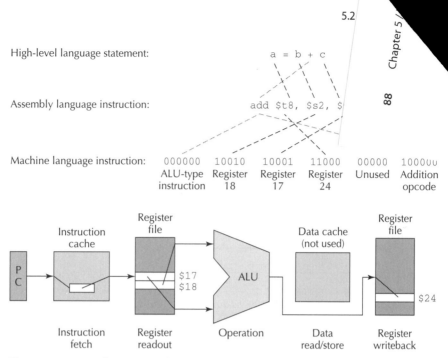

High-level language statement: a = b + c

Assembly language instruction: add $t8, $s2, $

Machine language instruction: 000000   10010   10001   11000   00000   100000
                                 ALU-type Register   Register   Register   Unused   Addition
                                 instruction   18   17   24   opcode

Figure 5.3 A typical instruction for MiniMIPS and steps in its execution.

```
add    $t8,$s2,$s3    # put the sum b + c in $t8
add    $t9,$s5,$s6    # put the sum e + f in $t9
sub    $s7,$t8,$t9    # set g to ($t8) - ($t9)
```

The preceding instruction sequence effectively computes g by performing the operations a = b + c, d = e + f, and g = a - d, with temporary values a and d held in registers $t8 and $t9, respectively.

In writing machine language programs, we need to supply integers that specify memory addresses or numerical constants. Such numbers are specified in *decimal* (radix-10) or *hexadecimal* (radix-16, or *hex* for short) format and are automatically converted to the binary format for machine processing. Here are some examples:

Decimal   25, 123456, -2873
Hexadecimal   0x59, 0x12b4c6, 0xffff0000

Hexadecimal numbers will be explained in Section 9.2. For now, just view them as a short-hand notation for bit patterns. The 4-bit patterns 0000 through 1111 correspond to the 16 hexadecimal digits 0-9, a, b, c, d, e, and f. So the hex number 0x59 represents the byte 0101 1001 and 0xffff0000 is shorthand for the word 1111 1111 1111 1111 0000 0000 0000 0000. The reason for using the prefix "0x" is to distinguish these numbers from both decimal numbers (e.g., 59 or 059) and variable names (e.g., x59).

A machine instruction for an arithmetic/logic operation specifies an opcode, one or more source operands, and, usually, one destination operand. Opcode is a binary code (bit pattern) that defines an operation. The operands of an arithmetic or logical instruction may come from a variety of sources. The method used to specify where the operands are to be found and where the result must go is referred to as the addressing mode (or scheme). For now, we assume that

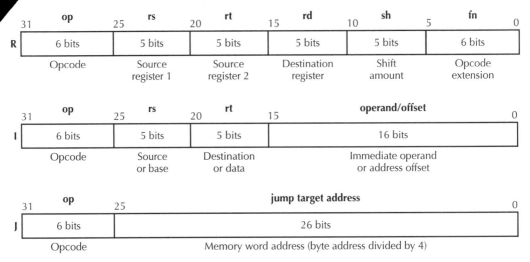

Figure 5.4 MiniMIPS instructions come in only three formats: register (R), immediate (I), and jump (J).

all operands are in registers $s0-$s7 and $t0-$t9, with other addressing modes discussed in Section 5.6.

The three MiniMIPS instruction formats are shown in Figure 5.4. Simplicity and uniformity of instruction formats is common in modern RISC (reduced instruction-set computer) designs that aim to execute the most commonly used operations as fast as possible, perhaps at the expense of the less common ones. Other approaches to instruction-set design, as well as the pros and cons of the RISC approach, will be discussed in Chapter 8. The operation code (*opcode*) field, which is common to all three formats, is used to distinguish the instructions in the three classes. Of the 64 possible opcodes, nonoverlapping subsets are assigned to the instruction classes in such a way that the hardware can easily recognize the class of a particular instruction and, thus, the proper interpretation for the remaining fields.

Register or R-type instructions operate on the two registers identified in the rs and rt fields and store the result in register rd. For such instructions, the function (fn) field serves as an extension of the opcode, to allow for more operations to be defined, and the shift amount (sh) field is used in instructions that specify a constant shift amount. Simple (logical) shift instructions will be covered in Chapters 6; arithmetic shifts will be discussed in Chapter 10.

Immediate or I-type instructions are really of two different varieties. In immediate instructions, the 16-bit operand field in bits 0–15 holds an integer that plays the same role as rt in R-type instructions; in other words, the specified operation is performed on the content of register rs and the immediate operand, with the result stored back in register rt. In load, store, or branch instructions, the 16-bit field is interpreted as an *offset,* or relative address, that is to be added to the *base* value in register rs (program counter) to obtain a memory address for reading or writing (transfer of control). For data accesses, the offset is interpreted as the number of bytes forward (positive) or backward (negative) relative to the base address. For branch instructions, the offset is in words, given that instructions always occupy complete 32-bit memory words.

Jump or J-type instructions cause unconditional transfer of control to the instruction in the specified address. Because MiniMIPS addresses are 32-bits wide, whereas only 26 bits are available in the address field of a J-type instruction, two conventions are used. First, the 26-bit field is assumed to carry a word address as opposed to a byte address; hence, the hardware attaches two 0s to the right end of the 26-bit address field to derive a 28-bit word address. The 4 bits still missing are attached to the left end of the 28-bit address in a manner to be described in Section 5.5.

■ 5.3 Simple Arithmetic and Logic Instructions

We introduced add and subtract instructions in Section 5.2. These instructions work on registers containing whole (32-bit) words. For example:

```
add     $t0,$s0,$s1     # set $t0 to ($s0)+($s1)
sub     $t0,$s0,$s1     # set $t0 to ($s0)-($s1)
```

Figure 5.5 depicts the machine representations of the foregoing instructions.

Logical instructions operate on a pair of operands on a bit-by-bit basis. Logical instructions in MiniMIPS include the following:

```
and     $t0,$s0,$s1     # set $t0 to ($s0)∧($s1)
or      $t0,$s0,$s1     # set $t0 to ($s0)∨($s1)
xor     $t0,$s0,$s1     # set $t0 to ($s0)⊕($s1)
nor     $t0,$s0,$s1     # set $t0 to (($s0)∨($s1))'
```

Machine representations for these logic instructions are similar to that in Figure 5.5, but with the function field holding 36 (100100) for and, 37 (100101) for or, 38 (100110) for xor, and 39 (100111) for nor.

Often, one operand of an arithmetic or logical operation is a constant. While it is possible to place this constant in a register and then perform the desired operation on two registers, it would be more efficient to use instructions that directly specify the desired constant in an I-format instruction. Of course, the constant must be small enough to fit in the 16-bit field that is available for this purpose. Thus, for signed integer values the valid range is from $-32,768$ to $32,767$, while for hex constants any 4-digit number in the range [0x0000, 0xffff] is acceptable.

```
addi    $t0,$s0,61      # set $t0 to ($s0)+61 (decimal)
```

The machine representation of addi is depicted in Figure 5.6. There is no corresponding "subtract immediate" instruction, given that its effect can be accomplished by adding a negative value. Because MiniMIPS has a 32-bit adder, the 16-bit immediate operand must be

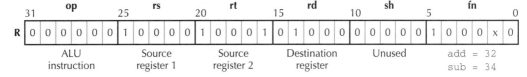

Figure 5.5 The arithmetic instructions add and sub have a format that is common to all two-operand ALU instructions. For these, the fn field specifies the arithmetic/logic operation to be performed.

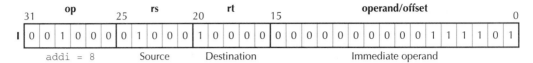

Figure 5.6 Instructions such as `addi` allow us to perform an arithmetic or logic operation for which one operand is a small constant.

converted to an equivalent 32-bit value before it is applied as input to the adder. We will see later in Chapter 9 that a signed number that is represented in 2's-complement format must be sign-extended if it is to result in the same numerical value in a wider format. *Sign extension* simply means that the most significant bit of a 16-bit signed value is repeated 16 times to fill the upper half of the corresponding 32-bit version. So, a positive number is extended with 0s while a negative number is extended with 1s.

Three of the logical instructions just introduced also have immediate or I-format versions:

```
andi    $t0,$s0,61      # set $t0 to ($s0)∧61
ori     $t0,$s0,61      # set $t0 to ($s0)∨61
xori    $t0,$s0,0x00ff  # set $t0 to ($s0)⊕ 0x00ff
```

Machine representations for these logic instructions are similar to that in Figure 5.6, but with the opcode field holding 12 (`001100`) for `andi`, 13 (`001101`) for `ori`, and 14 (`001110`) for `xori`.

One key difference between the `andi`, `ori`, and `xori` instructions and the `addi` instruction is that the 16-bit operand of a logical instruction is 0-extended from the left to turn it into 32-bit format for processing. In other words, the upper half of the 32-bit version of the immediate operand for logical instructions consists of 16 zeros.

Example 5.1: Extracting fields from a word   A 32-bit word in `$s0` holds a byte of data in bit positions 0–7 and a status flag in bit position 10. Other bits in the word have arbitrary (unpredictable) values. Unpack the information in this word, putting the data byte in register `$t0` and the status flag in register `$t1`. At the end, register `$t0` should hold an integer in [0, 255] corresponding to the data byte and register `$t1` should hold a nonzero value iff the status flag is 1.

Solution: Fields of a word can be extracted by ANDing the word with a predefined *mask,* a word that has 1s in bit positions of interest and 0s elsewhere. For example, ANDing a word with `0x000000ff` (which in binary has 1s only in its 8 least significant bit positions) has the effect of extracting the rightmost byte. Any desired flag bit can be similarly extracted through ANDing with a mask that has a single 1 in the desired position. Thus, the following two instructions accomplish what is required:

```
andi  $t0,$s0,0x00ff    # mask with eight 1s at right end
andi  $t1,$s0,0x0400    # mask with single 1 in position 10
```

Note that the nonzero value left in `$t1` in case the flag bit is 1 is equal to $2^{10} = 1024$. We will see later than a shift instruction can be used to leave 0 or 1 in `$t1` according to the flag bit value.

■ 5.4 Load and Store Instructions

Basic load and store instructions transfer whole words (32 bits) between memory and registers. Each such instruction specifies a register and a memory address. The register, which is the data destination for load and data source for store, is specified in the `rt` field of an I-format instruction. The memory address is specified in two parts that are added to yield the address: the 16-bit signed integer in the instruction is a constant offset which is added to the base value in register `rs`. In assembly language format, the source/destination register `rt` is specified first, followed by the constant offset and the base register `rs` in parentheses. Putting `rs` in parentheses is reminiscent of the indexing notation `A(i)` in high-level languages. Here are two examples:

```
lw      $t0,40($s3)      # load mem[40+($s3)] into $t0
sw      $t0,A($s3)       # store ($t0) into mem[A+($s3)]
                         # "($s3)" means "content of $s3"
```

The machine instruction format for `lw` and `sw` is shown in Figure 5.7 along with the memory addressing convention. Note that the offset can be specified as an absolute integer or via a symbolic name that has previously been defined. We will discuss defining symbolic names in Chapter 7.

Load and store instructions that deal with data types other than words will be covered in Section 6.4. Here, we only introduce one other load instruction that allows us to place an arbitrary constant in a desired register. A small constant, one that is representable in 16 bits or less, can be loaded into a register through a single `addi` instruction whose other operand is register `$zero` (which always holds 0). A larger constant must be placed in a register in two steps; the upper 16 bits are loaded into the upper half of the register through the "load upper

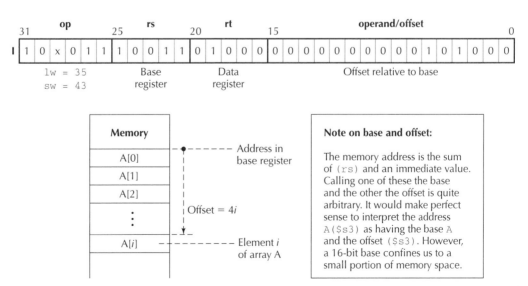

Figure 5.7 MiniMIPS `lw` and `sw` instructions and their memory addressing convention that allows for simple access to array elements via a base address and an offset (offset = 4i leads us to the ith word).

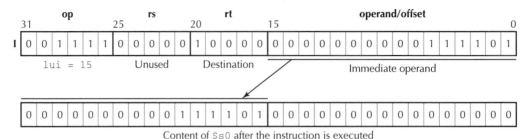

Content of $s0 after the instruction is executed

Figure 5.8 The `lui` instruction allows us to load an arbitrary 16-bit value into the upper half of a register while setting its lower half to 0s.

immediate" (`lui`) instruction and the lower 16 bits are then inserted through an "or immediate" (`ori`). This is possible because `lui` fills the lower half of the destination register with 0s, so that when these bits are ORed with the immediate operand, the immediate operand is simply copied into the lower half of the register.

```
lui       $s0,61       # The immediate value 61 (decimal)
                       # is loaded in the upper half of $s0
                       # with the lower 16 bits set to 0s
```

Figure 5.8 shows the machine representation of the foregoing `lui` instruction and its effect on the destination register $s0.

Note that even though the instruction pair `lui` and `addi` can sometimes accomplish the same effect as `lui` followed by `ori`, this may not be the case owing to sign extension before adding the 16-bit immediate operand to the 32-bit register value.

Example 5.2: Loading arbitrary bit patterns into registers   Consider the bit pattern shown in Figure 5.6, corresponding to an `addi` instruction. Show how this particular bit pattern can be loaded into register $s0. How about putting the bit pattern consisting of all 1s in $s0?

Solution: The upper half of the bit pattern in Figure 5.6 has the hex representation 0x2110, while the lower half is 0x003d. Thus, the following two instructions accomplish what is required:

```
lui       $s0,0x2110       # put upper half of pattern in $s0
ori       $s0,0x003d       # put lower half of pattern in $s0
```

These two instructions, with their immediate operands changed to 0xffff, could place the all-1s pattern in $s0. A simpler and faster way is through the `nor` instruction:

```
nor       $s0,$zero,$zero       # because (0V0)'=1
```

In 2's-complement representation, the all-1s bit pattern corresponds to the integer −1. Hence, after we learn, in Chapter 9, that MiniMIPS represents integers in 2's-complement format, alternate solutions for this latter part will emerge.

5.5 Jump and Branch Instructions

The following two unconditional jump instructions are available in MiniMIPS:

```
j    verify    # go to memory loc named "verify"
jr   $ra       # go to loc whose address is in $ra;
               # $ra may hold return address from
               # a procedure (see Section 6.1)
```

The first instruction is a simple jump, which causes program execution to proceed from the location whose numeric or symbolic address is provided, instead of continuing with the next instruction in sequence. Jump register, or `jr`, specifies a register as holding the jump target address. This register is often `$ra`, and the instruction `jr $ra` is used to effect a return from a procedure to the point from which the procedure was called. Procedures and their usage will be discussed in Chapter 6. Machine representations of the MiniMIPS jump instructions are shown in Figure 5.9.

For the `j` instruction, the 26-bit address field in the instruction is augmented with `00` to the right and 4 high-order bits of the program counter (PC) to the left to form a complete 32-bit address. This is called *pseudodirect addressing* (see Section 5.6).

Conditional branch instructions allow us to transfer control to a given address when a condition of interest is met. There are three basic comparison-based branch instructions in MiniMIPS for which the conditions are a register content being negative and the equality or inequality of the contents of two registers. Instead of providing a multitude of instructions for other comparisons, MiniMIPS provides an R-type comparison instruction "set less than" (`slt`) that sets the content of a specified destination register to 1 if the "less than" relationship holds between the contents of two given registers, and sets it to 0 otherwise. To allow comparison to a constant, the immediate version of this instruction, namely `slti`, is also provided.

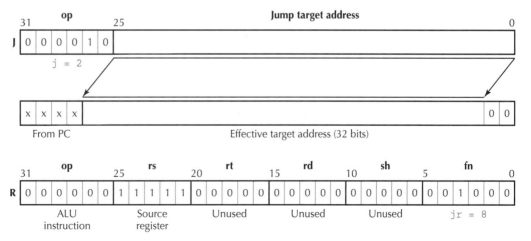

Figure 5.9 The jump instruction `j` of MiniMIPS is a J-type instruction which is shown along with how its effective target address is obtained. The jump register (`jr`) instruction is R-type, with its specified register often being `$ra`.

```
        bltz    $s1,L          # branch on ($s1)< 0
        beq     $s1,$s2,L      # branch on ($s1)=($s2)
        bne     $s1,$s2,L      # branch on ($s1)≠($s2)
        slt     $s1,$s2,$s3    # if ($s2)<($s3), set $s1 to 1
                               # else set $s1 to 0; this is
                               # usually followed by beq or bne
        slti    $s1,$s2,61     # if ($s2)<61, set $s1 to 1
                               # else set $s1 to 0
```

Figure 5.10 shows the machine representation of the three branch and two comparison instructions just discussed.

For the three instructions bltz, beq, and bne, PC-relative addressing is used whereby the 16-bit signed offset in the instruction is multiplied by 4 and the result added to the PC contents to get a 32-bit branch target address. If the label specified is too far to be reachable via a 16-bit offset (a very rare occurrence), the assembler automatically replaces beq $s0,$s1,L1 with a pair of Mini-MIPS instructions:

```
        bne     $s1,$s2,L2     # skip jump if (s1)≠(s2)
        j       L1             # goto L1 if (s1)=(s2)
L2:     ...
```

Here, the notation "L2:" defines the unspecified instruction appearing on that line as having the symbolic address L2. Therefore, in writing branch instructions, we can use symbolic

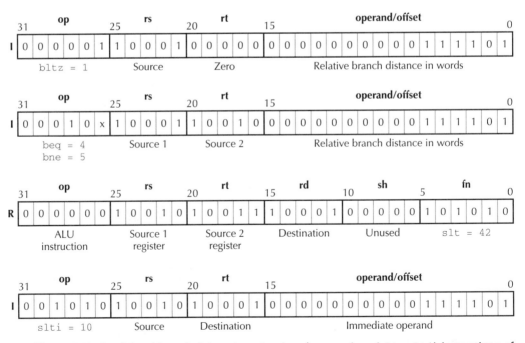

Figure 5.10 Conditional branch (bltz, beq, bne) and comparison (slt, slti) instructions of MiniMIPS.

names freely without worrying whether the corresponding address is reachable from the current instruction by means of a 16-bit offset.

Branch and jump instructions can be used to form conditional and repetitive computation structures akin to "if-then" and "while" of high-level languages. The if-then statement

```
if (i == j) x = x + y;
```

might be translated to the following MiniMIPS assembly language program fragment:

```
        bne     $s1,$s2,endif  # branch on i≠j
        add     $t1,$t1,$t2    # execute the "then" part
endif:  ...
```

If the condition in the "if" statement were i < j, then the first instruction in the sequence above would be replaced by the following two instructions (the rest would not change):

```
slt     $t0,$s1,$s2    # set $t0 to 1 if i<j
beq     $t0,$0,endif   # branch if ($t0)=0; i.e., i≥j
                       # which is the inverse of i<j
```

Many other conditional branches can be similarly synthesized.

Example 5.3: Compiling if-then-else statements   High-level languages contain an if-then-else construct that allows us to perform one of two computations depending on whether a condition is satisfied. Show a sequence of MiniMIPS instructions corresponding to the following if-then-else statement:

```
if (i <= j) x = x + 1; z = 1; else y = y - 1; z = 2 * z;
```

Solution: This is quite similar to the if-then statement, except that we need instructions corresponding to the "else" part and a way of skipping the else part after the "then" part has been executed.

```
       slt  $t0,$s2,$s1    # j<i? (inverse of condition)
       bne  $t0,$zero,else # branch on j<i to "else" part
       addi $t1,$t1,1       # begin "then" part: x=x+1
       addi $t3,$zero,1     # z=1
       j    endif           # skip "else" part
else:  addi $t2,$t2,-1      # begin "else" part: y=y-1
       add  $t3,$t3,$t3     # z=z+z
endif: ...
```

Note that each of the two instruction sequences corresponding to "then" and "else" parts of the conditional statement can be arbitrarily long.

The simple while loop

```
while (A[i] == k) i = i + 1;
```

might be translated to the following MiniMIPS assembly language program fragment, assuming that the index i, the starting address of array A, and the comparison constant k are found in registers $s1, $s2, and $s3, respectively:

```
loop:  add   $t1,$s1,$s1      # compute 2i in $t1
       add   $t1,$t1,$t1      # compute 4i in $t1
       add   $t1,$t1,$s2      # put address of A[i] in $t1
       lw    $t0,0($t1)       # load value of A[i] into $t0
       bne   $t0,$s3,endwhl   # exit loop if A[i] ≠ k
       addi  $si,$si,1        # i = i + 1
       j     loop             # stay in while loop
endwhl: ...
```

Note that testing of the while-loop condition needs five instructions: two to compute the offset 4i, one to add the offset to the base address in $s2, one to fetch the value of A[i] from memory, and one to check for equality.

Example 5.4: Loop with array index and explicit goto   In addition to while loops, high-level language programs may contain loops in which a (conditional or unconditional) goto statement initiates the next iteration. Show a sequence of MiniMIPS instructions that perform the function of the following loop of this type:

```
loop: i = i + step;
      sum = sum + A[i];
      if (i ≠ n) goto loop;
```

Solution: This is quite similar to a while loop and could in fact be written as one. Borrowing from our while-loop example, we write the following sequence of instructions, assuming that the index i, the starting address of array A, the comparison constant n, step, and sum are found in registers $s1, $s2, $s3, $s4, and $s5, respectively:

```
loop:  add   $s1,$s1,$s4      # i = i + step
       add   $t1,$s1,$s1      # compute 2i in $t1
       add   $t1,$t1,$t1      # compute 4i in $t1
       add   $t1,$t1,$s2      # put address of A[i] in $t1
       lw    $t0,0($t1)       # load value of A[i] into $t0
       add   $s5,$s5,$t0      # sum = sum + A[i]
       bne   $s1,$s3,loop     # if (i≠n) goto loop
```

It is assumed that repeatedly adding the increment step to the index variable i will eventually make it equal to n; otherwise, the loop will never terminate.

■ 5.6 Addressing Modes

Addressing mode is the method by which the location of an operand is specified within an instruction. MiniMIPS uses six addressing modes, depicted in Figure 5.11 in schematic form and described as follows.

1. *Implied addressing:* Operand comes from, or result goes to, a predefined place that is not explicitly specified in the instruction. An example is found in `jal` instruction (to be introduced in Section 6.1) which always saves the address of the next instruction in sequence into register `$ra`.

2. *Immediate addressing:* Operand is given in the instruction itself. Examples include `addi`, `andi`, `ori`, and `xori` instructions in which the second operand (or actually the lower half of it) is supplied as part of the instruction.

3. *Register addressing:* Operand is taken from, or result placed in, a specified register. R-type instructions in MiniMIPS specify up to three registers as locations of their operand(s) and/or result. Registers are specified by their 5-bit indices.

4. *Base addressing:* Operand is in memory and its location is computed by adding an offset (16-bit signed integer) to the contents of a specified base register. This is the addressing mode of `lw` and `sw` instructions.

5. *PC-relative addressing:* Same as base addressing, but with the register always being the program counter and the offset appended with two 0s at the right end (word

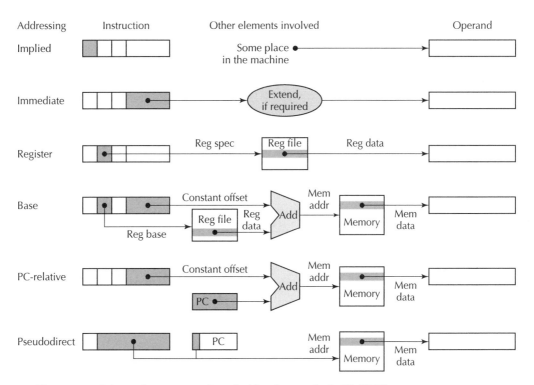

Figure 5.11 Schematic representation of addressing modes in MiniMIPS.

addressing is always used). This is addressing mode is used in branch instructions and allows for branching to other instructions within $\pm 2^{15}$ words of the current instruction.

6. *Pseudodirect addressing:* In direct addressing, the operand address is supplied as part of the instruction. For MiniMIPS, this is impossible, given that 32-bit instructions do not have enough room to carry full 32-bit addresses. The j instruction comes close to direct addressing because it contains 26 bits of the jump target address which is padded with 00 at the right end and 4 bits from the program counter at the left to form a full 32-bit address; hence the name "pseudodirect."

MiniMIPS has a load/store architecture: operands must be in registers before they can be processed. The only MiniMIPS instructions that refer to memory addresses are load, store, and jump/branch. This scheme, combined with the rather limited set of addressing modes, allows for efficient hardware to execute MiniMIPS instructions. Other addressing modes do exist. Some of these alternate modes will be discussed in Section 8.2. However, the addressing modes used in MiniMIPS are more than adequate for convenience in programming and efficiency in the resulting programs.

In all, 20 MiniMIPS instructions were introduced in this chapter. Table 5.1 summarizes these instructions for review and ready reference. This set of instructions is quite adequate for composing fairly complex programs. To make these programs modular and efficient, we need the additional mechanisms covered in Chapter 6. To make them complete assembly programs, we need assembler directives to be covered in Chapter 7.

■ **TABLE 5.1** The 20 MiniMIPS instructions covered in Chapter 5.

Class	Instruction	Usage		Meaning	op	fn
Copy	Load upper immediate	lui	rt,imm	rt ← (imm, 0X0000)	15	
Arithmetic	Add	add	rd,rs,rt	rd ← (rs) + (rt)	0	32
	Subtract	sub	rd,rs,rt	rd ← (rs) − (rt)	0	34
	Set less than	slt	rd,rs,rt	rd ← if (rs) < (rd) then 1 else 0	0	42
	Add immediate	addi	rt,rs,imm	rt ← (rs) + imm	8	
	Set less than immediate	slti	rd,rs,imm	rd ← if (rs) < imm then 1 else 0	10	
Logic	AND	and	rd,rs,rt	rd ← (rs) ∧ (rt)	0	36
	OR	or	rd,rs,rt	rd ← (rs) ∨ (rt)	0	37
	XOR	xor	rd,rs,rt	rd ← (rs) ⊕ (rt)	0	38
	NOR	nor	rd,rs,rt	rd ← ((rs) ∨ (rt))'	0	39
	AND immediate	andi	rt,rs,imm	rt ← (rs) ∧ imm	12	
	OR immediate	ori	rt,rs,imm	rt ← (rs) ∨ imm	13	
	XOR immediate	xori	rt,rs,imm	rt ← (rs) ⊕ imm	14	
Memory access	Load word	lw	rt,imm(rs)	rt ← mem[(rs) + imm]	35	
	Store word	sw	rt,imm(rs)	mem[(rs) + imm] ← (rt)	43	
Control transfer	Jump	j	L	goto L	2	
	Jump register	jr	rs	goto (rs)	0	8
	Branch less than 0	bltz	rs,L	if (rs) < 0 then goto L	1	
	Branch equal	beq	rs,rt,L	if (rs) = (rt) then goto L	4	
	Branch not equal	bne	rs,rt,L	if (rs) ≠ (rt) then goto L	5	

Example 5.5: Finding the maximum value in a list of numbers   A list of integers is stored in memory beginning in the address given in register $s1. The list length is provided in register $s2. Write a sequence of MiniMIPS instructions from Table 5.1 to find the largest integer in the list and to copy it into register $t0.

Solution: We scan all elements of the list A and use $t0 to hold the largest integer identified thus far (initially, A[0]). In each step, we compare a new list element to the value in $t0 and update the latter if needed.

```
        lw    $t0,0($s1)      # initialize maximum to A[0]
        addi  $t1,$zero,0     # initialize index i to 0
  loop: add   $t1,$t1,1       # increment index i by 1
        beq   $t1,$s2,done    # if all elements examined, quit
        add   $t2,$t1,$t1     # compute 2i in $t2
        add   $t2,$t2,$t2     # compute 4i in $t2
        add   $t2,$t2,$s1     # form address of A[i] in $t2
        lw    $t3,0($t2)      # load value of A[i] into $t3
        slt   $t4,$t0,$t3     # maximum < A[i]?
        beq   $t4,$zero,loop  # if not, repeat with no change
        addi  $t0,$t3,0       # if so, A[i] is the new maximum
        j     loop            # change completed; now repeat
  done: ...                   # continuation of the program
```

Note that the list has been assumed to be nonempty, containing at least the element A[0].

PROBLEMS

5.1 Instruction formats

In the MIPS instruction formats (Figure 5.4), we can reduce the opcode field from 6 to 5 bits and the function field from 6 to 4 bits. Given the number of MIPS instructions and different functions needed, these changes will not limit the design; that is, we will still have enough operation codes and function codes. The 3 bits thus gained can be used to extend the rs, rt, and rd fields from 5 to 6 bits each.

a. List two positive effects of these changes. Justify your answers.

b. List two negative effects of these changes. Justify your answers.

5.2 Other logic instructions

A number of other bitwise logic operations might be useful for certain applications. Show how the following logic operations can be synthesized by means of MiniMIPS instructions covered in this chapter. Try to use as few instructions as possible.

a. NOT
b. NAND
c. XNOR
d. NOR immediate

5.3 Overflow in addition

The sum of two 32-bit integers may not be representable in 32 bits. In this case, we say that an overflow has occurred. So far, we have not discussed how overflow is detected and dealt with. Write a sequence of MiniMIPS instructions that adds two numbers stored in registers $s1 and $s2, stores the sum (modulo 2^{32}) in register $s3, and sets register $t0 to 1 if an overflow occurs and to 0 otherwise. *Hint:* Overflow is possible only with operands of the same sign; for two nonnegative (negative) operands, if the sum obtained is less (greater) than either operand, overflow has occurred.

5.4 Multiplying by a small power of 2

Write a sequence of MiniMIPS instructions (using only those in Table 5.1) to multiply the integer *x* stored in register $s0 by 2^n, where *n* is a small nonnegative integer stored in $s1. The result should be placed in $s2. *Hint:* Use repeated doubling.

5.5 Compiling a switch/case statement

A switch/case statement allows multiway branching based on the value of an integer variable. In the following example, the switch variable s can assume one of the three values in [0, 2] and a different action is specified for each case.

```
switch (s) {
        case 0:   a = a + 1; break;
        case 1:   a = a - 1; break;
        case 2:   b = 2 * b; break;
}
```

Show how such a statement can be compiled into MiniMIPS assembly instructions.

5.6 Computing the absolute value

Write a sequence of MiniMIPS instructions to place the absolute value of a parameter that is stored in register $s0 into register $t0.

5.7 Swapping without intermediate values

Write a sequence of MiniMIPS instruction to swap the contents of registers $s0 and $s1 without disturbing the content of any other register. *Hint:* $(x \oplus y) \oplus y = x$.

5.8 Instruction set size

Suppose that in MiniMIPS, all instructions are to be encoded using only the opcode and function fields;

that is, no other part of the instruction should carry information about instruction type, even when it is not used for other purposes. Let n_R, n_I, and n_J be the allowable number of R-type, I-type, and J-type instructions, respectively. Write an equation from which we can obtain the maximum possible value of n_R, n_I, or n_J, when given the other two counts.

5.9 Conditional branching

Modify the solution to Example 5.3 so that the condition tested is:

a. i < j
b. i >= j
c. i + j <= 0
d. i + j > m + n

5.10 Conditional branching

Modify the solution to Example 5.4 so that the condition tested at the end of the loop is:

a. i < n
b. i <= n
c. sum >= 0
d. A[i] == 0

5.11 Mystery program fragment

The following program fragment computes a result *f(n)* in register $s1 when given nonnegative integer *n* in register $s0. Add appropriate comments to the instructions and characterize *f(n)*.

```
         add     $t2,$s0,$s0
         addi    $t2,$t2,1
         addi    $t0,$zero,0
         addi    $t1,$zero,1
loop:    add     $t0,$t0,$t1
         beq     $t1,$t2,done
         addi    $t1,$t1,2
         j       loop
done:    add     $s1,$zero,$t0
```

5.12 Other conditional branches

Using only instructions from Table 5.1, show how an effect equivalent to the following conditional branches can be obtained:

a. bgtz (branch on greater than 0)
b. beqz (branch on equal to 0)

c. `bnez` (branch on not equal to 0)

d. `blez` (branch on less than or equal to 0)

e. `bgez` (branch on greater than or equal to 0)

5.13 Identifying extreme values

Modify the solution to Example 5.5 so that it leads to the identification of:

a. The smallest integer in the list

b. The list element with the largest absolute value

c. The list element whose least significant byte is the largest

5.14 Adding a set of values stored in registers

Write the shortest possible sequence of MiniMIPS instructions from Table 5.1 to add the contents of the 8 registers $s0-$s7, storing the result in $t0. The original contents of the 8 registers should not be modified.

a. Assume that registers $t0 through $t9 can be used freely to hold temporary values.

b. Assume that no register other than $t0 should be modified in the process.

5.15 Modular reduction

Nonnegative integers x and y are stored in registers $s0 and $s1, respectively.

a. Write a sequence of MiniMIPS instructions that compute x mod y, storing the result in $t0. *Hint:* Use repeated subtractions.

b. Derive the number of instructions that are executed in the computation of part a in the best and worst cases.

c. Does your answer to part a lead to a reasonable outcome in the special case of $y = 0$?

d. Augment the instruction sequence in part a so that it also yields $\lfloor x/y \rfloor$ in $t1.

e. Derive the number of instructions that are executed in the computation of part d in the best and worst cases.

5.16 Ring buffer

A 64-entry ring buffer is stored in locations 5000 to 5252 of memory. The storage locations are called $L[0]$ to $L[63]$, with $L[0]$ viewed as following $L[63]$ in circular fashion. Register $s0 holds the address of the first entry $B[0]$ of the buffer. Register $s1 points to the entry just beyond the last one (i.e., where the next element $B[l]$ should be placed, assuming that the current buffer length is l). The fullness of the buffer is indicated by a flag in $s2 that holds 1 if the $l = 64$ and 0 otherwise.

a. Write a sequence of MiniMIPS instructions to copy the content of $t0 into the buffer if it is not full and adjusts the fullness flag if it becomes full afterward.

b. Write a sequence of MiniMIPS instructions to copy the first buffer element into $t1, provided that the buffer is not empty, and adjusts $s0 accordingly.

c. Write a sequence of MiniMIPS instructions to search the buffer to see if it contains an element x whose value if provided in $t2, setting $t3 to 1 if such an element is found and to 0 otherwise.

5.17 Instruction sequence optimization

Consider the following sequence of three high-level language statements: `X = Y + Z; Y = X + Z; W = X - Y`. Write an equivalent sequence of MiniMIPS instructions assuming that W is to be formed in $t0, and X, Y, and Z are in memory locations whose addresses are given in registers $s0, $s1, and $s2, respectively. Further assume the following.

a. The computation is to be performed exactly as specified, with each statement compiled independently of the others.

b. Any sequence of instructions is acceptable as long as the end results are the same.

c. Same as part b, but with the compiler having access to temporary registers that are reserved for its use.

5.18 Initializing a register

a. Identify all possible single MiniMIPS instruction from Table 5.1 that can be used to initialize a desired register to 0 (the all-0s bit pattern).

b. Repeat part a for the all-1s bit pattern.

c. Characterize the set of all bit patterns that can be placed in a desired register using a single instruction from Table 5.1.

REFERENCES AND FURTHER READINGS

[Kane92]   Kane, G., and J. Heinrich, *MIPS RISC Architecture,* Prentice Hall, 1992.

[MIPS]   MIPS Technologies Web site. Follow the architecture and documentation links at:
            http://www.mips.com/

[Patt98]   Patterson, D. A., and J. L. Hennessy, *Computer Organization and Design:
            The Hardware/Software Interface,* Morgan Kaufmann, 2nd ed., 1998.

[Sail96]   Sailer, P. M., and D. R. Kaeli, *The DLX Instruction Set Architecture Handbook,*
            Morgan Kaufmann, 1996.

[SPIM]   SPIM, a free downloadable software simulator for a subset of the MIPS instruction
            set; more information in Section 7.6.
            http://www.cs.wisc.edu/~larus/spim.html

[Swee99]   Sweetman, D., *See MIPS Run,* Morgan Kaufmann, 1999.

PROCEDURES AND DATA

"Mathematicians are like Frenchmen; if you talk to them, they translate it into their own language, and right away it is something entirely different."
—*Johann Wolfgang von Goethe, 1829*

"There are too goddammed many machines that spew out data too fast."
—*Robert Ludlum, Apocalypse Watch, 1996*

┌───┐
│ **TOPICS IN THIS CHAPTER** │
├───┤
│ **6.1** Simple Procedure Calls │
│ **6.2** Using the Stack for Data Storage │
│ **6.3** Parameters and Results │
│ **6.4** Data Types │
│ **6.5** Arrays and Pointers │
│ **6.6** Additional Instructions │
└───┘

In this chapter, we continue our study of the MiniMIPS instruction set by examining instructions needed for procedure calls and the mechanisms used to pass data between the caller and the called routines. In the process, we will learn other details of the instruction-set architecture and become familiar with some important ideas about data types, nested procedure calls, utility of a stack, access to array elements, and applications of pointers. By the end of this chapter, we will know enough instructions to be able to write nontrivial and useful programs.

■ 6.1 Simple Procedure Calls

A *procedure* is a subprogram that when *called (initiated, invoked)* performs a specific task, perhaps leading to one or more results, based on the *input parameters (arguments)* with which it is provided and returns to the point of call, having perturbed nothing else. In assembly language, a procedure is associated with a symbolic name that denotes its starting address. The `jal` instruction in MiniMIPS is intended specifically for procedure calls: it performs the control transfer (unconditional jump) to the starting address of the procedure, while also saving the return address in register `$ra`.

```
jal    proc            # jump to location "proc" and link;
                       # "link" means "save the return
                       # address" (PC)+4 in $ra ($31)
```

Note that while a `jal` instruction is executed, the program counter holds its address; therefore, (PC) + 4 designates the address of the next instruction after `jal`. The machine instruction format for `jal` is identical to that of the jump instruction shown at the top of Figure 5.9, except that the opcode field contains 3.

Using a procedure involves the following sequence of actions.

1. Put arguments in places known to the procedure (registers $a0-$a3).
2. Transfer control to the procedure, saving the return address (`jal`).
3. Acquire storage space, if required, for use by the procedure.
4. Perform the desired task.
5. Put results in places known to the calling program (registers $v0-$v1).
6. Return control to the calling point (`jr`).

The last step is performed via a jump register instruction (Figure 5.9):

```
jr     rs             # go to loc whose address is in rs
```

We will see later how procedures with more than four words of arguments and two words of results can be accommodated.

As a procedure is executed, it makes use of registers to hold operands and partial results. Upon returning from a procedure, the calling program might reasonably expect to find its own operands and partial results where they were prior to the procedure call. If this requirement were to be enforced for all registers, every procedure would need to save the original content of any register that it uses and then restore it prior to termination. Figure 6.1 depicts this saving and restoration within the called procedure as well as the preparation for calling the procedure and continuing in the main program.

To avoid the overhead associated with a large number of register save and restore operations during procedure calls, we use the following convention. A procedure can use registers $v0-$v1 and $t0-$t9 freely without having to save their original contents; in other words, a calling program should not expect any values placed in these 12 registers to remain unchanged after the procedure call. If the calling program has anything of value in these registers, it must save them to other registers or to memory before calling a procedure. This division of responsibility

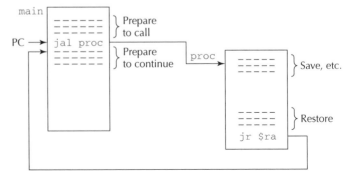

Figure 6.1 Relationship between the main program and a procedure.

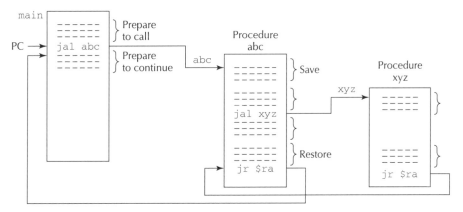

Figure 6.2 Example of nested procedure calls.

between the calling and called programs is quite sensible. It enables us, for example, to call a simple procedure without any saving and restoring overhead whatsoever. As indicated in Figure 5.2, the calling program (*caller*) can expect the values in the following registers undisturbed upon calling a procedure: $a0-$a3, $s0-$s7, $gp, $sp, $fp, $ra. A procedure (*callee* program) that modifies any of these must restore them to their original values before terminating. To summarize, the register saving convention in MiniMIPS is as follows:

Caller-saved registers:	$v0-$v1, $t0-$t9
Callee-saved registers:	$a0-$a3, $s0-$s7, $gp, $sp, $fp, $ra

Uses of the registers $gp, $sp, and $fp will be discussed in Section 6.2. In all cases, saving of a register's content is required only if it will be used in future by the caller/callee. For example, saving of $ra is required only if the callee will be calling another procedure that would then overwrite the current return address with its own return address. In Figure 6.2, the procedure abc in turn calls procedure xyz. Note that before the call to xyz, the calling procedure abc performs some preparatory actions, which include putting the arguments in registers $a0-$a3 and saving any of the registers $v0-$v1 and $t0-$t9 that contain useful data. After return from xyz, procedure abc may transfer any result in $v0-$v1 to other registers. This is needed, for example, before another procedure is called, to avoid overwriting the results of the previous procedure by the next procedure. Note that, with proper care, registers $v0 and $v1 can also be used to pass parameters to a procedure, thus allowing us to pass up to six parameters to a procedure without using the stack.

We illustrate the design of a procedure through two simple examples. More interesting and realistic procedures will be given later in this chapter.

Example 6.1: Procedure to find the absolute value of an integer   Write a MiniMIPS procedure that accepts an integer parameter in register $a0 and returns its absolute value in $v0.

Solution: The absolute value of x is $-x$ if $x < 0$ and x otherwise.

```
abs:    sub   $v0,$zero,$a0   # put -($a0) in $v0; in case ($a0)<0
        bltz  $a0,done        # if ($a0)<0 then done
        add   $v0,$a0,$zero    # else put ($a0) in $v0
done:   jr    $ra             # return to calling program
```

In practice, we seldom use such short procedures because of the excessive overhead that they entail. In this example, we have 3–4 instructions of overhead for 3 instructions of useful computation. The extra instructions are `jal`, `jr`, one instruction to put the parameter in $a0 before the call, and perhaps one instruction to move the returned result (we say "perhaps" because the result could be used directly out of register $v0, if done before the next procedure call).

Example 6.2: Procedure to find the largest of three integers   Write a MiniMIPS procedure that accepts three integer parameters in registers $a0, $a1, and $a2 and returns the maximum of the three values in $v0.

Solution: Begin by assuming that $a0 holds the largest value, compare this value against each of the other two values, and replace it when a larger value is found.

```
max:   add    $v0,$a0,$zero    # copy ($a0) in $v0; largest so far
       sub    $t0,$a1,$v0      # compute ($a1)-($v0)
       bltz   $t0,okay         # if ($a1)-($v0)<0 then no change
       add    $v0,$a1,$zero    # else ($a1) is largest thus far
okay:  sub    $t0,$a2,$v0      # compute ($a2)-($v0)
       bltz   $t0,done         # if ($a2)-($v0)<0 then no change
       add    $v0,$a2,$zero    # else ($a2) is largest overall
done:  jr     $ra              # return to calling program
```

The comments at the end of the solution to Example 6.1 apply here as well. See if you can derive the overhead in this case.

■ 6.2 Using the Stack for Data Storage

The mechanisms and conventions discussed in Section 6.1 are adequate for procedures that accept up to four arguments, return up to two results, and use a dozen or so intermediate values in the course of their computations. Beyond these limits, or when the procedure must itself call another procedure (thus necessitating the saving of some values), additional storage space is needed. A common mechanism for saving things or making room for temporary data that a procedure needs is the use of a dynamic data structure known as a *stack*.

Before discussing the stack and how it solves the data storage problem for procedures, let us look at the conventions for using the memory address space in MiniMIPS. Figure 6.3 shows a map of the MiniMIPS memory and the use of the three pointer registers $gp, $sp, and $fp. The second half of the MiniMIPS memory (beginning with the hex address 0x80000000) is used for memory-mapped I/O and is thus not available for storing programs or data. We will discuss memory-mapped I/O (input/output addressing) in Chapter 22. The first half of memory, extending from address 0 to address 0x7fffffff, is divided into four segments as follows:

The first 1M words (4 MB) are reserved for system use.

The next 63M words (252 MB) hold the text of the program being executed.

Beginning at hex address 0x10000000, the program's data is stored.

Beginning at hex address 0x7ffffffc, and growing backward, is the stack.

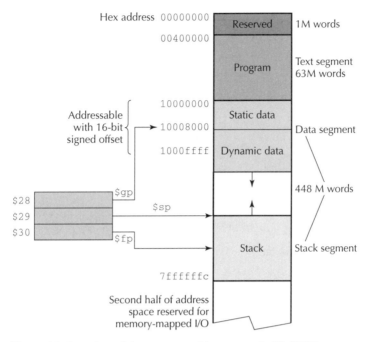

Figure 6.3 Overview of the memory address space in MiniMIPS.

The program's dynamic data and the stack can grow in size up to the maximum available memory. If we set the global pointer register ($gp) to hold the address 0x10008000, then the first 2^{16} bytes of the program's data become readily accessible through base addressing of the form imm($gp), where imm is a 16-bit signed integer.

This brings us to the use of the stack segment and its associated *top-of-stack pointer* register $sp (or *stack pointer,* for short). Stack is a dynamic data structure in which data can be placed and retrieved in last-in, first-out order. It can be likened to the stack of trays in a cafeteria. As trays are cleaned and become ready for use, they are placed on top of the stack of trays; customers likewise take their trays from the top of the stack. The last tray placed on the stack is the first one taken.

Data elements are added to the stack by pushing them onto the stack and are retrieved by popping them. The stack *push* and *pop* operations are illustrated in Figure 6.4 for a stack that has data elements *b* and *a* as its top two elements. The stack pointer points to the top element of the stack currently holding *b*. This means that the instruction lw $t0, 0($sp) causes the value *b* to be copied into $t0 and sw $t1, 0($sp) causes *b* to be overwritten with the content of $t1. Thus, a new element *c* currently in register $t4 can be pushed onto the stack by means of the following two MiniMIPS instructions:

```
push:   addi   $sp,$sp,-4
        sw     $t4,0($sp)
```

Note that the order of the two instructions could be reversed if the address -4($sp) were used instead of 0($sp). To pop the top element *b* from the stack in Figure 6.4, an lw

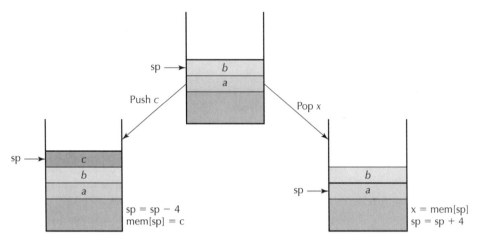

Figure 6.4 Effects of push and pop operations on a stack.

instruction is used for copying b into a desired register and the stack pointer is incremented by 4 to point to the next stack element:

```
pop:   lw      $t5,0($sp)
       addi    $sp,$sp,4
```

Again, we could adjust the stack pointer before copying its top element. Note that a pop operation does not erase the old top element b from the memory; b is still where it was before the pop operation and would in fact be accessible through the address -4($sp). However, the location holding b is no longer considered to be part of the stack, whose top element is now a.

Even though technically a stack is a last-in, first-out data structure, we can in fact access any element within the stack if we know its relative order from the top. For example, the element just below the top of the stack (its second element) can be accessed by using the memory address 4($sp), and the fifteenth stack element is at address 56($sp). Similarly, elements need not be removed one at a time. If we no longer need the top 10 elements of a stack, we can remove them all at once by incrementing the stack pointer by 40.

■ 6.3 Parameters and Results

In this section, we answer the following unresolved questions relating to procedures:

1. How can we pass more than four input parameters to a procedure or receive more than two results from it?
2. Where does a procedure save its own parameters and intermediate results when calling another procedure (nested calls)?

The stack is used in both cases. Before a procedure call, the calling program pushes the contents of any registers that need to be saved onto the top of the stack and follows these with any additional arguments for the procedure. The procedure can access these arguments in the stack. After the procedure terminates, the calling program expects to find the stack pointer undisturbed, thus allowing it to restore the saved registers to their original states and proceed

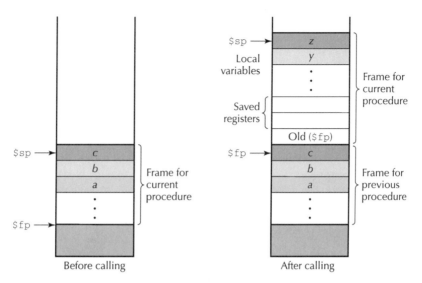

Figure 6.5 Use of the stack by a procedure.

with its own computations. Thus, a procedure that uses the stack by modifying the stack pointer must save the content of the stack pointer at the outset and, at the end, restore $sp to its original state. This is done by copying the stack pointer into the frame pointer register $fp. Before doing this, however, the old contents of the frame pointer must be saved. Hence, while a procedure is executing, $fp may hold the content of $fp right before it was called; $fp and $sp together "frame" the area of the stack that is in use by the current procedure (Figure 6.5).

In the example depicted in Figure 6.5, the three parameters a, b, and c are passed to the procedure by placing them on top of the stack right before the procedure is called. The procedure first pushes the contents of $fp onto the stack, copies the stack pointer into $fp, pushes the contents of registers that need to be saved onto the stack, uses the stack to hold those temporary local variables that cannot be held in registers, and so on. It may later call another procedure by placing arguments, such as y and z, on top of the stack. Each procedure in a nested sequence leaves the part of the stack belonging to the previous callers undisturbed and uses the stack beginning with the empty slot above the entry pointed to by $sp. Upon termination of a procedure, the process is reversed; local variables are popped from the stack, register contents are restored, the frame pointer is copied into $sp, and finally $fp is restored to its original state.

Throughout this process, the $fp provides a stable reference point for addressing memory words in the portion of the stack corresponding to the current procedure. It also provides a convenient way of returning $sp to its original value upon the termination of the procedure. The words in the current frame have addresses 4($fp), 8($fp), 12($fp), and so on. Whereas the stack pointer changes in the course of procedure execution, the frame pointer holds a fixed address throughout. Note that the use of $fp is entirely optional. A procedure that does not itself call another procedure can use the stack for whatever reason without ever changing the stack pointer. It simply stores data in, and accesses, the stack elements beyond the current top of stack by using the memory addresses -4($sp), -8($sp), -12($sp), and so on. In this way, the stack pointer need not be saved because it is never modified by the procedure.

For example, the following procedure saves the contents of $fp, $ra, and $s0 onto the stack at the outset and restores them just before termination:

```
proc: sw    $fp,-4($sp)    # save the old frame pointer
      addi  $fp,$sp,0      # save ($sp) into $fp
      addi  $sp,$sp,-12    # create 3 spaces on top of stack
      sw    $ra,4($sp)     # save ($ra) in 2nd stack element
      sw    $s0,0($sp)     # save ($s0) in top stack element
        .
        .
        .
      lw    $s0,0($sp)     # put top stack element in $s0
      lw    $ra,4($sp)     # put 2nd stack element in $ra
      addi  $sp,$fp,0      # restore $sp to original state
      lw    $fp,8($sp)     # restore $fp to original state
      jr    $ra            # return from procedure
```

If we knew that this procedure neither calls another procedure nor needs the stack for any purpose other than saving the contents of register $s0, we could accomplish the same end without saving $fp or $ra or even adjusting the stack pointer:

```
proc: sw    $s0,-4($sp)    # save ($s0) above top of stack
        .
        .
        .
      lw    $s0,-4($sp)    # put top stack element in $s0
      jr    $ra            # return from procedure
```

This reduces the procedure call overhead substantially.

■ 6.4 Data Types

In Section 5.1, and in Figure 5.2, we referred to various data sizes (*byte, word, doubleword*) in MiniMIPS. Subsequently, however, we considered only instructions dealing with word-size operands. For example, lw and sw transfer words between registers and memory locations, logical instructions operate on 32-bit operands that are viewed as bit strings, and arithmetic instructions operate on word-size signed integers. Other commonly used data sizes are *halfword* (16 bits) and *quadword* (128 bits). Neither of these two types is recognized in MiniMIPS. Even though immediate operands in MiniMIPS are halfwords, they are sign-extended (in the case of signed integers) or zero-extended (in the case of bit strings) to 32 bits before being operated upon. The only exception is in the lui instruction, which loads a 16-bit immediate operand directly into the upper half of a register.

While *data size* refers the number of bits in a particular piece of data, *data type* reflects the meaning assigned to a data element. MiniMIPS has the following data types, each given with all possible sizes that are available:

Signed integer:	byte	word	
Unsigned integer:	byte	word	
Floating-point number:		word	doubleword
Bit string:	byte	word	doubleword

Note that there is no doubleword integer or byte-size floating-point number: the former would be quite feasible and is excluded to simplify the instruction set, while the latter is infeasible. Floating-point numbers will be discussed in Chapter 9; until then, we will say nothing about this data type. So, in the rest of this section, we discuss the differences between signed and unsigned integers and some notions relating to bit strings.

In MiniMIPS, signed integers are represented in 2's-complement format. Integers can assume values in the interval $[-2^7, 2^7 - 1] = [-128, 127]$ in 8-bit format and $[-2^{31}, 2^{31} - 1] = [-2\ 147\ 483\ 648, 2\ 147\ 483\ 647]$ in 32-bit format. In machine representation, the sign of a signed integer is evident from its most significant bit: 0 for "+" and 1 for "−." We will study this representation in Section 9.4. Unsigned integers are just ordinary binary numbers with values in $[0, 2^8 - 1] = [0, 255]$ in 8-bit format and $[0, 2^{32} - 1] = [0, 4\ 294\ 967\ 295]$ in 32-bit format. The rules of arithmetic with signed and unsigned numbers are different; hence, MiniMIPS provides a number of instructions for unsigned arithmetic. These will be presented in Section 6.6. Changing the data size is also performed differently for signed and unsigned numbers. Going from a narrower format to a wider format is done by sign extension (repeating the sign bit in the additional positions) for signed numbers and by zero extension for unsigned numbers. The following examples illustrate the difference:

Type	8-bit number	Value	32-bit version of the same number
Unsigned	0010 1011	43	0000 0000 0000 0000 0000 0000 0010 1011
Unsigned	1010 1011	171	0000 0000 0000 0000 0000 0000 1010 1011
Signed	0010 1011	+43	0000 0000 0000 0000 0000 0000 0010 1011
Signed	1010 1011	−85	1111 1111 1111 1111 1111 1111 1010 1011

Sometimes, we want to process strings of bytes (e.g., small integers or symbols from an alphabet) as opposed to words. We will present, shortly, load and store instructions for byte-size data. It is evident from the preceding discussion that a signed byte and an unsigned 8-bit integer will be loaded differently into a 32-bit register. For this reason, the "load byte" instruction, like several other instructions with similar properties, will have two versions, for signed and unsigned values.

An important use for byte-size data elements is to represent the symbols of an alphabet consisting of letters (uppercase and lowercase), digits, punctuation marks, and other needed symbols. In hex notation, an 8-bit byte becomes a 2-digit number. Table 6.1 depicts how such 2-digit hex numbers (8-bit bytes) are assigned to represent the symbols of the American Standard Code for Information Interchange (ASCII). Table 6.1 actually defines a 7-bit code and leaves the right half of the code table unspecified. The unspecified half can be used for other needed symbols in various applications. Even though "8-bit/7-bit ASCII" is the correct usage, we sometimes talk about "8-bit/7-bit ASCII code" (i.e., repeating "code" for clarity).

When an alphabet with more than 256 symbols is involved, each symbol requires more than one byte for its representation. The next larger data size, a halfword, can be used to encode an alphabet with up to $2^{16} = 65,536$ symbols. This is more than adequate for virtually all applications of interest. Unicode, which is an international standard, uses 16-bit halfwords for representing each symbol.

■ **TABLE 6.1** ASCII (American Standard Code for Information Interchange)[1,2]

	0	1	2	3	4	5	6	7	8–9	a–f
0	NUL	DLE	SP[4]	0	@	P	`	p		
1	SOH	DC1	!	1	A	Q	a	q	M	M
2	STX	DC2	"	2	B	R	b	r	O	O
3	ETX	DC3	#	3	C	S	c	s	R	R
4	EOT	DC4	$[3]	4	D	T	d	t	E	E
5	ENQ	NAK	%	5	E	U	e	u		
6	ACK	SYN	&	6	F	V	f	v	C	S
7	BEL	ETB	'	7	G	W	g	w	O	Y
8	BS	CAN	(	8	H	X	h	x	N	M
9	HT	EM	)	9	I	Y	i	y	T	B
a	LF	SUB	*	:	J	Z	j	z	R	O
b	VT	ESC	+	;	K	[	k	{	O	L
c	FF	FS	,	<	L	\	l			L	S
d	CR	GS	-	=	M	]	m	}	S	
e	SO	RS	.	>	N	^	n	~		
f	SI	US	/	?	O	_	o	DEL[4]		

1: The 8-bit ASCII code is formed as $\texttt{(column\# row\#)}_{hex}$; for example, "+" is $\texttt{(2b)}_{hex}$.
2: Columns 0–7 define the 7-bit ASCII code; for example, "+" is $(010\ 1011)_{two}$.
3: The ISO code differs from ASCII only in the monetary symbol.
4: Columns 0–1 and 8–9 hold control characters, listed in alphabetical order:

ACK	Acknowledge	EM	End of medium	GS	Group separator
BEL	Bell	ENQ	Enquiry	HT	Horizontal tab
BS	Backspace	EOT	End of trans.	LF	Line feed
CAN	Cancel	ESC	Escape	NAK	Negative ack.
CR	Carriage return	ETB	End trans. block	NUL	Null
DCi	Device control i	ETX	End of text	RS	Record separator
DEL	Delete	FF	Form feed	SI	Shift in
DLE	Data link escape	FS	File separator	SO	Shift out

SOH	Start of heading
SP	Space
STX	Start of text
SUB	Substitute
SYN	Synchronous idle
US	Unit separator
VT	Vertical tab

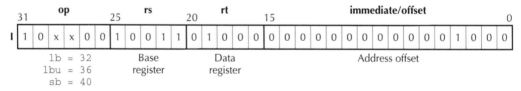

Figure 6.6 Load and store instructions for byte-size data elements.

In MiniMIPS, the "load byte," "load byte unsigned," and "store byte" instructions allow us to transfer bytes between memory and registers:

```
lb      $t0,8($s3)      # load rt with byte mem[8+($s3)];
                        # sign-extend to fill the register
lbu     $t0,8($s3)      # load rt with byte mem[8+($s3)];
                        # zero-extend to fill the register
sb      $t0,A($s3)      # store byte 0 of rt to mem[A+($s3)]
```

The machine instruction format for lb, lbu, and sbu instructions is depicted in Figure 6.6. As usual, the base address can be specified as an absolute value or by a symbolic name.

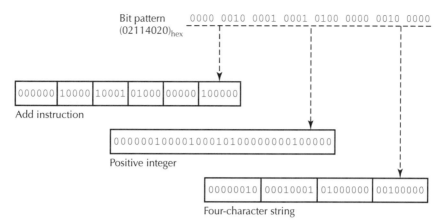

Figure 6.7 A 32-bit word has no inherent meaning and can be interpreted in a number of equally valid ways in the absence of other cues (e.g., context) for the intended meaning.

We conclude this section with a very important observation. A bit string, stored in memory or in a register, has no inherent meaning. A 32-bit word can mean different things depending on how it is interpreted or processed. For example, Figure 6.7 shows that the same word can mean three different things depending on how it is interpreted or used. The word represented by the hex pattern `0x02114020` becomes an add instruction if fetched from memory and executed. The same word, when used as an integer operand in an arithmetic instruction, represents a positive integer. Finally, as a string of bits, the word might represent a sequence of four ASCII symbols. None of these interpretations is more natural, or more valid, than others. Other interpretations are also possible. For example, we can view the bit string as a pair of Unicode symbols or the attendance record for 32 students in a particular class session, with 0 designating "absent" and 1 meaning "present."

■ 6.5 Arrays and Pointers

In a wide variety of programming tasks, it becomes necessary to step through an array or list, examining each of its elements in turn. For example, to determine the largest value in a list of integers, every element of the list must be examined. There are two basic ways of accomplishing this:

1. *Index:* Use a register that holds the index i and increment the register in each step to effect moving from element i of the list to element $i + 1$.
2. *Pointer:* Use a register that points to (holds the address of) the list element being examined and update it in each step to point to the next element.

Either approach is valid, but the second one is somewhat more efficient for MiniMIPS, given its lack of an indexed addressing mode that would allow the value in the index register i to be used in the address calculation. To implement the first scheme, the address must be computed by several instructions that essentially form $4i$ and then add the result to the register holding the base address of the array or list. In the second scheme, a single instruction that adds 4 to the pointer register accomplishes the advancement to the next array element. Figure 6.8 graphically represents the two methods.

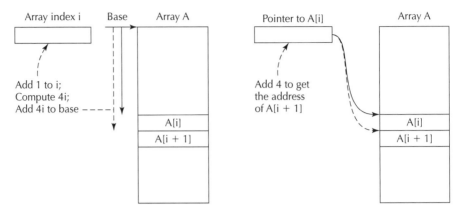

Figure 6.8 Using the indexing method and the pointer updating method to step through the elements of an array.

However, dealing with pointers is conceptually more difficult and error-prone, whereas use of array indices appears more natural and is thus easier to understand. So, the use of pointers just to improve the program efficiency is usually not recommended. Fortunately, modern compilers are intelligent enough to replace such indexed code with the equivalent (more efficient) code that uses pointers. So, programmers can relax and use whatever form is most natural for them.

We illustrate the use of these methods by means of two examples. Example 6.3 uses array indices while Example 6.4 takes advantage of pointers.

Example 6.3: Maximum-sum prefix in a list of integers   Consider a list of integers of length n. A *prefix* of length i for the given list consists of the first i integers in the list, where $0 \leq i \leq n$. A maximum-sum prefix, as the name implies, is a prefix for which the sum of elements is the largest among all prefixes. For example, if the list is $(2, -3, 2, 5, -4)$, its maximum-sum prefix consists of the first four elements and the associated sum is $2 - 3 + 2 + 5 = 6$; no other prefix of the given list has a larger sum. Write a MiniMIPS program to find the length of the maximum-sum prefix and the sum of its elements for a given list.

Solution: The strategy for solving this problem is rather obvious. We begin by initializing the max-sum prefix to length 0 with a sum of 0. We then gradually increase the length of the prefix, each time computing the new sum and comparing it with the maximum sum thus far. When a larger sum is encountered, the length and sum of the max-sum prefix are updated. We write the program in the form of a procedure that accepts the array base address A in $\$a0$ and its length n in $\$a1$, returning the length of the max-sum prefix in $\$v0$ and the associated sum in $\$v1$.

```
                                   # base A in $a0, length n in $a1
mspfx: addi  $v0,$zero,0           # initialize length in $v0 to 0
       addi  $v1,$zero,0           # initialize max sum in $v1 to 0
       addi  $t0,$zero,0           # initialize index i in $t0 to 0
       addi  $t1,$zero,0           # initialize running sum in $t1 to 0
loop:  add   $t2,$t0,$t0           # put 2i in $t2
       add   $t2,$t2,$t2           # put 4i in $t2
```

```
              addi   $t3,$t2,$a0    # put 4i+A (address of A[i]) in $t3
              lw     $t4,0($t3)     # load A[i] from mem[($t3)] into $t4
              add    $t1,$t1,$t4    # add A[i] to running sum in $t1
              slt    $t5,$v1,$t1    # set $t5 to 1 if max sum < new sum
              bne    $t5,$zero,mdfy # if max sum is less, modify results
              j      test           # done?
mdfy:         addi   $v0,$t0,1      # new max-sum prefix has length i+1
              addi   $v1,$t1,0      # new max sum is the running sum
test:         addi   $t0,$t0,1      # advance the index i
              slt    $t5,$t0,$a1    # set $t5 to 1 if i < n
              bne    $t5,$zero,loop # repeat if i < n
done:         jr     $ra            # return length=($v0), max sum=($v1)
```

Because the prefix data is modified only when a strictly larger sum is encountered, the procedure identifies the shortest prefix if there are several prefixes with the same maximum sum.

Example 6.4: Selection sort using a max-finding procedure A given list of n numbers can be sorted in ascending order as follows. Find a largest number in the list (there may be more than one) and swap it with the last element in the list. The new last element is now in its proper position in sorted order. Now, sort the remaining $n - 1$ elements using the same step repeatedly. When only one element is left, sorting is complete. This method is known as *selection sort*. Write a MiniMIPS program for selection sorting using a procedure to find the maximum element in a list.

Solution: Figure 6.9 illustrates one iteration of the algorithm. The unsorted part of the list is delimited by the two pointers first and last. The procedure max is called to identify a largest element in the unsorted part along with its location in the list. This element is then swapped with the last list element, the last pointer is decremented to point to the new last element, and the process is repeated until first = last.

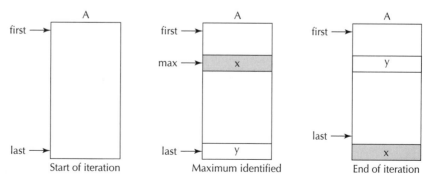

Figure 6.9 One iteration of selection sort.

```
# register usage in sort program
#    $a0    pointer to first element in unsorted part
#    $a1    pointer to last element in unsorted part
```

```
        #     $t0    temporary place for value of last element
        #     $v0    pointer to max element in unsorted part
        #     $v1    value of max element in unsorted part
sort: beq  $a0,$a1,done    # single-element list is sorted
      jal  max             # call the max procedure
      lw   $t0,0($a1)      # load last element into $t0
      sw   $t0,0($v0)      # copy last element to max location
      sw   $v1,0($a1)      # copy max value to last element
      addi $a1,$a1,-4      # decrement pointer to last element
      j    sort            # repeat sort for smaller list
done: ...                  # continue with rest of program
        # register usage in max procedure
        #     $a0    pointer to first element
        #     $a1    pointer to last element
        #     $t0    pointer to next element
        #     $t1    value of next element
        #     $t2    result of "(next) < (max)" comparison
        #     $v0    pointer to max element
        #     $v1    value of max element
max:  addi $v0,$a0,0       # init max pointer to first element
      lw   $v1,0($v0)      # init max value to first value
      addi $t0,$a0,0       # init next pointer to first
loop: beq  $t0,$a0,ret     # if next = last, return
      addi $t0,$t0,4       # advance to next element
      lw   $t1,0($t0)      # load next element into $t1
      slt  $t2,$t1,$v1     # (next)<(max)?
      bne  $t2,$zero,loop  # if (next)<(max), repeat with n/c
      addi $v0,$t0,0       # next element is new max element
      addi $v1,$t1,0       # next value is new max value
      j    loop            # change completed; now repeat
ret:  jr   $ra             # return to calling program
```

Because procedure max replaces a previously identified maximum element with a later one that has the same value, the maximum element identified is the last one among several equal values. Thus, our sorting algorithm preserves the original order of several equal elements in the list. Such a sorting algorithm is known as a *stable sorting algorithm*. It is instructive to compare the max procedure in this example with the program in Example 5.5, which essentially performs the same computation by means of indexed addressing.

■ 6.6 Additional Instructions

We introduced 20 instructions for MiniMIPS in Chapter 5 (see Table 5.1) and four additional instructions for procedure call (jal) and byte-oriented data (lb, lbu, sb) thus far in this chapter. As Examples 6.3 and 6.4 indicate, we can write useful and nontrivial programs using only these 24 instructions. However, MiniMIPS has additional instructions that allow us to perform more complex computations and to express programs more efficiently. A number of such instructions are presented in this section, bringing the total to 40 instructions. These 40 instructions complete the core part of the MiniMIPS instruction-set architecture. We have yet to cover instructions dealing with floating-point arithmetic and exceptions (i.e., the coprocessors shown in Figure 5.1). Floating-point instructions will be introduced in Chapter 12, whereas instructions relating to exception handling will be introduced as needed, beginning with Section 14.6.

We begin by introducing several additional arithmetic/logic instructions. The multiply (mult) instruction is an R-format instruction that places the doubleword product of the contents of two registers into the Hi (upper half) and Lo (lower half) registers. The div instruction computes the remainder and quotient of the contents of two source registers, placing them in the special Hi and Lo registers, respectively.

```
mult    $s0, $s1        # set Hi,Lo to ($s0)×($s1)
div     $s0, $s1        # set Hi to ($s0)mod($s1)
                        # and Lo to ($s0)/($s1)
```

Figure 6.10 depicts the machine representations of mult and div instructions.

To be able to use the results of mult and div, two special instructions, "move from Hi" (mfhi) and "move from Lo" (mflo) are provided to copy the contents of these two special registers into one of the general registers:

```
mfhi    $t0             # set $t0 to (Hi)
mflo    $t0             # set $t0 to (Lo)
```

Figure 6.11 depicts the machine representations of mfhi and mflo instructions.

Now that we have learned about the MiniMIPS multiply instruction, it may be tempting to use mult for computing the offset $4i$, which is needed when the ith element of an array is to be accessed in memory. However, as will become clear in Part III, multiplication and division are significantly more complex, and thus slower, operations than addition and subtraction. Thus, it is still advisable to compute $4i$ through two additions ($i + i = 2i$ and $2i + 2i = 4i$) rather than via a single multiplication.

Of course an even more efficient way of computing $4i$ is through a 2-bit left shift of i, provided i is an unsigned integer (as is usually the case in array indexing). Shifting of signed values will be discussed in Section 10.5. The MiniMIPS instruction that allows us to left-shift the content of a register by a known amount is called "shift left logical" (sll). Similarly, "shift right

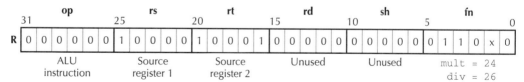

Figure 6.10 The multiply (mult) and divide (div) instructions of MiniMIPS.

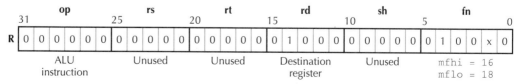

Figure 6.11 MiniMIPS instructions for copying the contents of Hi and Lo registers into general registers.

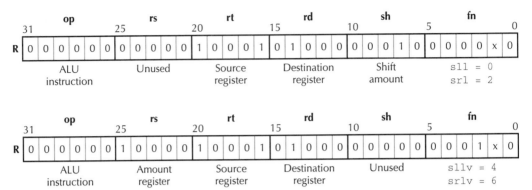

Figure 6.12 The four logical shift instructions of MiniMIPS.

logical" (srl) shifts a register's content to the right. The need for the qualification "logical" will become clear as we discuss arithmetic shifts in Section 10.5. For now, simply remember that logical shifts move the bits of a word to the left or right, filling the vacated positions with 0s and discarding any bit that moves out from the other end of the word. The sll and srl instructions deal with a constant shift amount that is given in the "sh" field of the instruction. For a variable shift amount that is given in a register, the relevant instructions are sllv and srlv.

```
sll     $t0,$s1,2       # $t0 = ($s1) left-shifted by 2
srl     $t0,$s1,2       # $t0 = ($s1) right-shifted by 2
sllv    $t0,$s1,$s0     # $t0 = ($s1) left-shifted by ($s0)
srlv    $t0,$s1,$s0     # $t0 = ($s1) right-shifted by ($s0)
```

An h-bit left shift multiplies the unsigned value x by 2^h, provided x is small enough that $2^h x$ is still representable in 32 bits. An h-bit right shift divides an unsigned value by 2^h, discarding the fractional part and keeping the integer quotient. Figure 6.12 shows the machine representation of the preceding four shift instructions.

Finally, because unsigned integers play such an important role in many computations, a number of MiniMIPS instructions have variations in which one or both operands are considered unsigned numbers. These instructions have the same symbolic names as the corresponding signed instructions, but with "u" added at the end.

```
addu    $t0,$s0,$s1     # set $t0 to ($s0)+($s1)
subu    $t0,$s0,$s1     # set $t0 to ($s0)-($s1)
multu   $s0,$s1         # set Hi,Lo to ($s0)×($s1)
divu    $s0,$s1         # set Hi to ($s0)mod($s1) and
                        # Lo to ($s0)/($s1)
addiu   $t0,$s0,61      # set $t0 to ($s0)+61 (decimal);
                        # the immediate operand is viewed
                        # as signed (it is sign extended)
```

Machine representations of these instructions are identical to those of the signed versions, except that the fn field value is 1 more for R-type instructions and the op field value is 1 more for addiu (see Figures 5.5, 6.10, and 5.6).

Note that the immediate operand in addiu is actually a 16-bit signed value that is sign-extended to 32 bits before being added to the unsigned operand in a specified register. This is one of those irregularities that must be remembered. Intuitively, one might think that both operands of `addiu` are unsigned values and this expectation is quite logical. However, because there in no "subtract immediate unsigned" instruction in MiniMIPS and there are occasions when we need to subtract something from an unsigned value, this seemingly illogical design choice has been made.

In all, 37 MiniMIPS instructions were introduced in Chapters 5 and 6. Table 6.2 summarizes these instructions for review and ready reference. At this point, you should have a complete

TABLE 6.2 The 40 MiniMIPS instructions covered in Chapters 5–7.*

Class	Instruction	Usage	Meaning	op	fn
	Move from Hi	`mfhi rd`	rd ← (Hi)	0	16
Copy	Move from Lo	`mflo rd`	rd ← (Lo)	0	18
	Load upper immediate	`lui rt,imm`	rt ← (imm, 0x0000)	15	
	Add	`add rd,rs,rt`	rd ← (rs) + (rt); with overflow	0	32
	Add unsigned	`addu rd,rs,rt`	rd ← (rs) + (rt); no overflow	0	33
	Subtract	`sub rd,rs,rt`	rd ← (rs) − (rt); with overflow	0	34
	Subtract unsigned	`subu rd,rs,rt`	rd ← (rs) − (rt); no overflow	0	35
	Set less than	`slt rd,rs,rt`	rd ← if (rs) < (rt) then 1 else 0	0	42
Arithmetic	Multiply	`mult rs,rt`	Hi, Lo ← (rs) × (rt)	0	24
	Multiply unsigned	`multu rs,rt`	Hi, Lo ← (rs) × (rt)	0	25
	Divide	`div rs,rt`	Hi ← (rs)mod(rt); Lo ← (rs) ÷ (rt)	0	26
	Divide unsigned	`divu rs,rt`	Hi ← (rs)mod(rt); Lo ← (rs) ÷ (rt) ·	0	27
	Add immediate	`addi rt,rs,imm`	rt ← (rs) + imm; with overflow	8	
	Add immediate unsigned	`addiu rt,rs,imm`	rt ← (rs) + imm; no overflow	9	
	Set less than immediate	`slti rd,rs,imm`	rd ← if (rs) < imm then 1 else 0	10	
	Shift left logical	`sll rd,rt,sh`	rd ← (rt) left-shifted by sh	0	0
	Shift right logical	`srl rd,rt,sh`	rd ← (rt) right-shifted by sh	0	2
Shift	Shift right arithmetic	`sra rd,rt,sh`	Like srl, but sign extended	0	3
	Shift left logical variable	`sllv rd,rt,rs`	rd ← (rt) left-shifted by (rs)	0	4
	Shift right logical variable	`srlv rd,rt,rs`	rd ← (rt) right-shifted by (rs)	0	6
	Shift right arith variable	`srav rd,rt,rs`	Like srlv, but sign extended	0	7
	AND	`and rd,rs,rt`	rd ← (rs) ∧ (rt)	0	36
	OR	`or rd,rs,rt`	rd ← (rs) ∨ (rt)	0	37
	XOR	`xor rd,rs,rt`	rd ← (rs) ⊕ (rt)	0	38
Logic	NOR	`nor rd,rs,rt`	rd ← ((rs) ∨ (rt))′	0	39
	AND immediate	`andi rt,rs,imm`	rt ← (rs) ∧ imm	12	
	OR immediate	`ori rt,rs,imm`	rt ← (rs) ∨ imm	13	
	XOR immediate	`xori rt,rs,imm`	rt ← (rs) ⊕ imm	14	
	Load word	`lw rt,imm(rs)`	rt ← mem[(rs) + imm]	35	
	Load byte	`lb rt,imm(rs)`	Load byte 0, sign-extend	32	
Memory access	Load byte unsigned	`lbu rt,imm(rs)`	Load byte 0, zero-extend	36	
	Store word	`sw rt,imm(rs)`	mem[(rs) + imm] ← rt	43	
	Store byte	`sb rt,imm(rs)`	Store byte 0	40	
	Jump	`j L`	goto L	2	
	Jump and link	`jal L`	goto L; $31 ← (PC) + 4	3	
	Jump register	`jr rs`	goto (rs)	0	8
Control transfer	Branch less than 0	`bltz rs,L`	if (rs) < 0 then goto L	1	
	Branch equal	`beq rs,rt,L`	if (rs) = (rt) then goto L	4	
	Branch not equal	`bne rs,rt,L`	if (rs) ≠ (rt) then goto L	5	
	System call	`syscall`	See Section 7.6 (Table 7.2)	0	12

*Arithmetic right-shift instructions (`sra`, `srav`), to be covered in Section 10.5, and `syscall` are also included for completeness.

understanding of Table 6.2, except for the phrases "set overflow" and "no overflow" in the "Meaning" column and the following three instructions:

```
sra      $t0,$s1,2      # shift right arith
srav     $t0,$s1,$s0    # shift right arith variable
syscall                 # system call
```

Arithmetic right shifts, and how they differ from logical right shifts, will be covered in Section 10.5. System call, including its use for performing input/output operations, will be discussed in Section 7.6, with details listed in Table 7.2.

PROBLEMS

6.1 Nested procedure calls

Modify the nested procedure call diagram in Figure 6.2 to correspond to the following changes:

a. Procedure xyz calls the new procedure def.
b. After calling xyz, procedure abc calls another procedure uvw.
c. Procedure abc calls xyz two different times.
d. After calling abc, the main program calls xyz.

6.2 Choosing one of three integers

Modify the procedure of Example 6.2 (finding the largest of three integers) so that it:

a. Also returns the index (0, 1, or 2) of the largest value in $v1
b. Finds the smallest of the three values instead of the largest
c. Finds the median of the three values instead of the largest

6.3 Divisibility by powers of 2

A binary integer that has h consecutive 0s at its right end is divisible by 2^h. Write a MiniMIPS procedure that accepts a single unsigned integer in register $a0 and returns the largest power of 2 by which it is divisible (an integer in [0, 32]) in register $v0.

6.4 Hamming distance between two words

The Hamming distance between two bit strings of the same length is the number of positions in which the strings have different bit values. For example, the Hamming distance between 1110 and 0101 is 3. Write a procedure that accepts two words in registers $a0 and $a1 and returns their Hamming distance (an integer in [0, 32]) in register $v0.

6.5 Meanings of a bit string

a. Decode the instruction, the positive integer, and the four-character ASCII string in Figure 6.7.
b. Repeat part a for the case when the instruction is andi $t1,$s2,13108.
c. Repeat part a for the case when the integer is 825,240,373.
d. Repeat part a for the case when the character string is '<US>'.

6.6 Determining the length of a character string

Write a procedure, howlong, that takes a pointer to a null-terminated ASCII string in register $a0 and returns the length of the string, excluding its null terminator, in register $v0. For example, if the argument to howlong points to the string 'not very long,' the returned value will be the integer 13.

6.7 Unpacking a character string

Write a sequence of MiniMIPS instructions (with comments) that would separate and put the 4 bytes of a character-string operand given in register $s0 into registers $t0 (least significant byte), $t1, $t2, and

$t3 (most significant byte). You can use $t4 and $t5 as temporaries if needed.

6.8 Recursive procedure for computing n!

a. The function $f(n) = n!$ can be defined recursively as $f(n) = n \times f(n-1)$. Write a recursive procedure, defined as a procedure that calls itself, to accept n in $a0 and return n! in $v0. Assume n small enough that the value of n! fits in the result register.

b. Repeat part a, but assume that the result is a doubleword and is returned in registers $v0 and $v1.

6.9 Prefix, postfix, and subsequence sums

Modify the procedure in Example 6.3 (finding the maximum-sum prefix in a list of integers) such that:

a. The longest prefix with maximum sum is identified.

b. The minimum-sum prefix is identified.

c. The maximum-sum postfix (elements at the end of the list) is identified.

d. The maximum-sum subsequence is identified. *Hint:* Any subsequence sum is the difference between two prefix sums.

6.10 Selection sort

Modify the procedure in Example 6.4 (selection sort) such that:

a. It sorts in descending order.

b. The keys that it sorts in ascending order are doublewords.

c. It sorts the list of key [...] also rearranges a list [...] the keys so that if a k [...] the list of keys is sor [...] is also in position j c [...] values.

6.11 Computing an XOR checksum

Write a procedure that accepts a byte string (base address in $a0, length in $a1) and returns its XOR checksum, defined as the exclusive-OR of all its bytes, in $v0.

6.12 Modifying the MiniMIPS ISA

Consider the following 32-bit instruction formats which are quite similar to those of MiniMIPS. The six fields are different in their widths and names, but have same roles as the corresponding fields of MiniMIPS.

Answer each of the following questions under two different assumptions: (1) register width remains at 32 bits and (2) registers are 64 bits wide. Assume that the action field holds 00xx for R-format, 1xxx for I-format, and 01xx for J-format instructions.

a. What is the maximum possible number of different instructions in each of the three classes R, I, and J?

b. Can we encode all the instructions shown in Table 6.2 with this new format?

c. Can you think of any new instruction that might be desirable to add in view of the changes?

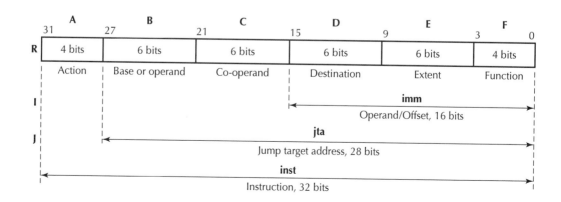

ng a procedure

sequence of MiniMIPS instructions to find
element of a list of integers with the largest
solute value, making use of the procedure of
Example 6.1. Assume that the starting address and
number of integers in the list are supplied in registers
$s0 and $s1, respectively.

6.14 Stack and frame pointers

Draw a schematic diagram of the stack (similar to
Figure 6.5), corresponding to the calling relationships
depicted in Figure 6.2, for each of the following cases,
showing the stack and frame pointers as arrows:

a. Within the main program, before calling the
   procedure abc
b. Within procedure abc, before calling the
   procedure xyz
c. Within procedure xyz
d. Within procedure abc, after return from the
   procedure xyz
e. Within the main program, after return from the
   procedure abc

6.15 ASCII/integer conversion

a. A decimal number is stored in memory in the
   form of a null-terminated ASCII string. Write a
   MiniMIPS procedure that accepts the starting

address of the ASCII string in register $a0 and
returns the equivalent integer value in register
$v0. Ignore the possibility of overflow and
assume that the number can begin with a digit
or a sign (+ or −).

b. Write a MiniMIPS procedure to perform the
   reverse of the conversion in part a.

6.16 Emulating shift instructions

Show how the effect of each of the following
instructions can be achieved using only instructions
introduced before Section 6.5.

a. Shift left logical, sll.
b. Shift left logical variable, sllv.
c. Shift right logical, srl. *Hint:* Use left rotation
   (circular shift) by an appropriate amount, followed
   by zeroing of some of the bits.
d. Shift right logical variable, srlv.

6.17 Emulating other instructions

a. Identify all instructions in Table 6.2 whose effect
   can be achieved through no more than two other
   instructions, using at most one register for
   intermediate values (use $at if needed).
b. Are there instructions in Table 6.2 whose effects
   cannot be achieved through other instructions, no
   matter how many instructions or registers we are
   allowed to use?

REFERENCES AND FURTHER READINGS

[Kane92]   Kane, G., and J. Heinrich, *MIPS RISC Architecture,* Prentice Hall, 1992.

[MIPS]   MIPS Technologies Web site. Follow the architecture and documentation links at:
http://www.mips.com/

[Patt98]   Patterson, D. A., and J. L. Hennessy, *Computer Organization and Design: The
Hardware/Software Interface,* Morgan Kaufmann, 2nd ed., 1998.

[Sail96]   Sailer, P. M., and D. R. Kaeli, *The DLX Instruction Set Architecture Handbook,*
Morgan Kaufmann, 1996.

[SPIM]   SPIM, a free downloadable software simulator for a subset of the MIPS instruction
set; more information in Section 7.6.
http://www.cs.wisc.edu/~larus/spim.html

[Swee99]   Sweetman, D., *See MIPS Run,* Morgan Kaufmann, 1999.

CHAPTER 7

ASSEMBLY LANGUAGE PROGRAMS

"The code says what the program is doing, the remarks (comments) say what it is supposed to be doing. Debugging is reconciling the differences."
—*Tony Amico, Tonyism*

"Software stands between the user and the machine."
—*Harlan D. Mills*

TOPICS IN THIS CHAPTER

To build and run efficient and useful assembly language programs, one needs more than a knowledge of machine instruction types and formats. For one thing, the assembler needs certain types of information about the program and its data that are not evident from the instructions themselves. For another, convenience dictates the use of certain pseudoinstructions and macros, which although not in one-to-one correspondence with machine instructions, are easily converted to the latter by the assembler. Rounding up the topics in this chapter are brief descriptions of the loading and linking processes and that of running assembly language programs.

■ 7.1 Machine and Assembly Languages

Machine instructions are represented as binary bit strings. In the case of MiniMIPS, all instructions have a uniform width of 32 bits and thus fit in a single word. In Chapter 8, we will see that certain other machines use variable-width instructions that lead to more efficient encoding of the intended actions. Whether fixed- or variable-width, binary *machine code,* or its equivalent hex representation, is ill-suited to human understanding. For this reason, *assembly*

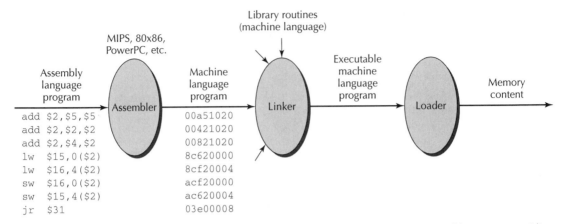

Figure 7.1 Steps in transforming an assembly language program to an executable program residing in memory.

languages have been developed that allow the use of symbolic names for instructions and their operands. Additionally, assemblers accept numbers in a variety of simple and natural representations and automatically convert them to the required machine formats. Finally, assemblers allow the use of *pseudoinstructions* and *macros* that serve the same purpose as abbreviations and acronyms in natural languages, that is, to allow more compact representations that are easier to write, read, and understand.

In Chapters 5 and 6, we introduced parts of the assembly language for the hypothetical MiniMIPS computer. Instruction sequences written in symbolic assembly language are translated to machine language by a program called "*assembler.*" Multiple program modules that are independently assembled are *linked* together and combined with (predeveloped) *library* routines to form a complete *executable program* which is then *loaded* into a computer's memory (Figure 7.1). Independently assembling program modules and then linking them is beneficial because when one module is modified, the other parts of the program do not have to be reassembled. The working of the linker and loader will be discussed in more detail in Section 7.5.

Instead of being loaded into a computer's memory, instructions of a machine language program may be *interpreted* by a *simulator:* a program that examines each instruction and carries out its function, updating variables and data structures that correspond to registers and other machine parts holding information. Such simulators are commonly used during the process of designing new machines to write and debug programs before any working hardware is available.

Most assembly language instructions are in one-to-one correspondence with machine instructions. The process of translating such an assembly language instruction into the corresponding machine instruction involves assigning appropriate binary codes to symbolically specified operations, registers, memory locations, immediate operands, and so on. Some pseudoinstructions and all macroinstructions correspond to multiple machine instructions. An assembler reads a *source file* containing the assembly language program and accompanying information (assembler directives or certain bookkeeping details) and in the process of producing the corresponding machine language program:

Keeps a *symbol table* containing name-address correspondences

Builds the program's text and data segments

Forms an *object file* containing header, text, data, and relocation information

The assembly process is often performed in two passes. The main function of the first pass is construction of the symbol table. A *symbol* is a string of characters that is used as an instruction label or as a variable name. As instructions are read, the assembler maintains an *instruction location counter* that determines the relative position of the instruction in the machine language program and, hence, the numeric equivalent of the instruction's label, if any. All this is done assuming that the program will be loaded beginning with address 0 in memory. Because the eventual placement of the program is often different, the assembler also compiles information about what needs to be done if the program is loaded beginning with another (arbitrary) address. This *relocation information* is part of the file produced by the assembler and will be used by the loader to modify the program according to its eventual location in memory.

Consider, for example, the assembly language instruction:

```
test:     bne      $t0,$s0,done
```

As the assembler reads this line, it detects the operation symbol "bne," two register symbols "$t0" and "$s0," and the instruction labels "test" and "done." The appropriate code for "bne" is read out from an opcode table (which also contains information about the number and types of operands that are expected), whereas the meanings of "$t0" and "$s0" are obtained from another reference table. The symbol "test" is entered in the symbol table along with the current content of the instruction location counter as its value. The symbol "done" may or may not be in the symbol table, depending on whether the branch is a backward (to a previous instruction) or forward branch. If it is a backward branch, then the numeric equivalent of "done" is already known and can be used in its place. In case of a forward branch, a symbol table entry is created for "done" with its value left blank; the value will be filled in on the second pass after all instruction labels have been assigned numeric equivalents.

This process of *resolving forward references* is the primary reason we need a second pass. It is also possible to perform the entire process in a single pass, but this would require leaving suitable markers for unresolved forward references so that their values can be filled in at the end.

Figure 7.2 shows a short assembly language program, its assembled version, and the symbol table created during the assembly process. The program is incomplete and does not make sense, but it does illustrate some of the concepts just discussed.

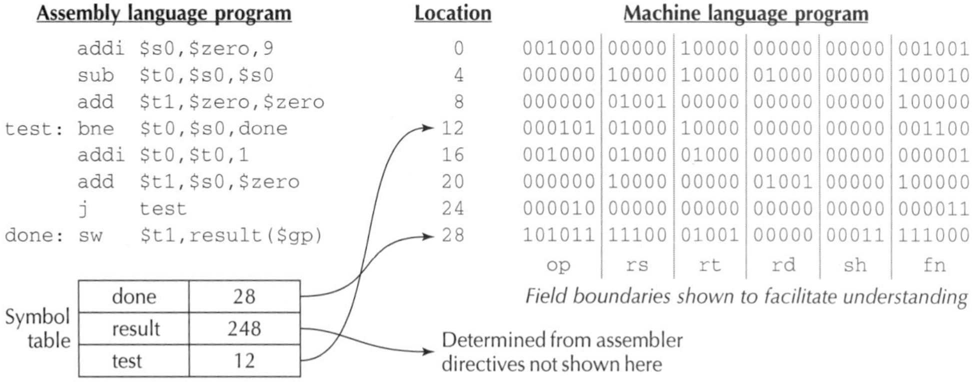

Assembly language program	Location	Machine language program
addi $s0,$zero,9	0	001000 00000 10000 00000 00000 001001
sub $t0,$s0,$s0	4	000000 10000 10000 01000 00000 100010
add $t1,$zero,$zero	8	000000 01001 00000 00000 00000 100000
test: bne $t0,$s0,done	12	000101 01001 10000 00000 00000 001100
addi $t0,$t0,1	16	001000 01000 01000 00000 00000 000001
add $t1,$s0,$zero	20	000000 10000 00000 01001 00000 100000
j test	24	000010 00000 00000 00000 00000 000011
done: sw $t1,result($gp)	28	101011 11100 01001 00000 00011 111000
		op rs rt rd sh fn

Field boundaries shown to facilitate understanding

Symbol table		
done	28
result	248
test	12

Determined from assembler
directives not shown here

Figure 7.2 An assembly language program, its machine language version, and the symbol table created during the assembly process.

■ 7.2 Assembler Directives

Assembler directives provide the assembler with information on how to translate the program but do not in themselves lead to the generation of corresponding machine instructions. For example, assembler directives may specify the layout of data in the program's data segment, or they may define variables with symbolic names and desired initial values. The assembler reads these directives and takes them into account in processing the rest of the program lines.

In MiniMIPS convention, assembler directives begin with a period to distinguish them from instructions. Following is a list of MiniMIPS assembler directives:

```
           .macro                  # start macro (see Section 7.4)
           .end_macro              # end macro (see Section 7.4)
           .text                   # start program's text segment
             ...                   # program text goes here
           .data                   # start program's data segment
  tiny:    .byte    156,0x7a       # name & initialize data byte(s)
  max:     .word    35000          # name & initialize data word(s)
  small:   .float   2E-3           # name short float (see Chapter 12)
  big:     .double  2E-3           # name long float (see Chapter 12)
           .align   2              # align next item on word boundary
  array:   .space   600            # reserve 600 bytes = 150 words
  str1:    .ascii   "a*b"          # name & initialize ASCII string
  str2:    .asciiz  "xyz"          # null-terminated ASCII string
           .global main            # consider "main" a global name
```

The directives ".macro" and ".end_macro" mark the start and end of the definition for a macroinstruction; they will be described in Section 7.4 and appear here only for completeness of the list. The directives ".text" and ".data" signal the beginning of a program's text and data segments, respectively. Thus, ".text" tells the assembler that the subsequent lines are to be interpreted as instructions. Within the text segment, instructions and pseudoinstructions (see Section 7.3) can be used at will.

In the data segment, data values can be assigned memory space, given symbolic names, and initialized to desired values. The assembler directive ".byte" is used to define one or more byte-size data elements with desired initial values and to assign a symbolic name to the first one. In our "tiny: .byte 156, 0x7a" example, a byte holding 156 followed by a second byte holding the hex value 0x7a (decimal 122) are defined, with the first one given the symbolic name "tiny." Within the program text, an address of the form tiny($s0) will refer to the first or second of these bytes if $s0 holds 0 or 1, respectively. The directives ".word" and ".float" and ".double" are similar to ".byte" except that they define words (e.g., unsigned or signed integers), short floating-point numbers, and long floating-point numbers, respectively.

The directive ".align h" is used to force the next data item's address to be a multiple of 2^h (aligned with 2^h-byte boundary). For example, ".align 2" forces the next address to be a multiple of $2^2 = 4$, thus aligning a word-size data element with the so-called word boundary. The directive ".space" is used to reserve a specified number of bytes in the data segment, typically to provide storage space for arrays. For example, "array: .space 600" reserves 600 bytes of space, which can then be used to store a string of bytes of length 600, a word vector or length 150, or a 75-element vector of long floating-point values. The type of usage is not specified in the directive itself but will be a function of what values are placed there and which instructions are applied to them. Preceding this directive with ".align 2" or ".align 3" allows us to use the array for words or doublewords, respectively. Note that arrays are typically not initialized by the directives in the data segment but rather by explicit "store" instructions as part of the program's execution.

Strings of ASCII characters could be defined using the ".byte" directive. However, to avoid having to obtain and list the numeric ASCII code for each character and to improve readability, two special directives are provided. The ".ascii" directive simply defines a sequence of bytes holding the ASCII codes for the characters that are listed between quotation marks. For example, the ASCII codes for "a", "*", and "b" can be placed in three consecutive bytes and the string given the symbolic name "str1" via the "str1: .ascii "a*b"" directive. It is common practice to terminate an ASCII string with the special "null" symbol (having the ASCII code 0x00); in this way, the end of the symbol string is easily recognizable. Hence, the directive ".asciiz" is provided that has the same effect as ".ascii," except that it appends the null symbol to the string and thus creates a string with one extra symbol at the end.

Finally, the directive ".global" defines one or more names as having global significance in the sense that they can be referenced from other files.

Example 7.1 shows the use of some of these directives in the context of a complete assembly language program. All subsequent programming examples in this chapter will make use of assembler directives.

Example 7.1: Composing simple assembler directives   Write an assembler directive to achieve each of the following objectives:

    a. Store the error message "Warning: The printer is out of paper!" in memory.
    b. Set up a constant called "size" with the value 4.
    c. Set up an integer variable called "width" and initialize it to 4.
    d. Set up a constant called "mill" with the value 1,000,000 (one million).
    e. Reserve space for an integer vector "vect" of length 250.

Solution

```
a. noppr: .asciiz "Warning: The printer is out of paper!"
b. size:  .byte  4          # small constant fits in one byte
c. width: .word  4          # byte could be enough, but ...
d. mill:  .word  1000000    # constant too large for byte
e. vect:  .space 1000       # 250 words = 1000 bytes
```

For part a, a null-terminated ASCII string is specified because with the null terminator, one does not need to know the length of the string during its use; if we decide to change the string, only this one directive will have to be modified. For part c, in the absence of information about the range of width, one word of storage is allocated to it.

■ 7.3 Pseudoinstructions

Although any computation or decision can be cast in terms of the simple MiniMIPS instructions covered thus far, it is sometimes easier and more natural to use alternative formulations. *Pseudoinstructions* allow us to formulate computations and decisions in alternative forms not directly supported by hardware. The MiniMIPS assembler takes care of translating these alternative forms to basic hardware-supported instructions. For example, MiniMIPS lacks a logical NOT instruction that would cause all the bits of a word to be inverted. Even though the same effect can be achieved by

```
nor      $s0,$s0,$zero      # complement ($s0)
```

it would be much more natural, and more easily understood, if we could write:

```
not      $s0                # complement ($s0)
```

We thus define "not" to be a pseudoinstruction of MiniMIPS; it is recognized just like ordinary instructions by the MiniMIPS assembler and is replaced by the equivalent "nor" instruction before conversion to machine language.

The "not" pseudoinstruction just defined translates to a single MiniMIPS machine language instruction. Some pseudoinstructions must be replaced with more than one instruction and may involve intermediate values that must be stored. For this reason, register $1 is devoted to use by the assembler and given the symbolic name $at (assembler temporary; see Figure 5.2). Clearly, the assembler cannot assume the availability of other registers and must thus limit its intermediate values to $at and, perhaps, the destination register(s) in the pseudoinstruction itself. An example is the "abs" pseudoinstruction that places the absolute value of the content of a source register into a destination register:

```
abs      $t0,$s0            # put |($s0)| into $t0
```

The MiniMIPS assembler might translate this pseudoinstruction into the following sequence of four MiniMIPS instructions:

```
add      $t0,$s0,$zero      # copy the operand x into $t0
slt      $at,$t0,$zero      # is x negative?
beq      $at,$zero,+4       # if not, skip next instruction
sub      $t0,$zero,$s0      # the result is 0 - x
```

Table 7.1 contains a complete list of pseudoinstructions for the MiniMIPS assembler. The arithmetic and logical NOT pseudoinstructions are self-explanatory. Rotate instructions are like shifts, except that bits spilling from one end of the word are reinserted at the other end. For example, the bit pattern 01000110, when left-rotated by 2 bits, becomes 00011001; that is, the two bits 01 shifted out from the left end occupy the two least significant positions in the left-rotated result. The "load immediate" pseudoinstruction allows any immediate value to be placed in a register, even if the value does not fit in 16 bits. The "load address" pseudoinstruction is quite useful for initializing pointers in registers. Suppose that we want to have a pointer to help us step through an array. This pointer must be initialized to point to the first element of the array. This cannot be done via regular MiniMIPS instructions. The instruction lw $s0, array would put the first array element, not its address, into register $s0, whereas the pseudoinstruction la $s0, array places the numerical equivalent of the label "array" into $s0. The remaining load/store and branch-related pseudoinstructions are also self-explanatory.

Because defining new pseudoinstructions constitutes a good way to practice assembly language programming, the problems at the end of this chapter hypothesize other pseudoinstructions and ask you to write the corresponding MiniMIPS instructions that must be produced by an assembler. Example 7.2 presents the machine language equivalents of some of the pseudoinstructions of Table 7.1 as a model. Example 7.3 shows how assembler directives and pseudoinstructions can help us create complete programs.

■ **TABLE 7.1** Pseudoinstructions accepted by the MiniMIPS assembler.

Class	Pseudoinstruction	Usage		Meaning
	Move	move	regd,regs	regd ← (regs)
Copy	Load address	la	regd,address	load computed address, not content
	Load immediate	li	regd,anyimm	regd ← arbitrary immediate value
	Absolute value	abs	regd,regs	regd ← |(regs)|
	Negate	neg	regd,regs	regd ← −(regs); with overflow
	Multiply (into register)	mul	regd,reg1,reg2	regd ← (reg1) × (reg2); no overflow
Arithmetic	Divide (into register)	div	regd,reg1,reg2	regd ← (reg1) ÷ (reg2); with overflow
	Remainder	rem	regd,reg1,reg2	regd ← (reg1)mod(reg2)
	Set greater than	sgt	regd,reg1,reg2	regd ← if (reg1) > (reg2) then 1 else 0
	Set less or equal	sle	regd,reg1,reg2	regd ← if (reg1) ≤ (reg2) then 1 else 0
	Set greater or equal	sge	regd,reg1,reg2	regd ← if (reg1) ≥ (reg2) then 1 else 0
Shift	Rotate left	rol	regd,reg1,reg2	regd ← (reg1) left-rotated by (reg2)
	Rotate right	ror	regd,reg1,reg2	regd ← (reg1) right-rotated by (reg2)
Logic	NOT	not	reg	reg ← (reg)′
Memory access	Load doubleword	ld	regd,address	load regd and the next register
	Store doubleword	sd	regd,address	store regd and the next register
	Branch less than	blt	reg1,reg2,L	if (reg1) < (reg2) then goto L
Control transfer	Branch greater than	bgt	reg1,reg2,L	if (reg1) > (reg2) then goto L
	Branch less or equal	ble	reg1,reg2,L	if (reg1) ≤ (reg2) then goto L
	Branch greater or equal	bge	reg1,reg2,L	if (reg1) ≥ (reg2) then goto L

Example 7.2: MiniMIPS pseudoinstructions For each of the following pseudoinstructions defined in Table 7.1, write the corresponding instruction(s) produced by the MiniMIPS assembler:

```
parta: neg    $t0,$s0          # $t0 = -($s0); set overflow
partb: rem    $t0,$s0,$s1      # $t0 = ($s0) mod ($s1)
partc: li     $t0,imm          # $t0 = arbitrary immediate value
partd: blt    $s0,$s1,label    # if ($s0)<($s1), goto label
```

Solution

```
parta: sub    $t0,$zero,$s0    # -($s0) = 0 - ($s0)
partb: div    $s0,$s1          # divide; remainder is in Hi
       mfhi   $t0              # copy (Hi) into $t0
partc: addi   $t0,$zero,imm    # if imm fits in 16 bits
partc: lui    $t0,upperhalf    # if imm needs 32 bits, the assembler
       ori    $t0,lowerhalf    # must extract upper and lower halves
partd: slt    $at,$s0,$s1      # ($s0)<($s1)?
       bne    $at,$zero,label  # if ($s0)<($s1), goto label
```

Note that for part c, the machine language equivalent of the pseudoinstruction differs depending on the size of the immediate operand supplied.

Example 7.3: Forming complete assembly language programs   Add assembler directives and make other necessary modifications in the partial program in Example 6.4 (selection sort using a max-finding procedure) to turn it into a complete program, excluding data input and output.

Solution: The partial program in Example 6.4 assumes an input list of words, with pointers to its first and last elements available in registers $a0 and $a1. The sorted list will occupy the same memory locations as the original list (*in-place sorting*).

```
        .global main        # consider "main" a global name
        .data               # start program's data segment
size:   .word  0            # space for list size in words
list:   .space 4000         # assume list has up to 1000 elements
        .text               # start program's text segment
main:   ...                 # input "size" and "list"
        la     $a0,list     # init pointer to first element
        lw     $a1,size     # put "size" into $a1
        addi   $a1,$a1,-1   # offset in words to last element
        sll    $a1,$a1,2    # offset in bytes to last element
        add    $a1,$a0,$a1  # init pointer to last element
sort:   ...                 # rest of program from Example 6.4
done:   ...                 # output sorted "list"
```

Note that the complete program is called "main" and includes as part of it the program "sort" from Example 6.4, including its "max" procedure.

◼ 7.4 Macroinstructions

A *macroinstruction* (*macro,* for short) is a mechanism to give a name to an oft-used sequence of instructions to avoid having to specify the sequence in full each time. As an analogy, one may write or type "ECE" in a draft document, instructing the typesetter or word processing software to replace all occurrences of "ECE" with the full name "Department of Electrical and Computer Engineering" in the final version. Because the same instruction sequence may involve different operand specifications (e.g., registers) each time used, a macro has a set of formal parameters that are replaced by actual parameters during the assembly process. Macros are delimited by special assembler directives:

```
.macro   name(arg list)    # macro and argument(s) named
...                        # instructions defining the macro
.end_macro                 # macro terminator
```

Two natural questions may arise at this point:

1. How is a macro different from a pseudoinstruction?
2. How is a macro different from a procedure?

Pseudoinstructions are incorporated in the design of an assembler and are thus fixed for the user; macros, on the other hand, are user-defined. Additionally, a pseudoinstruction looks exactly like an instruction, whereas a macro looks more like a procedure in a high-level language; for example, if you did not know that "move" is not a machine language instruction of MiniMIPS, you could not tell by its appearance. As for differences with a procedure, at least two jump instructions are used to call and return from a procedure, whereas a macro is just a shorthand notation for several assembly language instructions; after the macro has been replaced by its equivalent instructions, no trace of the macro itself remains in the program.

Example 7.4 provides definition and usage of a complete macro. It is instructive to compare Examples 7.4 and 6.2 (procedure to find the largest of three integers), both to see the differences between a macro and a procedure and to note the effects of pseudoinstructions in making programs easier to write and understand.

Example 7.4: Macro to find the largest of three values   Suppose we often need to determine the largest of three values in registers and to put the result in a fourth register. Write a macro mx3r for this purpose, with the parameters being the result register and the three operand registers.

Solution: The following macro definition uses only pseudoinstructions:

```
.macro mx3r(m,a1,a2,a3)   # macro and arguments named
move    m,a1              # assume (a1) is largest; m = (a1)
bge     m,a2,+4           # if (a2) is not larger, ignore it
move    m,a2              # else set m = (a2)
bge     m,a3,+4           # if (a3) is not larger, ignore it
move    m,a3              # else set m = (a3)
.end_macro               # macro terminator
```

If the macro is used as mx3r($t0,$s0,$s4,$s3), the assembler simply replaces the arguments m, a1, a2, and a3 in the text of the macro with $t0, $s0, $s4, $s3, respectively, producing the following seven instructions in lieu of the macro (note that the pseudoinstructions in the macro definition have been replaced with regular instructions):

```
addi    $t0,$s0,$zero     # assume ($s0) is largest; $t0 = ($s0)
slt     $at,$t0,$s4       # ($t0) < ($s4)?
beq     $at,$zero,+4      # if not, ignore ($s4)
addi    $t0,$s4,$zero     # else set $t0 = ($s4)
slt     $at,$t0,$s3       # ($t0) < ($s3)?
beq     $at,$zero,+4      # if not, ignore ($s3)
addi    $t0,$s3,$zero     # else set $t0 = ($s3)
```

At another place in the program, the macro may be used as mx3r($t5,$s2,$v0,$v1), leading to the same seven instructions being inserted in the program, but with different register specifications. This is very similar to procedure call; thus, the macro parameters are sometimes called "formal parameters," as is common for subroutines or procedures.

■ 7.5 Linking and Loading

A program, whether in assembly language or a high-level language, consists of multiple modules that are often designed by different groups at different times. For example, a software company designing a new application program may reuse many previously developed procedures as part of the new program. Similarly, *library routines* (e.g., those for computing common mathematical functions or performing useful services such as input/output) are incorporated into programs by simply referring to them where needed. To avoid having to reassemble (or recompile, in the case of high-level languages) all modules with each small modification in one of the components, a mechanism is provided that allows the modules to be built, assembled, and tested separately. Just before placing these modules in memory to form an *executable program,* the pieces are linked together, and references among them resolved, by a special *linker* program.

Each of the modules to be linked will have information in a special header section about the size of text segment (instructions) and data segment. It will also have sections containing relocation information and symbol table. These additional pieces of information will not be part of the executable program but are used to allow the linker to perform its job correctly and efficiently. Among other functions, the linker determines which memory locations each of the modules will occupy and adjusts (relocates) all addresses within the program to correspond to the modules' assigned locations. The combined linked program will also have size and other relevant information to be used by the *loader,* described shortly.

One of the most critical functions of the linker is to ensure that labels in all modules are properly interpreted (resolved). If, for example, a `jal` instruction specifies a symbolic target that is not defined in the module itself, the other modules being linked are searched to determine if any one of them has an external symbol that matches the unresolved symbolic name. If none of the modules resolves the undefined reference, the system's program libraries are consulted to see whether the programmer intended the use of a library routine. If any symbol remains unresolved at the end of this process, linking fails and an error is signaled to the user. Successful resolution of all such references by the linker is followed by:

Determining the placement of text and data segments in memory

Evaluating all data addresses and instruction labels

Forming an executable program with no unresolved references

The output of the linker does not go to the main memory where it can be executed. Rather, it takes the form of a file that is stored on secondary memory. It is the *loader* that transfers this file into main memory for execution. Because the same program may be placed in different areas of memory during each execution depending on where space is available, the loader is responsible for adjusting all addresses in the program to correspond to the program's actual location in memory. The linker essentially assumes that the program will be loaded beginning with location 0 in memory. If the starting location is L instead, then all absolute addresses must be shifted by L. This process, known as *relocation,* involves adding a constant amount to all absolute addresses within instructions as they are loaded into memory. Relative addresses, on the other hand, do not change, so a branch to 25 locations ahead, or 12 locations back, does not change during relocation.

The loader is thus in charge of the following:

Determining the memory needs of the program from its header

Copying text and data from the executable program file into memory

Modifying (shifting) addresses, where needed, during copying

Placing program parameters onto the stack (as in a procedure call)

Initializing all machine registers, including the stack pointer

Jumping to a start-up routine that calls the program's main routine

Note that the program is treated as a procedure that is called from an operating system routine. Upon termination, the program returns control to the same routine, which then executes an "exit" system call. This allows for passing of data and other parameters to the program via the same stack mechanism used for procedure calls. Initializing of machine registers usually means clearing them to 0, except for the stack pointer, which is set to point to the top of the stack after all the program parameters have been pushed onto it.

■ 7.6 Running Assembler Programs

In modern computing practice, programs in assembly or machine language are generated predominantly by compilers. Programmers seldom write directly in assembly language because it is a time-consuming and error-prone process. Nevertheless, in certain practical situations (e.g., for a program module that must be highly optimized for performance) one may want to program in assembly language. Of course, there is also the pedagogical reason: to learn enough about the machine language to be able to understand and appreciate issues in computer design, one must write at least some simple assembly language programs. It is in this latter spirit that we introduce the SPIM simulator that allows you to test your MiniMIPS assembly language programs by running them to completion, observing the results obtained, and tracing the execution in case of problems to facilitate debugging.

Readers who do not wish to design and run MiniMIPS assembly language programs can skip the rest of this section.

SPIM, which gets its name from reversing "MIPS," is a simulator for the MIPS R2000/R3000 assembly language. The instruction set accepted by SPIM is larger than the MiniMIPS subset covered in this book, but this obviously creates no problem for running our programs. We can liken this relationship to that of someone with a limited English vocabulary speaking to a listener who is fluent in the language; the latter will obviously understand what is spoken, provided the small subset of words is used correctly. Three versions of SPIM are available for free downloading:

PCSpim	for Windows machines
xspim	for Macintosh OS X
spim	for Unix or Linux systems

You can download SPIM by visiting http://www.cs.wisc.edu/~larus/spim.html and following the instructions provided there. Please read the copyright notice and conditions of use found at the bottom of the cited Web page before starting to use the program.

The following description is based on PCSpim which was adapted by David A. Carley from the other two versions developed by Dr. James R. Larus (formerly at University of Wisconsin, Madison, now with Microsoft Research).

Figure 7.3 shows the user interface of PCSpim. Besides the menu bar and the toolbar at the top and the status bar at the bottom of the PCSpim window, there are four panels in which information about the assembly program and its execution are displayed:

Register contents are shown in the top panel.

The program's text segment is shown in the second panel, with each line containing:

[hex memory address]   hex instruction content   opcode and parameters

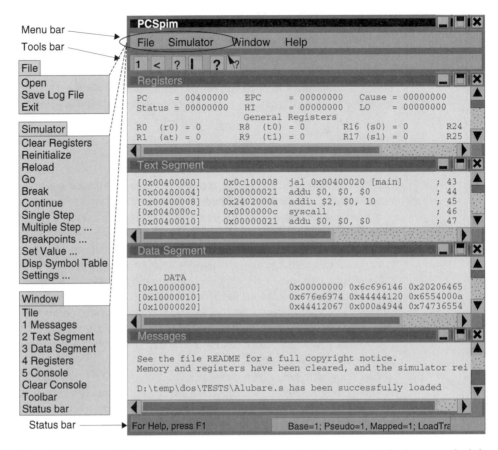

Figure 7.3 The graphical user interface of PCSpim. Menu selections are partially shown on the left.

The program's data segment is shown in the third panel, with each line typically containing a hex memory address and the contents of 4 words (16 bytes) in hex format.

Messages produced by SPIM are displayed in the fourth panel.

The simulator comes with certain default settings for its customizable features. These settings are fine for our purposes, so we will not discuss how they might be modified. Documentation for such modifications can be downloaded along with the simulator.

To load and run a MiniMIPS assembly language program on PCSpim, you must first compose the program in a text file. The file can then be opened through the "file" menu of PCSpim, and this will cause the program's text and data segments to appear in the middle two panels of the PCSpim window. Various simulator functions, such as "Go" for beginning program execution or "Break" for stopping, can then be accessed via PCSpim's "Simulator" menu.

We will study input/output and interrupts in some depth in Part IV of the book. Here, we supply a very brief overview of these concepts to allow the introduction of PCSpim mechanisms for data input and output and the meanings of "with overflow" and "no overflow" designations for some instructions in Tables 5.1 and 6.2. Instructions for data input and output will allow us to write complete programs that include automatic acquisition of the needed parameters (say, input from a keyboard) and presentation of computed results (say, output on a monitor screen).

Like many modern computers, MiniMIPS has memory-mapped I/O. This means that certain data buffers and status registers within I/O devices, which are required to initiate and control the I/O process, are viewed as memory locations. Thus, if we know the specific memory locations assigned to an input device such as the keyboard, we can inquire about the status of the device and transfer data from its data buffer to one of the general register using the "load word" instruction. However, this level of detail in I/O operations is only of interest in I/O routines known as *device handlers*. We will study some aspects of such I/O operations in Chapter 22. At the level of assembly language programming, I/O is often handled through system calls, meaning that the program requests the services of the operating system in performing the desired input or output operation.

The default I/O mode of PCSpim is via a system call instruction with the symbolic opcode `syscall`. The machine language instruction for `syscall` is R-type, with all fields set to 0, except the function field, which contains 12. A system call is characterized by an integer code in [1, 10] which is placed in register $v0 prior to the `syscall` instruction. Table 7.2 contains the functions associated with these 10 system calls.

Input and output operations cause PCSpim to open a new window named "Console." Any output from the program appears on the console; all inputs to the program must likewise be entered in this window. The "allocate memory" system call (`syscall` with 9 in $v0) results in a pointer to a block of memory containing n additional bytes, where the desired number n is supplied in register $a0. The "exit from program" system call (`syscall` with 10 in $v0) causes program execution to be terminated.

An arithmetic operation, such as addition, may produce a result that is too large to fit in the specified destination register. This event is called an "overflow," and it causes an invalid sum to be produced. Obviously, if we continue the computation with this invalid sum, there is a high probability of producing nonsensical results from our program. To avoid this, the hardware of MiniMIPS recognizes the occurrence of an overflow and calls a special operating system routine known as an interrupt handler. This interruption of the normal program flow and the ensuing transfer of control to the operating system is aptly referred to as an *interrupt* or *exception*. The interrupt handler can pursue several courses of action, depending on the nature or cause of the interrupt. These will be discussed in Chapter 24. Until then, it is sufficient for us to know that MiniMIPS assumes the interrupt handler to begin at the address

▪ **TABLE 7.2** Input/output and control functions of `syscall` in PCSpim.

Class	($v0)	Function	Argument(s)	Result
Output	1	Print integer	Integer in $a0	Integer displayed
	2	Print floating-point	Float in $f12	Float displayed
	3	Print double-float	Double-float in $f12,$f13	Double-float displayed
	4	Print string	Pointer in $a0	Null-terminated string displayed
Input	5	Read integer		Integer returned in $v0
	6	Read floating-point		Float returned in $f0
	7	Read double-float		Double-float returned in $f0,$f1
	8	Read string	Pointer in $a0, length in $a1	String returned in buffer at pointer
Control	9	Allocate memory	Number of bytes in $a0	Pointer to memory block in $v0
	10	Exit from program		Program execution terminated

0x80000080 in memory and will transfer control to it if an interrupt occurs. The control transfer is via an unconditional jump (much like jal) and the return address, or the value in the program counter at the time of interrupt, is automatically saved in a special register called "exception program counter" or EPC in coprocessor 0 (see Figure 5.1).

Some instructions are given the "no overflow" designation because they are often used when overflow is impossible or undesirable. For instance, one of the main uses of arithmetic with unsigned numbers is address calculation. Adding a base address to an offset in bytes (four times the offset in words) may yield an address in memory corresponding to a new array element. Under normal conditions, this computed address will not exceed the limit of the computer's address space. If it does, the hardware includes other mechanisms for detecting an invalid address and we do not need an overflow indication from the instruction execution unit.

From the viewpoint of writing assembly language programs, we can ignore the possibility of overflow, and the associated interrupt, provided we take care that results and intermediate values are not too large in magnitude. This is relatively easy to do for simple computations and programs that we deal with here.

PROBLEMS

7.1 Assembler directives

Write assembler directives to achieve each of the following objectives:

a. Set up four error messages, each of which is exactly 32 characters long, so that the program can print the ith error message ($0 \leq i \leq 3$) based on a numerical index in a register. *Hint:* The index in the register can be left-shifted by 5 bits before being used as an offset.

b. Set up integer constants least and most, with values 25 and 570, against which the validity of input data can be checked within the program.

c. Set aside space for a character string of length not exceeding 256 symbols, including a null terminator, if any.

d. Set aside space for a 20 × 20 integer matrix, to be stored in memory in row-major order.

e. Set aside space for an image with one million pixels, each of which is specified by an 8-bit color code and an 8-bit brightness code.

7.2 Defining pseudoinstructions

Of the 20 pseudoinstructions in Table 7.1, two (not, abs) were discussed at the beginning of Section 7.3 and four more (neg, rem, li, blt) were defined in Example 7.2. Supply equivalent MiniMIPS instructions or instruction sequences for the remaining 14 pseudoinstructions; these constitute parts a–n of the problem, in order of appearance in Table 7.1.

7.3 Additional pseudoinstructions

The following are some additional pseudo-instructions that one could define for MiniMIPS. In each case, supply an equivalent MiniMIPS instruction or sequence of instructions with the desired effect. In parth, mulacc is short for "multiply-accumulate."

```
parta: beqz    reg,L              # if (reg)=0, goto L
partb: bnez    reg,L              # if (reg)≠0, goto L
partc: bgtz    reg,L              # if (reg)>0, goto L
partd: blez    reg,L              # if (reg)≤0, goto L
parte: bgez    reg,L              # if (reg)≥0, goto L
partf: double  regd,regs          # regd = 2×(regs)
partg: triple  regd,regs          # regd = 3×(regs)
parth: mulacc  regd,reg1,reg2     # regd = (regd) + (reg1)×(reg2)
```

7.4 Complex pseudoinstructions

The pseudoinstructions in Problems 7.2 and 7.3 resemble regular MiniMIPS assembly instructions. In this problem, we propose a number of pseudoinstructions that perform more complex functions that do not resemble ordinary instructions and could not be implemented as such within the format constraints of MiniMIPS instructions. The following pseudoinstructions perform "increment memory word," "fetch and add," and "fetch and add immediate" functions. In each case, supply an equivalent MiniMIPS sequence of instructions with the desired effect.

```
parta: incmem reg,imm          # mem[(reg)+imm] = mem[(reg)+imm] + 1
partb: ftcha  reg1,reg2,imm    # mem[(reg1)+imm]=mem[(reg1)+imm]+(reg2)
partc: ftchai reg,imm1,imm2    # mem[(reg)+imm1]=mem[(reg)+imm1]+imm2
```

7.5 Input and output

a. Convert the selection sort program of Example 7.3 into a program that receives the list of integers to be sorted as input and displays its output.

b. Run the program of part a on the SPIM simulator using an input list of at least 20 numbers.

7.6 New pseudoinstructions

Propose at least two useful pseudoinstructions for MiniMIPS that do not appear in Table 7.1. Why do you think that your pseudoinstructions are useful? How are your pseudoinstructions convertible to equivalent MiniMIPS instructions or sequences of instructions?

7.7 Finding the *n*th Fibonacci number

Write a complete MiniMIPS program that accepts *n* as input and produces the *n*th Fibonacci number as output. Fibonacci numbers are defined recursively by the formula $F_n = F_{n-1} + F_{n-2}$, with $F_0 = 0$ and $F_1 = 1$.

a. Write your program using a recursive procedure.
b. Write your program without recursion.
c. Compare the programs or parts a and b and discuss.

7.8 Square-rooting program

Write a complete MiniMIPS program that accepts an integer x as input and produces $\lfloor x^{1/2} \rfloor$ as output.

The program should print a suitable message if the input is negative. Because the square root of a 31-bit binary number is no greater than 46,340, a binary search strategy in the interval [0, 65, 536] can lead to identification of the square root in 16 or fewer iterations. In binary search, the midpoint $(a + b)/2$ of the search interval $[a, b]$ is determined and the search is restricted to $[a, (a + b)/2]$ or $[(a + b)/2, b]$, depending on the outcome of a comparison.

7.9 Finding *max* and *min*

Write a complete MiniMIPS program that accepts a sequence of integers at input and after the receipt of each new input value, displays the largest and smallest integers thus far. An input of 0 indicates the end of input values and is not an input value itself. Note that you do not need to keep all integers in memory.

7.10 Symbol table

a. Show the symbol table constructed by the MiniMIPS assembler for the program in Example 7.3, ignoring the input and output portions.

b. Repeat part a, this time assuming that appropriate input and output operations have been included according to Problem 7.5.

7.11 Check-writing program

A company's checks are to be issued by writing the amount with words substituted for decimal digits (e.g., "five two seven dollars and five zero cents") to make forgery more difficult. Write a complete MiniMIPS program to read a nonnegative integer, representing an amount in cents, as input and produce the equivalent amount in words at output, as suggested by the example for $527.50 corresponding to the integer input 52,750.

7.12 Triangle formation

Write a complete MiniMIPS program to read three nonnegative integers, presented in arbitrary order, as inputs and determine if they can form the sides of:

a. A triangle
b. A right-angle triangle
c. An acute triangle
d. An obtuse triangle

7.13 Integer sequences

Write a complete MiniMIPS program to read three nonnegative integers, presented in arbitrary order, as inputs and determine if they can form consecutive terms of:

a. A Fibonacci sequence (in which each term is the sum of the preceding two terms)
b. An arithmetic progression
c. A geometric progression

7.14 Factoring and primality testing

Write a complete MiniMIPS program to accept a nonnegative integer x in the range [0, 1 000 000] as input and display its factors, from the smallest to the largest. For example, the output of the program for $x = 89$ should be "89" (indicating that x is a prime number) and its output for $x = 126$ should be "2, 3, 3, 7."

7.15 Decimal to hexadecimal conversion

Write a complete MiniMIPS program to read an unsigned integer with up to six decimal digits from the input and represent it in hexadecimal form at the output. Note that because the input integer fits in a single machine word, decimal-to-binary conversion takes place as part of the input process. All you need to do is to derive the hex representation from the binary word.

7.16 Substitution cipher

A substitution cipher changes a plaintext message to a ciphertext by substituting each of the 26 letters of the English alphabet by another letter according to a 26-entry table. For simplicity, we assume that the plaintext or ciphertext does not contain space, numerals, punctuation marks, or special symbols. Write a complete MiniMIPS program to read a 26-symbol string defining the substitution table (first symbol is the replacement for a, second one for b, and so on) and then repeatedly request plaintext inputs, producing the equivalent ciphertext as output. Each plaintext input is terminated by a period. Input of any symbol other than a lower case letter or period terminates the program's execution.

REFERENCES AND FURTHER READINGS

[Henn03]   Hennessy, J. L., and D. A. Patterson, *Computer Architecture: A Quantitative Approach,* Morgan Kaufmann, 3rd ed., 2003.

[Kane92]   Kane, G., and J. Heinrich, *MIPS RISC Architecture,* Prentice Hall, 1992.

[MIPS]   MIPS Technologies Web site. Follow the architecture and documentation links at: http://www.mips.com/

[Patt98]   Patterson, D. A., and J. L. Hennessy, *Computer Organization and Design: The Hardware/Software Interface,* Morgan Kaufmann, 2nd ed., 1998.

[Sail96]   Sailer, P. M., and D. R. Kaeli, *The DLX Instruction Set Architecture Handbook,* Morgan Kaufmann, 1996.

[Silb02]   Silberschatz, A., P. B. Galvin, and G. Gagne, *Operating System Concepts,* Wiley, 6th ed., 2002.

[SPIM]   SPIM, a free downloadable software simulator for a subset of the MIPS instruction set; more information in Section 7.6. http://www.cs.wisc.edu/~larus/spim.html

INSTRUCTION-SET VARIATIONS

"The engineers who pioneered the RISC movement had one advantage over their predecessors who designed the earlier instruction sets. In the interval, simulation techniques had matured, and the computer power needed for their exploitation had become readily available. It became possible to assess the efficiency of a design without actually implementing it. . . . It soon became apparent that unaided intuition was a very poor guide."
—*Maurice Wilkes, Computing Perspectives*

"Everything should be made as simple as possible, but not simpler."
—*Albert Einstein*

TOPICS IN THIS CHAPTER

8.1 Complex Instructions

8.2 Alternative Addressing Modes

8.3 Variations in Instruction Formats

8.4 Instruction Set Design and Evolution

8.5 The RISC/CISC Dichotomy

8.6 Where to Draw the Line

The MiniMIPS instruction set, though quite typical of those used for many modern processors, is only one example. In this chapter, we a discuss the ways in which the instruction-set architecture might be different from that of MiniMIPS, with the goal of arriving at a balanced and complete picture of the state of practice in instruction-set design. Among other things, we look at more elaborate addressing modes and variations in instruction formats. We then examine desirable features of an instruction set and discuss how the RISC and CISC philosophies fare in this respect. We conclude by describing an interesting single-instruction computer, the ultimate in RISC architecture.

■ 8.1 Complex Instructions

MiniMIPS instructions presented in Chapters 5–7 perform relatively simple tasks such as a single arithmetic/logic operation, copying of basic data elements, or transfer of control. This is true in virtually all modern computers. Conceptually, there is nothing to stop us from defining an instruction that performs a (very) complex task such as:

```
chksum regd,reg1,reg2    # set regd to checksum (i.e., XOR)
                         # of all bytes in array whose start
                         # (end) address is in reg1 (reg2)
sortup reg1,reg2         # arrange the integer words in array
                         # whose start (end) address is in
                         # reg1 (reg2) in nondescending order
```

Ultimately, however, any such complex instruction will be broken down to simpler steps for hardware execution. For example, the chksum instruction is likely executed by performing the equivalent of a software loop in hardware, that is, XORing the next byte to a running checksum, incrementing a pointer, comparing the pointer against the end address, and repeating if they are unequal. The question, then, is whether it is worthwhile to define such complex instructions.

On the positive side, use of more complex instructions leads to programs with shorter texts and thus lower memory requirements. In early computers, memories (both primary and secondary) were quite small, and this provided a strong incentive for using complex instructions. Also, performing a repetitive computation in hardware is likely to be faster than its software counterpart owing to the time saved as a result of fetching and decoding one instruction instead of many.

On the negative side, mastering a variety of complex instructions and using them in appropriate places, both in manual programming and in compiling, is quite a challenge. Also, as discussed at length in Section 8.5, inclusion of complex instructions in an instruction set could make even the simpler instructions take longer to execute, thus nullifying some of the potential gain. Finally, an instruction such as sortup is likely to have limited utility, given that the sorting algorithm implicit in its step-by-step hardware implementation may not be the best one in all possible situations.

Hence, computer architects use considerable care in choosing which complex instructions, if any, must be included in an instruction set to ensure that the benefits outweigh the drawbacks. Table 8.1 lists a number of complex instructions that exist in some popular processors.

Complexity of an instruction is of course a relative notion. What is complex in one application context, or with one implementation technology, may be rather simple in another setting. There are also different aspects to complexity. An instruction may be quite complex to describe and understand (and thus hard to use appropriately), but fairly easy to decode and execute. The CS instruction of IBM System/370 in Table 8.1 is one such instruction. Its inclusion in the instruction set was motivated by the need for handling of a shared queue in a multiprocessing environment [Giff87]. It is easily executed as the concatenation of three simple operations: load into a buffer, compare, and copy or store depending on the comparison outcome. On the other hand, an instruction that looks deceptively simple, and is quite easy to comprehend or use, may require fairly complex and time-consuming steps for its execution. The two instructions introduced at the beginning of this section provide good examples.

Although there is no agreed-upon standard definition for "complex instruction" in the computer architecture literature, the following more or less captures the essence of what most people mean by the term: a complex instruction is one that can potentially perform multiple memory accesses in the course of its execution. Because each memory access needs address calculation or updating, in addition to the physical memory read or write operation, the execution of such instructions can be significantly slower than those of MiniMIPS instructions listed in Table 6.2. However, complexity can be present without any memory access at all. The

■ **TABLE 8.1** Examples of complex instructions in two popular modern microprocessors (Pentium, PowerPC) and two computer families of historical significance (System/360–370, VAX).

Machine	Instruction	Effect
Intel Pentium	MOVS	Move one element in a string of bytes, words, or doublewords using addresses specified in two pointer registers; after the operation, increment or decrement the registers to point to the next element of the string.
	BOUND	Verify that operand 1 is within the lower and upper limits stored in two consecutive memory words referenced by operand 2 (useful for array index verification); an interrupt occurs if operand 1 is out of bounds.
	INVD, WBINVD	Flush the internal cache memory by invalidating all entries (for WBINVD, first write back all dirty cache lines to memory). These instructions will make more sense after we have studied cache memories in Chapter 18.
IBM/Motorola PowerPC	lmw	Load multiple words in consecutive memory locations into registers, from the specified target register through general-purpose register 31.
	lswx	Load a string of bytes into registers, 4 bytes per register, beginning with the specified target register; wrap around from register 31 to register 0.
	cntlzd	Count the number of consecutive 0s in a specified source register beginning with bit position 0 and place the count in a destination register.
	rldic	Rotate a specified doubleword register to the left, AND the result with a specified mask, and store in destination register.
IBM System/ 360–370	MVZ	Move zone: copy a specified number of bytes from one region of memory to another region; each of the two regions is defined by a starting address composed of a base register and an offset.
	TS	Test and set: read a control bit from memory and set the bit to 1 if it is 0, all in one atomic, uninterruptible action (used to control access to a shared resource, with 0/1 meaning the resource is available/locked).
	CS	Compare and swap: compare the content of a register to that of a memory location; if unequal, load the memory word into the register, else store the content of a different register into the same memory location.
Digital VAX	MOVTC	Move translated characters: copy a string of characters from one area of memory to another, translating each character by means of a lookup table whose location is specified as part of the instruction.
	POLYD	Polynomial evaluation with double floating-point arithmetic: evaluate a polynomial in x, with very high precision in intermediate results, using a coefficient table whose location in memory is given within the instruction.
	ADDP6	Add packed decimal strings (radix-10 integers, with two BCD digits stored per byte); each of the two source decimal strings and the destination string is specified by its length and location, for a total of six operands.

cntlzd instruction of the IBM/Motorola PowerPC in Table 8.1 provides an excellent example. This instruction is complex if bit counting is done through multiple cycles of conditional shifting. It is not complex, however, if a special leading-zeros counting circuit is implemented within the ALU.

■ 8.2 Alternative Addressing Modes

The addressing modes of MiniMIPS are limited in two ways. First, only six modes are used: implied, immediate, register, base (+offset), PC-relative, and direct (see Figure 5.11). Second, even these limited addressing modes cannot be used everywhere; for example, arithmetic instructions allow only the immediate and register modes. These limitations are found in many

RISC-type architectures, which aim to speed up the most commonly used combinations of operations and operand addressing (see Section 8.5).

The competing CISC-type architectures allow the preceding modes to be used more widely and may also have additional addressing modes. We first review how the six addressing modes of MiniMIPS might be used and then focus on two important addressing modes that are missing from MiniMIPS: indexed and indirect.

Implied addressing is much more versatile than one might think. There have been computers that used this mode exclusively for all arithmetic operations. In *stack machines,* all the required operands of an arithmetic/logic instruction are taken from the top of the stack and any result is also placed there. An instruction of this type needs only an opcode and is sometimes referred to as a *0-address instruction.* Of course, we need other forms of addressing to be able to move data in memory, such as from an arbitrary location to the top of the stack and vice versa (equivalents of load and store instructions in MiniMIPS). However, we still save a great deal of space in the instructions that would normally require specifications for operand and result locations. Other examples of implied addressing are found in increment and decrement instructions of some machines that are the equivalents of MiniMIPS' addi, with the immediate operand implicitly specified to be +1 or −1.

Immediate addressing is used for a constant operand that is small enough to fit in the instruction itself. Without immediate addressing, such constants would have to be stored in registers (thus, leaving fewer registers for other uses) or retrieved from memory (thus, requiring more bits for addressing and/or greater latency). The price paid for having immediate addressing is that there will be multiple forms of each arithmetic/logic instruction, which tends to complicate the instruction decoding and control circuitry. MiniMIPS allows only 16-bit immediate operands in general, although a 5-bit immediate operand, designating the shift amount, is used for shift instructions. Other, more complex, instruction sets may allow immediate operands of varying sizes, from bytes to doublewords. However, this complicates instruction decoding and control even further. Note that if we treat an instruction such as addi rd, rs, 8 like a 32-bit integer and add 4 to it, its immediate operand will change to 12. *Self-modifying programs* of this type, quite common in early days of digital computing, are no longer used because they greatly complicate user understanding and program debugging.

Register addressing is the most common addressing mode because register operands can be accessed faster, and require fewer bits to specify, than memory operands. An operation requiring two operands and producing one result, all in distinct registers, can easily fit in 32 bits (perhaps even in 16 bits, for a smaller number of registers). However, the result register does not have to be distinct from operand registers, leading to further economy in the number of bits needed. For instance, an operation such as $a = a + b$ requires only two register specifications. Early machines had a special register known as *the accumulator,* which always supplied one operand and received the result of any arithmetic/logic operation. Arithmetic/logic instructions in such machines required only one register specification. Note that the use of an accumulator, or a register doubling both as an operand source and as the result destination, is a form of implied addressing.

Base addressing, also known as "base plus offset" addressing, can take different forms. In MiniMIPS, the base value in a register is added to an offset specified as an immediate operand, producing a 32-bit memory address. Note that calling one value "base" and the other "offset" is a matter of convention; reversing the roles of the two values is not only possible but useful in practice. Practically speaking, base is a constant while offset is variable. So, if the register points to the beginning of an array or the top of a stack while the immediate value specifies which array or stack element is to be accessed, then the register holds the base and the immediate value is the offset. The reverse is also possible, provided the base can be specified as an immediate operand. The latter option provides a limited form of *index addressing* (considered shortly), with the register acting as an *index register*. When the immediate part is 0, the computed address is the same as the value in the specified register. This type of addressing is sometimes referred to as *register indirect,* implying that the memory is accessed indirectly via a register as opposed to directly by supplying a memory address. Again, the MiniMIPS restriction of having only 16-bit immediate operands is relaxed in some instruction-set architectures, leading to more versatile base addressing. In particular, with a 32-bit immediate operand, base addressing and index addressing may become indistinguishable.

Relative addressing is used when the address is specified relative to an agreed-upon reference address. The only difference from base addressing is that the reference address is implied rather than explicit. The most commonly used form of relative addressing takes the content of the program counter (corresponding to the current instruction or, more often, the next instruction) as the reference point and is known as *PC-relative addressing*. Most modern machines use PC-relative addressing for branches because branch target addresses are typically very close to the branch point, making it possible to specify the target with a small signed offset (negative offset for backward and positive offset for forward branches). In machines having special instructions for manipulating the stack, the stack pointer may be used as reference point. In some architectures, the program counter is part of the general register file; this makes PC-relative addressing even more similar to base addressing.

Direct addressing is the most basic form of addressing. The size of early computer memories was measured in thousands of locations, which meant that even a 16-bit instruction had enough room to hold a complete memory address; no one even suspected that a 32-bit instruction might some day be inadequate for direct addressing. Of course, one could solve the problem for the foreseeable future by making all instructions 64 bits wide, but this would be wasteful for instructions that do not require a direct memory address. Variable-width instructions used in some machines offer a solution, as do some of the addressing modes already discussed. MiniMIPS uses a scheme that allows us to almost achieve direct addressing with 32-bit addresses in 32-bit instructions. It uses two implied bits of 0 at the low end, along with 4 bits from the program counter at the high end to turn a 26-bit address field into a complete 32-bit address. Schemes that come close to direct addressing are referred to as *pseudodirect addressing*.

Indexed addressing takes its name from its main application in accessing the elements of an array. Some early computers had one or more registers that were dedicated to indexing. If the addressing mode were indexed, the content of one of these registers would be added to the base address, which was specified directly or via one of the preceding addressing modes. In some later models, any register in the general register file could be specified as an index register. As mentioned earlier, base addressing in MiniMIPS provides a limited form of indexing in which the base address is specified in 16 bits. Conventional indexed addressing requires that the base be a full address. Typically, the full address comprising the base is given via direct specification or is held in a register. In the latter case, the effective address is obtained as the sum of two register contents. Because it is very common to access the next element of an array after the current one, some machines provide a more elaborate form of indexed addressing known as *update addressing*.

Update addressing is any addressing scheme in which one of the registers involved in forming the address (typically a register used as index) is updated so that a new address computation yields the address of the next array element. Update addressing requires the addition of a constant (± 1 or $\pm$ a power of 2) to the designated register. This capability saves an instruction in many common loops and can also speed up execution if index updating is done in parallel with executing the main part of the instruction. Update addressing can also be used in conjunction with base addressing, provided the immediate component is regarded as the base and the register component as the offset.

Indirect addressing requires a two-stage process for obtaining an operand. In the first stage, the designated location (a register or a memory word) is consulted; it yields an address rather than an operand. In the second stage, this address is used to retrieve the operand itself. If the first stage specifies a register, the addressing mode is known as *register indirect,* which as stated earlier, is a special case of base addressing with an offset of 0. One of the most prominent uses of indirect addressing is the construction of *jump tables*. A jump table is an array whose elements are addresses. Suppose one of *n* sequences of actions must be performed depending on the value of an integer variable *j* (this is what the case statement does in some high-level programming languages). Then, placing the start addresses of *n* instruction sequences in an array of length *n* and executing an indirect jump to the *j*th array element accomplishes the desired task. Like most other complex addressing modes, the effect of indirect addressing can be accomplished via the simpler addressing modes.

Figure 8.1 depicts the new addressing modes just discussed (indexed, update, and indirect) in a format similar to Figure 5.11 (showing the implied, immediate, register, base, PC-relative, and pseudodirect addressing modes). Note that even though the instructions shown in Figure 8.1 resemble MiniMIPS instructions, these addressing modes are not supported in MiniMIPS.

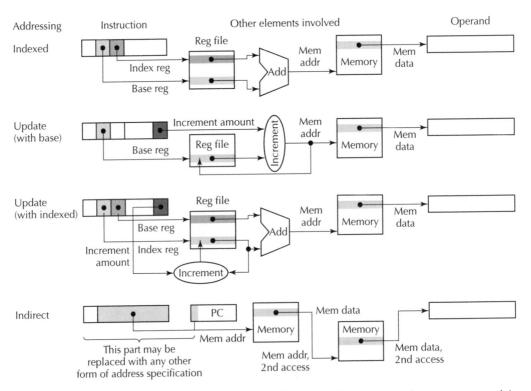

Figure 8.1 Schematic representation of more elaborate addressing modes not supported in MiniMIPS.

Like MiniMIPS, most machines place some restrictions on the types of addressing mode that can be used with each instruction or class of instructions. The VAX architecture, introduced in the mid-1970s, epitomized generality in addressing in the sense that each operand specified in an instruction could utilize any of the available addressing modes. This led to a highly variable instruction format, especially given that up to six operands could be specified for some instructions (see Table 8.1). Instruction formats are discussed in the next section.

8.3 Variations in Instruction Formats

Instructions can be variously classified with regard to format. One common classification is based on the number of addresses in the instruction (usually 0–3, although it is certainly possible to have more addresses). Here, "address" refers to the specification of an operand or other value and need not correspond to a location in memory. For example, a register specification, an immediate operand, or a relative offset qualifies as an "address" in the following discussion. A base and an offset, together specifying a single memory operand, are counted as two addresses. Similarly, an index register, when specified in an instruction, is viewed as a separate address even though its content may be combined with a base value, and even an offset, to define a single memory operand.

Zero-address instructions must rely on implicit addressing for their operands. Examples include incrementing an implied register (accumulator), popping the top element of the stack into an implied register, and skipping the next instruction in sequence (unconditionally or based on an implicit condition). MiniMIPS has only one such instruction: `syscall`.

One-address instructions carry one operand specification and use implicit addressing for any other needed operand or result destination. Examples include adding a value to the accumulator, pushing a specified value onto the stack, or jumping to specified location. Such instructions were predominant in early digital computers. The jump instruction `j` is an example of one-address instructions in MiniMIPS.

Two-address instructions allow arithmetic/logic operations of the form $a = g(b)$, involving a unary operator, or $a = f(a, b)$, with the result destination being the same as one of the operands of a binary operator. Alternatively, there may be three distinct operands as in three-address instructions, but with one of them implied. The `mult` instruction of MiniMIPS falls in this latter category. It is also possible for one address to specify a single operand, as in one-address instructions, with the other address used to supplement the former as an index or offset. In the latter case, the two "addresses" in the instruction are components of a single operand specification. Such instructions are sometimes said to belong to the one-plus-one-address format.

Three-address instructions are common in modern processors whose arithmetic/logic instructions take the form $a = f(b, c)$. Again, it is possible to have fewer distinct operands, with the extra address fields used for more complex addressing. For example, there may be two operands corresponding to the computation $a = f(a, b)$, with the operand b specified using base or indexed addressing. There are many examples of three-address instructions in MiniMIPS.

Even though instructions with four or more addresses are feasible and occasionally used (see, e.g., the `ADDP6` instruction of VAX in Table 8.1), they are too rare in modern architectures to warrant additional discussion in this book. Figure 8.2 depicts an example MiniMIPS instruction for each of the four categories described at the beginning of this section.

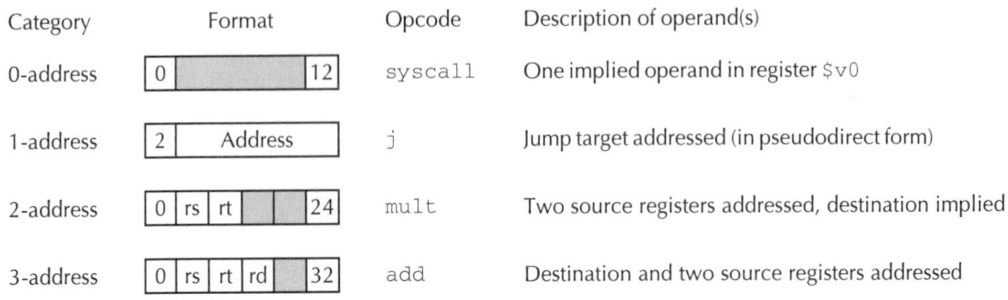

Category	Format	Opcode	Description of operand(s)
0-address	0 ▨ 12	syscall	One implied operand in register $v0
1-address	2 Address	j	Jump target addressed (in pseudodirect form)
2-address	0 rs rt ▨ 24	mult	Two source registers addressed, destination implied
3-address	0 rs rt rd ▨ 32	add	Destination and two source registers addressed

Figure 8.2 Examples of MiniMIPS instructions with 0 to 3 addresses; shaded fields are unused.

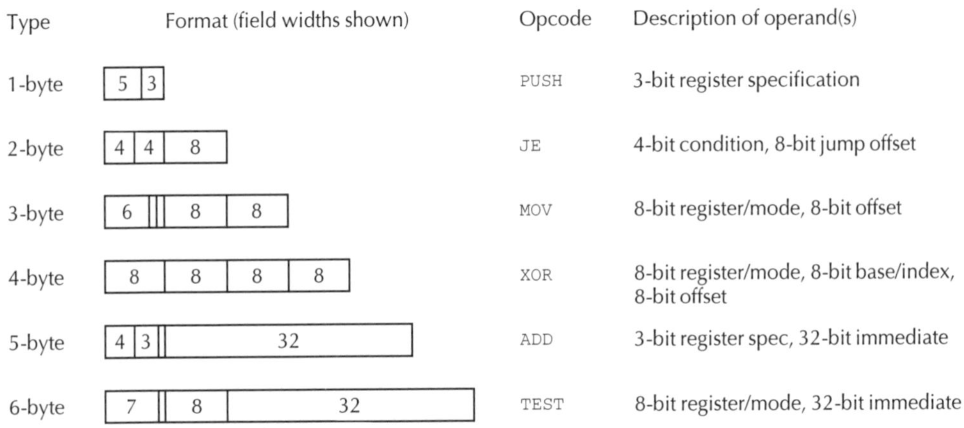

Type	Format (field widths shown)	Opcode	Description of operand(s)
1-byte	5 3	PUSH	3-bit register specification
2-byte	4 4 8	JE	4-bit condition, 8-bit jump offset
3-byte	6 ▨ 8 8	MOV	8-bit register/mode, 8-bit offset
4-byte	8 8 8 8	XOR	8-bit register/mode, 8-bit base/index, 8-bit offset
5-byte	4 3 ▨ 32	ADD	3-bit register spec, 32-bit immediate
6-byte	7 ▨ 8 32	TEST	8-bit register/mode, 32-bit immediate

Figure 8.3 Example 80x86 instructions ranging in width from 1 to 6 bytes; much wider instructions (up to 15 bytes) also exist.

All instructions in MiniMIPS are 32 bits wide. This uniformity, which simplifies many aspects of hardware implementation, is achieved at the expense of limiting the addressing modes. For example, three address instructions can specify only three registers, or two registers plus an immediate operand. Use of complex and flexible addressing modes often necessitates variable instruction formats to avoid extreme inefficiency resulting from unused fields in many instructions that do not need multiple memory addresses.

The Intel 80x86 instruction-set architecture, used for Pentium processors and their predecessors, provides a good example of variable-width instructions, ranging in width from 1 to 15 bytes. Even greater variability was provided in the instruction set of Digital VAX series of computers which were quite popular in the late 1970s and early 1980s (for example instructions, see Table 8.1). Advantages and drawbacks of complex addressing modes, and associated variable instruction formats, are similar to those listed for complex instructions. We will elaborate on the trade-offs in instruction-set design in Sections 8.4 and 8.5.

Figure 8.3 shows some of the more common formats in the now widely used Intel 80x86 instruction set. The instructions shown range from a single byte (which is either purely an opcode or an opcode plus a 3-bit register specification) to 6 bytes. In all cases, the leftmost field of the instruction, ranging in width from 4 to 7 bits, specifies the opcode. Of course, the opcodes must be chosen so that the longer ones do not have any of the shorter opcodes as a prefix. The hardware can determine by inspecting the first byte of an 80x86 instruction how many other bytes must be fetched and processed to complete the instruction. The 1-bit field(s) shown in some of the instructions serve functions whose description is beyond the scope of this book.

■ 8.4 Instruction-Set Design and Evolution

In the early days of digital computing, new machines were built from scratch, beginning with the choice of an instruction set. Over the years, certain instructions proved their usefulness and were thus included in many instruction sets. However, instruction sets remained incompatible. Assembly and machine language programs were not portable, even among machines built by the same company, and high-level language programs had to be recompiled for execution on each new machine. The introduction of IBM System/360 family of computers in the mid-1960s, and its subsequent commercial success, changed the scene. With this family, which shared the same instruction-set architecture but included machines with vastly different capabilities and performance, it became possible to run the same programs on several computers. The huge commercial success of IBM's personal computer, introduced in the early 1980s, and the attendant investment in system and application software for it, cemented the dominance of Intel's x86 instruction set, in much the same way that English became a de facto international standard for business and technical communication.

If given a blank slate, a computer architect might design an instruction set with the following desirable attributes:

Consistency, with uniform and generally applicable rules

Orthogonality, with independent features noninterfering

Transparency, with no visible side effect due to implementation details

Ease of learning/using (often a by-product of the three preceding attributes)

Extensibility, to allow the addition of future capabilities

Efficiency, in terms of both memory needs and hardware realization

These are generally recognized features of a good instruction set, but as in many other technical contexts, goodness cannot be defined or evaluated without reference to the design goals and intended applications. Over the years, with the growth of software in importance and cost relative to hardware, the aesthetics of instruction-set design has given way to the requirement for compatibility as the prime focus in hardware development. Today, instruction sets are seldom designed from scratch. Rather, new instruction sets are formed by modifying or extending existing ones. This incremental approach, essential for maintaining backward compatibility, protects huge investments in software and personnel by ensuring that previously developed software can run on new hardware.

Figure 8.4 depicts the process of rolling out a new processor. The task is given to a processor design team composed of a chief architect and tens or even hundreds of members with various subspecialties, from VLSI design and implementation technologies to performance evaluation and compiler design. If the project's goal is to introduce a somewhat faster version of an existing processor, perhaps with a number of discovered bugs fixed, then the lower path is taken, which involves minimal redesign followed by implementation and/or fabrication. On the other hand, introduction of a major new processor, or significant performance enhancement for an existing product, requires a more extensive and longer design process, often spanning several years.

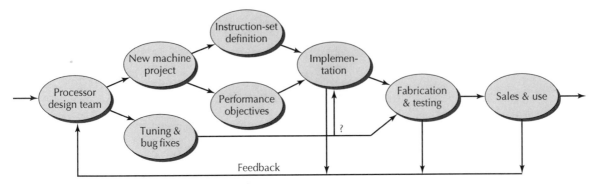

Figure 8.4 Processor design and implementation process.

■ **TABLE 8.2** Evolution of the x86 instruction set and architecture in some of the Intel microprocessors, and comparable products from AMD.

Intel	Year	Instruction set and other key modifications	AMD	Year
8086–8088	1978	Diverged from 8085 and its predecessors and began a new instruction-set architecture known as x86		
80286	1982	Continued with a 16-bit architecture and remained fully backward-compatible with 8086–8088		
80386	1985	Introduced the 32-bit extended architecture dubbed IA-32; was later augmented with the 80387 numeric coprocessor	Am386	1990
80486	1989	Integrated the 80386 with its 80387 numeric coprocessor and an on-chip cache memory	Am486	1994
Pentium	1993	Introduced a 64-bit data bus along with other performance boosters such as multiple instruction issue	K5	1996
Pentium II	1997	Incorporated 57 new machine instructions constituting the multimedia extensions (MMX) feature	K6	1997
Pentium III	1999	Incorporated 70 new machine instructions constituting the streaming SIMD extensions (SSE) feature	Athlon	1999
Pentium 4	2000	Incorporated a more advanced version of streaming SIMD extensions feature (SSE2) and wider internal buses	Athlon XP	2001

Table 8.2 exemplifies the evolutionary approach to instruction set design. The instruction-set architecture of the currently most popular processors offered by Intel and AMD for desktop applications has its roots in the Intel 8086 and 8088 microprocessors of a quarter-century ago. This instruction set was gradually extended to accommodate the move from 16-bit to 32-bit architectures and to allow efficient processing of multimedia and Web-based applications. A move to 64-bit architectures is in progress. Intel has introduced a completely new IA-64 architecture, with long instruction words and explicit parallelism (multiple operations packed in one instruction word), while AMD is pursuing x86-64, a 64-bit backward-compatible extension of the x86/IA-32 instruction-set architecture.

■ 8.5 The RISC/CISC Dichotomy

As computers grew in complexity, the limited instruction sets of early digital computers gave way to highly complex sets of operations with a rich variety of addressing modes. Between the 1940s and the 1970s, we went from a handful of instructions to hundreds of different instructions, in a variety of formats, leading to thousands of distinct combinations when addressing mode variations were taken into account. As early as 1971, however, it was recognized that only a small subset of available combinations were actually used within manually or automatically generated machine-language programs, leading to the conclusion that 32–64 operations would probably be sufficient [Fost71]. With the advent of VLSI, simplification of instruction sets and addressing modes, which had already proven quite successful in improving the performance of the CDC and Cray supercomputers, gained momentum in the early 1980s. The acronym RISC, for reduced instruction-set computer [Patt82], helped popularize this trend.

It appeared that instruction sets had become so complicated that the inclusion of mechanisms to interpret all the possible combinations of opcodes and operands was slowing down even very simple operations. Early VLSI chips simply did not have enough room to accommodate all the control circuitry, that took up roughly half of the chip area, and also hold the large number of registers required for good performance. To overcome this problem of complex instruction-set computers, or CISCs, a number of RISC-type machines were designed and built. The MIPS series of processors (on which our MiniMIPS machine of Chapters 5–7 is based) and Sun Microsystem's SPARC processor were two of the earliest products in this category. RISC machines lowered the control overhead from 50% of the chip area to less than 10%, thus opening up room for more registers, and eventually, larger on-chip caches. Moreover, the simplicity of control allowed a fully hardwired realization to replace the then common microprogrammed control, thus leading to execution speed that more than offset the effects of using several instructions to achieve the effects of a complex instruction. This last statement will make more sense to you after you have read Part IV of the book.

Of course "reduced" and "complex" are relative terms, and some processors are difficult to categorize as RISC or CISC. RISC must thus be viewed as a way of thinking corresponding to the "small is beautiful" philosophy, and an approach to instruction-set design, rather than a class of machines with concrete boundaries. Processor designs adhere to the RISC philosophy to varying degrees, forming almost a continuum from pure RISCs at one end to utter CISCs at the other. Features that define RISCs include the following.

1. Small set of instructions, each of which can be executed in approximately the same amount of time using hardwired control; a RISC instruction corresponds roughly to a *microinstruction,* which implements one of a sequence of steps in the execution of more complex instructions (see Section 14.5).

2. Load/store architecture that confines memory address calculations and access delays to a small set of load and store instructions, with all others obtaining their operands from faster, and more compactly addressable, registers (a larger number of which can be accommodated owing to control simplicity).

3. Limited addressing modes that eliminate or speed up address calculations for the vast majority of cases encountered in practice and yet offer enough versatility to allow the synthesis of other addressing modes in several steps. Note that because of the load/store architecture, an instruction needs either address calculation or manipulation of register operands, but never both.

4. Simple, uniform instruction formats that facilitate extraction/decoding of the various fields and allow overlap between opcode interpretation and register readout. Uniform word-width instructions simplify instruction prefetching and eliminate complications that arise from instructions crossing word, block, or page boundaries.

These four features collectively lead to faster execution of the most commonly used operations in computer programs. Of course, everyone agrees that faster is better; so, why do we have CISCs at all? There are two potential advantages to CISCs. First, economy in the number of instructions used (more compact programs) translates to smaller storage space requirements, fewer memory accesses, and more effective use of the cache space; all this can be beneficial, given that memory has become the bottleneck in modern computers. Second, closer correspondence between machine instructions and operations or constructs commonly found in high-level languages might facilitate program compilation, as well as understanding, troubleshooting, and modification of the resulting code.

In a way, the CISC style is a natural outcome of the way instruction sets are expanded and of the desire to maintain backward compatibility (ability to run existing programs). Some designs that start as pure RISCs grow more complex over time with the addition of new "features" to accommodate the needs of emerging applications. If a machine's instruction set is likened to its vocabulary, the problem becomes apparent. Suppose you were to expand a natural language to accommodate words proposed for new notions and gadgets. If people speaking the language were to be able to read previously published books, which in turn referred to older books, and so on, you would not be able to remove any existing word that is obsolete or incompatible with new discoveries. Imagine how funny modern English would sound, and how much thicker the typical collegiate dictionary would be, if we were required to understand every English word that has been used through the ages.

So, in the end, which is better, RISC or CISC? You will get different answers to this question depending on whom you ask or which book you read. RISC is certainly easier to describe in a textbook, or in class. This is why our exposition in this book is based on MiniMIPS, a simple RISC machine. Beyond this, one cannot make a general statement. We know from our discussion of performance in Chapter 4 that what ultimately counts is the running time of our application programs; what matters is not whether a computer executes 10 billion simple instructions or 5 billion complex instructions, but rather how much time it takes to perform the required tasks.

All else being equal, however, RISC has one undeniable advantage. Designing and building a processor are time-consuming and expensive undertakings. It literally takes years, and hundreds of hardware designers, to roll out the next model of a CISC processor. Much of this effort is devoted to design verification and testing. The RISC approach simplifies the design and testing of a new processor, thereby reducing development costs and shortening the time-to-market of new products. In today's business climate, these are important benefits. Also, if one is building a system on a chip, a RISC processor is more likely to fit on the chip along with all the other required subsystems and will be easier to integrate and test.

One can demonstrate why the RISC approach might be beneficial in terms of Amdahl's law.

Example 8.1: RISC/CISC comparison via generalized Amdahl's formula   An instruction-set architecture has two classes of simple (S) and complex (C) instructions. On an existing reference implementation of the ISA, class-S instructions account for 95% of the running time for programs of interest. A RISC version of the machine is being considered that executes only class-S instructions directly in hardware, with class-C instructions treated as pseudoinstructions (converted to sequences of class-S instructions by the assembler). It is estimated that in the RISC version, class-S instructions will run 20% faster and class-C instructions will be slowed down by a factor of 3. Does the RISC approach offer better or worse performance than the reference implementation?

> **Solution:** We use a generalized form of Amdahl's speedup formula that yields the overall speedup when 0.95 of the work is speeded up by a factor of $1.0/0.8 = 1.25$, while the remaining 5% is slowed down by a factor of 3. The overall RISC speedup is $1/[0.95/1.25 + 0.05 \times 3] = 1.1$. Thus, a 10% improvement in performance can be expected in the proposed RISC version of the machine. This is quite significant, given that it comes on top of cost and time savings in design, test, and manufacturing.

It is possible to combine the advantages of RISC and CISC in a single machine. In fact, current high-performance CISC processors, of which the devices in the Intel Pentium series are prime examples, are designed by using a front-end hardware translator that replaces each CISC instruction with a sequence of one or more RISC-like operations. These simpler operations are then executed at high speed, using all the benefits and speedup methods that are applicable to RISC-type instruction sets.

8.6 Where to Draw the Line

Having learned about RISC machines with a few dozens of instructions, you may legitimately wonder whether there is a limit to the simplicity of an instruction set and whether going below such a limit would compromise the machine's computational capabilities. In other words, how many instructions does the ultimate RISC (URISC) have? It turns out that, ignoring input/-output, interrupts, and other scheduling and bookkeeping operations that are needed in any computer, a single instruction would be adequate; that is, computationally, a computer can get by with just one instruction. This is quite surprising and enlightening. One consequence of learning about this one instruction is that extra instructions must be included in an instruction set only for good cause: that is, only if we can verify that they help, rather than hinder, the machine's performance.

Let's see if we can argue what the one instruction might be. First, we note that the instruction does not need an opcode. To be able to perform arithmetic, it needs two operands and a result; let's make the result destination the same as the second operand. The operands have to come from memory and the result must be stored back in memory, given that we do not have the luxury of separate instructions for loading into, or storing from, registers. So, thus far, we need two memory addresses in the instruction: source1 and source2/destination. Of course, nothing very useful can be accomplished without a branching capability to allow data-dependent conditional computations and loops. So, we postulate that the single instruction will incorporate a conditional branch that requires a third address for specifying the branch target. What about the branch condition? If we use subtraction as the arithmetic operation, we can take the sign of the result as our branch condition, thus requiring no additional specification for the condition.

The preceding leads to this single instruction for URISC:

```
subtract operand1 from operand2, replace operand2 with the
result, and jump to target address in case of negative
result
```

Although we do not need an opcode, we can write this one instruction in a format similar to that of MiniMIPS assembly language by using `urisc` as the only opcode:

```
label: urisc  dest,src1,target
```

We will use the conventions that program execution always starts at memory location 1 and that branching to location 0 stops the program's execution. Finally, we use the assembler directive `.word` to name and initialize one word of memory to be used as an operand. The following sample program fragment copies the contents of the memory location `src` to memory location `dest` and is thus equivalent to the MiniMIPS `move` pseudoinstruction; it uses another location `temp` for temporary storage.

```
stop:   .word  0
start:  urisc  dest,dest,+1    # dest = 0
        urisc  src,dest,+1     # temp = -(src)
        urisc  temp,dest,+1    # dest = -(temp)
        ...                    # rest of program
```

Note that in assembly language, every program begins with the directive `.word 0` to allow proper termination. Also, to avoid having to label every instruction in the program, the notation "$\pm i$" is used in the branch target address field to mean that the branch target is i instructions forward or backward.

Example 8.2: URISC pseudoinstructions For each of the following pseudoinstructions, write the corresponding instructions produced by URISC assembler. The prefix "u" is used to distinguish these instructions from MiniMIPS instructions.

```
parta: uadd  dest,src1,src2    # dest = (src1)+(src2)
partb: uswap src1,src2         # exchange (src1) and (src2)
partc: uj    label             # goto label
partd: ubge  src1,src2,label   # if (src1)≥(src2), goto label
parte: ubeq  src1,src2,label   # if (src1)=(src2), goto label
```

Solution: In the following, `at1` and `at2` are temporary memory locations for exclusive use by the assembler (similar to the role of register `$at` in MiniMIPS) and `one` is a memory location holding the constant 1.

```
parta: urisc at1,at1,+1     # at1 = 0
       urisc src1,at1,+1    # at1 = -(src1)
       urisc src2,at1,+1    # at1 = -(src1) - (src2)
       urisc dest,dest,+1   # dest = 0
       urisc at1,dest,+1    # dest = -(at1); that is, (src1)+(src2)
partb: urisc at1,at1,+1     # at1 = 0
       urisc at2,at2,+1     # at2 = 0
       urisc src1,at1,+1    # at1 = -(src1)
```

```
          urisc src2,at2,+1    # at2 = -(src2)
          urisc src1,src1,+1   # src1 = 0
          urisc src2,src2,+1   # src2 = 0
          urisc at2,src1,+1    # src1 = -(at2); that is, (src2)
          urisc at1,src2,+1    # src2 = -(at1); that is, (src1)
partc:    urisc at1,at1,+1     # at1 = 0
          urisc one,at1,label  # at1 = -1, to force jump
partd:    urisc src2,src1,+3   # if (src1)-(src2) < 0, skip 2 instr's
          urisc at1,at1,+1     # at1 = 0
          urisc one,at1,label  # at1 = -1, to force jump
parte:    urisc src2,src1,+4   # if (src1)-(src2) < 0, skip 3 instr's
          urisc src1,src2,+3   # if (src2)-(src1) < 0, skip 2 instr's
          urisc at1,at1,+1     # at1 = 0
          urisc one,at1,label  # at1 = -1, to force jump
```

In the solution to `parte`, we have used the fact that $x = y$ iff $x \geq y$ and $y \geq x$.

Figure 8.5 shows the elements needed to implement URISC in hardware. There are four registers, including the memory address and data registers (MAR, MDR), an adder, two condition flags N and Z (negative, zero) characterizing the adder's output, and a memory unit. The small shaded circles represent control points, with the control signal allowing the data transfer to take place written next to the circle. For example, the control signal PC_{in}, when asserted, causes the adder output to be stored in the program counter.

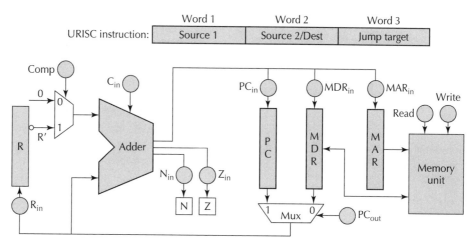

Figure 8.5 Instruction format and hardware structure for URISC.

PROBLEMS

8.1 Complex instructions

For each complex instruction listed in Table 8.1, estimate the number of MiniMIPS instructions that would be needed to achieve the same effect. Provide both the *static count* (number of machine instructions generated) and *dynamic count* (number of machine instructions executed). The 13 lines in Table 8.1 constitute parts a–m of this problem.

8.2 Instruction formats

Categorize each of the MiniMIPS instructions given in Table 6.2 according to the number of addresses in its format (0-, 1-, 2-, or 3-address instruction, as in Figure 8.2). For the sake of this problem, an address is any set of one or more fields that collectively specify the whereabouts of a distinct operand explicitly, be it in register or in memory.

8.3 Instruction formats

Does it make sense to talk about 0-, 1-, 2-, and 3-address pseudoinstructions as we do about instructions? Frame your discussion in terms of the MiniMIPS pseudoinstructions shown in Table 7.1.

8.4 Architecture versus implementation

Classify each of the following items as belonging to the instruction-set architecture, the user/application level above it, to the implementation level below it. Justify your answers.

a. Number representation format
b. Opcode map (table listing the binary encoding of each opcode)
c. Register usage conventions, as in Figure 5.2
d. Addressing modes
e. Carry-lookahead adder
f. Memory map, as in Figure 6.3
g. Character encoding for strings, as in Table 6.1 (ASCII)

8.5 Instruction-set attributes

Evaluate the MiniMIPS instruction set shown in Table 6.2 with regard to the attributes of a good instruction set enumerated in Section 8.4.

8.6 Attributes of good user interfaces

The attributes of a good instruction set, enumerated in Section 8.4, apply to other user interfaces as well. For each of the following system types, consider a pair of different instances with which you are familiar and discuss how their user interfaces fare with regard to these attributes relative to each other.

a. Elevators
b. Bank ATMs
c. Television remote controls
d. Alarm clocks
e. Telephone sets (regular or mobile)
f. Calculators
g. Web stores

8.7 Instruction-set encodings

A machine is being designed whose instructions range from 1 to 6 bytes in width, with 2-byte instructions being most common and 5- or 6-byte instructions rarely used. Compare the following encoding schemes for the instructions' opcode field.

a. The leftmost 3 bits in the first byte of every instruction contains a binary number in [1, 6] that indicates the width of the instruction in bytes.
b. One-byte instructions begin with 0 in the leftmost bit position of the first byte, 2-byte instructions begin with 10, and all other instructions begin with 11 followed by a 2-bit field that indicates the number of additional bytes (beyond the third) in the instruction.

8.8 The program counter

In MiniMIPS, the program counter is a dedicated register that always holds the address of the next instruction to be executed. Some processors embed the program counter into the general register file so that it can be treated like any other register. For example, in MiniMIPS, we can designate register $25 as $pc instead of $t9 (see Figure 5.2).

a. List two positive effects of this change, justifying your answers.
b. List two negative effects of this change, justifying your answers.

8.9 Hardware stack

It was mentioned in Section 8.2 that certain machines have been built that predominantly use 0-address instructions. These machines pop their required operands from the top of a stack and push their result to the top of that same stack. If the stack is a region in memory, such instructions would be quite slow, because each would require 2–3 data memory accesses. By supplying a complete logic design, show how a 33-entry hardware stack can be designed to speed up data accesses. Use a register to hold the top element of the stack and 32 bidirectional shift registers, each 32 bits wide, to hold the remaining 32 elements. In this way, the top two elements of the stack are easily accessible, and push and pop operations can be performed through shifting of the registers. Ignore the possibility of stack overflow (pushing a new element when the stack is full) or underflow (trying to pop an element when the stack is empty).

8.10 Memory-based operands

We are contemplating the addition of a new set of instructions to MiniMIPS that perform arithmetic and shift/logic operations on the content of a register and a memory location, storing the result in the same register. For example, `addm $t0,1000($s2)` would fetch the content of memory location `1000+($s2)` and add it to the content of register `$t0`. Each such instruction can potentially eliminate the need for one load instruction. On the negative side, this more complex instruction would lengthen the clock cycle of the machine to 1.1 times its original value (assume that CPIs for the various instruction classes are unaffected). Considering the instruction usage distributions in Table 4.3, under what conditions would the suggested modification lead to improved performance? In other words, what fraction of the load instructions must be eliminated for the new addressing mode to be beneficial?

8.11 MiniMIPS-64

A new model of MiniMIPS with 64-bit registers and arithmetic/logic unit is being designed. To maintain backward compatibility with the current 32-bit version, it has been decided to keep all current

instructions and to have them operate on the lower halves of the respective registers, while adding new 64-bit versions to deal with complete registers. With reference to Table 6.2, answer the following questions.

a. Which instructions require 64-bit versions?
b. Suggest appropriate modifications of the instruction encoding and the assembly language notation to accommodate the new instructions.
c. What problems are caused by the 16-bit immediate field, and how do you propose to handle them?
d. Can you identify any other problem resulting from this architectural extension?

8.12 Generalized Amdahl's formula in ISA design

Let instructions of a processor be divided into classes $C_1, C_2, \ldots, C_q$, with the fraction of time spent in executing class-C_i instructions being f_i. Clearly, $f_1 + f_2 + \cdots + f_q = 1$. Assume that starting from a reference implementation, the running time of class-C_i instructions is improved by a factor p_i, $1 \le i \le q$, and that $f_1 > f_2 > \cdots > f_q$. Further assume that the total cost of the improvements is proportional to $p_1 + p_2 + \cdots + p_q$. The following generalized form of Amdahl's formula denotes the overall speedup:

$$S = \frac{1}{f_1/p_1 + f_2/p_2 + \cdots + f_q/p_q}$$

Show that under these conditions, the hardware invested in speeding up class-C_i instructions must be proportional to f_i^2 for maximal overall speedup.

8.13 URISC

a. Characterize the single URISC instruction with respect to its format and addressing mode(s).
b. Would the single instruction be adequate for accommodating I/O operations if we use memory-mapped I/O? *Hint:* Look ahead to Section 22.2 for some ideas.
c. How many MiniMIPS instructions are needed to emulate the effect of a single URISC instruction?
d. If your answer to part c is x, does this mean that MiniMIPS is x times slower than URISC? Discuss.

8.14 URISC pseudoinstructions

For each of the URISC pseudoinstructions in Example 8.2, write an equivalent MiniMIPS instruction or sequence of instructions to accomplish the same effect.

8.15 Modified URISC

The design of URISC presented in Section 8.6 assumes that numbers and addresses each occupy one word of memory (say, 32 bits). Discuss how the instructions and design of URISC would change if addresses were half as wide as numbers (say, 32 vs 64 bits). State all your assumptions clearly.

8.16 Addressing modes for signal processing

Some digital signal processors implement special addressing modes that significantly speed up certain types of computation. Study the following special types of addressing mode and write a two-page report on the usefulness and implementation aspect of each.

a. Circular, or modulo, addressing (targeted for circular buffers)

b. Bit-reversal addressing (targeted for fast Fourier transform)

REFERENCES AND FURTHER READINGS

[Blaa97]   Blaauw, G. A., and F. P. Brooks Jr, *Computer Architecture: Concepts and Evolution,* Addison-Wesley, 1997.

[Fost71]   Foster, C., R. Gonter, and E. Riseman, "Measures of Op-Code Utilization," *IEEE Trans. Computers,* Vol. 20, No. 5, pp. 582–584, May 1971.

[Giff87]   Gifford, D., and A. Spector, "Case Study: IBM's System/360-370 Architecture," *Communications of the ACM,* Vol. 30, No. 4, pp. 292–307, April 1987.

[Henn03]   Hennessy, J. L., and D.A. Patterson, *Computer Architecture: A Quantitative Approach,* Morgan Kaufmann, 3rd ed., 2003.

[Kane92]   Kane, G., and J. Heinrich, *MIPS RISC Architecture,* Prentice Hall, 1992.

[Mava88]   Mavaddat, F., and B. Parhami, "URISC: The Ultimate Reduced Instruction Set Computer," *Int. J. Electrical Engineering Education,* Vol. 25, pp. 327–334, 1988.

[Patt82]   Patterson, D. A., and C. H. Sequin, "A VLSI RISC," *IEEE Computer,* Vol. 15, No. 9, pp. 8–21, September 1982.

[Patt98]   Patterson, D. A., and J. L. Hennessy, *Computer Organization and Design: The Hardware/Software Interface,* Morgan Kaufmann, 2nd ed., 1998.

[Siew82]   Siewiorek, D. P., C. G. Bell, and A. Newell, *Computer Structures: Principles and Examples,* McGraw-Hill, 1982.

[Stal03]   Stallings, W., *Computer Organization and Architecture,* Prentice Hall, 6th ed., 2003.

THE ARITHMETIC/LOGIC UNIT

"I only took the regular course." "What was that?" enquired Alice. "Reeling and Writhing, of course, to begin with," the Mock Turtle replied; "and then the different branches of Arithmetic—Ambition, Distraction, Uglification, and Derision."
—*Lewis Carroll, Alice's Adventures in Wonderland*

". . . even in such a tight, tidy, logical, and as it were entirely arithmetical system, it is possible to formulate theorems which cannot be shown to be either true or false."
—*J. Bronowski, The Common Sense of Science*

TOPICS IN THIS PART

9. Number Representation
10. Adders and Simple ALUs
11. Multipliers and Dividers
12. Floating-Point Arithmetic

Data manipulations in a digital computer fall under the categories of arithmetic operations (addition, subtraction, multiplication, division) and bit-manipulation or logic operations (NOT, AND, OR, XOR, shifting, rotation, etc.). Logic operations are more or less straightforward, but implementing arithmetic operations requires knowledge of computer arithmetic, the branch of computer design that deals with algorithms for manipulating numbers by means of hardware circuits or software routines. Discussion of computer arithmetic begins with number representation. This is because standard number representation in computers is different from what we use for pencil-and-paper calculation or with electronic calculators. Additionally, number representation affects the ease and speed of arithmetic in hardware and software. This has led to a variety of unconventional number representation formats. These unconventional formats are often invisible to the programmer and are used internally (along with their associated conversion algorithms to/from standard formats) for speed enhancement.

After reviewing the most important number representation schemes for digital computers in Chapter 9, we describe the design of counters, adders, logic operation units, and shifters (components possessed by every digital computer) in Chapter 10, multiplication and division schemes in Chapter 11, and floating-point arithmetic in Chapter 12. Readers interested only in basic integer ALU design can skip Sections 9.5 and 9.6 and Chapters 12 and 13. The general discussions in this part are related to specific MiniMIPS instructions where applicable.

CHAPTER 9

NUMBER REPRESENTATION

"Leibniz believed he saw the image of creation in his binary arithmetic in which he employed only the two characters, zero and unity. He imagined that unity can represent God, and zero nothing. . . ."
—*Pierre Laplace, Théorie Analytique des Probabilités, 1812*

"This can't be right . . . it goes into the red!"
—*Little boy, when asked to subtract 36 from 24 (caption on a cartoon by unknown artist)*

Number representation is arguably the most important topic in computer arithmetic. How numbers are represented affects compatibility between machines and their computation results and influences the implementation cost and latency of arithmetic circuits. In this chapter, we review the most important methods for representing integers (signed-magnitude and 2's-complement) and real numbers (ANSI/IEEE standard floating-point format). We also learn about other number representation methods, number-radix conversion, and binary encoding of arbitrary digit sets.

9.1 Positional Number Systems

When we think of numbers, it is usually the *natural numbers* that first come to our mind; the numbers that sequence book or calendar pages, mark clock dials, flash on stadium scoreboards, and guide deliveries to our houses. The set {0, 1, 2, 3, . . .} of natural numbers, also known as *whole numbers* or *unsigned integers,* forms the basis of arithmetic. Four thousand years ago, Babylonians knew about natural numbers and were proficient in arithmetic. Since then, representations of natural numbers have advanced in parallel with the evolution of language. Ancient civilizations used sticks and pebbles to record inventories or accounts. When the need for larger numbers arose, the idea of grouping sticks or pebbles simplified counting and comparisons. Eventually, objects of different shapes or colors were used to denote such groups, leading to more compact representations.

Numbers must be differentiated from their representations, sometimes called *numerals.* For example, the number "twenty-seven" can be represented in different ways using various numerals or *numeration systems;* these include the following:

‖‖‖ ‖‖‖ ‖‖‖ ‖‖‖ ‖‖‖ ‖	sticks or *unary* code
27	radix-10 or *decimal* code
11011	radix-2 or *binary* code
XXVII	roman numerals

However, we don't always make the distinction between numbers and numerals and often use "decimal numbers" in lieu of "decimal numerals" to refer to radix-10 representation.

Radices other than 10 have also appeared over the ages. Babylonians used radix-60 numbers, which make dealing with time easy. The radices 12 (*duodecimal*) and 5 (*quinary*) have also been used. The use of radix-2 (*binary*) numbers became popular with the onset of electronic computers because their use of binary digits, or *bits,* having only two possible values 0 and 1, is compatible with electronic signals. Radix-3 (*ternary*) numbers were given serious consideration early in the development of digital computers, but binary numbers eventually won. Radix-8 (*octal*) and radix-16 (*hexadecimal*) numbers are used as shorthand notation for binary numbers. For example, a 24-bit binary number can be represented as an 8-digit octal or a 6-digit hexadecimal number by taking the bits in groups of threes and fours, respectively.

In a general radix-r *positional number system,* with fixed word width k, a number x is represented by a string of k digits x_i, with $0 \le x_i \le r - 1$:

$$x = \sum_{i=0}^{k-1} x_i r^i = (x_{k-1} x_{k-2} \cdots x_1 x_0)_r$$

For example, using radix 2:

$$27 = (1 \times 2^4) + (1 \times 2^3) + (0 \times 2^2) + (1 \times 2^1) + (1 \times 2^0) = (11011)_{\text{two}}$$

In a k-digit radix-r number system, natural numbers from 0 to $r^k - 1$ can be represented. Conversely, given a desired representation range $[0, P]$, the required number k of digits in radix r is obtained from the following equation:

$$k = \lceil \log_r (P + 1) \rceil = \lfloor \log_r P \rfloor + 1$$

For example, representing the decimal number 3125 requires 12 bits in radix 2, six digits in radix 5, and four digits in radix 8.

The finiteness of number encodings in computers has important implications. Figure 9.1 shows 4-bit binary encodings for numbers 0 through 15. This encoding cannot represent the numbers 16 and higher (or −1 and lower). It is convenient to view the arithmetic operations of addition and subtraction as turning the cogwheel in Figure 9.1 counterclockwise and clockwise, respectively. For example, if the cogwheel is set so that the vertical arrow points to the number 3 and then is turned counterclockwise by 4 notches to add the number 4, the arrow will point to the correct sum 7. If we try the same procedure with the numbers 9 and 12, the wheel will wrap around past 0 and the arrow will point to 5, which is 16 units smaller than the correct sum 21. The result thus obtained is the modulo-16 sum of 9 and 12 and an *overflow* has occurred. Occasional overflows are inevitable in any finite number representation system.

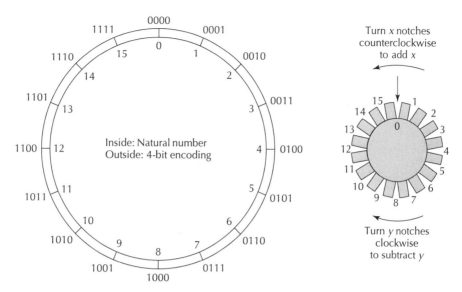

Figure 9.1 Schematic representation of 4-bit code for integers in [0, 15].

Figure 9.2 Overflow regions in finite number representation systems. For unsigned representations covered in this section, $max^- = 0$.

A similar situation arises in the subtraction $9 - 12$, because the correct result -3 is not representable in the encoding of Figure 9.1. The cogwheel interpretation in this case is setting the wheel so that the arrow points to 9 and then turning it clockwise by 12 notches, putting the arrow on the number 13. This result, which is 16 units too large, again represents the modulo-16 difference of 9 and 12. In this case, it is tempting to say that an underflow has occurred; however, the term *underflow* in computer arithmetic is reserved for numbers too small in magnitude to be distinguishable from 0 (see Section 9.6). When the range of the number system is exceeded from its lower end, we still say that an *overflow* has occurred. Figure 9.2 depicts the overflow regions of a finite number representation system.

> **Example 9.1: Fixed-radix positional number systems**   For each of the following conventional radix-r number representation systems, using the digit values 0 through $r - 1$, determine the largest number *max* that is representable with the indicated number k of digits and the minimum number K of digits required to represent all natural numbers under one million.
>
>   a. $r = 2, k = 16$
>   b. $r = 3, k = 10$
>   c. $r = 8, k = 6$
>   d. $r = 10, k = 8$

Solution: The largest natural number to be represented for the second part of the question is $P = 999{,}999$.

a. $max = r^k - 1 = 2^{16} - 1 = 65{,}535$; $K = \lceil \log_r (P + 1) \rceil = \lceil \log_2 (10^6) \rceil = 20$ $(2^{19} < 10^6)$

b. $max = 3^{10} - 1 = 59{,}048$; $K = \lceil \log_3 (10^6) \rceil = 13$ $(3^{12} < 10^6)$

c. $max = 8^6 - 1 = 262{,}143$; $K = \lceil \log_8 (10^6) \rceil = 7$ $(8^6 < 10^6)$

d. $max = 10^8 - 1 = 99{,}999{,}999$; $K = \lceil \log_{10} (10^6) \rceil = 6$

Example 9.2: Overflow in integer arithmetic   For each of the following k-digit conventional radix-r number representation systems, determine whether evaluating the arithmetic expression shown leads to overflow. All operands are given in radix 10.

a. $r = 2, k = 16$; $10^2 \times 10^3$

b. $r = 3, k = 10$; $15{,}000 + 20{,}000 + 25{,}000$

c. $r = 8, k = 6$; 555×444

d. $r = 10, k = 8$; $3^{17} - 3^{16}$

Solution: We do not need to represent the operands involved in the specified number systems; rather, we simply compare the values encountered in the course of expression evaluation with the maximum representable values derived in Example 9.1.

a. The result 10^5 is greater than $max = 65{,}535$, so overflow will occur.

b. The result $60{,}000$ is greater than $max = 59{,}048$, so overflow will occur.

c. The result $246{,}420$ is no greater than $max = 262{,}143$, so overflow will not occur.

d. The final result $86{,}093{,}442$ is no greater than $max = 99{,}999{,}999$. However, if we evaluate the expression by first computing $3^{17} = 129{,}140{,}163$ and then subtracting 3^{16} from it, overflow will be encountered and the computation cannot be completed correctly. Rewriting the expression as $3^{16} \times (3 - 1)$ removes the possibility of an unnecessary overflow.

■ 9.2 Digit Sets and Encodings

Digits of a binary number can be directly represented as binary signals, which can then be manipulated by logic circuits. Radices greater than 2 require digits sets that have more than two values. Such digit sets must be encoded as binary strings to allow their storage and processing within conventional two-valued logic circuits. An r-valued radix-r digit set requires at least b bits for its encoding, where

$$b = \lceil \log_2 r \rceil = \lfloor \log_2 (r - 1) \rfloor + 1$$

Decimal digits in [0, 9] thus require an encoding that is at least 4 bits wide. *Binary-coded decimal* (BCD) representation is based on the 4-bit binary representation of radix-10 digits. Two BCD digits can be packed into one 8-bit byte. Such *packed decimal* representations are common in some calculators whose circuits are designed for decimal arithmetic. Many computers offer special instructions to facilitate decimal arithmetic on packed BCD numbers. MiniMIPS, however, does not have any such instruction.

Of course, binary signals can be used to encode any finite set of symbols, not just digits. Such binary encodings are commonly used for input/output and data transfers. The *American Standard Code for Information Interchange* (ASCII), shown in Table 6.1, is one such convention that represents upper- and lowercase letters, numerals, punctuation marks, and other symbols in one byte. For example, the 8-bit ASCII codes for the 10 decimal digits are of the form 0011xxxx, where the "xxxx" part is identical to the BCD code discussed earlier. ASCII digits take twice as much space as BCD digits and thus are not used in arithmetic units. Even less compact than ASCII is the 16-bit *Unicode,* which can accommodate symbols from many different languages.

Hexadecimal numbers, with $r = 16$, use digits in [0, 15], which are written as 0–9, "a" for 10, "b" for 11, . . . , and "f" for 15. We have already seen that MiniMIPS assembly notation for hex numbers begins with "0x" followed by the hex number itself. Hex numbers can be viewed as shorthand notation for binary numbers, with each hex digit representing a block of 4 bits.

The use of digit values 0 through $r - 1$ in radix r is just a convention. We could use more than r digit values (e.g., digit values -2 to 2 in radix 4) or use r digit values that do not start with 0 (e.g., digit set $\{-1, 0, 1\}$ in radix 3). In the first instance, the resulting number system possesses redundancy in that some numbers will have multiple representations. The following examples illustrate some of the possibilities.

Example 9.3: Symmetric ternary numbers   If we had ternary as opposed to binary computers (with flip-flops replaced by flip-flap-flops), radix-3 arithmetic would be in common use today. The conventional radix-3 digit set is $\{0, 1, 2\}$. However, one can also use $\{-1, 0, 1\}$, which is an example of an unconventional digit set. Consider such a 5-digit *symmetric ternary* number system.

a. What is the range of representable values? (That is, find the boundaries max^- and max^+.)

b. Represent 35 and -74 as 5-digit symmetric ternary numbers.

c. Formulate an algorithm for adding symmetric ternary numbers.

d. Apply the addition algorithm of part c to finding the sum of 35 and -74.

Solution: We will denote the digit -1 as $^-1$, to avoid confusion with the subtraction symbol.

a. $max^+ = (1\,1\,1\,1\,1\,)_{three} = 3^4 + 3^3 + 3^2 + 3 + 1 = 121; max^- = -max^+ = -121$

b. To express an integer as a symmetric ternary number, we must decompose it into a sum of positive and negative powers of 3. We thus have:

$$35 = 27 + 9 - 1 = (0\,1\,1\,0\,^-1\,)_{three} \text{ and } -74 = -81 + 9 - 3 + 1 = (^-1\,0\,1\,^-1\,1\,)_{three}$$

c. The sum of two digits in $\{-1, 0, 1\}$ ranges from -2 to 2. Because $2 = 3 - 1$ and $-2 = -3 + 1$, we can rewrite these values as valid digits and transfer a carry of 1 or -1 (borrow), which is worth 3 or -3 units, respectively, to the next higher position. When the incoming ternary carry is included, the sum ranges from -3 to 3, which can still be handled in the same way.

d. $35 + (-74) = (0\,1\,1\,0\,^-1\,)_{three} + (^-1\,0\,1\,^-1\,1\,)_{three} = (0\,^-1\,^-1\,^-1\,0\,)_{three} = -39$.   In the addition process, positions 0 and 1 produce no carry, while positions 2 and 3 each produce a carry of 1.

Example 9.4: Carry-save numbers   Instead of the conventional digit set $\{0, 1\}$ for binary numbers, we can use the redundant digit set $\{0, 1, 2\}$. The result is called a *carry-save* number. Consider a 5-digit carry-save number system in which each digit is encoded in two bits, with both bits being 1 for the digit value 2, either bit being 1 for the digit value 1, and none for 0. Ignore overflow throughout, assuming that all results are representable in 5 digits.

a. What is the range of representable values? (That is, find the boundaries max^- and max^+.)
b. Represent 22 and 45 as 5-digit carry-save numbers.
c. Show that a 5-bit binary number can be added to a 5-digit carry-save number using only bitwise operations. That is, since there is no carry propagation, it would take the same amount of time to do the addition even if the operand widths were 64 instead of 5.
d. Show how using two carry-free addition steps of the type derived in part c, one can add two 5-digit carry-save numbers.

Solution

a. $max^+ = (2\,2\,2\,2\,2)_{two} = 2 \times (2^4 + 2^3 + 2^2 + 2 + 1) = 62; \ max^- = 0$
b. Because of redundancy, multiple representations may exist. We provide just one representation for each integer:

$$22 = (0\,2\,1\,1\,0)_{two} \quad \text{and} \quad 45 = (2\,1\,1\,0\,1)_{two}$$

c. This is best represented graphically as in Figure 9.3a. In each position, there are 3 bits: 2 from the carry-save number and 1 from the binary number. The sum of these 3 bits is a 2-bit number consisting of a sum bit and a carry bit that are schematically connected to each other by a line. Adding three bits x, y, and z to obtain the sum s and carry c is quite simple and leads to a simple logic circuit (a binary *full-adder*): $s = x \oplus y \oplus z$ and $c = xy \vee yz \vee zx$

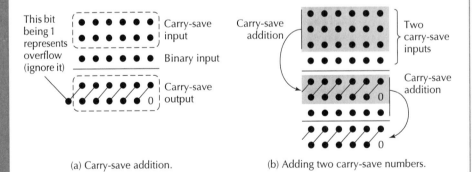

(a) Carry-save addition.   (b) Adding two carry-save numbers.

Figure 9.3 Adding a binary number or another carry-save number to a carry-save number.

d. Simply view the second carry-save number as two binary numbers. Add one of these binary numbers to the first carry-save number using the procedure of part c to get a carry-save number. Then, add the second binary number to the carry-save number just obtained. Again, the latency of this two-step process is independent of the width of the numbers involved. Figure 9.3b contains a graphical representation of this process.

Besides the use of unconventional and redundant digit sets, other variations of positional number representation have been proposed and do find occasional applications. For example, the radix r need not be positive, whole, or even real. *Negative-radix numbers* (known as *negabinary* for radix 2), representations with irrational radices (such as $\sqrt{2}$), and complex-radix number systems (e.g., $r = 2j$, where $j = \sqrt{-1}$) are all feasible [Parh00]. However, discussion of such number systems is beyond the scope of this book.

9.3 Number-Radix Conversion

Given a number x represented in radix r, one can obtain its radix-R representation in two ways. If we wish to perform arithmetic in the new radix R, we simply evaluate a polynomial in r whose coefficients are the digits x_i. This corresponds to the first equation in Section 9.1 and can be performed more efficiently by using Horner's rule, which involves alternating steps of multiplication by r and addition:

$$(x_{k-1}x_{k-2}\cdots x_1 x_0)_r = (\cdots((0 + x_{k-1})r + x_{k-2})r + \cdots + x_1)r + x_0$$

This method is particularly suitable for manual conversion from an arbitrary radix r to radix 10, given the relative ease with which we can perform radix-10 arithmetic.

To perform the radix conversion using arithmetic in the old radix r, we repeatedly divide the number x by the new radix R, keeping track of the remainder in each step. These remainders correspond to the radix-R digits X_i, beginning from X_0. For example, we convert the decimal number 19 to radix 3 as follows:

19 divided by 3 yields 6 with remainder 1

6 divided by 3 yields 2 with remainder 0

2 divided by 3 yields 0 with remainder 2

Reading the computed remainders from bottom to top, we find $19 = (201)_{\text{three}}$. Using the same process, we can convert 19 to radix 5 to get $19 = (34)_{\text{five}}$.

Example 9.5: Conversion from binary (or hex) to decimal   Find the decimal equivalent of the binary number $(1\,0\,1\,1\,0\,1\,0\,1)_{\text{two}}$ and outline how hexadecimal numbers can be converted to decimal.

Solution: Each 1 in the binary number corresponds to a power of 2 and the sum of these powers yields the equivalent decimal value.

1		0		1		1		0		1		0		1	
128	+	32	+	16	+	4	+	1	=	181					

We can arrive at the same answer using Horner's rule (read from left to right and top to bottom; e.g., start as $0 \times 2 + 1 \rightarrow 1 \times 2 + 0 \rightarrow 2$, etc.):

	1		0		1		1		0		1		0		1
	$\times 2 + \downarrow$	$\times 2 + \downarrow$	$\times 2 + \downarrow$	$\times 2 + \downarrow$	$\times 2 + \downarrow$	$\times 2 + \downarrow$	$\times 2 + \downarrow$	$\times 2 + \downarrow$						
0	1	2	5	11	22	45	90	181						

Hexadecimal to binary conversion is simple because it involves replacing each hex digit with its 4-bit binary equivalent; a k-digit hex number becomes a $4k$-bit binary number. Thus, we can convert from hex to decimal in two steps: (1) hex to binary and (2) binary to decimal.

Example 9.6: Conversion from decimal to binary (or hex)   Find the 8-bit binary equivalent of $(157)_{ten}$ and outline how the hexadecimal equivalent of a decimal number can be derived.

Solution: To convert $(157)_{ten}$ to binary, we need to divide by 2 repeatedly, noting the remainders. Figure 9.4 depicts a justification for this process.

157 divided by 2 yields 78 with remainder 1
78 divided by 2 yields 39 with remainder 0
39 divided by 2 yields 19 with remainder 1
19 divided by 2 yields 9 with remainder 1
9 divided by 2 yields 4 with remainder 1
4 divided by 2 yields 2 with remainder 0
2 divided by 2 yields 1 with remainder 0
1 divided by 2 yields 0 with remainder 1

Binary representation of $\lfloor x/2 \rfloor$

x_0

$x \bmod 2$

Figure 9.4 Justifying one step of the conversion of x to radix 2.

Reading the remainders from bottom to top, we get the desired binary equivalent $(10011101)_{two}$. Figure 9.4 shows why steps of the conversion process to radix 2 work. Once the binary equivalent of a number has been obtained, its hex equivalent is formed by simply taking groups of 4 bits, beginning with the least significant bit, and rewriting them as hex digits. For our example, the 4-bit groups are 1001 and 1101, leading to the hex equivalent $(9D)_{hex}$.

■ 9.4 Signed Integers

The set $\{\ldots, -3, -2, -1, 0, 1, 2, 3, \ldots\}$ of integers is also referred to as *signed or directed (whole) numbers*. The most straightforward representation of integers consists of attaching a sign bit to any desired encoding of natural numbers, leading to *signed-magnitude* representation. The standard convention is to use 0 for positive and 1 for negative and attach the sign bit to the left end of the magnitude. Here are some examples:

+27 in 8-bit signed-magnitude binary code   0 0011011
−27 in 8-bit signed-magnitude binary code   1 0011011
−27 in 2-digit decimal code with BCD digits   1 0010 0111

Another option for encoding signed integers in the range $[-N, P]$ is the *biased representation*. If we add the fixed positive value N (the bias) to all numbers in the desired range, unsigned integers in the range $[0, P + N]$ result. Any method for representing natural numbers in $[0, P + N]$ can then be used for representing the original signed integers in $[-N, P]$. This type of biased representation has only limited application in encoding of the exponents in floating-point numbers (see Section 9.6).

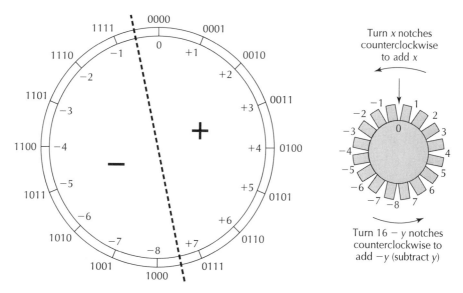

Figure 9.5 Schematic representation of 4-bit 2's-complement code for integers in $[-8, +7]$.

By far the most common machine encoding of signed integers is the *2's-complement representation*. In the k-bit 2's-complement format, a negative value $-x$, with $x > 0$, is encoded as the unsigned number $2^k - x$. Figure 9.5 shows encodings of positive and negative integers in the 4-bit 2's-complement format. Note that the positive integers 0 through 7 (or $2^{k-1} - 1$, in general) have the standard binary encoding, whereas negative values -1 through -8 (or -2^{k-1}) have been transformed to unsigned values by adding 16 (or 2^k) to them. The range of representable values in k-bit 2's-complement format is, thus, $[-2^{k-1}, 2^{k-1} - 1]$.

Two important properties of 2's-complement numbers are worth noting. First, the leftmost bit of the representation acts a the sign bit (0 for positive values, 1 for negative ones). Second, the value represented by a particular bit pattern can be derived without a need to follow different procedures for negative and positive numbers. We simply use polynomial evaluation or Horner's rule, as we did for unsigned integers, except that the sign bit is considered to have a negative weight. Here are two examples:

$$(01011)_{\text{2's-compl}} = (-0 \times 2^4) + (1 \times 2^3) + (0 \times 2^2) + (1 \times 2^1) + (1 \times 2^0) = +11$$
$$(11011)_{\text{2's-compl}} = (-1 \times 2^4) + (1 \times 2^3) + (0 \times 2^2) + (1 \times 2^1) + (1 \times 2^0) = -5$$

The reason for the popularity of 2's-complement representation can be understood from Figure 9.5. Whereas in signed-magnitude representation the addition of numbers with like and different signs involves two different operations (addition vs subtraction), both are performed in the same way with 2's-complement representation. In other words, addition of $-y$, which as usual involves clockwise rotation by y notches, can be accomplished via counterclockwise rotation by $2^k - y$ notches. Given that $2^k - y$ is simply the k-bit 2's-complement representation of $-y$, the common rule for both negative and positive numbers is to rotate counterclockwise by an amount equal to the number's representation. Thus, a simple binary adder can add numbers of either sign.

Example 9.7: Conversion from 2's-complement to decimal Find the decimal equivalent of the 2's-complement number $(1\,0\,1\,1\,0\,1\,0\,1)_{\text{2's-compl}}$.

Solution: Each 1 in the binary number corresponds to a power of 2 (with the sign bit considered to be negative) and the sum of these powers yields the equivalent decimal value.

$$
\begin{array}{ccccccccc}
1 & & 0 & 1 & & 1 & 0 & 1 & 0 & 1 \\
-128 & + & 32 & + & 16 & + & 4 & + & 1 & = -75
\end{array}
$$

We can arrive at the same answer using Horner's rule:

$$
\begin{array}{ccccccccc}
1 & 0 & 1 & 1 & 0 & 1 & 0 & 1 \\
\times 2- \downarrow & \times 2+ \downarrow & \times 2+ \downarrow & \times 2+ \downarrow & \times 2+ \downarrow & \times 2+ \downarrow & \times 2+ \downarrow & \times 2+ \downarrow \\
0 & -1 & -2 & -3 & -5 & -10 & -19 & -38 & -75
\end{array}
$$

If the 2's-complement number were given with its hexadecimal encoding, that is, as $(B5)_{\text{hex}}$, we could obtain its decimal equivalent by first converting to binary and then using the foregoing procedure.

Note that because $2^k - (2^k - y) = y$, changing the sign of a 2's-complement number is done via subtraction from 2^k in all cases, independent of whether the number is negative or positive. Practically, $2^k - y$ can be computed as $(2^k - 1) - y + 1$. Because $2^k - 1$ has the all-1s binary representation, the subtraction $(2^k - 1) - y$ is simple and consists of inverting the bits of y. So, as a rule, we change the sign of a 2's-complement number by inverting all its bits and then adding 1. The only exception is -2^{k-1} whose negation is not representable in k bits.

Example 9.8: Sign change for a 2's-complement number Given $y = (1\,0\,1\,1\,0\,1\,0\,1)_{\text{2's-compl}}$, find the 2's-complement representation of $-y$.

Solution: We need to invert all the bits in the representation of y and then add 1.

$$-y = (0\,1\,0\,0\,1\,0\,1\,0) + 1 = (0\,1\,0\,0\,1\,0\,1\,1)_{\text{2's-compl}}$$

Let us check the result by converting it to decimal:

$$
\begin{array}{ccccccc}
0 & 1 & 0 & 0 & 1 & 0 & 1 & 1 \\
& 64 & + & & 8 & + & 2 & + & 1 & = 75
\end{array}
$$

This is in agreement with $y = -75$ obtained in Example 9.7.

The preceding rule for sign change forms the basis of a 2's-complement adder/subtractor circuit depicted in Figure 9.6. Note that adding 1 to complete the sign change process is done by setting the carry-in of the adder to 1 when the operation to be performed is subtraction; during addition, c_{in} is set to 0. The simplicity of the adder/subtractor circuit of Figure 9.6 is one more advantage of the 2's-complement number representation.

Other complement representation systems can also be devised, but none is in widespread use. Choosing any *complementation constant M,* that is at least as large as $N + P + 1$, allows us to represent signed integers in the range $[-N, P]$, with the positive numbers in $[0, +P]$

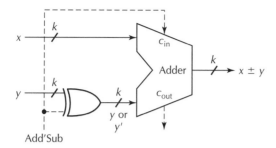

Figure 9.6 Binary adder used as 2's-complement adder/subtractor.

corresponding to the unsigned values in $[0, P]$ and negative numbers in $[-N, -1]$ repre-sented as unsigned values in $[M - N, M - 1]$, that is, by adding M to negative values. Some-times, M itself is recognized as an alternate code for 0 (actually, -0). For example, the k-bit *1's-complement* system is based on $M = 2^k - 1$ and includes numbers in the symmetric range $[-(2^{k-1} - 1), 2^{k-1} - 1]$, with 0 having two representations: the all-0s string and the all-1s string.

■ 9.5 Fixed-Point Numbers

A fixed-point number consists of a *whole or integral* part and a *fractional* part, with the two parts separated by a *radix point* (*decimal point* in radix 10, *binary point* in radix 2, etc.). The position of the radix point is almost always implied, and thus the point is not explicitly shown. If a fixed-point number has k whole digits and l fractional digits, its value is obtained from the formula:

$$x = \sum_{i=-l}^{k-1} x_i r^i = (x_{k-1} x_{k-2} \cdots x_1 x_0 \cdot x_{-1} x_{-2} \cdots x_{-l})_r$$

In other words, the digits to the right of the radix point are given negative indices and their weights are negative powers of the radix. For example:

$$2.375 = (1 \times 2^1) + (0 \times 2^0) + (0 \times 2^{-1}) + (1 \times 2^{-2}) + (1 \times 2^{-3}) = (10.011)_{two}$$

In a $(k + l)$-digit radix-r fixed-point number system with k whole digits, numbers from 0 to $r^k - r^{-l}$, in increments of r^{-l}, can be represented. The step size or resolution r^{-l} is often re-ferred to as *ulp*, or *unit in least position*. For example, in a $(2 + 3)$-bit binary fixed-point num-ber system, we have $ulp = 2^{-3}$, and the values $0 = (00.000)_{two}$ through $2^2 - 2^{-3} = 3.875 = (11.111)_{two}$ are representable. For the same total number $k + l$ of digits in a fixed-point number system, increasing k will lead to enlarged *range* of numbers, whereas increasing l leads to greater *precision*. Therefore, there is a trade-off between range and precision.

Signed fixed-point numbers can be represented by the same methods discussed for signed integers: signed-magnitude, biased format, and complement methods. In particular, for 2's-complement format, a negative value $-x$ is represented as the unsigned value $2^k - x$. Figure 9.7 shows encodings of positive and negative integers in the $(1 + 3)$-bit fixed-point 2's-complement format. Note that the positive values 0 to 7/8 (or $2^{k-1} - 2^{-l}$, in general) have the standard binary encoding, whereas negative values $-1/8$ to -1 (or -2^{-l} to -2^{k-1}, in gen-eral) are transformed to unsigned values by adding 2 (or 2^k, in general) to them.

The two important properties of 2's-complement numbers, mentioned earlier in connection with integers, are valid here as well; namely, the leftmost bit of the number acts a the sign bit,

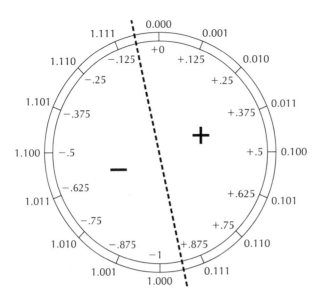

Figure 9.7 Schematic representation of 4-bit 2's-complement encoding for $(1 + 3)$-bit fixed-point numbers in the range $[-1, +7/8]$.

and the value represented by a particular bit pattern can be derived by considering the sign bit as having a negative weight. Here are two examples:

$$(01.011)_{2\text{'s-compl}} = (-0 \times 2^1) + (1 \times 2^0) + (0 \times 2^{-1}) + (1 \times 2^{-2}) + (1 \times 2^{-3}) = +1.375$$

$$(11.011)_{2\text{'s-compl}} = (-1 \times 2^1) + (1 \times 2^0) + (0 \times 2^{-1}) + (1 \times 2^{-2}) + (1 \times 2^{-3}) = -0.625$$

The process of changing the sign of a number is also the same: invert all bits and add 1 to the least significant position (i.e., add *ulp*). For example, given $(11.011)_{2\text{'s-compl}} = -0.625$, we change its sign by inverting all bits in 11.011 and adding *ulp* to get $(00.101)_{2\text{'s-compl}}$.

Conversion of fixed-point numbers from radix r to another radix R is done separately for the whole and fractional parts. To convert the fractional part, we can again use arithmetic in the new radix R or in the old radix r, whichever is more convenient. With radix-R arithmetic, we simply evaluate a polynomial in r^{-1} whose coefficients are the digits x_i. The simplest way to do this is to view the fractional part as an l-digit integer, convert this integer to radix R, and divide the result by r^l.

To perform radix conversion using arithmetic in the old radix r, we repeatedly multiply the fraction y by the new radix R, noting and removing the integer part in each step. These integer parts correspond to the radix-R digits X_{-i}, beginning from X_{-1}. For example, we convert .175 to radix 2 as follows:

.175 multiplied by 2 yields .350 with integer part 0
.350 multiplied by 2 yields .700 with integer part 0
.700 multiplied by 2 yields .400 with integer part 1
.400 multiplied by 2 yields .800 with integer part 0
.800 multiplied by 2 yields .600 with integer part 1
.600 multiplied by 2 yields .200 with integer part 1
.200 multiplied by 2 yields .400 with integer part 0
.400 multiplied by 2 yields .800 with integer part 0

Reading the recorded integer parts from top to bottom, we find $.175 \cong (.00101100)_{two}$. This equality is approximate because the result did not converge to 0. In general a fraction in one radix may not have an exact representation in another radix. In any case, we simply carry out the process until the required number of digits in the new radix has been obtained. It is also possible to continue the process past the last digit of interest so that the result can be rounded.

Example 9.9: Conversion from fixed-point binary to decimal   Find the decimal equivalent of the unsigned binary number $(1101.0101)_{two}$. What if the given number were in 2's-complement rather than unsigned format?

Solution: The integer part is easily seen to represent $8 + 4 + 1 = 13$. The fractional part, when viewed as a 4-bit integer (multiplied by 16), represents $4 + 1 = 5$. Therefore, the fractional part is really $5/16 = .3125$. Therefore, $(1101.0101)_{two} = (13.3125)_{ten}$. For the 2's-complement case, we can proceed as above: obtain the integer part $-8 + 4 + 1 = -3$ and fractional part $.3125$ and conclude that $(1101.0101)_{\text{2's-compl}} = (-2.6875)_{ten}$. Alternatively, recognizing that the number is negative, we can change its sign and then convert the resulting number:

$$(1101.0101)_{\text{2's-compl}} = -(0010.1011)_{two} = -(2 + 11/16) = (-2.6875)_{ten}$$

Example 9.10: Conversion from fixed-point decimal to binary   Find the $(4 + 4)$-bit binary fixed-point equivalents of $(3.72)_{ten}$ and $-(3.72)_{ten}$.

Solution: The 4-bit binary equivalent of 3 is $(0011)_{two}$.

.72 multiplied by 2 yields .44 with integer part 1
.44 multiplied by 2 yields .88 with integer part 0
.88 multiplied by 2 yields .76 with integer part 1
.76 multiplied by 2 yields .52 with integer part 1
.52 multiplied by 2 yields .04 with integer part 1

Reading the recorded integer parts from top to bottom, we find that $(3.72)_{ten} = (0011.1100)_{two}$. Note that the fifth fractional bit was obtained to allow rounding the representation to the closest $(4 + 4)$–bit fixed-point number. The same objective could have been achieved by noting that the remainder after the fourth step is .52, which is greater than .5, and thus rounding up. Had we obtained only 4 fractional bits with no rounding, the binary representation would have been $(0011.1011)_{two}$, whose fractional part of $11/16 = .6875$ is not as good an approximation to .72 as $12/16 = .75$. Using sign change for the result, we find $-(3.72)_{ten} = (1100.0100)_{\text{2's-compl}}$.

■ 9.6 Floating-Point Numbers

Integers in a prescribed range can be represented exactly for automatic processing, but most real numbers must be approximated within the machine's finite word width. Some real numbers can be represented as, or approximated by, $(k + l)$-bit fixed-point numbers, as discussed in Section 9.5. A problem with fixed-point representations is that they are not very good for dealing with very large and extremely small numbers at the same time. Consider the two $(8 + 8)$-bit fixed-point numbers shown below:

$x = (0000\ 0000\ .\ 0000\ 1001)_{two}$ Small number

$y = (1001\ 0000\ .\ 0000\ 0000)_{two}$ Large number

The relative representation error due to truncation or rounding of digits beyond the -8th position is quite significant for x, but it is much less severe for y. On the other hand, neither y^2 nor y/x is representable in this number format.

Fixed-point representation thus appears to be unsuitable for applications that manipulate numerical values in a wide range, from very small to extremely large, as it would need a very wide word to accommodate both the range and precision requirements simultaneously. *Floating-point numbers* constitute the primary mode of arithmetic in such situations. A floating-point value consists of a fixed-point signed-magnitude number and an accompanying scale factor. Following many years of experimentation with different floating-point formats and suffering from the resulting inconsistencies and incompatibilities, the computer industry has embraced the standard format proposed by the Institute of Electrical and Electronics Engineers (IEEE) and subsequently adopted by national and international standards organizations, including the American National Standards Institute (ANSI). We thus formulate our discussion of floating-point numbers and arithmetic exclusively in terms of this standard format. Other formats will differ in their parameters and representation details, but the basic trade-offs and algorithms remain the same.

A floating-point number in the ANSI/IEEE standard has three components: sign $\pm$, exponent e, and significand s, together representing the value $\pm 2^e s$. The *exponent* is a signed integer represented in biased format (a fixed bias is added to it to make it into an unsigned number). The *significand* is a fixed-point number in the range $[1, 2)$. Because the binary representation of the significand always starts with "1.", this fixed 1 is omitted (*hidden*) and only the fractional part of the significand is explicitly represented.

Table 9.1 and Figure 9.8 show the details of the ANSI/IEEE short (32-bit) and long (64-bit) floating-point formats. The short format has adequate range and precision for most common applications (magnitudes ranging from 1.2×10^{-38} to 3.4×10^{38}). The long format is used for highly precise computations or those involving extreme variations in magnitude (from about 2.2×10^{-308} to 1.8×10^{308}). Of course in both these formats, as explained thus far, zero has no proper representation, given that the significand is always nonzero. To remedy this problem, and to be able to represent certain other special values, the smallest and largest exponent codes (all 0s and all 1s in the biased exponent field) are not used for ordinary numbers. An all-0s word (0s in sign, exponent, and significand fields) represents $+0$; similarly, -0 and $\pm \infty$ have special representations, as does any nonsensical or indeterminate value, known as "not a number" (NaN). Certain other details of this standard are beyond the scope of this book; in particular, denormalized numbers (*denormals* for short), which are included in Table 9.1 for completeness, are not explained here.

When an arithmetic operation produces a result that is not exactly representable in the format being used, the result must be rounded to some representable value. The ANSI/IEEE standard prescribes four rounding options. The default rounding mode is "*round to nearest even*": choose the closest representable value and, in case of a tie, choose the value with its least-significant bit 0. There are also three *directed rounding* modes: "*round toward* $+\infty$" (choose

■ **TABLE 9.1** Some features of the ANSI/IEEE standard floating-point formats.

Feature	Single/Short	Double/Long
Word width in bits	32	64
Significand bits	23 + 1 hidden	52 + 1 hidden
Significand range	$[1, 2 - 2^{-23}]$	$[1, 2 - 2^{-52}]$
Exponent bits	8	11
Exponent bias	127	1023
Zero (± 0)	$e + \text{bias} = 0, f = 0$	$e + \text{bias} = 0, f = 0$
Denormalized number	$e + \text{bias} = 0, f \neq 0$	$e + \text{bias} = 0, f \neq 0$
	represents $\pm 0 \cdot f \times 2^{-126}$	represents $\pm 0 \cdot f \times 2^{-1022}$
Infinity ($\pm \infty$)	$e + \text{bias} = 255, f = 0$	$e + \text{bias} = 2047, f = 0$
Not-a-number (NaN)	$e + \text{bias} = 255, f \neq 0$	$e + \text{bias} = 2047, f \neq 0$
Ordinary number	$e + \text{bias} \in [1, 254]$	$e + \text{bias} \in [1, 2046]$
	$e \in [-126, 127]$	$e \in [-1022, 1023]$
	represents $1 \cdot f \times 2^e$	represents $1 \cdot f \times 2^e$
min	$2^{-126} \cong 1.2 \times 10^{-38}$	$2^{-1022} \cong 2.2 \times 10^{-308}$
max	$\cong 2^{128} \cong 3.4 \times 10^{38}$	$\cong 2^{1024} \cong 1.8 \times 10^{308}$

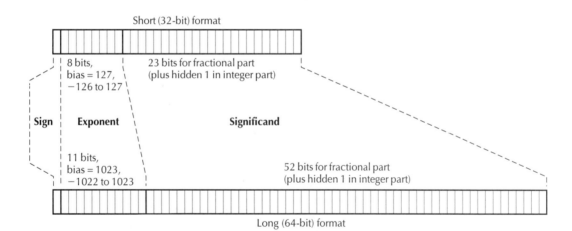

Figure 9.8 The two ANSI/IEEE standard floating-point formats.

the next higher value), "*round toward* $-\infty$" (choose the next lower value), and "*round toward* 0" (choose the closest value that is less than the value at hand in magnitude). With the round-to-nearest option, the maximum rounding error is 0.5 *ulp,* while with directed rounding schemes, the error can be up to 1 *ulp.* Rounding of floating-point values is discussed in more detail in Section 12.1.

PROBLEMS

9.1 Fixed-radix positional number systems

For each of the following conventional radix-r number systems, using the digit values 0 through $r-1$, determine: max^-, max^+, number b of bits needed to encode a digit, number K of digits needed to represent the equivalent of all 32-bit unsigned binary integers, and representational efficiency in the latter case.

a. $r = 2, k = 24$
b. $r = 5, k = 10$
c. $r = 10, k = 7$
d. $r = 12, k = 7$
e. $r = 16, k = 6$

9.2 Fixed-radix positional number systems

Prove the statements in parts a–c:

a. An unsigned binary integer is a power of 2 iff the bitwise logical AND of x and $x - 1$ is 0.
b. An unsigned radix-3 integer is even iff the sum of all of its digits is even.
c. An unsigned binary integer $(x_{k-1}x_{k-2} \cdots x_1 x_0)_{two}$ is divisible by 3 iff $\sum_{even\ i} x_i - \sum_{odd\ i} x_i$ is a multiple of 3.
d. Generalize the statements of parts b and c to obtain rules for divisibility of radix-r integers by $r - 1$ and $r + 1$.

*9.3 Overflow in arithmetic operations

Argue whether overflow will occur when each of the following arithmetic expressions is evaluated within the framework of the five number systems defined in Problem 9.1 (20 cases altogether). All operands are given in radix 10.

a. 3000×4000
b. $2^{24} - 2^{22}$
c. $9,000,000 + 500,000 + 400,000$
d. $1^2 + 2^2 + 3^2 + \cdots + 2000^2$

9.4 Unconventional digit sets

Consider a fixed-point symmetric radix-3 number system with k whole and l fractional digits, using the digit set $[-1, 1]$. The integer

version of this representation was discussed in Example 9.3.

a. Determine the range of numbers represented as a function of k and l.
b. What is the representational efficiency relative to binary representation, given that each radix-3 digit needs a 2-bit encoding?
c. Devise a simple, and fast, hardware procedure for converting from the representation above to a radix-3 representation using the redundant digit set [0, 3].
d. What is the representational efficiency of the redundant representation in part c?

9.5 Carry-save numbers

In Example 9.4:

a. Supply all possible alternate representations for part b.
b. Identify numbers, if any, that have unique representations.
c. Which integer has the largest possible number of different representations?

9.6 Carry-save numbers

Figure 9.3 can be interpreted as a way of compressing three binary numbers into two binary numbers having the same sum, and the same width, ignoring the possibility of overflow. Similarly, Figure 9.3b shows the compression of four binary numbers, first to three numbers and then to two numbers. A hardware circuit that converts three binary numbers to two binary numbers with the same sum is known as a *carry-save adder*.

a. Draw a diagram similar to Figure 9.3b representing the compression of six binary numbers to two binary numbers having the same sum and width.
b. Convert your solution to part a to a hardware diagram, using 3-input, 2-ouput blocks to represent carry-save adders.
c. Show that the hardware diagram of part b has a latency equal to that of three carry-save adders,

or else present an alternate hardware implementation with such a latency for compressing six binary numbers to two binary numbers.

9.7 Negabinary numbers

Negabinary numbers use the digit set $\{0, 1\}$ in radix $r = -2$. The value of a negabinary number is evaluated in the same way as a binary number, but with the terms containing odd powers of the radix being negative. Thus, both positive and negative numbers can be represented without a need for a separate sign bit or a complementation scheme.

a. What is the range of representable values in 9-bit and 10-bit negabinary representations?
b. Given a negabinary number, how do you determine its sign?
c. Devise a procedure for converting a positive negabinary number to a conventional unsigned binary number.

9.8 Compressed decimal numbers

One way to represent decimal numbers in memory is to pack two BCD digits into one byte. This representation is somewhat wasteful in that a byte that can encode 256 values is used to represent the digit pairs 00 through 99. One way of improving efficiency is to compress three BCD digits into 10 bits.

a. Devise a suitable encoding for this compression. *Hint:* Let the three BCD digits be $x_3x_2x_1x_0$, $y_3y_2y_1y_0$, and $z_3z_2z_1z_0$. Let the 10-bit encoding be $WX_2X_1x_0Y_2Y_1y_0Z_2Z_1z_0$. In other words the least significant bits (LSBs) of the three digits are used directly and the remaining 9 bits (3 from each digit) are encoded into 7 bits. Let $W = 0$ encode the case $x_3 = y_3 = z_3 = 0$. In this case, the remaining digits are simply copied in the new representation. Use $X_2X_1 = 00, 01, 10$ to encode the case of only one of the values x_3, y_3, or z_3 being 1. Note that when the most significant bit of a BCD digit is 1, the digit is completely specified by its LSB and no other information is needed. Finally, use $X_2X_1 = 11$ for all other cases.

b. Design a circuit to convert three BCD digits into the 10-bit compressed representation.
c. Design a circuit to decompress the 10-bit code to retrieve the three original BCD digits.
d. Suggest a similar encoding to compress two BCD digits into 7 bits.
e. Design the required compression and decompression circuits for the encoding of part d.

9.9 Number-radix conversion

Convert each of the following numbers from its indicated radix to radix-10 representation.

a. Radix-2 numbers: 1011, 1011 0010, 1011 0010 1111 0001
b. Radix-3 numbers: 1021, 1021 2210, 1021 2210 2100 1020
c. Radix-8 numbers: 534, 534 607, 534 607 126 470
d. Radix-12 numbers: 7a4, 7a4 539, 7a4 593 1b0
e. Radix-16 numbers: 8e, 8e3a, 8e3a 51c0

9.10 Fixed-point numbers

A fixed-point binary number system has 1 whole bit and 15 fractional bits.

a. What is the range of numbers represented, assuming an unsigned format?
b. What is the range of numbers represented, assuming 2's-complement format?
c. Represent the decimal fractions 0.75 and 0.3 in the format of part a.
d. Represent the decimal fractions −0.75 and −0.3 in the format of part b.

9.11 Number-radix conversion

Convert each of the following numbers from its indicated radix to radix-2 and radix-16 representations.

a. Radix-3 numbers: 1021, 1021 2210, 1021 2210 2100 1020
b. Radix-5 numbers: 302, 302 423, 302 423 140
c. Radix-8 numbers: 534, 534 607, 534 607 126 470
d. Radix-10 numbers: 12, 5 655, 2 550 276, 76 545 336, 3 726 755

e. Radix-12 numbers: 9a5, b0a, ba95, a55a1, baabaa

9.12 Number-radix conversion

Convert each of the following fixed-point numbers from its indicated radix to radix-10 representation.

a. Radix-2 numbers: 10.11, 1011.0010, 1011 0010.1111 0001
b. Radix-3 numbers: 10.21, 1021.2210, 1021 2210.2100 1020
c. Radix-8 numbers: 53.4, 534.607, 534 607.126 470
d. Radix-12 numbers: 7a.4, 7a4.539, 7a4 593.1b0
e. Radix-16 numbers: 8.e, 8e.3a, 8e3a.51c0

9.13 Number-radix conversion

Convert each of the following fixed-point numbers from its indicated radix to radix-2 and radix-16 representations.

a. Radix-3 numbers: 10.21, 1021.2210, 1021 2210.2100 1020
b. Radix-5 numbers: 30.2, 302.423, 302 423.140
c. Radix-8 numbers: 53.4, 534.607, 534 607.126 470
d. Radix-10 numbers: 1.2, 56.55, 2 550.276, 76 545.336, 3 726.755
e. Radix-12 numbers: 9a.5, b.0a, ba.95, a55.a1, baa.baa

9.14 Two's-complement format

a. Encode each of the following decimal numbers in 16-bit 2's-complement format with 0, 2, 4, or 8 fractional bits: 6.4, 33.675, 123.45

b. Check the correctness of your conversions in part a by applying Horner's formula to the resulting 2's-complement numbers to derive the decimal equivalents.
c. Repeat part a for the following decimal numbers: −6.4, 33.675, −123.45
d. Repeat part b for the results of part c.

9.15 Floating-point numbers

Consider the entries supplied for *min* and *max* in Table 9.1. Show how these values are derived and explain why the *max* values in the two columns are specified as being approximately equal to a power of 2.

9.16 Floating-point numbers

Show the representation of the following decimal numbers in the ANSI/IEEE short and long floating-point formats. When the number is not exactly representable, use the round to nearest even rule.

a. 12.125
b. 555.5
c. 333.3
d. −6.25
e. −1024.0
f. −33.2

REFERENCES AND FURTHER READINGS

[Gold91]   Goldberg, D., "What Every Computer Scientist Should Know About Floating-Point Arithmetic," *ACM Computing Surveys*, Vol. 23, No. 1, pp. 5–48, March 1991.

[IEEE85]   *ANSI/IEEE Standard 754-1985 for Binary Floating-Point Arithmetic*, available from IEEE Press.

[Knut97]   Knuth, D. E., *The Art of Computer Programming,* Vol. 2: *Seminumerical Algorithms,* Addison-Wesley, 3rd ed., 1997.

[Kore93]   Koren, I., *Computer Arithmetic Algorithms,* Prentice Hall, 1993.

[Parh00]   Parhami, B., *Computer Arithmetic: Algorithms and Hardware Designs,* Oxford University Press, 2000.

[Parh02]   Parhami, B., "Number Representation and Computer Arithmetic," in *Encyclopedia of Information Systems,* Academic Press, 2002, Vol. 3, pp. 317–333.

[Swar90]   Swartzlander, E. E., Jr, *Computer Arithmetic,* Vols. I and II, IEEE Computer Society Press, 1990.

10

ADDERS AND SIMPLE ALUs

"I wrote this book and compiled in it everything that is necessary for the computer, avoiding both boring verbosity and misleading brevity."

—*Ghiyath al-Din Jamshid al-Kashi, The Key to Computing (Miftah al-Hisabi), 1427*

"Thus it appears that whatever may be the number of digits the Analytical Engine is capable of holding, if it is required to make all the computations with k times that number of digits, then it can be executed by the same Engine, but in the amount of time equal to k^2 times the former."

—*Charles Babbage, Passages from the Life of a Philosopher, 1864*

Addition is the most important arithmetic operation in digital computers. Even the simplest embedded computers have an adder, whereas hardware multipliers and dividers are found only in higher performance microprocessors. In this chapter, we begin by considering the design of single-bit adders (half- and full adders) and show how these building blocks can be cascaded to build ripple-carry adders. We then proceed to the design of faster adders built by means of carry lookahead, the most widely used carry prediction method. Other topics covered include counters, shift and logic operations, and multifunction ALUs.

■ 10.1 Simple Adders

In this chapter, we cover only binary integer addition and subtraction. Fixed-point numbers that are both in the same format can be added or subtracted like integers by simply ignoring the implied radix point. Floating-point addition will be covered in Chapter 12.

When two bits are added, the sum is a value in the range [0, 2] that can be represented by a *sum bit* and a *carry bit*. The circuit that can compute the sum and carry bits is known as a

Inputs		Outputs	
x	y	c	s
0	0	0	0
0	1	0	1
1	0	0	1
1	1	1	0

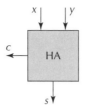

Figure 10.1 Truth table and schematic diagram for a binary half-adder.

Inputs			Outputs	
x	y	c_{in}	c_{out}	s
0	0	0	0	0
0	0	1	0	1
0	1	0	0	1
0	1	1	1	0
1	0	0	0	1
1	0	1	1	0
1	1	0	1	0
1	1	1	1	1

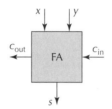

Figure 10.2 Truth table and schematic diagram for a binary full adder.

binary *half-adder* (HA), with its truth table and symbolic representation shown in Figure 10.1. The carry output is the logical AND of the two inputs, while the sum output is the exclusive OR (XOR) of the inputs. By adding a carry input to a half-adder, we get a binary *full adder* (FA) whose truth table and schematic diagram are depicted in Figure 10.2. Several implementations of a full adder are shown in Figure 10.3.

A full adder, connected to a flip-flop for holding the carry bit from one cycle to the next, functions as a *bit-serial adder*. The inputs of a bit-serial adder are supplied in synchrony with a clock signal, one bit from each operand per clock cycle, beginning from the least significant bits. One bit of the output is produced per clock cycle, and the carry from one cycle is held and used as input in the next cycle. A *ripple-carry adder*, on the other hand, unfolds this sequential behavior into space, using a cascade of k full adders to add two k-bit numbers (Figure 10.4).

The ripple-carry design of Figure 10.4 becomes a radix-r adder if each binary full adder is replaced by a radix-r full adder that accepts two radix-r digits (each encoded in binary) and a carry-in signal, producing a radix-r sum digit and a carry-out signal. Clearly, when all the intermediate carry signals c_i are known, the sum bits/digits are easily computed. For this reason, discussions of adder design usually focus on how all the intermediate carries can be derived, given the input operands and c_{in}. Because the carry signals are always binary and their propagation can be made independent of the radix r, as discussed in Section 10.2, from this point on, we often do not deal with radices other than 2.

Note that any binary adder design can be converted to a 2's-complement adder/subtractor through the scheme shown in Figure 9.6. For this reason, we will not discuss subtraction as a separate operation.

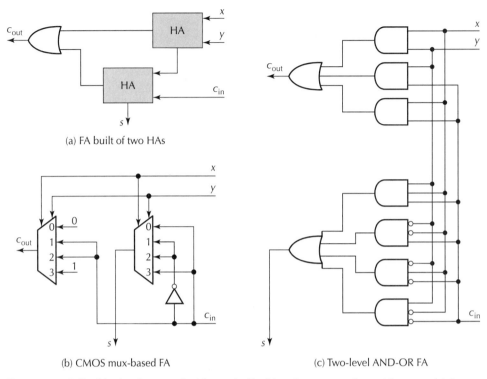

(a) FA built of two HAs

(b) CMOS mux-based FA   (c) Two-level AND-OR FA

Figure 10.3 Full adder implemented with two half-adders, by means of two 4-input multiplexers, and as two-level gate network.

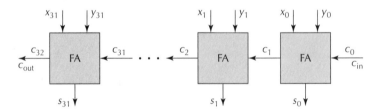

Figure 10.4 Ripple-carry binary adder with 32-bit inputs and output.

■ 10.2 Carry Propagation Networks

When we add two numbers, carries are generated at certain digit positions. For decimal addition, these are positions at which the sum of operand digits is 10 or more. In binary addition, carry generation requires that both operand bits be 1. We define the auxiliary binary signal g_i as being 1 for the positions at which a carry is generated and 0 elsewhere. For binary addition, $g_i = x_i y_i$; that is, g_i is the logical AND of the operand bits x_i and y_i. Similarly, there exist digit positions at which an incoming carry is propagated. For decimal addition, these are positions at which the sum of operand digits equals 9; an incoming carry makes the position sum 10, leading to an outgoing carry from that position. Of course, if there is no

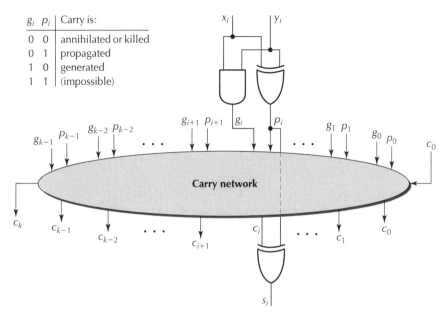

g_i	p_i	Carry is:
0	0	annihilated or killed
0	1	propagated
1	0	generated
1	1	(impossible)

Figure 10.5 The main part of an adder is the carry network. The rest is just a set of gates to produce the g and p signals and the sum bits.

carry-in, there won't be a carry-out for such positions. In binary addition, carry propagation requires that one operand bit be 0 and the other one be 1. The auxiliary binary signal p_i, derived as $p_i = x_i \oplus y_i$ for binary addition, is defined as being 1 iff digit position i propagates an incoming carry.

Now, given the carry-in c_0 of an adder and the auxiliary signals g_i and p_i for all of the k digit positions, the intermediate carries c_i and the outgoing carry c_k can be derived independently from input digit values. In a binary adder, the sum bit in position i is then derived as

$$s_i = x_i \oplus y_i \oplus c_i = p_i \oplus c_i$$

The general structure of a binary adder is shown in Figure 10.5. Variations in the carry network result in many designs that differ in their implementation costs, operational speed, energy consumption, and so on.

The ripple-carry adder of Figure 10.4 is quite simple and easily expandable to any desired width. It is rather slow, however, because carries may propagate across the full width of the adder. This happens, for example, when the two 8-bit numbers 10101011 and 01010101 are added. Each full adder requires some time to generate its carry output based on its carry input and the operand bits in that position. Cascading k such units together implies k times as much signal delay in the worst case. This linear amount of time becomes unacceptable for wide words (say, 32 or 64 bits) or in high-performance computers, though it might be acceptable in an embedded system that is dedicated to a single task and is not expected to be fast.

To view a ripple-carry adder in the general framework of Figure 10.5, we note that the carry network of a ripple-carry adder is based on the recurrence:

$$c_{i+1} = g_i \vee p_i c_i$$

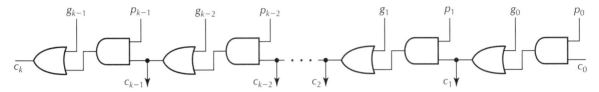

Figure 10.6 The carry propagation network of a ripple-carry adder.

This recurrence simply says that a carry will go into position $i + 1$ if it is generated in position i or if a carry that enters position i is propagated by position i. This observation leads to Figure 10.6 as the carry network of a ripple-carry adder. The linear latency of a ripple-carry adder ($2k$ gate levels for the carry network, plus a few more for deriving the auxiliary signals and producing the sum bits) is evident from Figure 10.6.

Example 10.1: Variations in adder design   We say that in digit position i, a transfer occurs if a carry is generated or propagated. For binary adders, the auxiliary transfer signal $t_i = g_i \vee p_i$ can be derived by an OR gate, given that $g_i \vee p_i = x_i y_i + (x_i \oplus y_i) = x_i \vee y_i$. Often, an OR gate is faster than an XOR gate, so t_i can be produced faster than p_i.

    a. Show that the carry recurrence $c_{i+1} = g_i \vee p_i c_i$ remains valid if we replace p_i with t_i.

    b. How does the change of part a affect the design of a carry network?

    c. In what other ways does the change of part a affect the design of a binary adder?

Solution

    a. We show that the two expressions $g_i \vee p_i c_i$ and $g_i \vee t_i c_i$ are equivalent by converting one to the other: $g_i \vee p_i c_i = g_i \vee g_i c_i \vee p_i c_i = g_i \vee (g_i \vee p_i)c_i = g_i \vee t_i c_i$. Note that in the first step of our conversion, inclusion of the additional term $g_i c_i$ is justified by $g_i \vee g_i c_i = g_i(1 \vee c_i) = g_i$; in other words, the term $g_i c_i$ is redundant.

    b. Because changing p_i to t_i does not affect the relationship between c_{i+1} and c_i, nothing in the carry network will change if we supply it with t_i instead of p_i. The small difference in speed between t_i and p_i leads to slightly faster production of the carry signals.

    c. We need to include k additional two-input OR gates to produce the signals t_i. We still need the signals p_i for the sake of producing the sum bits $s_i = p_i \oplus c_i$ once all the carries are known. Nonetheless, the adder will be slightly faster overall, because the p_i signals are derived concurrently with the functioning of the carry network, which is bound to take longer.

There are a number of ways to speed up carry propagation, leading to faster addition. One method, which is conceptually quite simple, is providing skip paths in a ripple-carry network. For example, a 32-bit carry network can be divided into eight 4-bit sections, with a 5-input AND gate allowing the incoming carry of position $4j$ to go directly to the end of the section in case $p_{4j} = p_{4j+1} = p_{4j+2} = p_{4j+3} = 1$. One 4-bit section of the resulting carry network, spanning bit positions $4j$ through $4j + 3$, is depicted in Figure 10.7. Note that the latency of such an adder with 4-bit skip paths is still linear in k, although it is much lower than that of a simple ripple-carry adder. Faster propagation of carries through skip paths can be likened to

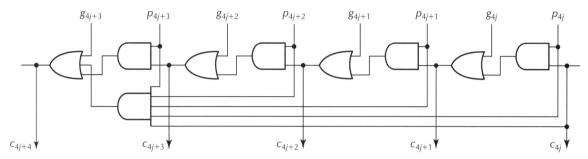

Figure 10.7 A 4-bit section of a ripple-carry network with skip paths.

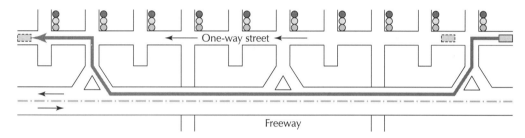

Figure 10.8 Driving analogy for carry propagation in adders with skip paths. Taking the freeway allows a driver who wants to travel a long distance to avoid excessive delays at many traffic lights.

drivers reducing their travel times by using a nearby freeway whenever the desired destination is more than a few blocks away (Figure 10.8).

> **Example 10.2: Carry equation for skip adders**   We saw that a ripple-carry adder directly implements the carry recurrence $c_{i+1} = g_i \vee p_i c_i$. What is the corresponding equation for the ripple-carry adder with 4-bit skip paths, depicted in Figure 10.7?
>
> **Solution:** It is evident from Figure 10.7 that the carry equation remains the same for any position whose index i is not a multiple of 4. The equation for the incoming carry into position $i = 4j + 4$ becomes $c_{4j+4} = g_{4j+3} \vee p_{4j+3} c_{4j+3} \vee p_{4j+3} p_{4j+2} p_{4j+1} p_{4j} c_{4j}$. This equation essentially says that there are three ways (not mutually exclusive) in which a carry can enter position $4j + 4$: by being generated in position $4j + 3$, through the propagation of a carry entering position $4j + 3$, or via the carry into position $4j$ being passed along the skip path.

10.3 Counting and Incrementation

Before discussing some of the common ways in which the process of addition is speeded up in modern computers, let us consider an important special case of addition, that of one of the two operands being a constant. If we initialize a register to a value x and then repeatedly add a constant a to it, the sequence of values $x, x + a, x + 2a, x + 3a, \ldots$ will be obtained. This process is known as counting by a. Figure 10.9 shows a hardware implementation of this

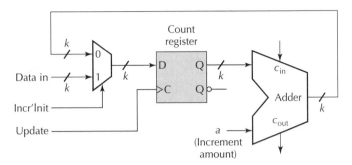

Figure 10.9 Schematic diagram of an initializable synchronous counter.

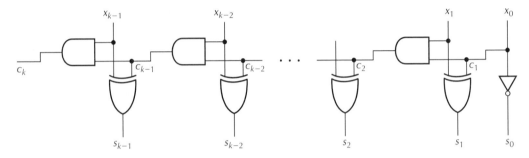

Figure 10.10 Carry propagation network and sum logic for an incrementer.

process using an adder whose lower input is permanently connected to the constant a. This counter can be updated in two different modes: *incrementation* causes the counter to step to the next value in the sequence above, and *initialization* causes an input data value to be stored in the register.

The special case of $a = 1$ corresponds to standard *up counter* whose sequence is $x, x + 1, x + 2, x + 3, \ldots$, whereas $a = -1$ produces a *down counter*, which proceeds in the order $x, x - 1, x - 2, x - 3, \ldots$; an *up/down counter* can count upward or downward, depending on the value of a direction control signal. If in the process of downward counting we go past 0, the counter is conveniently set to the appropriate 2's-complement negative value. Both up and down counters may overflow when the count becomes too large or too small to be represented within the number representation format used. In the case of unsigned up counters, overflow is indicated by the carry-out of the adder being asserted. In other cases, counter overflow is detected in the same manner as in adders (see Section 10.6).

Let us now focus on an up counter with $a = 1$. In this case, instead of connecting the constant 1 to the lower input of the adder as in Figure 10.9, we can set $c_{in} = 1$ and use 0 as the lower adder input. Then, the adder becomes an *incrementer* whose design is substantially simpler than an ordinary adder. To see why, note that in adding $y = 0$ to x, we have generate signals $g_i = x_i y_i = 0$ and propagate signals $p_i = x_i \oplus y_i = x_i$. Hence, referring to the carry propagation network of Figure 10.6, we see that all the OR gates as well as the rightmost AND gate can be eliminated, leading to the simplified carry network in Figure 10.10. We will see later that methods used to speed up carry propagation in adders can be adopted for designing faster incrementers as well.

A machine's program counter is an example of an up counter that is incremented to point to the next instruction as the current instruction is executed. The PC incrementation usually takes place early in the instruction execution cycle, so there is plenty of time for its completion, implying that a superfast incrementer may not be required. In the case of MiniMIPS, the PC is incremented not by 1 but rather by 4; however incrementation by any power of 2 such as 2^h is the same as ignoring the h least significant bits and adding 1 to the remaining part.

10.4 Design of Fast Adders

A variety of fast adders can be designed that require logarithmic, rather than linear, time. In other words, the delay of such fast adders grows as the logarithm of k. The best-known and most widely used such adders are *carry-lookahead adders* whose design is discussed in this section.

The basic idea in carry-lookahead addition is to form the required intermediate carries directly from the inputs g_i, p_i, and c_{in} to the carry network, rather than from the previous carries, as done in ripple-carry adders. For example, the carry c_3 of the adder in Figure 10.4, which was previously expressed in terms of c_2 using the carry recurrence

$$c_3 = g_2 \vee p_2 c_2$$

can be directly derived from the inputs based on the logical expression:

$$c_3 = g_2 \vee p_2 g_1 \vee p_2 p_1 g_0 \vee p_2 p_1 p_0 c_0$$

This expression is easily obtained by unrolling the original recurrence, that is, replacing c_2 with its equivalent expression in terms of c_1 and then expressing c_1 in terms of c_0. In fact, one could write this expression directly based on the following intuitive explanation. A carry into position 3 must have been originated at some point to the right of bit position 3 and propagated from there to bit position 3. Each term on the right-hand side of the foregoing equation covers one of the four possibilities.

Theoretically, one can unroll all carry equations and obtain each of the carries as a two-level AND-OR expression. However, the fully unrolled expression would grow quite large for a wider adder that requires c_{31} or c_{52}, say, to be derived. A variety of *lookahead carry networks* exist that systematize the preceding derivation for all the intermediate carries in parallel and make the computation efficient by sharing parts of the required circuits whenever possible. Various designs offer trade-offs in speed, cost, VLSI chip area, and energy consumption. Information on the design of lookahead carry networks and other types of fast adder can be found in books on computer arithmetic [Parh00].

Here, we present just one example of a lookahead carry network. The building blocks of this network consist of the *carry operator,* which combines the generate and propagate signals for two adjacent blocks $[i + 1, j]$ and $[h, i]$ of digit positions into the respective signals for the wider combined block $[h, j]$. In other words,

$$[i + 1, j] \ \mathfrak{c} \ [h, i] = [h, j]$$

where $\mathfrak{c}$ designates the carry operator and $[a, b]$ stands for $(g_{[a,b]}, p_{[a,b]})$ representing the pair of generate and propagate signals for the block extending from digit position a to digit

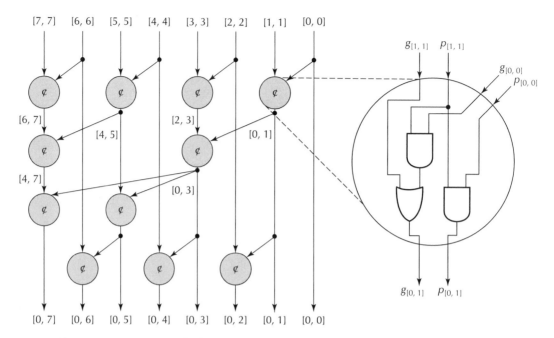

Figure 10.11 Brent-Kung lookahead carry network for an 8-digit adder, along with details of one of the carry operator blocks.

position b. Because the problem of determining all the carries c_{i+1} is the same as computing the cumulative generate signals $g_{[0,i]}$, a network built of ¢ operator blocks, such as the one depicted in Figure 10.11, can be used to derive all the carries in parallel. If a c_{in} signal is required for the adder, it can be accommodated as the generate signal g_{-1} of an extra position on the right; in this case, we would need a $(k + 1)$-bit carry network for a k-bit adder.

To better understand the carry network in Figure 10.11 and be able to analyze its cost and latency in general, we observe its recursive structure [Bren82]. The top row of carry operators combine bit-level g and p signals into g and p signals for blocks of 2 bits. The latter signals essentially correspond to generate and propagate signals for a radix-4 addition, where each radix-4 digit consists of 2 bits in the original binary number. The remaining rows of carry operators, except the last row, compute all the required intermediate carries for the radix-4 addition, which basically consist of every other carry (even-numbered ones) in the original radix-2 addition. All that remains is for the bottom row of carry operators to supply the missing odd-numbered carries.

Figure 10.12 accentuates this recursive structure by showing how the 8-input Brent-Kung network of Figure 10.11 is composed of a 4-input network of the same type plus two rows of carry operators, one row at the top and one at the bottom. This leads to a latency corresponding to roughly $2 \log_2 k$ carry operators (2 rows, times $\log_2 k$ levels of recursion) and an approximate cost of $2k$ operator blocks (roughly k blocks in the two rows at the outset, then $k/2$ blocks, $k/4$ blocks, etc.). The exact values are slightly less: $2 \log_2 k - 2$ levels for latency and $2k - \log_2 k - 2$ blocks for cost.

Instead of combining the auxiliary carry signals two at a time, leading to $2 \log_2 k$ levels, one can do four-way combining for faster operation. Within a 4-bit group, spanning bit positions

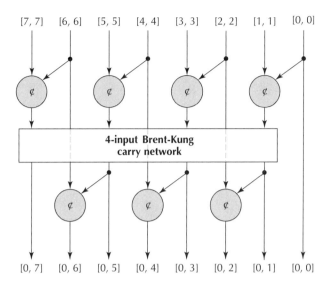

Figure 10.12 Brent-Kung look-ahead carry network for an 8-digit adder, with only its top and bottom rows of carry operators shown.

0 to 3, the group generate and propagate signals are derived as:

$$g_{[0,3]} = g_3 \vee p_3 g_2 \vee p_3 p_2 g_1 \vee p_3 p_2 p_1 g_0$$
$$p_{[0,3]} = p_3 p_2 p_1 p_0$$

Once g and p signals for 4-bit groups are known, the same process is repeated for the resulting $k/4$ signals pairs. This eventually leads to the derivation of the intermediate carries c_4, c_8, c_{12}, c_{16}, and so on; that is, one in every four positions. The remaining problem is determining the intermediate carries within 4-bit groups. This can be done with full lookahead. For example, the carries c_1, c_2, and c_3 in the rightmost group are derived as:

$$c_1 = g_0 \vee p_0 c_0$$
$$c_2 = g_1 \vee p_1 g_0 \vee p_1 p_0 c_0$$
$$c_3 = g_2 \vee p_2 g_1 \vee p_2 p_1 g_0 \vee p_2 p_1 p_0 c_0$$

The resulting circuit will be very similar in structure to the Brent-Kung carry network, except that the top half of rows will consist of group g and p production blocks and the bottom half will be intermediate carry production blocks just defined. Figure 10.13 shows the designs of these two block types.

An important method for fast adder design, which often complements the carry-lookahead scheme, is *carry-select*. In the simplest application of the carry-select method, a k-bit adder is built of a $(k/2)$-bit adder in the lower half, two $(k/2)$-bit adders in the upper half (forming two versions of the $k/2$ upper sum bits with $c_{k/2} = 0$ and $c_{k/2} = 1$), and a multiplexer for choosing the correct set of values once $c_{k/2}$ becomes known. A hybrid design, in which some of the carries (say, c_8, c_{16}, and c_{24} in a 32-bit adder) are derived via carry-lookahead and are then used to select one of two versions of the sum bits that are produced for 8-bit blocks concurrently with the operation of the carry network, is quite popular in modern arithmetic units. Figure 10.14 shows one part of such a carry-select adder, which chooses the correct version of the sum for bit positions a through b after the intermediate carry c_a becomes known.

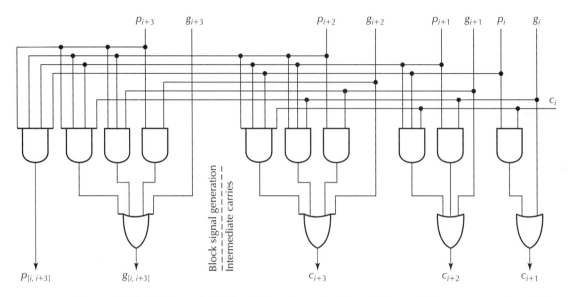

Figure 10.13 Blocks needed in the design of carry-lookahead adders with four-way grouping of bits.

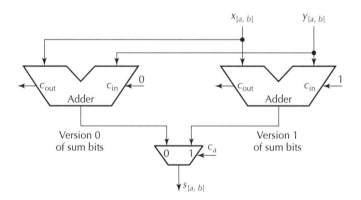

Figure 10.14 Carry-select addition principle.

■ 10.5 Logic and Shift Operations

Implementing logic operations within an ALU is quite simple, given that the ith bits of the two operands are combined to yield the ith bit of the result. Such bitwise operations can be implemented by an array of gates, as depicted in Figure 1.5. For example, the and, or, nor, xor, and other logic instructions of MiniMIPS are easily implemented in this way. Controlling which of these operations is performed by the ALU is another matter that will be discussed in Section 10.6.

Shifting involves a rearrangement of bits within a word. For example, when a word is logically shifted to the right by 4 bits, bit i of the input word will constitute bit $i - 4$ of the output word, with the most significant 4 bits of the output word filled with 0s. Suppose we want to shift a 32-bit word to the right or left (right/left control signal) by an amount given as a

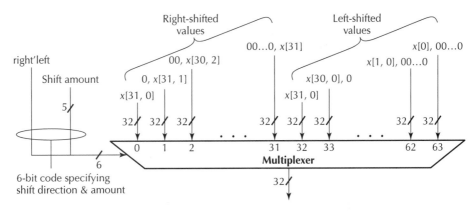

Figure 10.15 Multiplexer-based logical shifting unit.

5-bit binary number (0 to 31 bits). Conceptually, this can be accomplished by using a 64-to-1 multiplexer with 32-bit inputs (Figure 10.15). Practically, however, the resulting circuit is too complex, particularly when other types of shift (arithmetic, cyclic) are also included. Practical shifters use a multilevel implementation. After discussing the notion of arithmetic shifts, we will describe such an implementation.

Shifting a k-bit unsigned number x to the left by h bits multiplies its value by 2^h, provided of course that $2^h x$ is representable in k bits. This is because each 0 appended to the right of a binary number doubles its value (in the same way that decimal numbers are multiplied by 10 with each 0 appended to their right end). Somewhat surprisingly, this observation applies to k-bit 2's-complement numbers as well. Given that the sign of a number should not change when multiplying it by 2^h, the 2's-complement number must have $h + 1$ identical bits at its left end if it is to be multiplied by 2^h in this manner. This will ensure that after h bits have been discarded as a result of left shifting, the bit value in the sign position will not change.

Logical right shifting affects unsigned and 2's-complement numbers differently. An unsigned number x is divided by 2^h when it is right-shifted by h bits. This is akin to moving the decimal point to the left by one position to divide a decimal number by 10. However, this method of dividing by 2^h does not work for negative 2's-complement numbers; such numbers become positive when 0s are inserted from the left in the course of logical right shifting. Proper division of a 2's-complement number by 2^h requires that the bits that enter from the left be the same as the sign bit (0 for positive and 1 for negative numbers). This process is known as arithmetic right shift. Given that dividing numbers by powers of 2 is quite useful, and very efficient when done through shifting, most computers have provisions for two types of right shift: logical right shift, which views the number as a bit-string whose bits are to be repositioned via shifting, and arithmetic right shift, whose purpose is to divide the numerical value of the operand by a power of 2.

MiniMIPS has two arithmetic shift instructions: "shift right arithmetic" and "shift right arithmetic variable." These are defined similarly to logical right shifts, except that sign extension occurs during shifting, as discussed earlier.

```
sra  $t0, $s1, 2    # set $t0 to ($s1) right-shifted by 2
srav $t0, $s1, $s0  # set $t0 to ($s1) right-shifted by ($s0)
```

Figure 10.16 shows the machine representations of these two instructions.

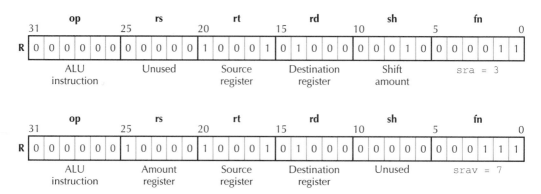

Figure 10.16 The two arithmetic shift instructions of MiniMIPS.

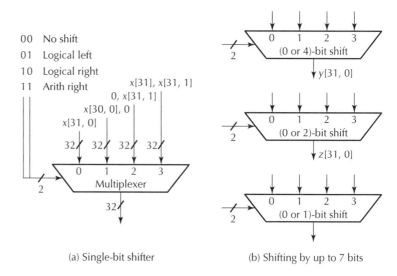

(a) Single-bit shifter   (b) Shifting by up to 7 bits

Figure 10.17 Multistage shifting in a barrel shifter.

We are now ready to discuss the design of a shifter for both logical and arithmetic shifts. First, consider the case of single-bit shifts. We want to design a circuit that can perform 1-bit logical left shift, 1-bit logical right shift, or 1-bit arithmetic right shift based on control signals provided. It is convenient to consider the case of no shifting as a fourth possibility and use the encoding shown in Figure 10.17a to distinguish the four cases. If the input operand is $x[31, 0]$, the output should be $x[31, 0]$ for no shift, $x[30, 0]$ appended with 0 for logical left shift, $x[31, 1]$ preceded by 0 for logical right shift, and $x[31, 1]$ preceded by $x[31]$ (i.e., a copy of the sign bit) for arithmetic right shift. Hence, a 4-input multiplexer can be used to perform any of these shifts, as depicted in Figure 10.17a.

Multibit shifts can be performed in several stages using replicas of the circuit shown in Figure 10.17a for each stage. For example, suppose logical and arithmetic shifts are to be performed with shift amounts between 0 and 7, provided as a 3-bit binary number. The three stages shown in Figure 10.17b realize the desired shifts by first performing a 4-bit shift, if required, based on the most significant bit of the shift amount. This converts the input $x[31, 0]$

32-pixel (4 × 8) block of black-and-white image:

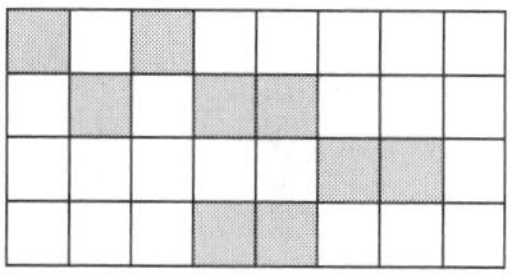

	Row 0		Row 1		Row 2		Row 3	
Representation as 32-bit word:	1010	0000	0101	1000	0000	0110	0001	0111

Hex equivalent: 0xa0a80617

Figure 10.18 A 4 × 8 block of a black-and-white image represented as a 32-bit word.

to $y[31, 0]$. The intermediate value y is then subjected to a 2-bit shift if the middle bit of the shift amount is 1, leading to the result z. Finally, z is shifted by 1 bit if the least significant bit of the shift amount is 1. The multistage design of Figure 10.17b is known as a *barrel shifter*. It is a simple matter to add cyclic shifts, or rotations, to the designs of Figure 10.17.

Logical and shift instructions find many applications. For example, they can be used for identifying and manipulating fields or individual bits within words. Suppose that you want to isolate bits 10 through 15 in a 32-bit word. One way to do it is to AND the word with the "mask"

$$0000\ 0000\ 0000\ 0000\ 1111\ 1100\ 0000\ 0000$$

which has 1s in the bit positions of interest and 0s elsewhere, and then shift the result right (logically) by 10 bits to bring the bits of interest to the right end of the word. At this point, the resulting word will have a numerical value in the range $[0, 63]$ depending on the contents of the original word in bit positions 10–15.

As a second example, consider a 32-bit word as representing a 4 × 8 block of a black-and-white image, with 1 representing a dark pixel and 0 a white pixel (Figure 10.18). The pixel values can be individually identified by alternately performing 1-bit left shifts and checking the sign of the number. An initial test identifies the first pixel (a negative number means 1). After one left shift, the second pixel can be identified by testing the sign. This can be continued until all the pixel values are known.

10.6 Multifunction ALUs

We can now put everything we have discussed in this chapter together and present the design of a multifunction ALU that can perform add/subtract, logic, and shift operations. We consider only the arithmetic/logic operations needed for executing the instructions in Table 5.1; that is, add, subtract, AND, OR, XOR, NOR. The overall structure of the ALU is shown in Figure 10.19. It consists of three subunits for shifting, addition/subtraction, and logic operations. The output of one of these subunits, or the MSB of the adder output (the sign bit), 0-extended to a full 32-bit word, can be chosen as the ALU output by asserting the "function class" control signals of the 4-input multiplexer. In the remainder of this section, we describe each of the three subunits in the ALU.

First, let us focus on the adder. This is the 2's-complement adder described in Figure 9.6. What has been added here is a 32-input NOR circuit whose output is 1 iff the adder output is

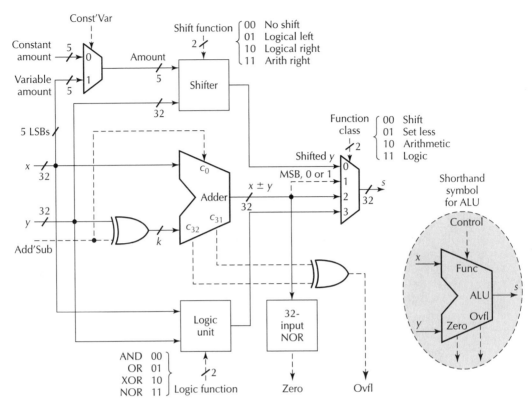

Figure 10.19 A multifunction ALU with 8 control signals (2 for function class, 1 arithmetic, 3 shift, 2 logic) specifying the operation.

0 (all-0s detector) and an XOR gate that serves to detect overflow. Overflow in 2's-complement arithmetic occurs only when the input operands are of the same sign and the adder output is of the opposite sign. Thus, denoting the signs of the inputs and output by x_{31}, y_{31}, and s_{31}, the following expression for the overflow signal is easily derived:

$$\text{Ovfl} = x_{31} y_{31} s'_{31} \vee x'_{31} y'_{31} s_{31}$$

An equivalent formulation, whose proof is left as an exercise, is that an overflow occurs when the next to the last carry of the adder (c_{31}) is different from its carry-out (c_{32}). This is the way overflow detection is implemented in Figure 10.19.

Next, we consider again the barrel shifter (Figure 10.17). Because MiniMIPS has two classes of shift instruction with constant shift amount (given in the "sh" field of the instruction) or variable shift amount (supplied in a designated register), a multiplexer is used to direct the appropriate amount to the shifter. Note that when the shift amount is given in a register, only the least significant 5 bits of the amount are relevant (why?).

The logic unit realizes one of the four bitwise logical operations of AND, OR, XOR, NOR. So, the design of the logic unit essentially consists of four arrays of gates computing these logic functions and a 4-input multiplexer that allows us to choose which set of results is forwarded to the unit's output.

Finally, supplying the MSB of the adder's output as one of the inputs to the 4-input multiplexer needs some explanation. The sign bit is 0-extended to form a full 32-bit word whose value is 0 if the sign bit is 0 and 1 if the sign bit is 1. This allows us to use our ALU for implementing the `slt` instruction of MiniMIPS, which requires that 1 or 0 be stored in a register depending on whether or not $x < y$. This condition can be checked by computing $x - y$ and looking at the sign bit of the result: if the sign bit is 1, then $x < y$ holds and 1 must be stored in the designated register; otherwise, 0 must be stored. This is exactly what the ALU provides as its output when its "function class" signals that control the output multiplexer are set to 01.

PROBLEMS

10.1 Design of half-adders

A half-adder can be realized with an AND gate and an XOR gate. Show that it can also be realized with:

a. Four 2-input NAND gates and an inverter (or with no inverter if the c_{out} signal is produced in inverted form)

b. Three 2-input NOR gates and two inverters (or with no inverter if x and y inputs are available in both true and complement forms)

10.2 Ripple-carry adders

a. Assume that each FA block in Figure 10.4 is implemented as in Figure 10.3c and that 3-input gates are slightly slower than 2-input gates. Draw a line representing the critical path on Figure 10.4.

b. Now, assume that FAs are implemented as in Figure 10.3b and derive the delay of the critical path of Figure 10.4 in terms of mux and inverter delays.

10.3 Counter with unit decrement

In Section 10.3, it was shown that inserting an increment value of 1 through the adder's carry-in simplifies the design. Show that similar simplifications are possible for unit decrement (addition of -1).

10.4 Adders as versatile building blocks

A 4-bit binary adder can be used to realize many logic functions besides its intended function of addition. For example, the adder implementing $(x_3x_2x_1x_0)_{two} + (y_3y_2y_1y_0)_{two} + c_0 = (c_4s_3s_2s_1s_0)_{two}$ can be used as a 5-input XOR realizing the function

$a \oplus b \oplus c \oplus d \oplus e$ by setting $x_0 = a$, $y_0 = b$, $c_0 = c$ (these lead to $s_0 = a \oplus b \oplus c$), $x_1 = y_1 = d$ (these lead to $c_2 = d$), $x_2 = e$, $y_2 = s_0$, and using s_2 as the output. Show how a 4-bit binary adder can be used as:

a. A 5-input AND circuit

b. A 5-input OR circuit

c. A circuit to realize the 4-variable logic function $ab \lor cd$

d. Two independent single-bit full adders, each with its own carry-in and carry-out

e. A multiply-by-15 circuit for a 2-bit unsigned binary number $(u_1u_0)_{two}$

f. A 5-input "parallel counter" producing the 3-bit sum of five 1-bit numbers

10.5 Two's-complement numbers

Prove the following for k-bit 2's-complement numbers x and y.

a. A 1-bit arithmetic right shift of x always produces $\lfloor x/2 \rfloor$, regardless of the sign of x.

b. In the addition $s = x + y$, overflow occurs iff $c_{k-1} \neq c_k$.

c. In an adder computing $s = x + y$ but not producing a carry-out signal c_k, the latter can be derived externally as $c_k = x_{k-1}y_{k-1} \lor s'_{k-1}(x_{k-1} \lor y_{k-1})$.

10.6 Brent-Kung carry network

Draw a diagram similar to Figure 10.11 that corresponds to the carry network of a 16-digit adder. *Hint:* Use the recursive construction depicted in Figure 10.12.

10.7 Borrow-lookahead subtractor

Any carry network producing the carries c_i based on g_i and p_i signals can be used, with no modification, as a borrow propagation circuit to find the borrows b_i.

a. Define the borrow-generate γ_i and borrow-propagate π_i signals for binary input operands.
b. Design a circuit to compute the difference digit d_i from γ_i, π_i, and the incoming borrow b_i.

10.8 Carry-lookahead incrementer

a. In Section 10.3, we noted that an incrementer, computing $x + 1$, is much simpler than an adder and presented the design of a ripple-carry incrementer. Design a carry-lookahead incrementer, taking advantage of any simplification due to one operand being 0.
b. Repeat part a for a borrow-lookahead decrementer.

10.9 Fixed-priority arbiter

A fixed-priority arbiter has k request input lines $R_{k-1}, \ldots, R_1, R_0$, and k grant output lines G_i. At each arbitration cycle, at most one of the grant signals is 1 and that corresponds to the highest priority request signal; i.e., $G_i = 1$ iff $R_i = 1$ and $R_j = 0$ for $j < i$.

a. Design a synchronous arbiter using ripple-carry techniques. *Hint:* Consider $c_0 = 1$, along with carry propagation and annihilation rules; there is no carry generation.
b. Discuss the design of a faster arbiter using carry-lookahead techniques. Present a complete fixed-priority arbiter design for $k = 64$.

10.10 Lookahead with overlapping blocks

The equation $[i + 1, j] \; \xcancel{c} \; [h, i] = [h, j]$, presented in Section 10.4, symbolizes the function of the carry operator that yields g and p signals for the block $[h, j]$ composed of two smaller blocks $[h, i]$ and $[i + 1, j]$. Show that the carry operator still yields the correct g and p values for a block $[h, j]$ if it is applied to two overlapping subblocks $[h, i]$ and $[i - a, j]$, where $a \geq 0$.

10.11 Alternate lookahead carry network

A carry network for $k = 2^a$ can be recursively defined as follows. A carry network of width 2 is built

of a single carry operator. To build a carry network of width 2^{h+1} from two carry networks of width 2^h, simply combine the last output of the lower (less significant part of the) network with every output of the upper network using a carry operator. Thus, given two carry networks of width 2^h, a carry network of width 2^{h+1} can be synthesized using 2^h additional carry operator blocks.

a. Draw a carry network of width 16 using the recursive construction just defined.
b. Discuss any problems that might arise in implementing the design of part a.

10.12 Variable-block carry-skip adder

Consider a 16-bit carry network built by cascading 4 copies of the 4-bit skip block in Figure 10.7.

a. Show the critical path of the resulting carry network and derive its latency in terms of gate delays.
b. Show that using the block widths 3, 5, 5, 3, rather than 4, 4, 4, 4, leads to a faster carry network.
c. Formulate a general principle about variable-block carry-skip adders based on the results of part b.

10.13 Wide adders built from narrow ones

Suppose you have a supply of 8-bit adders that also provide outputs for the block g and p signals. Use a minimal amount of additional components to build the following types of adder for a width of $k = 24$ bits. Compare the resulting 24-bit adders in terms of latency and cost, taking the cost and latency of an a-input gate as a units each and the cost and latency of an 8-bit adder as 50 and 10 units, respectively.

a. Ripple-carry adder.
b. Carry-skip adder with 8-bit blocks.
c. Carry-select adder with 8-bit blocks. *Hint:* The select signal for the multiplexer in the upper 8 bits can be derived from c_8 and the two carry outputs in the middle 8 bits assuming $c_8 = 0$ and $c_8 = 1$.

10.14 Adders for media processing

Many media signal processing applications are characterized by narrower operands (say, 8 or 16 bits wide). In such applications, 2 or 4 data elements can be packed in a single 32-bit word. It would be more efficient if adders were designed to handle parallel operations on several such narrow operands at once.

a. Suppose we want to design a 32-bit adder so that when a special "Halfadd" signal is asserted, it treats each of the two input operands as a pair of independent 16-bit unsigned integers and adds the corresponding subwords of the two operands together, producing two 16-bit unsigned sums. For each of the adder types introduced in this chapter, show how the design can be modified to accomplish our goal. Ignore overflow.

b. How can the adders of part a be modified to accommodate four independent 8-bit additions besides two 16-bit or one 32-bit addition already allowed? *Hint:* Consider using a "Quarteradd" signal that is asserted when independent 8-bit additions are desired.

c. In some applications, we need *saturating addition,* in which the output is set to the largest unsigned integer when an overflow occurs. Discuss how the adder designs of parts a and b can be modified to perform saturating addition whenever the control signal "Saturadd" is asserted.

10.15 Carry completion detection

By using two carry networks, one for the propagation of 1 carries and another for the propagation of 0 carries, we can detect the termination of the carry propagation process in an asynchronous ripple-carry adder. Not having to wait for the worst-case carry propagation delay in every addition results in a simple ripple-carry adder with an average latency that is competitive with more complex carry-lookahead adders. A 0 carry is "generated" in a position where both operand bits are 0s and is propagated in the same way as a 1 carry. Carry into position i is known when either the 1 carry or the 0 carry signal has been asserted. Carry propagation is complete when carries into all positions are known. Design a carry-completion detection adder based on the foregoing discussion.

10.16 Three-operand addition

a. Address calculation in some machines may require the addition of three components: A base value, an index value, and an offset. Assuming 32-bit unsigned base and index values and a 16-bit 2's-complement offset, design a fast address calculation circuit. *Hint:* See Figure 9.3a.

b. If the sum of the three address components cannot be represented as a 32-bit unsigned number, an "invalid address" exception signal must be asserted. Augment the design of part a to produce the required exception signal.

10.17 Unpacking the bits of a number

a. Write a MiniMIPS procedure for taking a 32-bit word x as input and producing a 32-word array, beginning with a specified address in memory, whose elements are 0 or 1 according to the value of the corresponding bit in x. The most significant bit of x should appear first.

b. Modify the procedure of part a so that it also returns the number of 1s in x. This operation, known as *population count,* is quite useful and is sometimes provided as a machine instruction.

10.18 Rotations and shifts

a. Draw the counterpart of Figure 10.15 for right and left rotations, as opposed to logical shifts.

b. Repeat part a for arithmetic shifts.

10.19 ALU for MiniMIPS-64

A 64-bit backward-compatible version of MiniMIPS was defined in Problem 8.11. Discuss how the ALU design of Figure 10.19 should be modified for use in this new 64-bit machine.

10.20 Decimal adder

Consider the design of a 15-digit decimal adder for unsigned numbers, with each decimal digit encoded in 4 bits (for a total width of 60 bits).

a. Design the required circuits for carry-generate and carry-propagate signals, assuming BCD encoding for the input operands.

b. Complete the design of the decimal adder of part a by proposing a carry-lookahead circuit and the sum computation circuit.

10.21 Multifunction ALU

For the multifunction ALU of Figure 10.19, specify the values of all control signals for each ALU-type instruction in Table 6.2. Present your answer in tabular form, using "x" for don't-care entries.

REFERENCES AND FURTHER READINGS

[Bren82]   Brent, R. P., and H. T. Kung, "A Regular Layout for Parallel Adder," *IEEE Trans. Computers,* Vol. 31, No. 3, pp. 260–264, March 1982.

[Goto02]   Goto, G., "Fast Adders and Multipliers," in *The Computer Engineering Handbook,* V. G. Oklobdzija, ed., pp. 9-22 to 9-41, CRC Press, 2002.

[Lee02]   Lee, R., "Media Signal Processing," Section 39.1 in *The Computer Engineering Handbook,* V. G. Oklobdzija, ed., pp. 39-1 to 39-38, CRC Press, 2002.

[Kore93]   Koren, I., *Computer Arithmetic Algorithms,* Prentice Hall, 1993.

[Parh00]   Parhami, B., *Computer Arithmetic: Algorithms and Hardware Designs,* Oxford University Press, 2000.

[Parh02]   Parhami, B., "Number Representation and Computer Arithmetic," in *Encyclopedia of Information Systems,* Academic Press, 2002, Vol. 3, pp. 317–333.

[Patt98]   Patterson, D. A., and J. L. Hennessy, *Computer Organization and Design: The Hardware/Software Interface,* Morgan Kaufmann, 2nd ed., 1998.

[Swar90]   Swartzlander, E. E., Jr, *Computer Arithmetic,* Vols. I and II, IEEE Computer Society Press, 1990.

11

MULTIPLIERS AND DIVIDERS

"So this is everything that is necessary for men concerning the division and multiplication with an integer, . . . Having completed this, we now begin to discuss the multiplication of fractions and their division, and the extraction of roots, if God so wills."

—*Abu Jafar Muhammad al-Khwarizmi, Arithmetic, ca. 830*

"At least one good reason for studying multiplication and division is that there is an infinite number of ways of performing these operations and hence there is an infinite number of PhDs (or expenses-paid visits to conferences in the USA) to be won from inventing new forms of multiplier."

—*Alan Clements, The Principles of Computer Hardware, 1986*

Multiplication and division are extensively used, even in applications that are not commonly associated with numerical computation. Prime examples include data encryption for privacy/security, certain image compression methods, and graphic rendering. Hardware multipliers and dividers have thus become virtual requirements for all but the most limited processors. In this chapter, beginning with the shift-add binary multiplication algorithm, we show how the algorithm is mapped to hardware and how the speed of the resulting unit is further improved. We also show how the shift-add multiplication algorithm can be programmed on a machine that does not have a multiplication instruction. Our discussion of division follows the same pattern: shift-subtract binary algorithm, hardware realization, speedup methods, and programmed division.

■ 11.1 Shift-Add Multiplication

The simplest machine multipliers are designed to follow a variant of the pencil-and-paper multiplication algorithm depicted in Figure 11.1, where each row of dots in the *partial products bit-matrix* is either all 0s (if the corresponding $y_i = 0$) or the same as x (if $y_i = 1$). When

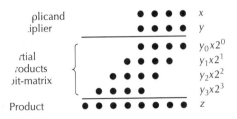

plicand
iplier

rtial
roducts
bit-matrix

Product

$y_0 x 2^0$
$y_1 x 2^1$
$y_2 x 2^2$
$y_3 x 2^3$
z

Figure 11.1 Multiplication of 4-bit numbers in dot notation.

we perform a $k \times k$ multiplication manually, we form all of the k partial products and add the resulting k numbers to obtain the product p.

For machine execution, it is easier if a *cumulative partial product* is initialized to $z^{(0)} = 0$, each row of the bit-matrix added to it as the corresponding term is generated, and the result of addition shifted to the right by one bit to achieve proper alignment with the next term, as depicted in Figure 11.1. In fact, this is exactly how *programmed multiplication* is performed on a machine that does not have a hardware multiply unit. The recurrence equation describing the process is:

$$z^{(j+1)} = \left(z^{(j)} + y_j x 2^k\right)2^{-1} \quad \text{with } z^{(0)} = 0 \text{ and } z^{(k)} = z$$
$$|\!\!-\!\!- \text{ add } -\!\!-\!|$$
$$|\!\!-\!\!- \text{ shift right } -\!\!-\!|$$

Because by the time we are done, the right shifts will have caused the first partial product to be multiplied by 2^{-k}, we premultiply x by 2^k to offset the effect of these right shifts. This is not an actual multiplication but is done by aligning x with the upper half of the $2k$-bit cumulative partial product in the addition steps. This *shift-add multiplication* algorithm can be directly realized in hardware, as we will see in Section 11.2. The shifting of the partial product need not be done in a separate step but can be incorporated in the connecting wires that go from the adder output to the doublewidth register holding the cumulative partial product (see Figure 11.5).

After k iterations, the multiplication recurrence leads to:

$$z^{(k)} = 2^{-k} z^{(0)} + \sum_{j=0}^{k-1} (y_j x 2^j) = xy + 2^{-k} z^{(0)}$$

Thus if $z^{(0)}$ is initialized to $2^k s$ (s padded with k zeros) instead of 0, the expression $xy + s$ will be evaluated. This *multiply-add operation* is quite useful for many applications and is performed at essentially no extra cost in comparison to plain shift-add multiplication.

Radix-r multiplication is quite similar to the foregoing, except that all occurrences of the number 2 in the equations are replaced by r.

Example 11.1: Binary and decimal multiplication

    a. Assuming unsigned operands, perform the binary multiplication 1010×0011, showing all algorithm steps and intermediate cumulative partial products.

    b. Repeat part a for the decimal multiplication 3528×4067.

Solution: In the following, the term $2z^{(j+1)} = z^{(j)} + y_j x 2^k$ is computed with one extra digit at the left end to avoid losing the carry-out. This extra digit moves into the 8-digit cumulative partial product once it has been right-shifted.

    a. See Figure 11.2a. We verify the result by noting that it represents $30 = 10 \times 3$.

    b. See Figure 11.2b. The only difference with the binary multiplication of part a is that the partial product term $y_j x 10^4$ needs one extra digit. Thus, if we were to draw the dot-notation diagram of Figure 11.1 for this example, each row of the partial product bit-matrix would contain 5 dots.

Position	7 6 5 4	3 2 1 0
$x2^4$	1 0 1 0	
y		0 0 1 1
$z^{(0)}$	0 0 0 0	
$+y_0 x 2^4$	1 0 1 0	
$2z^{(1)}$	0 1 0 1 0	
$z^{(1)}$	0 1 0 1	0
$+y_1 x 2^4$	1 0 1 0	
$2z^{(2)}$	0 1 1 1 1	0
$z^{(2)}$	0 1 1 1	1 0
$+y_2 x 2^4$	0 0 0 0	
$2z^{(3)}$	0 0 1 1 1	1 0
$z^{(3)}$	0 0 1 1	1 1 0
$+y_3 x 2^4$	0 0 0 0	
$2z^{(4)}$	0 0 0 1 1	1 1 0
$z^{(4)}$	0 0 0 1	1 1 1 0

(a) Binary

Position	7 6 5 4	3 2 1 0
$x10^4$	3 5 2 8	
y		4 0 6 7
$z^{(0)}$	0 0 0 0	
$+y_0 x 10^4$	2 4 6 9 6	
$10z^{(1)}$	2 4 6 9 6	
$z^{(1)}$	2 4 6 9	6
$+y_1 x 10^4$	2 1 1 6 8	
$10z^{(2)}$	2 3 6 3 7	6
$z^{(2)}$	2 3 6 3	7 6
$+y_2 x 10^4$	0 0 0 0 0	
$10z^{(3)}$	0 2 3 6 3	7 6
$z^{(3)}$	0 2 3 6	3 7 6
$+y_3 x 10^4$	1 4 1 1 2	
$10z^{(4)}$	1 4 3 4 8	3 7 6
$z^{(4)}$	1 4 3 4	8 3 7 6

(b) Decimal

Figure 11.2 Step-by-step multiplication examples for 4-digit unsigned binary and decimal numbers.

Signed-magnitude numbers can be multiplied by using the shift-add algorithm discussed earlier to multiply their magnitudes and separately deriving the sign of the product as XOR of the two input sign bits.

For 2's-complement inputs, a simple modification of the shift-add algorithm is required. We first note that if the multiplier y is positive, the shift-add algorithm still works for a negative multiplicand x. The reason can be understood by examining Figure 11.2a, where $3x$ is computed essentially by evaluating $x + 2x$. Now if x is negative (in 2's-complement format), we would be adding the negative values x and $2x$, which should lead to the correct result $3x$. All that remains now is to show how a negative 2's-complement multiplier y must be handled.

Consider the multiplication of x by $y = (1011)_{\text{2's-compl}}$. Recall from our discussion in Section 9.4 that the sign bit of a 2's-complement number can be viewed as being negatively weighted. Thus, the negative 2's-complement number y is $-8 + 2 + 1 = -5$, whereas as an unsigned number, it is $8 + 2 + 1 = 11$. Just as we can multiply x by $y = 11$ via computing $8x + 2x + x$, we can perform multiplication by $y = -5$ by computing $-8x + 2x + x$. We see that the only major difference between an unsigned and a 2's-complement multiplier y is that in the last multiplication step, we must subtract, rather than add, the partial product $y_{k-1}x$.

Example 11.2: Two's-complement multiplication

    a. Assuming 2's-complement operands, perform the binary multiplication 1010×0011, showing all algorithm steps and intermediate cumulative partial products.

    b. Repeat part a for the 2's-complement multiplication 1010×1011.

Solution: In the following, all partial products are written with an extra bit at the left to ensure that the sign information is preserved and correctly handled. In other words, the 4-bit multiplicand x must be written as $(11010)_{\text{2's-compl}}$ or else its value would change. Similarly, sign extension (arithmetic shift) must be used when $2z^{(i)}$ is right-shifted to obtain $z^{(i)}$.

    a. See Figure 11.3a. We verify the result by noting that it represents $-18 = (-6) \times 3$.

    b. See Figure 11.3b. We verify the result by noting that it represents $30 = (-6) \times (-5)$.

Position	7 6 5 4	3 2 1 0		Position	7 6 5 4	3 2 1 0
$x2^4$	1 0 1 0			$x2^4$	1 0 1 0	
y		0 0 1 1		y		1 0 1 1
$z^{(0)}$	0 0 0 0 0			$z^{(0)}$	0 0 0 0 0	
$+y_0x2^4$	1 1 0 1 0			$+y_0x2^4$	1 1 0 1 0	
$2z^{(1)}$	1 1 0 1 0			$2z^{(1)}$	1 1 0 1 0	
$z^{(1)}$	1 1 1 0 1	0		$z^{(1)}$	1 1 1 0 1	0
$+y_1x2^4$	1 1 0 1 0			$+y_1x2^4$	1 1 0 1 0	
$2z^{(2)}$	1 0 1 1 1	0		$2z^{(2)}$	1 0 1 1 1	0
$z^{(2)}$	1 1 0 1 1	1 0		$z^{(2)}$	1 1 0 1 1	1 0
$+y_2x2^4$	0 0 0 0 0			$+y_2x2^4$	0 0 0 0 0	
$2z^{(3)}$	1 1 0 1 1	1 0		$2z^{(3)}$	1 1 0 1 1	1 0
$z^{(3)}$	1 1 1 0 1	1 1 0		$z^{(3)}$	1 1 1 0 1	1 1 0
$+(-y_3x2^4)$	0 0 0 0 0			$+(-y_3x2^4)$	0 0 1 1 0	
$2z^{(4)}$	1 1 1 0 1	1 1 0		$2z^{(4)}$	0 0 0 1 1	1 1 0
$z^{(4)}$	1 1 1 0	1 1 1 0		$z^{(4)}$	0 0 0 1	1 1 1 0

      (a) Positive multiplier y (b) Negative multiplier y

Figure 11.3 Step-by-step multiplication examples for 4-digit 2's-complement numbers.

11.2 Hardware Multipliers

The shift-add algorithm of Section 11.1 can be directly converted into the hardware multiplier shown in Figure 11.4. There are k cycles for $k \times k$ multiplication. In the jth cycle, x or 0 is added to the upper half of the doublewidth partial product, depending on the jth bit y_j of the multiplier, and the new partial product is right-shifted before the start of the next cycle. The multiplexer in Figure 11.4 allows subtraction to be performed in the last cycle, as required for 2's-complement multiplication. In a multiplier that is used only with unsigned operands, the multiplexer can be replaced by an array of AND gates that collectively multiply the bit y_j by the multiplicand x.

Rather than store y in a separate register, as shown in Figure 11.4, we can keep it in the lower half of the partial product register. This is because as the partial product expands to occupy more and more bits of the lower half in the register, bits of the multiplier are retired due to it being right-shifted. The binary multiplication examples in Figures 11.2a and 11.3 clearly show how the lower half of the partial product register is initially unused and then bits are shifted into it at the rate of one per cycle.

Rather than treating shifting as something that is to be performed after the adder output has been stored in the partial product register, we can incorporate shifting in how data is stored in the register. Recall from Figure 2.1 that to store a word in a register, bits of the word must be supplied to the individual flip-flops comprising the register. It is an easy matter to move the bits to the right by one position before supplying them to the register and asserting the load signal. Figure 11.5 shows how the connections to the register input data lines are made to accomplish the objective of right-shifted loading.

Radix-2 multiplication is fairly straightforward to implement and involves little additional hardware complexity in an ALU that already has an adder/subtractor. However, the k clock cycles needed to perform a $k \times k$ multiplication makes this operation much slower than addition and logic/shift operations, which typically take just a single clock cycle. One way to speed up the multiplication hardware is to perform the multiplication in radix 4 or higher radices.

In radix 4, every operation cycle takes care of 2 bits of the multiplier, thus cutting the number of cycles in half. Considering unsigned multiplication for simplicity, the 2 bits of the

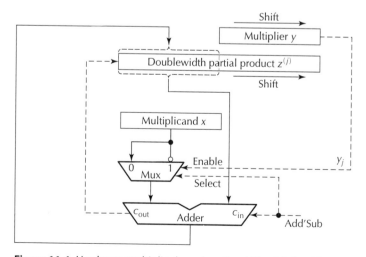

Figure 11.4 Hardware multiplier based on the shift-add algorithm.

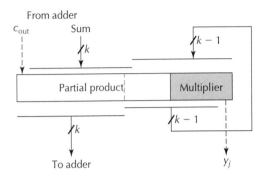

Figure 11.5 Shifting incorporated in the connections to the partial product register rather than as a separate phase.

multiplier examined in a given cycle are used to select one of four values to be added to the cumulative partial product: 0, x, $2x$ (shifted x), $3x$ (precomputed through the addition $2x + x$ and stored in a register before the iterations begin). In actual implementations, precomputation of $3x$ is avoided through special recoding methods such as Booth recoding. Additionally, the cumulative partial product is kept in carry-save form, making the addition of the next partial product to it quite fast (Figure 9.3a). In this way, only one regular addition is required at the very last step, leading to significant speedup. Implementation details for recoded and *high-radix multipliers* are beyond the scope of this book and can be found in books on computer arithmetic [Parh00].

Fast hardware multiplication units in high-performance processors are based on *tree multiplier* designs. Instead of forming the partial products one at a time in radix 2 or h at a time in radix 2^h, we can form all of them simultaneously, thus reducing the multiplication problem to n-operand addition, where $n = k$ in radix 2, $n = k/2$ in radix 4, and so on. For example, 32×32 multiplication becomes a 32-operand addition problem in radix 2 or a 16-operand addition problem in radix 4. In tree multipliers, the n operands thus formed are added in two stages. In stage 1, a tree built of *carry-save adders* is used to reduce the n operands to 2 operands that have the same sum as the original n numbers. A carry-save adder (see Figure 9.3a) reduces three values to two values, for a reduction factor of 1.5, thus leading to a $\lceil \log_{1.5}(n/2) \rceil$-level circuit for reducing n numbers to 2. The two numbers thus derived are then added by a fast logarithmic-time adder, leading to an overall logarithmic latency for the multiplier (Figure 11.6a).

The *full-tree multiplier* of Figure 11.6a is rather complex, and its speed may not be needed for all applications. In such cases, more economical *partial-tree multipliers* might be implemented. For example, if about half the partial products are accommodated by the tree part, then two passes through the tree can be used to form the two numbers representing the desired product, with the results of the first pass fed back to the inputs and combined with the second set of partial products (Figure 11.6b). A partial-tree multiplier can be viewed as a (very-) high-radix multiplier. For example, if 12 partial products are combined in each pass, then a radix-2^{12} multiplication is effectively performed.

An *array multiplier* uses the same two-stage computation scheme of a tree multiplier, with the difference that the tree of carry-save adders is one-sided (has the maximum possible depth of k for $k \times k$ multiplication) and the final adder is of ripple-carry type (quite slow). An example 4×4 array multiplier is depicted in Figure 11.7, where the HA and FA cells are half- and full adders defined in Figures 10.1 and 10.2, respectively; MA cells are modified full adders, one of whose inputs is internally formed as the logical AND of x_i and y_j.

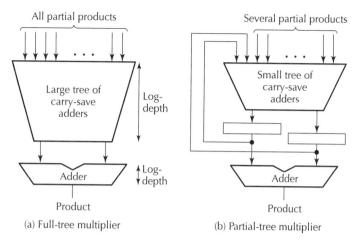

Figure 11.6 Schematic diagrams for full-tree and partial-tree multipliers.

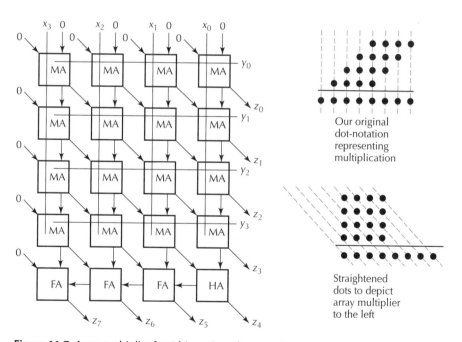

Figure 11.7 Array multiplier for 4-bit unsigned operands.

You may well ask why such a slow tree-type multiplier is of any interest at all. The answer is that array multipliers are quite suitable for VLSI realization, given their highly regular design and efficient wiring pattern. They can also be readily pipelined by inserting latches between some of the rows of cells, thus allowing several multiplications to be performed on the same hardware structure.

■ 11.3 Programmed Multiplication

MiniMIPS has two multiply instructions that perform 2's-complement and unsigned multiplication, respectively. They are:

```
mult    $s0, $s1    # set Hi,Lo to ($s0)×($s1); signed
multu   $s2, $s3    # set Hi,Lo to ($s2)×($s3); unsigned
```

These instructions leave the double-width product in the Hi and Lo special registers, with Hi holding the upper half and Lo the lower half of the 64-bit product. Why, like other R-type instructions of MiniMIPS, the product is not placed in a pair of registers in the register file will become clear as we discuss instruction execution and control sequencing in Part IV of the book. For now, we just mention that the reason has to do with the much longer latency of multiplication relative to addition and logic/shift operations. Because the product of two 32-bit numbers is always representable in 64 bits, there can be no overflow in either type of multiplication.

To allow access to Hi and Lo contents, the following two instructions are provided for copying their contents into desired registers in the general register file:

```
mfhi    $t0    # set $t0 to (Hi)
mflo    $t1    # set $t1 to (Lo)
```

For machine representation of these four instructions, see Section 6.6.

Note that if a 32-bit product is desired, it can be retrieved from the Lo register. However, the content of Hi must be examined to make sure that the correct product is in fact representable in 32 bits; that is, it has not exceeded the range of 32-bit numbers.

Example 11.3: Using multiplication in MiniMIPS programs   Show how to obtain the 32-bit product of 32-bit signed integers that are stored in registers $s3 and $s7, placing the product in register $t3. If the product is not representable in 32 bits, control must be transferred to movfl. Assume that registers $t1 and $t2 are available for scratch results if needed.

Solution: If the product of signed integers is to fit in a 32-bit word, the special register Hi is expected to hold 32 identical bits equal to the sign bit of Lo (if this were an unsigned multiplication, Hi would need to be checked for 0). Thus, if the value in Lo is positive, Hi must hold 0 and if the value in Lo is negative, Hi must hold −1, which has the all-1s representation.

```
mult $s3,$s7        # product formed in Hi,Lo
mfhi $t2            # copy upper half of product into $t2
mflo $t3            # copy lower half of product into $t3
slt  $t1,$t3,$zero  # set (LSB of) $t1 to the sign of Lo
sll  $t1,$t1,31     # set sign bit of $t1 to the sign of Lo
sra  $t1,$t1,31     # set $t1 to all-0s/1s via arith shift
bne  $t1,$t2,movfl  # if (Hi) ≠ ($t1), we have overflow
```

On machines that do not have a hardware-supported multiply instruction, multiplication can be performed in software by means of the shift-add algorithm of Section 11.1. It is instructive to develop such a program for MiniMIPS because it helps us understand the algorithm better. In what follows, we consider unsigned multiplication and leave it to the reader to develop the signed version.

Example 11.4: Shift-add multiplication of unsigned numbers   Using the shift-add algorithm, define a MiniMIPS procedure that multiplies two unsigned numbers (passed to it in registers $a0 and $a1) and leaves the double-width product in $v0 (high part) and $v1 (low part).

Solution: The following procedure, named "shamu" for "shift-add multiplication" uses both instructions and pseudoinstructions. Registers Hi and Lo, holding the upper and lower half of the cumulative partial product z, are represented by $v0 and $v1, respectively. The multiplicand x is in $a0 and the multiplier y is in $a1. Register $t2 is used as a counter that is initialized to 32 and decremented by 1 in each iteration until it reaches 0. The jth bit of y is isolated in $t1 by repeatedly right-shifting y and looking at its LSB after each shift. Register $t1 is also used to isolate the LSB of Hi so that it can be shifted into Lo during right shift. Finally, $t0 is used to compute the carry-out of the addition which must be shifted into Hi during right shifts. Register usage in this example is depicted in Figure 11.8 for ready reference.

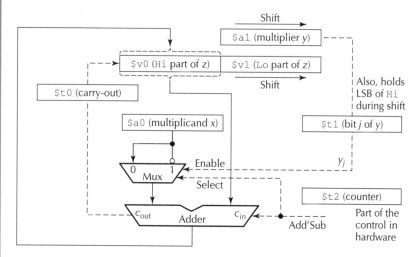

Figure 11.8 Register usage for programmed multiplication superimposed on the block diagram for a hardware multiplier.

```
shamu:  move $v0,$zero        # initialize Hi to 0
        move $v1,$zero        # initialize Lo to 0
        addi $t2,$zero,32     # initialize repetition counter to 32
```

```
mloop:  move $t0,$zero          # set carry-out to 0 in case of no add
        move $t1,$a1            # copy ($a1) into $t1
        srl  $a1,1             # halve the unsigned value in $a1
        subu $t1,$t1,$a1       # subtract ($a1) from ($t1) twice to
        subu $t1,$t1,$a1       # obtain LSB of ($a1), or y[j], in $t1
        beqz $t1,noadd         # no addition needed if y[j]=0
        addu $v0,$v0,$a0       # add x to upper part of z
        sltu $t0,$v0,$a0       # form carry-out of addition in $t0
noadd:  move $t1,$v0           # copy ($v0) into $t1
        srl  $v0,1             # halve the unsigned value in $v0
        subu $t1,$t1,$v0       # subtract ($v0) from ($t1) twice to
        subu $t1,$t1,$v0       # obtain LSB of Hi in $t1
        sll  $t0,$t0,31        # carry-out converted to 1 in MSB of $t0
        addu $v0,$v0,$t0       # right-shifted $v0 corrected
        srl  $v1,1             # halve the unsigned value in $v1
        sll  $t1,$t1,31        # LSB of Hi converted to 1 in MSB of $t1
        addu $v1,$v1,$t1       # right-shifted $v1 corrected
        addi $t2,$t2,-1        # decrement repetition counter by 1
        bne  $t2,$zero,mloop   # if counter > 0, repeat multiply loop
        jr   $ra               # return to the calling program
```

Note that because the carry-out of addition is not recorded in MiniMIPS, we have devised a scheme to derive it in $t0 by noting that the carry-out is 1 (an unsigned addition overflows) iff the sum is less than either operand.

When a multiplicand x is to be multiplied by a constant multiplier a, using the multiply instruction, or its software version in Example 11.4, may not be the best option. Multiplication by a power of 2 can obviously be done through shifting, which is faster and more efficient than a full-blown multiply instruction. Less obviously, multiplication by other small constants can also be performed through shift and add instructions. For example, to compute $5x$, one can form $4x$ by a left-shift instruction and then add x to the result. On many machines, one shift and one add instruction take less time than a multiply instruction. As another example, $7x$ can be computed as $8x - x$, although in this case there is a danger of encountering overflow in computing $8x$ even though $7x$ itself is within the representation range of our machine. Most modern compilers are smart enough to avoid spewing out multiply instructions when a short sequence of add/subtract/shift instructions can accomplish the same goal.

11.4 Shift-Subtract Division

Like multipliers, the simplest machine dividers are designed to follow a variant of the pencil-and-paper division algorithm depicted in Figure 11.9. Each row of dots in the subtracted bit-matrix of Figure 11.9 is either all 0s (if the corresponding $y_i = 0$) or the same as x (if $y_i = 1$). When we perform a $2k/k$ division manually, we form the subtracted terms one at a time by "guessing" the value of the next *quotient digit*, subtract the appropriate term (0 or a suitably

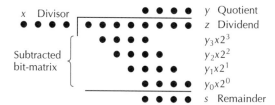

Figure 11.9 Division of an 8-bit number by a 4-bit number in dot notation.

shifted version of x) from the *partial remainder,* which is initialized to the value of the dividend z, and proceed until all k bits of the quotient y have been determined. At this time, the partial remainder becomes the final remainder s.

For hardware or software implementation, a recurrence equation describing the process above is used:

$$z^{(j)} = 2z^{(j-1)} - y_{k-j}x2^k \quad \text{with } z^{(0)} = z \text{ and } z^{(k)} = 2^k s$$
$$\quad\text{|-shift-|}$$
$$\quad\text{|—— subtract ——|}$$

Because by the time we are done, the left shifts will have caused the partial remainder to be multiplied by 2^k, the true remainder is obtained by multiplying the final partial remainder by 2^{-k} (shifting it to the right by k bits). This is justified as follows:

$$z^{(k)} = 2^k z - \sum_{j=1}^{k} 2^{k-j}(y_{k-j}x2^k) = 2^k(z - xy) = 2^k s$$

As in the case of partial products for multiplication, the shifting of the partial remainder need not be performed in a separate step but can be incorporated in the connecting wires that go from the adder output to the double-width register holding the partial remainder (see Section 11.5).

Radix-r division is quite similar to binary division except that all occurrences of the number 2 in the equations are replaced by r.

Example 11.5: Integer and fractional division

    a. Assuming unsigned operands, perform the binary division 0111 0101/1010, showing all algorithm steps and partial remainders.

    b. Repeat part a for the fractional decimal division .1435 1502/.4067.

Solution: In the following, the term $2z^{(j)}$ is formed with one extra digit at the left end to avoid losing the additional digit created by doubling.

    a. See Figure 11.10a. We verify the results by noting that they represent $117 = 10 \times 11 + 7$.

    b. See Figure 11.10b. The only differences from the binary division of part a are that the dividend x is not premultiplied by a power of the radix and the subtracted terms $y_j x$ need one extra digit. Thus, if we were to draw the dot-notation diagram of Figure 11.9 for this example, each row of the subtracted bit-matrix would contain 5 dots.

```
Position    7 6 5 4  3 2 1 0          Position    -1 -2 -3 -4 -5 -6 -7 -8

z           0 1 1 1  0 1 0 1          z           . 1  4  3  5  1  5  0  2
x2⁴         1 0 1 0                   x           . 4  0  6  7

z⁽⁰⁾        0 1 1 1  0 1 0 1          z⁽⁰⁾        . 1  4  3  5  1  5  0  2
2z⁽⁰⁾     0 1 1 1 0  1 0 1            10z⁽⁰⁾     1. 4  3  5  1  5  0  2
-y₃x2⁴      1 0 1 0         y₃ = 0    -y₋₁x      1. 2  2  0  1              y₋₁ = 3

z⁽¹⁾        0 1 0 0  1 0 1            z⁽¹⁾        . 2  1  5  0  5  0  2
2z⁽¹⁾     0 1 0 0 1  0 1              10z⁽¹⁾     2. 1  5  0  5  0  2
-y₂x2⁴      0 0 0 0         y₂ = 0    -y₋₂x      2. 0  3  3  5              y₋₂ = 5

z⁽²⁾        1 0 0 1  0 1              z⁽²⁾        . 1  1  7  0  0  2
2z⁽²⁾     1 0 0 1 0  1                10z⁽²⁾     1. 1  7  0  0  2
-y₁x2⁴      1 0 1 0         y₁ = 1    -y₋₃x      0. 8  1  3  4              y₋₃ = 2

z⁽³⁾        1 0 0 0  1                z⁽³⁾        . 3  5  6  6  2
2z⁽³⁾     1 0 0 0 1                   10z⁽³⁾     3. 5  6  6  2
-y₀x2⁴      1 0 1 0         y₀ = 0    -y₋₄x      3. 2  5  3  6              y₋₄ = 8

z⁽⁴⁾        0 1 1 1                   z⁽⁴⁾        . 3  1  2  6
s                    0 1 1 1          s           . 0  0  0  0  3  1  2  6
y                    1 0 1 1          y           . 3  5  2  8


       (a) Integer binary                        (b) Fractional decimal
```

Figure 11.10 Step-by-step division examples for 8/4-digit unsigned binary integers and decimal fractional numbers.

Example 11.6: Division with same-width operands   Often, the division z/x is performed with operands of the same width rather than z being twice as wide as x. The algorithm, however, remains the same.

    a. Assuming unsigned operands, perform the binary division 1101/0101, showing all algorithm steps and partial remainders.

    b. Repeat part a for the fractional binary division .0101/.1101.

Solution

    a. See Figure 11.11a. Note that because z is 4 bits wide, left shifting can never produce a nonzero bit in position 8; so unlike the example in Figure 11.10, an extra bit in position 8 is not needed. We verify the results by noting that they represent $13 = 5 \times 2 + 3$.

    b. See Figure 11.11b. The only differences from the binary division of part a are that the dividend x is not premultiplied by a power of the radix and that both the shifted partial remainders and the subtracted terms $y_{-j}x$ need one extra bit at the left (position 0). We verify the results by noting that they represent $5/16 = (13/16) \times (6/16) + 2/256$. Comparing Figures 11.11b and 11.10b, we note that in Figure 11.11b, positions –5 through –8 are not used, except in the final remainder s. Given that in fractional division the remainder is usually not of interest, positions to the right of the operands' LSB can be completely ignored, both in manual computation and in hardware implementation.

(a) Integer binary

	7	6	5	4	3	2	1	0	
z	0	0	0	0	1	1	0	1	
$x2^4$	0	1	0	1					
$z^{(0)}$	0	0	0	0	1	1	0	1	
$2z^{(0)}$	0	0	0	1	1	0	1		
$-y_3x2^4$	0	0	0	0					$y_3=0$
$z^{(1)}$	0	0	0	1	1	0	1		
$2z^{(1)}$	0	0	1	1	0	1			
$-y_2x2^4$	0	0	0	0					$y_2=0$
$z^{(2)}$	0	0	1	1	0	1			
$2z^{(2)}$	0	1	1	0	1				
$-y_1x2^4$	0	1	0	1					$y_1=1$
$z^{(3)}$	0	0	0	1	1				
$2z^{(3)}$	0	0	1	1					
$-y_0x2^4$	0	0	0	0					$y_0=0$
$z^{(4)}$	0	0	1	1					
s					0	0	1	1	
y					0	0	1	0	

(b) Fractional binary

		-1	-2	-3	-4	-5	-6	-7	-8	
z	.	0	1	0	1					
x	.	1	1	0	1					
$z^{(0)}$	.	0	1	0	1					
$2z^{(0)}$	0.	1	0	1	0					
$-y_{-1}x$	0.	0	0	0	0					$y_{-1}=0$
$z^{(1)}$	.	1	0	1	0					
$2z^{(1)}$	1.	0	1	0	0					
$-y_{-2}x$	0.	1	1	0	1					$y_{-2}=1$
$z^{(2)}$	.	0	1	1	1					
$2z^{(2)}$	0.	1	1	1	0					
$-y_{-3}x$	0.	1	1	0	1					$y_{-3}=1$
$z^{(3)}$	.	0	0	0	1					
$2z^{(3)}$	0.	0	0	1	0					
$-y_{-4}x$	0.	0	0	0	0					$y_{-4}=0$
$z^{(4)}$	.	0	0	1	0					
s	.	0	0	0	0	0	0	1	0	
y	.	0	1	1	0					

Figure 11.11 Step-by-step division examples for 4/4-digit unsigned binary integers and fractional numbers.

Because the quotient of dividing a $2k$-digit number by a k-digit number may not fit in k digits, division can lead to overflow. Fortunately, there exist simple tests for overflow detection prior to division. In integer division, overflow will not occur iff $z < 2^k x$, since this will guarantee $y < 2^k$; that is, we require that x be strictly greater than the upper half of z. In fractional division, avoiding overflow requires $z < x$. So, in either case, the upper half of the double-width dividend z must be less than the divisor x.

When dividing signed numbers, the remainder s is defined to have the same sign as the dividend z and a magnitude that is less than $|x|$. Consider the following examples of integer division with all possible combinations of signs for z and x:

Dividend	Divisor		Quotient	Remainder
$z = 5$	$x = 3$	$\Rightarrow$	$y = 1$	$s = 2$
$z = 5$	$x = -3$	$\Rightarrow$	$y = -1$	$s = 2$
$z = -5$	$x = 3$	$\Rightarrow$	$y = -1$	$s = -2$
$z = -5$	$x = -3$	$\Rightarrow$	$y = 1$	$s = -2$

We see from the preceding examples that the magnitudes of the quotient y and remainder s are unaffected by the input signs and that the signs of y and s are easily derivable from the signs of z and x. Hence, one way to do signed division is through an indirect algorithm that converts the operands into unsigned values and, at the end, accounts for the signs by adjusting the sign bits or via complementation. This is the method of choice with the restoring division algorithm, discussed in this section. Direct division of signed numbers is quite possible via the nonrestoring division algorithm, whose discussion is beyond the scope of this book. Interested readers can refer to any book on computer arithmetic [Parh00].

■ 11.5 Hardware Dividers

The shift-subtract algorithm of Section 11.4 can be directly converted into the hardware divider shown in Figure 11.12. There are k cycles for $2k/k$ or k/k division. In the jth cycle, x is subtracted from the upper half of the double-width partial remainder. The result, known as the *trial difference,* is loaded into the partial remainder register only if it is positive. The sign of the trial difference essentially tells us whether 1 is the correct choice for the next quotient digit y_{k-j} or is too large (0 is the correct choice). Note that the trial difference is positive if the MSB of the previous partial remainder is 1, making the shifted partial remainder large enough to guarantee a positive difference, or else if the c_{out} of the adder is 1. This is the reason for supplying these two bits to the quotient digit selector block.

The multiplexer in Figure 11.12 allows either addition or subtraction to be performed in each cycle. Addition of x is never required for the *restoring division algorithm* presented in Section 11.4. The qualifier "restoring" means that whenever the trial difference becomes negative, it is taken to be an indication that the next quotient digit is 0 and the trial difference is not loaded into the partial remainder register, causing the original value to remain intact at the end of the cycle. In *nonrestoring division,* which we do not cover in this book, the computed difference, whether positive or negative, is stored as the partial remainder, which is thus not

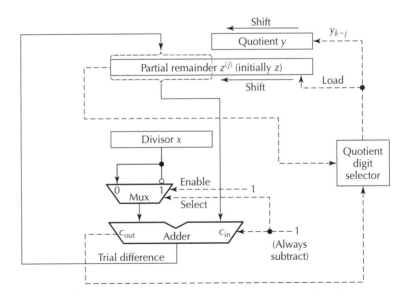

Figure 11.12 Hardware divider based on the shift-subtract algorithm.

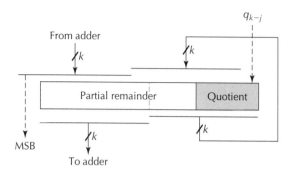

q_{k-j}

From adder

k

k

Partial remainder

Quotient

MSB

k

k

k

To adder

Figure 11.13 Shifting incorporated in the connections to the partial remainder register rather than as a separate phase.

restored to its correct value when it goes negative. However, appropriate actions in subsequent steps will lead to the correct result. These corrective actions require that x be added to, rather than subtracted from, the partial remainder. The nonrestoring approach makes the control circuits simpler and also has the side benefit of rendering direct signed division possible.

Rather than inserting the bits of y into a separate register, as shown in Figure 11.12, we can insert them into the lower half of the partial remainder register. This is because as the partial remainder is shifted to the left, bit positions at the right end of the register are freed up and can be used to store the quotient bits as they are developed. The division examples in Figure 11.10 clearly show how the lower half of the partial remainder register, which is fully occupied at the outset, is freed up at the rate of one bit/digit per cycle.

Rather than treat shifting as something that is to be performed after the adder output is stored in the partial remainder register, we can incorporate shifting in how data is stored in the register. Recall from Figure 2.1 that to store a word in a register, bits of the word must be supplied to the set of flip-flops comprising the register. It is an easy matter to move the bits to the left by one position before supplying them to the register and asserting the load signal. Figure 11.13 shows how the connections to the register input data lines are made to accomplish the objective of left-shifted loading.

A comparison of Figures 11.4 and 11.12 reveals that multipliers and dividers are quite similar and can be implemented with shared hardware within an ALU that performs different operations based on an externally supplied function code. In fact, given that *square-rooting* is quite similar to division, it is fairly common to implement a single unit that realizes all three operations of multiplication, division, and square-rooting.

As in the case of multipliers, *high-radix dividers* speed up the division process by producing several bits of the quotient in each cycle. For example, in radix 4, every operation cycle generates 2 bits of the quotient, thus cutting the number of cycles in half. However, there is one complication that makes the process somewhat more difficult than radix-4 multiplication: because radix-4 digits have 4 possible values, a similarly simple selection scheme such as the one for radix 2 (i.e., try 1 and choose 0 if it doesn't work) cannot be used for quotient digit selection in radix 4. Details of how this problem is resolved and how, as for partial products in multiplication, the partial remainder in division can be kept in carry-save form, are beyond the scope of this book.

Whereas there is no counterpart to tree multipliers for performing division, *array dividers* do exist and are structurally quite similar to array multipliers. Figure 11.14 shows an array divider that divides an 8-bit dividend z by a 4-bit divisor x, producing a 4-bit quotient

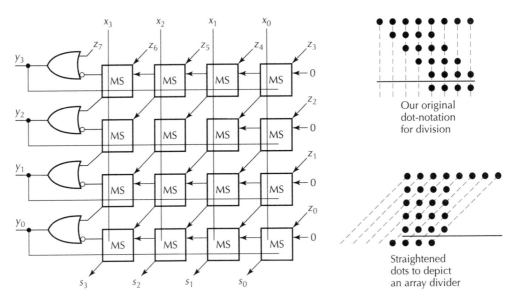

Figure 11.14 Array divider for 8/4-bit unsigned integers.

y and a 4-bit remainder s. The MS cells in Figure 11.14 are modified full subtractors. They receive a borrow-in bit from the right and two operand bits from above, subtract the vertical operand from the diagonal operand, and produce a difference bit that goes down diagonally and a borrow-out bit that goes to the left. There is a multiplexer at the diagonal output that lets the difference through if the y_i, presented to the cells as a horizontal control line coming from the left, is 1 and lets z through if $y_i = 0$. This serves the function of using the trial difference as the next partial remainder or restoring the partial remainder to the previous value.

It is also possible to perform division by using a sequence of multiplications instead of additions. Even though multiplications are slower and more complex than additions, an advantage over additive schemes may be gained because far fewer multiplications are needed to perform division. So, in such *convergence division algorithms,* we trade off iteration complexity for fewer iterations. Very briefly, in convergence division, we derive the quotient $y = z/x$ by first computing $1/x$ and then multiplying it by z. To compute $1/x$, we start with a crude approximation obtained on the basis of a few high-order bits of x, using a specially designed logic circuit or a small lookup table. The approximation $u^{(0)}$ will have a small relative error of ϵ, say, meaning that $u^{(0)} = (1 + \epsilon)(1/x)$. We then obtain successively better approximations to $1/x$ by using an existing approximation $u^{(i)}$ in the formula

$$u^{(i+1)} = u^{(i)} \times (2 - u^{(i)} \times x)$$

So, each iteration in refining the value of $1/x$ involves two multiplications and one subtraction. If the initial approximation is accurate to 8 bits, say, the next one will be accurate to 16 bits and the one after that to 32 bits. Hence, 2–4 iterations suffice in practice. Details of implementing such convergence division schemes and analysis of the number of iterations needed can be found in books on computer arithmetic [Parh00].

◼ 11.6 Programmed Division

MiniMIPS has two divide instructions that perform 2's-complement and unsigned division, respectively. They are:

```
div     $s0, $s1        # Lo=quotient, Hi=remainder
divu    $s2, $s3        # unsigned version of div
```

For machine representation of the preceding instructions, see Section 6.6. These instructions leave the quotient and remainder in the special registers Lo and Hi, respectively. Note that unlike much of our discussion in Sections 11.4 and 11.5, the dividend for MiniMIPS divide instructions is single-width. For this reason, the quotient, which is always smaller in magnitude than the dividend, is guaranteed to fit in one word. As in the case of multiplication, once the results have been obtained in Hi and Lo, they can be copied into general registers, by means of the instructions mfhi and mflo, for further processing.

Why, like other R-type instructions of MiniMIPS, the quotient and remainder are not placed in the general register file will become clear as we discuss instruction execution and control sequencing in Part IV of the book. For now, we just mention that the reason has to do with the much longer latency of division compared to addition and logic/shift operations.

Example 11.7: Using division in MiniMIPS programs   Show how to obtain the residue of z modulo x (z mod x), where z and x are 32-bit signed integers in registers $s3 and $s7, respectively. The result must be placed in register $t2. Note that for signed numbers, the residue operation is different from the remainder in division; whereas the sign of the remainder is defined to be the same as the sign of the dividend z, residues are by definition always positive. Assume that register $t1 is available for scratch results if needed.

Solution: The result of z mod x is a positive integer s^{pos} that satisfies $s^{pos} < |x|$ and $z = x \times y + s^{pos}$ for some integer y. It is easy to see that s^{pos} is the same as the remainder s of the division z/x when $s \geq 0$ and can be obtained as $s + |x|$ when $s < 0$.

```
        div   $s3,$s7        # remainder formed in Hi
        mfhi  $t2            # copy remainder into $t2
        bgez  $t2,done       # positive remainder is the residue
        move  $t1,$s7        # copy x into $t1; this is |x| if x ≥ 0
        bgez  $s7,noneg      # |x| is in $t1; no negation needed
        sub   $t1,$zero,$s7  # put -x into $t1; this is |x| if x < 0
noneg:  add   $t2,$t2,$t1    # residue is computed as s + |x|
done:   ...
```

On machines that do not have a hardware-supported divide instruction, division can be performed in software by means of the shift-subtract algorithm discussed in Section 11.4. It is instructive to develop such a program for MiniMIPS because it helps us understand the algorithm better. In what follows, we consider unsigned division and leave it to the reader to develop the signed version.

Example 11.8: Shift-subtract division of unsigned numbers Use the shift-subtract algorithm to define a MiniMIPS procedure that performs the unsigned division z/x, with z and x passed to it in registers $a2-$a3 (upper and lower halves of the double-width integer z) and $a0, respectively. The results should be returned in $v0 (remainder) and $v1 (quotient).

Solution: The following procedure, named "shsdi" for "shift-subtract division" uses both instructions and pseudoinstructions. Registers Hi and Lo, holding the upper and lower half of the partial remainder z, are represented by $v0 and $v1, respectively. The divisor x is in $a0 and the quotient y is formed in $a1. The $(k - j)$th bit of y is formed in $t1 and is then added to a left-shifted $a1, effectively inserting the next quotient bit as the LSB of $a1. Register $t1 is also used to isolate the MSB of Lo so that it can be shifted into Hi during left shift. Register $t0 holds the MSB of Hi during left shift, so that it can be used in choosing the next quotient digit. Register $t2 is used as a counter that is initialized to 32 and decremented by 1 in each iteration until it reaches 0. Register usage in this example is depicted in Figure 11.15 for ready reference.

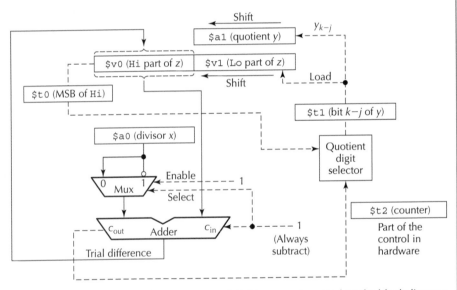

Figure 11.15 Register usage for programmed division superimposed on the block diagram for a hardware divider.

```
shsdi: move $v0,$a2        # initialize Hi to ($a2)
       move $v1,$a3        # initialize Lo to ($a3)
       addi $t2,$zero,32   # initialize repetition counter to 32
dloop: slt  $t0,$v0,$zero  # copy MSB of Hi into $t0
       sll  $v0,$v0,1      # left-shift the Hi part of z
       slt  $t1,$v1,$zero  # copy MSB of Lo into $t1
       or   $v0,$v0,$t1    # move MSB of Lo into LSB of Hi
       sll  $v1,$v1,1      # left-shift the Lo part of z
       sge  $t1,$v0,$a0    # quotient digit is 1 if (Hi) ≥ x,
       or   $t1,$t1,$t0    # or if MSB of Hi was 1 before shifting
```

```
        sll   $a1,$a1,1        # shift y to make room for new digit
        or    $a1,$a1,$t1      # copy y[k-j] into LSB of $a1
        beq   $t1,$zero,nosub  # if y[k-j] = 0, do not subtract
        subu  $v0,$v0,$a0      # subtract divisor x from Hi part of z
nosub:  addi  $t2,$t2,-1       # decrement repetition counter by 1
        bne   $t2,$zero,dloop  # if counter > 0, repeat divide loop
        move  $v1,$a1          # copy the quotient y into $v1
        jr    $ra              # return to the calling program
```

Note that in the subtraction of x from the Hi part of z, we ignore the most significant bit of the partial remainder which is in $t3. This does not create a problem because subtraction is performed only if the partial remainder z (including its hidden MSB) is no less than the divisor x.

Division by powers of 2 can be done through shifting, which tends to be a much faster operation than division on virtually any computer. Just as one can avoid using a multiply instruction or software routine for certain small constant multipliers (see the last paragraph in Section 11.3), one can divide numbers by small constant divisors using a handful of shift/add/subtract instructions. The theory for deriving the required steps is somewhat more complicated than that used for multiplication and is thus not discussed in this book. Most modern compilers are smart enough to recognize opportunities for avoiding the use of a slow divide instruction. Optimizations that avoid division operations are even more important than those that eliminate multiplications. This is because on modern microprocessors, division is typically 4–10 times slower than multiplication [Etie02].

PROBLEMS

11.1 Multiplication algorithm

Draw dot diagrams similar to Figure 11.1 for the following variations:

a. Integer 8×4-digit unsigned decimal multiplication. *Hint:* Number of dots will change.
b. Fractional 8×4-bit unsigned binary multiplication. *Hint:* Alignment of dots will change.
c. Fractional 8×4-digit unsigned decimal multiplication.

11.2 Unsigned multiplication

Multiply the following 4-bit unsigned binary numbers. Present your work in the format of Figure 11.2a.

a. $x = 1001$ and $y = 0101$
b. $x = 1101$ and $y = 1011$
c. $x = .1001$ and $y = .0101$

11.3 Unsigned multiplication

Multiply the following 4-bit unsigned decimal numbers. Present your work in the format of Figure 11.2b.

a. $x = 8765$ and $y = 4321$
b. $x = 1234$ and $y = 5678$
c. $x = .8765$ and $y = .4321$

11.4 Two's-complement multiplication

Represent the following signed-magnitude binary numbers in 5-bit 2's-complement format and then multiply them. Present your work in the format of Figure 11.3.

a. $x = +.1001$ and $y = +.0101$
b. $x = +.1001$ and $y = -.0101$
c. $x = -.1001$ and $y = +.0101$
d. $x = -.1001$ and $y = -.0101$

11.5 Multiplication algorithm

a. By redoing the multiplication steps in Figure 11.2, verify that if the cumulative partial product is initialized to 1011 instead of 0000, a multiply-add operation is performed

b. Show that regardless of the initial value of $z^{(0)}$, the multiply-add result with k-digit operands is always representable in $2k$ digits.

11.6 Array multiplier

a. On the array multiplier of Figure 11.7, label the input lines with bit values corresponding to the multiplication example in Figure 11.2a. Then, determine all the intermediate and output signal values on the diagram and verify that the correct product is obtained.

b. Repeat part a for $x = 1001$ and $y = 0101$.

c. Repeat part a for $x = 1101$ and $y = 1011$.

d. Will the multiplier yield the correct product for fractional inputs (e.g., $x = .1001$ and $y = .0101$)?

e. Show how a multiply-add operation can be performed on the array multiplier.

f. Verify your method of part e, using the input values given in Problem 11.5a.

11.7 Multiplication with left shifts

The shift-add multiplication algorithm presented in Section 11.1 and exemplified in Figure 11.2, corresponds to processing rows of the partial products bit-matrix (Figure 11.1) from top to bottom. An alternative multiplication algorithm goes in the reverse bottom-to-top direction and requires left shifting of the partial product before each addition step.

a. Formulate this new shift-add multiplication algorithm in the form of a recurrence equation.

b. Apply your algorithm to the examples in Figure 11.2, verifying that it yields the correct answers.

c. Compare the new algorithm based on left shifts with our original algorithm with right shifts in terms of hardware implementation.

11.8 Multiplication in MiniMIPS

Can you accomplish the task performed in Example 11.3 without using any register other than $t3 and without changing the operand registers?

11.9 Programmed multiplication

It was stated in Section 11.2 that the registers holding the multiplier y and the lower half of the cumulative partial product z can be merged in Figure 11.4. Is a similar merger of registers $a1 and $v1 (Figure 11.8) beneficial in Example 11.4? Fully justify your answer, either by presenting an improved procedure or showing that the merger complicates the multiplication process.

11.10 Multiplication by constants

Using shift and add/subtract instructions only, devise efficient procedures for multiplication by each of the following constants. Assume 32-bit unsigned operands and ensure that intermediate results do not exceed the range of 32-bit unsigned numbers. Do not modify the operand registers, and use only one other register for partial results.

a. 13

b. 43

c. 63

d. 135

11.11 Multiplication by constants

a. Intel's new 64-bit architecture (IA-64) has a special shladd (shift left and add) instruction that can shift one operand by 1–4 bits to the left before adding it to another operand. This allows multiplication by 5, say, to be performed with one shladd instruction. What other multiplications by constants can be done via a single shladd instruction?

b. Repeat part a for shlsub (shift left and subtract), assuming that the first operand is shifted.

c. What is the smallest positive constant, multiplication by which requires at least three of the instructions defined in parts a and b?

11.12 Division algorithm

Draw dot diagrams similar to Figure 11.9 for the following variations:

a. Integer 8/4-digit unsigned decimal division. *Hint:* Number of dots will change.

b. Fractional 8/4-bit unsigned binary division. *Hint:* Alignment of dots will change.

c. Fractional 8/4-digit unsigned decimal division.

11.13 Unsigned division

Perform the division z/x for the following unsigned binary dividend/divisor pairs, obtaining the quotient y and remainder s. Present your work in the format of Figures 11.11 and 11.10.

a. $z = 0101$ and $x = 1001$
b. $z = .0101$ and $x = .1001$
c. $z = 1001\ 0100$ and $x = 1101$
d. $z = .1001\ 0100$ and $x = .1101$

11.14 Unsigned division

Perform the division z/x for the following unsigned decimal dividend/divisor pairs, obtaining the quotient y and remainder s. Present your work in the format of Figures 11.11 and 11.10.

a. $z = 5678$ and $x = 0103$
b. $z = .5678$ and $x = .0103$
c. $z = 1234\ 5678$ and $x = 4321$
d. $z = .1234\ 5678$ and $x = .4321$

11.15 Signed division

Perform the division z/x for the following signed binary dividend/divisor pairs, obtaining the quotient y and remainder s. Present your work in the format of Figures 11.11 and 11.10.

a. $z = +0101$ and $x = -1001$
b. $z = -.0101$ and $x = -.1001$
c. $z = +1001\ 0100$ and $x = -1101$
d. $z = -.1001\ 0100$ and $x = +.1101$

11.16 Array divider

a. On the array divider of Figure 11.14, label the input lines with bit values corresponding to the division example in Figure 11.10a. Then, determine all the intermediate and output signal values on the diagram and verify that the correct quotient and remainder are obtained.
b. Show that the OR gates at the left edge of the array divider of Figure 11.14 can be replaced by MS cells, leading to a more uniform structure.
c. Rotate the array divider counterclockwise by 90 degrees, observe that the structure is similar to array multiplier, and suggest how the two circuits can be combined to obtain one circuit that can

multiply or divide according to the state of the Mul'Div signal.

11.17 Analysis of convergence division

At the end of Section 11.5, we presented a convergence scheme for division based on iteratively refining an approximation to $1/x$ until a good approximation $u \cong 1/x$ is obtained and then computing $q = z/x$ via the multiplication $z \times u$. Show that the method of refining the approximation u using the recurrence $u^{(i+1)} = u^{(i)} \times (2 - u^{(i)} \times x)$ has quadratic convergence in the sense that if $u^{(i)} = (1 + \epsilon)(1/x)$, then $u^{(i+1)} = (1 - \epsilon^2)(1/x)$. Then starting with the approximation 0.75 for the reciprocal of 1.5, derive successive approximations based on the recurrence just given (using decimal arithmetic and a calculator) and verify that the error is indeed reduced quadratically in each step.

11.18 Programmed division

a. Describe how the programmed unsigned division procedure in Example 11.8 can be used to perform a division in which both operands are 32 bits wide.
b. Would any simplification in the procedure result from the knowledge that it will always be used with a single-width (32-bit) dividend z?
c. Modify the procedure in Example 11.8 so that it performs signed division.

11.19 Programmed division

It was stated in Section 11.5 that the registers holding the quotient y and the lower half of the partial remainder z can be merged in Figure 11.12. Is a similar merger of registers $\$a1$ and $\$v1$ (Figure 11.15) beneficial in Example 11.8? Fully justify your answer, either by presenting an improved procedure or by showing that the merger complicates the division process.

11.20 Division by 255

If $z/255 = y$, then $y = 256y - z$. This observation leads to a procedure for dividing a number z by 255, using one subtraction to obtain each byte of the quotient. Because $256y$ ends in eight 0s, the least significant byte of y is easily obtained through a byte-width subtraction, for which the borrow is saved. The lowest byte of y just obtained is the second lowest byte in $256y$, thus leading to the determination of the second lowest byte of y through another subtraction, with the saved borrow used as borrow-in. This process is continued until all the bytes of y have been found. Write a MiniMIPS procedure for implementing this divide-by-255 algorithm without any multiplication or division instruction.

REFERENCES AND FURTHER READINGS

[Etie02]   Etiemble, D., "Computer Arithmetic and Hardware: 'Off the Shelf' Microprocessors versus 'Custom Hardware,'" *Theoretical Computer Science,* Vol. 279, Nos. 1–2, pp. 3–27, May 2002.

[Goto02]   Goto, G., "Fast Adders and Multipliers," in *The Computer Engineering Handbook,* V. G. Oklobdzija, ed., pp. 9-22 to 9-41, CRC Press, 2002.

[Knut97]   Knuth, D. E., *The Art of Computer Programming,* Vol. 2: *Seminumerical Algorithms,* Addison-Wesley, 3rd ed., 1997.

[Kore93]   Koren, I., *Computer Arithmetic Algorithms,* Prentice Hall, 1993.

[Parh00]   Parhami, B., *Computer Arithmetic: Algorithms and Hardware Designs,* Oxford University Press, 2000.

[Parh02]   Parhami, B., "Number Representation and Computer Arithmetic," in *Encyclopedia of Information Systems,* Academic Press, 2002, Vol. 3, pp. 317–333.

[Patt98]   Patterson, D. A., and J. L. Hennessy, *Computer Organization and Design: The Hardware/Software Interface,* Morgan Kaufmann, 2nd ed., 1998.

[Swar90]   Swartzlander, E. E., Jr, *Computer Arithmetic,* Vols. I and II, IEEE Computer Society Press, 1990.

CHAPTER 12

FLOATING-POINT ARITHMETIC

TOPICS IN THIS CHAPTER

Signal processing requirements of multimedia and applications of other types have transformed floating-point arithmetic from an exclusive tool for scientific and engineering programs to a necessary capability for all computer users. Main attributes of the ANSI/IEEE standard floating-point format were presented in Chapter 9. In this chapter, we discuss some of the details of the standard format and discuss how arithmetic operations are performed on floating-point numbers. Basic arithmetic operations (add, subtract, multiply, divide, square root) as well as general function evaluation are considered. In addition, number conversions, rounding, exceptions, and issues relating to result precision and errors are reviewed. Also included are MiniMIPS instructions for floating-point arithmetic.

■ 12.1 Rounding Modes

The ANSI/IEEE standard floating-point format was described in terms of its components and main attributes in Section 9.6. In this and the next section, we cover other features of the standard, including how it deals with rounding and exceptions, in preparation for our discussion of floating-point arithmetic in the rest of this chapter.

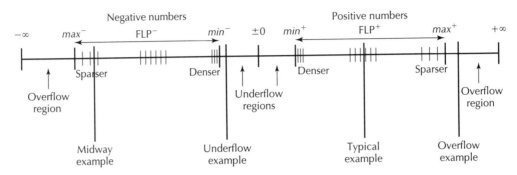

Figure 12.1 Distribution of floating-point numbers on the real line.

First, consider Figure 12.1, which shows the real number line extending from $-\infty$ on the left to $+\infty$ on the right. Floating-point numbers (except denormals, to be discussed later) are represented by short tick marks on the line. The special values ± 0 and $\pm\infty$ are depicted using heavy tick marks, as are the extreme representable numbers max^+, max^-, min^+, and min^- that delimit the range of ordinary positive (FLP$^+$) and negative (FLP$^-$) floating-point numbers. A few tick marks within each of the two ranges FLP$^+$ and FLP$^-$ show examples of representable numbers. We see that these tick marks are closer to each other near $min^{\pm}$ and further apart near $max^{\pm}$. This is because the same minimal change of 1 *ulp* in the significand leads to a larger magnitude change with larger exponents than with smaller exponents. So the density of floating-point numbers along the line is reduced as their magnitudes increase. This is a key to the usefulness of floating-point numbers, since they can represent small numbers with good precision while sacrificing precision for larger numbers to achieve greater range. Note that even though the precision is reduced as we move away from 0, the error in representation (difference between an exact value that we need to represent and the closest tick mark in Figure 12.1) increases in absolute terms but stays approximately constant when considered in relative terms.

Unlike integers, floating-point numbers are by nature inexact. For example, 1/3 does not have an exact representation in the ANSI/IEEE floating-point format (of course real numbers such as π, e, and $\sqrt{2}$ do not have exact representations either). Even when operands are exact, results of floating-point arithmetic operations may be inexact. This happens, for example, if we divide 1 by 3 or extract the square root of 2. Such numbers correspond to points on the real line that do not coincide with any of the tick marks in Figure 12.1. When this happens, the closest tick mark to the actual value is chosen as its floating-point representation. The process of obtaining the best possible floating-point representation for a given real value is known as *rounding*.

Four examples of rounding are shown in Figure 12.1. In the typical case, our real number falls between two tick marks and is closer to one than the other. Here the closer of the two adjacent floating-point numbers is chosen as the rounded value to minimize the rounding error. This *round-to-nearest* scheme is also the one we use in manual computation. When the real number is midway between two tick marks, the distance to the two tick marks is exactly the same and either one could legitimately be considered to be the best approximation. In mathematical calculations, the midway cases are always rounded up (so, 3.5 is rounded to 4 and 4.5 to 5). The ANSI/IEEE standard prescribes rounding to the floating-point number whose significand has an

LSB of 0 (of two adjacent floating-point number, the significand of one must end in 0 and the other in 1). This *round-to-nearest-even* procedure tends to result in more symmetric negative and positive errors and in greater probability that the errors cancel each other out in the course of a long computation. Note that a significand that ends in 0 is "even" when regarded as an integer. When this scheme is applied to rounding values to integers, 3.5 and 4.5 are both rounded to 4, the closest even number.

The two cases just described cover most of the situations that occur in practice. Occasionally, numbers in the overflow and underflow regions must be represented. In these cases, rounding is a bit trickier. Consider positive overflow (negative overflow is similar). In this region, virtually all numbers are rounded to $+\infty$; the only exceptions are values that are close enough to max^+ that they would have been rounded down if there were a next floating-point number after max^+. Similarly, in the positive underflow region, only numbers that are very close to the right boundary would be rounded to min^+. All other values are rounded down to $+0$ (they would be rounded up to -0 in the negative underflow region). Hence, $+0$ and -0, though numerically equivalent, may carry information about how they were produced in the course of our computation. This *flush-to-zero* option is used in floating-point units that do not recognize denormals, to which we now turn.

All ANSI/IEEE floating-point numbers are represented in Figure 12.1 except for denormals, which fall between ±0 and $min^{\pm}$. Note that the width of each of the two underflow regions in Figure 12.1 is 2^{-126} for short format and 2^{-1022} for long format. These are extremely small numbers, yet if a number that falls in one of the underflow regions is flushed to zero, the relative representation error will be quite significant. Denormals soften this blow by allowing us to represent values in these two regions more precisely. For this reason, we sometimes say that denormals allow gradual or *graceful underflow*. With denormals, the underflow regions in Figure 12.1 are filled with tick marks that are the same distance apart as the tick marks immediately to the other side of $min^{\pm}$. The smallest number representable is now $2^{-23} \times 2^{-126} = 2^{-149}$ (smallest possible significand without a hidden 1, multiplied the lowest possible power of 2) in short format and 2^{-1074} in long format, making underflow a less serious problem.

Example 12.1: Rounding to the nearest integer
   a. Consider the rounded even integer corresponding to a real signed-magnitude number x as a function $rtnei(x)$. Plot this round-to-nearest-even-integer function for x in the range $[-4, 4]$.
   b. Repeat part a for the function $rtni(x)$, that is, round-to-nearest-integer function, where midway values are always rounded up.

Solution
   a. See Figure 12.2a. Heavy dots indicate how the midway values are rounded. Note that all the heavy dots appear on horizontal grid lines associated with even integers. The dashed diagonal line is the identity function $f(x) = x$ corresponding to the ideal (error-free) representation of x. Deviations from this line represent rounding errors.
   b. See Figure 12.2b. The only difference from part a is in how some of the midway values are treated. For example, 2.5 is rounded to 3 and -0.5 to -1.

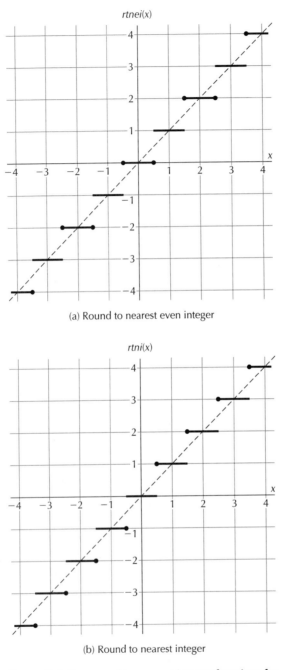

(a) Round to nearest even integer

(b) Round to nearest integer

Figure 12.2 Two round-to-nearest-integer functions for
x in $[-4, 4]$.

Besides round-to-nearest-even, which is the default rounding mode for the ANSI/IEEE standard, three *directed rounding* modes are defined that allow users to control the direction of rounding errors:

1. *Round inward (toward 0):* Choose the nearest value in the same direction as 0.
2. *Round upward (toward $+\infty$):* Choose the larger of the two possible values.
3. *Round downward (toward $-\infty$):* Choose the smaller of the two possible values.

Inward-directed, upward-directed, and downward-directed rounding modes are listed here for completeness. In most run-of-the-mill floating-point calculations, the default round-to-nearest-even mode is satisfactory. We may use directed rounding, for example, when we want to be sure that an imprecise result is guaranteed to be less than the correct value (it is a lower bound for the actual result). If we need to compute z/x in this way, where z and x are results of other computations, then we must derive z with downward-directed rounding, x with upward-directed rounding, and also round the floating-point division result downward.

Example 12.2: Directed rounding

    a. Consider the inward-directed rounded integer corresponding to a real signed-magnitude number x as a function *ritni(x)*. Plot this round-inward-to-nearest-integer function for x in the range $[-4, 4]$.

    b. Repeat part a for the round-upward-to-nearest-integer function *rutni(x)*.

Solution

    a. See Figure 12.3a. The dashed diagonal line is the identity function $f(x) = x$ corresponding to the ideal (error-free) representation of x. Deviations from this line represent rounding errors.

    b. See Figure 12.3b. The difference from part a is in positive numbers being rounded upward.

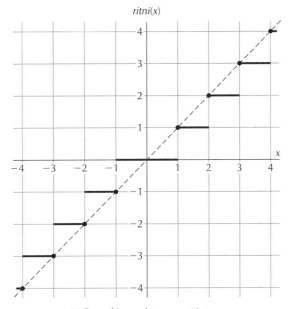

(a) Round inward to nearest integer

Figure 12.3 Two directed round-to-nearest-integer functions for x in $[-4, 4]$.

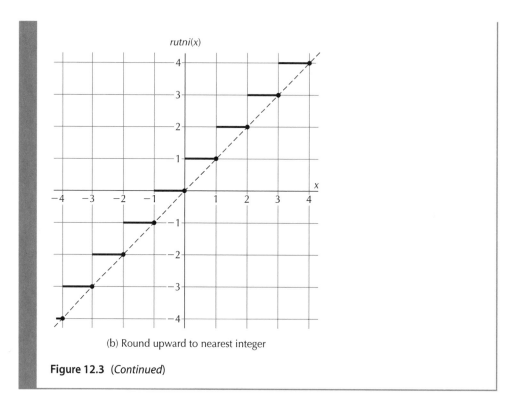

(b) Round upward to nearest integer

Figure 12.3 (*Continued*)

■ 12.2 Special Values and Exceptions

The ANSI/IEEE floating-point standard specifies five special values:

±0	Biased exponent = 0, significand = 0 (no hidden 1)
±∞	Biased exponent = 255 (short) or 2047 (long), significand = 0
NaN	Biased exponent = 255 (short) or 2047 (long), significand ≠ 0

NaN actually specifies a class of special values, with the nonzero significand potentially carrying additional information about what is being represented. However, in this book we do not distinguish between different NaNs and treat them all as a single special type. Denormals are also, in a sense, special values. However, after noting that they do not have a hidden 1 and that their exponent is coded differently, we essentially treat them like ordinary floating-point numbers in the context of various arithmetic operations. So, we do not discuss denormals in this section.

It is somewhat surprising that 0 is considered a special value. However, this is a consequence of our use of a hidden 1, requiring that all leading 0 bits of a significand be eliminated via left shifts until its leftmost 1 bit becomes the hidden 1. This makes it impossible to represent a significand of 0 in the normal way, as it has no leftmost 1 to shift and hide. In floating-point arithmetic operations, 0 is treated in a manner consistent with the rules of algebra. For example, $x \pm 0 = x$ for any ordinary floating-point number x. If x itself is a special value, then things become interesting, as we shall see shortly.

It is also puzzling that there are two types of 0. This is convenient because of the dual roles played by 0: the true mathematical 0 arising from an operation such as $2 - 2$, with both operands assumed to be exact, and the approximate 0 obtained by flushing an underflowed result to 0. To preserve mathematical identities, $+0$ and -0 are considered equal, so that the equality test $+0 = -0$ yields "true" and $-0 < +0$ yields "false" (note that it is tempting to consider the latter result "true"). When a result x underflows from the negative (positive) side, it is flushed to -0 $(+0)$ to preserve the sign information. If, subsequently, we compute $1/x$ for $x = +0$ or -0, we get $+\infty$ or $-\infty$, respectively. Note that even though tiny negative and positive values are not much different and little harm results from considering them equal, $+\infty$ and $-\infty$ are very different. So, having $+0$ and -0 does serve a useful purpose. Preserving the sign information requires that we define, for example,

$$(+0) + (+0) = (+0) - (-0) = +0$$
$$(+0) \times (+5) = +0$$
$$(+0)/(-5) = -0$$

The special operands $+\infty$ and $-\infty$ have their standard mathematical meanings. As noted, 1 divided by $+0$ yields $+\infty$ and 1 divided by -0 yields $-\infty$, as expected. Equally logical are the following sample rules, where x is any nonspecial floating-point number:

$$(+\infty) + (+\infty) = +\infty$$
$$x - (+\infty) = -\infty$$
$$(+\infty) \times x = \pm\infty, \text{ depending on the sign of } x$$
$$x/(+\infty) = \pm 0, \text{ depending on the sign of } x$$
$$\sqrt{+\infty} = +\infty$$

In comparison tests, $+\infty$ is greater than any value (except for $+\infty$ and NaN) and $-\infty$ is less than any value (other than $-\infty$ and NaN).

The last special operand type, NaN, is useful because some operations do not yield a valid numerical value and it is convenient to have a special representation for such otherwise unrepresentable results. For example $y = z/x$ is undefined, in a mathematical sense, when $z = x = 0$. If a program tries to perform this operation, we may choose to halt its execution and produce an error message for the user. However, it may turn out that the value of y is never actually used later on in the program. As an example, consider the following program fragment, with current variable values supplied in comments:

$y = z/x$	# currently, $z = 0, x = 0$
$v = w/u$	# currently, $w = 2, u = 3$
if $a < b$ then $c = v$ else $c = y$	# currently, $a = 4, b = 5$

It is clear that even though y is undefined, the outcome of the program fragment in the current setting does not depend on y; thus, assigning the special value NaN to y allows the computation to proceed and come to a successful completion. Here are a few other situations that yield NaN as a result:

$$(+\infty) + (-\infty) = \text{NaN}$$
$$(\pm 0) \times (\pm\infty) = \text{NaN}$$
$$(\pm\infty)/(\pm\infty) = \text{NaN}$$

In arithmetic operations, the value NaN propagates to the result. This is consistent with the intuitive notion of an undefined value. For example:

$\text{NaN} + x = \text{NaN}$

$\text{NaN} + \text{NaN} = \text{NaN}$

$\text{NaN} \times 0 = \text{NaN}$

$\text{NaN} \times \text{NaN} = \text{NaN}$

The special value NaN is unordered with respect to any other value, including itself. Thus, comparison tests such as $\text{NaN} < 2$, $\text{NaN} = \text{NaN}$, or $\text{NaN} \le +\infty$ all return "false," whereas $\text{Nan} \ne 2$ or $\text{NaN} \ne \text{NaN}$ return "true."

Example 12.3: Special floating-point values   Consider the computation $v = z/x + w/x$.
  a. What is the result of this computation if currently $z = +2$, $w = -1$, and $x = +0$?
  b. What would the result be if we used the algebraically equivalent form $v = (z + w)/x$?
  c. How would the results of parts a and b change if $x = -0$ instead of $+0$?

Solution
  a. We get $z/x = +\infty$ and $w/x = -\infty$, leading to $v = (+\infty) + (-\infty) = \text{NaN}$.
  b. The result of the equivalent computation is $v = (2 - 1)/0 = +\infty$. Note that this result is "better" than that of part a. If we subsequently compute $u = 1/v$, the $+\infty$ result here leads to $1/(+\infty) = 0$, which is consistent with what we would get from the direct computation $x/(z + w)$. With the NaN result of part a, we would get $1/v = 1/\text{NaN} = \text{NaN}$.
  c. In part a, we still get $v = \text{NaN}$. In part b, the result becomes $v = -\infty$.

Besides the exception signaled in comparing unordered values, the ANSI/IEEE standard also defines exceptions associated with divide-by-zero, overflow, underflow, inexact result, and invalid operation. The first three of these are self-explanatory. The "inexact exception" is signaled when the unrounded exact result of an operation or conversion is not representable. The "invalid operation" exception occurs in the following situations, among others:

Addition	$(+\infty) + (-\infty)$
Multiplication	$0 \times \infty$
Division	$0/0$ or ∞/∞
Square root	Operand < 0

A more complete description is given in the ANSI/IEEE standard document [IEEE85]. A working group of experts is discussing some revisions and clarifications to the standard.

12.3 Floating-Point Addition

We discuss only floating-point addition because subtraction can be converted to addition by changing the sign of the subtrahend. To perform addition, the exponents of the two floating-point operands must be equalized, if needed. Consider the addition of $\pm 2^{e1}s1$ and $\pm 2^{e2}s2$, with $e1 > e2$. By making both exponents equal to $e1$, the addition becomes:

$$(\pm 2^{e1}s1) + (\pm 2^{e1}(s2/2^{e1-e2})) = \pm 2^{e1}(s1 \pm s2/2^{e1-e2})$$

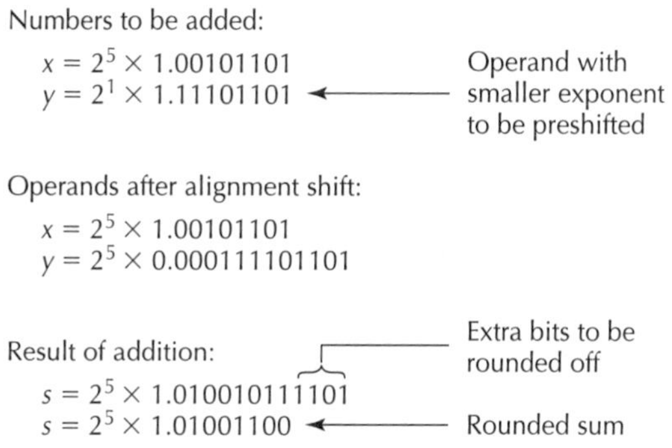

Numbers to be added:

$x = 2^5 \times 1.00101101$
$y = 2^1 \times 1.11101101$ ◄——— Operand with smaller exponent to be preshifted

Operands after alignment shift:

$x = 2^5 \times 1.00101101$
$y = 2^5 \times 0.000111101101$

Result of addition: ┌——— Extra bits to be rounded off

$s = 2^5 \times 1.010010111101$
$s = 2^5 \times 1.01001100$ ◄——— Rounded sum

Figure 12.4 Alignment shift and rounding in floating-point addition.

We thus see that $s2$ must be right-shifted by $e1 - e2$ bits before being added to $s1$. This *alignment shift* is also called *preshift* (to distinguish it from the *postshift* needed for normalizing a floating-point result). Figure 12.4 shows a complete example of floating-point addition, including preshift, addition of aligned significands, and final rounding. In this example, no postshift is needed because the result is already normalized. In general, though, the result may need a 1-bit right shift, when it is in [2, 4), or a multibit left shift when the addition of operands with different signs leads to *cancellation* or *loss of significance* and one or more leading 0s appear in the result.

From the simplified block diagram for a hardware floating-point adder in Figure 12.5, we see that once the operands are unpacked, their exponents and significands are processed in two separate tracks whose functions are coordinated by the block labeled "Control & sign logic." For example, based on the difference of the two exponents, this unit decides which operand must be preshifted. To economize on hardware, usually only one preshifter is provided, say for the left operand of the adder. If the other operand needs to be preshifted, the operands are physically swapped. Also, in adding operands with unlike signs, the operand that is not preshifted is complemented. This time-saving strategy may lead to the computation of $y - x$ when in fact $x - y$ is the desired result. The control unit corrects this problem by forcing the complementation of the result if needed. Finally, normalization and rounding are preformed, and the exponent is adjusted accordingly.

The significand adder in Figure 12.5 can have any design, but in practice it is always one of the faster types, such as carry-lookahead adder, discussed in Section 10.4. The swap circuit consists of two multiplexers that allow either significand to be sent to either side of the adder. The alignment shifter is designed according to the methods discussed in Section 10.5 (see, in particular, Figure 10.17). Given that alignment shifting is always to the right, the resulting shifter will be simpler and faster than the more general version shown in Figure 10.17. For example, any shift from 0 to 31 bits can be performed in three stages:

0, 8, 16, or 24 bits in stage 1 (4-input mux)

0, 2, 4, or 6 bits in stage 2 (4-input mux)

0 or 1 bit in stage 3 (2-input mux)

The normalizer may have to shift the result one bit to the right or an arbitrary number of bits to the left. In the following, we limit our discussion to a positive output from the adder for the sake of simplicity. One-bit right shift is needed when the adder output equals or exceeds 2. In this case, the result is guaranteed to be less than 4 (why?), thus requiring a 1-bit right shift to make the whole part of the number, which is 10 or 11, equal to 1; this 1 will then constitute the hidden 1. Left shifting is needed when the result has one or more leading 0s. Many leading

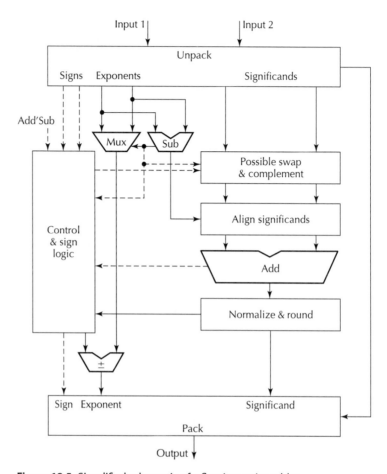

Figure 12.5 Simplified schematic of a floating-point adder.

0s may exist when we add numbers of different signs with significands of roughly comparable values. If all bits of the result are 0s, then special treatment is needed to encode the result as 0 at the output. Otherwise, the number of leading 0s must be counted and the result given to the postshifter as its control input.

Finally, as shown in the example of Figure 12.4, the sum output of the adder may have extra bits as a result of the preshifting of one operand. These bits must be discarded and the remaining bits adjusted accordingly for proper rounding. Note that in the worst case, rounding may require full carry propagation across the width of the result. Thus, rounding is potentially a slow process that adds to the latency of floating-point addition. For this reason, and because so many different operations must be performed in sequence in floating-point addition, many clever design methods have been developed to make the operations faster. For example, the number of leading 0s in the result may be predicted by a special circuit rather than determined after the sum becomes available. Discussion of these methods is beyond the scope of this book [Parh00].

Note that when a significand is normalized through shifting, the exponent must be adjusted accordingly. For example, when the significand is right-shifted by 1 bit (hence divided by 2), the exponent must be incremented by 1 to compensate for the change. This is why we have the final small adder on the exponent path in Figure 12.5.

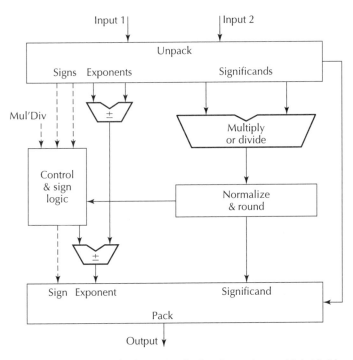

Figure 12.6 Simplified schematic of a floating-point multiply/divide unit.

■ 12.4 Other Floating-Point Operations

The floating-point operations of multiplication and division (Figure 12.6) are not much different from their fixed-point counterparts. For multiplication, exponents of the two operands are added and their significands are multiplied:

$$(\pm 2^{e1}s1) \times (\pm 2^{e2}s2) = \pm 2^{e1+e2}(s1 \times s2)$$

Thus, a hardware floating-point multiplier consists of a significand multiplier and an exponent adder that together compute $2^e s$, with $e = e1 + e2$ and $s = s1 \times s2$. The result's sign is easily obtained from the signs of the operands. This is not all, however. With $s1$ and $s2$ in $[1, 2)$, their product will lie in $[1, 4)$ and may thus be outside the permitted range for a significand. If the product of the two significands is in $[2, 4)$, dividing it by 2 via a 1-bit right shift will put it back into the desired range. When this *normalization* is needed, the exponent e must be incremented by 1 to compensate for the halving of s.

Floating-point division is similar and is governed by the equation

$$(\pm 2^{e1}s1)/(\pm 2^{e2}s2) = \pm 2^{e1-e2}(s1/s2)$$

Again, given that the ratio $s1/s2$ of the two significands lies in $(0.5, 2)$, normalization may be required for results that are less than 1. This normalization consists of multiplying the significand by 2 via a 1-bit left shift and decrementing the resulting exponent by 1 to compensate for the doubling of the significand. Of course, throughout the operation and ensuing adjustments, for both multiplication and division, the hardware must check for exceptions such as *overflow* (exponent too large) and *underflow* (exponent too small).

Square-rooting is also quite simple and can be converted to extracting the square root of s or $2s$ and a simple right shift of the exponent via the following rules:

$$(2^e s)^{1/2} = 2^{e/2}(s)^{1/2} \qquad \text{when } e \text{ is even}$$
$$= 2^{(e-1)/2}(2s)^{1/2} \quad \text{when } e \text{ is odd}$$

Note that both $e/2$ for e even and $(e-1)/2$ for e odd are easily formed through a 1-bit right shift of e. Also, both $s^{1/2}$ and $(2s)^{1/2}$ are already normalized and no postnormalization is required (why?).

Besides the arithmetic operations discussed thus far, a number of conversions are needed for floating-point computations. The first type of conversion is from input values (usually supplied in decimal) to the internal floating-point representation. These conversions must be performed in such a way that the result is properly rounded; that is, it is the closest possible floating-point number to the actual input value. The inverse conversion, from the internal floating-point format to decimal format, is clearly needed for output.

Other conversions that are of interest pertain to changing from one floating-point format to another (single to double or vice versa) or between floating-point and integer formats. For example, single-to-double conversion is needed when outputs of a single-precision program must be further processed by another program that expects double-precision inputs. The reverse conversion, from double to single, is somewhat trickier because it requires rounding of the wider significand and checking for possible overflow.

12.5 Floating-Point Instructions

The floating-point unit in MiniMIPS is a separate coprocessor (Figure 5.1) with its own registers and arithmetic unit capable of performing floating-point operations. There are 32 floating-point registers that are named $f0 to $f31. Unlike registers in the CPU's general register file, there is no convention for using the floating-point registers, and no register is dedicated to holding the constant 0; the 32 floating-point registers are truly general-purpose units in this respect. The MiniMIPS floating-point instructions are divided into four categories of arithmetic operations, format conversions, data transfers, and conditional branches.

There are 10 floating-point arithmetic instructions consisting of five different operations (add, subtract, multiply, divide, negate), each with single or double operands. Each of these instructions in assembly language consists of its operation name, followed by a dot (ignore or read "float") and the letter "s" (for single) or "d" (for double). Single operands can be in any of the floating-point registers, while double operands must be specified to be in even-numbered registers (they occupy the specified register and the next one in sequence, for the upper and lower half of the long floating-point number, respectively). Here are some example floating-point arithmetic instructions:

```
add.s    $f0,$f8,$f10      # set $f0 to ($f8) +fp ($f10)
sub.d    $f0,$f8,$f10      # set $f0 to ($f8) -fp ($f10)
mul.d    $f0,$f8,$f10      # set $f0 to ($f8) ×fp ($f10)
div.s    $f0,$f8,$f10      # set $f0 to ($f8) /fp ($f10)
neg.s    $f0,$f8           # set $f0 to -($f8)
```

The first instruction is read "add (float) single" and the third one "multiply (float) double." The "float" part is optional because "single" and "double" imply that floating-point operations are meant. The format for these five pairs of MiniMIPS instructions is shown in Figure 12.7.

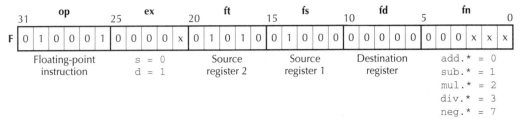

Figure 12.7 The common floating-point instruction format for MiniMIPS and components for arithmetic instructions. The extension (ex) field distinguishes single (* = s) from double (* = d) operands.

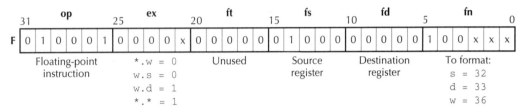

Figure 12.8 Floating-point instructions for format conversion in MiniMIPS.

There are six format conversion instructions: integer to single/double, single to double, double to single, and single/double to integer. As before, single operands can be in any of the floating-point registers, while double operands must be specified to be in even-numbered registers. Here are some example format conversion instructions:

```
cvt.s.w $f0,$f8      # set $f0 to single(integer $f8)
cvt.d.w $f0,$f8      # set $f0 to double(integer $f8)
cvt.d.s $f0,$f8      # set $f0 to double($f8)
cvt.s.d $f0,$f8      # set $f0 to single($f8,$f9)
cvt.w.s $f0,$f8      # set $f0 to integer($f8)
cvt.w.d $f0,$f8      # set $f0 to integer($f8,$f9)
```

In these instructions, integer is designated as "w" (for word), while single and double have the usual symbols "s" and "d," respectively. Note that the destination format appears first, so that the first instruction above is read "convert to (float) single from integer." The format for these six MiniMIPS instructions is shown in Figure 12.8.

MiniMIPS has six data transfer instructions: load/store word to/from coprocessor 1, move single/double from one floating-point register to another, and move (copy) between floating-point registers and CPU general registers. Typical usage of these instructions is as follows:

```
lwc1    $f8,40($s3)      # load mem[40+($s3)] into $f8
swc1    $f8,A($s3)       # store ($f8) into mem[A+($s3)]
mov.s   $f0,$f8          # load $f0 with ($f8)
mov.d   $f0,$f8          # load $f0,$f1 with ($f8,$f9)
mfc1    $t0,$f12         # load $t0 with ($f12)
mtc1    $f8,$t4          # load $f8 with ($t4)
```

The first two instructions have the same format as lw and sw, shown in Figure 5.7 (i.e., I format), except that the op field contains 49 for lwc1 and 50 for swc1 and the data register

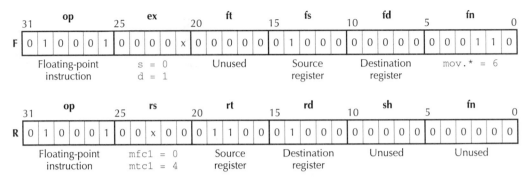

Figure 12.9 Instructions for floating-point data movement in MiniMIPS.

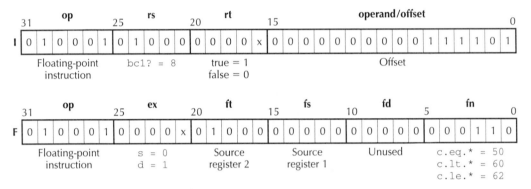

Figure 12.10 Floating-point branch and comparison instructions in MiniMIPS.

specified in the `rt` field is a floating-point register. The middle two instructions are F-format instructions that allow single or double floating-point values to be transferred from one floating-point register to another (Figure 12.9). Note that general registers do not have such a move instruction because its effect can be achieved through adding ($0) to the source register and storing the result in the destination register. Given that floating-point addition is a much slower operation than integer addition, it would have been rather wasteful to follow the same strategy here. Finally, the last two instructions are R-format instructions, as shown in Figure 12.9. They allow transfer of words between floating-point and general CPU registers.

The final set of MiniMIPS instructions related to the floating-point unit consists of two branch and six comparison instructions. The floating-point unit has a condition flag that is set to "true" or "false" by any one of six comparison instructions: three comparison types (equal, less than, less or equal) for two data types (single, double). The two instructions "branch on floating-point true/false" allow conditional branching to be based on the status of this flag.

```
bc1t    L                # branch on fp flag true
bc1f    L                # branch on fp flag false
c.eq.*  $f0,$f8          # if ($f0)=($f8), set flag to "true"
c.lt.*  $f0,$f8          # if ($f0)<($f8), set flag to "true"
c.le.*  $f0,$f8          # if ($f0)≤($f8), set flag to "true"
```

Figure 12.10 depicts the machine representations of these instructions. Table 12.1 lists all the MiniMIPS floating-point instructions covered in this section.

TABLE 12.1 The 30 MiniMIPS floating-point instructions: because the op field contains 17 fc
tions (49 for lwc1 and 50 for swc1), it is not shown.

Class	Instruction	Usage	Meaning		
Copy	Move s/d registers	mov.* fd,fs	fd ← fs		
	Move fm coprocessor 1	mfc1 rt,rd	rt ← rd; move f		
	Move to coprocessor 1	mtc1 rd,rt	rd ← rt; move C. ᵕ reg to fp	4	
Arithmetic	Add single/double	add.* fd,fs,ft	fd ← (fs) + (ft)	#	0
	Subtract single/double	sub.* fd,fs,ft	fd ← (fs) − (ft)	#	1
	Multiply single/double	mul.* fd,fs,ft	fd ← (fs) × (ft)	#	2
	Divide single/double	div.* fd,fs,ft	fd ← (fs) / (ft)	#	3
	Negate single/double	neg.* fd,fs	fd ← −(fs); change sign bit	#	7
	Compare equal s/d	c.eq.* fs,ft	if (fs) = (ft), set fp flag to true	#	50
	Compare less s/d	c.lt.* fs,ft	if (fs) < (ft), set fp flag to true	#	60
	Compare less or equal s/d	c.le.* fs,ft	if (fs) ≤ (ft), set fp flag to true	#	62
Conversion	Convert integer to single	cvt.s.w fd,fs	fd ← sflp(fs); (fs) is integer	0	32
	Convert integer to double	cvt.d.w fd,fs	fd ← dflp(fs); (fs) is integer	0	33
	Convert single to double	cvt.d.s fd,fs	fd ← dflp(fs); even fd	1	33
	Convert double to single	cvt.s.d fd,fs	fd ← dflp(fs); even fs	1	32
	Convert single to integer	cvt.w.s fd,fs	fd ← int(fs)	0	36
	Convert double to integer	cvt.w.d fd,fs	fd ← int(fs); even fs	1	36
Memory access	Load word coprocessor 1	lwc1 ft,imm(rs)	ft ← mem[(rs) + imm]	rs	
	Store word coprocessor 1	swc1 ft,imm(rs)	mem[(rs) + imm] ← (ft)	rs	
Control transfer	Branch coprocessor 1 true	bc1t L	if (fp flag) = "true", goto L	8	
	Branch coprocessor 1 false	bc1f L	if (fp flag) = "false", goto L	8	

* is s/d for single/double
# is 0/1 for single/double

Note that even though an instruction that compares floating-point values for equality is provided, it is best to avoid using it wherever possible. The reason is that floating-point results are
inexact; thus if we evaluate the same function in two different ways, say as $ab + ac$ or
$a(b + c)$, we may get slightly different results. This is elaborated upon in Section 12.6.

12.6 Result Precision and Errors

Results of floating-point computations are inexact for two reasons. First, many numbers do not
have exact binary representations within a finite word format. This is referred to as *representation error*. Second, even for values that are exactly representable, floating-point arithmetic
produces inexact results. For example, the exactly computed product of two short floating-
point numbers will have a 48-bit significand that must be rounded to fit in 23 bits (plus the
hidden 1). The latter is characterized as *computation error*. It is important both for the designers of arithmetic circuits and for the users of machine arithmetic to be mindful of these errors
and to learn methods for estimating and controlling them. There are documented instances of
arithmetic errors leading to disasters in computer-controlled critical systems. Even a small
per-operation error of 0.5 *ulp*, when compounded over many millions, perhaps billions, of operations needed in some applications, can lead to highly inaccurate or totally incorrect results.

We limit our discussion of errors, their sources, and countermeasures to a few examples.
Collectively, these examples show that despite its obvious advantages, floating-point arithmetic can be quite dangerous and must thus be used with proper care.

Example 12.4: Violation of laws of algebra in floating-point arithmetic   In algebra, the two expressions $(a + b) + c$ and $a + (b + c)$ are equivalent. This is known as the *associative law of addition*. By evaluating these two expressions for the operands $a = -2^5 \times (1.10101011)_{two}$, $b = 2^5 \times (1.10101110)_{two}$, and $c = -2^{-2} \times (1.01100101)_{two}$, using the rules of floating-point arithmetic, show that the associative law of addition does not hold in general for floating-point arithmetic.

Solution: Steps of the computation $(a + b) + c$, and its final result $2^{-6} \times (1.10110000)_{two}$ are shown in Figure 12.11a. The computation $a + (b + c)$, on the other hand, leads to the final result of 0, as shown in Figure 12.11b. The second computation is less precise because during its course, some of the bits of $b + c$ are rounded off, whereas no such loss occurs in the first computation. Generally speaking, significant digits are lost owing to preshifting whenever operands with different exponents are added. These lost digits, which are relatively unimportant to the accuracy of the result of that particular step, may later become crucial owing to cancellation of most or all of the remaining digits when a subtraction with comparable operand magnitudes is performed.

Numbers to be added first

```
a    =-2⁵  × 1.10101011
b    = 2⁵  × 1.10101110
```

Compute $a + b$

```
       2⁵  × 0.00000011
a+b = 2⁻²  × 1.10000000
  c =-2⁻²  × 1.01100101
```

Compute $(a + b) + c$

```
     2⁻²  × 0.00011011
Sum = 2⁻⁶  × 1.10110000
```

(a) $(a +_{fp} b) +_{fp} c$

Numbers to be added first

```
b    = 2⁵  × 1.10101110
c    =-2⁻² × 1.01100101
```

Compute $b + c$ (after preshifting c)

```
        2⁵  × 1.1010101100011011
b+c =  2⁵  × 1.10101011  (Round)
  a  =-2⁵  × 1.10101011
```

Compute $a + (b + c)$

```
     2⁵  × 0.00000000
Sum =  0  (Normalize to special code for 0)
```

(b) $a +_{fp} (b +_{fp} c)$

Figure 12.11 Algebraically equivalent computations may yield different results with floating-point arithmetic.

One way to avoid excessive error accumulation is to carry extra precision in the course of a computation. Even inexpensive calculators use extra digits that are invisible to the user but help ensure greater accuracy for the results. Without these *guard digits,* the computation of 1/3 will produce 0.333 333 333 3, assuming a 10-digit calculator. Multiplying this value by 3 will yield 0.999 999 999 9, instead of the expected 1. In a calculator with two guard digits, the value of 1/3 is evaluated and stored as 0.333 333 333 333, but still displayed as 0.333 333 333 3. If we now multiply the stored value by 3, and use rounding to derive the result to be displayed, the expected value 1 will be obtained.

Use of guard digits improves the accuracy of floating-point arithmetic but does not totally eliminate some incorrect and highly surprising results such as the violation of the associative law of addition discussed in Example 12.4. Many other laws of algebra do not hold for floating-point arithmetic, causing difficulties in result predictability and certification. An optimizing compiler that switches the order of evaluation for the sake of computation speedup may inadvertently change the result obtained!

One of the sources of difficulties is loss of precision that occurs when subtraction is performed with operands of comparable magnitudes. Such a subtraction produces a result that is close to 0, making the effect of previous rounding operations performed on the operands quite significant in relative terms. Such an event is referred to as *catastrophic cancellation*. For example, when the algebraically correct equation

$$A = [s(s-a)(s-b)(s-c)]^{1/2}$$

with $s = (a+b+c)/2$, is used to calculate the area of a needlelike triangle (a triangle for which one side a is approximately equal to the sum $b+c$ of the other two sides), a large error can be produced owing to the catastrophic cancellation in computing $s-a$. A user or programmer who is aware of this problem can use an alternate formula that is not prone to producing such large errors.

Because of the anomalies and surprises associated with floating-point arithmetic, there is some interest in *certifiable arithmetic*. An example is offered by *interval arithmetic* whereby each number is represented by a pair of values, a lower bound and an upper bound. We represent x by the interval $[x_l, x_u]$ if we are certain that $x_l \le x \le x_u$. Given interval representations of x and y, arithmetic operations can be defined in such a way as to ensure containment of the result in the interval that is produced as output. For example:

$$[x_l, x_u] +_{\text{interval}} [y_l, y_u] = [x_l +_{\text{fp}\nabla} y_l, x_u +_{\text{fp}\Delta} y_u]$$

The subscripts "interval," "fp∇," and "fpΔ" in the preceding expression qualify the operations as "interval addition," "floating-point addition with downward rounding," and "floating-point addition with upward rounding." This is one place where the downward- and upward-directed rounding modes come in handy. With interval arithmetic, we always have a guaranteed error bound and will know when a result is too imprecise to be trusted.

The ultimate in result certification is *exact arithmetic,* which may be feasible in some applications through the use of *rational numbers* or other forms of exact representation. For example, if each value is represented by a sign and a pair of integers for the numerator and denominator, then numbers such as 1/3 will have exact representations and an expression such as $(1/3) \times 3$ will always produce the exact result. However, besides limited applicability, exact rational arithmetic also implies significant hardware and/or time overhead.

In many numeric calculations, there is a need to evaluate functions such as logarithm, sine, or tangent. One approach to function evaluation is the use of an *approximating function* that is easier to evaluate than the original function. Polynomial approximations, derived from Taylor-series and other expansions, allow function evaluation by means of addition, multiplication, and division. Here are a few examples:

$$\ln x = 2(z + z^3/3 + z^5/5 + z^7/7 + \cdots) \quad \text{where } z = (x-1)/(x+1)$$
$$e^x = 1 + x/1! + x^2/2! + x^3/3! + x^4/4! + \cdots$$
$$\cos x = 1 - x^2/2! + x^4/4! - x^6/6! + x^8/8! - \cdots$$
$$\tan^{-1} x = x - x^3/3 + x^5/5 - x^7/7 + x^9/9 - \cdots$$

A second approach is *convergence computation*: begin with a suitable approximation and proceed to refine the value with iterative evaluation. For example, if $q^{(0)}$ is an approximation to

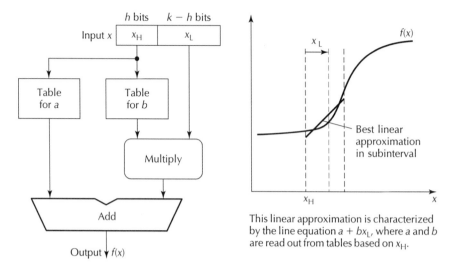

Figure 12.12 Function evaluation by table lookup and linear interpolation.

the square root of x, the following recurrence can be used to refine the value, using one addition, one division, and a 1-bit right shift per iteration:

$$q^{(i+1)} = 0.5\big(q^{(i)} + x/q^{(i)}\big)$$

The initial approximation can be obtained via table lookup based on a few high-order bits of x; alternatively, it can simply be taken to be a constant.

With both series expansion and convergence computation, several floating-point operations are needed for deriving one function value. This value will have an error that may be quite large because in the worst case, the small errors committed in various computation steps add up (they are in the same direction). Such errors are carefully analyzed, and bounds for them are established, in an effort to guarantee reasonable accuracy for function evaluation as part of widely available program libraries.

An alternative to the use of long computation sequences is the use of tables of precomputed values. These tables are then consulted whenever function values for given input arguments are needed. Of course, a table holding the values of sin x for all possible double or even single floating-point inputs x would be impractically large. For this reason, a mixed approach involving much smaller tables and a few arithmetic operations is often preferred. This mixed approach is based on the fact that within a reasonably narrow interval $[x^{(i)}, x^{(i+1)})$, an arbitrary function $f(x)$ can be approximated by the linear function $a + b(x - x^{(i)})$. This *interpolation scheme* leads to the hardware implementation depicted in Figure 12.12. The range of x values is divided into 2^h intervals based on the h high-order bits of x, which define the value x_H. For each of these intervals $[x_H, x_H + 2^{-h})$, the corresponding a and b values of the approximating linear function $a + b(x - x_H) = a + bx_L$ are stored in two tables. Function evaluation with this method thus involves two table accesses, one multiplication, and one addition.

PROBLEMS

12.1 Rounding modes

Represent each of the values 1/3, 1/4, and 1/5 in the ANSI/IEEE short format, rounding inexact values:

a. To nearest value
b. To nearest even
c. Inward
d. Downward
e. Upward

12.2 Rounding modes

This problem is a continuation of Example 12.1.

a. Draw new versions of the diagrams in Figure 12.2 if values in the range $[-4, 4]$ are to be rounded to fixed-point binary format with one fractional bit.
b. Plot the round-to-nearest-odd-integer function $rtnoi(x)$ for x in $[-4, 4]$.
c. Show that $rtnoi(x)$ is easier to implement in hardware than $rtnei(x)$ in the sense that only the LSB is affected during the rounding process.
d. Jamming, or von Neumann rounding, is performed by discarding any extra bits and forcing the LSB of the remaining part to 1. The process is almost as easy as simple chopping. Compare this rounding mode with chopping and those in parts a–c in terms of the errors introduced.

12.3 Rounding modes

This problem is a continuation of Example 12.2.

a. Draw new versions of the diagrams in Figure 12.3 if values in the range $[-4, 4]$ are to be rounded to fixed-point binary format with one fractional bit.
b. Plot the round-downward-to-nearest-integer function $rdtni(x)$ for x in $[-4, 4]$.
c. Compare these three directed rounding modes with simple chopping and round-to-nearest modes in terms of the errors introduced.

12.4 Operations on special values

For each of the following floating-point operations, draw a 5×5 table, labeling the rows and columns with the special values $-\infty, -0, +0, +\infty$, NaN. In each box, write down the result of the given operation when applied to the operands labeling the corresponding row and column. For example, in the case of $+_{\text{fp}}$, the entry for row $+\infty$ and column $-\infty$ should be NaN.

a. Addition
b. Subtraction
c. Multiplication
d. Division

12.5 Floating-point operations

Show the results of the following floating-point operations. Justify your answers.

a. $min +_{\text{fp}} max$
b. $min -_{\text{fp}} max$
c. $min \times_{\text{fp}} max$
d. $min /_{\text{fp}} max$
e. $(min)^{1/2}$

12.6 Floating-point operations

Represent each of the decimal operands in the following expressions in the ANSI/IEEE short floating-point format. Then, perform the operation and derive the result using the round-to-nearest-even rounding mode.

a. $1.5 +_{\text{fp}} 2^{-23}$
b. $1.0 -_{\text{fp}} (1.5 \times 2^{-23})$
c. $(1 + 2^{-11}) \times_{\text{fp}} (1 + 2^{-12})$
d. $2^5 /_{\text{fp}} (2 - 2^{-23})$
e. $(1 + 2^{-23})^{1/2}$

12.7 Toy floating-point format

Consider a toy 8-bit floating-point format with a sign bit, a 4-bit exponent field, and a 3-bit significand field. Exponents 0000 and 1111 are reserved for special values, and the rest are used to encode exponents -7 (0001) to $+6$ (1110). The exponent base is 2. The significand has a hidden 1 to the left of the radix point, with the 3-bit field constituting its fractional part.

a. What is the exponent bias in the floating-point format defined?
b. Determine the largest (max) and smallest nonzero (min) values represented.
c. Excluding the special values, how many different values are represented with this format?

d. Represent the numbers $x = 0.5$ and $y = -2$ in this format.

e. Compute the sum $x + y$ using the rules of floating-point arithmetic. Show all the steps.

12.8 Floating-point operations

Represent each of the decimal operands in the following expressions in the ANSI/IEEE short floating-point format. Then, perform the operation and derive the result in the same format, normalizing if necessary.

a. $(+41.0 \times 2^{+0}) \times_{fp} (+0.875 \times 2^{-16})$
b. $(-4.5 \times 2^{-1}) /_{fp} (+0.0625 \times 2^{+12})$
c. $(+1.125 \times 2^{+11})^{1/2}$
d. $(+1.25 \times 2^{-10}) +_{fp} (+0.5 \times 2^{+11})$
e. $(-1.5 \times 2^{-11}) -_{fp} (+0.0625 \times 2^{-10})$

12.9 Floating-point representations

Consider the ANSI/IEEE short floating-point format.

a. Ignoring $\pm\infty$, ± 0, NaN, and denormals, how many distinct real numbers are representable?
b. What is the minimum number of bits needed to represents this many distinct values? What is the encoding or representation efficiency of this format?
c. Discuss the consequences (in terms of range and precision) of shortening the exponent field by 2 bits and adding 2 bits to the significand field.
d. Repeat part d, this time assuming that the exponent base is increased from 2 to 16.

12.10 Fixed- vs floating-point

Find the largest value of n for which $n!$ can be represented exactly in the following 32-bit formats. Explain the counterintuitive result.

a. Two's-complement integer format
b. The ANSI/IEEE short format

12.11 Floating-point exceptions

a. Give examples of ANSI/IEEE short-format numbers x and y such that they lead to overflow in the rounding stage of the operation $x +_{fp} y$.
b. Repeat part a for $x \times_{fp} y$.
c. Show that rounding overflow is impossible in the normalization phase of floating-point division.

12.12 Rounding to nearest even

This example shows one advantage of rounding to nearest even over ordinary rounding. All numbers are decimal. Consider the floating-point numbers $u = .100 \times 10^0$ and $v = -.555 \times 10^{-1}$. Start with $u^{(0)} = u$ and use the recurrence $u^{(i+1)} = (u^{(i)} -_{fp} v) +_{fp} v$ to compute $u^{(1)}, u^{(2)}$, and so on.

a. Show that with ordinary rounding, successive values of u will be different, an occurrence known as *drift*.
b. Verify that drift does not occur in our example if we round to nearest even.

12.13 Double rounding

Consider the multiplication of two-digit, single-precision decimal values .34 and .78, yielding .2652. If we round this exact result to an internal three-digit format, we get .265, which when subsequently rounded to single-precision by means of round-to-nearest even, produces .26. However, if the exact result were directly rounded to single precision, it would yield .27. Can double-rounding lead to a similar problem if we always round up the halfway cases instead of using the round-to-nearest-even mode?

12.14 Rounding of ternary numbers

If we had ternary as opposed to binary computers, radix-3 arithmetic would be in common use today. Discuss the effects such a change would have on rounding in floating-point arithmetic. *Hint:* What happens to midway cases, or to numbers that are equally spaced from the floating-point numbers on either side?

12.15 Computation errors

Consider the sequence $\{u^{(i)}\}$ defined by the recurrence $u^{(i+1)} = i \times u^{(i)} - i$, with $u^{(1)} = e$.

a. Use a calculator or write a program to determine the values of $u^{(i)}$ for i in [1, 25].
b. Repeat part a with a different calculator or with a different precision in your program.
c. Explain the results.

12.16 Interval arithmetic

You are given the decimal floating-point numbers
$u = .100 \times 10^0$ and $v = -.555 \times 10^{-1}$.

a. Use interval arithmetic to compute the mean of x
   and y via the expression $(x +_{fp} y)/_{fp} 2$.
b. Repeat part a, but use the expression
   $x +_{fp} [(y -_{fp} x)/_{fp} 2]$. Explain any difference
   with part a.
c. Use interval arithmetic to compute the expression
   $(x \times_{fp} x) -_{fp} (y \times_{fp} y)$.
d. Repeat part c, but use the expression
   $(x -_{fp} y) \times_{fp} (x +_{fp} y)$. Explain any difference
   with part c.

12.17 Floating-point performance

In Chapter 4, MFLOPS was suggested as a measure
of computer performance for floating-point-intensive
applications. In this part of the book, we learned that
some arithmetic operations are intrinsically more
difficult, and thus slower, than others. For example,
two machines exhibiting the same MFLOPS
performance on two different applications may have
substantially different computational powers if one
application performs only floating-point additions
and multiplications while the other one has a heavy
dose of divisions, square-rooting, and exponentiation.
To make the comparison fairer, it has been suggested
that each addition/subtraction (including comparison)
or multiplication be counted as 1 operation, each
division or square-rooting as 4 operations, and each
exponentiation or other function evaluation as
8 operations. For an application that executes
200 billion floating-point operations in 100 seconds,
with the number of different operations, in billions,
given within parentheses, compute the MFLOPS
rating without and with the weightings suggested. The
operation mix is load (77), store (23), copy (4), add
(41), subtract (21), multiply (32), divide (1), other
functions (1). State all your assumptions clearly.

REFERENCES AND FURTHER READINGS

[Etie02]   Etiemble, D., "Computer Arithmetic and Hardware: 'Off the Shelf' Microprocessors
            versus 'Custom Hardware,'" *Theoretical Computer Science,* Vol. 279, Nos. 1–2,
            pp. 3–27, May 2002.

[Gold91]   Goldberg, D., "What Every Computer Scientist Should Know About Floating-Point
            Arithmetic," *ACM Computing Surveys,* Vol. 23, No. 1, pp. 5–48, March 1991.

[IEEE85]   *ANSI/IEEE Standard 754-1985 for Binary Floating-Point Arithmetic,* available from
            IEEE Press.

[Knut97]   Knuth, D. E., *The Art of Computer Programming,* Vol. 2: *Seminumerical Algorithms,*
            Addison-Wesley, 3rd ed., 1997.

[Parh00]   Parhami, B., *Computer Arithmetic: Algorithms and Hardware Designs,* Oxford
            University Press, 2000.

[Parh02]   Parhami, B., "Number Representation and Computer Arithmetic," in *Encyclopedia of
            Information Systems,* Academic Press, 2002, Vol. 3, pp. 317–333.

[Patt98]   Patterson, D. A., and J. L. Hennessy, *Computer Organization and Design: The
            Hardware/Software Interface,* Morgan Kaufmann, 2nd ed., 1998.

[Ster74]   Sterbenz, P. H., *Floating-Point Computation,* Prentice-Hall, 1974.

[Swar90]   Swartzlander, E. E., Jr, *Computer Arithmetic,* Vols. I and II, IEEE Computer Society
            Press, 1990.

PART FOUR

DATA PATH AND CONTROL

"Truth is a river that is always splitting up into arms that reunite. Islanded between the arms, the inhabitants argue for a lifetime as to which is the main river."
—*Cyril Connolly*

"Computers can figure out all kinds of problems, except the things in the world that just don't add up."
—*Anonymous*

The data path is the part of a CPU through which data signals flow as they are manipulated according to the instruction's definition (e.g., from two registers, through the ALU, and back to a register). The simplest computers have a linear data path that is used for all instructions, with control signals determining the action, or lack thereof, in each part of the path. This uniformity simplifies the hardware's design and implementation. More advanced computers have data paths that branch out, thus allowing concurrent execution of instructions in different parts of the datapath. The control unit is responsible for guiding the data signals along the data path, indicating to each part what transformation, if any, is to be performed on data elements as they pass through.

After choosing a small subset of MiniMIPS instructions to make our discussion and hardware implementation diagrams manageable, we embark on a simple data path and associated single-cycle control in Chapter 13. In Chapter 14, we show that multicycle control allows for more flexibility, as well as potentially greater performance and efficiency. Virtually all modern processors use pipelining to achieve greater performance. This topic is discussed in the second half of Part 4, with basics of pipelining covered in Chapter 15 and complications (along with solutions to avoid loss of performance) presented in Chapter 16.

13

INSTRUCTION EXECUTION STEPS

"In a mechanical computer [the overhead of administrative instructions] would have been only too obvious to the bystander and if Babbage had hit on the stored program principle, he would undoubtedly have rejected it for that reason. With electronics, what the eye does not see, the heart does not grieve over."

—*Maurice Wilkes, Computing Perspectives*

"For entry into the operating room, emergency patients please follow these steps: (1) Swipe credit card, (2) Choose operation from menu, (3) Wait for authorization."

—*Anonymous, Fictitious hospital sign*

TOPICS IN THIS CHAPTER
13.1 A Small Set of Instructions
13.2 The Instruction Execution Unit
13.3 A Single-Cycle Data Path
13.4 Branching and Jumping
13.5 Deriving the Control Signals
13.6 Performance of the Single-Cycle Design

The simplest digital computers execute instructions one by one, following a control flow from a completed instruction to the next one in sequence, unless explicitly directed to alter this flow (by a branch or jump instruction) or to terminate instruction execution. Thus, such a computer can be viewed as being in a loop, each iteration of which leads to the completion of one instruction. Part of the instruction execution process, which begins by fetching the instruction from memory at the address given in the program counter, is determining where the next instruction is located and updating the program counter accordingly. In this chapter, we examine instruction execution steps in such a simple computer. We will see later that to achieve higher performance, this naive approach must be substantially modified.

■ 13.1 A Small Set of Instructions

The CPU data path and control unit designs presented in Chapters 13–16 are based on the MiniMIPS instruction-set architecture introduced in Part II. To make the design problem manageable, and our diagrams and tables less cluttered, we base our hardware realizations on a 22-instruction version of MiniMIPS, which we call "MicroMIPS." The MicroMIPS instruction set is virtually identical to that in Table 5.1 at the end of Chapter 5, with the only differences being the inclusion of jal and syscall instructions from Table 6.2. The latter pair of instructions turn MicroMIPS into a complete computer that can run simple, yet useful, programs. To make this chapter self-contained and also for ease of reference, the complete MicroMIPS instruction set is listed in Table 13.1. Handling of the remaining MiniMIPS instructions, given in Table 6.2 at the end of Chapter 6, forms the subjects of several end-of-chapter problems.

Also for reference, we reproduce in Figure 13.1 a more compact version of Figure 5.4, that shows the R, I, and J instruction formats and their various fields. Recall that in arithmetic and logic instructions with two register source operands, rd specifies the destination register. For ALU-type instructions with an immediate operand or for the load word instruction, the rd field becomes part of the 16-bit immediate operand. In this case, rt designates the destination register. Note that because there is no shift instruction in MicroMIPS, the sh (shift amount) filed is unused.

■ **TABLE 13.1** The MicroMIPS instruction set.*

Class	Instruction	Usage		Meaning	op	fn
Copy	Load upper immediate	lui	rt,imm	rt ← (imm, 0x0000)	15	
	Add	add	rd,rs,rt	rd ← (rs) + (rt)	0	32
	Subtract	sub	rd,rs,rt	rd ← (rs) − (rt)	0	34
Arithmetic	Set less than	slt	rd,rs,rt	rd ← if (rs) < (rd) then 1 else 0	0	42
	Add immediate	addi	rt,rs,imm	rt ← (rs) + imm	8	
	Set less than immediate	slti	rt,rs,imm	rt ← if (rs) < imm then 1 else 0	10	
	AND	and	rd,rs,rt	rd ← (rs) ∧ (rt)	0	36
	OR	or	rd,rs,rt	rd ← (rs) ∨ (rt)	0	37
	XOR	xor	rd,rs,rt	rd ← (rs) ⊕ (rt)	0	38
Logic	NOR	nor	rd,rs,rt	rd ← ((rs) ∨ (rt))'	0	39
	AND immediate	andi	rt,rs,imm	rt ← (rs) ∧ imm	12	
	OR immediate	ori	rt,rs,imm	rt ← (rs) ∨ imm	13	
	XOR immediate	xori	rt,rs,imm	rt ← (rs) ⊕ imm	14	
Memory access	Load word	lw	rt,imm(rs)	rt ← mem[(rs) + imm]	35	
	Store word	sw	rt,imm(rs)	mem[(rs) + imm] ← (rt)	43	
	Jump	j	L	goto L	2	
	Jump register	jr	rs	goto (rs)	0	8
	Branch on less than 0	bltz	rs,L	if (rs) < 0 then goto L	1	
Control transfer	Branch on equal	beq	rs,rt,L	if (rs) = (rt) then goto L	4	
	Branch on not equal	bne	rs,rt,L	if (rs) ≠ (rt) then goto L	5	
	Jump and link	jal	L	goto L; $31 ← (PC) + 4	3	
	System call	syscall		See Section 7.6 (Table 7.2)	0	12

*Note: Except for jal and syscall instructions at the bottom which turn MicroMIPS into a complete computer, this table is the same as Table 5.1.

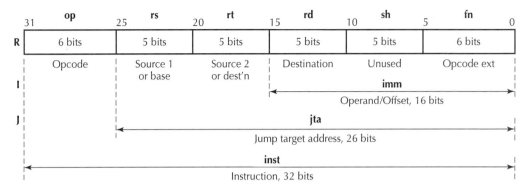

Figure 13.1 MicroMIPS instruction formats and naming of the various fields.

The instructions in Table 13.1 can be divided into five categories with respect to the steps needed for their execution:

Seven R-format ALU instructions (add, sub, slt, and, or, xor, nor)

Six I-format ALU instructions (lui, addi, slti, andi, ori, xori)

Two I-format memory access instructions (lw, sw)

Three I-format conditional branch instructions (bltz, beq, bne)

Four unconditional jump instructions (j, jr, jal, syscall)

The seven R-format ALU instructions have the following common execution sequence:

1. Read out the contents of source registers rs and rt and forward them as inputs to the ALU.
2. Tell the ALU what operation to perform.
3. Write the output of the ALU in destination register rd.

Five of the six I-format ALU instructions require steps similar to the three just listed, except that the contents of rs and the immediate value in the instruction are forwarded as inputs to the ALU and the result is stored in rt (rather than rd). The only exception is lui, which needs only the immediate operand, but even in this case, reading out the content of rs will do no harm, as the ALU can simply ignore it. The preceding discussion covers 13 of the 21 MicroMIPS instructions.

The execution sequence for the two I-format memory access instructions is as follows:

1. Read out the content of rs.
2. Add the number read out from rs to the immediate value in the instruction to form a memory address.
3. Read from or write into memory at the specified address.
4. In the case of lw, place the word read out from memory into rt.

Note that the first two steps of this sequence are identical to those of the I-format ALU instructions, as is the last step of lw, involving the writing of a value in rt (only data read from memory, rather than the result computed by the ALU, is written).

The final set of instructions in Table 13.1 deals with conditional or unconditional transfer of control to an instruction other than the next one in sequence. Recall that branch target address is specified by an offset relative to the incremented program counter value, or (PC) + 4. Therefore, if the intent of the branch is to skip the next instruction conditionally, the offset value +1 will appear in the immediate field of the branch instruction. This is because the offset is specified in terms of words relative to the memory address (PC) + 4. On the other hand, to branch back to the previous instruction, the offset value supplied in the immediate field of the instruction will be −2, which results in the branch target address (PC) + 4 − 2 × 4 = (PC) − 4.

For two of the three branch instructions (beq, bne), contents of rs and rt are compared to determine whether the branch condition is satisfied. If the condition holds, the immediate field is added to (PC) + 4 and the result is written back into PC; otherwise, (PC) + 4 is written back in PC. The remaining branch instruction, bltz, is similar, except that the branch decision is based on the sign bit of the content of rs rather than comparison of two register contents. For the four jump instructions, PC is unconditionally modified to allow the next instruction to be fetched from the jump target address. The jump target address comes from the instruction itself (j, jal), is read out from register rs (jr), or is a known constant associated with the location of an operating system routine (syscall). Note that even though syscall is in effect a jump instruction, it has an R format.

■ 13.2 The Instruction Execution Unit

MicroMIPS instructions can be executed in a hardware unit like the one whose structure and components are depicted in Figure 13.2. Beginning at the left end, the content of the program counter (PC) is supplied to the instruction cache and an instruction word is read out from the specified location. We will discuss cache memories in Chapter 18. For now, just view the instruction and data caches as small, extremely fast SRAM memory units that can keep up with the high speeds of the other components in Figure 13.2. As shown in Figure 2.10, an SRAM memory unit has data and address input ports and a data output port. The data input port of the instruction cache is not used within the data path and is thus not shown in Figure 13.2.

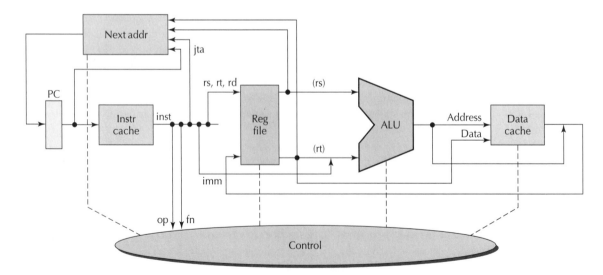

Figure 13.2 Abstract view of the instruction execution unit for MicroMIPS. For naming of instruction fields, see Figure 13.1.

Once an instruction has been read out from the instruction cache, its various fields are separated and each is dispatched to the appropriate place. For example, op and fn fields go to the control unit, whereas rs, rt, and rd are sent to the register file. The upper input of the ALU always comes from register rs, whereas its lower input can be either the content of rt or the immediate field of the instruction. For many instructions, the output of the ALU is stored in a register; in such cases, the data cache is bypassed. In the case of lw and sw instructions, the data cache is accessed, with the content of rt written into it for sw and its output sent to the register file for lw.

The register file in Figure 13.2 has a design similar to Figure 2.9b, with $h = 5$ and $k = 32$. Details of the register file implementation are depicted in Figure 2.9a. In one clock cycle, contents of any two (rs and rt) of the 32 registers can be read out through the read ports, while at the same time, a third register, not necessarily distinct from rs or rt, is being modified via the write port. The flip-flops constituting the registers are edge-triggered, so that reading from and writing into the same register in a single clock cycle does not cause a problem (see Figure 2.3). Recall that register $0 is a special register that always contains 0 and cannot be modified.

The ALU used for our MicroMIPS implementation has the same design as that shown in Figure 10.19, except that the shifter and its associated logic as well as the zero detection block (32-input NOR circuit) are not needed. The output of the shifter going into the final mux in Figure 10.19 can be replaced by the upper half of y (the lower ALU input), padded with 16 zeros at the right, to allow the implementation of the lui (load upper immediate) instruction. Treating lui as an ALU instruction leads to simplification in our execution unit because we do not need a separate path for writing the right-extended immediate value into the register file. Because the effect of lui can be viewed as logical left shift of the immediate value by 16 bit positions, using the shift option of the ALU for this instruction is not inappropriate.

To conclude our preliminary discussion of the instruction execution unit, we must specify the data flow associated with branch and jump instructions. For beq and bne instructions, contents of rs and rt are compared to determine whether the branch condition is satisfied. This comparison is performed within the "Next addr" box in Figure 13.2. In the case of bltz, the branch decision is based on the sign bit of the content of rs rather than comparison of two register contents. Again, this is done within the "Next addr" box, which is also responsible for choosing the jump target address under guidance from the control unit. Recall that the jump target address comes from the instruction itself (j, jal), is read out from register rs (jr), or is a known constant associated with the location of an operating system routine (syscall).

Note that some details are missing from Figure 13.2. For example, it is not shown how the register file is notified which register, if any, is to be written into (rd or rt). These details will be supplied in Section 13.3.

▣ 13.3 A Single-Cycle Data Path

We now begin the process of refining the abstract execution unit of Figure 13.2 until it has turned into a concrete logic circuit capable of executing all 22 MicroMIPS instructions. In this section, we ignore the "Next addr" and "Control" blocks of Figure 13.2 and focus on the middle part composed of the program counter, instruction cache, register file, ALU, and data cache. This part is known as the *data path*. The next address logic will be covered in Section 13.4 and the control circuit in Section 13.5.

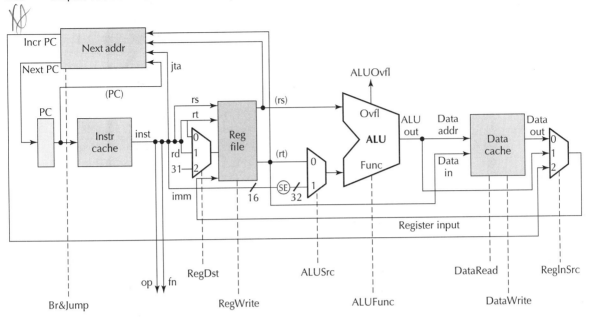

Figure 13.3 Key elements of the single-cycle MicroMIPS data path.

Figure 13.3 shows some the details of the data path that are missing from the abstract version in Figure 13.2. Everything that follows in this section is keyed to the data path portion of Figure 13.3 through which instruction execution steps proceed from left to right. We have already described the four main blocks that appear on this data path. Now we explain the function of the three multiplexers used at the input to the register file, at the lower input of the ALU, and at the outputs of the ALU and data cache. Grasping the roles played by these multiplexers is a key to understanding not only the data path of Figure 13.3 but any data path in general.

The multiplexer at the input to the register file allows rt, rd, or $31 to be used as the index of the destination register into which a result will be written. A pair of logic signals RegDst, supplied by the control unit, direct the selection. RegDst is set to 00 for selecting rt, 01 for rd, and 10 for $31; this last option is needed for executing jal. Of course, not every instruction writes a value into a register. Writing into a register requires that the Reg-Write control signal be asserted by the control unit; otherwise, regardless of the state of RegDst, nothing is written into the register file. Note that the two registers rs and rt are read out for every instruction, even though they may not be needed in all cases. Hence, no read control signal for the register file is shown. For the same reason, the instruction cache does not receive any control signal, because an instruction is read out in every cycle (i.e., the clock signal serves as read control for the instruction cache).

The multiplexer at the lower input to the ALU allows the control unit to choose the content of rt or the 32-bit sign-extended version of the 16-bit immediate operand to be used as the second ALU input (the first or top input always comes from rs). This is controlled by asserting or deasserting the control signal ALUSrc. If this signal is deasserted (has a value 0), the content of rt is used as the lower input to the ALU; otherwise, the immediate operand, sign-extended to 32 bits, is used. Sign extension of the immediate operand is performed by the circular block labeled "SE" in Figure 13.3. (See also Problem 13.17.)

Finally, the rightmost multiplexer in Figure 13.3 allows the word supplied by the data cache, output from the ALU, or the incremented PC value to be sent to the register file for writing (the last option is needed for `jal`). The choice is effected by a pair of control signals, RegInSrc, which are set to 00 for choosing the data cache output, 01 for the ALU output, and 10 for the incremented PC value coming from the next-address block.

The data path in Figure 13.3 is capable of executing one instruction per clock cycle; hence the name "single-cycle data path." With every clock tick, a new address is loaded into the program counter, causing a new instruction to appear at the output of the instruction cache after a short access delay. Contents of the various fields in the instruction are sent to the relevant blocks, including the control unit which decides (based on the `op` and `fn` fields) what operation is to be performed by each block.

As the data from `rs` and `rt`, or `rs` and sign-extended `imm`, pass through the ALU, the operation specified by the control signals ALUFunc is performed and the result eventually appears at the ALU output. Ignoring the shift-related control signals (Const'Var, Shift function) of Figure 10.19 that are not needed for MicroMIPS, the ALUFunc control signal bundle contains 5 bits: 1 bit for adder control (Add'Sub), 2 bits for controlling the logic unit (Logic function), and 2 bits for controlling the rightmost multiplexer in Figure 10.19 (Function class). The ALU output signal indicating overflow in addition or subtraction is shown in Figure 13.3, although it is not used in this chapter.

In the case of arithmetic and logic instructions, the ALU result must be stored in the destination register and is thus forwarded to the register file through the feedback path near the bottom of Figure 13.3. In the case of memory access instructions, the ALU output is a data address for writing into the data cache (DataWrite asserted) or reading from it (DataRead asserted). In the latter case, the data cache output, which appears after a short latency, is sent through the lower feedback path to the register file for writing. Finally, when the instruction executed is `jal`, the incremented program counter value, $(PC) + 4$, is stored in register $\$31$.

■ 13.4 Branching and Jumping

This section is devoted to the design of the next-address block that appears in the upper left part of Figure 13.3.

The next address to be loaded into the program counter is derived in one of five ways, depending on the instruction being executed and the contents of registers on which the branch condition is based. Because instructions are words stored in memory locations with addresses that are multiples of 4, the two LSBs of the program counter are always set to 0. Hence, in the following discussion, $(PC)_{31:2}$ refers to the upper 30 bits of the program counter which is the part of PC that is modified by the next-address logic. With this convention, adding 4 to the content of the program counter is done by computing $(PC)_{31:2} + 1$. Also, the immediate value, which by definition must be multiplied by 4 before being added to the incremented program counter value, is simply added to this upper part unchanged. The five options for the next $(PC)_{31:2}$ content are as follows:

$(PC)_{31:2} + 1$	Default option
$(PC)_{31:2} + 1 + \text{imm}$	When the instruction is a branch and the condition is met
$(PC)_{31:28} \mid \text{jta}$	When the instruction is `j` or `jal`
$(\text{rs})_{31:2}$	When the instruction is `jr`
SysCallAddr	Start address of an operating system routine

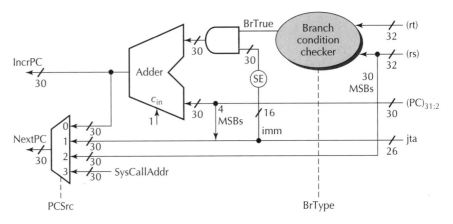

Figure 13.4 Next-address logic for MicroMIPS (see the top part of Figure 13.3).

The first two options are combined by using an adder with its lower input tied to $(PC)_{31:2}$, its upper input connected to `imm` (sign-extended to 30 bits) or 0 depending on whether or not a branch is to be performed, and its carry-in signal permanently asserted (Figure 13.4). This *address adder* thus computes $(PC)_{31:2} + 1$ or $(PC)_{31:2} + 1 + \text{imm}$, which is written into PC unless a jump instruction is executed. Note that when the instruction is not a branch, the output of this adder is $(PC)_{31:2} + 1$. Hence, this output, with two 0s attached to its right, can be used as the incremented program counter value that must be stored in $31 as part of executing the `jal` instruction.

Referring to Figure 13.4, the branch condition checker verifies the branch predicate, which is $(\text{rs}) = (\text{rt})$, $(\text{rs}) \neq (\text{rt})$, or $(\text{rs}) < 0$, and asserts its BrTrue output if one of these conditions is satisfied *and* the corresponding branch instruction is being executed. The latter information is supplied by the pair of signals BrType from the control unit. Finally, the pair of signals PCSrc, also supplied by the control unit, direct the multiplexer at the left edge of Figure 13.4 to send one of its 4 inputs to be written into the upper 30 bits of PC. These signals are set to 00 most of the time (for all instructions other than the four jumps); they are set to 01 for both j and jal, 10 for jr, and 11 for syscall.

■ 13.5 Deriving the Control Signals

Proper execution of MicroMIPS instructions requires that the control circuit assign appropriate values to the control signals shown in Figure 13.3 and in part further elaborated in Figure 13.4. The value to be assigned to each signal is a function of the instruction being executed and is thus uniquely determined by its `op` and `fn` fields. Table 13.2 contains a list of all the control signals and their definitions. In the leftmost column of Table 13.2, the block in Figure 13.3 to which the signals relate is named. Column 2 lists the signals as they appear in Figure 13.3 and, if applicable, assigns names to components of the signals. For example, ALUFunc has three components (see Figure 10.19): Add′Sub, LogicFn, and FnClass. The latter two are 2-bit signals, with their bits indexed 1 (MSB) and 0 (LSB). The remaining columns of Table 13.2 specify the meaning associated with each control signal value or setting. For example, the next to the last line in the table assigns distinct bit patterns or codes to the three different branch types (beq, bne, bltz) and to all other cases in which no branching is to occur.

■ **TABLE 13.2** Control signals for the single-cycle MicroMIPS implementation.

Block	Control signal	0	1	2	3
Reg file	RegWrite	Don't write	Write		
	RegDst$_1$, RegDst$_0$	rt	rd	$31	
	RegInSrc$_1$, RegInSrc$_0$	Data out	ALU out	IncrPC	
ALU	ALUSrc	(rt)	imm		
	ALUFunc — Add'Sub	Add	Subtract		
	ALUFunc — LogicFn$_1$, LogicFn$_0$	AND	OR	XOR	NOR
	ALUFunc — FnClass$_1$, FnClass$_0$	lui	Set less	Arithmetic	Logic
Data cache	DataRead	Don't read	Read		
	DataWrite	Don't write	Write		
Next addr	Br&Jump — BrType$_1$, BrType$_0$	No branch	beq	bne	bltz
	Br&Jump — PCSrc$_1$, PCSrc$_0$	IncrPC	jta	(rs)	SysCallAddr

■ **TABLE 13.3** Control signal settings for the single-cycle MicroMIPS instruction execution unit.*

Instruction	op	fn	RegWrite	RegDst	RegInSrc	ALUSrc	Add'Sub	LogicFn	FnClass	DataRead	DataWrite	BrType	PCSrc
Load upper immediate	001111		1	00	01	1			00	0	0	00	00
Add	000000	100000	1	01	01	0	0		10	0	0	00	00
Subtract	000000	100010	1	01	01	0	1		10	0	0	00	00
Set less than	000000	101010	1	01	01	0	1		01	0	0	00	00
Add immediate	001000		1	00	01	1	0		10	0	0	00	00
Set less than immediate	001010		1	00	01	1	1		01	0	0	00	00
AND	000000	100100	1	01	01	0		00	11	0	0	00	00
OR	000000	100101	1	01	01	0		01	11	0	0	00	00
XOR	000000	100110	1	01	01	0		10	11	0	0	00	00
NOR	000000	100111	1	01	01	0		11	11	0	0	00	00
AND immediate	001100		1	00	01	1		00	11	0	0	00	00
OR immediate	001101		1	00	01	1		01	11	0	0	00	00
XOR immediate	001110		1	00	01	1		10	11	0	0	00	00
Load word	100011		1	00	00	1	0		10	1	0	00	00
Store word	101011		0			1	0		10	0	1	00	00
Jump	000010		0							0	0		01
Jump register	000000	001000	0							0	0		10
Branch on less than 0	000001		0							0	0	11	00
Branch on equal	000100		0							0	0	01	00
Branch on not equal	000101		0							0	0	10	00
Jump and link	000011		1	10	10					0	0	00	01
System call	000000	001100	0							0	0		11

*Note: Blank entries constitute don't-cares.

Based on the definitions in Table 13.2, and our understanding of what needs to be done to execute each instruction, we construct Table 13.3, in which the values of all 17 control signals are specified for each of the 22 MicroMIPS instructions.

Table 13.2 essentially defines each of the 17 control signals as a logic function of 12 input bits (op and fn). It is an easy matter to derive logic expressions for these signals in terms of

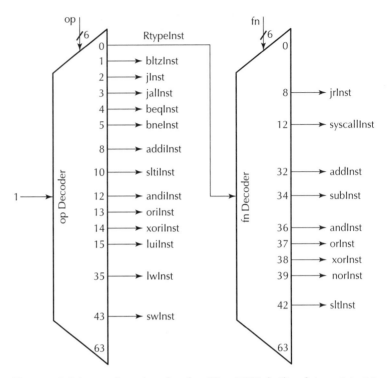

Figure 13.5 Instruction decoder for MicroMIPS built of two 6-to-64 decoders.

the 12 input bits op_5, op_4,..., op_0, fn_5, fn_4,..., fn_0. The drawback of such an ad hoc approach is that if we later decide to modify the instruction set of the machine or add new instructions to it, the entire design must be modified.

For this reason, a two-step approach to the synthesis of control circuits is often preferred. In the first step, the instruction set is decoded and a different logic signal is asserted for each instruction. Figure 13.5 shows a decoder for the instruction set of MicroMIPS. The 6-bit `op` field is provided to a 6-to-64 decoder which asserts one of its outputs depending of the value of `op`. For example, output 1 of the `op` decoder corresponds to the instruction `bltz` and is thus given the symbolic name "bltzInst." This makes it easy to remember when each signal will be asserted. Output 0 of the `op` decoder goes to a second decoder. Again, the outputs of this `fn` decoder are labeled with names that correspond to the instructions they represent.

Now, each of the 17 required control signals can be formed simply as the logical OR of a subset of the decoder outputs in Figure 13.5. Because some of the signals in Table 13.3 have a large number of 1 entries in their truth tables, thus requiring multilevel ORing anyway, it is convenient to define several auxiliary signals that are then used in forming the main control signals. Let us define three auxiliary signals as follows:

arithInst = addInst ∨ subInst ∨ sltInst ∨ addiInst ∨ sltiInst

logicInst = andInst ∨ orInst ∨ xorInst ∨ norInst ∨ andiInst ∨ oriInst ∨ xoriInst

immInst = luiInst ∨ addiInst ∨ sltiInst ∨ andiInst ∨ oriInst ∨ xoriInst

Then, for example:

$$\text{RegWrite} = \text{luiInst} \vee \text{arithInst} \vee \text{logicInst} \vee \text{lwInst} \vee \text{jalInst}$$
$$\text{ALUSrc} = \text{immInst} \vee \text{lwInst} \vee \text{swInst}$$
$$\text{Add}'\text{Sub} = \text{subInst} \vee \text{sltInst} \vee \text{sltiInst}$$
$$\text{DataRead} = \text{lwInst}$$
$$\text{PCSrc}_0 = \text{jInst} \vee \text{jalInst} \vee \text{syscallInst}$$

Deriving logic expressions for the remaining control signals in Figures 13.3 and 13.4 is left as an exercise.

13.6 Performance of the Single-Cycle Design

The single-cycle MicroMIPS implementation discussed in the preceding sections might also be referred to as a single-state or stateless implementation in that the control circuit is purely combinational and does not need to remember anything from one clock cycle to the next. All the information that is needed for proper operation in the next clock cycle is carried in the program counter. Because a new instruction is executed in each clock cycle, we have CPI = 1. All instructions share the fetch and register access steps. Instruction decoding is fully overlapped with register access, so it involves no additional latency.

The clock cycle is determined by the longest execution time for an instruction which in turn depends on the signal propagation latency through the data path of Figure 13.3. With our simple instruction set, the `lw` instruction, which needs an ALU operation, data cache access, and register writeback is likely to be the slowest instructions. No other instruction needs all three steps. Let us assume the following worst-case latencies for the blocks in our data path, the sum of which yields the execution latency for the `lw` instruction:

Instruction access	2 ns
Register read	1 ns
ALU operation	2 ns
Data cache access	2 ns
Register write-back	1 ns
Total	8 ns

This corresponds to a clock rate of 125 MHz and a performance of 125 MIPS. If we could make the cycle time variable to match the actual time needed by each instruction, we would get a somewhat better average instruction execution time. Figure 13.6 depicts the critical signal propagation paths for the various instruction classes in MicroMIPS. We shall assume here that all jump instructions are of the fastest variety that need no register access (`j` or `syscall`). This leads to a best-case estimate for the average instruction execution time, but the true average will not be much different, given the small percentage of jump instructions. With the following typical instruction mix, an average instruction execution time can be derived.

R-type	44%	6 ns	No data cache access
Load	24%	8 ns	See the preceding analysis
Store	12%	7 ns	No register writeback
Branch	18%	5 ns	Fetch + Register read + Next-address formation
Jump	2%	3 ns	Fetch + Instruction decode

Weighted average $\cong$ 6.36 ns

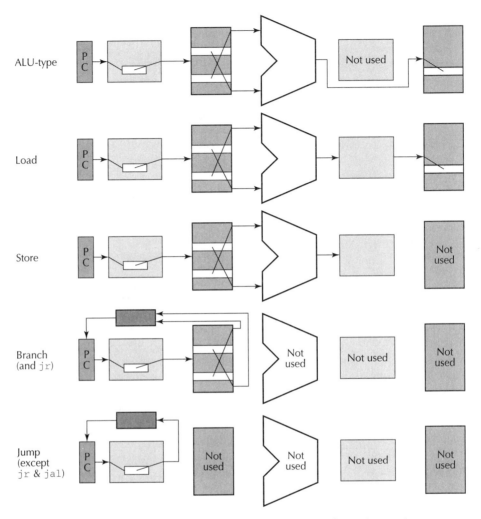

ALU-type

Load

Store

Branch
(and jr)

Jump
(except
jr & jal)

Figure 13.6 The MicroMIPS data path unfolded (by depicting the register write step as a separate block) to allow better visualization of the critical-path latencies for various instruction classes.

So, the single-cycle implementation with a fixed cycle time is slower than the ideal implementation with variable cycle time which could achieve an average performance of 157 MIPS. The latter, however, is not practical and is discussed here only to show that we cannot hope to obtain a MicroMIPS hardware implementation with fundamentally higher performance based on the single-cycle control philosophy. Drawbacks of the single-cycle design are discussed next.

As noted earlier, the clock cycle time of a machine with single-cycle control is determined by the most complex or slowest instruction. Thus, with such an implementation, we would be increasing the delays of simple operations to accommodate complex operations in one clock cycle. In the case of MicroMIPS, we were forced to set the clock period to 8 ns, which corresponds to the execution time of lw, the slowest MicroMIPS instruction. This caused faster instructions, which could theoretically be executed in 3, 5, 6, or 7 ns, to also take 8 ns.

In fact, we are rather fortunate in that, except for jump instructions that account for a minute fraction of those encountered, the execution times of MicroMIPS instructions do not significantly deviate from the average, making single-cycle control with fixed cycle duration quite competitive with an ideal variable-cycle-time implementation. If the instruction mix provided earlier in this section is typical of applications to be run on our machine, more than a third of the single-cycle MicroMIPS instructions are executed at or close to their minimal latencies when we use a clock cycle time of 8 ns, whereas some 80% suffer no more than 33% slowdown as a result of single-cycle implementation.

Had MicroMIPS included more complex instructions, such as multiplication, division, or floating-point arithmetic, the disadvantage of single-cycle control would have been more pronounced. For example, if the latency of a more complex instruction such as division were four times that of addition, single-cycle control implementation would imply that the very common operation of addition must be slowed down by a factor of at least 4, thus hurting performance. As we know from our discussion in Section 8.5, this is in direct conflict with the RISC design philosophy. We can now appreciate why MiniMIPS relegates the execution of multiplication and division instructions to a unit other than the main ALU (see Figure 5.1). The multiply/divide unit can perform these more complex operations, while the ALU continues to fetch and execute simpler instructions. As long as adequate time is allowed before copying multiplication or division results from the Hi and Lo registers into the general register file, no problem will arise between these two independent arithmetic units.

The following analogy helps direct us to the multicycle control implementation in Chapter 14. Consider a dentist's appointment book. Rather than arrange all appointments on the hour because some patients require a full hour's worth of work, appointments may be given in standard increments of, say, 15 minutes. A patient coming in for a routine checkup could be assigned only 15 minutes of the dentist's time, while those requiring more attention or complex procedures may be given multiple time increments. In this way, the dentist can attend to more patients and will have less idle time between patients.

PROBLEMS

13.1 Details of data path

a. Label each of the lines in Figure 13.2 with the number of binary signals it represents.
b. Repeat part a for Figure 13.3.

13.2 Data path selection options

Let the three multiplexers in Figure 13.3 be M_1, M_2, and M_3, from left to right.

a. M_1 has three settings, while M_2 has two settings; thus, there are six combinations when M_1 and M_2 settings are taken together. For each of these six combinations, indicate whether it is ever used and, if so, for executing which MicroMIPS instruction(s).
b. Repeat part a for M_2 and M_3 (six combinations).
c. Repeat part a for M_1 and M_3 (nine combinations).

13.3 Branch condition checker

Based on the description in Section 13.4 and the signal encodings defined in Table 13.2, present a complete logic design for the branch condition checker of Figure 13.4.

13.4 Next-address logic

Consider the following alternate design for the next-address logic of MicroMIPS. The array of 30 AND gates shown near the top of Figure 13.4 is eliminated and the immediate value, sign-extended to 30 bits, is connected directly to the top adder input. A separate incrementer is introduced to compute $(PC)_{31:2} + 1$. The BrTrue signal is then used to control a multiplexer that allows the IncrPC output to be taken from the adder or the newly introduced incrementer. Compare this alternate design with the original design of Figure 13.4 in terms of potential advantages and disadvantages.

13.5 MicroMIPS instruction format

Suppose that you are given a blank slate to redesign the instruction format for MicroMIPS. The instruction set is defined in Table 13.1. The only requirement is for each instruction to contain the appropriate number of 5-bit register specification fields and a 16-bit immediate/offset field where needed. In particular, the width of the jta field can change. What is the minimum number of bits required to encode all MicroMIPS instructions in a fixed-width format? *Hint:* Since there are seven different instructions that need two register fields and an immediate field, you can establish a lower bound on the width.

13.6 Control signal values

a. Examining Table 13.3, we note that for any pair of rows, there exists at least one column in which the control signal settings are different (one is set to 0, the other to 1). Why is this not surprising?
b. Identify three pairs or rows, with each pair differing in exactly one control bit value. Explain how these differing control bit values cause distinct execution behaviors.

13.7 Deriving the control signals

Logic expressions for 5 of the 17 control signals listed in Tables 13.2 and 13.3 are provided at the end of Section 13.5. Supply logic expressions defining the other 12 control signals.

13.8 Performance of the single-cycle design

Discuss the effects of the following changes in the performance results obtained in Section 13.6:

a. Reducing the register access time from 1 ns to 0.5 ns
b. Improving the ALU latency from 2 ns to 1.5 ns
c. Using cache memories with access time of 3 ns instead of 2 ns

13.9 Exception handling

a. Suppose ALU overflow is to cause a special operating system routine at location "ExcepHandler" of the memory to be invoked. Discuss changes in the MicroMIPS instruction execution unit to accommodate this change.
b. Discuss how a similar provision can be made for overflow in address computation (note that addresses are unsigned numbers).

13.10 Instruction decoding

Suppose that the instruction decoder of our single-cycle MicroMIPS implementation were to be designed from Table 13.3 directly, rather than based on the two-stage process of full decoding followed by ORing (Figure 13.5). Write down the simplest possible logic expression for each of the 17 control signals listed in Table 13.3 (parts a–q of the problem, in order from left to right). Blank and missing entries in the table can be considered to be don't-cares.

13.11 Instruction decoding

a. Show how by using only one extra 3-input AND gate, the operation decoder on the left side of Figure 13.5 can be replaced by a much smaller 4-to-16 decoder. *Hint:* Subtract 32 from 35 and 43.
b. Show how the function decoder on the right side of Figure 13.5 can be replaced by a 4-to-16 decoder.

13.12 Control signals for shift instructions

Extend Table 13.3 with lines corresponding to the following new instructions from Table 6.2 that might be added to the single-cycle MicroMIPS implementation. Justify your answers.

a. Shift left logical (sll)
b. Shift right logical (srl)
c. Shift right arithmetic (sra)
d. Shift left logical variable (sllv)
e. Shift right logical variable (srlv)
f. Shift right arithmetic variable (srav)

13.13 Handling other instructions

Explain changes needed in the single-cycle data path and associated control signal settings to add the following new instructions from Table 6.2 to our MicroMIPS implementation. Justify your answers.

a. Load byte (`lb`)
b. Load byte unsigned (`lbu`)
c. Shift right arithmetic (`sra`)

13.14 Handling multiply/divide instructions

Suppose we want to augment MicroMIPS with a multiply/divide unit to enable it to execute the multiplication and division instructions in Table 6.2 along with the associated `mfhi` and `mflo` instructions. Besides `Hi` and `Lo`, the multiply/divide unit has a register `Md`, which holds the multiplicand/divisor during instruction execution. The multiplier/dividend is stored, and quotient developed, in `Lo`. The multiply/divide unit must be supplied with its operands and a few control bits that indicate which operation is to be performed. The unit then operates independently from the main data path over several clock cycles and eventually obtains the required results. You need not be concerned with the unit's operation beyond the initial setup. Propose changes in the single-cycle execution unit design to accommodate these changes.

13.15 Adding other instructions

Certain other instructions can be added to the instruction set of MicroMIPS if desired. Consider the following pseudoinstructions from Table 7.1 and assume that we want to include them in MicroMIPS

as regular instructions. In each case, choose an appropriate encoding for the instruction and specify all modifications required in the single-cycle data path and associated control circuits. Make sure that the chosen encodings are not in conflict with other MiniMIPS instructions listed in Tables 6.2 and 12.1.

a. Move (`move`)
b. Load immediate (`li`)
c. Absolute value (`abs`)
d. Negate (`neg`)
e. Not (`not`)
f. Branch less than (`blt`)

13.16 URISC

Consider the URISC processor described in Section 8.6 [Mava88]. How many clock cycles are needed for URISC to execute one instruction, assuming that memory can be accessed in one clock cycle?

13.17 ALU for MicroMIPS

The description of the MicroMIPS ALU at the end of Section 13.2 omits one detail: that the logic unit must undo the effect of sign extension on an immediate operand.

a. Present the design of the logic unit within the ALU with this provision.
b. Speculate on possible reasons for this design choice (i.e., sign extension in all cases, followed by possible undoing).

REFERENCES AND FURTHER READINGS

[Mava88]   Mavaddat, F., and B. Parhami, "URISC: The Ultimate Reduced Instruction Set Computer," *Int. J. Electrical Engineering Education,* Vol. 25, pp. 327–334, 1988.

[MIPS]   MIPS Technologies, Web site. Follow the architecture and documentation links at: http://www.mips.com/

[Patt98]   Patterson, D. A., and J. L. Hennessy, *Computer Organization and Design: The Hardware/Software Interface,* Morgan Kaufmann, 2nd ed., 1998.

[Wake01]   Wakerly, J. F., *Digital Design: Principles and Practices,* updated 3rd ed., Prentice Hall, 2001.

14

CONTROL UNIT SYNTHESIS

"Not to have control over the senses is like sailing in a rudderless ship, bound to break to pieces on coming in contact with the very first rock."
—*Mahatma Gandhi*

"Microprogramming is the implementation of hopefully reasonable systems through interpretation on unreasonable machines."
—*R. F. Rosin*

TOPICS IN THIS CHAPTER
14.1 A Multicycle Implementation
14.2 Clock Cycle and Control Signals
14.3 The Control State Machine
14.4 Performance of the Multicycle Design
14.5 Microprogramming
14.6 Dealing with Exceptions

The memoryless control circuit for the single-cycle implementation of Chapter 13 forms all the control signals as functions of certain bits within the instruction. This is fine for a limited set of instructions, most of which execute in about the same length of time. When instructions are more varied in complexity or when some resource must be used more than once during the same instruction, a multicycle implementation is called for. The control circuit of such a multicycle implementation is a state machine, with a number of states for normal execution and additional states for exception handling. In this chapter, we derive a multicycle implementation of control for MicroMIPS and show that the execution of each instruction now becomes a "hardware program" (or microprogram) that, like a normal program, has sequential execution, branching, and, perhaps, even loops and procedure calls.

■ 14.1 A Multicycle Implementation

As we learned in Chapter 13, the execution of each MicroMIPS instruction encompasses a set of actions such as memory access, register readout, and ALU operation. According to our assumptions in Section 13.5, each of these actions takes 1–2 ns to complete. Single-cycle operation requires that the worst-case sum of these latencies be taken as the clock period.

With multicycle design, a subset of actions required for an instruction is performed in one clock cycle. Hence, the clock cycle can be made much shorter, with several cycles needed to execute a single instruction. This is analogous to a dental office allotting time to patients in multiples of 15 minutes, depending on the amount of work that is anticipated. To allow multicycle operation, the intermediate values from one cycle must be kept in registers so that they are available for examination in any subsequent clock cycle where they are needed.

One might use a multicycle implementation for reasons of greater speed and/or economy. Faster operation results from picking a shorter clock period and using a variable number of clock cycles per instruction; hence, each instruction takes as much time as needed for the various execution steps rather than as much time as the slowest instruction (Figure 14.1). Lower implementation cost results from being able to use some resources more than once in the course of instruction execution; for example, the same adder that is used for executing the add instruction might be used for computing the branch target address or to increment the program counter.

An abstract view of a multicycle datapath is shown in Figure 14.2. Several features of the multicycle data path are noteworthy. First, the two memory blocks (instruction cache and data cache) of Figure 13.2 have been merged into a single cache block. When a word is read from the cache, it must be held in a register for use in subsequent cycles. The reason for having two registers (instruction register and data register) between the cache and the register file is that once the instruction has been read out, it must be kept for all the remaining cycles in its execution to generate the control signals appropriately. So, a second register is needed for data readout associated with `lw`. Three other registers (x, y, and z) also serve the purpose of holding information between cycles. Note that except for PC and instruction register, all registers are loaded in every clock cycle; hence the absence of explicit control for loading of these registers. Because the content of each of these registers is needed only in the immediately following clock cycle, the redundant loads into these registers do no harm.

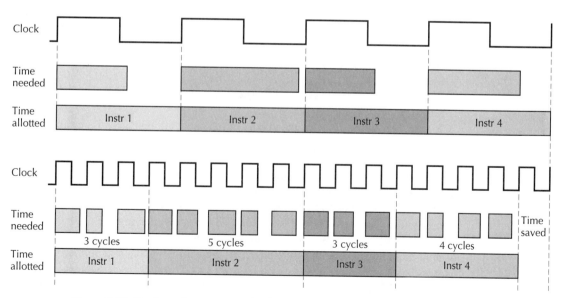

Figure 14.1 Single-cycle versus multicycle instruction execution.

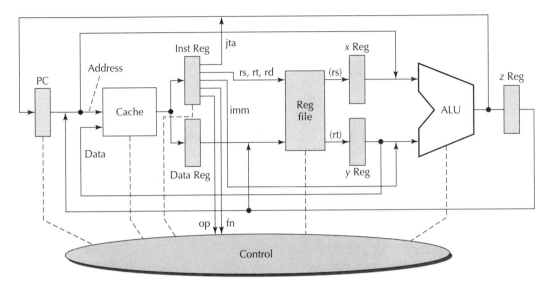

Figure 14.2 Abstract view of a multicycle instruction execution unit for MicroMIPS. For naming of instruction fields, see Figure 13.1.

The data path in Figure 14.2 is capable of executing one instruction every 3–5 clock cycles; hence the name "multicycle data path." Execution of all instructions starts the same way in the first cycle: the content of PC is used to access the cache and the retrieved word is placed in the instruction register. This is known as the *instruction fetch* cycle. The second cycle is devoted to decoding the instruction and also accessing the registers rs and rt. Note that not every instruction requires two operands from the registers and at this point we do not yet know what instruction has been fetched. However, reading rs and rt will do no harm, even if it turns out that we do not need the contents of either or both registers. If the instruction at hand is one of the four jump instructions (j, jr, jal, syscall), its execution terminates in the third cycle by simply writing the appropriate address into PC. If it is a branch instruction (beq, bne, bltz), the branch condition is checked and the appropriate value is written into PC in the third cycle. All other instructions proceed to the fourth cycle, where they are completed. There is only one exception: lw requires a fifth cycle to write the data retrieved from the cache into a register.

Figure 14.3 shows some of the details of the data path that are missing from the abstract version in Figure 14.2. The multiplexers serve essentially the same functions as those used in Figure 13.2. The 3-input multiplexer at the input to the register file allows rt, rd, or $31 to be used as the index of the destination register into which a result is to be written. The 2-input multiplexer at the lower part of the register file allows data read out from the cache or output of the ALU to be written into the selected register. This one serves the same function as the 3-input mux at the right edge of Figure 13.3. The reason for having one fewer input here is that the incremented PC is now formed by the ALU rather than by a separate unit. The 2-input and 4-input multiplexers near the right edge of Figure 14.3 corresponds to the mux in the next-address block of Figure 13.3 (see also Figure 13.4). The address of the next instruction to be written into PC can come from five possible sources. The first two are the suitably modified jta and SysCallAddr, corresponding to j and syscall instructions. One of these two values is selected and sent to the top input of the 4-input "PC source" multiplexer. The other three

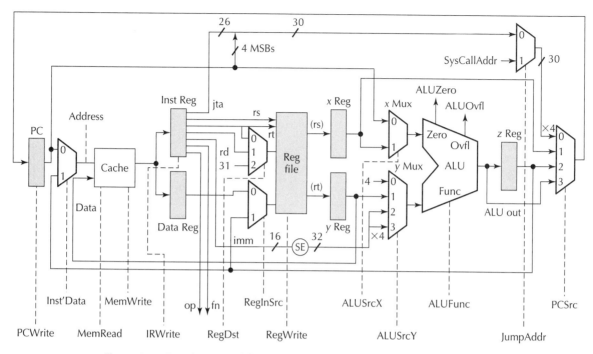

Figure 14.3 Key elements of the multicycle MicroMIPS data path.

inputs of this multiplexer are (rs) from x register, ALU output in the preceding cycle from z register, and ALU output in the current cycle.

In comparison to Figure 13.3, we have added a mux for the upper input to the ALU (x mux) and expanded the lower ALU input multiplexer (y mux) from 2 to 4 inputs. This is because the ALU must now also compute (PC) + 4 and (PC) + 4 + imm. To compute (PC) + 4, the x mux is supplied with the control signal 0 and the y mux with 00. This is done in the first cycle of instruction execution for every instruction. Then, the incremented PC value may be added in a subsequent cycle to 4 × imm by using the control settings 0 and 11 for x and y muxes, respectively. Note that two versions of the sign-extended immediate value can be used as the lower input to the ALU: the regular version, which is needed for instructions such as addi, and the left-shifted version (multiplied by 4), which is needed for dealing with the offset in branch instructions.

14.2 Clock Cycle and Control Signals

In multicycle control, the actions needed for executing each instruction are divided up, with a subset of these actions assigned to each clock cycle. The clock period should be chosen to balance the work done in each cycle, with the goal of minimizing the amount of idle time; excessive idle time leads to performance loss. As in Section 13.5, we assume the following latencies for the basic steps in instruction execution:

Memory access (read or write)   2 ns
Register access (read or write)   1 ns
ALU operation   2 ns

■ **TABLE 14.1** Control signals for the multicycle MicroMIPS implementation.

Block	Control signal		0	1	2	3
Program counter	JumpAddr		jta	SysCallAddr		
	$PCSrc_1$, $PCSrc_0$		Jump addr	x reg	z reg	ALU out
	PCWrite		Don't write	Write		
Cache	Inst'Data		PC	z reg		
	MemRead		Don't read	Read		
	MemWrite		Don't write	Write		
	IRWrite		Don't write	Write		
Register file	RegWrite		Don't write	Write		
	$RegDst_1$, $RegDst_0$		rt	rd	$31	
	RegInSrc		Data reg	z reg		
ALU	ALUSrcX		PC	x reg		
	$ALUSrcY_1$, $ALUSrcY_0$		4	y reg	imm	$4 \times$ imm
	ALUFunc	Add'Sub	Add	Subtract		
		$LogicFn_1$, $LogicFn_0$	AND	OR	XOR	NOR
		$FnClass_1$, $FnClass_0$	lui	Set less	Arithmetic	Logic

A clock cycle of 2 ns would thus allow us to perform each of the basic steps of an instruction in one clock cycle. This leads to a clock frequency of 500 MHz. If the numbers do not include a safety margin, then a somewhat longer clock period (say, 2.5 ns, for a clock frequency of 400 MHz) might be needed to accommodate the added overhead of storing values in registers in each cycle. We proceed with the assumption that a clock period of 2 ns is sufficient.

Table 14.1 contains a listing and definitions of all control signals shown in Figure 14.3, grouped by the block in the diagram that is affected by the signal. The first three entries in Table 14.1 relate to the program counter. PCSrc selects on of the four alternative values for loading into the PC and PCWrite specifies when PC is to be modified. The four sources for the new PC content are:

00   Direct address (PC_{31-28}|jta|00 or SysCallAddr), as selected by JumpAddr
01   Content of x register, which holds the value read out from `rs`
10   Content of z register, which holds the ALU output from the preceding cycle
11   ALU output in the current cycle

Note that in Figure 14.3, right-extending PC_{31-28}|jta with 00 is shown as multiplication by 4.

Four binary signals are associated with the cache. The MemRead and MemWrite signals are self-explanatory. The Inst'Data signal indicates whether memory is accessed to fetch an instruction (address coming from the PC) or to read/write data (address computed by the ALU in the preceding cycle). The IRWrite signal, which is asserted in the instruction fetch cycle, indicates that the memory output is to be written into the instruction register. Note that the data register has no corresponding write control signal. This is because its write control input is tied to the clock, causing it to load the memory output in every cycle, even in the instruction fetch cycle. As noted earlier, redundant loads cause no problem, provided the data loaded into this register is always used in the immediately following cycle before being overwritten by something else.

Control signals affecting the register file are virtually identical to those for single-cycle design in Figure 14.3, except that RegInSrc is two- rather than three-valued because the incremented PC content now emerges from the ALU.

Finally, the control signals associated with the ALU specify the sources of its two operands and the function to be performed. The top ALU operand can come from PC or x register, under the control of ALUSrcX signal. The lower ALU operand has four possible sources as follows:

00 The constant 4 for incrementing the program counter
01 Content of y register holding (rt), which was read out in the preceding cycle
10 The immediate field of the instruction, sign-extended to 32 bits
11 The offset field of the instruction, sign-extended and left-shifted by 2 bits

Again, appending the sign-extended offset with 00 at the right is shown as multiplication by 4. The signals comprising ALUFunc have the same meanings as those of single-cycle design (Table 13.2).

Table 14.2 shows the control signal settings in each clock cycle during the execution of one instruction. The first two cycles are common to all instructions. In cycle 1, the instruction is fetched from the cache and placed in the instruction register. Because the ALU is free in this cycle, we use it to increment the PC. In this way, the incremented PC value will also be available for adding to the branch offset. In cycle 2, registers rs and rt are read out, with their contents written into x and y registers, respectively. Also, the instruction is decoded and the branch target address is formed in z register. Even though in most cases the instruction will turn out to be something other than a branch, using the ALU's idle cycle to precompute the branch address does no harm. Note that we are assuming here that the 2 ns clock cycle provides enough time for register readout and addition latency through the ALU.

■ **TABLE 14.2** Execution cycles for the multicycle MicroMIPS implementation.

Clock cycle	Instruction	Operations	Signal settings
1 Fetch and PC increment	Any	Read out the instruction and write it into instruction register; increment PC	Inst'Data = 0, MemRead = 1 IRWrite = 1, ALUSrcX = 0 ALUSrcY = 0, ALUFunc = '+' PCSrc = 3, PCWrite = 1
2 Decode and register readout	Any	Read out rs and rt into x and y registers; compute branch address and save in z register	ALUSrcX = 0, ALUSrcY = 3 ALUFunc = '+'
3 ALU Operation and PC update	ALU type	Perform ALU operation and save the result in z register	ALUSrcX = 1, ALUSrcY = 1 or 2 ALUFunc: Varies
	Load/Store	Add base and offset values; save in z register	ALUSrcX = 1, ALUSrcY = 2 ALUFunc = '+'
	Branch	If $(x$ reg) $= \neq <(y$ reg), set PC to branch target address	ALUSrcX = 1, ALUSrcY = 1 ALUFunc = '−', PCSrc = 2 PCWrite = ALUZero or ALUZero' or ALUOut$_{31}$
	Jump	Set PC to the target address jta, SysCallAddr, or (rs)	JumpAddr = 0 or 1 PCSrc = 0 or 1, PCWrite = 1
4 Register write or memory access	ALU type	Write back z reg into rd	RegDst = 1, RegInSrc = 1 RegWrite = 1
	Load	Read memory into data reg	Inst'Data = 1, MemRead = 1
	Store	Copy y reg into memory	Inst'Data = 1, MemWrite = 1
5 Register write for lw	Load	Copy data register into rt	RegDst = 0, RegInSrc = 0 RegWrite = 1

Beginning with cycle 3, the instruction at hand is known because decoding is completed in cycle 2. Control signal values in cycle 3 depend on the instruction category: ALU type, load/store, branch, and jump. The latter two categories of instructions are completed in cycle 3, while others move on to cycle 4, where ALU-type instructions terminate and different actions for load and store are prescribed. Finally, `lw` is the only instruction that needs cycle 5 for its completion. During this cycle, the content of the data register is written in register `rt`.

14.3 The Control State Machine

The control unit must distinguish between the five cycles of the multicycle design and additionally be able to perform different operations depending on the instruction. We note that the setting of any control signal is uniquely determined if we know what instruction is being executed and which of its cycles is currently in progress. The control state machine carries the required information along by moving from state to state, where each state is associated with a particular set of values for the control signals.

Figure 14.4 depicts the control states and state transitions. The control state machine is set to state 0 when program execution begins. It then moves from state to state until one instruction has been completed, at which time it returns to state 0 to begin the execution of another instruction. This looping through the states of Figure 14.4 continues until a `syscall` instruction is executed with the number 10 in register `$v0` (see Table 7.2). This instruction terminates program execution.

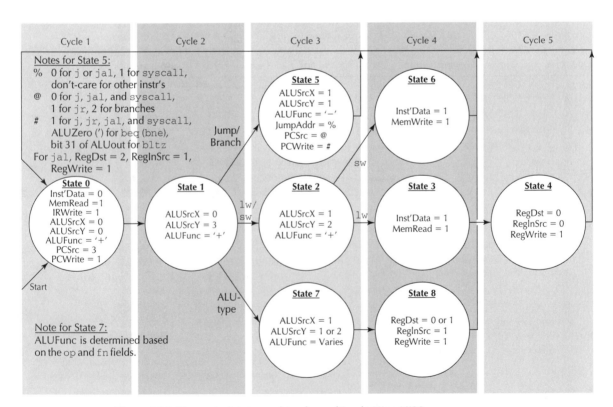

Figure 14.4 The control state machine for multicycle MicroMIPS.

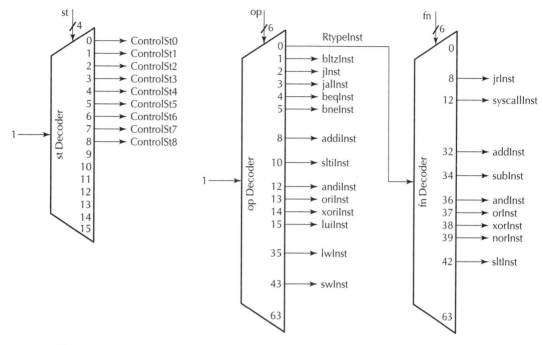

Figure 14.5 State and instruction decoders for multicycle MicroMIPS.

The control state sequences for various MicroMIPS instruction classes are as follows:

ALU-type	0, 1, 7, 8
Load word	0, 1, 2, 3, 4
Store word	0, 1, 2, 6
Jump/branch	0, 1, 5

In each state, except for states 5 and 7, the control signal settings are uniquely determined. Information about the current control state and the instruction being executed is supplied by the decoders shown in Figure 14.5. Note that the instruction decoder portion of Figure 14.5 (composed of op and fn decoders) is identical to that in Figure 13.5, with the outputs of this decoder used in determining the control signals in states 5 and 7 as well as controlling the state transitions according to Figure 14.4. What has been added is a state decoder that asserts the signal ControlSti whenever the control state machine is in state i.

Logic expressions for the control signals of our multicycle MicroMIPS implementation can be easily derived based on Figures 14.4 and 14.5. Examples of control signals that are uniquely determined by control state information include:

$$\text{ALUSrcX} = \text{ControlSt2} \lor \text{ControlSt5} \lor \text{ControlSt7}$$

$$\text{RegWrite} = \text{ControlSt4} \lor \text{ControlSt8}$$

The settings of ALUFunc signals depend not only on the control state but also on the specific instruction being executed. Let us define a couple of auxiliary control signals:

$$\text{addsubInst} = \text{addInst} \lor \text{subInst} \lor \text{addiInst}$$

$$\text{logicInst} = \text{andInst} \lor \text{orInst} \lor \text{xorInst} \lor \text{norInst} \lor \text{andiInst} \lor \text{oriInst} \lor \text{xoriInst}$$

Then, the ALU control signals can be set as follows:

$\text{Add}'\text{Sub} = \text{ControlSt5} \lor (\text{ControlSt7} \land \text{subInst})$

$\text{FnClass}_1 = \text{ControlSt7}' \lor \text{addsubInst} \lor \text{logicInst}$

$\text{FnClass}_0 = \text{ControlSt7} \land (\text{logicInst} \lor \text{sltInst} \lor \text{sltiInst})$

$\text{LogicFn}_1 = \text{ControlSt7} \land (\text{xorInst} \lor \text{xoriInst} \lor \text{norInst})$

$\text{LogicFn}_0 = \text{ControlSt7} \land (\text{orInst} \lor \text{oriInst} \lor \text{norInst})$

Control state 5 is similar to state 7 in that control signal settings for it depend on the instruction being executed and a number of other conditions. For example:

$\text{JumpAddr} = \text{syscallInst}$

$\text{PCSrc}_1 = \text{ControlSt0} \lor \text{ControlSt5} \land (\text{beqInst} \lor \text{bneInst} \lor \text{bltzInst})$

$\text{PCSrc}_0 = \text{ControlSt0} \lor \text{ControlSt5} \land \text{jrInst}$

$\text{PCWrite} = \text{ControlSt0} \lor \text{ControlSt5} \land [\text{jInst} \lor \text{jrInst} \lor \text{jalInst} \lor \text{syscallInst} \lor$
$\quad\quad (\text{ALUZero} \land \text{beqInst}) \lor (\text{ALUZero}' \land \text{bneInst}) \lor (\text{ALUout}_{31} \land \text{bltzInst})]$

The control circuits just derived would be somewhat simpler if states 5 and 7 of the control state machine were expanded into multiple states corresponding to identical or similar signal settings. For example, we could decompose state 5 into states 5b (for branches) and 5j (for jumps), or into multiple states, one for each different instruction. However, this would complicate the control state machine and the associated state decoder and might be cost-ineffective.

14.4 Performance of the Multicycle Design

The multicycle MicroMIPS implementation discussed in the preceding sections might also be referred to as a multistate implementation. This is in contrast to the single-state or memoryless control implementation of Chapter 13. Single-cycle control is memoryless in the sense that the execution of each cycle starts anew, with signals and events during a cycle based only on the current instruction being executed; they are unaffected by what transpired in previous cycles.

We noted, in Section 13.6, that the single-cycle MicroMIPS has a CPI of 1, given that a new instruction is executed in each clock cycle. To evaluate the performance of our multicycle MicroMIPS, we calculate the average CPI using the same instruction mix as used in Section 13.6. The contribution of each instruction class to the average CPI is obtained by multiplying its frequency by the number of cycles needed to execute instructions in that class:

			Contribution to CPI
R-type	44%	4 cycles	1.76
Load	24%	5 cycles	1.20
Store	12%	4 cycles	0.48
Branch	18%	3 cycles	0.54
Jump	2%	3 cycles	0.06
Average CPI $\cong$			4.04

Note that the number of cycles for each instruction class is dictated by the steps needed for its execution (Table 14.2).

With the clock rate of 500 MHz, derived at the beginning of Section 14.2, our CPI of 4.04 corresponds to a performance of $500/4.04 \cong 123.8$ MIPS. This is virtually the same as the 125 MIPS performance of our single-cycle implementation derived in Section 13.6. Hence, the two implementations of MicroMIPS in Chapters 13 and 14 have comparable performance, in part because the instruction latencies are not very different from each other; the slowest instruction has a latency that is $8/5 = 1.6$ times that of the fastest one. Had the instruction latencies been more varied, the multicycle design would have led to a performance gain over the single-cycle implementation.

Example 14.1: Larger variability in instruction execution times   Consider a multicycle implementation of MicroMIPS++, a machine that is similar to MicroMIPS except that its R-type instructions fall into three categories.

    a. R_a-type instructions, constituting half of all R-type instructions executed, take 4 cycles.

    b. R_b-type instructions, constituting a quarter of all R-type instructions executed, take 6 cycles.

    c. R_c-type instructions, constituting a quarter of all R-type instructions executed, take 10 cycles.

With the instruction mix given at the beginning of Section 14.4, and assuming that the slowest R-type instructions will take 16 ns to execute in a single-cycle implementation, derive the performance advantage of multicycle implementation over single-cycle implementation.

Solution: The 16 ns worst-case execution time assumed leads to a clock rate of 62.5 MHz and performance of 62.5 MIPS for the single-cycle design. For the multicycle design, the only change in the average CPI calculation is that the contribution of R-type instructions to the average CPI increases from 1.76 to $0.22 \times 4 + 0.11 \times 6 + 0.11 \times 10 = 2.64$. This raises the average CPI from 4.04 to 4.92. The performance of multicycle MicroMIPS++ thus becomes $500/4.92 \cong 101.6$ MIPS. The performance improvement factor of the multicycle design over the single-cycle implementation is, therefore, $101.6/62.5 = 1.63$. Note that the inclusion of more complex R-type instructions taking 6 and 10 cycles to execute has a relatively small effect on the performance of the multicycle design (from 123.8 MIPS to 101.6 MIPS, for a reduction of about 18%), whereas they cut the performance of the single-cycle design in half.

▊ 14.5 Microprogramming

The control state machine of Figure 14.4 resembles a program that has instructions (the states), branching, and loops. We call such a hardware program a *microprogram* and its basic steps, *microinstructions*. Within each microinstruction, different actions, such as asserting the MemRead control signal or setting ALUFunc to "+," are prescribed. Each such action is a *microorder*. Instead of implementing the control state machine in custom hardware, we can store microinstructions in locations of a control ROM, fetching and executing a sequence of microinstructions for each machine language instruction. So, in the same way that a program or procedure is broken down into machine instructions, a machine instruction is in turn broken down into a sequence of microinstructions. Thus, each microinstruction defines a step in the execution of a machine language instruction.

    ROM-based implementation of control has several advantages. It makes the hardware simpler, more regular, and less dependent on the details of the instruction-set architecture so that the same hardware can be used for different purposes simply by modifying the ROM contents. Also, as the design of hardware progresses from planning to implementation, it may be possible to correct errors and omissions by simply changing the microprogram as opposed to costly redesign and remanufacturing of integrated circuits. Finally, instruction sets can be fine-tuned, and new instructions added, by simply changing and expanding the microprogram. A machine with this type of control is *microprogrammed*. Designing a suitable sequence of microinstructions to realize a particular instruction set architecture is *microprogramming*. If the microprogram can be easily modified, perhaps even by the user, the machine is *microprogrammable*.

Are there drawbacks to microprogramming? In other words, does the flexibility offered by microprogrammed control implementation come at a cost? The main drawback is lower speed than is achievable with *hardwired* control implementation. With microprogrammed implementation, execution of a MicroMIPS instruction requires 3–5 ROM accesses to fetch the microinstructions corresponding to the states in Figure 14.4. After each microinstruction has been read out and placed in a *microinstruction register,* sufficient time must be allowed for all signals to stabilize and actions (such as memory read or write) to take place. Thus, all previous latencies associated with register readout, memory access, and ALU operation are still in effect; on top of these, a few gate delays previously needed for control signal generation has been replaced by a ROM access delay which is typically much longer.

The design of a microprogrammed control unit begins by devising a suitable microinstruction format. For MicroMIPS, we can use the 22-bit microinstruction format shown in Figure 14.6. Other than the rightmost 2 bits labeled "Sequence control," the bits in our microinstruction are in one-to-one correspondence with the control signals in the multicycle data path of Figure 14.3. Thus, each microinstruction explicitly defines the setting for each of the control signals.

The 2-bit sequence control field allows for the control of microinstruction sequencing in the same way that "PC control" affects the sequencing of machine language instructions. Figure 14.7 shows that there are four options for choosing the next microinstruction. Option 0 is to advance to the next microinstruction in sequence by incrementing the microprogram counter. Options 1 and 2 allow branching to occur depending on the opcode field in the machine instruction being executed. Option 3 is to go to microinstruction 0 corresponding to state 0 in Figure 14.4. This initiates the fetch phase for the next machine instruction. Each of the two dispatch tables translates the opcode into a microinstruction address. Dispatch table 1 corresponds to the multiway branch in going from cycle 2 to cycle 3 in Figure 14.4. Dispatch table 2 implements the branch between

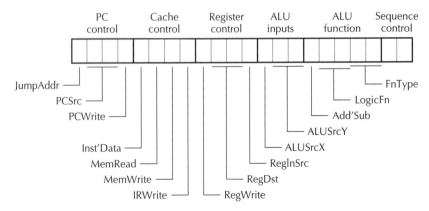

Figure 14.6 Possible 22-bit microinstruction format for MicroMIPS.

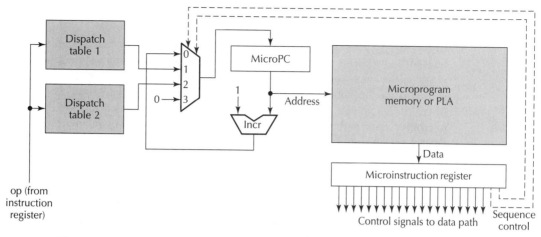

Figure 14.7 Microprogrammed control unit for MicroMIPS.

■ **TABLE 14.3** Microinstruction field values and their symbolic names: the default value for each unspecified field is the all-0s bit pattern.

Field name	Possible field values and their symbolic names				
PC control	0001 PCjump	1001 PCsyscall	x011 PCjreg	x101 PCbranch	x111 PCnext
Cache control	0101 CacheFetch	1010 CacheStore	1100 CacheLoad		
Register control	1000 rt ← Data	1001 rt ← z	1011 rd ← z	1101 $31 ← PC	
ALU inputs*	000 PC ⊗ 4	011 PC ⊗ 4imm	101 x ⊗ y	110 x ⊗ imm	
ALU function*	0xx10 + x1011 ⊕	1xx01 < x1111 ~∨	1xx10 − xxx00 lui	x0011 ∧	x0111 ∨
Sequence control	01 μPCdisp1	10 μPCdisp2	11 μPCfetch		

*Note: The operator symbol ⊗ stands for any one of the ALU functions defined above (except for "lui").

cycles 3 and 4. Collectively, the two dispatch tables allow for two instruction-dependent multiway branches in the course of instruction execution, thus enabling the sharing of microinstructions within classes of instructions that follow more or less similar steps in their executions.

We can now proceed to write the microprogram for our multicycle MicroMIPS implementation. To make the microprogram more readable, we use the symbolic names shown in Table 14.3 to designate combinations of bit values in the various fields of the microinstruction. As an example, the microinstruction

```
x111   0101   0000   000   0xx10   00
```

is written in much more readable symbolic form as:

```
PCnext, CacheFetch, PC + 4
```

Note that two of the fields ("register control" and "sequence control"), which have the default all-0s settings, do not appear in this symbolic representation. These default settings simply specify that no register writing occurs and the following microinstruction is executed next. Also, settings of the two fields "ALU inputs" and "ALU function" are combined into an expression that identifies the inputs applied to the ALU, and the operation performed by it, much more clearly.

Based on the notation in Table 14.3, the complete microprogram for the multicycle MicroMIPS implementation is shown in Figure 14.8. Note that each line represents one microinstruction and that microinstruction labels ending in 1 (2) are arrived at from the dispatch 1 (2) table of Figure 14.7.

The microprogram in Figure 14.8, consisting of 37 microinstructions, completely defines the operation of MicroMIPS hardware for instruction execution. If the topmost microinstruction labeled "fetch" is stored at ROM address 0, then starting the machine with the μPC cleared to 0 will cause program execution beginning at the instruction specified in PC. Thus, part of the booting process for MicroMIPS consists of clearing μPC to 0 and setting PC to the address of the system routine that initializes the machine.

```
fetch:       PCnext, CacheFetch, PC + 4          # State 0 (start)
             PC + 4imm, µPCdisp1                  # State 1
lui1:        lui(imm)                             # State 7lui
             rt ← z, µPCfetch                     # State 8lui
add1:        x + y                                # State 7add
             rd ← z, µPCfetch                     # State 8add
sub1:        x - y                                # State 7sub
             rd ← z, µPCfetch                     # State 8sub
slt1:        x - y                                # State 7slt
             rd ← z, µPCfetch                     # State 8slt
addi1:       x + imm                              # State 7addi
             rt ← z, µPCfetch                     # State 8addi
slti1:       x - imm                              # State 7slti
             rt ← z, µPCfetch                     # State 8slti
and1:        x ∧ y                                # State 7and
             rd ← z, µPCfetch                     # State 8and
or1:         x ∨ y                                # State 7or
             rd ← z, µPCfetch                     # State 8or
xor1:        x ⊕ y                                # State 7xor
             rd ← z, µPCfetch                     # State 8xor
nor1:        x ~∨ y                               # State 7nor
             rd ← z, µPCfetch                     # State 8nor
andi1:       x ∧ imm                              # State 7andi
             rt ← z, µPCfetch                     # State 8andi
ori1:        x ∨ imm                              # State 7ori
             rt ← z, µPCfetch                     # State 8ori
xori:        x ⊕ imm                              # State 7xori
             rt ← z, µPCfetch                     # State 8xori
lwsw1:       x + imm, µPCdisp2                    # State 2
lw2:         CacheLoad                            # State 3
             rt ← Data, µPCfetch                  # State 4
sw2:         CacheStore, µPCfetch                 # State 6
j1:          PCjump, µPCfetch                     # State 5j
jr1:         PCjreg, µPCfetch                     # State 5jr
branch1:     PCbranch, µPCfetch                   # State 5branch
jal1:        PCjump, $31 ← PC, µPCfetch           # State 5jal
syscall1:    PCsyscall, µPCfetch                  # State 5syscall
```

Figure 14.8 The complete microprogram for MicroMIPS. The comments on the right show that each microinstruction corresponds to a state or substate in the control state machine of Figure 14.4.

```
regreg1:      x ⊗ y                          # State 7regreg
              rd ← z, µPCfetch               # State 8regreg
regimm1:      x ⊗ imm                        # State 7regimm
              rt ← z, µPCfetch               # State 8regimm
```

Figure 14.9 Alternate MicroMIPS microinstructions representing states 7 and 8 in the control state machine of Figure 14.4.

Note that there is a great deal of repetition in the microprogram of Figure 14.8. These correspond to substates of states 7 and 8 of the control state machine of Figure 14.4. If the 5-bit function code, which now forms part of the microinstruction, is provided directly to the ALU by a separate decoder, we need just two microinstructions for each of the states 7 and 8 of the control state machine. The changes are depicted in Figure 14.9, suggesting that the complete microprogram now consists of 15 microinstructions, with each microinstruction being 17 bits wide (the 5-bit ALU function field is removed from the 22-bit microinstruction of Figure 14.6).

Further reduction in the number of microinstructions is still possible (see the end-of-chapter problems for some examples).

It is also possible to reduce the width of the microinstructions further through more efficient encoding of the control signal values. Note that the microinstruction format of Figure 14.6 holds one bit for each of the 20 control signals in the data path of Figure 14.3, plus 2 bits to control microinstruction sequencing. Such an approach leads to *horizontal microinstructions*. Referring to Table 14.3, we note that the 4-bit cache control field can hold only one of four possible bit patterns: the default bit pattern 0000 and the three patterns listed in Table 14.3. These four possibilities can be efficiently encoded in 2 bits, thus reducing the microinstruction width by 2 bits. All other fields, except for sequence control, can be similarly compacted. Such compact encodings require the use of decoders to derive the actual control signal values from their encoded forms in microinstructions. Microinstructions in which signal value combinations are compactly encoded are known as *vertical microinstructions*. In the extreme case of a vertical encoding, each microinstruction specifies a single microoperation using a format that is quite similar to that of a machine language instruction. Clearly, the designer has a spectrum of choices from purely horizontal to extreme vertical format. Microinstruction formats that are close to purely horizontal, are faster (because they do not need much decoding), and allow concurrent operations among the data path components.

14.6 Dealing with Exceptions

The control state diagram of Figure 14.4, and its associated hardwired or microprogrammed control implementation, specify the behavior of the MicroMIPS hardware in the course of normal instruction execution. As long as nothing unusual occurs, the instructions are executed one by one and the intended effect of the program is observed in updated register and memory contents. However, things can and do go wrong within the machine. The following are some of the problems, or *exceptions*, that must be dealt with:

- ALU operation leads to overflow (incorrect result is obtained).
- Opcode field holds a pattern that does not represent a legal operation.
- Cache error-detecting code checker deems an accessed word invalid.
- Sensor or monitor signals a hazardous condition (e.g., overheating).

A common way of dealing with such exceptions is to force immediate control transfer to an operating system routine known as *exception handler*. This routine either initiates remedial action to correct or circumvent the problem or, in the extreme, terminates the execution of the program to prevent further corruption of data and/or damage to system components.

Besides exceptions, caused by events internal to the machine's CPU, the control unit must deal with *interrupts,* defined as external events that must be dealt with promptly. Whereas exceptions are often undesirable events, interrupts may be due to anticipated completion of tasks by input/output devices, notification of data availability from sensors, arrival of messages over a network, and so on. However, a processor's reaction to an interrupt is quite similar to its handling of exceptions. Therefore, in what follows, we focus on the overflow and illegal-operation exceptions to demonstrate the procedures and mechanisms required. Interrupts will be discussed more thoroughly in Chapter 24. Figure 14.10 shows how overflow and illegal-operation

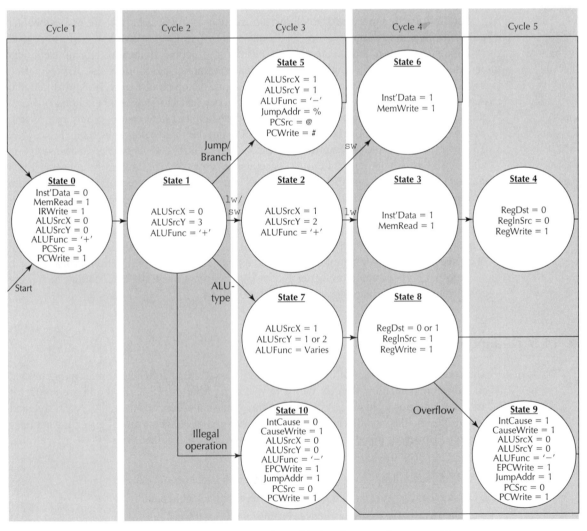

Figure 14.10 Exception states 9 and 10 added to the control state machine.

exceptions can be incorporated into the control state machine of our multicycle MicroMIPS implementation.

An arithmetic overflow is observed in state 8, following the ALU operation in state 7. Assertion of the overflow output signal of the ALU forces the state machine into the special state 9. So that the cause of the exception can be later determined by the exception handling routine, the "Cause" register is set to 1 (a code for overflow), the current value of the program counter, minus 4 (to nullify its advancement to the next instruction), is saved in the exception program counter (EPC) register, and control is transferred to the address "SysCallAddr," the entry point of an operating system routine. For the place of Cause and EPC registers in the machine hardware, refer to Figure 5.1.

An illegal operation in the opcode field is detected in state 1, where the instruction is decoded. A corresponding signal is asserted by the detecting circuit, which then forces the control state machine into the special state 10. Again a code for cause of the exception, and the address of the current instruction that led to it, are saved before control is transferred to the exception handler.

The two examples we have discussed show the general procedure for dealing with an exception or interrupt. A code showing the cause of the exception or interrupt is saved in the Cause register for the benefit of the operating system. The address of the current instruction being executed is saved in the EPC register so that program execution can resume from that point once the problem has been dealt with. An mfc0 instruction (similar to mfc1 of Table 12.1) allows us to examine the contents of registers in Coprocessor 0. Returning from the exception handling routine to the interrupted program is quite similar to returning from a procedure, as discussed in Section 6.1.

PROBLEMS

14.1 Details of multicycle data path

a. Label each of the lines in Figure 14.2 with the number of binary signals it represents.
b. Repeat part a for Figure 14.3.

14.2 Data path selection options

There are three pairs of related multiplexers in Figure 14.3. In order from left to right, the first pair feeds the register file, the second pair supplies operands to the ALU, and the third pair, located near the right edge of the diagram, selects the PC input.

a. The multiplexers feeding the register file have three and two settings, respectively; thus, there are six combinations when the settings are taken together. For each of these six combinations, indicate whether it is ever used and, if so, for executing which MicroMIPS instruction(s).
b. Repeat part a for the pair of multiplexers supplying the ALU operands (eight combinations).

c. Repeat part a for the pair of multiplexers selecting the PC input (eight combinations).

14.3 Extending the multicycle data path

Suggest some simple changes (the simpler, the better) in the multicycle data path of Figure 14.3 so that the following instructions can be included in the machine's instruction set:

a. Load byte (lb)
b. Load byte unsigned (lbu)
c. Store byte (sb)

14.4 Adding other instructions

Certain other instructions can be added to the instruction set of MicroMIPS if desired. Consider the following pseudoinstructions from Table 7.1 and assume that we want to include them in MicroMIPS as regular instructions. In each case, choose an appropriate encoding for the instruction and specify all modifications required in the multicycle data path and associated control circuits. Make sure that the chosen encodings are not in conflict with other MiniMIPS instructions listed in Tables 6.2 and 12.1.

a. Move (`move`)
b. Load immediate (`li`)
c. Absolute value (`abs`)
d. Negate (`neg`)
e. Not (`not`)
f. Branch less than (`blt`)

14.5 Control state machine

In the control state machine of Figure 14.4, state 5 does not completely specify the values to be used for the control signals; rather, the use of external circuits is assumed to derive control signal values in accordance with the notes in the upper left corner of Figure 14.4. Divide state 5 into a minimal number of substates, called 5a, 5b, and so on, so that within each substate, all control signal values are completely determined (as is the case for all other states, except for states 7 and 8).

14.6 Control state machine

In the control state machine of Figure 14.4, states 7 and 8 do not completely specify the values to be used for all control signals. Incomplete specifications, to be resolved by means of external control circuits, consist of the values assigned to control signals ALUSrcY and ALUFunc in state 7 and RegDst in state 8. Show that ignoring ALUFunc, which is still to be determined externally, the specifications of ALUSrcY and RegDst can be rendered complete by using two pairs of states: 7a/8a and 7b/8b.

14.7 Instruction decoding in MicroMIPS

The use of two 6-to-64 decoders in Figure 14.5 appears wasteful, since only a small subset of the 64 outputs in each decoder is useful. Show how each of the 6-to-64 decoders in Figure 14.5 can be replaced by a 4-to-16 decoder and a small amount of additional logic circuitry (the smaller, the better). *Hint:* In the op decoder of Figure 14.5, most of the first 16 outputs are useful, but only 2 of the remaining 48 outputs are used.

14.8 Control signals for multicycle MicroMIPS

Logic expressions for a number of the 20 control signals, shown in Figure 14.3, were derived in

Section 14.3 based on the outputs of various decoding circuits. Derive logic expressions for all remaining signals, aiming to simplify and share circuit components to the extent possible.

14.9 Performance of multicycle control

In Example 14.1, let the relative frequencies of R_a-, R_b-, and R_c-type instructions be f_a, f_b, and f_c, respectively, with $f_a + f_b + f_c = 1$.

a. Find a relationship between the three relative frequencies if the multicycle design is to be 1.8 times as fast as the single-cycle design.
b. Compute the actual frequencies from the result of part a assuming $f_b = f_c$.
c. What is the maximum speedup factor of the multicycle design relative to the single-cycle design over all possible values for the three relative frequencies?

14.10 Performance of multicycle control

An instruction set is composed of h different instruction classes, with the execution time of class-i instructions being $3 + i$ ns, $1 \leq i \leq h$. Single-cycle control clearly implies a clock cycle of $3 + h$ ns. Consider a multicycle control implementation with a clock cycle of 1 ns and assume that class-i instructions can then be executed in $3 + i$ clock cycles; that is, ignore any overhead associated with multicycle control.

a. Derive the performance advantage (speedup factor) of multicycle control relative to single-cycle control, assuming that the various instruction classes are used with the same frequency.
b. Show that the performance benefit derived in part a is an increasing function of h, thereby proving that any speedup factor is possible for a suitably large h.
c. Repeat part a for the case when the relative frequency of class-i instructions is proportional to $1/i$.
d. How does the performance benefit of part c vary with h, and does the speedup factor grow indefinitely with increasing h, as was the case in part b?

14.11 Performance of multicycle control

Repeat the Problem 14.10, this time assuming a clock cycle of 2 ns for the multicycle design, leading to class-i instructions requiring $\lceil (3 + i)/2 \rceil$ clock cycles.

14.12 Single-cycle versus multicycle control

a. Discuss conditions under which a multicycle implementation of control would be decidedly inferior to single-cycle implementation.
b. How does varying the memory access latency affect the performance of single-cycle versus multicycle control implementation, assuming that the number of cycles and the actions performed within each cycle do not change?
c. Discuss the implications our your answers to parts a and b in the specific case of MicroMIPS.

14.13 Microinstructions

a. Construct a table with 6 columns and 37 rows that contains the binary field contents for the microprogram shown in Figure 14.8.
b. Repeat part a, assuming the microprogram of Figure 14.8 has been modified according to Figure 14.9 and the associated discussion.

14.14 Microprogrammed control

a. How would the microprogram in Figure 14.8 change if the controller hardware in Figure 14.7 contained only one dispatch table instead of two?
b. What changes are needed in Figure 14.7 if we were to include a third dispatch table?
c. Argue that the change in part b offers no advantage with regard to the microprogram in Figure 14.8.
d. Under what circumstances would the change in part b be advantageous?

14.15 Microprogramming

a. In connection with Figure 14.8, we noted that a simple modification allows us to have two substates for each of states 7 and 8, namely, 7regreg, 7regimm, 8regreg, 8regimm. Is it possible to remove these substates altogether and have only one microinstruction for each of the states 7 and 8?
b. What does it take to allow merging all the substates of state 5, corresponding to the last five

microinstructions in the microprogram of Figure 14.8, into a single microinstruction?

14.16 Microinstruction formats

Our discussion at the end of Section 14.5 indicates that the width of a microinstruction can be reduced if we use a more compact encoding for the valid combinations of signal values in each field.

a. Assuming that we keep the same six fields in the microinstruction as those in Figure 14.6, and that the most compact encoding is used for each field, determine the width of the microinstruction.
b. Show that it is possible to reduce the microinstruction width further by combining two or more of its fields into a single field. Argue that the savings achieved in microinstruction width is not worth the added decoding complexity and associated delay.

14.17 Exception handling

Upon encountering an exception, we could save the current contents of PC, rather than (PC) − 4, in the exception program counter, letting the operating system figure out the address of the offending instruction. Would this modification simplify the multicycle MicroMIPS data path or its associated control state machine? Fully justify your answer.

14.18 Exception handling

Assume that instructions and data are stored in the cache of the multicycle MicroMIPS using an error-detecting code. Each time cache memory is accessed, a special error detection circuit checks the validity of the encoded word and asserts the "CacheError" signal if it is an invalid codeword. Add exception states to Figure 14.10 to deal with a detected error in:

a. Instruction word
b. Memory data word

14.19 URISC

Consider the URISC processor described in Section 8.6 [Mava88].

a. Design a hardwired control unit for URISC.
b. Describe a microprogrammed implementation of URISC and provide the complete microprogram using a suitable notation.

REFERENCES AND FURTHER READINGS

[Andr80]   Andrews, M., *Principles of Firmware Engineering in Microprogram Control,* Computer Science Press, 1980.

[Bane82]   Banerji, D. K., and J. Raymond, *Elements of Microprogramming,* Prentice-Hall, 1982.

[Mava88]   Mavaddat, F., and B. Parhami, "URISC: The Ultimate Reduced Instruction Set Computer," *Int. J. Electrical Engineering Education,* Vol. 25, pp. 327–334, 1988.

[Patt98]   Patterson, D. A., and J. L. Hennessy, *Computer Organization and Design: The Hardware/Software Interface,* Morgan Kaufmann, 2nd ed., 1998.

15

PIPELINED DATA PATHS

"There is no easy way around the branch delay penalty [because] processor cycle time is decreasing at a faster rate than the memory cycle time. . . . These trends tend to increase the number of cycles involved in instruction execution, and also increase the relative size of the branch penalty."

—*Michael J. Flynn, Computer Architecture: Pipelined and Parallel Processor Design, 1995*

"The HMO maternity ward, drive-through procedure: (1) Pull up to the delivery window, (2) Push, (3) Pay at the cashier window, (4) Pick up baby. Have a nice day!"

—*Based on a "Non Sequitur" cartoon by Wiley*

TOPICS IN THIS CHAPTER

15.1 Pipelining Concepts

15.2 Pipeline Stalls or Bubbles

15.3 Pipeline Timing and Performance

15.4 Pipelined Data Path Design

15.5 Pipelined Control

15.6 Optimal Pipelining

Pipelining, once an exotic technique reserved for top-of-the-line computers, has become commonplace in computer design. Pipelining in processors is based on the same principle as assembly lines in manufacturing: there is no need to wait until one unit is fully assembled before beginning work on the next one. There are some differences, though, that form the core of our discussions in this and the following chapter. For example, whereas one car is a completely independent entity from those preceding and following it on the assembly line, the same cannot be said about instructions; there exist data and control dependencies that must be honored to ensure correct operation. In this chapter, we lay the foundation for pipelined instruction execution, discussing how control signals are handled, and pointing out some of the challenges. Solutions to the more difficult challenges will be covered in the next chapter.

■ 15.1 Pipelining Concepts

We have completed two designs for MicroMIPS; the single-cycle design of Chapter 13 with a clock rate of 125 MHz and CPI of 1 and the multicycle design of Chapter 14 with a clock rate of 500 MHz and CPI of approximately 4. Both designs offered roughly the same performance of about 125 MIPS. Is there any way of exceeding the performance of 125 MIPS? There are at least two strategies for achieving greater performance:

Strategy 1: Use multiple independent data paths that can accept several instructions that are read out at once: this leads to *multiple-instruction-issue* or *superscalar* organization.

Strategy 2: Overlap the execution of several instructions in the single-cycle design, starting the next instruction before the previous one has run to completion: this leads to *pipelined* or *super-pipelined* organization.

Let us postpone the discussion of the first strategy to Section 16.6 and focus on the second one in the rest of this chapter.

Consider a 5-stage process for registration at the start of an academic term. Students, after completing their course selection forms, must proceed through these steps: (1) seek approval from an academic counselor, (2) pay at the cashier's window, (3) turn in the signed course selection form and evidence of payment to the registrar, (4) be photographed for the picture ID, (5) pick up the ID card, receipt, and class schedule. Suppose each of these stages takes about 2 minutes and is performed at a booth or window located in a large room. We could admit one student to the room, let him or her finish the registration process in about 10 minutes, and admit another student once the first one has left the room. This corresponds to our single-cycle design in Chapter 13. A better approach is to admit one student to the room every 2 minutes, because once the first student has moved from the approval stage to the payment stage, the academic counselor can help the next student, and so on down the line. This assembly line strategy, known as *pipelining,* allows us to increase the processing throughput without using any additional resources. The improvement is achieved by simply making full use of resources that would otherwise remain idle in the single-cycle approach.

The five steps in the student registration process depicted in Figure 15.1 can be likened to the five instruction execution steps in MicroMIPS: (1) instruction fetch, (2) instruction decode and register access, (3) ALU operation, (4) data memory access, and (5) register writeback. Given that each of these steps takes 1–2 ns, as assumed in Section 13.6, we can initiate the execution of a new instruction every 2 ns, provided the state of each instruction and its partial results are saved in pipeline registers located between pipeline stages. Figure 15.2 shows the execution of five instructions in such a pipelined fashion. The similarity of this approach to the industrial assembly line is quite obvious. In the case of the assembly line in an automobile factory, one auto may take hours to assemble, but after the first auto has rolled off the assembly line, subsequent ones emerge within minutes of each other.

Figure 15.1 Pipelining in the student registration process.

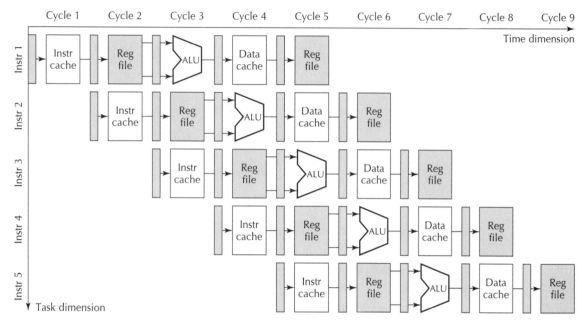

Figure 15.2 Pipelining in the MicroMIPS instruction execution process.

Like most analogies, the correspondence between instruction execution and student registration or automobile assembly is imperfect. For example, whereas automobiles on an assembly line are totally independent of each other, instructions can and do depend on the outcome of previous instructions. An instruction that reads the content of a register is fully dependent on a previous instruction that loads a value into the same register. Similarly, the execution of an instruction that follows a branch instruction in the pipeline is dependent on whether the branch condition was satisfied.

The graphical representation of a pipeline in Figure 15.2 is known as task-time diagram. In a task-time diagram, stages of each task are horizontally aligned and their positions along the horizontal axis represent the timing of their execution. A second graphical representation for a pipeline is the space-time diagram which is shown in Figure 15.3b alongside a more abstract form of the corresponding task-time diagram in Figure 15.3a. In a space-time diagram, the vertical axis represents stages in the pipeline (the space dimension) and boxes representing the various stages of a task are diagonally aligned.

When a finite number of tasks are executed in a pipeline, the space-time diagram clearly shows the pipeline *start-up region,* where all stages are not yet fully utilized, and the pipeline *drainage region,* composed of stages that have become idle because the last task has left them. If a pipeline executes many tasks, the overhead of start-up and drainage can be ignored and the effective throughput of the pipeline taken to be 1 task per cycle. In terms of instruction execution, this corresponds to an effective CPI of 1. If the 5-stage pipeline has to be drained after executing 7 instructions (as in Figure 15.3b), then 7 instructions are executed in 11 cycles, making the effective CPI equal to $11/7 = 1.57$. Hence, gaining the full benefit of a pipeline requires that it not be drained too often. As we will see later, this is quite hard to ensure for instruction execution owing to data and control dependencies.

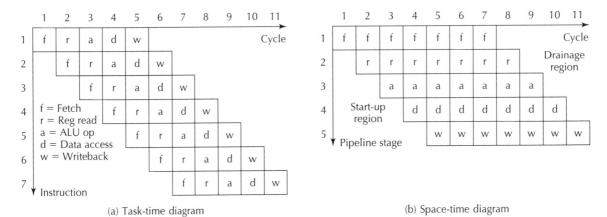

(a) Task-time diagram   (b) Space-time diagram

Figure 15.3 Two abstract graphical representations of a 5-stage pipeline executing 7 tasks (instructions).

Ideally, a q-stage pipeline can increase instruction execution throughput by a factor of q. This is not quite the case because of the following:

1. Effects of pipeline start-up and drainage
2. Wastage due to unequal stage delays
3. Time overhead of saving stage results in registers
4. Safety margin in clock period necessitated by clock skew

We will discuss the first factor later in this chapter and will mostly ignore the last two factors. Wastage due to unequal stage delays is evident from the MicroMIPS pipeline in which stage delays are 2, 1, 2, 2, and 1 ns. Even ignoring all other overheads, this leads to a clock rate of 500 MHz for the 5-stage pipelined implementation and a speedup factor of at most 4 rather than the ideal factor of 5 relative to the single-cycle implementation.

Example 15.1: Throughput of a photocopier   A photocopier with a document feeder capable of holding x sheets copies the first sheet in 4 s and each subsequent sheet in 1 s. The copier's paper path can be viewed as a 4-stage pipeline with each stage having a latency of 1 s. The first sheet goes through all 4 pipeline stages and emerges at the output after 4 s. Each subsequent sheet is also copied in 4 s, but emerges 1 s after the previous sheet. Discuss how the throughput of this photocopier varies with x, assuming that loading the document feeder and removing the copies takes 15 s altogether. Also, compare the photocopier's throughput with that of a non-pipelined unit that copies each sheet in 4 s.

Solution: Loading the document feeder with input sheets and unloading the output copies constitute parts of start-up and drainage overheads. The larger the value of x, the smaller the effect of these overheads on the throughput. Ideally, when x approaches infinity, a steady-state throughput of 1 copy per second is achieved, leading to a speedup of 4 over a nonpipelined copier. Performance under more realistic conditions can be easily derived. For example, with the given assumptions, each batch of x sheets will be copied in $15 + 4 + (x - 1) = 18 + x$ seconds. This should be compared to $4x$ seconds for a copier with no pipelining. Thus, for $x > 6$, a performance gain is achieved and for $x = 50$, the speedup is $200/68 = 2.94$.

■ 15.2 Pipeline Stalls or Bubbles

Data dependency in pipelines (execution of one instruction depending on completion of a previous instruction) can cause pipeline stalls which diminish the performance. There are two types of data dependency for our MicroMIPS pipeline:

Read-after-compute: register access after updating it with a computed value

Read-after-load: register access after updating it with data from memory

Two examples of read-after-compute data dependency appear in Figure 15.4 where the third instruction uses the value that the second instruction writes into register $8 and the fourth instruction needs the result of the third instruction in register $9. Note that writing into register $8 is completed in cycle 6; hence, reading of the new value from register $8 is possible beginning with cycle 7. The third instruction, however, reads out registers $8 and $2 in cycle 4 and will thus not get the intended value for register $8. This data dependency problem can be solved by *bubble insertion* or via *data forwarding*.

Bubble Insertion

The first solution is for the assembler to detect this type of data dependency and insert three redundant but harmless instructions (adding 0 to a register or shifting a register by 0 bit) before the next instruction. Such an instruction, exemplified by the all-0s instruction in MicroMIPS, is sometimes referred to as a "*no-op*" (short for *no operation*). Because they perform no useful work and just take up memory locations to space out the data-dependent instructions, such no-op instructions essentially have the role of *bubbles* in a water pipe. We say that the assembler inserts three bubbles in the pipeline to resolve a read-after-compute data dependency. Actually, inserting two bubbles might suffice if we note that writing into and reading out of a register each take 1 ns; so it is feasible to design the register file to make the value written into a register in the first half of a 2 ns cycle available at the output in the second half of the same cycle.

Insertion of bubbles in a pipeline implies reduced throughput; inserting three bubbles obviously hurts the performance more than inserting two bubbles. Therefore, an objective of pipeline designers

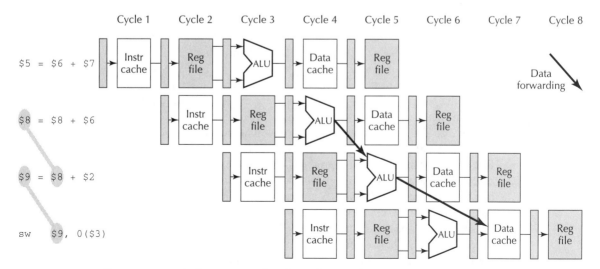

Figure 15.4 Read-after-compute data dependency and its possible resolution through data forwarding.

is to minimize the instances of bubble insertion. An intelligent compiler can also help mitigate the performance penalty. If instructions i and $i + 1$ have a read-after-compute data dependency, the compiler might look before instruction i or after instruction $i + 1$ in the program to see whether any instruction exists that can be relocated between the two data-dependent instructions without changing the correct functioning of the program. If, for example, two such instructions are found and moved, only one bubble needs to be inserted, leading to improved performance.

Data Forwarding

Note that in Figure 15.4, even though the result of the second instruction is not yet stored in register $8 by the time the third instruction needs it, the result is in fact available at the output of the ALU. Thus, if a bypass path is provided from the output of the ALU to one of its inputs, the needed value can be passed from the second instruction to the third one and used by the latter even though register $8 does not yet contain the correct value. This approach is known as *data forwarding*. Implementation details for data forwarding will be provided in Section 16.2.

Example 15.2: Bubble insertion   How many bubbles must be inserted for the second read-after-compute data dependency, involving register $9, in Figure 15.4? What if the last instruction in Figure 15.4 were changed to sw $3, 0($9)?

Solution: We still need three bubbles because register read is performed two cycles before the corresponding write, whereas it must be done one cycle after. As before, if register write and read can occur in the same 2 ns cycle, two bubbles would suffice. Data forwarding can of course obviate the need for bubbles (see Figure 15.4). If the last instruction is replaced by sw $3, 0($9), content of register $9 would be needed as input to the ALU for address calculation. This would still involve insertion of three (or two) bubbles.

A read-after-load data dependency is shown in Figure 15.5 where the third instruction uses the value that the second instruction loads into register $8. Without data forwarding, the third instruction must read register $8 in cycle 7, one cycle after the second instruction completes the load process. This implies the insertion of three bubbles into the pipeline to avoid using the wrong value in the third instruction. Note that data forwarding alone cannot solve the problem in this case. The value needed by the ALU in the third instruction becomes available at the end of cycle 5; so even if a data forwarding mechanism (to be discussed in Section 16.2) is available, we still need one bubble to ensure correct operation. An intelligent compiler might look before the lw instruction to see whether there exists any instruction that can be placed after lw without affecting the program semantics. If so, the bubble slot would not go to waste. This type of instruction reordering is quite common in modern compilers.

Another form of dependency between instructions is *control dependency*. This is exemplified by a conditional branch instruction. When a conditional branch is executed, the location of the next instruction depends on whether the branch condition is satisfied. However, because branch instructions in MicroMIPS are based on testing the contents of registers (sign of one or comparison of two), the earliest we can hope to resolve the branch condition is at the end of the second pipeline stage. Therefore, one bubble is required after every conditional branch instruction. This might even be true for an unconditional jump instruction if instruction decoding begins in the second cycle, preventing us from learning that the instruction is a jump in time to modify the PC for the next instruction fetched. In the case of data dependencies, we

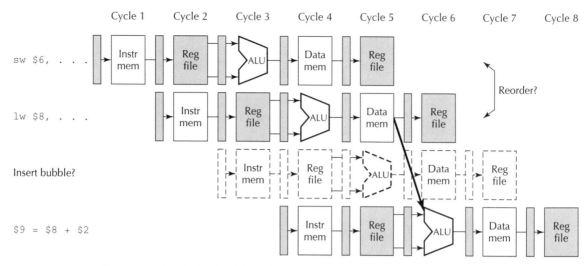

Figure 15.5 Read-after-load data dependency and its possible resolution through bubble insertion and data forwarding.

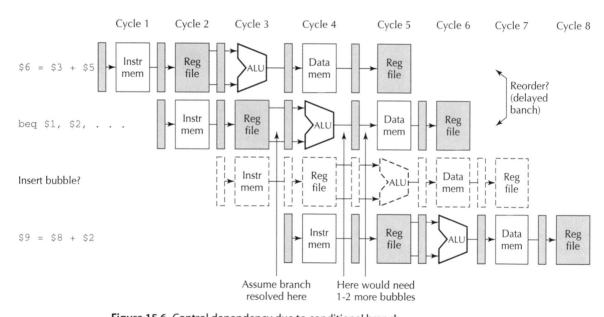

Figure 15.6 Control dependency due to conditional branch.

noted that data forwarding obviates the need for most of the bubbles that would otherwise be needed. Is there a corresponding method for avoiding bubbles after branch instructions?

A possible method is the use of delayed branches. In other words, the definition of a branch instruction is modified so that beq . . . means "check the condition, execute the next instruction in sequence, then branch to the indicated address if the branch condition is satisfied." The extra instruction that is executed before branching occurs is said to occupy the *branch delay slot*. In the example of Figure 15.6, reordering the first two instructions and considering the branch to be of the delayed variety obviates the need for inserting a bubble.

Note that checking the branch condition in stage 2 of the pipeline requires the provision of a comparator to signal the equality or inequality of register contents in the case of beq or bne instructions, respectively. We could avoid this extra circuitry, opting instead to use the ALU to perform a subtraction and then deducing equality or inequality based on the ALU's "zero" output flag. This, however, would increase the branch penalty to two or three bubbles, depending on whether, after the ALU operation, there is still enough time left in stage 3 of the pipeline to set the PC to the branch target address. This is too high a price to pay for avoiding a relatively simple comparator circuit.

■ 15.3 Pipeline Timing and Performance

As stated earlier, a q-stage pipeline ideally increases instruction execution throughput by a factor of q. This is because without any overhead or dependency of any kind, and assuming that a task of latency t is divisible into q stages having equal latencies t/q, a new task can be initiated every t/q time units instead of every t time units without pipelining. In this section, we aim to determine the actual performance gain by modeling the effects of overheads and dependencies.

The overhead due to unequal stage latencies and latching of signals between stages can be modeled by taking the stage delay to be $t/q + \tau$ instead of the ideal t/q, as in Figure 15.7. Then, the increase in throughput will drop from the ideal of q to

$$\text{Throughput increase in a } q\text{-stage pipeline} = \frac{t}{t/q + \tau} = \frac{q}{1 + q\tau/t}$$

So, the ideal throughput enhancement factor of q can be approached, provided the cumulative pipeline latching overhead $q\tau$ is considerably smaller than t. Figure 15.8 plots the throughput improvement as a function of q for different overhead ratios τ/t.

The pipeline throughput equation and Figure 15.8 are reminiscent of Amdahl's law (see Section 4.3). In fact, we can write Amdahl's speedup formula as follows to expose the similarities further:

$$\text{Speed-up with } p\text{-fold improvement in fraction } 1 - f = \frac{1}{f + (1 - f)/p} = \frac{p}{1 + (p-1)f}$$

We note that τ/t (the relative magnitude of the per-stage time overhead τ) plays roughly the same role as Amdahl's unaffected or unimproved fraction f; both limit the maximum performance that can be attained.

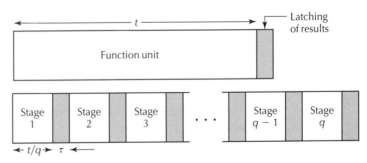

Figure 15.7 Pipelined form of a function unit with latching overhead.

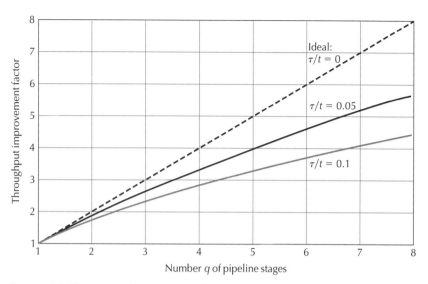

Figure 15.8 Throughput improvement due to pipelining as a function of the number of pipeline stages for different pipelining overheads.

For our pipelined MicroMIPS implementation, we have $t = 8$ ns (corresponding to the latency in single-cycle implementation), $q = 5$, and $q\tau = 2$ ns. This leads to a throughput improvement factor of 4 with our 5-stage pipeline. Thus, performance of the pipelined implementation is 500 MIPS versus 125 MIPS for the single-cycle design. Note, however, that we have not yet considered the effects of data and control dependencies.

We next try to model the effects of data and control dependencies. To keep our analysis simple, we assume that most data dependencies are resolved through data forwarding, with a single bubble inserted in the pipeline only for a read-after-load data dependency (Figure 15.5). Similarly, a fraction of branch instructions (those for which the compiler does not succeed in filling the branch delay slot with a useful instruction) lead to insertion of a single bubble in the pipeline. In any case, no type of dependency results in the insertion of more than one bubble. Let the fraction of all instructions that are followed by a bubble in the pipeline be β. Such bubbles effectively reduce the throughput by a factor of $1 + \beta$, making the throughput equation

$$\text{Throughput increase with dependencies} = \frac{q}{(1 + q\tau/t)(1 + \beta)}$$

Now consider the instruction mix used earlier in our evaluation of the single-cycle and multi-cycle designs:

R-type	44%
Load	24%
Store	12%
Branch	18%
Jump	2%

It is reasonable to assume that about a quarter of our branch and load instruction will be followed by bubbles in the pipeline. This corresponds to $0.25(0.24 + 0.18) = 0.105 = \beta$ or 10.5% of all instructions. With these and our previous assumptions, the performance of the pipelined MicroMIPS implementation is estimated to be:

$$\frac{500 \text{ MIPS}}{1.105} = 452 \text{ MIPS}$$

Even if we proceed with the more pessimistic assumption that half rather than a quarter of load and branch instructions will be followed by bubbles in the pipeline, the performance would still be $500/1.21 = 413$ MIPS, which is more than 3.3 times that of the single-cycle or multi-cycle design.

Example 15.3: Effective CPI   Calculate the effective CPI for the pipelined MicroMIPS implementation with the overhead assumptions given in the preceding discussion.

Solution: Except for the effect of bubbles, a new instruction is initiated in every clock cycle. Because a fraction β of the instructions are followed by a single bubble in the pipeline, the effective CPI is $1 + \beta$. This leads to a CPI of 1.105 or 1.21 for $\beta = 0.105$ or 0.21, respectively. Based on this result, we observe that the pipelined implementation essentially combines the benefits of the single-cycle and multicycle implementations in that it nearly achieves the low CPI of the former with the higher clock frequency of the latter.

Our discussion thus far was based on the assumption that a function with a latency of t can be readily subdivided into q stages of equal latency t/q. In practice, this is often not the case. For example, the single-cycle MicroMIPS data path had a latency of 8 ns, which we divided into 5 stages, each with a latency of 2 ns (not $8/5 = 1.6$ ns). The effect of this function subdivision overhead on performance is exactly the same as that of the latching overhead τ. In other words, the increase in stage delay from the ideal of 1.6 ns to 2.0 ns can be viewed as corresponding to a stage overhead of $\tau = 0.4$ ns. Hence, the parameter τ can be used to incorporate both the latching overhead and the function subdivision overhead.

■ 15.4 Pipelined Data Path Design

The pipelined data path for MicroMIPS is obtained by inserting latches or registers in the single-cycle data path of Figure 13.3. The result is shown in Figure 15.9. The five pipeline stages are (1) instruction fetch, (2) register access and instruction decode, (3) ALU operation, (4) data cache access, and (5) register writeback.

Comparing the pipelined data path of Figure 15.9 with the nonpipelined version in Figure 13.3 reveals a number of changes and additions besides interstage latches:

Inclusion of an incrementer and a mux within the logic of stage 1

Change in placement for the mux originally feeding the register file

Change in the number of inputs for the mux feeding the ALU

Splitting of the rightmost mux into two muxes in stages 4 and 5

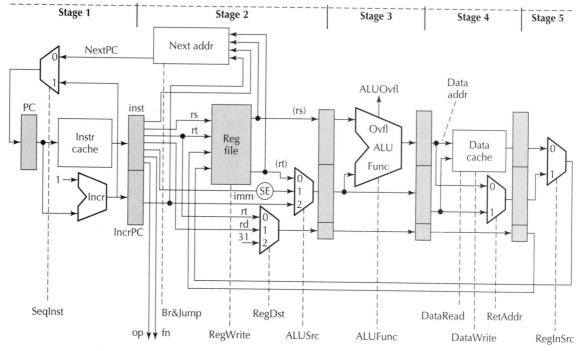

Figure 15.9 Key elements of the pipelined MicroMIPS data path.

Reasons for these differences will become clear as the roles of the five pipeline stages are described in the following paragraphs.

Pipeline stage 1 (instruction fetch): This stage is very similar to the instruction fetch segment of the single-cycle data path in Figure 13.3. One key difference is that an incrementer has been included to compute (PC) + 4, by adding 1 to the upper 30 bits in the program counter. In the single-cycle data path, this incrementation was combined with the branch address logic. Here, given that branching decision and address calculation is performed in the second pipeline stage, we need to increment the PC in stage 1 to be able to fetch the next instruction. This incremented PC value is saved in a special register between stages 1 and 2 for use in stage 2. The control signal SeqInst is deasserted unless the instruction currently in the second pipeline stage is a branch or jump, in which case the NextPC output of the "Next addr" box at the top of Figure 15.9 must be written into the PC.

Pipeline stage 2 (register read and instruction decode): Comparing this stage with the corresponding segment of the single-cycle data path in Figure 13.3, we note a number of changes. First, the multiplexer that chooses the register to be written into is not directly connected to the register file but rather to a special register between stages 2 and 3. This is because the action of writing into the chosen register occurs not in this stage but rather in stage 5. For this reason, the index of the register to be written into is carried along with the instruction as it moves from stage to stage and is used eventually in stage 5 for the writeback operation. The upper multiplexer in this second stage allows us to carry (rt) or the sign-extended immediate operand or the incremented PC value to the next stage. Options 0 and 1 correspond to the function of the multiplexer located between the register file and the ALU in Figure 13.3. Option 2 is needed only for the jal and syscall instructions which require the incremented PC value to be written into register $31.

Pipeline stage 3 (ALU operation): This stage is quite straightforward. The ALU is instructed, via the ALUFunc control signals, to perform an operation on its two inputs. Unlike in the single-cycle data path of Figure 13.3, no selection is involved for the ALU's lower input because this was done in stage 2 before the chosen input was saved.

Pipeline stage 4 (data memory access): This stage is very similar to its corresponding segment in the single-cycle data path of Figure 13.3. One key difference is the addition of a multiplexer to allow the incremented PC value to be sent on to stage 5 where it is written into register $31. This is needed only for jal and syscall instructions.

Pipeline stage 5 (register writeback): In this stage, data is written into a register if required by the instruction being executed. The need for writeback is indicated through the assertion of the RegWrite control signal. The register to be written into was previously selected in stage 2 of the pipeline, with its index passed on between stages in a 5-bit field (the bottom part of the pipeline registers between stages 2–3, 3–4, and 4–5 in Figure 15.9). The data to be written is the output of the data cache or one of the two values chosen in stage 4 and saved in a register between stages 4–5.

The "Next addr" block in Figure 15.9 is quite similar to the corresponding block in the single-cycle data path of Figure 13.3 (depicted in Figure 13.4), the only difference being that the $(PC)_{31:2}$ input to the circuit is now in incremented form owing to the incrementer used in stage 1. This change leads to the carry-in of the adder in Figure 13.4 being set to 0 instead of 1 and the top output of the circuit not being used.

Example 15.4: Contents of pipeline registers   The following sequence of MicroMIPS instructions is stored in memory beginning at the hex address 0x00605040:

```
lw    $t0,4($t1)      # $t0 ← mem[4+($t1)]
add   $t2,$s2,$s3     # $t2 ← ($s2) + ($s3)
xor   $t3,$s4,$s5     # $t3 ← ($s4) ⊕ ($s5)
```

Determine the successive contents of the pipeline registers in Figure 15.9 as these instructions are executed, beginning with an empty pipeline. Assume that register $si holds the integer 4i, register $t1 holds 0x10000000, and the content of location 0x10000004 in memory is 0x10203040.

Solution: The first instruction loads the word 0x10203040 into register $8 (see Figure 5.2 for register naming conventions). The second instruction puts the sum 0x00000008 + 0x0000000c = 0x00000014 into register $10. The third instruction places 0x00000010 ⊕ 0x00000014 = 0x00000004 into register $11. Table 15.1 shows the pipeline register contents in the course of executing these three instructions. The blank table entries following the three instructions represent unknown register contents corresponding to instructions that come afterwards. The column headings consist of register names and the stages between which the registers appear.

■ **TABLE 15.1** Pipeline register contents for Example 15.4.

Clock cycle	PC(0–1)	Inst(1–2) IncrPC(1–2)	Top(2–3) Bottom(2–3) Reg(2–3)	Top(3–4) Bottom(3–4) Reg(3–4)	Top(4–5) Bottom(4–5) Reg(4–5)
1	0x00605040				
2	0x00605044	lw $t0,4($t1) 0x00605044			
3	0x00605048	add $t2,$s2,$s3 0x00605048	0x10000000 0x00000004 $8		
4		xor $t3,$s4,$s5 0x0060504c	0x00000008 0x0000000c $10	0x10000004 0x10000000 $8	
5			0x00000010 0x00000014 $11	0x00000014 0x0000000c $10	0x10203040 0x10000004 $8
6				0x00000004 0x00000014 $11	0x00000000 0x00000014 $10
7					0x00000000 0x00000004 $11

15.5 Pipelined Control

As an instruction moves through the pipeline, it must carry along sufficient control information to allow the determination of all subsequent actions needed to complete its execution. Referring to Figure 15.9, when the instruction is decoded in stage 2, the following control signals are directly asserted by the instruction decoder:

Stages 1 and 2: SeqInst, Br&Jump, RegDst, ALUSrc

The remaining control signals will be needed in future stages and must thus be saved and sent along with the data in the interstage pipeline registers. So, the interstage pipeline registers must have room to store the following control signals generated in stage 2:

Interstage 2–3: ALUFunc, DataRead, DataWrite, RetAddr, RegInSrc, RegWrite
Interstage 3–4: DataRead, DataWrite, RetAddr, RegInSrc, RegWrite
Interstage 4–5: RegInSrc, RegWrite

Thus, control signals for stages 1 and 2 are generated in stage 2 and used right away, whereas the control signals for stages 3–5 are generated in stage 2 and passed on, along with any required data for the instruction, to subsequent stages in which they are used. Figure 15.10 shows the required extensions of the interstage pipeline registers to hold the needed control information at the end of stages 2, 3, and 4.

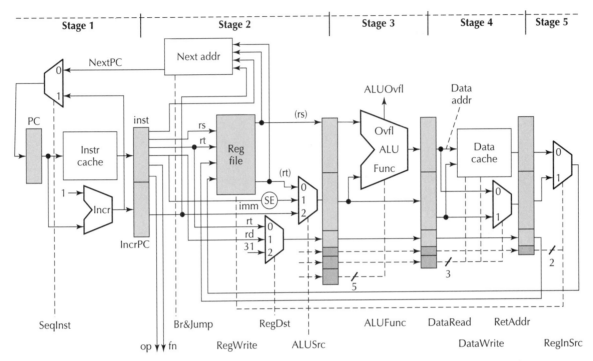

Figure 15.10 Pipelined control signals.

Example 15.5: Specifying control signals For the instruction sequence given in Example 15.4, specify the control signals that are held in the extended pipeline registers of Figure 15.10 as the three instructions are executed.

Solution: Referring to Table 14.3, we obtain the 5-bit ALU function code used in stage 3 (Add'Sub, LogicFn, FnClass), the 3 control bits for stage 4 (DataRead, DataWrite, RetAddr), and the 2 control bits for stage 5 (RegInSrc, RegWrite). The results are summarized in Table 15.2, where clock cycles are the same as in Table 15.1. The column headings consist of the unit or function being controlled and the stages between which the control signals are stored.

■ **TABLE 15.2** Pipelined control signal values for Example 15.5.

Cycle	ALU(2–3), Cache(2–3), Writeback(2–3)	Cache(3–4), Writeback(3–4)	Writeback(4–5)
3	0xx10, 10x, 01		
4	0xx10, 000, 11	10x, 01	
5	x1011, 000, 11	000, 11	01
6		000, 11	11
7			11

■ 15.6 Optimal Pipelining

We now know that the performance of a processor can be improved by executing the instructions in a pipelined data path. A pipeline that has only a few stages is a *shallow pipeline,* while a pipeline with many stages is a *deep pipeline*. Of course, shallowness and depth are relative terms, so the boundary between the two classes of pipelines is rather fuzzy (like the distinction between short and tall people). As a rule, a pipeline with half a dozen or fewer stages is deemed shallow, whereas one having a dozen or more stages is considered deep. Increasing the number σ of pipeline stages, or the *depth of pipelining,* generally leads to performance improvement. However, performance does not increase linearly with σ. We have already discussed some of the reasons for this sublinear scaling of performance.

1. Clocking uncertainties and latch setup requirements impose a time overhead τ per stage. Given this overhead, the pipeline throughput improves with finer subdivisions of the data path, but the impact of τ becomes more and more pronounced as σ increases; even at the extreme of pipeline stages with negligible latency, the throughput can never exceed $1/\tau$.

2. If the σ stages of a pipeline do not have exactly the same latency, which is often the case owing to the irregularity of natural boundaries at which latches can be inserted, then even with no overhead, throughput will improve by a factor less than σ.

3. Data dependencies and branch/jump hazards sometimes make it impossible to keep pipelines full at all times. Instruction reordering by compilers can reduce the performance penalty of such dependencies and hazards, but there are always situations in which loss of throughput cannot be totally avoided.

In our pipelined implementation of MicroMIPS, we had the following stage latencies:

2 ns	Access to instruction memory
1 ns	Register readout and decoding
2 ns	ALU operation
2 ns	Data memory access
1 ns	Register writeback

We see that a 5-stage pipeline improves the MicroMIPS instruction execution throughput by a factor 4 in the best case (no stage time overhead of any kind and no stall).

Is there any way to achieve a better-than-fourfold throughput improvement for our pipelined MicroMIPS? As a first step, we note that, at least theoretically, performance can be increased by a factor of 8 if we build a pipeline with 1 ns stages. This would require that the 2 ns memory access and ALU operations be spread over two pipeline stages. For the ALU, the required two stages are readily formed by inserting latches midway through the critical path of the logic circuit. Referring to the analogy given in Figure 15.1, this is akin to dividing the function of the registrar's window into two subfunctions because it takes twice as much time as any of the other four stages. Spreading the memory access latency across two pipeline stages is not as clear-cut. Understanding how this might be done requires more knowledge of how the memory operates. So, here we accept that a two-stage pipelined memory is feasible and defer the discussion of implementation issues to Section 17.4.

Figure 15.11 contains an abstract representation of the resulting 8-stage pipeline for MicroMIPS and also shows how consecutive instructions are executed in it. Again, we have assumed that pipelining overhead is negligible, and thus when a 2 ns operation is divided into two pipeline stages, each stage will have a latency of 1 ns.

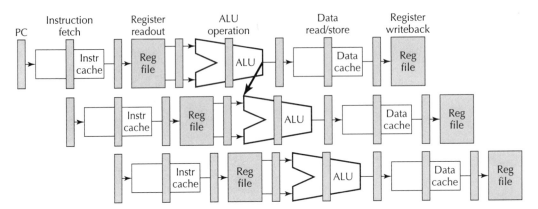

Figure 15.11 Higher-throughput pipelined data path for MicroMIPS and the execution of consecutive instructions in it.

Note that with the deeper pipeline of Figure 15.11, the branch condition is decided no earlier than the end of the third stage, as opposed to the second stage for Figure 15.2. This implies the insertion of two bubbles, or the provision of two delay slots, after each branch instruction. Whereas experience has shown that a single branch delay slot can almost always be filled by a compiler, the second of two delay slots is somewhat harder to use and may lead to the insertion of a bubble in the pipeline. Note that the preceding analysis is based on the optimistic assumption that the 1 ns cycle time still leaves enough time to compare contents of two registers in the same cycle when they are read out. This may not be feasible, leading to an additional bubble or delay slot. The situation for jump instructions is similar in that they also need at least two bubbles. However, this is a less serious problem, given that jumps are far less frequent than branches.

Data dependencies also have more serious consequences in a deeper pipeline. Consider, for example, a register read after a previous instruction that writes into the same register following an ALU operation. The heavy arrow in Figure 15.11 shows that even if data is forwarded directly from one instruction to the next, the foregoing dependency cannot be resolved without the insertion of at least one bubble. Reading a register after a preceding load instruction is more problematic and requires three bubbles (why?).

Example 15.6: Comparing pipelined implementations   Compare the performance of the 8-stage pipelined implementation of MicroMIPS in Figure 15.11 with the 5-stage implementation discussed earlier in this chapter. Assume that the compiler can eliminate all data dependencies via proper scheduling of instructions. Ignore jump instructions and assume that 20% of instructions are conditional branches for which there are 3 delay slots with the 8-stage pipeline: the compiler can always fill the first delay slot with a useful instruction, but of the remaining 2 delay slots, 1.5 go unused on average.

Solution: The 5-stage pipeline executes instructions with no waste due to bubbles. This leads to 100 instructions being executed in 200 ns, for a performance of 500 MIPS. The 8-stage pipeline wastes 1.5 cycles for 20 out of every 100 instructions. So, it executes 100 instructions in 130 ns, for a performance of $1000/1.3 \cong 770$ MIPS. Note that the ratio $770/500 = 1.54$ of throughputs is very close to the ratio $8/5 = 1.6$ of the number of pipeline stages in the two designs. This is only an indication of the branch bubbles for the 8-stage pipeline more than nullifying the gains from a reduction in the allotted time for register read and writeback operations from 2 ns (one clock cycle in the 5-stage pipeline) to 1 ns. More revealing is a comparison of the 770 MIPS throughput of the 8-stage pipeline to the ideal throughput of 1000 MIPS for a pipeline operating with a 1 ns cycle.

We end this section with an idealized analysis that demonstrates some of the pitfalls of very deep pipelining. Suppose, for the sake of argument, that we can divide the total latency t ns of one instruction into any arbitrary number σ of pipeline stages, with a time overhead of τ ns per stage. This leads to a pipeline stage latency of $t/\sigma + \tau$ ns, or a clock rate of $1/(t/\sigma + \tau)$ GHz. Further, assume that a branch decision can be made near the midpoint of the pipeline, so that for each branch that is taken, roughly $\sigma/2$ bubbles must be inserted into the pipeline. Finally, assume that taken branches constitute a fraction b of all instructions that are executed. With these assumptions, the average number of cycles per instruction is:

$$CPI = 1 + \frac{b\sigma}{2}$$

The average throughput is then:

$$Throughput = \frac{\text{Clock rate}}{\text{CPI}} = \frac{1}{(t/\sigma + \tau)(1 + b\sigma/2)} \text{ Instructions/ns}$$

Computing the derivative of throughput with respect to σ and equating it with 0, we find the optimal number of pipeline stages:

$$\sigma^{opt} = \sqrt{\frac{2t/\tau}{b}}$$

Based on the foregoing analysis, the optimal number of pipeline stages increases as the ratio t/τ increases and decreases with an increase in the fraction b. Designing a pipeline with more than σ^{opt} stages would only hurt the performance.

PROBLEMS

15.1 Student registration pipeline

Suppose that in the student registration pipeline (Figure 15.1) the latency at each window is not constant but varies from 1 to 2 minutes. When a student is done with a particular window, he or she stays there until the next window becomes available. Movement from one window to the next is instantaneous (i.e., you can ignore this overhead).

a. How should this pipeline be used to maximize its throughput?
b. Is the method of part a applicable to a processor's data path?
c. What would be the throughput of the scheme in part a if the latency of each window were uniformly distributed in [1, 2]?

d. Discuss a method for improving the throughput of this pipeline beyond that obtained in part c (obviously, you must modify one or more of the assumptions).

15.2 Pipelined photocopier

The photocopier of Example 15.1 is provided with two document feeders and two output trays, so that one document feeder can be filled and one output tray emptied while the other pair is in use. This effectively eliminates the 15 s loading and unloading overhead. Plot the speedup of this new photocopier and the original copier of Example 15.1, relative to a nonpipelined copier, as functions of x and discuss the observed differences. Relate your findings to Amdahl's law.

15.3 Graphical representation of pipelines

Figure 15.3 depicts two different representations of a 5-stage pipeline, plotting instructions versus cycles and stages versus cycles. Discuss whether the third combination, stages versus cycles, leads to a useful representation.

15.4 Pipelined data path concepts

Consider the 5-stage pipelined data path for MicroMIPS (Figure 15.9).

a. Explain what happens in each stage for load, store, add, and jump instructions.
b. What is stored in each of the pipeline registers at the boundary between consecutive stages?
c. Can the instruction and data caches be merged into a single unit? If so, what would be the effect of this action on the control unit? If not, why not?

15.5 Pipeline dependencies and bubbles

a. Identify all data dependencies in the following sequence of instructions, when executed on the pipelined MicroMIPS implementation shown in Figure 15.9.

```
        addi  $9,$zero,0
        addi  $12,$zero,5000
Loop:   addi  $12,$12,4
        lw    $8,40($12)
        add   $9,$9,$8
        addi  $11,$11,-1
        bne   $11,$zero,Loop
```

b. Determine the number and places of bubbles that must be inserted to correctly execute the instruction sequence in part a. Explain your reasoning in each step.
c. Can you suggest any reordering of instructions that would reduce the number of bubbles?

15.6 Pipeline dependencies and bubbles

Repeat Problem 15.5 for each of the sequences of instructions appearing in:

a. Solution to Example 5.3
b. Solution to Example 5.4
c. Solution to Example 5.5
d. Problem 5.11
e. Solution to Example 6.2
f. Figure 7.2

15.7 Pipelined data path performance

Consider the following loops executed on the 5-stage pipelined data path for MicroMIPS (Figure 15.9). Which of these uses the pipeline most efficiently and why? State all your assumptions clearly.

a. Copying the contents of array A into array B
b. Traversing a linearly linked list while counting its elements
c. Traversing a binary search tree to find a desired element

15.8 Effects of instruction mix on pipelining

Consider the instruction mix assumed at the end of Section 15.3 (and used in Example 15.3). Now, consider a second "compute-intensive" instruction mix derived from that one by increasing the R-type fraction to 56% and decreasing the branch fraction to 6%. Calculate the effective CPI for the new instruction mix and compare pipeline performance in the two cases.

15.9 Selection options in pipelined data path

Consider the pair of 3-input multiplexers appearing in stage 2 of the pipeline shown in Figure 15.9. For each of the nine possible combinations of settings of these multiplexers:

a. Indicate whether it is ever used and, if so, for executing which MicroMIPS instruction(s).

b. List the possible setting of the multiplexers in stages 4 and 5 that would make sense.

15.10 Pipelined data path

One of the four changes in the pipelined data path of Figure 15.9 relative to the nonpipelined counterpart in Figure 13.3, as outlined at the beginning of Section 15.4, is avoidable. Which one is it, and what are possible drawbacks of not making that change?

15.11 Pipeline register contents

Repeat Example 15.4, but use the sequences of instructions appearing in each of the following. Make reasonable assumptions about register and memory contents where needed.

a. Solution to Example 5.3
b. Solution to Example 5.4
c. Solution to Example 5.5
d. Problem 5.11
e. Solution to Example 6.2
f. Figure 7.2

15.12 Pipeline register contents

In Example 15.4, the blank entries of the associated Table 15.1 are said to be unknown. Actually, we can specify some of these entries without knowing the subsequent instructions. Which ones and why?

15.13 Pipelined control

Repeat Example 15.5, but use the sequences of instructions appearing in each of the following. Make reasonable assumptions about register and memory contents where needed.

a. Solution to Example 5.3
b. Solution to Example 5.4
c. Solution to Example 5.5
d. Problem 5.11
e. Solution to Example 6.2
f. Figure 7.2

15.14 Pipelining alternatives

a. Suppose that in the pipeline depicted in Figure 15.11, the ALU occupies 3 rather than 2 stages. Discuss the effects of data and control dependencies in terms of the minimum number of bubbles or delay slots needed.

b. Repeat part a, this time assuming a 2-stage ALU and 3-stage cache memories (for both caches).

15.15 Performance of alternative pipelines

With the assumptions of Example 15.6, compare the performance of the 9- and 10-stage pipelined implementations of MicroMIPS defined in Problem 15.14 to those of the previous 5- and 8-stage pipelines.

15.16 Nonlinear or branching pipelines

In the pipelining analogy of Figure 15.1, suppose we find out that a student must spend twice as much time at the registrar's window as at any other window. One remedy, suggested in Section 15.6, is to divide the function of that window into two subfunctions, thus increasing the number of pipeline stages to 6. Suppose such a subdivision is not possible because the function cannot be suitably subdivided.

a. Show how providing two registrar's windows can help solve the problem.
b. Describe the operation of the new pipeline, demonstrating that its throughput would be the same as that corresponding to the first solution suggested.
c. Is the idea suggested in part a applicable to a processor's data path? How or why not?

15.17 Nonlinear or branching pipelines

In our discussion of optimal pipelining at the end of Section 15.6:

a. How would the result change if the branch decision could be made near the one-third point or one-quarter point of the pipeline?
b. We understand quite intuitively that σ^{opt} increases with an increase in t/τ, or with a decrease in b. Supply an intuitive explanation for the nonlinear relationship between σ^{opt} and the two entities t/τ and $1/b$.

REFERENCES AND FURTHER READINGS

[Crag96]   Cragon, H. G., *Memory Systems and Pipelined Processors,* Jones and Bartlett, 1996.

[Flyn95]   Flynn, M. J., *Computer Architecture: Pipelined and Parallel Processor Design,* Jones and Bartlett, 1995.

[Hart02]   Hartstein, A., and T. R. Puzak, "The Optimum Pipeline Depth for a Microprocessor," *Proceedings of the 29th International Symposium on Computer Architecture,* May 2002, pp. 7–13.

[Spra02]   Sprangle, E., and D. Carmean, "Increasing Processor Performance by Implementing Deeper Pipelines," *Proceedings of the 29th International Symposium on Computer Architecture,* May 2002, pp. 25–34.

16

PIPELINE PERFORMANCE LIMITS

"It would appear that we have reached the limits of what it is possible to achieve with computer technology, although one should be careful with such statements, as they tend to sound pretty silly in five years."
—*John von Neumann, circa 1949*

"Caution: Cape does not enable user to fly."
—*Warning label on a Batman costume*

Data and control dependencies prevent a pipeline from achieving its full performance potential. In this chapter, we discuss how a combination of hardware provisions (data forwarding, branch prediction) and software/compiler methods (delayed branch, instruction reordering) can help us recover most of the performance that could be lost to such dependencies. We also look at more advanced pipelining methods, including nonlinear pipelines and the scheduling considerations associated with them. We conclude the chapter by discussing how exceptions arising for one instruction might be handled without contaminating other partially executed instructions.

■ 16.1 Data Dependencies and Hazards

In Section 15.2, we learned that data dependency is the phenomenon of one instruction requiring data generated by a previous instruction. This generated data may reside in a register or memory location, where the subsequent instruction expects to find it. Several examples of data dependencies are shown in Figure 16.1, where each of the second through fifth instructions reads a register written into by the first instruction. The fifth instruction needs the content of register $2 after the

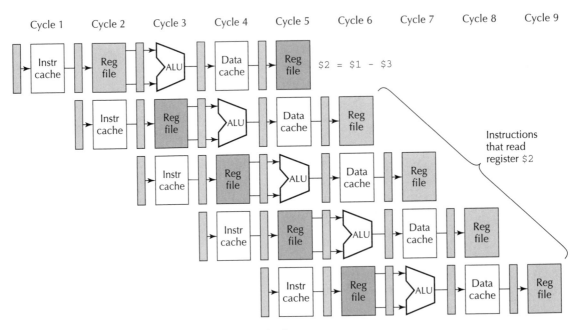

Figure 16.1 Data dependency in a pipeline.

completion of register writeback by the first instruction. So, this data dependency presents no problem whatsoever. The fourth instruction needs the new content of register $2 in the same cycle that the first instruction produces it. This may or may not present a problem, depending on the design of the register file. The second and third instructions need the content of register $2 before it is made available by the writeback stage of the first instruction. These two cases are definitely problematic!

One way to deal with these problems is for the assembler or compiler to insert an appropriate number of bubbles in the pipeline to ensure that no register is read out before its updated value has been written back. This implies the insertion of 0–3 bubbles, depending on the location of the instruction that uses a register value relative to a previous one that writes into that register.

In the following, we consider the two possible types of data dependency in our pipelined implementation of MicroMIPS:

a. *Read-after-compute* dependency exists when one instruction updates a register with a computed value and a subsequent instruction uses the content of that register as an operand.

b. *Read-after-load* dependency arises when one instruction loads a new value from memory into a register and a subsequent instruction uses the content of that register as an operand.

In both cases, the worst case occurs when the register is read by the instruction immediately following the one that modified its content.

Figure 16.2 depicts read-after-compute dependencies between an instruction that updates register $2 with the result of a subtraction operation and the three following instructions, each of which uses register $2 as an operand. Considering the worst case of the immediately following instruction, we note that we need:

3 bubbles if a register must be read one cycle after it is updated

2 bubbles if register can be written and read in the same cycle

0 bubble with data forwarding

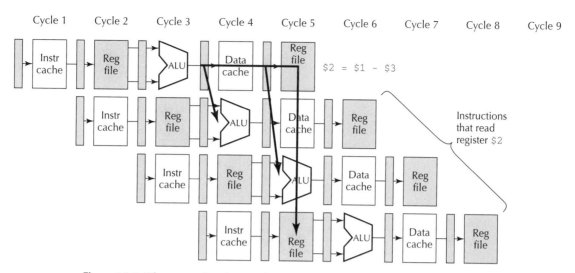

Figure 16.2 When a previous instruction writes back a value computed by the ALU into a register, the data dependency can always be resolved through forwarding.

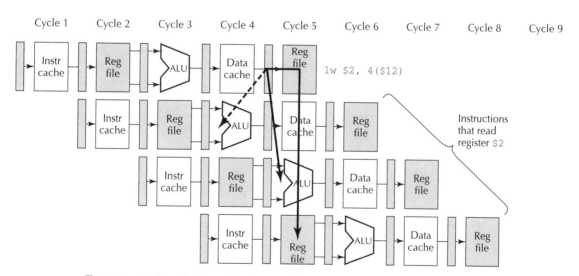

Figure 16.3 When the immediately preceding instruction writes a value read out from the data memory into a register, the data dependency cannot be resolved through forwarding (i.e., we cannot go back in time), and a bubble must be inserted in the pipeline.

We will see, in Section 16.2, that a simple mechanism allows us to forward the computed result of one instruction to subsequent instructions that need the updated value before it has been written back into the destination register. Hence, read-after-compute data dependencies are not problematic in pipelined MicroMIPS because they lead to no performance degradation.

Figure 16.3 depicts read-after-load dependencies between loading of register $2 and the three following instructions, each of which uses register $2 as an operand. Considering the worst case of the immediately following instruction, we note that we need:

3 bubbles if register must be read one cycle after it is written

2 bubbles if register can be written and read in the same cycle

1 bubble with data forwarding

Hence with the forwarding mechanism to be discussed in Section 16.2, the compiler must insert a single bubble into the pipeline only when a load instruction is immediately followed by an instruction that uses the loaded register as an operand. Frequently, such a situation can be avoided by moving another instruction between the load and its immediately following data-dependent instruction. Hence, with proper design of the compiler, read-after-load data dependencies do not present serious problems in pipelined MicroMIPS, because they have a negligible effect on performance.

To summarize, data dependencies in pipelined processors can be handled by software, hardware, or hybrid methods. A pure software solution leaves it to the compiler to ensure that data-dependent instructions are sufficiently spaced out to ensure the availability of each data element before its actual use. The compiler handles this by instruction reordering, when possible, or through the insertion of bubbles. A pure hardware solution requires the incorporation of a data forwarding mechanism that intercepts data values already available in the data path but not yet properly stored in a register, and sends them to the units that require them. When forwarding is not possible, the hardware blocks the dependent instruction until its required data can be supplied. The latter option is known as *pipeline interlock* and amounts to run-time insertion of bubbles when needed. A hybrid solution uses a mix of hardware and software methods that are deemed most cost-effective; for example, data forwarding may be used for the most common dependencies, which also do not unduly complicate the hardware (thus potentially slowing it down), with the handling of rare or complex instances relegated to software.

16.2 Data Forwarding

Data forwarding obviates the need for inserting bubbles in the pipeline, and thus reduces or eliminates the associated loss in performance, through routing the results of partially completed instructions to where they are needed by subsequent instructions. In the pipelined MicroMIPS data path of Figure 15.9, consider an instruction I2 that has just completed its register reading phase in stage 2 and is about to move to stage 3. At this instant, instructions I3 and I4 are ahead of the aforementioned instruction, with their partial results and control signals stored at the end of stages 3 and 4, respectively. The task of the forwarding unit (Figure 16.4) is to determine whether either of these two instructions will write a value into the rs and rt registers whose contents were just read into registers $x2$ and $y2$ and if so, to forward the more recent value to the ALU in lieu of $x2$ or $y2$.

Consider $x2$, for example, which has been loaded from rs, with the index rs saved as $s2$ in the pipeline register. From the signals RegWrite3 and RegWrite4, we know whether either of the instructions I3 or I4 will write something in a register. If neither instruction will write in a register, then there is no reason for concern and $x2$ can be directed to the ALU. If either instruction has its RegWrite signal asserted, then a comparison of its register index ($d3$ or $d4$) with $s2$ will indicate whether the register rs that was just read out will be overwritten by a partially completed instruction. If so, then one of the values $x3$, $y3$, $x4$, or $y4$ must be directed to the ALU in lieu of $x2$. We can easily tell which one by taking the two comparison results s2matchesd3 (asserted if $s2 = d3$) and s2matchesd4 (asserted if $s2 = d4$), as well as the five control signals stored at the end of stages 3 and 4, into account. A partial truth table for the upper forwarding unit of

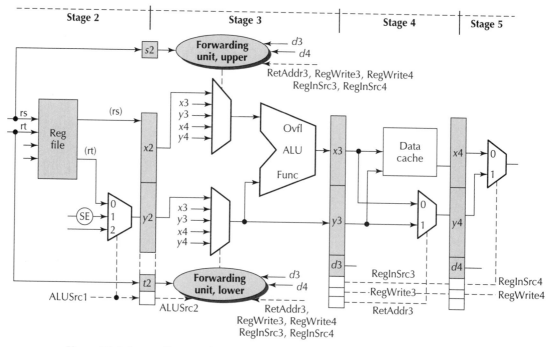

Figure 16.4 Forwarding unit for the pipelined MicroMIPS data path.

■ **TABLE 16.1** Partial truth table for the upper forwarding unit in the pipelined MicroMIPS data path.

RegWrite3	RegWrite4	s2matchesd3	s2matchesd4	RetAddr3	RegInSrc3	RegInSrc4	Choose
0	0	x	x	x	x	x	$x2$
0	1	x	0	x	x	x	$x2$
0	1	x	1	x	x	0	$x4$
0	1	x	1	x	x	1	$y4$
1	0	0	x	0	1	x	$x3$
1	0	0	x	1	1	x	$y3$
1	1	1	1	0	1	x	$x3$

Figure 16.4 is given in Table 16.1. Note that if both I3 and I4 happen to write into the same register, the value written by I3 must be used because it represents the most recent update to the register.

The lower forwarding unit in Figure 16.4 is similar to the upper unit, except that the comparison results and control signals are relevant only if ALUSrc2 = 0 (i.e., content of rt was actually placed in the pipeline register y2 in stage 1). If not, y2 is directed to the ALU regardless of the status of other inputs to the forwarding unit. (See also Problem 16.7.)

As noted earlier, data dependency in MicroMIPS cannot be resolved through data forwarding when a load instruction is immediately followed by an instruction that uses the value just loaded (see Figure 16.3). It is important for proper instruction execution to detect this case and insert a bubble in the pipeline. The bubble causes the dependent instruction to be delayed by one cycle, enabling the forwarding unit to supply its required data. Bubble insertion is done by a data hazard detector shown in Figure 16.5.

The data hazard detector has a simple task. It must examine the instruction at the end of stage 2 of the pipeline to determine whether it is a load instruction (DataRead2 signal is

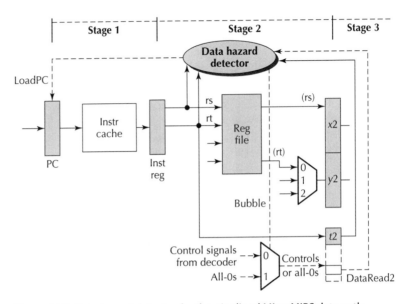

Figure 16.5 Data hazard detector for the pipelined MicroMIPS data path.

asserted). If it is a load instruction, and register $t2$, into which it will write, matches either register rs or register rt of the instruction at the end of the first stage, the latter instruction in nullified (turned into a no-op) by setting all the control signals to 0s as the instruction advances to the next stage (the mux at the bottom of Figure 16.5) and LoadPC signal is deasserted so that PC is not updated. This leads to the same instruction being fetched a second time and executed with the requisite one cycle of delay. The no-op instruction thus inserted is the pipeline bubble that resolves the data dependency problem. In all other cases, the Bubble signal is deasserted and the LoadPC signal is asserted, causing the next instruction to be fetched as usual.

Note that in the original pipelined data path of Figure 15.9, there is no LoadPC signal because the PC is loaded on every clock cycle. Thus, the original pipelined data path would not work correctly unless the compiler or assembler automatically inserts a bubble (no-op) after every load instruction that is immediately followed by an instruction using the just-loaded value. Any instruction that does not use the result of the load instruction can follow it in the pipeline without endangering correct operation. Consequently, the compiler has the option of moving an instruction that is independent of both the load and its dependent instruction between the two, thus effectively preventing the loss of one instruction slot to the no-op.

Note that the bubble insertion scheme of Figure 16.5 is somewhat pessimistic: even though every instruction causes the contents of rs and rt to be read out, not all instructions actually use the values thus obtained.

◼ 16.3 Pipeline Branch Hazards

Recall that a branch instruction must be immediately followed by a bubble in the MicroMIPS pipeline. This is because branching decisions and address formation occur in stage 2 of the pipeline (see Figure 15.9). The instruction being fetched in stage 1 while a branching decision is being made in stage 2 may, therefore, not be the right instruction. However, inserting a bubble after every branch is unnecessarily pessimistic because often the branch condition is not satisfied. For example, a branch that is used inside a loop to cause exit from the loop when a termination condition has been met is taken only once and is not taken for the remaining iterations (which may number in the thousands). Inserting a no-op after such a branch instruction leads to an unnecessary loss of performance.

Solutions for this problem, like the data hazard problem, fall into the software- and hardware-based categories. As noted earlier, one popular software-based solution is to change the definition of branch to include execution of the immediately following instruction before control is actually transferred to the branch target address. More generally, under such a *delayed branch* scheme, if the data path is such that branch decision is made in stage β, then $\beta - 1$ instructions following the branch are always executed before control transfer occurs. If there are instructions before the branch that are independent of it and do not alter the branch condition, they can be moved to the *branch delay slots* following the branch instruction to avoid wasting of these slots. In the worst case, if the compiler or programmer cannot identify any useful work that can be done in some branch delay slots, it simply fills them with no-ops as a last resort. In practice, this last option is rarely exercised.

In MicroMIPS, we take this simple software-based approach, redefining the branch as being a delayed one with one branch delay slot. This may take some getting used to if you had always thought of a branch instruction as taking effect right away. However, given that machine language programs are predominantly generated by compilers, this is not an unreasonable burden. In rare cases when it is necessary to hand-code an assembly language program or procedure, you can begin by automatically inserting a no-op after every branch and, near the end of the design process, look for instructions that can be moved into these delay slots. Of course if there is more than one delay slot to fill, the task may become more difficult for the compiler or programmer, and the probability of some delay slots going unused may increase. But this is not of concern to us with regard to MicroMIPS.

The same consideration applies to the three jump instructions, although for `j` and `jal`, it might be feasible to modify the pipelined data path so that PC is modified in the first stage right after the instruction has been read out and determined to be `j` or `jal`. In other words, for these two jump instructions, the PC and the pipeline register between the first and second stage will be written into at the same time, allowing the instruction at the jump target address to follow the jump instruction without any delay.

Hardware-based solutions extend the data hazard detector of Figure 16.5 to detect and deal with branch (and possibly jump) hazards. Note that if the instruction in stage 2 is not a branch, or if it is a branch but the branch condition is not satisfied, then all is well and the extended hazard detector of Figure 16.5 need do nothing. On the other hand if the instruction is a branch, and the branch condition is satisfied, the instruction just fetched in stage 1 must be nullified. This can be achieved by the hazard detector (which now deals with both data and branch hazards) asserting a ClearIR signal to reset the instruction register to all-0s, which effectively represents a no-op instruction. Again if more than one instruction were to be affected because branch decisions are made in stage β, where $\beta > 2$, then $\beta - 1$ of the interstage pipeline registers would have to be reset to all 0s, corresponding to the insertion of $\beta - 1$ bubbles.

The strategy discussed in the preceding paragraph may be viewed as a rudimentary form of branch prediction (see Section 16.4). Essentially, instruction execution continues by predicting or assuming that the branch will not be taken. If this prediction proves correct, then no performance penalty is paid; otherwise, the following instruction, which is not the one that should be executed anyway, is nullified and its space in the pipeline becomes a bubble. Alternatively, one can view this approach as a dynamic or run-time, as opposed to static or compile-time, bubble insertion strategy.

■ 16.4 Branch Prediction

Most modern processors have some form of branch prediction, that is, a method for predicting whether a branch will or will not be taken and to fetch instructions from the more likely path while the branch condition is being evaluated. This approach reduces the probability of needing to flush the pipeline, thus boosting performance. Branch prediction strategies range from very simple to highly complex (and correspondingly more accurate). Some example strategies follow.

1. Always predict that the branch will not be taken, flushing the instruction(s) fetched if it is established otherwise. This is what we have been doing thus far.
2. Use program context to decide which path is more likely: a branch at the end of a loop (*backward branch*) is more likely to be taken, while one at the beginning (*forward branch*) is usually not taken. Branches used in if-then-else constructs are harder to predict.
3. Allow the programmer or compiler to supply clues to which is the more likely path and encode these clues in the instruction.
4. Decide based on past history: maintain a small history table for the behavior of each branch instruction in the past and use this information to decide which alternative is more likely. Some implementations of this method will be detailed later in this section.
5. Apply a combination of factors: modern high-performance processors use very elaborate schemes for branch prediction because with deep pipelines (superpipelining), the penalty for a wrong prediction is quite high.

Let us focus on the fourth, or history-based, method. This is an example of a *dynamic branch prediction* strategy, in contrast to *static branch prediction* methods that rely on the branch instruction itself or on its program context. The least amount of history is, of course, a single bit that indicates whether a particular branch instruction was or was not taken the last time it was executed. This very simple strategy is remarkably accurate for branches that control loop repetitions or exits; the former type is almost always taken, the only exception being in the last iteration of the loop, while the latter is taken but once. Hence, in a loop that is executed 100 times, this very simple branch prediction strategy would be 98–99% accurate. Branches associated with if-then-else constructs are not as uniform and thus cannot be predicted as accurately.

Note that the use of a single bit of history causes two mispredictions for each instance of a loop. Consider, for example, a backward branch at the end of a loop. This branch will be mispredicted once at the end of the first iteration (because the last time it was not taken) and again at the end of the last iteration. We can easily cut this penalty in half (i.e., reduce it to only one misprediction per loop execution) by not allowing a single change of behavior to alter our prediction. Figure 16.6 shows a four-state branch prediction scheme that corresponds to keeping

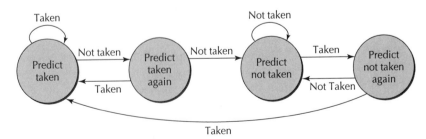

Figure 16.6 A four-state branch prediction scheme.

2 bits of history. As long as a branch continues to be taken, we predict that it will be taken the next time (the leftmost state in Figure 16.6). After the first misprediction, the state is changed, but we continue to predict that the branch will be taken. A second misprediction causes another change of state, this time to a state that causes the opposite prediction.

Example 16.1: Comparing branch prediction strategies   A program consists of two nested loops, with a single branch instruction at the end of each loop and no other branch instruction anywhere. The outer loop is executed 10 times and the inner loop 20 times. Determine the accuracy of the following three branch prediction strategies: (a) always predict taken, (b) use 1 bit of history, (c) use 2 bits of history according to Figure 16.6.

Solution: From the viewpoint of branch prediction, we have 210 loop iterations or branch instruction executions: $10 \times 20 = 200$ for the inner loop (190 taken, 10 not taken) and 10 for the outer loop (9 taken, 1 not taken). Option (a) yields 11 mispredictions and thus has an accuracy of $199/210 = 94.8\%$. Option (b) causes 1 misprediction for the outer loop and 19 for the inner loop (once in its first execution and twice for each subsequent execution), assuming that the 1-bit history for each loop is initialized to "taken." The accuracy in this case is $190/210 = 90.5\%$. Option (c) leads to the same result as option (a). We see that in this example, the simplest strategy is also the best one; however, this is because all branches are of the same backward type.

Such dynamic branch prediction strategies can be made quite elaborate. The more elaborate schemes tend to have greater accuracy, but also involve more overhead in terms of hardware complexity. The time overhead of branch prediction is generally not an issue because it can be removed from the critical path of instruction execution. As processor pipelines get deeper, the use of branch delay slots is falling out of favor and reliance is placed on more accurate branch prediction strategies.

Consider the following example, which uses several ideas for more accurate branch prediction and faster prefetching from the predicted path (Figure 16.7). A few low-order bits of the address in PC are used to index a table that stores information about the latest branch instruction encountered that had the same low-order address bits. This information includes the full address of the branch instruction, its target address, and history bits, as discussed earlier. If the history bits indicate that the branch will likely be taken, the stored branch target address is immediately loaded into the PC without waiting for address calculation or even decoding of the instruction.

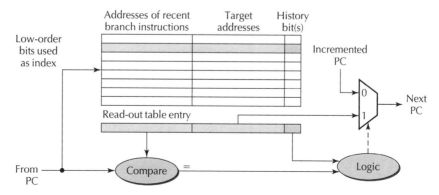

Figure 16.7 Hardware elements for a branch prediction scheme.

■ 16.5 Advanced Pipelining

Most high-performance processors today are superpipelined. However, there is a limit to performance improvement through deeper pipelines. For one thing, deeper pipelines imply greater overhead. As stages are made faster, the overhead of latching and the safety margin allowed for clock skew and other uncertainties come to comprise a significant fraction of the time spent doing the computation. This overhead, combined with the more severe penalty of pipeline flush and the requirement for a greater number of bubbles due to data and control dependencies, places an upper limit on the pipeline depth. Currently, pipelines of 20–30 stages are at the boundary of practicality. Besides dependencies of the types already discussed, cache misses (see Chapter 18) inflict an even greater performance penalty. An instruction encountering a data cache miss cannot advance until the required data has been brought into the cache. This typically stalls the pipeline for tens of cycles, sometimes dwarfing the branch misprediction penalty.

> **Example 16.2: Effective CPI with branching and cache misses**   In a 20-stage superpipeline, four bubbles must be inserted for conditional branch instructions, which constitute 15% of all instructions executed. About 2% of all instructions encounter a cache miss when accessing the data memory, causing the pipeline to stall for 25 cycles. What is the effective CPI for this pipeline?
>
> **Solution:** A pipeline that is always full (no bubbles or stalls), leads to a CPI of 1 in the long run. To this CPI of 1, we must add the average (expected) number of cycles per instruction lost to bubbles or stalls. Thus: average CPI $= 1 + 0.15 \times 4 + 0.02 \times 25 = 2.1$. We see that more than half the theoretically maximum performance of the pipeline is lost to bubbles and stalls.

Given the limitations on improving performance through deeper pipelining while maintaining the linear and static structure of the processor pipeline, other architectural methods have been devised.

The first method is the use of branching pipelines as opposed to strictly linear ones. Figure 16.8 shows such a pipeline with multiple function units that may be of the same type or specialized

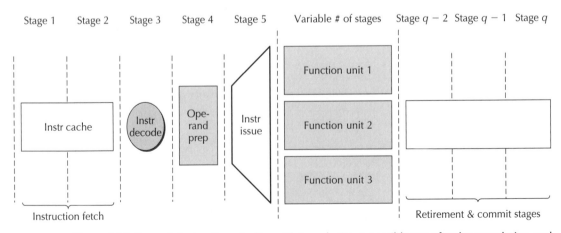

Figure 16.8 Dynamic instruction pipeline with in-order issue, possible out-of-order completion, and in-order retirement.

(e.g., separate integer and floating-point ALUs). As in a linear pipeline, in the absence of data and control dependencies, one instruction is initiated in every clock cycle. Different instruction may take different paths in the branching portions of the pipeline and may emerge at the other end out of order. The out-of-order completion may be due to different numbers of stages in the function units or to different data-dependent latencies in the same function unit. Thus, for example, instructions I1, I2, I3, I4 entering the pipeline may be completed in the order I1, I3, I4, I2. The retirement and commit stages at the end of the pipeline are charged with the task of judging when all instructions that preceded a given instruction have been completed and only then commit the temporary results of such an instruction to permanent (register or cache) storage. In this way, if an interrupt occurs, partially completed instructions and those completed ahead of others will not lead to inconsistencies in register or memory contents.

A more advanced version of the scheme depicted in Figure 16.8 allows the instruction issue logic to look ahead and issue instructions beyond those that are known, or expected, to stall in the pipeline.

The second method prescribes the use of multiple independent pipelines that allow several instructions to be initiated at once (2–4 is typical). In such *superscalar processors*, CPI may become less than 1. Let us look at a two-way superscalar design. In such a processor, the register file must be modified to allow up to 4 register readouts and 2 register write operations to be performed in each cycle. Alternatively, one may allow only one write operation and restrict the concurrently issued instructions to pairs of instructions that do not both write in a register.

Of course the instruction sequence might be such that superscalar execution offers no benefit, but this situation is rare. Consider the following loop as an example:

```
Loop:   lw    $t0,0($s1)      # load $t0 with array element
        add   $t0,$t0,$s2     # add scalar in $s2
        sw    $t0,0($s3)      # save the result in memory
        addi  $s1,$s1,-4      # decrement pointer
        bne   $s1,$zero,Loop  # branch if $s1 not zero
```

The only concurrency possible is to issue the sw and bne instructions at the same time.

Cycle 1: lw
Cycle 2: addi
Cycle 3: add
Cycle 4: sw, bne

If this situation (5 instructions issued in 4 clock cycles) were to continue, a CPI of 0.8 would result. More typically, both instruction issue slots are used in most cycles and a CPI much closer to the lower bound of 0.5 is obtained.

Based on what we have learned thus far, Table 16.2 summarizes the effect of various processor architectures and associated implementation strategies on CPI, and thus on performance. We began our discussion of processor architecture with the single-cycle data path in Chapter 13 and proceeded to a more practical multicycle implementation in Chapter 14. A simple, static pipeline was introduced in Chapter 15. Even though a static pipeline can theoretically achieve a CPI of 1, the actual CPI is often in the range of 2–3 once the penalties due to data dependencies, branch misprediction, and cache misses (see Chapter 18) have been taken into account. Dynamic pipelining with out-of-order execution can get us pretty close to

■ **TABLE 16.2** Effect of processor architecture, branch prediction methods, and speculative execution on CPI.

Architecture	Methods used in practice	CPI
Nonpipelined, multicycle	Strict in-order instruction issue and execution	5–10
Nonpipelined, overlapped	In-order issue, with multiple function units	3–5
Pipelined, static	In-order execution, simple branch prediction	2–3
Superpipelined, dynamic	Out-of-order execution, advanced branch prediction	1–2
Superscalar	2- to 4-way issue, interlocking and speculation	0.5–1
Advanced superscalar	4- to 8-way issue, aggressive speculation	0.2–0.5

a CPI of 1. To go beyond this, we must rely on multiple instruction issue (superscalar design), and perhaps more advanced speculative execution.

Software-based methods go hand-in-hand with the aforementioned hardware techniques to ensure maximum performance with a given processor architecture. This is why as pipeline depth and other features of processor implementation evolve, new versions of software must be introduced to take full advantage of the new hardware's capabilities. Older versions might run correctly, but are unlikely to lead to optimal performance.

A software technique that has been found helpful in increasing the likelihood of multiple independent instructions being available for superscalar execution is *loop unrolling*. Consider the following loop shown in abstract form:

> Loop: Do certain computations involving the index value i
> Increment the loop index i by 1
> Check termination condition and repeat if required

Unrolling this loop once results in the following:

> Loop: Do some computations involving the index value i
> Do some computations involving the index value $i + 1$
> Increment the loop index i by 2
> Check termination condition and repeat if required

The unrolled loop will be executed half as many times, doing twice as much computation in each iteration. Of course we could unroll the loop three times, four times, or more. Unrolling increases the number of instructions in the program text but leads to a reduction in the number of instructions executed. This is due to the lower overhead of index checking and branching in the unrolled version. More importantly, unrolling reduces the number of branch instructions executed and creates more instructions within the body of the loop that may be independent of each other and thus capable of being issued together in a superscalar architecture.

We end this section with a brief overview of the architectural development of Intel microprocessors [Hint01], the latest of which are now in common use in desktop and laptop computers (see Table 8.2). The Intel Pentium processor, and its immediate predecessors (known as 286, 386, 486) all had similar pipeline depths, with performance enhancement achieved mainly through advances in technology. The Pentium Pro started a series of products that roughly doubled the pipeline depth and led to Pentium II, III, and Celeron processors. This increase in pipeline depth, and the associated improvement in clock frequency (though not quite by a factor of 2), was achieved by breaking IA32 instructions into micro-ops and using out-of-order execution. Pentium 4 (for some reason, Intel abandoned the use of roman numerals for numbering of its Pentium family of processors) further doubled the pipeline depth, leading to the need for more aggressive speculation and many associated architectural enhancements.

16.6 Exceptions in a Pipeline

In a nonpipelined processor, the occurrence of an exception, such as arithmetic overflow, causes a transfer of control to an operating system routine (see Figure 14.10). Interrupts are treated in much the same way in that, after the completion of the current instruction, control is transferred to an interrupt handling routine. In a pipelined processor, exceptions and conditional branches present problems of the same kinds. An overflow exception is essentially equivalent to "branch to a special address if overflow occurs." However, given that exceptions are rare, it is sufficient to ensure correct handling of the exception; performance and other issues relating to branch prediction are not involved.

When the effects of exceptions in a pipelined processor are identical to those of a nonpipelined processor with purely sequential execution, we say that the pipelined implementation supports *precise exceptions*. A precise exception is desirable because it allows the program to be later resumed from the point of interruption with no ill effect. Some early high-performance machines had *imprecise exceptions,* meaning that in some cases, the results observed were inconsistent with simple sequential execution. This was done for cost and performance reasons, given that the cost of ensuring precise exceptions, and their associated performance penalty, was deemed not justified. *Precise and imprecise interrupts* have similar connotations. We devote the rest of this section to a study of implementation options for precise exceptions in pipelined processors, leaving a discussion of interrupts to Chapter 24.

When an exception occurs during the execution of an instruction in a pipelined processor, the instruction itself and all subsequent instructions in the program order whose processing has already started must be flushed from the pipeline, while instructions ahead of the one leading to an exception must be allowed to run to completion before control is transferred to an exception handling routine. In a simple linear pipeline, such as the one used in MicroMIPS, this is done by asserting the "clear" control signal for each set of interstage pipeline registers preceding the stage in which the exception occurred. This simple strategy works as long as none of the flushed instructions has updated the value in a register or memory location. It is also necessary for the exception handling routine to know which instruction led to the exception. Thus, the content of PC associated with the exception-causing instruction should be made available by writing it to a special register or memory location. MicroMIPS has a special EPC (exception PC) register into which the PC value of the instruction producing the exception is written (Figure 5.1).

In a processor with dynamic pipelining or multiple instruction issue per cycle, providing precise exceptions is more complicated. Referring to Figure 16.8, we note that when the operation in one of the function units leads to an exception, the other function units may be executing instructions that are ahead of, or behind, that instruction in the normal program sequence. Those that are ahead must be allowed to run to completion, while those that are behind must be flushed. The retirement and commit stages at the end of the pipeline accomplish this in a rather natural way. These stages retire instructions in strict sequential order so that an instruction is not retired, and thus its results are not permanently committed, unless all previous instructions have already been retired. Hence, when it is the turn of the exception-causing instruction to be retired, the unit takes note of the exception and does not retire any further instructions; the partial uncommitted results of such instructions will thus have no effect on the permanent state of the processor.

The hardware implementation of the instruction retirement and commit mechanism may take two forms:

1. *History files:* In the course of instruction execution, update registers with new values but keep the previous values so that when a rollback is needed due to an exception, the older values can be restored.

2. *Future files:* Do not write new register contents in the register file itself but keep them in a future file, copying these updated values into the main register file only when all previous instructions have been retired.

When the execution latencies of various instructions are significantly different, a large number of nonretired instructions and their results must be buffered in the retirement and commit unit as they await the completion of other instructions. This leads to high implementation cost and, possibly, nonnegligible speed penalty. For this reason, some processors provide precise exceptions as a selectable option to avoid the associated performance penalty when imprecise exceptions would do.

A viable alternative to hardware-based precise exceptions is to allow the exception handling routine to finish the in-progress instructions using software execution based on information that has been saved or is obtained from various parts of the pipeline. In this way, a significant speed penalty is paid when an exception does occur, but this may be acceptable given that exceptions are rare.

PROBLEMS

16.1 Load-after-store data dependency
In Section 16.1, we discussed read-after-compute and read-after-load data dependencies having to do with ensuring that a register operand supplied to each unit holds the latest value written into the corresponding register. Discuss whether the same concerns arise for memory contents. In other words, do we need mechanisms to properly deal with *load-after-store* data dependencies?

16.2 Store-after-load data dependency
Consider copying a list of n words from one area in memory to another area. This can be accomplished by placing a pair of `lw` and `sw` instructions in a loop, with each loop iteration copying one word. In the current implementation of pipelined MicroMIPS with forwarding, as depicted in Figures 16.4 and 16.5, this leads to one bubble between `lw` and `sw`. Is it possible to avoid this stalling via additional data forwarding

hardware? Discuss how this can be done or explain why the problem is unavoidable.

16.3 Pipeline performance
A 10-stage instruction pipeline runs at a clock rate of 1 GHz. The data forwarding scheme and the instruction mix are such that for 15% of instructions one bubble, for 10% two bubbles, and for 5% four bubbles must be inserted in the pipeline. The equivalent single-cycle implementation would lead to a clock rate of 150 MHz.

a. What is the reduction in pipeline throughput over the ideal pipeline as a result of bubbles?
b. What is the speedup of the pipelined implementation over the single-cycle implementation?

16.4 CPI calculation for pipelined processors
Assume that all data hazards can be eliminated by forwarding and/or appropriate scheduling of machine instructions. Consider two instruction mixes

corresponding to the programs "gcc" (branch 19%, jump 2%, other 79%) and "spice" (branch 6%, jump 2%, other 92%). Find the average CPI for each instruction mix, assuming a 5-stage pipelined data path, average probability of 30% that a branch will be taken, and:

a. Total stalling for both branch and jump instructions
b. Continuing the execution assuming that branch is not taken

Explain all your assumptions completely. In each case, compare the resulting MIPS rating assuming a 500 MHz pipelined clock rate with a nonpipelined, single-cycle implementation using a 125 MHz clock.

16.5 Data forwarding unit operation

Consider the data forwarding unit of Figure 16.4. Given a sequence of instructions, you can trace their progress in the pipeline, determining if and when either forwarding unit is activated and causes an input other than the topmost one of the associated multiplexer to be sent to the ALU. Perform the foregoing analysis on the instruction sequence found in:

a. Solution to Example 5.3
b. Solution to Example 5.4
c. Solution to Example 5.5
d. Problem 5.11
e. Solution to Example 6.2
f. Figure 7.2

16.6 Data forwarding unit design

The design of the data forwarding unit depends on the details of the pipeline.

a. Present the complete logic design for the upper and lower data forwarding units of Figure 16.4.
b. Present a block diagram for a data forwarding unit for the modified pipeline of Figure 15.11. State all your assumptions clearly.

16.7 Data forwarding and hazard detection

In our discussion of data forwarding (Figure 16.4) we considered supplying the most recent or up-to-date version of register data only to the ALU. Because register contents are also used in the "next address"

box depicted in Figure 15.9, forwarding must be extended to that unit also.

a. Discuss the design of a forwarding unit to ensure correct branching and jumping.
b. Do we need to extend the data hazard detector of Figure 16.5 for this purpose as well?

16.8 Delayed branching

We considered moving an instruction that originally appeared before the branch instruction to the branch delay slot. Is it feasible to fill the branch delay slot with an instruction that is at the target address of the branch? Explain. What about not doing anything, so that the branch delay slot is occupied by the instruction that follows the branch and constitutes the one to be executed if the branch is not taken?

16.9 Change of addressing in MicroMIPS

Suppose load and store instructions of MicroMIPS were redefined to require the full memory address to be given in a register. In other words, the redefined memory access instructions would contain no offset and thus would require no address calculation. Describe the effects of this change on:

a. Design of the pipelined data path
b. Performance of the pipelined implementation
c. Placement and design of data forwarding unit(s)
d. Design of the data hazard detection unit

16.10 Avoiding branches

Consider adding conditional copying instructions to the instruction set of MicroMIPS. The instruction cpyz rd,rs,rt performs the operation rd ← (rs) if(rt) = 0. The instruction cpyn is similar, except that the condition used is (rt) ≠ 0.

a. Show that the new instructions allow us to place the larger of two register values into a third register without using a branch instruction. You can use $at as a temporary register.
b. Write an equivalent sequence of MicroMIPS instructions to accomplish the same task as in part a, but without using the new instructions.
c. What modifications in the pipelined data path are needed to implement these new instructions?
d. Compare the pipeline performance for the instruction sequences of parts a and b.

16.11 Branch prediction

a. Solve Example 16.1 after the following change: the outer loop has a branch at the end, as before, but the inner loop has a forward exit branch near the beginning and a jump at the end.

b. Repeat part a, with the type of branches used in the inner and outer loops reversed (forward branch in the outer loop and backward branch in the inner loop).

16.12 Implementation of branch prediction

Figure 16.7 shows the block diagram for a history-based branch prediction unit.

a. Explain why the comparator is needed.
b. Present the design of the logic block below the multiplexer, assuming 1 bit of history.
c. Repeat part b with 2 bits of history in accordance with the state diagram of Figure 16.6.

16.13 History-based branch prediction

Consider the branch prediction scheme defined by the state diagram of Figure 16.6.

a. How does the method defined by the following diagram compare with that of Figure 16.6?

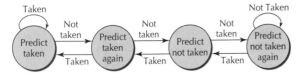

b. Repeat part a for the following scheme:

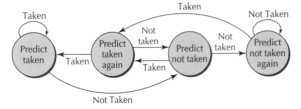

c. Compare and contrast the branch prediction schemes defined in parts a and b.
d. Discuss which of the four states would be chosen as the initial state in each scheme.

16.14 Loop unrolling

Loop unrolling was discussed near the end of Section 16.5 as a way of reducing branch penalty

and providing greater opportunity for issuing multiple instructions. For loops in each of the following program fragments, show how unrolling the loop once or twice affects the pipeline performance with 1 or 2 instructions issued in each cycle (5 cases to be compared: no unrolling, plus the 4 combinations above).

a. Solution to Example 5.4
b. Solution to Example 5.5
c. Problem 5.11
d. Figure 7.2

16.15 Special-purpose pipelines

Consider the following 15-stage computation pipeline that accepts a sequence of numbers on successive clock cycles and produces a sequence of numbers at output. The shaded boxes are pipeline registers and each of the big blocks is a 4-stage pipelined adder. Explain how the output sequence is related to the inputs.

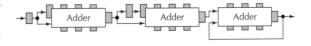

16.16 Pipelining performance and its limit

A linear data path being designed consists of parts with the following latencies, in order from left to right: 0.2 ns, 0.6 ns, 0.5 ns, 0.6 ns, 0.3 ns, 0.8 ns. These parts are indivisible, so that any pipeline latches must be inserted between consecutive components. Insertion of latches introduces a stage overhead of 0.1 ns. Determine the latency and throughput of the data path with no pipelining (only one set of latches at the output), and with 2, 3, 4, . . . stages in the pipeline, continuing until the maximum throughput is reached.

16.17 Exceptions due to faults or errors

In some computers, when an instruction does not execute properly, or its results are suspected of being incorrect, the control unit attempts to execute the instruction again in case the problem was due to a transient fault in hardware or some rare combination of operating conditions. This is known as *instruction retry*. Assuming that there is special hardware that signals the need for instruction retry, discuss how this feature might be implemented in nonpipelined and pipelined processors.

REFERENCES AND FURTHER READINGS

[Crag96] Cragon, H. G., *Memory Systems and Pipelined Processors,* Jones and Bartlett, 1996.

[Dube91] Dubey, P., and M. Flynn, "Branch Strategies: Modeling and Optimization," *IEEE Trans. Computers,* Vol. 40, No. 10, pp. 1159–1167, October 1991.

[Flyn95] Flynn, M. J., *Computer Architecture: Pipelined and Parallel Processor Design,* Jones and Bartlett, 1995.

[Hint01] Hinton, G., et al., "The Microarchitecture of the Pentium 4 Processor," *Intel Technology J.,* 12 pp., First quarter, 2001.

[Lilj88] Lilja, D., "Reducing the Branch Penalty in Pipelined Processors," *IEEE Computer,* Vol. 21, No. 7, pp. 47–55, July 1988.

[Smit81] Smith, J. E., "A Study of Branch Prediction Strategies," *Proceedings of the Eighth International Symposium on Computer Architecture,* pp. 135–148, May 1981.

[Smit88] Smith, J. E., and A. R. Pleszkun, "Implementing Precise Interrupts in Pipelined Processors," *IEEE Trans. Computers,* Vol. 37, No. 5, pp. 562–573, May 1988.

[Yeh92] Yeh, T.-Y., and Y. N. Patt, "Alternative Implementations of Two-Level Adaptive Branch Prediction," *Proceedings of the 19th International Symposium on Computer Architecture,* pp. 124–134, May 1992.

MEMORY SYSTEM DESIGN

"Always design a thing by considering it in its next larger context—a chair in a room, a room in a house, a house in an environment, an environment in a city plan."
—*Eliel Saarinen*

"The fancy is indeed no other than a mode of memory emancipated from the order of time and space."
—*Samuel Taylor Coleridge*

A computer's memory system is just as important as the CPU in determining its performance and usability. In Part 4, we used memory components that were just as fast as the ALU and the other data path elements. While such memories can in fact be built, their size is quite limited by technological and economic constraints. The paradox in memory system design is that we want a large amount of memory to accommodate complex programs as well as extensive data sets, and we want this huge memory to be fast enough not to slow down the flow of data through the data path. The gist of this part of the book is to show how this paradox is resolved through architectural methods.

After reviewing technologies and organizational structures for a computer's main memory in Chapter 17, we conclude that the current technology is incapable of providing a single-level memory that is both fast enough and large enough for our needs. In Chapter 18, we show how the use of one or two levels of cache memory helps bridge the speed gap between the CPU and our large main memory. Because even a large main memory is still not large enough to accommodate all our storage needs, we study technologies and organizations for secondary or mass memories in Chapter 19. Chapter 20, dealing with virtual memory, explains how by automating data transfers between primary and secondary memories we can provide the illusion of a multigigabyte main memory at modest cost.

MAIN MEMORY CONCEPTS

"It's a poor sort of memory that only works backwards."
—*Lewis Carroll*

"The existence of forgetting has never been proven; we only know that some things do not come to mind when we want them."
—*Friedrich W. Nietzsche*

TOPICS IN THIS CHAPTER
17.1 Memory Structure and SRAM
17.2 DRAM and Refresh Cycles
17.3 Hitting the Memory Wall
17.4 Pipelined and Interleaved Memory
17.5 Nonvolatile Memory
17.6 The Need for a Memory Hierarchy

The main memory technology now in use is quite different from the magnetic drums and core memories of early digital computers. Today's semiconductor memories are at the same time faster, denser, and cheaper than their predecessors. This chapter is devoted to a review of memory organization, including both SRAM and DRAM technologies typically used for fast cache memories and slower main memory, respectively. We show that memory has already become a severely limiting factor in computer performance and discuss how certain organizational techniques, such as interleaving and pipelining, can mitigate some of the problems. We conclude by showing the need for a memory hierarchy, in preparation for our discussions on cache and virtual memories.

■ 17.1 Memory Structure and SRAM

Static random-access memory (SRAM) is basically a large array of storage cells that are accessed like registers. An SRAM memory cell typically requires 4–6 transistors per bit and holds the stored data as long as it is powered on. This is in contrast to dynamic random-access memory (DRAM), to be discussed in Section 17.2, which uses only one transistor per

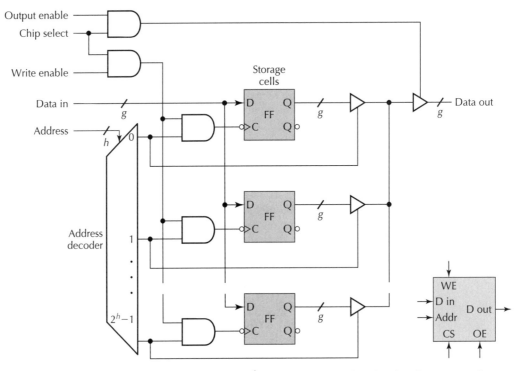

Figure 17.1 Conceptual inner structure of a $2^h \times g$ SRAM chip and its shorthand representation.

bit and must be periodically refreshed to prevent loss of the stored data. Both SRAM and DRAM would lose data if disconnected from power; hence their designation as *volatile* memory. As depicted in Figure 2.10, a $2^h \times g$ SRAM chip has an h-bit input that carries the address. This address is decoded and used to select one of 2^h locations, indexed 0 through $2^h - 1$, each of which is g bits wide. During a write operation, g bits of data are supplied to the chip for copying into the addressed location. For a read operation, g bits of data are read out from the addressed cell. The "Chip select" signal must be asserted for both read and write operations, whereas "Write enable" is asserted for writing and "Output enable" for reading (Figure 17.1). A chip that is not selected does not perform any operation, regardless of the values of its other input signals.

For ease of understanding, the storage cells in Figure 17.1 are depicted as edge-triggered D flip-flops. In practice, D latches are employed because using flip-flops would lead to additional complexity in the cells and thus fewer cells on a chip. The use of latches causes no special difficulty during read operations; however, for write operations, more stringent timing requirements must be met to ensure that data is properly written into the desired location and only in that location. Detailed discussion of such timing considerations are beyond the scope of this book [Wake01].

A synchronous SRAM (SSRAM) provides a cleaner interface to the designer while still using D latches internally. The synchronous behavior is achieved by providing internal registers to hold address, data, and control inputs (and perhaps the data output). Because input signals are provided in one clock cycle while memory is accessed in the next cycle, there is no danger of the inputs to the memory array changing at inopportune times.

If the size of a $2^h \times g$ SRAM chip is inadequate for our storage needs, multiple chips might be used. We use k/g chips in parallel to get k-bit data words. We use $2^m/2^h = 2^{m-h}$ rows of chips to get a capacity of 2^m words.

Example 17.1: Multiple-chip SRAM   Show how 128K × 8 SRAM chips can be used to build a 256K × 32 memory unit.

Solution: Because the desired word width is four times that of the SRAM chip, we must use four chips in parallel. We need two rows of chips to double the number of words from 128K to 256K. The requisite structure is shown in Figure 17.2. The most significant bit of the 18-bit address is used to choose row 0 or row 1 of the SRAM chips. All other chip control signals are externally tied to the common input control signals of the memory unit.

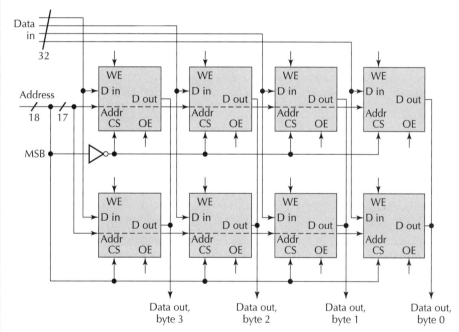

Figure 17.2 Eight 128K × 8 SRAM chips forming a 256K × 32 memory unit.

Often, the data input and output pins of an SRAM chip are shared, or nonshared input and output pins are connected to the same bidirectional data bus. This makes sense because unlike a register file, which is read from and written into during the same clock cycle, a memory unit performs a read or a write operation, but not both at the same time. To make sure that output data from the SRAM does not interfere with the input data supplied during a write operation, the control circuitry shown at the top of Figure 17.1 must be slightly modified. This modification, which entails disabling the data output when "Write enable" is asserted, is shown in Figure 17.3.

Early memory chips were invariably organized as $2^h \times 1$ memories. This is because chip capacities were quite limited then and any practically sized memory required many RAM chips anyway. Having one bit of each data word in one chip provided the advantage of error isolation; a failed chip would affect no more than one bit in each word, thus allowing codes

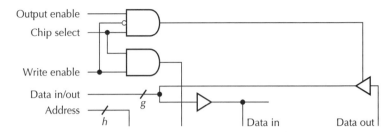

Figure 17.3 When data input and output of an SRAM chip are shared or connected to a bidirectional data bus, output must be disabled during write operations.

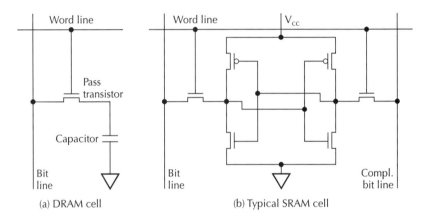

Figure 17.4 Single-transistor DRAM cell, which is considerably simpler than SRAM cell, leads to dense, high-capacity DRAM memory chips.

for detecting and correcting errors to effectively signal or mask the error. At present, it is not uncommon for the entire memory needs of an application to fit on one or a handful of chips. Hence, chips with byte-size words have become quite common. Beyond 8-bit data input and output, however, pin limitation makes further widening of the memory words unattractive. Note that, as depicted in Figure 2.10, a random-access memory array is built with very wide words that are read out into an internal buffer, where the portion corresponding to one external memory word is selected for output. So, other than pin limitation, there is no real impediment to having wider memory words.

■ 17.2 DRAM and Refresh Cycles

It is impossible to build a bistable element with only one transistor. To allow single-transistor memory cells, which lead to the highest possible storage density on a chip and thus very low per-bit cost, dynamic random-access memory (DRAM) stores data as electric charge on tiny capacitors, each accessed via a MOS pass transistor. Figure 17.4 shows such a cell in schematic form. When the word line is asserted, low (high) voltage on the bit line causes the capacitor to be discharged (charged), thus storing 0 (1). To read a DRAM cell, the bit line is first *precharged* to a halfway voltage. This voltage is then pulled slightly lower or higher upon

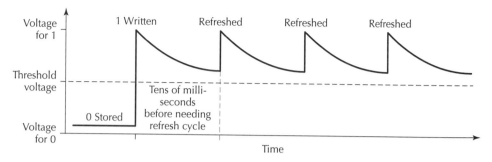

Figure 17.5 Variations in the voltage across a DRAM cell capacitor after writing a 1 and subsequent refresh operations.

the assertion of the word line, depending on whether the cell stores 0 or 1. This change of voltage is detected by a sense amplifier, which recovers a 0 or 1 accordingly. Because the act of reading destroys the cell content, such a *destructive readout* of data must be followed immediately by a write operation to restore the original values.

Leakage of charge from the tiny capacitor shown in Figure 17.4 causes data to be erased after a fraction of a second. Hence, DRAMs must be equipped with special circuitry that periodically refreshes the memory contents. Refreshing takes place for entire memory rows through reading each row out and writing it back to restore the charge to the original value. Figure 17.5 shows how leakage leads to the decaying of charge in a DRAM cell storing 1, and how periodic refreshing restores the charge just before the voltage across the capacitor falls below a certain threshold. DRAMs are much less expensive, but also slower, than SRAMs. In addition, some of the potential memory bandwidth in DRAMs is lost to writeback operations to restore data destroyed during readout and to refresh cycles.

Example 17.2: Loss of bandwidth to refresh cycles   A 256 Mb DRAM chip is organized as a 32M × 8 memory externally and as a 16K × 16K square array internally. Each row must be refreshed at least once every 50 ms to forestall loss of data; refreshing one row takes 100 ns. What fraction of the total memory bandwidth is lost to refresh cycles?

Solution: Refreshing all 16K rows takes $16 \times 1024 \times 100$ ns = 1.64 ms. Thus, out of every 50 ms period, 1.64 ms is lost to refresh cycles. This amounts to $1.64/50 = 3.3\%$ of the total bandwidth.

In part because of the large capacity of DRAM chips, which would require a large number of address pins, and partly because within the chip, the readout process occurs in two steps (row access, column selection) anyway, DRAMs usually have half as many address pins as are dictated by their word capacity. For example, a $2^{18} \times 4$ DRAM chip might have only 9 address pins. To access a word, its row address within the memory array is provided first, along with a *row address strobe* (RAS) signal that indicates the availability of the row address to the memory unit, which copies it into an internal register. Shortly thereafter, the column address is supplied via the same address lines, concurrently with the *column address strobe* (CAS) signal. Figure 17.6 shows a typical 24-pin DRAM package with 11 address and 4 data pins.

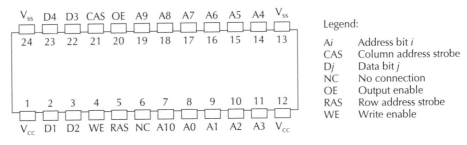

Figure 17.6 Typical DRAM package housing a 16M × 4 memory.

We next describe the timing of events in a DRAM chip during the three operations of refresh, read, and write. Refreshing can be performed by simply supplying a row address to the chip. In this RAS-only refresh mode, the leading edge of RAS causes the corresponding row to be read out into an internal row buffer and the trailing edge causes the row buffer contents to be written back. The operations are asynchronous and no clock is involved. For this reason, the RAS signal's timing is quite critical. A read cycle begins like a refresh cycle, but the CAS signal is used to enable the chip output bits, which are selected from the row buffer content by the column address supplied concurrently with CAS. A write cycle also begins like a refresh cycle. However, before the trailing edge of RAS triggers a writeback operation, the data in the row buffer is modified by asserting the "Write enable" and CAS signals concurrently with the application of the column address. This causes the data in the appropriate part of the row buffer to be modified before the entire buffer is written back.

Typical DRAMs have other modes of operation besides RAS-only refresh, read, and write. One of the most useful of these variations is known as *page mode*. In page mode, once a row has been selected and read out into the internal row buffer, subsequent accesses to words within the same row do not require the full memory cycle. Each subsequent access to a word in the same row is accomplished by simply supplying the corresponding column address and is thus significantly faster.

It is evident from the discussion thus far that timing of signals is quite critical for DRAM operation. This not only makes the design process difficult but also leads to lower performance owing to the need for providing adequate safety margins. For this reason, synchronous DRAM (SDRAM) variations have become quite popular. As was the case for SSRAM, internal operation of the SDRAM remains asynchronous. However, the external interface is synchronous. Typically, the row address is supplied in one clock cycle and the column address on the next. Also supplied in the first cycle is a command word, which specifies the operation to be performed. The actual access to memory contents takes several clock cycles. However, the memory is internally organized into multiple banks so that when access to one bank is initiated, the wait time may be used to process further input commands that may involve access to other banks. In this way, a much higher throughput can be supported. This is particularly true because modern DRAMs are typically accessed in bursts to read out sequences of instructions or multiword cache blocks. A *burst length* is often allowed as part of the input command to the DRAM controller, which then causes the specified number of words to be transferred, one per clock cycle, once the row has been read into the row buffer.

Two enhanced implementations of SDRAM are presently in widespread use. The first is known as double data rate DRAM (DDR-DRAM), which doubles the transfer rate from the DRAM by using both edges of the clock signal to trigger actions. Another, Rambus DRAM

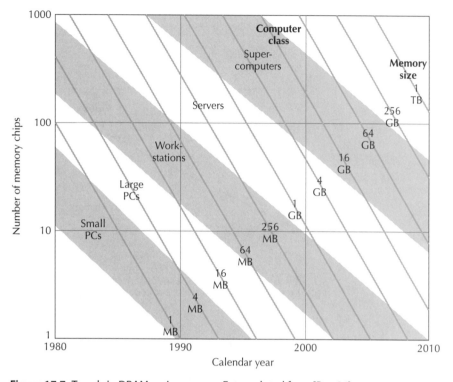

Figure 17.7 Trends in DRAM main memory. Extrapolated from [Przy94].

(RDRAM), combines double-edge operation with a very fast, but relatively narrow, channel between the DRAM controller and memory array. The narrowness of the channel is intended to facilitate the production of a high-quality, skew-free link that can be driven at extremely high clock rates. RDRAMs are expected to adhere to the Rambus channel specifications for timing and pinout [Shri98], [Cupp01].

Figure 17.7 presents an interesting view of the progress of DRAM densities and chip capacities since 1980. It shows, for example, that a 512 MB main memory, which would have required hundreds of DRAM chips in 1990, could be built with a handful of chips in 2000 and now requires but one DRAM chip. Beyond this, the same memory unit may be integrated on a VLSI chip with a CPU and other required devices to form a powerful single-chip computer.

■ 17.3 Hitting the Memory Wall

Whereas both SRAM and DRAM densities and chip capacities have increased dramatically since the invention of integrated circuits, speed improvements have not been as impressive. So, faster and faster processors and ever greater clock speeds have led to a widening of the gap between CPU performance and memory bandwidth. In other words, processor performance and density, as well as memory density, increase exponentially as predicted by Moore's law. This is represented by the upper sloped line in the semilogarithmic graph of Figure 17.8. Memory performance, however, has improved with a much more modest slope. This CPU-memory performance gap is particularly troublesome for DRAMs. SRAM speeds have shown

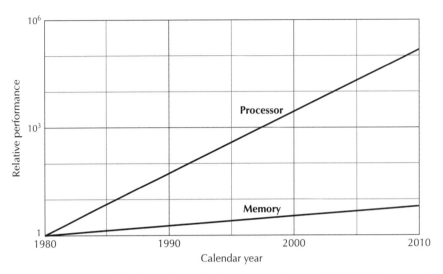

Figure 17.8 Memory density and capacity have grown along with the CPU power and complexity, but memory speed has not kept pace.

greater improvement, not only for memory chips but also because cache memories, which constitute a primary application for SRAMs, are now routinely integrated with the processor on the same chip, reducing signal propagation times and other access overheads typically involved when an off-chip unit must be accessed.

For these reasons, memory latency has become a serious bottleneck in modern computers. It has been argued that even now, further improvements in processor speed and clock rate do not translate to any noticeable gain in performance at the application level because user-perceived performance is entirely limited by the memory access time. This condition has been dubbed "hitting the memory wall," which pinpoints memory as a barrier to further progress [Wulf95]. It is noted, for example, that if the trends depicted in Figure 17.8 continue, by 2010 each memory access will have an average latency equivalent to hundreds of processor cycles. Thus, even if only 1% of instructions require access to DRAM main memory, it is the DRAM latency, not the processor speed, that dictates program execution time.

The arguments just presented are quite discouraging, but all hope is not lost. Even if a major breakthrough discovery does not solve the performance gap problem, several existing and proposed methods can be used to move the memory wall further away.

One way to bridge the gap between processor and memory speeds is to use extremely wide words so that each access to the slow memory retrieves a large amount of data; a mux is then used to select the appropriate word to be forwarded to the processor (Figure 17.9). The remaining words fetched may then be useful for subsequent instructions. We will see later that data is transferred between main memory and cache in multiple words known as a cache line. Such wide-word accesses are thus ideal for modern system with caches. Two other approaches, namely interleaved and pipelined memories, have special significance and need more detailed descriptions; hence they are discussed separately in Section 17.4.

Even assuming that the growing performance gap cannot be overcome through the architectural methods already named, the only conclusion we can draw is that the performance of a single processor will be limited by the memory latency. In theory, we can apply the power of tens, perhaps even thousands, of processors to the solution of our problems. While each of

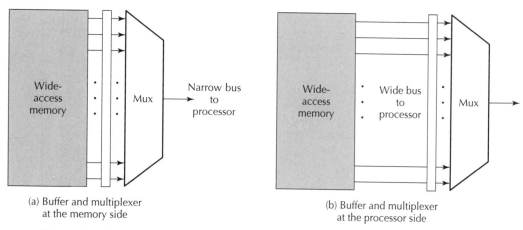

(a) Buffer and multiplexer
at the memory side

(b) Buffer and multiplexer
at the processor side

Figure 17.9 Two ways of using a wide-access memory to bridge the speed gap between the processor and memory.

these processors might be limited by the memory bottleneck, collectively they supply a level of performance that can be viewed as going right through the memory wall. Parallel processing methods will be covered in Part VII.

■ 17.4 Pipelined and Interleaved Memory

Simple memory units allow sequential accesses to their locations (one at a time). Whereas register files can be, and are, provided with multiple ports to allow several simultaneous accesses, this multiported approach to raising the bandwidth would be too expensive for memories. How then can we increase memory throughput so that more data can be accessed per unit time? The two main schemes for this purpose are pipelined and parallel data access.

Pipelining of memory allows the memory access latency to be spread over several pipeline stages, thus increasing the memory throughput. Without pipelining of the instruction and data accesses in a processor's data path, performance will be severely limited by the pipeline stages that contain memory references. Memory pipelining is possible because access to a memory bank consists of several sequential events or steps: row-address decoding, row readout from the memory matrix, writing into a word or forwarding it to output (based on the column address), and writing back the modified row buffer into the memory matrix if needed. By separating some of these steps and viewing them as different stages of a pipeline, a new memory access can be initiated once the previous one has moved to the second pipeline stage. As usual, pipelining may increase the latency somewhat but improves the throughput by allowing several memory accesses to be "in flight" through the memory pipeline stages.

Besides access to the physical memory, as discussed earlier, memory access may involve other supporting operations that can form extra stages in the memory pipeline. These include possible address translation prior to accessing the memory (cache or main) and tag comparison following access to a cache memory to ensure that the data word read out from the cache is indeed the one requested (why the two may be different is not clear at this point). Concepts related to cache memory access are covered in Chapter 18, while address translation for virtual memory is discussed in Chapter 20.

Figure 17.10 shows a pipelined cache memory based on the notions just discussed. There are four stages in the pipeline: an address translation stage, two stages for the actual memory

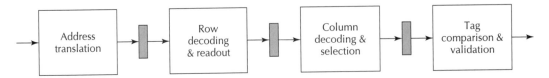

Figure 17.10 Pipelined cache memory.

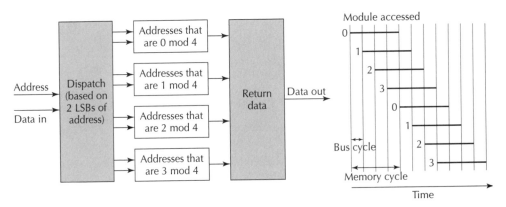

Figure 17.11 Interleaved memory is more flexible than wide-access memory in that it can handle multiple independent accesses at once.

access, and one stage for tag comparison to ensure the validity of the data fetched. The address translation stage is not always needed. For one thing, caches do not always require address translation; for another, translation can sometimes be overlapped with the physical memory access (we will understand these points in Chapter 18). In the case of an instruction cache, the tag comparison stage can be overlapped with instruction decoding and register access, so that its latency becomes transparent, whereas for a data cache, which is usually followed by register writeback, no overlap is possible. Thus, if the pipelined memory were to be used in the data path of Figure 15.11, an extra pipeline stage between data cache access and register writeback would have to be included.

Interleaved memory allows multiple accesses to occur in parallel, but they must be to addresses located in different memory banks. Figure 17.11 shows the block diagram for a *four-way interleaved* memory unit. Each of the four memory banks holds addresses that have the same residue when divided by 4; so, bank 0 has addresses that are of the form $4j$, bank 1 has addresses $4j + 1$, and so on. As each memory access request arrives, it is forwarded to the appropriate memory bank based on the 2 LSBs in the address. A new request can be accepted in every clock cycle, even though a memory bank takes many clock cycles to supply the requested data or write a word. Because all banks have the same latency, requested data words emerge from the output side in arrival order.

Under ideal conditions, an m-way interleaved memory achieves a bandwidth that is m times that of a single memory bank. This happens, for example, when enough memory addresses are accessed sequentially to allow each bank to complete one access before the next access to the same bank comes along. At the other extreme, if all accesses are to the same bank, interleaving does not provide any performance benefit. Even when the addresses are random, the performance benefit is quite limited if accesses must be forwarded to banks in the order received to ensure that the output words do not appear out of order. This is best understood in terms of the common birthday problem in elementary probability: even though there are 365 days in a year, it takes only 50 people in a room to make it very likely (probability of more than 95%) that at least two individuals have a common birthday. Statistical analysis shows that with random accesses and in-order processing of access requests, m-way interleaving leads to a throughput improvement by a factor of $\sqrt{m}$, which is much less than the ideal factor m. However, practical memory addresses are not randomly distributed but exhibit a definite sequential pattern, so much better performance can be expected.

An interleaved memory unit can form the core of a pipelined memory implementation. Consider the 4-way interleaved memory of Figure 17.11 as a 4-stage pipelined memory unit. Figure 17.11 shows that as long as accesses to the same memory bank are 4 clock cycles apart, the memory pipeline operates with no problem. However, within a processor's data path, such spacing of accesses cannot be guaranteed, and a special conflict detection mechanism is needed to ensure correct operation via stalling when necessary. Such a mechanism is fairly easy to implement. An incoming access request is characterized by a 2-bit memory bank number. This bank number must be checked against the bank numbers of up to three accesses that may still be in progress (the ones that may have begun in each of the three preceding clock cycles). If any of these three comparisons leads to a match, the pipeline must be stalled by disallowing the new access. Otherwise, the request is accepted and forwarded to the appropriate bank, while its bank number is shifted into a 4-position shift register for comparison with incoming requests in the next three cycles.

The pipelining scheme discussed early in this section can accommodate a limited number of stages. Pipelined memory based on interleaving can conceptually be used with an arbitrary number of stages. However, except in applications with highly regular memory access patterns, the complexity of the control circuitry and the stalling penalty place a practical upper bound on the number of stages. For this reason, large-scale interleaving is used only in vector supercomputers, which are optimized for operating on long vectors whose layout in memory ensures that temporally close memory accesses are routed to different banks (see Chapter 26).

17.5 Nonvolatile Memory

Both SRAMs and DRAMs require power to keep stored data intact. This type of *volatile* memory must be supplemented with *nonvolatile* or *stable* memory if data and programs are not to be lost when power is interrupted. For most computers, this stable memory consists of two parts: a relatively small *read-only memory* (ROM) to hold critical system programs that are needed to start up the machine and a *hard disk* that can keep stored data virtually indefinitely without requiring power. The low cost and high storage density of modern disk memories make them ideal stable memory devices. Because of their high capacities, disk memories play the dual roles of stable and *mass storage* (see Chapter 19).

In small, portable devices with limited space and battery capacity, the size and power requirements of disk memories are serious handicaps, as are their moving mechanical parts. For these reasons, nonvolatile semiconductor memory devices are preferred for use in such systems. Available options span a wide range from old, and well-established, read-only memory devices to newer read-write devices exemplified by flash memory.

Read-only memories are built in a variety of ways, all of which share the property of having a specific pattern of 0s and 1s wired in at the time of manufacture. For example,

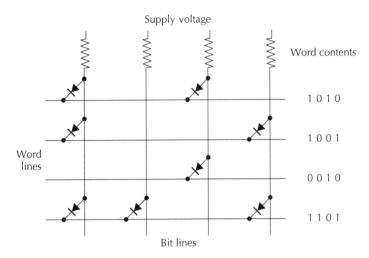

Figure 17.12 Read-only memory organization, with the fixed contents shown on the right.

Figure 17.12 shows a 4-word segment of a ROM in which a normally high bit line assumes low voltage when a selected word line is pulled low and there is a diode at the intersection of the bit line and the selected word line. Diodes are placed in bit cells that must store 1; no diode then corresponds to 0. If diodes are placed at all intersections and a mechanism is provided to selectively disconnect each unneeded diode by blowing a fuse, a *programmable ROM,* or PROM, results. Programming of a PROM is done by putting it in a special device (*PROM programmer*) and applying currents to blow selected fuses.

An erasable PROM (EPROM) uses a transistor in each cell that acts as a programmable switch. The contents of an EPROM can be erased (set to all 1s) by exposing the device to ultraviolet light for a few minutes. Because ROMs and PROMs are simpler and thus cheaper than EPROMs, the latter are used during system development and debugging, with the contents placed into ROMs once data or programs have been finalized. Erasure of data in electrically erasable PROMs (EEPROMs) is both more convenient and selective. Any given bit in the memory matrix can be erased by applying an appropriate voltage across the corresponding transistor. There is often a limit (typically, many thousands) on how many times an EEPROM cell can be erased before it loses the ability to retain information. This limits the range of applications and/or useful life of such devices as writable storage media.

A currently popular type of EEPROM, in which erasure is performed in large blocks rather than bit by bit, is known as *flash EPROM,* or *flash memory* (because erasure occurs quickly, or in a flash). Erasure in large blocks reduces the overhead circuitry, thus leading to greater density and lower cost. Figure 17.13 depicts a 4-word segment of a flash memory unit. A bit is stored by placing an electric charge on the floating gate of a transistor. Unlike in DRAM, however, this charge is trapped so that it cannot escape, thus requiring no refreshing and no power to keep it in place for several years. Because erasure occurs in blocks and is relatively slow, flash memories are not replacements for SRAMs or DRAMs; rather, they are used mainly to store information about configuration or default setup of digital systems that change rather infrequently and should be preserved when the system is unpowered.

Other technologies for nonvolatile random-access memory that look promising include ferroelectric RAM, magnetoresistive RAM, and ovonic unified memory [Gepp03].

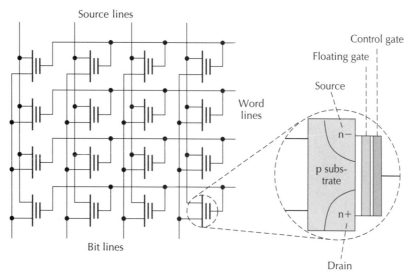

Figure 17.13 EEPROM or flash memory organization. Each memory cell is built of a floating-gate MOS transistor.

■ 17.6 The Need for a Memory Hierarchy

To match the processor speed, the memory holding the program's instructions and data must be accessible in 1 ns or less. We can build such a memory, but only in small sizes (e.g., a register file). The bulk of the program and its data must be kept in slower, and correspondingly larger, memory. The challenge is to design the overall memory system so that it appears to have the speed of the fastest component and the cost of the cheapest one. While increasing the bandwidth of slow memory can help bridge the speed gap, this approach requires increasingly sophisticated methods for hiding the memory latency and eventually falls apart when the gap grows sufficiently wide. Example 17.3 shows that increasing the bandwidth may run into problems even in the absence of limits on latency hiding methods.

Example 17.3: Relationship between memory bandwidth and performance Estimate the minimum required main memory bandwidth to sustain an instruction execution rate of 10 GIPS. Assume that there is no cache memory or other fast buffer for instructions or data. Would this bandwidth be feasible with a memory latency of 100 ns and a bus frequency of 200 MHz?

Solution: The no-cache assumption means that every instruction executed must be fetched from main memory. So, the execution rate of 10 GIPS implies at least 10 billion instruction accesses per second. Assuming 4-byte instructions, this implies a minimum memory bandwidth of 40 GB/s, even if no data is ever fetched or stored. Extracting from memory 40 B/ns at an access latency of 100 ns would require that 4000 B be read out in every access. This access width, while not completely infeasible, is rather impractical. Note that our analysis is based on three highly optimistic assumptions: total lack of data references, the ability to spread memory accesses uniformly over time, and perfect latency hiding. Transferring 40 GB/s from memory to processor over a 200 MHz bus would require a bus width of 200 B. Again the assumption that no bus cycle ever goes to waste is optimistic.

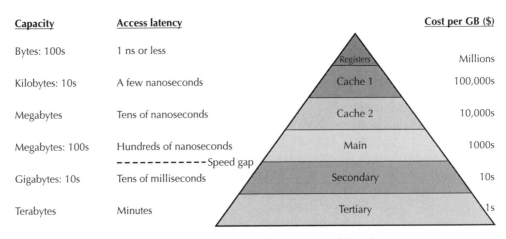

Capacity	Access latency		Cost per GB ($)
Bytes: 100s	1 ns or less	Registers	Millions
Kilobytes: 10s	A few nanoseconds	Cache 1	100,000s
Megabytes	Tens of nanoseconds	Cache 2	10,000s
Megabytes: 100s	Hundreds of nanoseconds	Main	1000s
Gigabytes: 10s	Tens of milliseconds	Secondary	10s
Terabytes	Minutes	Tertiary	1s

Figure 17.14 Names and key characteristics of levels in a memory hierarchy.

The fact that we can build small memories with access times of no more than a few nanoseconds leads naturally to the idea of a *buffer memory* that holds the currently most useful program segments and data (those that are frequently referenced or known to be needed in the near future), in much the same way that registers hold some of the currently active data elements for rapid access by the processor. This buffer or *cache memory* is likely to be too small to hold all of our programs and required data, so items must be brought into it from the main memory. Such a cache does not completely bridge the speed gap between the processor and main memory, so a second-level cache memory is often used. These two cache levels, along with registers, main memory, secondary memory (usually disk), and tertiary or archival memory are depicted in Figure 17.14.

Collectively, interacting memories of varying capacities, speeds, and costs depicted in Figure 17.14 are said to constitute a *memory hierarchy* within which the most useful data and program components somehow move to the top levels, where they are more readily accessible. Practically, every modern computer system has a *hierarchical memory,* although not all levels depicted in Figure 17.14 are present in every case.

The pyramidal shape of Figure 17.14 is intended to convey the smaller size of the memory units near the top and the higher capacities of the ones near the bottom. Fast register files have capacities that are measured in hundreds or at most thousands of bytes. Currently, multi-terabyte tertiary memories are practical, and the introduction of petabyte units is under consideration. Of course, cost and speed vary in the opposite direction, with the smaller memories near the top being faster and more expensive. Examining the access latencies given in Figure 17.4, we note that the ratios of latencies for successive levels are fairly small near the top (10 or less). The ratio suddenly grows to about 10^5 between main and secondary memories and is also large, though not as bad, between secondary and tertiary memories. This *speed gap* between semiconductor and magnetic/optical memories is an important impediment to high performance in data-intensive applications.

Levels in the memory hierarchy of Figure 17.14 are numbered: 0 for registers, 1 and 2 for caches (known as L1 and L2 caches), 3 for main memory, and so on. Registers are sometimes excluded from the memory hierarchy, in part because the mechanisms for moving data into and out of registers (explicit load/store instructions) are different from those used for data transfers between other levels. Also, in some architectures, certain data elements are never moved into registers and are processed directly out of the cache memory. However, given that our focus in this book is on load/store architectures in which data must be loaded into registers before they can be manipulated, it is appropriate to include registers as level 0 of the memory hierarchy. Note that the register file is used as a high-speed buffer only for data. However, many modern processors use instruction buffers that have the same role with regard to instructions as that played by the register file for data.

The register level, or cache-1 level, is sometimes considered the *highest level* of the memory hierarchy; while this nomenclature is consistent with the pyramidal view shown in Figure 17.4, it may cause some confusion when, for example, level 1 is viewed as being higher than level 3. We will thus refrain from characterizing the memory hierarchy levels as "high" or "low" and instead use the level's name or number. When relative positions must be specified, we characterize one as faster or closer to the processor (respectively, slower or further from the processor). For example, when a required item is not found in a given level of the memory hierarchy, the next slower level is consulted. This process of moving the focus of attention to the next slower level continues until the item is found. An item thus located is then copied through successively faster levels on its journey toward the processor until it reaches level 0, where it is accessible to the processor.

In this chapter, we dealt with the technology and basic organization of memory units that comprise the main and cache components in Figure 17.14. Registers and register files were covered in Chapter 2. What remains to be discussed is how information is transparently moved between cache and main memories (Chapter 18), the technology and data storage schemes of mass memories employed as secondary and tertiary components in the memory hierarchy (Chapter 19), and the management of information transfers between mass and main memories (Chapter 20).

PROBLEMS

17.1 SRAM memory organization

Two SRAM chips, each forming a b-bit wide, w-word memory are given, with both b and w even. Show how to use a minimum amount of external logic to form a memory with the following properties, or argue that it is impossible to do so.

a. w words that are $2b$ bits wide
b. $2w$ words that are b bits wide
c. $w/2$ words that are $4b$ bits wide
d. $4w$ words that are $b/2$ bits wide
e. Storing duplicate copies of w words that are b bits wide and comparing the two copies during each access for error detection

17.2 SRAM memory organization

Consider 4 Mb SRAM chips of three different internal organizations, offering data widths of 1, 4, and 8 bits. How many of each type of chip would be needed to build a 16 MB memory unit with the following word widths and how should they be interconnected?

a. 8-bit words
b. 16-bit words
c. 32-bit words

17.3 DRAM memory organization

A survey of desktop and laptop PCs in an organization has revealed that they have from 256 MB to 1 GB of DRAM main memory, in increments of 128 MB. We have been told that these machines use DRAM chips with capacities of 256 Mb or 1 Gb, with the two types never intermixed in the same machine. What do these pieces of information reveal about the number of memory chips in the PCs? In each case, specify possible data width for the chips used if the DRAM memory word width is 64 bits.

17.4 DRAM technology trends

Assuming that the trends in Figure 17.7 continue for the foreseeable future, what would be the expected range of values for the number of memory chips used and the overall memory capacity for:

a. Workstations in the year 2008
b. Servers in the year 2015
c. Supercomputers in the year 2020
d. Large PCs in the year 2010

17.5 Design of a wide-word DRAM

An SDRAM unit supplies 64-bit data words, taking four clock cycles for the first word and one cycle for each subsequent word (up to 7 more) within the same memory row. How could you use this unit as a component to build a wide-word SDRAM with a fixed access time, and what would be the resulting memory latency for word widths of 256, 512, and 1024 bits?

17.6 Pipelined DRAM operation

In the description of DRAMs, we noted that a DRAM chip needs half as many address pins as an SRAM of the same size because the row and column addresses do not have to be provided simultaneously. Why does the pipelined operation depicted in Figure 17.10 change this?

17.7 Processor-in-memory architectures

The argument has been advanced that because external memory bandwidth has become a serious bottleneck, perhaps one can exploit the high internal bandwidth (due to reading an entire row of the memory matrix at once) by implanting many simple processors on a DRAM memory chip. The multiple processors can manipulate segments of the long internal memory word that can be accessed in each memory cycle. Briefly discuss the positive points, and disadvantages or implementation problems, of this approach to bulldozing the memory wall.

17.8 Pipelined memory with interleaving

Supply the detailed design for the conflict detection and stalling mechanism needed to turn a 4-way interleaved memory unit into a 4-stage pipelined memory, as discussed in Section 17.4.

17.9 Data organization in interleaved memories

Suppose that elements of two 1000×1000 matrices A and B are stored in the 4-way interleaved memory unit of Figure 17.11 in row-major order. Thus, the 1000 elements of a row of A or B are spread evenly among the banks while elements of a column all fall in the same bank.

a. Assuming that computation time is negligible compared with memory access time, derive the memory throughput when elements of A are added to the corresponding elements of B in row-major order.
b. Repeat part a, this time assuming that additions are performed in column-major order.
c. Show that for some $m \times m$ matrices, the computations of parts a and b lead to comparable memory throughputs.
d. Repeat part a, this time assuming that B is stored in column-major order.

17.10 Access stride in interleaved memories

A convenient way of analyzing the effects of data organization in interleaved memories on the memory throughput is via the notion of *access stride*. Consider an $m \times m$ matrix that is stored in an h-way interleaved memory in row-major order. When we access the elements in a particular row of such a matrix, memory locations $x, x + 1, x + 2, \ldots$ are addressed; we say that the access stride is 1. Elements of a column fall in locations $y, y + m, y + 2m, \ldots$, for an access stride of m. Accessing elements on the main diagonal leads to an access stride of $m + 1$, while the antidiagonal elements produce a stride of $m - 1$.

a. Show that memory throughput is maximized as long as the access stride s is relatively prime with respect to h.
b. One way to ensure maximum memory throughput for all strides is to choose h to be a prime number. Why is this not a particularly good idea?
c. Instead of storing each row of the matrix beginning with its 0th element, we can begin the storage of row i with its ith element, wrapping around to the beginning of the row after the last element of the row has appeared. Show that this type of *skewed storage* is helpful for

improving the memory throughput in some cases.

17.11 Read-only memory

One application of read-only memories is in function evaluation. Suppose we want to evaluate a function $f(x)$, where x is an 8-bit fraction and the result is to be obtained with 16 bits of precision.

a. What size ROM do we need and how must it be organized?
b. Given that memories are slower than logic circuits, is this method ever faster than conventional function evaluation using ALU-type arithmetic circuits?

17.12 Choice of memory technology

a. The specs for a digital camera indicate that its photo storage subsystem contains an SRAM memory unit large enough to hold a couple of photos and a flash memory module that can store some 100 photos. Discuss the reasons that you think might have motivated the choices of technologies and capacities for the two memory components.
b. Repeat part a for an electronic organizer, capable of storing a few thousand names and associated contact information, with the same combination of memories: a relatively small SRAM memory unit and a fairly large flash memory module.

17.13 Flash memory organization

Flash memory is random-access memory as far as reading is concerned. For writing, however, an arbitrary data element cannot be modified in place because single-word erasure is not possible. Study alternative data organizations in flash memory to allow selective write operations.

17.14 Memory hierarchy characteristics

Augment Figure 17.14 with a column specifying the approximate peak data rates at the various levels of the hierarchy. For example, a three-ported 32-bit register file (two reads and one write per cycle) with access time of about 1 ns supports a data rate of $3 \times 32 \times 10^9$ b/s $= 12$ GB/s $\cong 0.1$ Tb/s. This rate could perhaps increase by a factor of 10, to 1 Tb/s, if the registers were twice as fast and twice as wide, and

could be accessed through a few more read/write ports.

17.15 Memory hierarchy characteristics

Based on Figure 17.14, which level of a hierarchical memory is likely to have the highest cost? Note that the total cost, not the cost per byte, is in question.

17.16 Analogy for a computer's hierarchical memory

Consider the hierarchical way in which a person deals with telephone numbers. He has a handful of important phone numbers memorized. Numbers for other key contacts are kept in a pocket phone book or electronic organizer. Proceeding further down the equivalent of Figure 17.14 in this case, we arrive at the city phone directory and, finally, to the collection of directories from around the country available in the local library. Draw, and appropriately label, a pyramidal diagram to represent this hierarchical system, listing the important characteristics of each level.

17.17 History of main memory technology

Today, we take fast, high-capacity, random-access memories for granted. Modern desktop and laptop computers have RAM capacities that exceed those of secondary memories of the most powerful early digital computers. The first digital computers did not have random-access memories but rather used serial memories in which data items moved in a circular path; access to a particular item required long waits until that item appeared in the right position to be readable. Even when random-access capability appeared in *magnetic core* memories, the manufacturing process was complicated and expensive, leading to the use of very small main memories by today's standards. Other examples of now abandoned memory technologies include *plated-wire* memories, *sonic delay-line* memories, and *magnetic bubble* memories. Pick one of these, or some other pre-1970s memory technology, and write a report describing the technology, associated memory organizations, and range of practical applications in digital computers and elsewhere.

REFERENCES AND FURTHER READINGS

[Crag96]   Cragon, H. G., *Memory Systems and Pipelined Processors,* Jones and Bartlett, 1996.

[Cull99]   Culler, D. E., and J. P. Singh, *Parallel Computer Architecture: A Hardware/Software Approach,* Morgan Kaufmann, 1999, Sec. 12.1, pp. 936–955.

[Cupp01]   Cuppu, V., B. Jacob, B. Davis, and T. Mudge, "High-Performance DRAMS in Workstation Environments," *IEEE Trans. Computers,* Vol. 50, No. 11, pp. 1133–1153, November 2001.

[Gepp03]   Geppert, L., "The New Indelible Memories," *IEEE Spectrum,* Vol. 40, No. 3, pp. 49–54, March 2003.

[Kush91]   Kushiyama, N., Y. Watanabe, T. Ohsawa, K. Muraoka, Y. Nagahama, and T. Furuyama, "A 12-MHz Data Cycle 4-Mb DRAM with Pipeline Operation," *IEEE J. Solid-State Circuits,* Vol. 26, No. 4, pp. 479–482, 1991.

[Przy94]   Przybylski, S., *New DRAM Technologies,* MicroDesign Resources, 1994.

[Shri98]   Shriver, B., and B. Smith, *The Anatomy of a High-Performance Microprocessor: A Systems Perspective,* IEEE Computer Society Press, 1998, Chap. 5, pp. 427–461.

[Wake01]   Wakerly, J. F., *Digital Design: Principles and Practices,* 3rd ed., Prentice Hall, 2001.

[Wulf95]   Wulf, W. A., and S. A. McKee, "Hitting the Memory Wall: Implications of the Obvious," *Computer Architecture News,* pp. 20–24, March 1995.

CHAPTER 18

CACHE MEMORY ORGANIZATION

"The use is discussed of a fast core memory . . . as slave to a slower core memory . . . in such a way that in practical cases the effective access time is nearer that of the fast memory than that of the slow memory."

—*Maurice Wilkes, Slave Memories and Dynamic Storage Allocation, 1965.*

"Memory is the cabinet of imagination, the treasury of reason, the registry of conscience, and the council chamber of thought."

—*Saint Basil*

The quotation from Maurice Wilkes shows that the idea of using a fast (slave or cache) memory to bridge the speed gap between a processor and a slower, but larger, main memory has been around for quite some time. Even though in the intervening years, memories have become much faster, the processor-memory speed gap has in fact widened so much that the use of a cache memory is almost mandatory now. The relationship of cache to main memory is the same as that of a desk drawer to a file cabinet: a more readily accessible place to hold data of current interest for the duration of time when the data is very likely to be accessed. In this chapter, we review strategies for moving data between main and cache memories and learn ways of quantifying the resulting improvement in performance.

■ 18.1 The Need for a Cache

Memory access latency is a major performance hindrance in modern computers. Improvements in memory access time (currently hundreds of nanoseconds for large off-chip memories) have not kept pace with processor speeds (<1 ns to a few nanoseconds per operation).

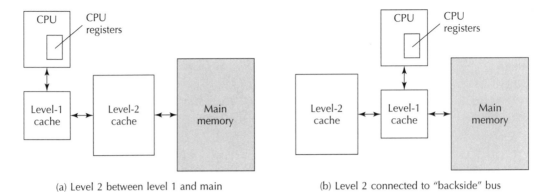

(a) Level 2 between level 1 and main   (b) Level 2 connected to "backside" bus

Figure 18.1 Cache memories act as intermediaries between the superfast processor and the much slower main memory.

Because larger memories tend to be slower, the problem has been worsening by the ever increasing memory sizes. For this reason, most processors use a fast, relatively small memory for keeping instructions and data so that most of the time access to the slow main memory is avoided. Data must still be moved from the slower/larger memory to the smaller/faster memory and vice versa, but this can (conceivably) be overlapped with computation. The name "cache" (safe hiding place) is used for this small/fast memory because it is usually invisible to the user except through its effect on performance.

Recently, using a second-level cache memory to reduce accesses to the main memory even further has become common. Figure 18.1 shows the relationship between cache and main memories. Level-2 cache can be added to a system with cache and main memories in two ways. The first option (Figure 18.1a) is to insert the level-2 cache between level-1 cache and main memory. The second option is to connect the level-1 cache unit to both level-2 cache and main memory directly through two different memory buses (sometimes called backside and frontside buses).

Consider a single level of cache memory. To access a required data word, the cache is consulted first. Finding the required data in the cache is referred to as a *cache hit;* not finding it is a *cache miss.* An important parameter in evaluating the effectiveness of cache memories is the *hit rate,* defined as the fraction of data accesses that can be satisfied from the cache as opposed to the slower memory that sits beyond it. A hit rate of 95%, for example, means that only one in 20 accesses, on the average, will not find the required data in the cache. With a hit rate h, cache access cycle of C_{fast}, and slower memory access cycle of C_{slow}, the effective memory cycle time is

$$C_{eff} = hC_{fast} + (1 - h)(C_{slow} + C_{fast}) = C_{fast} + (1 - h)C_{slow}$$

This equation is derived with the assumption that when data is not found in the cache, it must first be brought into the cache (in C_{slow} time) and then accessed from the cache (in C_{fast} time). Simultaneous forwarding of data from the slow memory to both the processor and the cache reduces the effective delay somewhat, but the simple formula for C_{eff} is adequate for our purposes, especially given that we have not accounted for the overhead of determining whether the required data is in the cache. We see that when the hit rate h is close to 1, an effective memory cycle close to C_{fast} is achieved. Therefore, the cache provides the illusion that the entire memory space consists of fast memory.

In typical microprocessors, accessing the cache memory is part of the instruction execution cycle. As long as the required data is in the cache, instruction execution continues at full speed. When a cache miss occurs and the slower memory must be accessed, instruction execution is interrupted. The *cache miss penalty* is usually specified in terms of the number of clock cycles that will be wasted because the processor has to stall until the data becomes available. In a microprocessor that executes an average of 1 instruction per clock cycle when there is no cache miss, a cache miss penalty of 8 cycles means that 8 cycles of delay will be added to the instruction execution time. If 5% of instructions encounter a cache miss, corresponding to a cache hit rate of 95%, and assuming an average of one memory access per instruction executed, the effective CPI will be $1 + 0.05 \times 8 = 1.4$.

When we have a second-level or L2 cache, we can associate a local hit or miss rate with it. For example, a local hit rate of 75% for the L2 cache means that 75% of accesses that were referred to the L2 cache (due to a miss in the L1 cache) can be satisfied there, with 25% needing a reference to the main memory.

Example 18.1: Performance of a two-level cache system   A computer system has L1 and L2 caches. The local hit rates for L1 and L2 are 95 and 80%, respectively. The miss penalties are 8 and 60 cycles, respectively. Assuming a CPI of 1.2 without any cache miss and an average of 1.1 memory accesses per instruction, what is the effective CPI after cache misses are factored in? Taking the two levels of caches as a single cache memory, what are its miss rate and miss penalty?

Solution: We can use the formula $C_{eff} = C_{fast} + (1 - h_1)[C_{medium} + (1 - h_2)C_{slow}]$. Because C_{fast} is already included in the CPI of 1.2, we must account for the rest. This leads to an effective CPI of $1.2 + 1.1(1 - 0.95)[8 + (1 - 0.8)60] = 1.2 + 1.1 \times 0.05 \times 20 = 2.3$. When the two caches are lumped together, we have a hit rate of 99% (95% hit rate in level 1, plus 80% of the 5% misses of level 1 found in level 2) or a miss rate of 1%. The effective access time of this imaginary single-level cache is $1 + 0.05 \times 8 = 1.4$ cycles and its miss penalty is 60 cycles.

A cache memory is characterized by several design parameters that influence its implementation cost and performance (hit rate). The following description is with the assumption of a single cache level; that is, there is no level-2 cache. The most important cache parameters are as follows.

a. *Cache size* in bytes or words. A larger cache can hold more of the program's useful data but is more costly and likely to be slower.

b. *Block size* or *cache line width,* defined as the unit of data transfer between the cache and main memory. With a larger cache line, more data is brought into the cache with each miss. This can improve the hit rate but also tends to tie up parts of the cache with data of lesser utility.

c. *Placement policy*. Determining where an incoming cache line can be stored. More flexible policies imply higher hardware cost and may or may not have performance benefits in view of their more complex, and thus slower, process for locating the required data in the cache.

d. *Replacement policy*. Determining which of several existing cache blocks (into which a new cache line can be mapped) should be overwritten. Typical policies include choosing a random block and choosing the least recently used block.

e. *Write policy*. Determining whether updates to cache words are immediately forwarded to the main memory (*write-through* policy) or modified cache blocks are copied back to main memory in their entirety if and when they must be replaced in the cache (*writeback* or *copy-back* policy).

These parameters are closely interrelated, and changing one often necessitates changes in the others to ensure optimal memory performance. The impact of these parameters on memory system performance will be explored in Section 18.6.

18.2 What Makes a Cache Work?

Caches are so successful in improving the performance of modern processors mainly because of two locality properties of memory access patterns in typical programs. *Spatial locality* of memory accesses results from consecutive accesses usually referring to nearby memory locations. For example, a 9-instruction program loop that is executed 1000 times causes instruction accesses to be concentrated in a 9-word region of the address space for a relatively long period of time (Figure 18.2). Similarly, as a program is being assembled, the symbol table, which occupies a fairly small region in the address space, is consulted frequently. *Temporal locality* indicates that once an instruction or data element has been accessed, future accesses to the same item tend to occur mostly in the near future. In other words, programs tend to focus in one region of memory for getting instructions and/or data and then move on to other regions as phases of computation are completed.

The two locality properties of memory access patterns cause the most useful instructions and data elements at any given point in a program's execution (sometimes called the

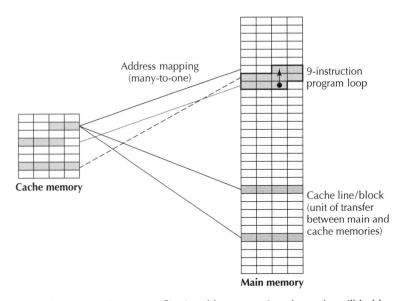

Figure 18.2 Assuming no conflict in address mapping, the cache will hold a small program loop in its entirety, leading to fast execution.

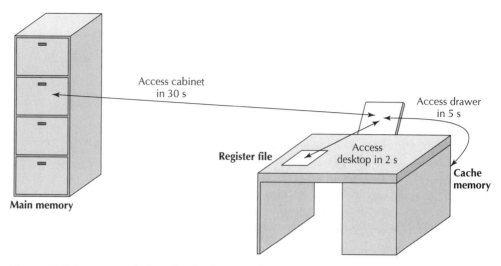

Figure 18.3 Items on a desktop (register) or in a drawer (cache) are more readily accessible than those in a file cabinet (main memory).

program's *working set*) to reside in the cache. This leads to high cache hit rates, which are typically in the range 90–98%, or, equivalently, low miss rates in the range 2–10%.

The following analogy is quite useful (see Figure 18.3). You work on documents by placing them on your desktop. The desktop corresponds to a CPU's registers. Among documents or files that are not needed right away, the most useful ones may be in a desk drawer (analog of cache memory) and the rest in file cabinets (main memory) or perhaps in a storage room (secondary memory). Most of the time, you find what you need in your drawer. Once in a while, you have to get up to fetch less frequently used documents or files from the file cabinet; on rare occasions, you may have to go to the storage room to fetch a seldom referenced document or file. With the latencies given in Figure 18.3, if the hit rate in the drawer is 90%, the average document access time becomes $5 + (1 - 0.90)30 = 8$ s.

Example 18.2: Drawer and file cabinet analogy   Assuming a hit rate of h in the drawer, formulate the situation shown in Figure 18.2 in terms of Amdahl's law and the speedup resulting from the use of a drawer.

Solution: Without the drawer, a document is accessed in 30 s. So, fetching 1000 documents, say, would take 30,000 s. The drawer causes a fraction h of the cases to be done 6 times as fast, with the access time unchanged for the remaining $1 - h$. Speedup is thus $1/(1 - h + h/6) = 6/(6 - 5h)$. Improving the drawer access time can increase the speedup factor, but as long as the miss rate remains at $1 - h$, the speedup can never exceed $1/(1 - h)$. Given $h = 0.9$, for instance, the speedup achieved is 4, with the upper bound being 10 for an extremely short drawer access time. If everything in the drawer could be placed on the desktop, then a speedup factor of $30/2 = 15$ could be achieved in 90% of the cases. The overall speedup would then be $1/(0.1 + 0.9/15) = 6.25$. Note, however, that this is a hypothetical analysis; stacking documents and files on your desktop is not a good way to improve access speed!

It is instructive to briefly review cache miss types and categorize them as compulsory, capacity, and conflict misses.

Compulsory misses: The first access to any cache line results in a miss. Some "compulsory" misses can be avoided by predicting future access to items and prefetching them into the cache. So, such misses are truly compulsory only if we use an *on-demand fetching policy*. These misses are sometimes referred to as *cold-start misses*.

Capacity misses: Because cache size is finite, we have to discard some cache lines to make room for others; this leads to misses in future that might not have been incurred with an infinitely large cache.

Conflict misses: Occasionally, there is free room, or space occupied by useless data, in the cache, but the mapping scheme used for placing items in the cache forces us to displace useful data to bring in other required data. This may lead to misses in future. These misses are sometimes referred to as *collision misses*.

Compulsory misses are quite easy to understand. If a program accesses 3 different cache lines, it encounters 3 compulsory misses. To see the difference between capacity and conflict misses, consider a 2-line cache and the access pattern *A B C A C A B*, where each letter represents a line of data. First *A* and *B* are loaded into the cache. Then *C* is loaded (the third and last compulsory miss) and must replace *A* or *B*. If the cache mapping is such that *C* replaces *A*, and vice versa, then the next three misses are conflict misses. In this case there are 6 misses in all (3 compulsory, 3 conflict). On the other hand, if *C* replaced *B*, there would be 4 misses in all (3 compulsory, 1 capacity). One could argue that one of the three extra misses in the first instance must be viewed as a capacity miss, given that a 2-line cache cannot possibly hold three different data lines through their second accesses. So, please do not take this categorization too seriously!

Example 18.3: Compulsory, capacity, and conflict misses   A program accesses each element of a 1000×1000 matrix 10 times in the course of its execution. Only 1% of this matrix fits in the data cache at any given time. A cache line holds four matrix elements. How many compulsory data cache misses will be caused by this program's execution? If all 10^6 matrix elements are accessed once in round i before accesses in round $i + 1$ begin, how many capacity misses will there be? Is it possible to have no conflict misses at all, regardless of the mapping scheme used?

Solution: Bringing all matrix elements into the cache requires the loading of $10^6/4$ cache lines; thus, there will be 250,000 compulsory misses. It is of course possible to have a cache miss upon the first access to each of the 10^6 matrix elements. This would happen if when a line is brought in, only one of its four elements is accessed before the line is replaced. However, not all these misses are truly compulsory. As for capacity misses, each of the 10 rounds of accesses generates at least 250,000 misses. Thus, there will be $250,000 \times 9 = 2.25 \times 10^6$ capacity misses. Though rather unlikely, it is possible that all accesses to each matrix element will occur while it resides in cache after it is first brought in. In this case, there is no conflict (or even capacity) miss.

Given a fixed-size cache, dictated for example by cost factors or availability of space on the processor chip, compulsory and capacity misses are pretty much fixed. Conflict misses, on the other hand, are influenced by the data mapping scheme, which is under our control. In the next two sections, we discuss two popular mapping schemes.

18.3 Direct-Mapped Cache

For simplicity, we assume that the memory is word-addressable. For a byte-addressable memory, of the type used in our MiniMIPS and MicroMIPS, "word(s)" must be replaced by "byte(s)" in the following discussion.

In the simplest mapping scheme, each line from main memory has a unique place in the cache where it can reside. Let the cache contain 2^L lines, each with 2^W words. Then, the least significant W bits in each address specify the word index within a line. Taking the next L bits in the address as the line number in the cache will cause successive lines to be mapped to successive cache lines. All words whose addresses are the same modulo 2^{L+W} will be mapped to the same word in cache. In the example of Figure 18.4, we have $L = 3$ and $W = 2$; so, the least significant 5 bits of the address identify a cache line and a word in that line $(3 + 2 \text{ bits})$ from which the desired word must be read. Because many main memory lines map onto the same cache line, the cache stores the tag part of the address to indicate which of the many possible lines is actually present in the cache. Of course, a particular cache line may hold no useful data; this is indicated by resetting the "valid bit" associated with the cache line.

When a word is read out from the cache, its tag is also fetched and compared with the tag of the desired word. If they match, and the valid bit of the cache line is set (this is equivalent to matching $\langle 1, \text{Tag} \rangle$ against $\langle x, y \rangle$ read out from the valid-bit/tag store), a cache hit is indicated and the word just read out is used. Otherwise, we have a cache miss and the accessed word is ignored. Note that this reading out and matching of the tags is required even for a write operation. In the case of write operation, if the tags match, we modify the word and write it

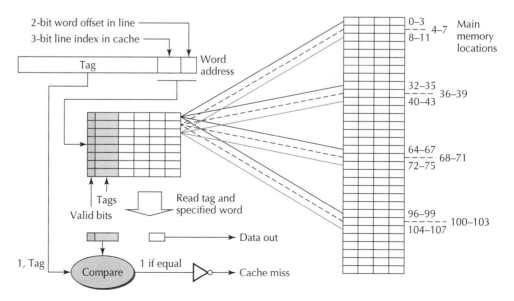

Figure 18.4 Direct-mapped cache holding 32 words within eight 4-word lines. Each line is associated with a tag and a valid bit.

back as usual. In the case of mismatch, referred to as a "write miss," a new cache line containing the desired word must be brought into the cache (just as for read miss) and the process is performed with the new line.

The process of deriving the cache address to be read out from the word address supplied is known as address translation. With direct mapping, this translation process is essentially trivial and consists of taking the least significant $L + W$ bits of the word address and using it as the cache address. This is why in Figure 18.4, the least significant 5 bits of the word address are used as the cache address.

Conflict misses can be a problem for direct-mapped caches. For example, if memory is accessed with a *stride* that is a multiple of 2^{L+W}, every access leads to a cache miss. This would happen, for example, if an m-column matrix is stored in row-major order and m is a multiple of 2^{L+W} (32 in the example of Figure 18.4). Given that strides that are powers of 2 are quite common, such an occurrence is not rare.

Example 18.4: Accessing a direct-mapped cache   Assume that memory is byte-addressable, memory addresses are 32 bits wide, a cache line contains $2^W = 16$ bytes, and the cache size is $2^L = 4096$ lines (64 KB). Show the various parts of the address and identify which portion of the address is used to access the cache.

Solution: Byte offset in a line is $\log_2 16 = 4$ bits wide and cache line index is $\log_2 4096 = 12$ bits wide. This leaves $32 - 12 - 4 = 16$ bits for the tag. Figure 18.5 shows the result.

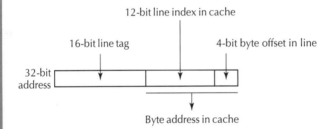

Figure 18.5 Components of the 32-bit address in an example direct-mapped cache with byte addressing.

The first quotation at the beginning of this chapter is from a short paper that described a direct-mapped cache for the first time, although the term "cache" and actual implementations of the idea did not appear until a few years later. Direct-mapped caches were common in early implementations; most modern caches use the set-associative mapping scheme, described next.

18.4 Set-Associative Cache

An *associative cache* (sometimes called fully associative) is one in which a cache line can be placed in any cache location, thus eliminating conflict misses altogether. Such a cache is quite difficult to implement because it needs to compare thousands of tags against the desired tag

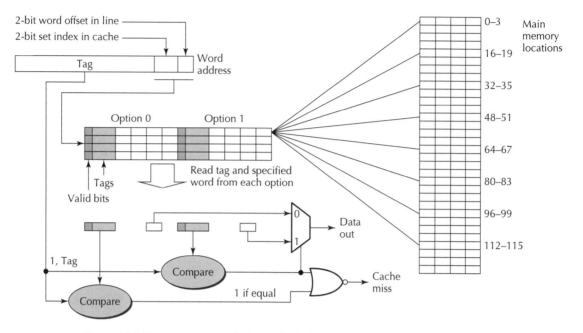

Figure 18.6 Two-way set-associative cache holding 32 words of data within 4-word lines and 2-line sets.

for each access. In practice, a compromise between fully associative and direct-mapped cache works quite well. It is known as *set-associative cache*.

Set-associative mapping is the most commonly used mapping scheme in processor caches. At the extreme of single-block sets, a set-associative cache degenerates into a direct-mapped cache. A read operation from a set-associative cache with a set size $2^S = 2$ is depicted in Figure 18.6. The memory address supplied by the processor is composed of tag and index parts. The index part, itself consisting of a block address and word offset within the block, identifies a set of 2^S cache words that can potentially hold the required data, while the tag specifies one of the many cache lines in the address space that map into the same set of 2^S cache lines via the set-associative placement policy. For each memory access, all 2^S candidate words, along with the tags associated with their respective lines, are read out. The 2^S tags are then simultaneously compared with the desired tag, leading to two possible outcomes:

1. None of the stored tags matches the desired tag: the data parts are ignored, and a cache miss signal is asserted to initiate a cache line transfer from main memory.

2. The ith stored tag, which corresponds to the placement option i ($0 \leq i < 2^S$), matches the desired tag: the word read out from the block corresponding to the ith placement option is chosen as the data output.

As in a direct-mapped cache, each cache line has a *valid bit* that indicates whether it holds valid data. This valid bit is also read out along with the tag and used in the comparison to ensure that a match occurs only with the tag of valid data. A line of a writeback cache may also have a *dirty bit* that is set to 1 with every write update to the line and is used at the time of line replacement to decide whether a line to be overwritten needs to be copied back into main memory. Because of multiple placement options for each cache line, conflict misses are less problematic here than in direct-mapped caches.

A remaining question is the choice of one of the 2^S cache lines in a set to be replaced with an incoming line. In practice, random selection and selection based on which line was least recently used (LRU) work well. Effects of the replacement policy on cache performance are discussed in Section 18.6.

Example 18.5: Accessing a set-associative cache Assume that memory is byte-addressable, memory addresses are 32 bits wide, a cache line contains $2^W = 16$ bytes, sets contain $2^S = 2$ lines, and the cache size is $2^L = 4096$ lines (64 KB). Show the various parts of the address and identify which portion of the address is used to access the cache.

Solution: Byte offset in a line is $\log_2 16 = 4$ bits wide and cache set index is $\log_2 (4096/2) = 11$ bits wide. This leaves $32 - 11 - 4 = 17$ bits for the tag. Figure 18.7 shows the result.

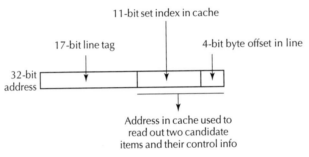

Figure 18.7 Components of the 32-bit address in an example two-way set-associative cache.

Example 18.6: Cache address mapping A 64 KB four-way set-associative cache memory is byte-addressable and contains 32 B lines. Memory addresses are 32 b wide.

   a. How wide are the tags in this cache?

   b. Which main memory addresses are mapped to set number 5 in the cache?

Solution: The number of sets in the cache is $64 \text{ KB}/(4 \times 32 \text{ B}) = 512$.

   a. A 32-bit address is divided into a 5-bit byte offset, a 9-bit set index, and an 18-bit tag.

   b. Addresses that have their 9-bit set index equal to 5 map into set number 5. These addresses are of the form $2^{14}a + 2^5 \times 5 + b$, where a is a tag value $(0 \leq a \leq 2^{18} - 1)$ and b is a byte offset $(0 \leq b \leq 31)$. So, the addresses mapped to set number 5 include 160 through 191, 16,544 through 16,575, 32,928 through 32,959, and so on.

As evident from Figure 18.6, two-way set-associative caches are easily implemented. The LRU replacement policy requires a single bit associated with each set that designates which of the two slots or options was used least recently. Increasing the degree of associativity improves the cache performance by reducing conflict misses but also complicates the design and potentially lengthens the access cycle. Thus, in practice, the degree of associativity seldom exceeds 16 and is often kept at 4 or 8. More on this in Section 18.6.

◼ 18.5 Cache and Main Memory

Caches are variously organized to meet the memory performance requirements of particular machines. We have already referred to single-level and multilevel caches (L1, L2, and, perhaps, L3), with the latter laid out in different ways (see Figure 18.1). A *unified cache* is one that holds both instructions and data, whereas a *split cache* consists of separate instruction and data caches. Because early machines designed at Harvard University had separate instruction and data memories, a machine with split cache is said to follow the *Harvard architecture*. Unified caches are embodiments of the *von Neumann architecture*. Each cache level can be unified or split, but the most common combination in high-performance processors consists of a split L1 cache and a unified L2 cache.

In what follows, we explore the relationship between a fast memory (cache) and a relatively slower memory (main). Similar issues apply to data transfer methods and requirements between L1 and L2, or L2 and L3, if the additional cache levels exist. Note that it is commonly the case that the contents of a level within the memory hierarchy is a subset of the contents of the next slower level. Thus, searching for data elements proceeds in the direction of slower memories, away from the processor, because whatever is not available in a given level certainly would not exist in any of the faster levels. If a cache level, say L1, is split, then each of the two parts has a similar relationship to the next slower cache level or to main memory, with the additional complication of the two parts competing for the bandwidth of the slower memory.

Because main memory is so much slower than cache memory, many methods have been developed for making data transfers between main and cache memories faster. Note that DRAMs have extremely high bandwidths internally (Figure 18.8). However, this bandwidth is lost as a result of the I/O pin limitations on memory chips, and to a lesser extent, because of relatively narrow buses that connect the main memory to the CPU cache.

Consider a 4-chip, 128 MB main memory built of the chip shown in Figure 18.8. This memory can access 32-bit words and transmit them over a bus of the same width to the cache.

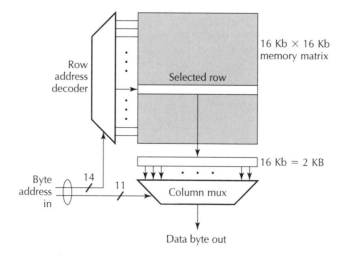

Figure 18.8 A 256 Mb DRAM chip organized as a 32 M × 8 memory module: four such chips could form a 128 MB main memory unit.

Suppose the cache line is 4 words wide. These 4 words will be contained in the same row of our 4 chips. Thus, once the first word has been transferred, subsequent words can be read out faster because they will be read out from the row buffer rather than the memory matrix. Because a cache miss occurs when a particular word is accessed, it is possible to design the data transfer mechanism to have the main memory read out the requested word first so that the cache can supply the word to the CPU while the remaining 3 words are being transferred. Optimizations such as this are in common use in high-performance designs.

Higher-performance processors tend to utilize larger main memories composed of many DRAM chips. In this case, the chips collectively provide access to several words (super-words), making it feasible to use a single or a small number of cycles on a wide bus to trans-fer an entire cache line to the CPU.

Writing modified cache entries to main memory presents a special design challenge in high-performance systems. The write-through policy (see the end of Section 18.1) is particularly problematic because, unless write operations are very infrequent, they slow the cache down significantly while the main memory is catching up. With writeback or copy-back, the prob-lem is less severe, given that writing to main memory occurs only when a modified cache line needs to be replaced. In the latter case, at least two main memory accesses are needed: one to copy back the old cache line and another to read the new line. A commonly used method to avoid this performance penalty due to write operations is to provide the cache with *write buffers*. Data to be written to main memory is placed in one of these buffers and cache opera-tion continues without regard to whether writing to main memory can occur immediately. As long as there is no further cache miss, the main memory is not required to catch up right away. The write operations can be performed using idle cycles of the bus until all write buffers have been emptied. In the case of another cache miss before all write buffers have been emptied, we can either flush the buffers before attempting to look for the data in main memory or provide a special mechanism to search the write buffers for the desired data, proceeding to main mem-ory only if the required location is not in one of the write buffers.

18.6 Improving Cache Performance

In this chapter, we learned that cache memory bridges the speed gap between the CPU and main memory. Cache hit rates in the range of 90–98%, and occasionally even higher, are com-mon, leading to high performance by eliminating most accesses to main memory. Because the fastest caches are quite expensive, some computers use two or three levels of cache memory, with the additional cache level(s) being larger, slower, and cheaper, per byte, than the first. A major design decision in introducing a new machine is the number, capacities, and types of cache memories to be used. For example, split caches generally produce higher performance by allowing concurrency in access to data and instructions. However, for a given total cache capacity, split caches imply a smaller capacity for each unit, thus potentially leading to a higher miss rate than a unified cache when a large program is run with little need for data or, conversely, a fairly small program operates on a very large data set.

A common way of evaluating the relative merits of various cache design alternatives is simulation using publicly available data sets that characterize memory accesses in typical ap-plications of interest. A *memory address trace* contains information about the sequence and timing of memory addresses generated in the course of executing particular sets of programs. If we supply an address trace of interest to a cache system simulator that has also been pro-vided with design parameters for a particular cache system, it produces a record of hits and misses in the various cache levels, and thus a fairly accurate indicator of performance. To get a feel for the interplay of the various parameters, we present the results of some empirical studies based on the approach just outlined.

Generally speaking, larger caches produce better performance. However, there is a limit to the validity of this statement. Very large caches tend to be somewhat slower; so if the larger capacity is not truly needed, one might be better off with a smaller cache. Also, a cache that fits on the processor chip is faster owing to shorter wiring and communication distances and the lack of need for off-chip signal transmission, which is rather slow. The requirement that the cache fit on the same chip with the processor clearly limits its size, although this size limit is less and less problematic with the phenomenal growth in the number of transistors that can be placed on an IC chip. It is not uncommon to have 90% or more of the transistors on a CPU chip allocated to cache memories.

Other than cache size, typically given in bytes or words, important cache parameters are:

1. Line width 2^W
2. Set size (associativity) 2^S
3. Line replacement policy
4. Write policy

Issues relevant to the choice of these parameters, and the associated trade-offs, are outlined in the rest of this section.

Line width 2^W: Wider lines cause more data to be brought into the cache with each miss. If transferring a larger block of data into the cache can be accomplished at a higher rate, wider cache lines have the positive effect of making words that will likely be accessed in future (owing to locality) readily available without further misses. On the other hand, it is quite possible that a significant part of a very wide cache line is never accessed by the processor, leading to waste of cache space (which could otherwise be allocated to more useful items) and data transfer time. Because of these opposing effects, there is often an optimal cache line width that leads to best performance.

Set size (associativity) 2^S: The trade-off here is between the simplicity, and thus speed, of direct mapping and the lower conflict misses generated by set-associative caches. The larger the associativity, the lower the effect of conflict misses. However, beyond 4-way or 8-way associativity, the performance effect of greater associativity is negligible and easily nullified by the more complex, and thus slower, addressing mechanisms. Figure 18.9 shows experimental results on the effects of associativity on performance. Given that higher levels of associativity require hardware overhead that slows down the cache and also uses some chip area for the needed comparison and selection mechanisms, it is often the case that low levels of associativity with a larger capacity (enabled by using the space freed up by the removal of more complex control mechanisms for more cache entries) provide better performance overall.

Line replacement policy: Usually LRU (least recently used) or some approximation thereof is used to simplify the process of keeping track of which line in each set should be replaced next. For two-way associativity, LRU implementation is fairly simple; a single bit of state is kept with each set to indicate which of the two lines in the set was last accessed. Upon each access to a line, the hardware automatically updates the set's LRU state bit. As associativity increases, it becomes harder to keep track of usage times. Some ideas for implementing LRU with higher-associativity caches are given in the end-of-chapter problems. Somewhat surprisingly, random selection of the line to be replaced can work quite well in practice.

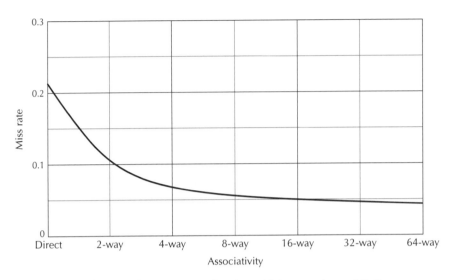

Figure 18.9 Performance improvement of caches with increased associativity.

Write policy: With the write-through scheme, the main memory is always consistent with the cache data so that cache lines can be replaced freely without losing any information. A writeback cache is often more efficient because it minimizes the number of accesses to main memory. With writeback caches, a "dirty bit" is associated with each cache line to indicate whether the cache line has been modified since being brought in from main memory. If a line is not dirty, its replacement would create no problem. Otherwise, the cache line must be copied back to main memory before it can be replaced. As mentioned earlier, the actual writing to main memory does not have to occur right away; rather, the lines to be written back are placed in write buffers and are gradually copied back as bus availability and memory bandwidth permit.

Note that the choice of cache parameters is dictated by the dominant pattern and timing of memory accesses. Because these characteristics are often significantly different for instruction streams and data streams, optimal choices of parameters for instruction caches, data caches, and unified caches are often not the same. Thus, for example, it is not uncommon to have varying degrees of associativity, or different replacement policies, in multiple cache units within the same system.

PROBLEMS

18.1 Spatial and temporal locality

Describe a realistic application program whose data accesses exhibit each of the following patterns or argue that the postulated combination is impossible.

a. Almost no spatial or temporal locality
b. Good spatial locality but virtually no temporal locality

c. Good temporal locality but very little or no spatial locality
d. Good spatial and temporal locality

18.2 Two-level cache performance

A processor with two levels of caches has a CPI of 1 when there is no level-1 cache miss. At level 1, the hit rate is 95% and a miss incurs a 10-cycle penalty. For the two-level cache as a whole, the hit rate is 98% (meaning that 2% of the time the main memory must be accessed) and the miss penalty is 60 cycles.

a. What is the effective CPI after cache misses are factored in?
b. If a single-level cache were to be used in lieu of this two-level cache system, what hit rate and miss penalty would be needed to provide the same performance?

18.3 Two-level cache performance

A computer system uses two levels of caches L1 and L2. Level L1 is accessed in one clock cycle and supplies the data in case of an L1 hit. For an L1 miss, occurring 3% of the time, L2 is consulted. An L2 hit incurs a penalty of 10 clock cycles while an L2 miss implies a 100-cycle penalty.

a. Assuming pipelined implementation with a CPI of 1 when there is no cache miss whatsoever (i.e., ignoring data and control dependencies), calculate the effective CPI if L2's local miss rate is 25%.
b. If we were to model the two-level cache system as a single cache, what miss rate and miss penalty should we use?
c. Changing the mapping scheme of L2 from direct to two-way set-associative can improve its local miss rate to 22% while increasing its hit penalty to 11 clock cycles owing to the more complex access scheme. Ignoring cost issues, is this change a good idea?

18.4 Cache memory hits and misses

The following sequence of numbers represents memory addresses in a 64-word main memory: 0, 1, 2, 3, 4, 15, 14, 13, 12, 11, 10, 9, 0, 1, 2, 3, 4, 56, 28, 32, 15, 14, 13, 12, 0, 1, 2, 3. Classify each of the accesses as a cache hit, compulsory miss, capacity miss, or conflict miss, given the following cache parameters. In each case, also provide the final cache contents.

a. Direct-mapped, 4-word lines, 4-line capacity
b. Direct-mapped, 2-word lines, 4-line capacity
c. Direct-mapped, 4-word lines, 2-line capacity
d. Two-way set-associative, 2-word lines, 4-set capacity, LRU replacement
e. Two-way set-associative, 4-word lines, 2-set capacity, LRU replacement
f. Four-way set-associative, 2-word lines, 2-set capacity, LRU replacement

18.5 Cache memory hits and misses

A program has a 9-instruction loop that is executed many times. Only the last loop instruction is a branch whose target is the first loop instruction at memory address 5678. The first loop instruction reads the content of a different memory location each time, beginning with the memory address 8760 and going up by 1 in each new iteration. Determine the cache memory hit rate, as a whole and separately for instructions and data, given the following cache parameters.

a. Unified direct-mapped, 4-word lines, 4-line capacity
b. Unified two-way set-associative, 2-word lines, 4-set capacity, LRU replacement
c. Split direct-mapped caches, each having 4-word lines and 2-line capacity
d. Split two-way set-associative caches, each having 2-word lines, 2-set capacity, LRU replacement

18.6 Cache memory design

Characterize the address trace produced by the execution of the loop defined in Problem 18.5, assuming an infinite number of loop iterations and cache sizes that are powers of 2. Find the smallest possible cache (or smallest total cache capacity in the case of split caches) to achieve a miss rate not exceeding 5% with each of the following constraints on cache organization. You are free to choose any parameter that is not explicitly specified.

a. Unified direct-mapped cache
b. Unified two-way set-associative cache
c. Split direct mapped caches
d. Split two-way set-associative caches

18.7 Cache memory design

a. Consider the cache memory depicted in Figure 18.4. For a main memory capacity of 2^x words, determine the total number of bits in the cache array and derive the contribution of nondata bits as a percentage overhead relative to actual data bits.
b. Repeat part a for the cache memory depicted in Figure 18.6.

18.8 Cache memory design

A computer system has 4 GB of byte-addressable main memory and a 256 KB unified cache memory with 32-byte blocks.

a. Draw a diagram showing each of the components of a main memory address (i.e., how many bits for tag, set index, and byte offset) for a four-way set-associative cache.

b. Draw a diagram showing the tag comparison circuits, generation of the cache miss signal, and the data output for the cache.

c. The performance of the computer system with four-way set-associative cache architecture proves unsatisfactory. Two redesign options are being considered, implying roughly the same additional design and production costs. Option A is to increase the size of the cache to 512 KB. Option B is to increase the associativity of the 256 KB cache to 16-way. In your judgment, which option is more likely to result in greater overall performance and why?

18.9 Cache address in a byte-addressable memory

An address for a byte-addressable memory presented to the cache unit is divided as follows: 13-bit tag, 14-bit line index, 5-bit byte offset.

a. What is the cache size in bytes?

b. What is the cache mapping scheme?

c. For a given byte in cache, how many different bytes in the 2^{32}-byte main memory can occupy it?

18.10 Relationships between cache parameters

For each of the cache memories partially specified in the accompanying table, find the values for the missing parameters where possible or explain why they cannot be uniquely deduced. Assume word-addressable main and cache memories.

18.11 Relationships between cache parameters

Using a for address bits, c_w for words in cache, l_w for words per line, s_l for lines per set, c_s for sets in cache, t for tag bits, i for set index bits, and o for offset bits, write equations that interrelate the parameters listed in Problem 18.10, so that when values are assigned to a subset of the parameters, unique values, or feasible set of values, for other parameters can be obtained.

18.12 Trade-offs in cache design

Three design options for a 16-word direct-mapped cache memory are being considered. These options C1, C2, and C4 correspond to using 1-word, 2-word, and 4-word cache lines, respectively. The miss penalties for options C1, C2, and C4 are 6, 7, and 9 clock cycles, respectively. Supply relatively short memory address traces that lead to each of the following outcomes or show that the outcome is impossible.

a. C2 has more misses than C1.

b. C4 has more misses than C2.

c. C1 has more misses than C4.

d. C2 has fewer misses than C1 but wastes more cycles on cache misses.

e. C4 has fewer misses than C2 but wastes more cycles on cache misses.

18.13 Cache-aware programming

A problem encountered with direct or even set-associative caches is *thrashing,* defined as excessive conflict misses resulting from the nature of particular memory address patterns. Consider a direct-mapped cache containing two 4-word lines used in the course of computing the inner product of two vectors of length 8 in a way that involves reading A_i and B_i, multiplying them, and adding the product to a running total in a register.

Problem part	Address bits	Words in cache	Words per line	Lines per set	Sets in cache	Tag bits	Set index bits	Offset bits
a	16	1024	4	1				
b	24	4096	8	2				
c					64	12	6	0
d					128	23	7	2
e			16	8			5	3
f	12	256			32	6		

a. Show that thrashing occurs when the starting addresses of A and B are both multiples of 4.
b. Suggest ways of preventing thrashing in this example.
c. For this particular example, would thrashing be possible if the cache were two-way set-associative?

18.14 Cache behavior during matrix transposition

Matrix transposition is an important operation in many signal processing and scientific computations. Consider transposing a 4×4 matrix A, stored in row-major order starting at address 0, and placing the result in B, stored in row-major order beginning at address 16. We use two nested loops (indices i and j), copying $A_{i,j}$ into $B_{j,i}$ within the inner loop j. Assume word-addressed cache and main memory units. Note that each matrix element is accessed exactly once. Draw two 4×4 tables representing the matrix elements and place "H" (for hit) or "M" (for miss) in each entry for the following organizations of an 8-word cache.

a. Direct-mapped, 2-word lines
b. Direct-mapped, 4-word lines
c. Two-way set-associative, 1-word lines, LRU replacement policy
d. Two-way set-associative, 2-word lines, LRU replacement policy

18.15 Implementing the LRU policy

One way to implement the LRU replacement policy for a four-way set-associative cache is to store 6 state bits for each set: bit $b_{i,j}$, $0 \le i < j \le 3$, is set to 1 iff line i has been accessed more recently than line j in the set. Provide implementation details for this scheme, including logic circuit that update the 6 state bits and select the line to be replaced.

18.16 Cache for avoiding repeated computations

In a number of applications (notably multimedia) certain instructions are executed repeatedly with the same arguments, yielding the same results. Most instructions, such as addition or multiplication, are executed so rapidly that repeating them is probably more prudent than trying to detect their repetition for the sake of using previously calculated results. Other instructions, such as load or store, may yield different results even when the memory and register addresses

involved are the same. However, in the case of division, which takes 20–40 clock cycles to execute on many modern microprocessors, significant savings can be achieved if the results of previously performed divisions are stored in a buffer, which is consulted in one clock cycle to see whether the needed result is available there. If a hit occurs, the previously computed quotient is sent to the appropriate register. Only in the case of a miss, say in 10–20% of the cases, are the operands sent to the divide unit for calculation. We refer to this method as "*memoing*" and to the buffer holding the arguments and results for recent division instructions as the "*division memo table*" (DMT).

a. Draw a block diagram for a 64-entry direct-mapped DMT and show how it might work; that is, show what must be stored in it, how it is consulted, and how the miss/hit signal is obtained and used.
b. Repeat part a for a four-way set-associative DMT and outline the advantages and drawbacks of the modified scheme, if any.
c. Assuming a 22-cycle divide instruction (one preparation/decode cycle, DMT lookup cycle, and 20 execution cycles if there is a DMT miss), express the average number of clock cycles per divide operation, and the attendant division speedup factor s, as a function of the hit rate h in the DMT. What DMT hit rate h is needed for a division speedup of at least 3?
d. Draw and explain another hardware diagram for the memoing scheme that does not involve the one-cycle penalty in case of misses in the DMT (i.e., division takes 21 cycles in the worst case).
e. Repeat part c for the implementation of part d. What fraction of the running time must have been spent on division if division speedup by an average factor of 3 yields a 5% overall speedup?

18.17 Trace cache for instructions

A trace cache holds instructions not in address order but in dynamic execution order. This increases the instruction fetch bandwidth because a block of instructions fetched is likely to be executed in its entirety. Study design issues for, and advantages of, a trace cache and write a two-page report on it [Rote99].

REFERENCES AND FURTHER READINGS

[Crag96]   Cragon, H. G., *Memory Systems and Pipelined Processors,* Jones and Bartlett, 1996.

[Lipt68]   Liptay, J. S., "Structural Aspects of the System/360 Model 85, Part II: The Cache," *IBM Systems J.,* Vol. 7, No. 1, pp. 15–21, 1968.

[Patt98]   Patterson, D. A., and J. L. Hennessy, *Computer Organization and Design: The Hardware/Software Interface,* Morgan Kaufmann, 2nd ed., 1998.

[Rote99]   Rotenberg, E., S. Bennett, and J. E. Smith, "A Trace Cache Microarchitecture and Evaluation," *IEEE Trans. Computers,* Vol. 48, No. 2, pp. 111–120, February 1999.

[Shri98]   Shriver, B., and B. Smith, *The Anatomy of a High-Performance Microprocessor: A Systems Perspective,* IEEE Computer Society Press, 1998, Chap. 5, pp. 427–461.

[Smit82]   Smith, A. J., "Cache Memories," *ACM Computing Surveys,* Vol. 14, No. 3, pp. 473–530, September 1982.

MASS MEMORY CONCEPTS

"I think Silicon Valley was misnamed. If you look back at the dollars shipped in products in the last decade there has been more revenue from magnetic disks than from silicon. They ought to rename the place Iron Oxide Valley."

—*Al Hoagland, 1982*

"A memex is a device in which an individual stores all his books, records, and communications, and which is mechanized so that it may be consulted with exceeding speed and flexibility. It is an enlarged intimate supplement to his memory."

—*Vannevar Bush, As We May Think, 1945*

TOPICS IN THIS CHAPTER
19.1 Disk Memory Basics
19.2 Organizing Data on Disk
19.3 Disk Performance
19.4 Disk Caching
19.5 Disk Arrays and RAID
19.6 Other Types of Mass Memory

The size of main memory in a modern computer is beyond the wildest dreams of early computer programmers, yet today it is deemed too small to hold all the data and programs of interest to a typical user. In addition, the volatility of semiconductor memories, that is, the erasure of data in the event of power loss, would necessitate a form of backup storage, even if size were not an issue. Over the years, disk memories have played this dual role of extended and backup storage. Improvements in capacity and storage density, and reductions in the cost of disk memories, have been just as phenomenal as the advances in integrated circuits. In this chapter, we study disk memory organization and performance and see how disk caching and redundant array organization of multiple disks lead to speed and reliability enhancements. We also review a number of other mass storage technologies.

■ 19.1 Disk Memory Basics

The bulk of this chapter is devoted to a discussion of hard magnetic-recording disk memories, which we will refer to as "disk memory" for short. Floppy disks, optical disks (CD-ROM, CD-RW, DVD-ROM, DVD-RW), and other disk variants have similar organizations and

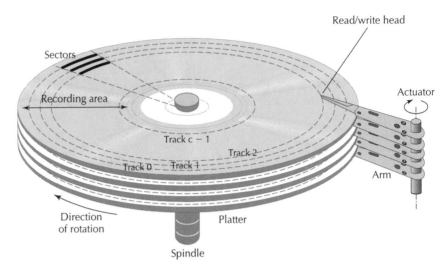

Figure 19.1 Disk memory elements and key terms.

operating principles but differ in their recording and access technologies, application areas, and performance criteria. These variants are discussed in Section 19.6, along with a number of other mass storage options.

Modern hard disks are marvels of electrical and mechanical design. It is rather curious that such disks are used at all. It appears that electronic memories should replace the relatively slow disk memory in short order, as cheerfully predicted more than once over the past few decades. Yet, the phenomenal improvement in data recording density, rapid decline in cost, and the very high reliability of modern disk systems has led to their continued use in virtually every computer, beginning with laptops and desktops.

Figure 19.1 shows a typical disk memory configuration and the terminology associated with its design and use. There are 1–12 *platters* mounted on a *spindle* that rotates at speeds of 3600 to well over 10,000 revolutions per minute. Data is recorded on both surfaces of each platter along circular *tracks*. Each track is divided into several *sectors,* with a sector being the unit of data transfer into and out of the disk. The recording density is a function of the *track density* (tracks per centimeter or inch) and the *linear bit density* along the track (bits per centimeter or inch). In the year 2000, the *areal recording density* of inexpensive commercial disks was in the vicinity of 1–3 Gb/cm^2. Early computer disks had diameters of up to 50 cm, but modern disks are seldom outside the range of 1.0–3.5 inches (2.5–9 cm) in diameter.

The *recording area* on each surface does not extend all the way to the center of the platter because the very short tracks near the middle cannot be efficiently utilized. Even so, the inner tracks are a factor of 2 or more shorter than the outer tracks. Having the same number of sectors on all tracks would limit the track (and, hence, disk capacity) by what it is possible to record on the short inner tracks. For this reason, modern disks put more sectors on the outer tracks. Bits recorded in each sector include a sector number at the beginning, followed by a gap to allow the sector number to be processed and noted by the read/write head logic, the sector data, and error detection/correction information. There is also a gap between adjacent sectors. It is because of these gaps, the sector number, and error coding overhead, plus spare tracks that are often used to allow for "repairing" bad tracks discovered in the course of disk memory operation, that a disk's *formatted capacity* is much lower than its raw capacity based on data recording density.

An *actuator* can move the arms holding the read/write heads, of which we have as many as there are recording surfaces, to align them with a desired *cylinder* consisting of tracks with same diameter on different recording surfaces. Reading of very closely spaced data on the disk necessitates that the head travel very close to the disk surface (within a fraction of a micrometer). The heads are prevented from crashing onto the surface by a thin cushion of air. Note that even the tiniest dust particle is so large in comparison to the head separation from the surface that it will cause the head to crash onto the surface. Such *head crashes* damage the mechanical parts and destroy a great deal of data on the disk. To prevent these highly undesirable events, hard disks are typically sealed in airtight packaging.

The access time to the data in a desired sector on the disk consists of three components:

1. *Seek time*, or the time to align the heads with the cylinder containing the track in which the sector resides.
2. *Rotational latency*, or the time for the disk to rotate until the beginning of the sector data arrives under the read/write head.
3. *Data transfer time*, consisting of the time for the sector to pass under the head which reads the bits on the fly.

Table 19.1 contains data on the key characteristics of three modern disks with different physical parameters and intended application domains. The capacity of a disk memory is related to some of these parameters, as follows:

$$\text{Disk capacity} = \text{Surfaces} \times \text{Tracks/surface} \times \text{Sectors/track} \times \text{Bytes/sector}$$

The number of recording surfaces is often twice the number of platters. For this reason, the highest capacity disks are of the multiplatter variety. Number of tracks per surface is affected by both the disk diameter and the track density. Bytes per track, which is the product of the last two terms, is proportional to the track length (and thus track diameter) and the linear bit density. When all tracks do not contain the same number of sectors, the average number of sectors per track is used in the disk capacity equation.

Example 19.1: Disk memory parameters   Calculate the capacity of a two-platter disk unit with 18,000 cylinders, an average of 520 sectors per track, and a sector size of 512 B.

Solution: With two platters, there are four recording surfaces. The maximum raw capacity of the disk is thus $4 \times 18{,}000 \times 520 \times 512 \text{ B} = 1.917 \times 10^{10} \text{ B} = 1.917 \times 10^{10}/2^{30} \text{ GB} = 17.85 \text{ GB}$. Allowing 10% overhead or capacity wastage for gaps, sector numbers, and coding for cyclic redundancy check (CRC), we arrive at a formatted capacity of about 16 GB.

Based on the foregoing observations, one can deduce that *hard disks* hold more data and are faster than *floppy disks* because they can:

Have larger diameters (although very wide disks are no longer built)
Spin faster
Record at higher densities (due to more precise control)
Have multiple platters

Optical disks use a laser beam and its reflection on a single recording surface, rather than magnetization and magnetic field detection, to write and read data. The more precise control

■ **TABLE 19.1** Key attributes of three representative magnetic disks, from the highest capacity to the smallest physical size (circa early 2003).

	Manufacturer	Seagate	Hitachi	IBM
Identity of disk	Series	Barracuda	DK23DA	Microdrive
	Model	180 SCSI	ATA-5	1 GB
	Model number	ST1181677LW	40	DSCM-11000
	Typical application domain	Server/desktop	Laptop	Pocket device
Storage attributes	**Formatted capacity, GB**	**180**	**40**	**1**
	Recording surfaces	24	4	2
	Cylinders	24,247	33,067	7167
	Sector size, B	512	512	512
	Avg sectors/track	604	591	140
	Max recording density, Kb/cm	198	236	171
	Max track density, tracks/cm	12,280	21,700	13,780
	Max areal density, Gb/cm^2	2.4	5.1	2.4
	Buffer size, MB	16	2	1/8
Access attributes	Min seek time, ms	1	3	1
	Avg seek time, ms	8	13	12
	Max seek time, ms	17	25	19
	Min internal data rate, MB/s	25.3	18.7	2.6
	Max internal data rate, MB/s	47.0	34.7	4.2
	External data rate, MB/s	160	100	13
Physical attributes	Diameter, inches	3.5	2.5	1
	Platters	12	2	1
	Rotation speed, rpm	7200	4200	3600
	Package $W \times H \times D$, cm	$10.2 \times 4.1 \times 14.6$	$7.0 \times 1.0 \times 10.0$	$4.3 \times 0.5 \times 3.6$
	Package weight, kg	1.04	0.10	0.04
	Typical operating power, W	14.1	2.3	0.8
	Idle power, W	10.3	0.7	0.5

of the light mechanism allows for denser recording and, thus, higher capacity. Floppy and optical disks will be discussed in more detail in Section 19.6.

■ 19.2 Organizing Data on Disk

Data bits on a track appear as small regions of the magnetic coating on the disk surface that are magnetized in opposite directions to record 0 or 1 (Figure 19.2). As the areas associated with different bits pass under the read mechanism, the direction of magnetization is sensed and the bit value is deduced. Recording occurs when the write mechanism forces the magnetization into a desired direction by passing a current through a coil attached to the head. This scheme is referred to as *horizontal recording*. It is also possible to use *vertical recording,* in which direction of magnetization is perpendicular to the recording surface. Vertical recording allows the bits to be placed closer together but requires specially designed magnetic recording media along with more complex read and write mechanisms, and is thus not in common use.

The 0s and 1s corresponding to magnetization directions within small cells on the disk surface, as shown in Figure 19.2, usually do not represent data bit values directly because special encoding techniques are used to maximize the storage density and to make the correct functioning of read and write mechanisms more probable. For example, rather than let data bit

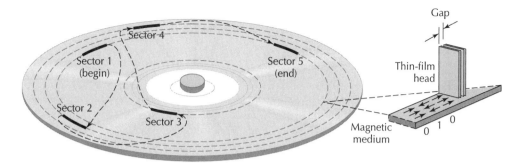

Figure 19.2 Magnetic recording along the tracks and the read/write head.

values dictate the direction of magnetization, one can magnetize based on whether there is a change in the bit value from one cell to the next. This type of *nonreturn-to-zero* (NRZ) encoding, which allows a doubling of data recording capacity relative to *return-to-zero* (RTZ) encoding, was the first widely used encoding technique. Discussion of such codes is beyond the scope of this book. The simplified view that the string "0 1 0" shown in Figure 19.2 represents the values of three consecutive data bits on the disk track is sufficient for our purposes.

In addition to the intricacies of the codes used for magnetic recording, each data sector is preceded by a recorded sector number and followed by a *cyclic redundancy check,* which allows certain recording anomalies and read/write errors to be detected and/or corrected. This is essential because at very high recording densities, magnetization and detection errors are inevitable. Additionally, there are intersector gaps and gaps within sectors to separate the various sector components to allow the processing of one part to be completed before the next part arrives. Again, the simplified view that sectors follow each other, with no recording overhead and no gap, is adequate for our purposes.

The unit of data transfer to/from the disk is a sector, typically containing 512 to a few thousand bytes. The address of a sector on disk consists of three components:

Disk address = Cylinder #,	Track #,	Sector #
17–31 bits 10–16 bits,	1–5 bits,	6–10 bits

With a sector size of $512 = 2^9$ B, this translates to a disk capacity of:

$$\text{Disk capacity} = 2^{13\pm3} \times 2^{3\pm2} \times 2^{8\pm2} \times 2^9 = 2^{33\pm7} \text{ B} = 0.06 - 1024 \text{ GB}$$

Of course, current disks do not allow all these parameters to be simultaneously at their maximum values. Cylinder number is supplied to the actuator mechanism to align the read/write heads with the desired cylinder. Track number selects one of the read/write heads (or the associated recording surface). Finally sector number is compared against recorded sector indices as they pass under the selected read/write head, with a match indicating that the desired sector has arrived under the head. The head then reads the actual sector data and its associated error detection/correction information.

The sectors on a disk are logically independent and any collection of sectors can be used to hold various parts of a file or other data structure. For example, Figure 19.2 shows a file composed of five sectors that are scattered on different tracks. Addresses of these sectors may be listed in a file directory so that any piece of the file can be retrieved when needed; alternatively, only the first file sector may be listed in the directory, with a link provided within each sector to the next sector. Of course, given that pieces of a file are likely to be accessed in close proximity of each other, it makes sense to try to allocate sectors that would reduce the amount of head movement (seek time) and rotational latency in the course of file access.

Example 19.2: Making a backup copy of a full disk   A disk with $t = 100,000$ tracks (the total number on all recording surfaces) rotates at 7200 rpm and its track-to-track seek time is 1 ms. What is the minimum amount of time needed to make a backup copy of the entire contents of the disk? Assume that the disk is completely full and that the device doing the backup can accept data at the rate provided by the disk.

Solution: The disk makes 120 revolutions per second, or one revolution in $1/120$ s. We ignore the one-time rotational latency at the outset, which lasts an average of 4.17 ms. To copy the entire contents of the disk, we need $t - 1 = 99,999$ track-to-track seeks and 100,000 complete revolutions for data transfer. The total time is thus $(t - 1)/10^3 + t/120 \cong 933$ s $\cong 15.5$ min. This calculation assumes that the sectors can be read in order of their physical appearance on the track. In other words, the data read from one sector is offloaded immediately so that the next sector can be read without any delay. We will see shortly that this may not be the case.

Because seek time is much smaller when going from one cylinder to an adjacent cylinder (as opposed to a distant one), data elements that are typically accessed together must be placed on the same or on adjacent cylinders. However, consecutively accessed data should not be assigned to successive sectors on the same track. The reason is that often some amount of processing on one sector is needed before the next sector is to be accessed. Thus, placing the next part of data on the immediately following sector leads to the possibility of just missing the opportunity to read it and having to wait for almost a full rotation of the disk. For this reason, consecutive *logical sector numbers* are assigned to *physical sectors* that are separated by a few intermediate sectors. In this way, placing the pieces of a file on consecutive logical sectors would not lead to the problem just described. Additionally, logical sector numbers in adjacent tracks may be skewed. Suppose that we have just completed reading the last logical sector on one track and must now move to the first logical sector on the next track to obtain the next piece of our file. It may take the head a couple of milliseconds to complete the move from one track to the next, by which time the disk may have rotated by a fairly large angle. Figure 19.3 shows a possible numbering scheme for sectors on several adjacent tracks based on the foregoing observations.

Fortunately the user need not be concerned with the actual data placement scheme on the disk surface. The disk controller maintains the required mapping information to translate a

0	16	32	48	1	17	33	49	2		Track i
30	46	62	15	31	47	0	16	32		Track $i + 1$
60	13	29	45	61	14	30	46	62		Track $i + 2$
27	43	59	12	28	44	60	13	29		Track $i + 3$

Figure 19.3 Logical numbering of sectors on several adjacent tracks.

simple sequential sector number, presented by the operating system, into a physical disk address that identifies the surface, track, and sector. The controller then plans and performs all the required activities to collect the sector data into a local buffer before transferring it into a designated area in main memory.

19.3 Disk Performance

Disk performance is related to *access latency* and *data transfer rate*. Access latency is the sum of cylinder seek time (or simply *seek time*) and *rotational latency,* the time needed for the sector of interest to arrive under the read/write head. Thus:

Disk access latency = Seek time + Rotational latency

Seek time depends on how far the head has to travel from its current position to the target cylinder. Because this involves a mechanical motion, consisting of an acceleration phase, a uniform motion, and a deceleration or braking phase, one can model the seek time for moving by c cylinders as follows, where α, β, and γ are constants:

Seek time = $\alpha + \beta(c - 1) + \gamma\sqrt{c - 1}$

The linear term $\beta(c - 1)$, corresponding to the uniform motion phase, is a rather recent addition to the seek-time equation; older disks simply did not have enough tracks, and/or a high enough acceleration, for uniform motion to kick in.

Rotational latency is a function of where the desired sector is located on the track. In the best case, the head is aligned with the track just as the desired sector is arriving. In the worst case, the head just misses the sector and must wait for nearly one full revolution. So, on average, the rotational latency is equal to the time for half a revolution:

Average rotational latency = (30/rpm) s = (30,000/rpm) ms

Hence, for a rotation speed of 10,000 rpm, the average rotational latency is 3 ms and its range is 0–6 ms.

The data transfer rate is related to the rotational speed of the disk and the linear bit density along the track. For example, suppose that a track holds roughly 2 Mb of data and the disk rotates at 10,000 rpm. Then, every minute, 2×10^{10} bits pass under the head. Because bits are read on the fly as they pass under the head, this translates to an average data transfer rate of about 333 Mb/s = 42 MB/s. The overhead induced by gaps, sector numbers, and CRC encoding causes the peak transfer rate to be somewhat higher than the average transfer rate thus computed.

Attempts at eliminating the seek time, which according to Table 9.1 constitutes a significant fraction of the disk access latency, have not been successful. *Head-per-track disks,* which had one head permanently aligned with each track of every recording surface (typically 1–2), were not successful because of their complexity and limited market, which made design and manufacturing costs unacceptably high. Because rotation speed affects both the rotational latency and data transfer rate, disk manufacturers are motivated to increase it to the extent possible. Beyond this, efforts to cut the average rotational latency by a factor of 2–4, through the placement of multiple sets of read/write heads around the periphery of the platters, were doomed for the same reasons cited for head-per-track disks.

Hence, we must learn to live with seek and rotational latencies and design around them. Paying attention to how data is organized on disk, as discussed at the end of Section 19.2, can

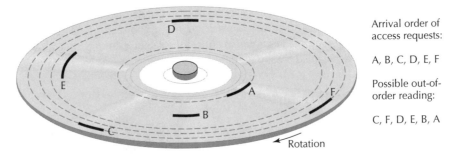

Figure 19.4 Reducing average seek time and rotational latency by performing disk accesses out of order.

reduce both the seek time and rotational latency for commonly encountered access patterns. Queuing the requests for disk access and performing them out of order is another useful method. The latter method is applicable when multiple independent programs share a disk memory (*multiprogramming*) or when some applications issue independent disk access requests that can be returned out of order (*transaction processing*). In Figure 19.4, six sectors are requested in the order A, B, C, D, E, F. If the head happens to be close to sector C, the sectors may be read out in the order C, F (on the same track), D (on a nearby track), E, B, A, with the optimal order calculated by taking into account the head movement times and rotation latencies based on the physical locations of the various sectors.

■ 19.4 Disk Caching

Disk cache is a random-access memory unit that is used to reduce the number of disk accesses in much the same way that a CPU cache reduces accesses to the slower main memory. For example, when a particular disk sector is needed, one might read out several adjacent sectors, or perhaps an entire track, into a disk cache. If subsequent accesses to the disk happen to be to the extra sectors that were read out, they can be satisfied from the much faster cache, obviating the need for several additional disk accesses. Before the emergence of dedicated hardware caches or buffers in disk controllers, a form of software buffering was prevalent, where a similar caching or *read-ahead* function was performed by the operating system using a portion of the main memory that was set aside for holding disk sectors. The three disk memories listed in Table 19.1 have dedicated caches/buffers ranging in size from 0.125 to 16 MB.

Because the disk is orders of magnitude slower than main memory, the operation of a disk cache can be entirely software controlled. When a request for disk access is received by the disk controller, the disk cache directory is consulted to find out whether the requested sector is in the disk cache. If it is, the sector is supplied from the disk cache (read) or modified therein (write); if not, a regular access to the disk is initiated. Given that the time to search the disk cache directory is much smaller than the average time for a disk access, the overhead is very small, while the payoff in case of finding the sector in the disk cache is quite significant. Hit/miss rates for disk caches are quite difficult to come by because manufacturers use proprietary designs for their disk caches and are reluctant to share detailed performance data. For initial design purposes, a reasonable estimate for the miss rate of a disk cache is 0.1 [Crag96].

Note that when an entire track is read into a disk cache, rotational latency is almost completely eliminated. This is because as soon as the head is aligned with the desired track, reading can begin, regardless of which sector happens to arrive under the head next. The sectors thus accessed can simply be stored in the random-access cache memory in their corresponding positions within the space allocated to the track. Similarly, when a track must be written back to the disk to make room for a new track, the sectors can be copied in the order that they are encountered by the head. Note that the use of a writeback policy for disk caches, which is a natural choice to minimize the number of disk accesses, requires a form of backup power source to ensure that updates are not lost in the event of power outage or other forms of disruption.

Example 19.3: Performance benefit of disk caching   A 40 GB disk with 100,000 tracks contains 512 B sectors, rotates at 7200 rpm, and has an average seek time of 10 ms. Assuming that entire tracks are brought into the disk cache, what is the performance benefit or speedup due to disk caching in an application whose running time is completely dominated by disk access? In other words, assume that processing time and other aspects of the application are negligible relative to data access time from the disk. Use a disk cache miss rate of 0.1 in your calculation.

Solution: An average track on this disk contains $40 \times 2^{30}/(100,000 \times 512) \cong 839$ sectors. Thus a sector access requires an average time of 10 ms plus the time needed for $1/2 + 1/839$ rotations. This amounts to 18.35 ms. Reading of an entire sector involves the average seek time plus one full rotation, or 26.67 ms. Disk caching with a miss rate of 0.1 allows us to replace ten 18.35 ms sector accesses with one 26.67 ms track access, yielding a speedup of $10 \times 18.35/26.67 \cong 6.88$. The actual speedup is somewhat less, not only because processing time and other aspects of the application were ignored but also because a disk access that is satisfied from the disk cache still has to go through several intermediaries such as channels, storage controllers, and device controllers, each contributing some latency.

In the preceding discussion, we assumed that the disk cache is incorporated in the disk controller. There are several drawbacks to this approach:

1. The cache is linked to the CPU via intermediaries such as buses, I/O channel, storage controller, and device controller. So, even in the case of a disk cache hit, some nontrivial latency is incurred.

2. In systems with many disks, there will be multiple caches, with some units underutilized when the associated disks are not very active, and others not having enough space to keep all the useful tracks.

An approach to solving these remoteness and imbalance problems is to use a large cache that is placed closer to the CPU and has its space shared by data coming from several disks. For a given total disk cache capacity, this latter approach is bound to be more efficient. Such a shared cache may be included in addition to the ones in the disk controllers, leading to a multilevel caching structure.

■ 19.5 Disk Arrays and RAID

Despite dramatic improvements in the capacity and performance of hard disk drives over the past few decades, there still exist applications that require greater capacity and/or higher bandwidth than even the largest and fastest available disk drives can deliver. Building larger and faster disks, though technically possible, is not economically viable because such high-capacity and ultrahigh-performance disks are not needed in large enough quantities to engender economy of scale. It would be preferable to find a solution based on using arrays of inexpensive disks that are built in high volumes, and thus at extremely low cost, for the personal computer market to offer expanded capacity and improved performance. This is referred to as the "*disk array*" approach.

It is, of course, a simple matter to solve the capacity problem by using a disk array. Overcoming the performance limit is not as simple and requires more effort. Furthermore, applications that use vast amounts of data typically also require assurances on data availability, integrity, and security. Take a large bank or e-commerce Web site that uses 500 disks to store its databases and other information. Each of the 500 disks may fail very infrequently, say once per 100,000 hours (11^+ years). Taken together, however, the 500-disk system has a failure rate that is about 500 times as large (one failure every 8 days). It is, therefore, imperative that fault tolerance through redundancy be incorporated into any disk array solution.

The term RAID, for redundant array of inexpensive (or independent) disks, was coined in the late 1980s to refer to a class of solutions to capacity and reliability problems for applications requiring vast data sets [Patt88]. Prior to formulation of the RAID concept, it had been recognized that disk arrays, with their many independent read/write mechanisms, could offer improved data bandwidth for vector or parallel computers whose performance was potentially limited by the rate at which data was fed to their highly pipelined and/or multiple processing units. This use of disk arrays to take advantage of the aggregate bandwidth of a large number of disks by *striping* data across them is sometimes referred to as "RAID level 0," although it was not included in the original taxonomy [Patt88] and has no redundancy to justify the RAID designation.

RAID0 disk arrays can be designed to operate in synchronous or asynchronous mode. In a synchronous disk array, rotation of the multiple disks and their head movements are synchronized so that all disks access the same local logical sector on the same track at the same time. Externally, such a *d*-unit disk array appears as a single disk that has a bandwidth equal to *d* times that of a single disk. Designing such disk arrays requires expensive modifications to commodity disk units and is thus cost-effective only for use with high-performance supercomputers. In asynchronous disk arrays, the disks are accessed in much the same way as memory banks in interleaved memory. Because multiple disk accesses can be in progress at the same time, the effective bandwidth increases. Some higher level RAID systems can be configured to operate as RAID0 units when the user does not require the added reliability offered through redundancy.

Use of *mirroring,* the storing a backup copy of a disk's contents on another *mirror disk*, allows the tolerance of any single disk failure with a very simple recovery procedure: detecting the disk failure via its built-in error-detection encoding and switching to the corresponding mirror disk while the failed disk is being replaced. The mirroring scheme of RAID1 implies 100% redundancy, which is a high price to pay for single-disk failure tolerance when tens or hundreds of disks are used. RAID2 represents an attempt at reducing the degree of redundancy through the use of error-correcting codes instead of duplication. For example, a Hamming single-bit error-correcting code requires 4 check bits for 11 data bits. Thus, if data is striped across the 11 disks, 4 disks will suffice to hold the check information (vs 11 in the case of mirroring). With more data disks, the relative redundancy of RAID2 is further reduced.

It turns out that even the redundancy of Hamming code is too much, and the same effect can be accomplished with just two extra disks: a *parity disk* that stores the XOR of data bits from all other disks and a spare disk that can take the place of a failed disk when required

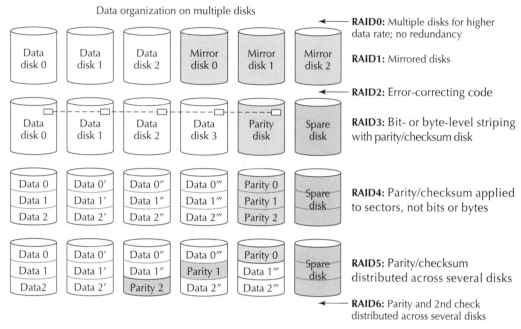

Figure 19.5 RAID levels 0–6, with a simplified view of data organization in the more common variants.

(RAID3). This is possible owing to the built-in error detection capability at the sector level based on the routinely included cyclic redundancy check. If there are d data disks holding bit values b_i, $0 \le i \le d - 1$, in a particular position on the disk surface, the parity disk will hold the following bit value in the same position:

$$p = b_0 \oplus b_1 \oplus \cdots \oplus b_{d-1} = \overset{d-1}{\underset{i=0}{\oplus}} b_i$$

Upon the failure of data disk j, its corresponding bit value b_j can be reconstructed from the contents of the remaining data disks and the parity disk, as follows:

$$b_j = \left(\overset{d-1}{\underset{i=0, i \ne j}{\oplus}} b_i \right) \oplus p$$

Each of the RAID levels 1–3 (Figure 19.5) has shortcomings that limit its usefulness or domain of applicability.

1. Besides 100% redundancy, which may not be a major issue with truly inexpensive disks, RAID level 1 involves a performance penalty regardless of whether striping is used. Each update operation on a file must also update the backup copy. If updating of the backup is done right away, the larger of the two disk access times will dictate the delay. If backup updates are queued and performed when convenient, the probability of data loss due to a disk failure increases.

2. RAID level 2 improves on the redundancy factor of level 1 through the use of striping along with Hamming single-error-correcting code. However, because all disks must be accessed to read out or write one block of data, severe performance penalties are incurred for reading or writing small amounts of data.

3. RAID level 3 also has the drawback that all disks must participate in every read and write operation, thus reducing the number of disk accesses that can be performed in unit time and hurting the performance for small reads and writes. With a special controller that computes the required parity for write operations and a nonvolatile write buffer to hold the blocks while parity is computed, RAID3 can achieve performance close to that of RAID0.

Because disk data is commonly accessed in units of sectors rather than bits or bytes, RAID level 4 applies the parity or checksum to disk sectors. In this case, striping does not affect small files that fit entirely on one sector. Read operations are performed from data disks with no need to access the parity disk. When a disk fails, its data is reconstructed from the contents of other disks and the parity disk in much the same way as for RAID3, except that the XOR-ing is performed on sectors rather than bits. A write operation requires that the associated parity sector also be updated with every sector update and thus involves two accesses to the parity disk. Using uppercase letters to denote data and parity sector contents, we have:

$$P_{\text{new}} = D_{\text{new}} \oplus D_{\text{old}} \oplus P_{\text{old}}$$

This equation shows an advantage of RAID4 over RAID3 but also reveals one of its key drawbacks: unless write operations are quite rare, accesses to the parity disk create a severe performance bottleneck.

RAID level 5 removes the preceding performance bottleneck by distributing the parity sectors on all disks instead of putting them on a dedicated disk. As seen in the example depicted in Figure 19.5, the parity data for the 4 sectors of file 0 is stored on the rightmost disk, whereas parity sectors for files 1 and 2 are placed on different disks. This scheme distributes the parity accesses and thus eases the performance bottleneck resulting from parity updates. Read operations are independent as before. Thus, multiple read and write operations can be in progress at the same time in RAID5. For example, the sectors labeled Data0 and Data1' can be updated at the same time, given that the sectors and their associated parities are on different disks.

Note that RAID levels 3–4, and the more commonly used RAID5, provide adequate protection against single disk failures under the assumption that a second disk failure does not occur while recovery from one failure is in progress. To protect against double failures, RAID level 6 adds a second form of error checking to the parity/checksum scheme of level 5, using the same distribution scheme, but with the two check sectors placed on different disks. For this reason, RAID6 is said to use "P+Q redundancy," where P stands for the parity scheme and Q for the second scheme. The second scheme can be more complex because it is rarely, if ever, invoked for data reconstruction. With RAID6, only if a third disk failure occurs before the first failed disk has been replaced is there any danger of data loss.

The efficiency of RAID can be significantly improved by combining the idea with that of a log-structured file system. In a log-structured file, data is not modified in place; rather, a fresh copy of any modified record is created in a different location, with the file directory appropriately updated to reflect the new location. Suppose that a RAID controller has a large enough writeback cache to hold an entire cylinder's worth of data. Then, as a sector is modified, it is marked for deletion from its current location. The updated version is not immediately written back but is kept in the nonvolatile cache until the cached cylinder is completely full. At this point, the cylinder is written to any disk that happens to be available. Given that cylinder contents become sparse upon deletion of their sectors, a form of automatic garbage collection is required to read out two or more such cylinders during times when disks are not used and to compress them into a new cylinder. An added benefit of this approach is that cylinder data can be written in compressed format, with decompression occurring during readout which involves copying an entire cylinder into the disk cache.

Commercial RAID products are offered by virtually every major mass storage vendor. These include IBM, Compaq-HP, Data General, EMC, and Storage Tek. Most RAID products offer some flexibility in selecting the RAID level based on application needs.

■ 19.6 Other Types of Mass Memory

Even though magnetic recording dominates as the technology of choice for secondary memory in modern computers, other options are available. One important feature of disk memory, which makes it a necessary component even if main memory is large enough for all our programs and data, is its nonvolatility (see also the discussion of nonvolatile memory in Section 17.5). Magnetic disks can keep data almost indefinitely, whereas main memory loses its data when the computer is turned off or power is interrupted for any other reason. Of course, secondary memory is not limited to on-line storage of data so that its contents are continuously available to a computer; some mass memory technologies are used as backup storage or as recording media for distribution of software, documents, music, images, films, and other types of content.

Before proceeding to review optical disks and other secondary and tertiary memory technologies, we should note that *floppy disks* (or *diskettes*) and several other rotating magnetic memories use fundamentally the same principles as hard disks for data recording and access. In other words, they have tracks and sectors, actuators to effect radial movement of a head assembly for alignment with a desired track, and read/write heads that magnetize small areas of the surface or sense the magnetization direction. What distinguishes 1.2 MB floppy disks (see Figure 3.12b), or the higher capacity 100/250 MB zip disks, from hard disks is the former's lower recording density and less precise read/write mechanisms arising from the flexibility, and thus wider tolerances, in the recording media and the lack of airtight enclosures to keep dust and other fine particles away from the recording surface.

Magnetic tapes record data along straight tracks, in lieu of the circular tracks of a rotating disk memory. A key advantage of magnetic tapes is that they can be removed and placed in permanent archives, although in the past, many types of tape drive were lost to obsolescence, making such archives unavailable long before the recordings showed any sign of deterioration. Typically, 9 bits are recorded across the tape (one byte of data, plus a parity bit), with the linear bit density along the tape being much lower than that of hard disks (for the same reasons cited for floppy disks). As the tape unwinds from one spool and winds on another one, the read/write head (and possibly a separate *erase head*) fly over the recorded data, with read and write technique being quite similar to those for disk memories. Magnetic tapes come in many different varieties: from small cassettes or cartridges (see Figure 3.12b) to large reels with expensive transport mechanisms that can move the tape at very high speeds and also have almost instantaneous start and stop capabilities. The latter tape drives use a vacuum buffer that holds a loose segment of the tape to prevent damage to the tape material and the recorded data during high-speed mechanical movement or acceleration/deceleration.

As floppy and zip disks, along with magnetic tapes, gradually lose importance and are replaced by other media such as writable CDs, hard disks will likely become the only widely used magnetic-recording memory in computers. There is some speculation that eventually even hard magnetic disks will be displaced by optical and semiconductor memories. However, given past and ongoing advances in disk memory technology, this will not happen in the short term.

Optical disks (CD-ROM, DVD-ROM, and their writable and rewritable varieties) have become increasingly popular since the 1990s. In a way, these devices are similar to magnetic disk units in that they hold blocks of data on the surface of a round platter that must be spun to make the data available to an access mechanism. The *compact disc* (CD) format was developed first and quickly took over as the preferred method for distributing music and software products requiring hundreds of megabytes of capacity. Subsequent advances in substrate materials, semiconductor lasers, head positioning methods, and optical components led to the creation of the higher-capacity *digital versatile disc* (DVD) format whose multigigabyte capacity is more than enough to accommodate a full-length feature film. CD and DVD data are extensively protected via sophisticated error-correcting codes. Thus the obliteration of many recorded bits (due to material defects or scratches) will not affect the correctness of the retrieved data.

Read-only optical disks (CD, DVD) are descendants of primitive optical storage systems that recorded data by placing marks or punching holes on cards, paper tapes, and similar media. Optical disks record data by creating micrometer-size *pits* in a thin layer of optical material (placed on a plastic substrate) along a continuous spiral track that begins somewhere inside the disk and ends near the outside edge; for those who are old enough to remember, this is the opposite of the spiral direction used in vinyl phonograph records. Data is recorded by creating pits of varying sizes during the production of a CD or DVD. A laser light beam is focused on the surface of the platter, and differences in the reflection from the unaffected surface and the pits are detected for reading purposes. Note that the foregoing account is highly simplified and does not explain the workings of the laser diode, the beam splitter, the lenses, and the detector in Figure 19.6 [Clem00].

Writable CDs and DVDs may be write-once or rewritable. In the write-once versions, pits are created by blasting away a special coating placed on top of a reflecting surface (this is different from the protective coating in Figure 19.6), melting holes in a thin layer of special material using a more powerful write laser, or a variety of other methods. Rewritable versions

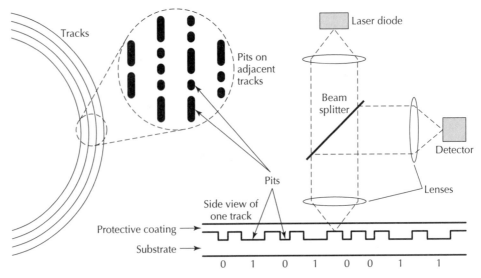

Figure 19.6 Simplified view of recording format and access mechanism for data on a CD-ROM or DVD-ROM.

typically rely on reversible modification of the optical or magnetic properties of material through selective exposure to laser light [Clem00].

Microelectromechnical (MEM) devices are being developed that can provide mass memory on IC chips, perhaps as early as 2005. One technology, pursued by IBM, operates like a phonograph, using sharp tips of tiny silicon cantilevers to inscribe data on, and to read it from, a polymer medium [Vett02]. Development of such a technology will take us a step closer to building truly single-chip computer systems.

As noted earlier, *on-line* mass memory units, such as hard disks, are directly accessible to the computer, whereas *off-line* storage media, such as CDs and tapes, must be placed or mounted on an on-line device to become accessible. Intermediate between these two are the so-called *near-line* mass memories that provide vast amount of storage without the need for human intervention in mounting the media. Such devices are often used as tertiary storage to hold rarely used databases and other information that must, nevertheless, be readily available when the need arises. For example, *automated tape libraries* provide many terabytes of storage capacity with an access time of under one minute. Typically, thousands of tape cartridges are housed in a large cabinet, with robotic arms capable of choosing a cartridge, loading it into a read/write assembly, and later putting it back into its home slot.

No matter what type of mass storage is used, the problem of permanence for digital data remains. Magnetic tapes last no more than a few decades. CDs are better, since their lifetimes are measured in centuries. Coming up with devices to read centuries-old CDs is of course a different challenge, given the rapid pace of technological progress. Programming languages and database formats also face extinction, making data preservation even more difficult [Tris02].

PROBLEMS

19.1 Disk capacity maximization

Consider the following optimization problem in designing a disk memory system. The diameter D of the outermost track is a given constant. You must choose the diameter xD of the innermost track, where $x < 1$. The trade-off is that the capacity of all tracks must be the same so that the shorter the innermost track, the less data can be recorded on each track, but there will be more tracks. How can one derive the optimal value of x and which disk or data recording parameters influence this optimal value? State all your assumptions clearly.

19.2 Parameters of commercial disk units

For each of the three disks listed in Table 19.1:

a. Derive the approximate average number of complete disk tracks that can be held in its cache. Ignore the overhead resulting from the storage of identifying information, such as track or sector numbers, in the buffer.

b. Calculate the time needed to read a 10 MB file that is stored on adjacent tracks according to the scheme of Figure 19.3 so that there is no wasted time due to rotational latency between the reading of successive logical sectors of the file.

19.3 Disk cost trends

Price data for disk memories are available at www.cs.utexas.edu/users/dahlin/techTrends/data/ diskPrices.

a. Plot price variations for personal computer disks using the time frame 1980–2010 on the horizontal axis and price range $0–$3000 on the vertical axis. Plot a separate curve for each of the capacities 10 MB, 20 MB, 80 MB, 210 MB, 420 MB, 1.05 GB, 2.1 GB, 4.2 GB, 9.1 GB, 18.2 GB, 36.4 GB, and 72.8 GB, where a curve extends in time from first commercial availability to discontinuation of the product. Where multiple prices are listed for a given disk capacity, choose the lowest one.

b. Produce a scatter plot based on the data in part a, where the horizontal axis again covers the time frame 1980–2010 and the vertical axis shows the price per gigabyte of capacity, ranging from $1 to $1M in a logarithmic scale (each grid line is a factor of 10 larger than the one below).

c. Discuss the general trends observed in parts a and b and try to extrapolate into the future beyond the available data.

19.4 Average seek distance

The average seek distance is the average number of cylinders to be crossed to get to the next cylinder that is of interest. Consider a c-cylinder disk, which thus has a maximum seek distance of $c - 1$.

a. If the head is retracted to home cylinder 0 (the outermost cylinder) after each access, then what is the average seek distance per access?

b. If you could choose a home cylinder other than cylinder 0, which one would you choose and why? What is the average seek distance from your chosen cylinder?

c. Show that if the head is allowed to stay on the last accessed cylinder rather than being retracted to a home cylinder, then the average seek distance with completely random accesses is about $c/3$.

19.5 Disk seek time formula

Derive a simplified form of the disk seek time formula (Section 19.3) for which $\beta = 0$, assuming that the head accelerates at a constant rate for the first half of the seek distance and then decelerates at the same rate for the second half. *Hint:* At a constant acceleration a, the distance traveled is related to time t by $d = \frac{1}{2}at^2$.

19.6 Disk seek time

For each of the disk memories listed in Table 19.1, determine the coefficients of the seek time formula (see Section 19.3), assuming that the average seek time cited is for half of the maximum cylinder distance.

19.7 Disk access scheduling

A disk with a single recording surface and 10,000 tracks has a controller that optimizes the performance via out-of-order processing of access requests. The access request queue is currently holding the following track numbers (in arrival order): 173, 2939, 1827, 3550, 1895, 3019, 2043, 3502, 259, 260. The head has just completed reading track 250 and is on its way to track 285 for a read access. Determine the total travel distance of the head (in tracks) for each of the following scheduling alternatives.

a. First come, first served (FCFS).

b. Shortest seek time first (SSTF).

c. Shortest seek time among the oldest three requests first.

d. Maintain scan direction (if the head is moving inward, say, continue moving in the same direction until the innermost requested track is accessed; then reverse the direction of head motion).

19.8 Disk caching and access scheduling

In many applications, the tracks on a disk are not uniformly accessed; rather, a small number of frequently used tracks account for a large fraction of disk accesses. Suppose we know that 50% of all disk accesses are made to 5% of the tracks.

a. Can this information be used to make the disk caching scheme more effective?

b. Which of the disk scheduling algorithms given in Problem 19.7 will likely perform better in optimizing disk accesses and why?

c. Can you devise a different scheduling algorithm that does even better than the one in part b?

19.9 Disk performance parameters

A single-platter disk spins at 3600 rpm and has 256 cylinders, each storing 256 Mb. Seek time is given by the formula $s + tc$, where $s = 0.5$ ms is the start-up time, $t = 0.05$ ms is the head travel time from one cylinder to an adjacent one, and c is the cylinder distance; for example, if the head must travel 5 cylinders inward, then it needs 0.75 ms to get there.

a. Ignoring the gaps between cylinders and other overhead, compute the peak data transfer rate.

b. Assuming an average cylinder distance of 85 from one access to a randomly chosen cylinder, compute the average access time for a 4 KB sector.

c. Based on your answer to part b, on average how much faster is it to access a random sector on the same track than a random sector anywhere on the disk?

d. What is the minimum time needed to back up the entire contents of the disk on a tertiary storage?

19.10 Disk memory technology

An intermediate solution between disks with a single moving head per platter and head-per-track disks, that have a dedicated head for each track to eliminate seek time completely, can be envisaged. Imagine a disk that has 8 heads mounted on an assembly. The heads move together and are aligned with different tracks so that the data rate during read and write can be 8 times that of a single-head disk.

a. What would be the best arrangement of the heads with respect to the tracks? In other words, should the heads read/write adjacent tacks or tracks that are spaced apart?

b. Enumerate the performance benefits, if any, of your disk design of part a.

c. Speculate about why such disks are not used in ordinary PCs.

19.11 RAID systems

Suppose each of the disks listed in Table 19.1 were to be used to build a RAID level 5 system that fits in a large cabinet having a volume of 1 m^3. About half the cabinet's space will be taken by ventilation gaps, fans, and power supply equipment. For each disk type:

a. Estimate the maximum total storage capacity that can be achieved.

b. Derive the maximum read throughput of the RAID system; state all your assumptions.

c. Repeat part b for the write throughput.

19.12 RAID systems

Consider the RAID4 and RAID5 data organizations depicted in Figure 19.5.

a. If each access to the disk for reading data involves a single sector, which organization leads to a higher bandwidth for reading? Quantify the difference for random distribution of read addresses.

b. Repeat part a for write accesses.

c. Suppose one of the disks fails and its data must be reconstructed on the spare disk. Which organization offers better performance for reads during the reconstruction process?

d. Repeat part c for write accesses.

19.13 Floppy disk parameters and performance

Consider a 3.5-inch floppy disk drive that uses two-sided disks with 80 tracks per side. Each track contains nine 512 B sectors. The disk spins at 360 rpm and seek time is $s + tc$, where $s = 200$ ms is the start/stop overhead and $t = 10$ ms is the track-to-track travel time.

a. Compute the capacity of the floppy disk.

b. Determine the average access time to a random sector if the head's home position is on the outermost track.

c. What is the data transfer rate once the sector has been located?

19.14 Floppy disk parameters

Take a floppy disk, note its capacity, and see whether it is one- or two-sided. Then dismantle it to measure the parameters (inner radius, outer radius) of its recording area. Then, assuming that the floppy has 80 equal-capacity tracks per side, determine its parameters such as track density, linear recording density, and average areal recording density.

19.15 Magnetic tape parameters

Data is written on magnetic tape using contiguously recorded blocks with a linear recording density of 1000 b/cm and a 1.2 cm gap between blocks. Recall that a tape typically has 8 data recording tracks and one parity track.

a. What fraction of the tape's total raw capacity holds useful data if each block contains a 512 B record?

b. Repeat part a, this time assuming that 4 records are packed into a tape block.

19.16 CD parameters

A CD has a recording area with approximate outer (inner) radius of 6 cm (2 cm). It holds 600 MB of data on a spiral track with fixed bit density and track separation of 1.6 μm. Ignore the effects of housekeeping and error-checking overheads. Derive the linear bit density and areal recording density for such a CD.

19.17 DVD parameters

A DVD has a recording area with approximate outer (inner) radius of 6 cm (2 cm). It holds 3.6 GB of data on a spiral track with fixed bit density and track separation of 1.6 μm. Ignore the effects of housekeeping and error-checking overheads.

a. Derive the linear bit density and areal recording density for such a DVD.
b. Assuming no data compression, how long a video can we store on this DVD if each image is 500 × 800 pixels, each pixel requires 2 B of storage, and the image must be refreshed 30 times per second?
c. Based on the result of part b, what can you say about the average compression ratio for the formats of common DVD movies?
d. At what speed should the DVD spin if the data rate required for parts c is to be achieved?

19.18 Jukebox-style tertiary memory

Consider a jukebox that stores up to 1024 optical cartridges and has a mechanism for choosing and "playing" any arbitrary cartridge. The selection and setup time is 15 s. High-speed playback to read out the data on the cartridge takes 120 s. The cartridge has a useful recording area of 100 cm^2.

a. Derive the required areal recording density if this system is to offer 1 TB of capacity.
b. What data transfer rate is implied by the information given for the system of part a?
c. What is the effective average data rate when many cartridges are read out in succession?
d. Suggest an application for this jukebox-style tertiary memory and discuss what other components would be needed to make it work for your suggested application.
e. Speculate on the possibility of a petabyte storage system using the same jukebox-style operation.

REFERENCES AND FURTHER READINGS

[Asha97]   Ashar, K., *Magnetic Disk Drive Technology,* IEEE Press, 1997.

[Clem00]   Clements, A., *The Principles of Computer Hardware,* Oxford, 3rd ed., 2000.

[Crag96]   Cragon, H. G., *Memory Systems and Pipelined Processors,* Jones and Bartlett, 1996.

[Dani99]   Daniel, E. D., C. D. Mee, and M. H. Clark, eds., *Magnetic Recording: The First 100 Years,* IEEE Press, 1999.

[Gang94]   Ganger, G. R., B. R. Worthington, R. Y. Hou, and Y. N. Patt, "Disk Arrays: High-Performance, High-Reliability Storage Subsystems," *IEEE Computer,* Vol. 27, No. 3, pp. 30–36, March 1994.

[Henn03]   Hennessy, J. L., and D. A. Patterson, *Computer Architecture: A Quantitative Approach,* Morgan Kaufmann, 3rd ed., 2003.

[Patt88]   Patterson, D. A., G. A. Gibson, and R. H. Katz, "A Case for Redundant Arrays of Inexpensive Disks (RAID)," *Proceedings of the ACM SIGMOD Conference,* Chicago, June 1988, pp. 109–116.

[Sier90]   Sierra, H. M., *An Introduction to Direct Access Storage Devices,* Academic Press, 1990.

[Tris02]   Tristram, C., "Data Extinction," *Technology Review,* Vol. 105, No. 8, pp. 36–42, 2002.

[Vett02]   Vettiger, P., et al., "The 'Millipede'—Nanotechnology Entering Data Storage," *IEEE Trans. Nanotechnology,* Vol. 1, No. 1, pp. 39–55, March 2002. See also IBM's Web site at: www.research.ibm.com/pics/nanotech

CHAPTER 20

VIRTUAL MEMORY AND PAGING

> "Ideally one would desire an indefinitely large memory capacity such that any particular word would be immediately available. . . . We are . . . forced to recognize the possibility of constructing a hierarchy of memories, each of which has greater capacity than the preceding but which is less quickly accessible."
> —*A. Burkes, H. Goldstine, and J. von Neumann, in a now classic report, 1946*

> "Virtually everywhere, this Friday."
> —*From prerelease ads for the movie* S1m0ne, *which features a virtual movie star, 2002*

TOPICS IN THIS CHAPTER

When main memory does not have the capacity to hold a very large program along with its associated data, or several smaller programs that need to coexist in the machine, we are forced to break things down into pieces and move the pieces into and out of main memory according to their access patterns. In a virtual memory, the process of data movement into and out of main memory is automated so that the programmer or compiler need not worry about it. What the programmer/compiler sees is a vast address space, even though, at any given time, only a small portion of this space is mapped to main memory. In this chapter, we review strategies for moving data between secondary and primary memories, look at the problem of virtual-to-real address translation and ways of speeding it up, and discuss virtual memory performance.

■ 20.1 The Need for Virtual Memory

Whereas caches are used to boost performance in a transparent fashion, virtual memory is used solely for convenience. In some cases, disabling virtual memory (if allowed) can lead to better performance. Virtual memory provides the illusion of a main memory that is much

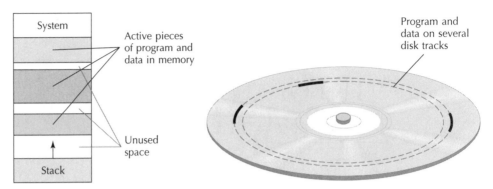

Figure 20.1 Program segments in main memory and on disk.

larger than the available physical memory. Programs that are written using a large virtual address space can be executed on systems with varying amounts of real (physical) memory. For example, MiniMIPS uses 32-bit addresses, but the system almost never has 4 GB of main memory. Yet, the virtual memory management hardware provides the illusion of a 4 GB physical address space with, say, a 64 MB main memory unit.

In the absence of virtual memory, a programmer or system software must explicitly manage the available memory space, moving pieces of a large program and its data set in and out of main memory as needed. This is a cumbersome and error-prone process and creates nontrivial storage allocation problems because program and data units are unequal in size. With virtual memory, the programmer or compiler generates code pretending that the main memory is as large as the available address space suggests. As pieces of the program or its data are referenced, the virtual memory system brings those pieces from the secondary (disk) memory into the much smaller main memory and, perhaps, takes other pieces out. Figure 20.1 shows a large program occupying several tracks on a disk, with three pieces (designated by heavy arcs on the disk surface) residing in main memory. As was the case for processor caches, the transfer of data between main and secondary memories is entirely automatic and transparent.

In virtual memory, data transfer between disk and main memories is done via fixed-size units known as *pages*. A page is typically in the range of 4-64 KB. On a disk with 512 B sectors, a page corresponds to 8-128 sectors. Virtual memory can be, and has been, implemented by means of variable-size data units known as *segments*. However, because the implementation of virtual memory through *paging* is both simpler and more prevalent than through *segmentation,* we limit our discussion to the former.

Figure 20.2 puts the ideas of virtual memory and cache memory together, depicting data movements between various levels of the memory hierarchy and the names associated with units of data transfers. From Figure 20.2, the reason behind the choice of the terms "line" and "page" is quite evident.

Virtual memory is a good idea for virtually (no pun intended) the same reasons that have made caches successful: that is, spatial and temporal locality of memory references (we return to this point in Section 20.4). Because of the much larger units (pages) brought into main memory and the larger size of the main memory, hit rate in main memory (99.9% or greater) is usually much better than hit rate in caches (typically 90–98%). When a page is not found in main memory, we say that a *page fault* has occurred. The use of "page fault" is purely for historical reasons; "main memory miss" (analog of "cache miss") would have been more appropriate.

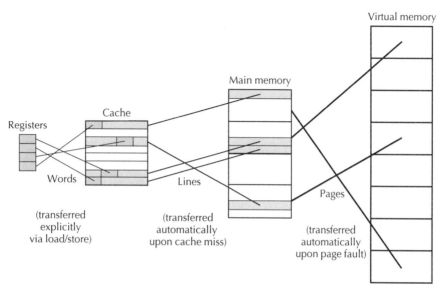

Figure 20.2 Data movement in a memory hierarchy.

How does virtual memory relate to cache memory, which we studied in Chapter 18? Cache is used to make the main memory appear faster. Virtual memory is used to make the main memory appear bigger. Hence, the hierarchical combination of cache, main, and secondary memories, with automatic transfer of data among them, creates the illusion of very a fast main memory (comparable in speed to SRAM) whose cost per gigabyte is a small multiple of the corresponding cost for a disk.

■ 20.2 Address Translation in Virtual Memory

Under virtual memory, a program being executed generates virtual addresses for memory accesses. These virtual addresses must be *translated* to physical memory addresses before instructions or data are retrieved and sent to the processor. If pages contain 2^P bytes and memory is byte-addressable, a V-bit virtual address can be divided into a P-bit byte offset within the page and a $V - P$ bit virtual page number. Because pages are brought into main memory in their entirety, the P-bit byte offset never changes. Thus, it is sufficient to translate the virtual page number to a physical page number corresponding to the location of the page in main memory. Figure 20.3 depicts the *virtual-to-physical address translation* parameters.

> **Example 20.1: Virtual memory parameters**   A virtual memory system with 32-bit virtual addresses uses 4 KB pages and a 128 MB byte-addressable main memory. What are the address parameters in Figure 20.3?
>
> **Solution:** Physical memory addresses for a 128 MB unit are 27 bits wide ($\log_2 128M = 27$), and byte offset in page is 12 bits wide ($\log_2 4K = 12$). This leaves $32 - 12 = 20$ bits for the virtual page number and $27 - 12 = 15$ bits for the physical page number. The 128 MB main memory has room for $2^{15} = 32K$ pages, whereas the virtual address space contains $2^{20} = 1M$ pages.

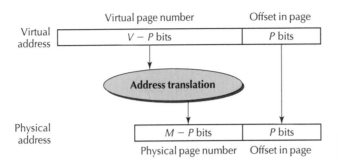

Figure 20.3 Virtual-to-physical address translation parameters.

The mapping scheme used to place pages in main memory is usually *fully associative,* meaning that each page can be mapped to anywhere in main memory. This eliminates *conflict misses* and minimizes page faults, which are extremely expensive in terms of time penalty (a few milliseconds may span millions of clock cycles). There are however *compulsory misses* and *capacity misses,* just as discussed for caches near the end of Section 18.2.

Because parallel comparison of the page tag with many thousands of tags is quite complex, a two-stage process is often used for memory access: a page table is consulted to find out whether a required page is in memory and if so, where it is located; then the actual memory access is performed or, in the event of a page fault, access from disk is initiated. Because disk access is quite slow, the operating system usually saves all program context and switches to a different task (*context switch*) rather than forcing the processor to wait idly for millions of cycles until disk access is complete and the required page has been brought into main memory. In the case of cache misses, however, the processor simply stalls for several clock cycles until data has been brought into the cache.

Figure 20.4 shows a page table and how it is used in the address translation process. While a program is in execution, the start address of its page table is stored in a special *page table register.* The virtual page number is used as an index into the page table and the corresponding entry is read out. The memory address for the desired page table entry is obtained by adding the virtual page number (offset) to the base address held in the page table register. As shown in Figure 20.4, each page table entry has a valid bit, several other flags, and a pointer to the page's whereabouts.

The page table entry thus obtained can be one of two types. If the valid bit is set, the address part of the entry is a physical page number identifying the location of the page in main memory (page hit). If the valid bit is reset, the address part points to the location of the virtual page on disk memory (page miss or page fault). Besides valid and invalid pages, distinguished via the valid bit, a page within the virtual memory address space may be *unallocated*. This is because the virtual address space is typically huge and most programs do not use their entire address space. An unallocated page is completely void of information; it does not even occupy space on the disk.

Each page table entry is typically one word (4 bytes), which is adequate for specifying a physical page number or a sector address on disk. Each time a page is copied into main memory or is sent to the disk to make room for another page, its associated page table entry is updated to reflect the new location of the page.

Besides the "valid bit," the page table entry may have a "dirty bit" (to indicate that the page has been modified since it was brought into main memory and must thus be written back to the disk if it needs to be replaced) and a "use bit," which is set to 1 whenever the page is accessed.

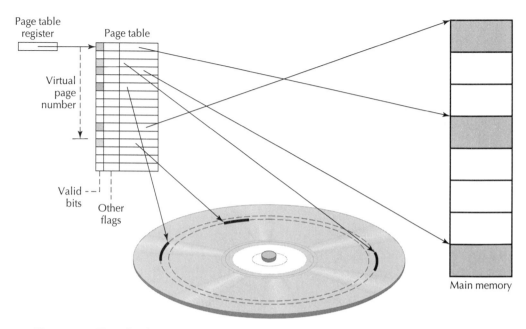

Figure 20.4 The role of page table in the virtual-to-physical address translation process.

The use bit finds application in implementing an approximate version of the least recently used (LRU) replacement policy (see Section 20.4).

It is evident from the preceding discussion that the convenience of virtual memory comes with some overhead, which consists of storage space for page tables and a page-table access (address translation) for every memory reference. We will see in Section 20.3 that the extra memory reference can be avoided in most cases, thus making the time overhead negligible. Storage overhead for page tables can also be reduced substantially. Note that the page table can be huge: in a 2^{32} B virtual address space with 4 KB pages, there are 2^{20} pages and, potentially, the same number of page table entries. Rather than allocate 4 MB of memory to the page table, one can organize it as a variable-size structure that grows to its maximum size only if needed. For example, instead of a directly addressed page table, with entry address determined by adding the page table base address to the virtual page number, a hash table can be used that needs far fewer entries for most programs.

Besides simplifying memory management (including allocation, linking, and loading), virtual memory offers advantages that may make its use worthwhile even when an expanded memory address space is not needed. Two of the most important among these additional benefits are *sharing* and *memory protection* (Figure 20.5):

1. Sharing of a page by two or more processes is straightforward and simply requires making entries in the associated page tables point to the same page in main memory or on disk. The shared page can, and often does, occupy different parts in the virtual address spaces of the sharing processes.

2. The page table entry can be augmented with *permission bits* that specify what types of access to the page are allowed and what other privileges are granted. Because all memory accesses go through the page table, pages that are off-limits to a process automatically become inaccessible to it.

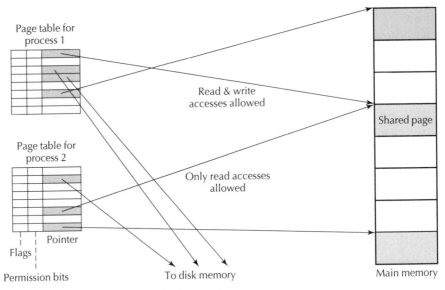

Figure 20.5 Virtual memory as a facilitator of sharing and memory protection.

Even though the virtual address space is usually much larger than the physical (main memory) address space, based on the benefits just discussed, it makes sense to have a virtual address that is narrower than, or of the same width as, the physical address.

■ 20.3 Translation Lookaside Buffer

Page table access for virtual-to-physical address translation essentially doubles the main memory access delay. This is because reading or writing a memory word requires two accesses: one to the page table and one to the word itself. To avoid this time penalty, which reduces the efficiency of virtual memory, we take advantage of spatial and temporal locality properties of programs. Because consecutive addresses generated by a program often reside in the same page, it is quite likely that the address translation process consults the same entry, or a small number of entries, in the page table over a period of time. Thus, we can use a cache-like structure, know as *translation lookaside buffer* (TLB), to keep a record of the most recent address translations.

When a virtual address is to be translated to a physical address, the TLB is consulted first. Just as in the processor cache, a portion of the virtual page number specifies where in the TLB to look, and the remainder is compared against the tag of the stored entry or entries. If the tags match and the associated entry is valid, then the physical page number is read out and used. Otherwise, we have a TLB miss, which is handled in a manner similar to a processor cache miss. In other words, the page table is consulted, the physical address is obtained, and the translation result is recorded in the TLB for future use, possibly replacing an existing TLB entry.

Typically, a TLB has tens to thousands of entries, with the smaller sizes being fully associative and larger ones having lower degrees of associativity. A TLB is essentially a cache memory dedicated to page table entries. When a TLB entry is to be replaced, its flags must be

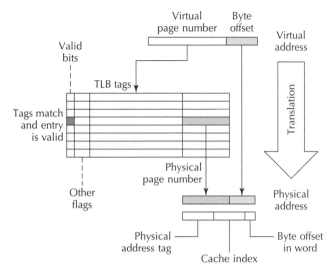

Figure 20.6 Virtual-to-physical address translation by a translation lookaside buffer, showing how the resulting physical address is used to access the cache memory.

copied into the page table. Fortunately, however, this does not involve much time penalty because TLB misses are extremely rare. Figure 20.6 depicts the TLB and its use for address translation.

Example 20.2: Address translation via TLB   A particular address translation process converts a 32-bit virtual address to a 32-bit physical address. Memory is byte-addressable and uses 4 KB pages. A 16-entry, direct-mapped TLB is used. Specify the components of the virtual and physical addresses and the width of various fields in the TLB.

Solution: Byte offset takes 12 bits in both virtual and physical addresses. The remaining 20 bits in the virtual (physical) address form the virtual (physical) page number. The 20-bit virtual page number is decomposed into a 4-bit index to address the 16-entry TLB and a 16-bit tag; the latter is compared against the tag read out from the TLB to determine whether there was a hit in the TLB. Besides the 16-bit tag, each TLB entry must hold a 20-bit physical page number, a valid bit, and other flags that are copied over from the corresponding page table entry.

We began our discussion of TLB with a virtual address that was presented to the main memory and showed how the first access to memory for consulting the page table can be avoided. It remains to describe how TLB, or virtual-to-physical address translation, works in the presence of a processor cache. There are two approaches for combined use of virtual memory and a processor cache.

In a *virtual-address cache,* the cache is organized according to virtual addresses. When a virtual address is presented to the cache controller, it is divided into various fields (offset, line/set index, virtual tag), and the cache is accessed as usual. If the result is a hit, nothing further is needed. For a cache miss, address translation and main memory access is required. Thus, TLB access time and other overheads of address translation are incurred only in the event of a cache miss, which is a rare event.

In a *physical-address cache,* TLB is accessed before the cache. The physical address obtained from the TLB, or from the page table in the event of a TLB miss, is presented to the cache, in turn leading to a cache hit or miss. For a miss, the main memory is accessed with the physical address that was obtained prior to cache access. Because the TLB is just like a cache, it appears that with this approach the time to access data in the cache is doubled, even ignoring the TLB misses (which are rare). However, the TLB access can be incorporated into a separate pipeline stage so that the increased latency produces little or no reduction in throughput (see Figure 17.10). The throughput is reduced only to the extent that the deeper pipeline may require more frequent bubbles.

Given that a *virtual-address cache* eliminates the address translation overhead in most cases, one may wonder why physical-address caches are used at all. The answer is that even though virtual-address caches reduce the overhead of address translation, they lead to complications elsewhere. In particular, when data must be shared among multiple processes (including application and I/O processes), the same data may have different virtual addresses in the address spaces of several processes, leading to "aliasing" or the existence of multiple (potentially inconsistent) copies of the same data in the cache.

It is possible to use a *hybrid-address cache* to gain the speed of a virtual-address cache while avoiding its aliasing problems. One commonly used hybrid approach is to make the location of data in the cache a function of only the page offset bits that do not change during address translation. For example, if the page size is 4 KB (12-bit offset) and the cache line size is 32 B (5-bit offset), there will be $12 - 5 = 7$ bits in the virtual address that are invariant during address translation and can be used to determine the cache line or cache set in which the accessed word resides.

The preceding method, combined with the use of physical tags in the cache leads to a hybrid scheme, which may be referred to as *virtually indexed, physically tagged.* Upon presentation of a virtual address, the processor cache and TLB are accessed in parallel. If the physical tag retrieved from the processor cache matches the tag read out from the TLB, then the cache data can be used. Otherwise, we have a cache miss. Even in this case, however, the address translation result is already available, unless of course we had a TLB miss. Figure 20.7 shows this hybrid and the pure addressing options in graphic form.

Note that with the processor cache, TLB, and virtual memory, a memory access can lead to misses of three types: cache miss, TLB miss, and page fault. Not all eight possible combinations of hit/miss in these three entities make sense, however.

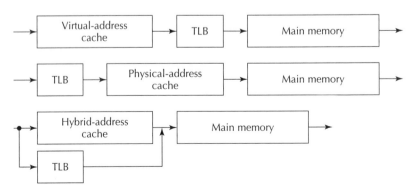

Figure 20.7 Options for where virtual-to-physical address translation occurs.

20.4 Page Replacement Policies

Based on our discussion thus far, the designer of a virtual memory system must resolve the following key questions, which are fundamentally the same as those encountered for cache memories:

1. *Fetch policy:* when to bring a particular page into main memory.
2. *Placement policy:* where to place a newly brought-in page (and where to find it when needed).
3. *Replacement policy:* how to choose among the placement options (which of the existing pages currently occupying those locations to overwrite).

The most common fetch policy is *demand paging,* bringing a page in upon the first access to it. An alternative is *prepaging,* which means that pages may be brought in before they are needed by a running program. This may be beneficial, for example, if when a particular page is accessed, nearby pages on the same disk track are also brought in, given that doing so incurs very little time penalty as far as disk access is concerned. Because most modern disk systems employ special caches to hold nearby sectors or even complete tracks upon each disk access (see Section 19.4), we do not need to consider prepaging any further.

The fully associative nature of the page mapping scheme in main memory implies that page placement is not an issue (a page can be placed anywhere in main memory). It is this unrestricted placement that necessitates the use of indirect access via a page table to locate a page, and the use of a TLB to avert this extra access in most cases. By contrast, in direct and set-associative mappings used in caches, the single slot, or a handful of possible locations, for a cache line allow it to be found quickly by means of simple hardware aids. We will thus ignore the issue of placement in virtual memory altogether. We note, however, that in more advanced computer systems having a multitude of local (quickly accessible) and remote (high-latency) memory units available, placement does become an issue.

We devote the remainder of this section to *page replacement* policies used to choose a page to be overwritten when there is no empty *page frame* available in main memory to accommodate an incoming page. Because fetching a page from disk takes millions of clock cycles, the operating system can afford to use a sophisticated page replacement policy that takes reference history and other factors into account. The running time of even a fairly complex decision process is likely to be small in comparison to the several milliseconds spent on a single disk access. This is in contrast to the replacement policies in a processor cache or TLB, which must be extremely simple.

Ideally, a page replacement policy minimizes the number of page faults over the course of a program's execution. Such an ideal policy cannot be implemented because it would require perfect knowledge about all future page accesses. Practical replacement policies are designed to come close to an ideal policy using knowledge about the past behavior of a program to predict its future course. The *least recently used* (LRU) algorithm is one such policy. Implementing the LRU policy is rather difficult; it requires that each page be time-stamped with each access and the time stamps be compared to find the smallest among them at the time of replacement. For this reason, an approximate version of the LRU policy, which does quite well in practice, is often implemented.

One way to implement LRU in an approximate fashion is as follows. A *use bit* is associated with each page; it specifies whether access has been made to that page in the recent past (since the use bit was last reset by the operating system). The use bit essentially divides the pages into two groups, recently accessed and not recently accessed. Only pages in the latter category

(a) Before replacement

(b) After replacement

Figure 20.8 A scheme for the approximate implementation of LRU.

are candidates for replacement. Various methods can be used for selection among the candidates and for periodically resetting the use bits. One such scheme, sometimes referred to as the *clock policy,* is depicted in Figure 20.8, where the 0s and 1s are use bits for the various pages, and the arrow is a pointer that marks one of the pages. When a page must be selected for replacement, the arrow moves clockwise, resetting to 0s all 1s that are encountered and stopping at the first 0, which is where the new page will be placed, with its use bit set to 1. A page whose use bits is changed from 1 to 0 will be replaced when the arrow has made one full rotation, unless of course it is used again before then and thus its use bit is set to 1. It is easily seen that frequently accessed pages will never be replaced under this policy.

Virtual memory works because it takes full advantage of both the spatial and temporal locality of memory accesses in typical programs. *Spatial locality* is what justifies bringing thousands of bytes into main memory when a page fault is encountered during an attempt to access a single byte or word. Because of spatial locality, much of the rest of the page will likely be used in future, perhaps more than once, amortizing the latency of a single disk access over many memory references. *Temporal locality* is what makes the LRU replacement policy successful in keeping the more useful instructions and data (from the viewpoint of future memory references) in main memory and overwriting the less useful parts. If an instruction or data element has not been used for a while, chances are that the program has moved on to doing other things and will not need that item in the near future. Of course it is not hard to write a program that exhibits neither spatial nor temporal locality. Such a program will make the virtual memory perform very poorly. But most of the time it does quite well.

Example 20.3: LRU isn't always the best policy   Consider the following program fragment that deals with a table T with 17 rows and 1024 columns, computing an average for each table column and printing it to the screen (i is row index and j is column index):

```
for j = [0 ... 1023] {
       temp = 0;
       for i = [0 ... 16]
            temp = temp + T[i][j]
       print(temp/17.0); }
```

T[i][j] and temp are 32-bit floating-point values and memory is word-addressable. The temporary variable temp is kept in a processor register, so access to temp does not involve a memory reference. The main memory is paged and holds 16 pages of size 1024 words. The page replacement policy is "least recently used."

  a. Assuming that T is stored in the virtual address space in row-major format, how many page faults will be encountered and what is the main memory hit ratio?
  b. What fraction of the page faults in part a are compulsory? Capacity? Conflict?
  c. Repeat part a, this time assuming that T is stored in column-major format.
  d. What fraction of the page faults in part c are compulsory? Capacity? Conflict?

Solution: Figure 20.9 offers a visualization of how elements of T are divided among 17 pages for the two cases of row-major and column-major storage.

  a. After row 0 has been brought into main memory, 16 other rows are accessed before row 0 is needed again. The LRU policy forces each page out right before its next use! Thus, every access causes a page fault. There are a total of $1024 \times 17 = 17{,}408$ page faults and the hit ratio is 0.
  b. Because there are only 17 pages, 17 or approximately 0.1% of the misses can be considered compulsory. There is no conflict miss with a fully associative mapping scheme. The remaining 17,391, or 99.9%, of the misses are capacity misses.
  c. Each page contains $1024/17 \cong 60$ columns of T. A page is never used again once its columns have been processed. Thus, there are only 17 misses and the hit ratio is 99.9%.
  d. All 17 misses are compulsory; there is no capacity or conflict miss.

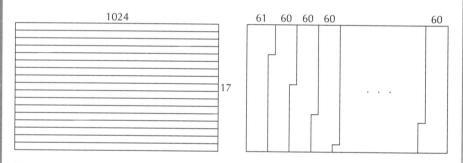

Figure 20.9 Pagination of a 17 × 1024 table when stored in row-major or column-major order.

A page may have been modified since it was brought into main memory. Thus, to ensure that no information is lost, pages must be copied back to disk before being overwritten with new incoming pages. Because this writeback is time-consuming, a "dirty bit" is associated with each page that is set whenever the page is modified. If a page is not dirty, no writeback is needed and time is saved. Note that because of the extreme time penalty of disk access, use of write-through scheme is not an option here. With writeback, however, the number of disk accesses is minimized and the overhead becomes acceptable, as it was between cache and main memory. To avoid tacking the writeback penalty to the already long disk access time upon a page fault, the operating system may preselect pages for replacement and initiate the writeback process before an actual need arises. Additionally, certain useful or frequently needed pages may be locked into main memory by the operating system so that they are never replaced.

The following analogy might be helpful. You have bookcases of limited capacity for your technical books and have decided that you buy or keep a new technical book only if you can discard an old book that has ceased to be useful. Certain books are very useful in your work and you mark them as nonreplaceable. If you discard books ahead of time, space is more likely to be available for new books when they arrive; otherwise, you might be forced to stack books on your desk until you find time to decide which books to discard. Such a time often never comes, making the stacks on your desk taller and taller, until they topple and hurt you upon the slightest disturbance.

20.5 Main and Mass Memories

Virtual memory not only makes it possible for one process to expand beyond the size of the available main memory but also allows multiple processes to share the main memory with significantly simplified memory management. Upon encountering a page fault, a process is normally put into a dormant state and the processor is assigned to some other activity. In other words, a page fault is treated as an exception that triggers a context switch. The dormant process is later awakened when its required page is already in main memory. In this way, control may be transferred continually among several processes, with each one becoming dormant as it encounters a page fault or another situation requiring it to wait for the availability of a resource. When many processes are available for execution, the processor can always find something useful to do during long wait periods created by page faults. On the other hand, putting more processes in main memory means that each one gets fewer pages, potentially leading to frequent page faults and thus lower performance. Thus, a balance must be struck between reducing the processor idle time through the availability of more active processes and having enough pages of each process in main memory to ensure a low page fault rate.

A useful notion in this regard is that of the *working set* of a process. As a program executes, its memory accesses tend to be concentrated in a few pages for some time. Then, some of these pages are abandoned and focus of interest shifts to other pages. The working set of duration x for a process is the set of all pages that have been referenced in the course of executing the last x instructions. The working set changes over time, so we denote it as $W(t, x)$. The principle of locality ensures that $W(t, x)$ remains rather small for large values of x. Figure 20.10 shows

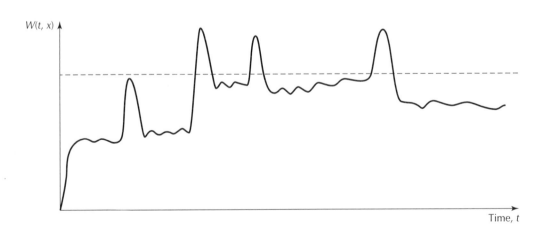

Figure 20.10 Variations in the size of a program's working set.

typical variations in the size of a program's working set over time, with the narrow peaks corresponding to shifts in the program's memory references from one locality to another locality (during the shifts, both the old locality and the new locality have been accessed in the recent past).

If the working set of a process is resident in main memory, then few page faults are encountered. At this point, allocating more memory to the process may not have a significant effect on performance. If the dashed line in Figure 20.10 represents the amount of main memory allocated to the program, then the program will run without a page fault for long stretches of time.

If we knew exactly what the working set of a process would be at any given time, we could prefetch its members into main memory and avoid most page faults. Unfortunately, since the past behavior of a program does not always accurately reflect what will happen in future, this is impossible to do. So, the notion of working set is often used as a conceptual tool in memory allocation. If we monitor the page faults generated by a process, we get a fairly accurate indication of whether the amount of memory allocated to the process is sufficient to accommodate its working set. Frequent page faults indicate that the allocated memory is inadequate. If a process must be suspended to improve the memory performance, the one producing the most page faults is a good candidate. On the other hand, if all active processes are producing a low level of page faults, then perhaps a new process can be activated and brought into main memory.

Processes are typically created by placing their pages on the secondary memory. When a process is to begin execution, a certain number of main memory pages are allocated to it and its pages are gradually brought in (demand paging). Some of these pages that are expected to be frequently accessed may be locked in main memory. When the initially allocated pages are used up, several options are available upon the next page fault encountered. With a *local replacement policy,* one of the nonlocked pages of the process is chosen for replacement. This causes the number of main memory pages allocated to the process to remain constant over time. A *global replacement policy* chooses the page to be replaced without regard to which process owns it. This will cause more active processes, or the ones with larger working sets, to gradually occupy more pages at the expense of other processes, thus leading to a form of automatic memory allocation and balancing; as a process stops using certain pages, it may lose the space to other processes that are more active, and then regain some space as it produces more activity itself.

■ 20.6 Improving Virtual Memory Performance

The implementation and performance of virtual memory are affected by a number of parameters whose impact and interrelationships must be well understood, not only by designers, but also by users. These include:

    Main memory size
    Page size
    Replacement policy
    Address translation scheme

The first three parameters and their interrelationships are quite similar to those of processor caches. Thus, in Table 20.1, we list parameters relating to hierarchical memory schemes (of which cache and virtual memories are examples) and their effects of performance. We are

■ **TABLE 20.1** Memory hierarchy parameters and their effects on performance.

Parameter variation	Potential advantages	Possible disadvantages
Larger main or cache size	Fewer capacity misses	Longer access time
Longer pages or lines	Fewer compulsory misses (prefetching effect)	Greater miss penalty
Greater associativity (for cache only)	Fewer conflict misses	Longer access time
More sophisticated replacement policy	Fewer conflict misses	Longer decision time, more hardware
Write-through policy (for cache only)	No writeback time penalty, easier write-miss handling	Wasted memory bandwidth, longer access time

already familiar with the assertions in Table 20.1 in relation to caches. In what follows, we will justify the same for virtual memory and also discuss some issues relating to page table implementation for address translation.

The performance impact of the main memory size is obvious. In the extreme when main memory is large enough to hold an entire program and its data, we have only compulsory misses. However, a very large main memory is not only more expensive but also slower. So, there is a hidden speed penalty that must be considered, along with cost-effectiveness issues, in choosing a main memory size.

The choice of a page size is a function of the typical program behavior as well as the difference in the latencies and data rates of main and mass memories. When program accesses have a great deal of spatial locality, a larger page size tends to reduce the number of compulsory misses due to the prefetching effect. However, the same larger pages will waste memory space and bandwidth when there is little or no spatial locality. So, there is often an optimum page size that leads to the best average performance for programs that are typically run on a given computer. The greater the ratio of disk access time to main memory latency, the larger the optimum page size. Figure 20.11 shows how disk seek time (which varies roughly in proportion to the total disk latency) and main memory access time have changed over the years. We see that the ratio of the two parameters has stayed pretty much constant. This fact, along with faster cache memories effectively hiding some of the DRAM latency, explains why page sizes have hovered around 4 KB.

It is interesting to note that in the early 1980s, as the speed gap between disk and DRAM memories seemed destined to grow (while their storage densities got closer), predictions that disks would gradually give way to semiconductor memories were commonplace. In part as a result of this challenge, disk manufacturers intensified their research and development efforts and succeeded in actually narrowing the gap over the next decade (see Figure 20.11).

The impact of the replacement policy on performance has been extensively studied, and many novel policies and refinements to older methods have been offered in an effort to reduce the page fault frequency. Figure 20.12 depicts experimental results on the page fault rate of LRU and approximate LRU, compared against the ideal algorithm and the very simple first-in, first-out (FIFO) algorithm. This is based on a fairly old study conducted by running a Fortran program using a fixed page size of 256 words [Baer80]. However, substantially similar results have been reported by other investigators in different contexts. The number of pages allocated to a process is shown along the horizontal axis and can simply be viewed as representing the main memory size in a single-process environment. Based on the trends depicted

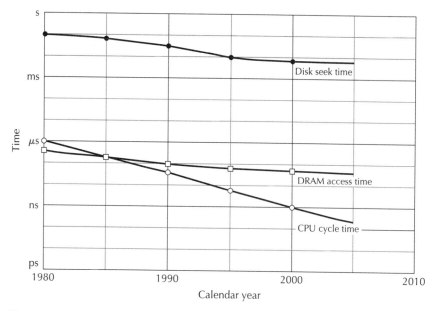

Figure 20.11 Trends in disk, main memory, and CPU speeds.

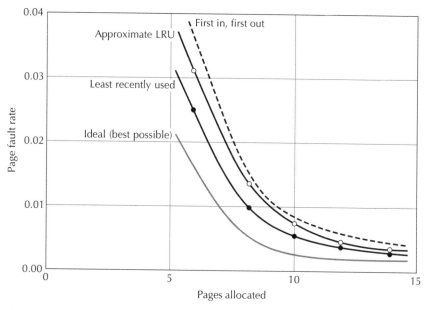

Figure 20.12 Dependence of page faults on the number of pages allocated and the page replacement policy.

in Figure 20.12, we can conclude that the relative effect of replacement policy on the page fault rate is confined to the neighborhood of a small constant factor (around 2). The difference is quite significant in absolute terms when a small set of pages is allocated to a process (or, equivalently, the main memory is rather limited), with the difference becoming less pronounced when memory is plentiful.

Conceptually, address translation is implemented via a page table, with its performance impact softened by using a TLB. As noted earlier, page tables can be huge. For example, 32-bit virtual addresses imply 1M-entry page tables when the page size is 4 KB. Of course the page table must reside in main memory if the required address translation in case of a TLB miss is to be performed quickly. This can be accomplished without having to set aside large, sparsely used areas of main memory for the page tables. The trick is to let pages of the page table to be swapped in and out of memory like all other pages. The principle of locality would ensure that the most useful chunks of the page table will remain in main memory and thus can be accessed quickly.

An alternative to having a large monolithic page table is to use a two-level structure. For 20-bit virtual page numbers, for example, the upper 10 bits might be used as an index into a page directory (level-1 page table) with 1024 entries. Each entry in this page directory contains a pointer to a 1024-entry level-2 table. With 32-bit entries, each such table fits in a 4096 B page. The page directory might be locked in main memory, with level-2 tables swapped in and out as needed. One advantage of this scheme is that for typical programs that use a number of contiguous pages at the beginning of their virtual address space and one or more pages at the end to hold a stack, only a few level-2 tables are ever needed, making it possible for all of them to reside in main memory. A drawback of two-level page tables is the need for two table accesses for address translation. However, the use of a TLB mitigates this to a large extent.

PROBLEMS

20.1 Analogs of paging in everyday life

Describe what each of the following situations has in common with virtual memory and paging, elaborating on the counterparts of fetch, placement, and replacement policies, as well as address translation, where applicable.

a. Supermarket manager assigning shelf space to products
b. Movies chosen for screening in theaters worldwide
c. Cars parked along a street equipped with parking meters

20.2 Parts of a memory hierarchy

Consider the following diagram of a hierarchical memory system.

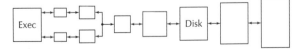

a. Assign an appropriate label to each unlabeled box and explain its function.
b. Name hardware technologies that might be used at each level.
c. Supply an approximate value for the latency ratios between successive levels.
d. Provide a ballpark figure for the hit ratio at each level.
e. Name typical placement and replacement schemes at each level.
f. Describe the address translation mechanism, if any, at each level.

20.3 Virtual memory concepts

Answer true or false, with full justification.

a. The numerical difference between a virtual address and the corresponding physical address is always nonzero.

b. The size of a virtual address space can exceed the total disk capacity in bytes.

c. It is not possible to run an address translation mechanism backward, obtaining a corresponding virtual address from a physical address.

d. Pages should be made as large as possible to minimize the size of page tables.

e. When several processes share a page, their corresponding page table entries must be identical.

f. An optimal replacement policy that always leads to the fewest possible page faults is not implementable.

20.4 Virtual and physical addresses

A byte-addressed virtual memory system with 4096 B pages has 8 virtual pages and 4 physical page frames in main memory. Virtual pages 1, 3, 4, and 7 reside in page frames 3, 0, 2, and 1, respectively.

a. Specify the virtual address ranges that would lead to page faults.

b. Find the physical addresses that correspond to virtual addresses 5,000; 16,200; 17,891; and 32,679.

20.5 Data movement in memory hierarchy

a. Draw, and appropriately label all components of, a diagram similar to Figure 20.2 that shows two caching levels.

b. Repeat part a, this time assuming single-level caching with split caches.

c. Draw a diagram that combines parts a and b; that is, split L1 and unified L2 caches.

20.6 Address translation via TLB

a. Show how each of the translation options in Figure 20.7 would work with the TLB specified in Example 20.2.

b. Redo Example 20.2 with a 64-entry, two-way set-associative TLB.

c. Repeat part a for the TLB specified in part b.

20.7 Approximate LRU replacement algorithm

How would the program fragment in Example 20.3 behave under the approximate LRU replacement algorithm? State all your assumptions clearly.

20.8 MRU replacement algorithm

A friend suggests that replacing the *most recently used* (MRU) page may be a viable alternative. You try to convince him that this is the worst possible idea, given the spatial and temporal locality properties of programs. He insists that MRU can outperform LRU in some cases.

a. Does your friend's claim have any merit?

b. Is MRU any easier to implement than LRU?

20.9 Approximate LRU replacement algorithm

Figure 20.8 exemplifies the application of "use bits" in implementing an approximate version of the LRU algorithm.

a. Under what conditions will this approximate version exhibit exactly the same behavior as LRU?

b. A variation of this method also uses "dirty bits" (also known as "modified bits") in making a replacement decision. Describe how this more sophisticated form of the algorithm might work.

c. What are the benefits of using a 2-bit "use counter" instead of a single "use bit" for this algorithm?

20.10 Working sets

a. Ignoring the print statement, convert the program fragment in Example 20.3 into a sequence of MiniMIPS instructions.

b. Plot the working set variations for the program of part a based on the last 20, 40, 60, . . . instructions and assuming that the table is stored in row-major format.

c. Repeat part b, this time assuming that the table is stored in column-major format.

20.11 Page fault frequency

Consider the execution of the following loop with arrays A, B, and C stored in separate 1024-word pages:

```
for i in 0 ... 1023 do
    C[i]:= A[i] + B[i]
endfor
```

Indicate the sequence of page references and discuss the frequency of page faults with various amounts of main memory assigned to the program containing the loop. State all your assumptions clearly.

20.12 Page replacement policy

A process accesses its 5 pages in the following order: A B C D A B E A B C D E.

a. Determine which page accesses cause a page fault if there are 3 page frames in main memory and the replacement policy is FIFO, LRU, or approximate LRU (three cases).

b. Repeat part a for 4 page frames.

20.13 Optimal page replacement policy

Show that an optimal replacement policy is obtained if the page whose next reference is furthest in future is replaced [Matt70].

20.14 Average main memory access time

In a demand paging system, main memory cycle time is 150 ns and average disk access time is 15 ms. Address translation requires 1 memory access in the case of a TLB miss and negligible time otherwise. The TLB hit rate is 90%. Of TLB misses, 20% lead to a page fault (2% of total accesses). Compute an average access time for this virtual memory system. In what way is the computed average access time misleading?

20.15 Reducing page faults via blocking

Example 20.3 showed us that, depending on whether a table is stored in row-major order or column-major order, excessive page faults or very few page faults are generated. Consider the problem of matrix multiplication with 256×256 square matrices. Assume a total main memory allocation of 64 pages, each holding 1024 words, to the two operand matrices and the result matrix.

a. Assuming row-major storage of the three matrices involved, derive the number of page faults when matrix multiplication is performed via the simple

algorithm with three nested loops computing c_{ij} as the sum of the product terms $a_{ik} \times b_{kj}$ over all values of k and the LRU replacement algorithm is used.

b. Repeat part a with column-major storage of the three matrices.

c. Show that if the matrices are viewed as consisting of 32×32 blocks and matrix multiplication is performed on the resulting 8×8 block matrices, the number of page faults is significantly reduced.

20.16 Two-level page tables

As mentioned at the end of Section 20.6, two-level page tables are used to reduce the memory requirements of a large monolithic page table which typically have large blocks of unused entries.

a. Draw a diagram similar to Figure 20.4, but with a two-level page table.

b. Repeat part a for Figure 20.5.

c. How is the TLB organized when we have two-level page tables?

d. Explain why it makes sense to have the second-level page tables occupy one page each.

e. Study the two-level page table structure of Intel's Pentium and prepare a two-page summary of its address translation scheme, including the way it uses the TLB.

20.17 Virtual memory performance

Given a sequence of numbers representing virtual page numbers in order of their being accessed, you can evaluate the performance of a virtual memory system with known parameters by figuring out which accesses lead to page faults. Now consider reversing the given sequence so that accesses to virtual pages occur in exactly the opposite order (say, C B B A A C B A instead of A B C A A B B C). Can you deduce anything about the number of page faults encountered with this reverse ordering relative to the original access sequence? Fully justify any assumptions that you make and your conclusion.

REFERENCES AND FURTHER READINGS

[Baer80]   Baer, J.-L., *Computer Systems Architecture,* Computer Science Press, 1980.

[Brya03]   Bryant, R. E., and D. O'Hallaron, *Computer Systems: A Programmer's Perspective,* Prentice Hall, 2003.

[Denn70]   Denning, P. J., "Virtual Memory," *ACM Computing Surveys,* Vol. 2, No. 3, pp. 153–189, September 1970.

[Hand93]   Handy, J., *The Cache Memory Book,* Academic Press, 1993.

[Henn03]   Hennessy, J. L., and D. A. Patterson, *Computer Architecture: A Quantitative Approach,* Morgan Kaufmann, 3rd ed., 2003.

[Kilb62]   Kilburn, T. D., B. G. Edwards, M. J. Lanigan, and F. H. Sumner, "One-Level Storage System," *IRE Trans. Electronic Computers,* Vol. 11, pp. 223–235, April 1962.

[Matt70]   Mattson, R. L., J. Gecsei, D. R. Slutz, and I. L. Traiger, "Evaluation Techniques for Storage Hierarchies," *IBM Systems J.,* Vol. 9, No. 2, pp. 78–117, 1970.

[Silb02]   Silberschatz, A., P. B. Galvin, and G. Gagne, *Operating Systems Concepts,* Wiley, 6th ed., 2002.

PART SIX

INPUT/OUTPUT AND INTERFACING

"If you put garbage in a computer nothing comes out but garbage. But this garbage, having passed through a very expensive machine, is somehow ennobled and none dare criticize it."
—*Source unknown (from the days when inexpensive personal computers could not be imagined)*

"I knew we were getting phone service through our cable TV and transmitting our documents through our copier, but when did we start getting faxes through our toaster oven?"
—*Caption of a cartoon by unknown artist*

TOPICS IN THIS PART

21. Input/Output Devices
22. Input/Output Programming
23. Buses, Links, and Interfacing
24. Context Switching and Interrupts

Much of the data to be processed by a computer originates outside the machine, and computation results obtained by executing programs must often go to external sources for interpretation, archiving, and/or further processing. It follows that the latency of input and output operations can have a significant impact on our perception of a computer's performance; it matters little that a CPU runs a program in a fraction of a second if it takes several minutes to supply the data to be processed and get the results back. It is therefore imperative, for effective computer design and use, that we understand how input/output devices work, how they interact with the memory and CPU, and how a computer can be used to collect data from external sources or to drive and control external devices.

In Chapter 21, we review the types of input/output devices and their implementation details that have a bearing on cost, performance, or the required data rates to support their interactions with memory and CPU. We then examine the issue of I/O programming, and cost/performance implications of alternative approaches such as polling, interrupts, and DMA, in Chapter 22. Buses and links of other types are the primary mechanisms for connecting computer components to each other and to peripheral devices. These mechanisms, and associated standards, are discussed in Chapter 23. Chapter 24 deals with interrupts, which form important mechanisms for implementing efficient asynchronous input/output processes and also lead us to methods for switching between computation threads in an effort to avoid idle times due to data dependencies and access delays.

21

INPUT/OUTPUT DEVICES

"When the user is building a trail, he names it, inserts the name in his code book, and taps it out on his keyboard. . . . It is exactly as though the physical items had been gathered together from widely separated sources and bound together to form a new book. It is more than this, for any item can be joined into numerous trails."

—*Vannevar Bush, As We May Think, 1945 (Prophesying what is now the Worldwide Web)*

"The value of a program is proportional to the weight of its output."

—*Sixth law of computer programming*

In this chapter, we review the structure and working principles of a number of common input/output devices, both devices that offer or display data on the fly and those that capture data for archiving or further processing. In addition to the type of data presentation or recording, I/O devices might be categorized by their data rates, from very slow data entry devices (keyboards) to high-bandwidth storage subsystems. We will see that the required data rate may dictate the way in which CPU, memory, and I/O devices interact. Increasingly, the source of input, or the recipient of output, for one computer is another computer that is linked to it via a network. For this reason, networking of I/O devices is also discussed in this chapter.

■ 21.1 Input/Output Devices and Controllers

The processor and memory are much faster than most I/O devices. In general, the closer a unit is to the CPU, the faster it can be accessed. For example, if main memory is 15 cm away from the CPU (see Figure 3.11a), signal propagation alone takes about 1 ns each way, given that electronic signals travel at about half the speed of light; to this 2 ns round-trip signal propagation delay we must add various logic delays, buffering time, bus arbitration delay, and, of

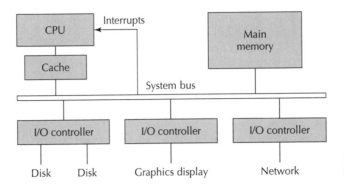

Figure 21.1 Input/output via a single common bus.

course, the memory access latency. Besides additional delays due to increased distance from the CPU, many I/O devices are also slower because of their electromechanical nature.

In Table 3.3 we listed a number of I/O devices along with their approximate data rates and application domains. Besides the type of input or output data, used in Table 3.3 as the primary classification criterion, I/O devices can be categorized based on other technology or application characteristics. The medium used for data presentation (hard copy vs electronic or soft copy), extent of human involvement (manual vs automatic), and production quality (preliminary draft vs publication or photo quality) are some of the relevant characteristics.

Modern I/O devices are quite intelligent and often contain their own CPU (typically a micro-controller or low-end general-purpose processor), memory, and communication capabilities, which increasingly include network connectivity. Interfacing with such devices, which may have several megabytes of memory for buffering, is fundamentally different from the control of early I/O devices, which had to be fed with information, or directed to send data, one byte at a time.

Devices typically communicate with the CPU and memory via I/O controllers connected to a shared bus. Simple low-end systems may use the same bus for I/O that is used for sending data back and forth between CPU and memory (Figure 21.1). Because the common bus in Figure 21.1 contains a number of address lines for main memory accesses, it is an easy matter to let the same lines select devices for I/O operations by assigning a portion of the memory address space to them. This type of *memory-mapped I/O,* and other strategies for I/O control through programming, will be covered in Chapter 22. More elaborate or high-performance systems may have a separate I/O bus to ensure that no bandwidth is taken away from CPU-memory transfers (Figure 21.2). When multiple buses exist in a system, they are interfaced with each other through *bus adapters.* Buses, relevant standards, and interfacing methods will be covered in Chapter 23.

The I/O controllers in Figures 21.1 and 21.2 fulfill the following roles:

1. Isolate the CPU and memory from details of I/O device operation and specific interface requirements.
2. Facilitate expansion in capabilities and innovation in I/O device technology without impacting the CPU design and operation.
3. Manage the (potentially wide) speed mismatch between processor/memory on one side and I/O devices on the other, through buffering.
4. Convert data formats or encodings and enforce data transfer protocols.

I/O controllers are essentially computers in their own right. When activated, they run special programs to guide them through the required data transfer operations and associated protocols.

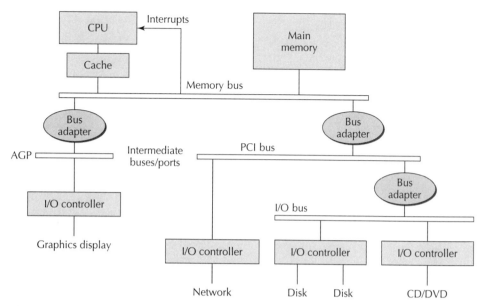

Figure 21.2 Input/output via intermediate and dedicated I/O buses (to be explained in Chapter 23); AGP (accelerated graphic port) is a shared port, not a bus.

For this reason, they introduce to I/O operations nontrivial latencies that must be considered in determining I/O performance. Depending on system and device types, I/O controller latencies on the order of a few milliseconds are not uncommon.

21.2 Keyboard and Mouse

A *keyboard* consists of an array of keys used to enter information into a computer or other digital device. Smaller keyboards, such as the ones found on telephones, or in a separate area on many desktop computers, are referred to as *keypads*. Physically, almost all alphanumeric keyboards follow the QWERTY layout, a name derived from the labels of the first few keys on the top row of letters on a standard typewriter keyboard. Over the years, serious attempts have been made to introduce other key layouts that would make it easier to reach more frequently used letters of the alphabet, thereby increasing data entry speed. Ironically, it is said that the QWERTY layout was chosen to deliberately reduce typing speed in an effort to prevent the mechanical hammers of early typewriters from jamming. Unfortunately, familiarity of the QWERTY layout and the vast existing expertise in using it have prevented the adoption of these more sensible layouts. However, some progress has been made in the area of unconventional key placements to add to user comfort during typing. Keyboards following such designs are known as *ergonomic keyboards*.

Figure 21.3 shows two specific designs for a key that is capable of closing an electrical circuit upon depression of the key cap attached to a plunger assembly or a membrane mounted over shallow pits. Many other designs exist and are in use. Membrane switches are inexpensive and are thus in common use in embedded system applications such as the control panel of a microwave oven. Mechanical switches such as the one depicted in Figure 21.3a are used in standard desktop keyboards in view of the tactile feedback they provide and their more sturdy construction. Because the contacts can get dirty with the passage of time, other forms

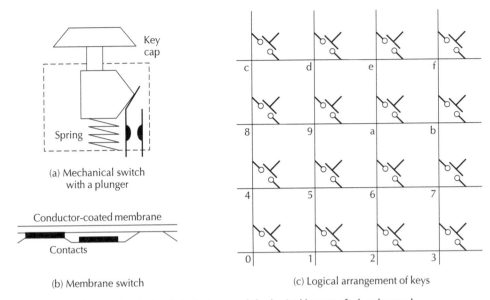

(a) Mechanical switch
with a plunger

(b) Membrane switch

(c) Logical arrangement of keys

Figure 21.3 Two mechanical switch designs and the logical layout of a hex keypad.

of switches rely on force induced magnetically rather then mechanically to close a pair of contacts. In this way, the contacts can be placed in a sealed enclosure for increased reliability. No matter what type of contact is used, the circuit may reopen and reclose several time with each key depression. This effect, known as *contact bounce,* can be avoided by not using the signal from the key directly but letting it set a flip-flop, whose output goes high with a key depression and stays high regardless of the length or severity of contact bounce. It is also possible to deal with the contact bounce effect through proper design of the software that handles data acquisition from the keyboard.

Regardless of the physical layout, the keys of a keyboard or keypad are often arranged into a square or rectangular 2D array from a logical standpoint. Each key is at the intersection of a row and a column circuit. Depressing a key causes electrical changes in row and column circuits associated with the key, thus allowing identification of the key that was depressed (Figure 21.3c). An encoder then converts the row and column identities into a unique symbol code (usually ASCII), or sequence of codes, to be transmitted to the computer. The physical layout of the keyboard and the ordering of keys are not relevant to the detection and encoding process.

To obtain the 4-bit output representing the depressed key on the hex keypad of Figure 21.3c, row signals are asserted in turn, perhaps using a 4-bit ring counter that follows the counting sequence 0001, 0010, 0100, and 1000. As a signal is asserted on a particular row, the column signals are noted. The 2-bit encoding of the row number attached to the 2-bit encoding of the column number supplies the 4-bit output. A 64-key keyboard may be logically arranged into an 8×8 array (even though the physical arrangement of the keys may be nonsquare). The 6-bit output code is then produced in a manner similar to the procedure for the hex keyboard. If the ASCII representation of the symbol is desired, a lookup table with 64 entries may be used.

Besides a keyboard, most desktop and laptop computers have pointing devices that allow the user to choose options from menus, select text and graphic objects for editing, and perform a variety of other operations. In fact, some keyboardless devices rely exclusively on pointing for control and data capture functions. The most commonly used pointing device is a *mouse,* so named

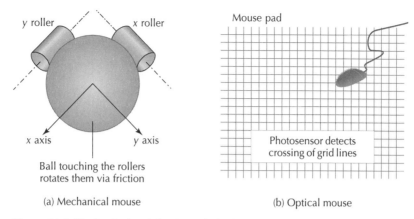

y roller   x roller

x axis   y axis

Ball touching the rollers
rotates them via friction

(a) Mechanical mouse

Mouse pad

Photosensor detects
crossing of grid lines

(b) Optical mouse

Figure 21.4 Mechanical and simple optical mice.

because of its shape in some early designs and the taillike wire connecting it to the computer. Modern mice come in a variety of shapes, and many of them use wireless links to the computer.

In a mechanical mouse, two counters are associated with the x and y rollers (Figure 21.4a). Lifting the mouse resets the counters to zero. When the mouse is dragged, the counters are incremented or decremented according to the direction of movement. The computer uses the counter values to determine the direction and extent of movement to be applied to the cursor. Optical mice are more accurate and less prone to failure due to dust and lint gathering on their parts. The simplest optical mice detect grid lines on a special mouse pad (Figure 21.4b). New, more advanced, versions use tiny digital cameras that allow them to detect motion on any surface.

A *touchpad* often replaces a mouse for laptop computer applications. The location of a finger touching the pad is sensed (via row and column circuits) and the cursor movement is determined according to how far, how fast, and in which direction the finger is moved. A *touchscreen* is similar, but instead of a separate pad, the surface of the display screen is used for pointing. Other pointing devices include the *trackball* (essentially an upside-down mechanical mouse whose large ball is manipulated by hand) and the *joystick,* which finds applications in many computer games as well as industrial control settings. Some laptop computers use a tiny joystick embedded in the keyboard for pointing.

Keyboards and pointing devices are nowadays quite intelligent and often have dedicated processors (microcontrollers) built in.

21.3 Visual Display Units

The visual display of symbols and images is the primary output method for most computers. Available options range from small, monochrome displays (of the types used on inexpensive cellular phones and calculators) to large, high-resolution, and rather expensive display devices aimed for use by graphic artists and professional publishers. Until recently, the *cathode ray tube* (CRT) was the main type of visual display device for desktop computers, with flat-panel displays reserved for use in laptops and other portable digital devices. It is widely anticipated that most of the bulky, heavy, and power-hungry CRTs will be gradually replaced by flat-panel display units, whose costs are becoming almost competitive and whose small footprints and much lower heat generation are important advantages in both office and home settings.

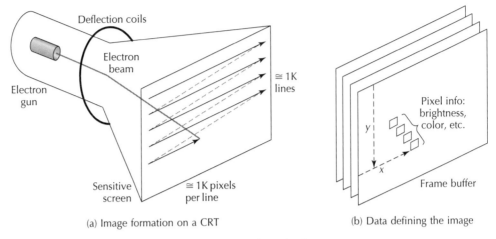

(a) Image formation on a CRT

(b) Data defining the image

Figure 21.5 CRT display unit and image storage in frame buffer.

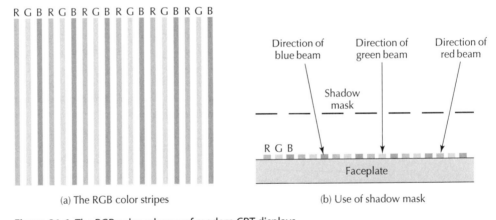

(a) The RGB color stripes

(b) Use of shadow mask

Figure 21.6 The RGB color scheme of modern CRT displays.

CRT displays work through an electron beam sweeping the surface of a sensitive screen, creating a dark or light pixel as it passes each point (Figure 21.5a). Early CRTs were *monochromic*. In such CRTs, the electron beam hits a phosphor layer on the back side of the display glass. This phosphor layer emits light because it is being hit by a stream of electrons traveling at a very high speed, with the intensity of the electron beam as it passes a given point determining the brightness level. To protect the phosphor layer from direct bombardment by electrons, an aluminum layer is placed behind it; this metallic layer also acts as an electrical contact. The technology of color CRTs went through several stages. The earliest attempts actually used a monochromic CRT that was viewed through rotating color filters while pixels associated with various colors were displayed in turn. Other designs included replacing the mechanical filters with electronically controlled ones and using multiple phosphor layers, each emitting light of a different color.

Modern CRTs in common use today are based on the tricolor "shadow-mask" method introduced for RCA television sets in the 1950s. Design details vary, but the scheme used in Sony's Trinitron tubes is representative. As shown in Figure 21.6, narrow stripes of phosphor producing three different colors of light are deposited on the backside of the tube's glass face. The three colors are typically red, green, and blue, giving rise to the name "RGB" for the resulting scheme. Three separate electron beams scan the display surface, each coming in at a slightly different angle. A shadow mask, which is essentially a metal plate with openings or holes, forces each beam to hit only phosphor stripes of a particular color. The separation of two consecutive stripes of the same color, known as the *display pitch,* dictates the resulting image resolution.

The three electron beams are controlled based on a representation of the desired image to be displayed. Every pixel is associated with 4 (simple 16-color image) to 32 bits of data in a *frame buffer*. If the display resolution is 1K × 1K pixels, say, and each pixel has 64K possible colors, then the frame buffer needs 2 MB of space. This space may be provided in a dedicated *video memory* or as part of the main memory address space (*shared memory*). Dedicated video memories are often dual-ported to allow simultaneous access by the CPU to modify the image and by the display driver to display it. Such video memories are sometime referred to as VRAM. Figure 21.5 depicts the sweeping motion of the electron beam, as it covers the entire surface of the sensitive screen 30–75 times per second (known as the *refresh rate*), and a frame buffer storing 4 bits of data per pixel. In practice, up to 32 bits of data are needed per pixel:

  32 bits, 8 bits each for R, G, B, A ("true color")

  16 bits, 5 bits each for R and B, 6 bits for G ("high color")

  8 bits or 256 different colors in VGA format

In the descriptions listed, "A" stands for "alpha" (a fourth component which is used to control color blending), and VGA is an old video graphics array format that is still supported for compatibility.

Example 21.1: Video memory throughput   Consider a display unit with a resolution of 1024 × 768 pixels and a refresh rate of 70 Hz. Compute the throughput required of the video memory to support this display, assuming 8, 16, or 32 bits of data per pixel.

Solution: The number of pixels accessed per second is $1024 \times 768 \times 70 \cong 55\text{M}$. This implies a throughput of 55 MB/s, 110 MB/s, or 220 MB/s, depending on the pixel data width. With 55M pixels accessed per second, around 18 ns is available for each pixel readout, even ignoring the wasted time due to left and right margins and the beam's flyback time. Therefore, if the desired data rates are to be achieved with typical VRAMs, multiple pixels must be read out with each access.

Physically, CRT displays are bulky, require high power, and generate a great deal of heat. Also, the image displayed by a CRT suffers from distortion as well as nonuniform focus and color. For these reasons, flat-panel liquid-crystal displays (LCDs) are gaining ground, especially in light of their continually improving image quality and rapidly declining cost. Figure 21.7a shows a *passive display* screen. Each intersection point between a row and column line represents a tiny optical shutter that is controlled by the difference between row and column voltages. Because the row voltage is given to every cell in a row and additionally cells receive cross talk voltage from other rows, contrast and resolution tend to be low. *Active displays* are similar, except that a tiny thin-film transistor is planted at each intersection. A transistor that is

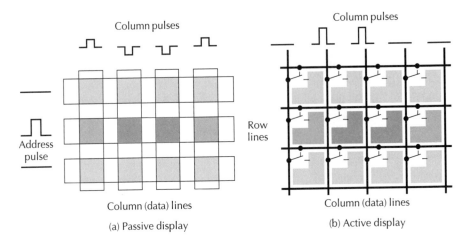

Figure 21.7 Passive and active LCD displays.

switched on allows the associated liquid crystal cells to be charged to the voltages on the column lines. In this way, an image that is "written" row by row is maintained until the next refresh cycle.

Other flat-panel display technologies include those based on light-emitting diodes (LEDs) and the plasma phenomenon. LED displays consist of arrays of LEDs of one or more colors, with each LED addressed via a row index and a column index. Electronic LEDs are particularly suitable for displays that must be viewed outdoors and thus require a high degree of brightness. A relatively recent development in LED displays is the emergence of organic LEDs (OLEDs), which require less power than ordinary LEDs and offer a range of colors, including white. The operation of plasma displays is quite similar to that of a neon lamp. They exploit the property of certain gas mixtures that break down into plasma when subjected to a sufficiently strong electric field. The plasma conducts electricity and also converts a part of the electrical energy into visible light. At present, plasma displays are quite expensive and thus have limited applications.

Many computers also provide output that is compatible with the television display format, allowing for any TV set to act as a display unit. The same TV-compatible signal can be supplied to a *video projector* that produces a replica of the image on the CRT or flat-panel display unit of the computer on a wall-size screen. These display technologies are helpful for computer-based presentations everywhere, from small boardrooms or classrooms to large lecture halls.

■ 21.4 Hard-Copy Input/Output Devices

Despite numerous predictions over the years that the paperless office, or perhaps a paperless society, will make hard-copy I/O devices obsolete, the need for such equipment remains. Paper documents, far from disappearing into oblivion, have proliferated with increased use of computers in business and home settings.

Hard-copy input is accepted through *scanners*. A scanner works like a CRT display unit, but in the reverse direction. Whereas a CRT display converts electronic signals into color and brightness levels in a sweeping motion, a scanner senses color and intensity and converts them

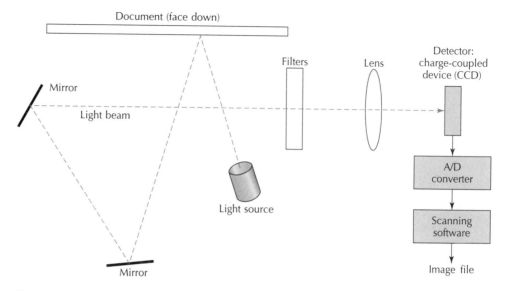

Figure 21.8 Scanning mechanism for hard-copy input.

to electronic signals as it sweeps an image line by line and point by point within each line (Figure 21.8). This information is then stored in memory in one of many standard formats. Scanners are characterized by spatial resolution, expressed in number of pixels or dots per inch (e.g., 1200 dpi), and color fidelity (number of colors). With regard to the type of document input into the scanner, such devices are divided into *sheet-feed, flatbed, overhead,* and *handheld* types. Flatbed scanners have the advantage of not causing damage to the original document due to curling and also allowing the scanning of book and periodical pages. Overhead and handheld scanners can scan large documents without becoming bulky or expensive. Inexpensive scanners now available are making the office fax machines more or less obsolete.

In the case of scanned text, the image may be converted to symbolic form through the use of *optical character recognition* (OCR) software and stored as a text file. This type of image to text conversion through scanning and OCR is commonly used for bringing older books and other documents on line. Handwriting recognition is also becoming increasingly important as applications of *personal digital assistants* (PDAs) and keyboardless *handheld computers* proliferate.

The development of modern printers is one the most awe-inspiring success stories in the computer industry. Early computer printers worked very much like old mechanical typewriters; they used character formation devices that were struck over a cloth or plastic ribbon by a hammerlike mechanism to imprint the characters on paper one by one (*character printers*). To increase the speed of such printers, special mechanisms were developed that allowed complete lines to be imprinted at once, leading to a wide variety of *line printers*. Gradually, line printers evolved from noisy and bulky (refrigerator-size) machines to smaller, quieter units. It was realized early on that forming characters by selecting a subset of dots in a 2D dot matrix (Figure 21.9) leads to greater flexibility in supporting arbitrary character sets as well as in image formation. Hence, *dot-matrix printers* gradually replaced a multitude of impact-type printer technologies.

Modern printers basically print a large dot-matrix image of the page which is composed from text and/or graphic files, via *postscript* or other intermediate printer file formats. Each dot in the page image is characterized by intensity and color. Relatively slow, inexpensive *ink-jet printers* (Figure 21.10a) print the dots one or a few at a time. Ink droplets are ejected from

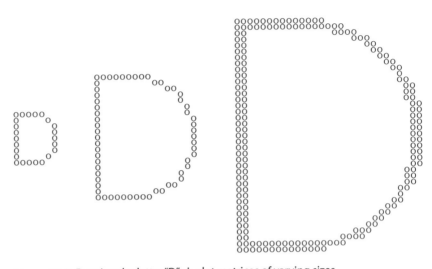

Figure 21.9 Forming the letter "D" via dot matrices of varying sizes.

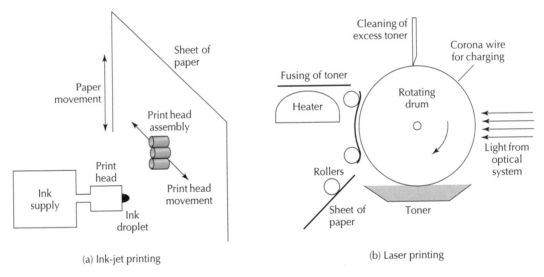

(a) Ink-jet printing   (b) Laser printing

Figure 21.10 Ink-jet and laser printers.

the print head by various mechanisms such as heating (which leads to the expansion of an air bubble inside the head) or shock wave generation via a piezoelectric crystal transducer in the side of the reservoir. Larger and faster *laser printers* (Figure 21.10b) form a copy of the image to be printed in the form of electric charge patterns on a rotating drum and print the entire page at high speed.

Like a scanner, a dot-matrix printer is characterized by its spatial resolution, expressed in number of pixels or dots per inch (e.g., 1200 dpi), and color fidelity (number of colors). Printing throughput, another key performance characteristic for computer printers, ranges from a few to several hundred pages per minute (ppm), sometimes varying even for the same printer depending on resolution and color requirements. Many older printers required special paper that was covered with chemicals and/or was packaged in rolls to simplify the paper feed mechanism. Modern printers use ordinary paper and are know as *plain-paper printers*.

Black-and-white printers deposit ink droplets or fuse toner particles on the paper according to the requirements of the document being printed. Gray levels are created by letting some of the underlying white paper show through. Color printers work quite similarly to color CRTs in that they create various colors from three colors. However, the three colors used in printers are cyan (blue-green), magenta, and yellow, together forming the CMY color scheme, which is certainly different from the CRT's RGB. The reasons for the difference have to do with the way color is perceived by the human eye. The CMY color scheme represents the absence of the RGB colors (cyan is the absence of red, and so on). So, cyan absorbs red, magenta absorbs green, and yellow absorbs blue. The RGB color scheme is additive, meaning that a desired color is created by adding the appropriate amount of each of the three primary colors. The CMY scheme, on the other hand, is subtractive, forming a desired color by removing the appropriate components from white light. Mixing these three colors in equal amounts would absorb all three primary colors, leaving black. However, the black thus produced is rather unsatisfactory, especially in view of the human eye's extreme sensitivity to any color shift in black. For this reason, most color printers use the CMYK scheme, where K stands for black.

Color printing is much more tricky than color display. Reasons include the difficulty in exactly controlling the size and alignment of the dots of various colors and the possibility of colors running if they are placed too close together. Further problems arise from reduced resolution when different intensity levels (gray scales in black and white) are to be supported. For example, one way of creating the illusion of 5 gray levels (0, 25, 50, 75, and 100%) is to divide the print area into 2×2 blocks of pixels, placing 0–4 black pixels in a block to create the five levels. This, however, reduces the resolution by a factor of 2 in each direction (fourfold overall).

Although modern printers can produce very high quality hard-copy output, specialized hard-copy output devices are also available for particular requirements. Examples include *plotters,* used for producing technical, architectural, and other drawings, typically on oversize paper, and *photo printers,* which differ from ordinary printers only in the quality of their print mechanisms and the types of paper that they accept.

The use of combination scanner/printer office machines is becoming quite common. Such machines can be provided with fax transmission and photocopying capabilities with little additional hardware. Fax machines scan documents into image files before transmission, so when scanning capability is present, the rest is easy. In fact, documents are increasingly being sent through scanning followed by transmission as attachment to e-mail, rather than via fax machines. Copying is essentially scanning followed by printing.

Example 21.2: Data throughput of a digital copier   Assuming a resolution of 1200 dpi, copying area of $8^{1}/_{2}$ inches $\times$ 11 inches, and 32-bit color in a digital copier that is composed of a scanner followed by a laser printer, derive the data throughput needed to support a copying throughput of 20 ppm (pages per minute).

Solution: The data rate for a third of a page to be printed per second is $8^{1}/_{2} \times 11 \times 1200^2 \times 4/3 \cong$ 180 MB/s. Assuming that the data from the scanner is stored in a memory and is then retrieved for printing, the data rate to be supported by the memory is 360 MB/s. This is well within the capabilities of modern DRAMs. However, it is possible to substantially reduce this rate by taking advantage of significant white space that exists on most documents (data compression).

■ 21.5 Other Input/Output Devices

Besides secondary and tertiary memories that constitute commonly used I/O devices for stable storage and data archiving (see Chapter 19), many other types of input and/or output units are available. The most important such options are reviewed in this section to complete our discussion of I/O devices.

A digital still or video camera captures images for input to a computer in much the same way as a scanner. Incoming light from outside the camera is converted to pixels and stored in flash memory or some other type of nonvolatile memory unit. Still digital cameras are characterized by their resolution in terms of the number of pixels in each image captured. A megapixel camera, for example, may have a resolution of 1280 × 960. Cameras with resolutions of 5 or more megapixels are quite expensive and usually not needed in run-of-the-mill applications, given that a 2-megapixel camera can deliver photo-quality 20 cm × 25 cm prints on an ink-jet printer. Digital cameras can use traditional optical zooms to bring objects closer; they can also have digital zooms, using software algorithms to zoom on a particular part of the digital image but in the process reducing the image quality. Some still digital cameras can take short movies of rather low resolution. Digital camcorders are capable of capturing high-quality videos, whereas Webcams are used to capture moving pictures for monitoring, videoconferencing, and similar applications in which the image quality and smoothness of motion are not critical. Photos and movies are stored in computers in a variety of standard formats, usually in compressed form to reduce the storage requirements. The most common examples include JPEG (due to the Joint Photographic Experts Group) and GIF (graphic interchange format), for images, and MPEG and Quick Time for movies.

Three-dimensional images can be captured for computer processing by means of volume scanners. One method is to project a laser line onto the 3D object to be scanned and capture the image of the line where it intersects the object via high-resolution cameras. The surface coordinates of the object are then computed from the captured images and information about the position and orientation of the scanning head.

Audio input is captured via microphones. Most desktop and laptop computers come with a microphone, or a stereo pair, and contain a sound card that can capture sound through a microphone port. For storage in a computer, sound is digitized by taking samples of the waveform at regular intervals. Sound fidelity is improved by increasing the sampling rate and by using more bits to represent each sample (say, 24 bits for professional results, instead of 16 bits). Because both these provisions lead to an increase in storage requirements, sound is often compressed before storage. Example standard formats for compressed audio include MP3 (short for MPEG-1, layer 3), Real Audio, Shockwave Audio, and the Microsoft Windows WAV format. MP3 compresses audio files to about 1 MB per minute and leads to CD-quality audio because in the course of compression it removes only sound components that are beyond the human hearing range. Besides the formats just mentioned, MPEG and Quick Time movie formats can be used to store sound by simply ignoring the video component.

Sensors are increasingly being used to provide information about the environment and other conditions of interest to computers. For example, there are scores of sensors in an automobile and many thousands in a modern industrial plant. Following is a partial list of commonly used sensors and their applications.

- Photocells constitute the simplest *light sensors* used to control night lights, street-lights, security systems, cameras, and even toys. A photocell incorporates a variable resistance that changes with light (from many thousands of ohms in the dark to about one kilohm in bright light), making it relatively easy to detect the amount of light via an analog-to-digital converter.

- Temperature sensors are of two types. A contact sensor measures its own temperature, thus deducing the temperature of an object with which it is in contact, assuming thermal equilibrium. Measurement is based on variation in material properties (such as electrical resistance) with temperature. Noncontact sensors measure the infrared or optical radiation they receive from an object.

- Pressure sensors convert the deformation or strain in materials to changes in some measurable electrical property. For example, the zigzag wire embedded in a plastic substrate in a *strain gauge* stretches owing to deformation, whereupon its resistance changes slightly. Microelectromechanical pressure sensors offer greater sensitivity and accuracy. Pressure sensors are used in pipelines, engine control, aircraft wings, and the like.

Innovations in sensor design are of immense current interest as a result of increasing demand in embedded control, security systems, and military applications. New technologies being pursued include microelectromechanical (MEM) sensors, particularly for pressure, and biosensors, which incorporate biological components, either in the mechanisms used for sensing or in the phenomena sensed. MEM sensors offer greater sensitivity and accuracy as well as small size. Biosensor advantages include low cost, greater sensitivity, and power economy. They are used in pollution control, bacterial analysis, medical diagnosis, and mining, to name a few applications.

Image output is produced by computers for rendering on various types of visual display devices (see Section 21.3) or printing/plotting on paper (see Section 21.4). Additionally, images can be transferred directly to microfilm for archival storage or projected on a screen for audiovisual presentations. The latter is typically done by connecting a video projector to a desktop or laptop computer's display output port or a special port that provides TV-format output. More exotic graphic outputs include stereo images for virtual reality applications and holographic images.

Audio output is produced from audio files, with the sound card converting possibly compressed stored files to appropriate electrical waveforms to be sent to one or more speakers. In addition to the audio file formats mentioned earlier in connection with audio input, sound output may be produced from much more compact MIDI (musical instrument digital interface) files. MIDI files contain not recorded audio but instructions for the sound card to produce particular notes for certain musical instruments. For this reason, MIDI files are typically 100 or more times smaller than comparable MP3 files, but have much lower fidelity. Speech synthesis is also an area of great interest because it allows a more natural user interface in many contexts. Speech synthesis can be done by means of putting together prerecorded fragments or via algorithmic text-to-speech conversion.

Increasingly, computers are used for direct control of a variety of mechanical devices. This is done by *actuators* that convert electronic signals to force and movement. *Stepper motors* (also called *step motors*) are the most commonly used components in this regard. A stepper motor is capable of small rotations upon receiving one or more control pulses. This rotation can then be converted to linear motion, if desired, or used directly to move cameras, robotic arms, and many other types of devices. Figure 21.11 shows the workings of a typical stepper motor. The rotor consists of magnets spaced 60° apart. The stator is divided into eight sections with 45° spacing. Assume that half the stator segments are magnetized as shown in Figure 21.11a. Now, if the remaining half of the stator segments are magnetized as in Figure 21.11b and the magnetizing current is removed from the first set, the rotor turns by 15° (the difference between the 60° spacing on the rotor and the 45° spacing on the stator).

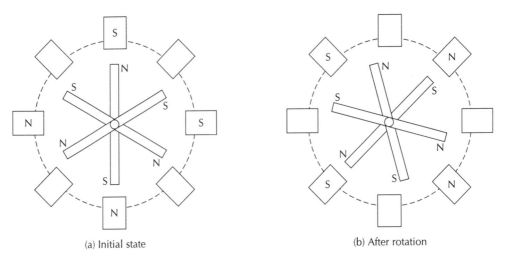

(a) Initial state   (b) After rotation

Figure 21.11 Stepper motor principles of operation.

There is some hope that eventually devices with no mechanical parts will allow the construction of smaller, lighter, more robust, and lower-power movement generators. Musclelike *electroactive polymers* that expand and contract in response to electrical stimulation constitute one potentially useful technology currently being pursued [BarC01].

■ 21.6 Networking of Input/Output Devices

Increasingly, input and output involve file transfers over a network. For example, sending a print document to a printer that has a large data buffer and a CPU is not much different from sending a file to another computer. Network-based peripheral devices allow for sharing of unusual or rarely used resources and also provide backup options in the event of failure or overload of a local resource (Figure 21.12). In an office setting, for example, a workgroup may share an expensive color laser printer, with another printer, perhaps located in a different department, designated as a backup in case of breakdown. Networked I/O also provides flexibility in placement of I/O devices according to dynamically changing needs and allows for simple upgrading or replacement, while reducing wiring and connectivity problems. Furthermore, given the universality of network communication standards, such as IP and Ethernet (see Section 23.1), networked I/O improves compatibility and facilitates interoperability.

Nowhere are the benefits of networked I/O more evident than in industrial process control. In such systems, scores to hundreds, perhaps thousands, of sensors, actuators, and controllers must interact with a central computer or with nodes of a distributed platform. Using a network with a tree or loop topology, in lieu of point-to-point connections, leads to significant reduction in wiring, with an attendant reduction in operation and maintenance costs. The same network can be used for data exchange, diagnostics, configuration, and calibration, leading to further cost savings. Clearly, even such a reduced level of wiring can be avoided if wireless networking is used.

In the foregoing context, input/output is thoroughly mixed with processing and control functions, with the boundaries between the various functions becoming quite fuzzy. A sensor with a built-in processor and network adapter, perhaps integrated on a single chip using MEM and other technologies, can be viewed as an input device or as a node in a distributed processing system (see Section 28.4). It is an input device in the sense that its main function and ultimate goal is to

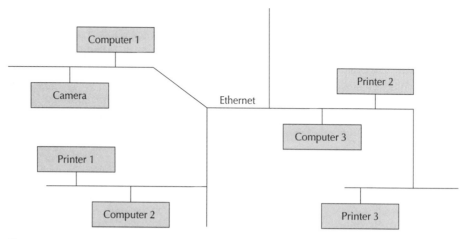

Figure 21.12 With network-enabled peripherals, I/O is done via file transfers.

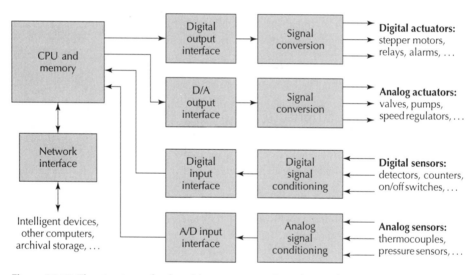

Figure 21.13 The structure of a closed-loop, computer-based control system.

supply information about its environment to a control process or algorithm. It is a node in the sense of being capable of cooperating with other nodes, running self-diagnostics, performing self- or mutual calibration, and carrying out various functions related to data collection traditionally relegated to a central processor. The latter include tasks related to reliable and accurate operation: filtering of noise, transmission retry, adaptation to changes in the environment, and so on.

Figure 21.13 shows the structure of a closed-loop, computer-based control system with specialized interfaces to handle sensors and actuators of various types. With network-enabled devices, most of these disappear or are incorporated in the sensor/actuator subsystem. Everything goes to the controlling computer via the network interface, thus simplifying its task immensely. The designer of the software for such a computer-based control system can then focus on the relevant algorithmic and performance requirements, rather than on the specific interface needs of each device type.

PROBLEMS

21.1 Keyboards and their switches

a. The mechanical switches depicted in Figure 21.3a appear to require a great deal of vertical movement to close the electrical contact. If you examine the keyboard on a modern ultrathin notebook computer, you will note that the keys move very little. Investigate the design of such small-movement switches.

b. Some keyboards are advertised as "spill-proof." What are the implications of this property on the design of switches and other parts of a keyboard?

c. List two other physical properties of a keyboard that you consider important to a user.

d. List two negative properties of a keyboard that would lead to user dissatisfaction or rejection.

21.2 Keyboard encoding

Design an encoder for the keypad of Figure 21.3c, assuming that the output should be:

a. A 4-bit hex digit

b. An 8-bit ASCII character representing the hex digit

21.3 Keyboard encoding

a. The discussion of keyboard encoding in Section 21.2 tacitly assumed that at most one key is depressed at any given time. Most keyboards support double key depressions (e.g., one ordinary key, plus one of the special keys "shift," "alt," or "control") to allow a larger set of symbols. Speculate on how encoding is accomplished in this case.

b. On Windows-based machines, at least one triple key depression ("Alt" + "Control" + "Delete") is also supported. Can you think of a good reason for including this feature, which certainly complicates the encoding process?

c. In the provisions of parts a and b, multiple key depressions lead to the transmission of one symbol from the keyboard to the computer. The opposite may also be true for some keyboards: multiple symbols sent as a result of a single key depression. Why is this feature useful? Describe one way for realizing the required encoder.

21.4 Pointing devices

The following experiment is performed on the 5×6 cm^2 touchpad of a laptop computer. The cursor is moved to the upper left corner of the 21×28 cm^2 screen. A finger is placed on the upper left corner of the touchpad and dragged quickly to the lower right corner of the pad. The new cursor position is near the lower right corner of the screen. Now, the finger is moved in the opposite direction along the same diagonal path, but much more slowly. When the finger gets to the upper left corner of the touchpad, the cursor is close to the center of the screen. What does this experiment tell you about how position data from the touchpad is processed? Justify your conclusions and discuss their practical implications.

21.5 Video memory throughput

In Example 21.1 the data rate was derived with the assumption that all pixels in the frame buffer must be updated in every frame.

a. List three applications in which typically only a very small fraction of the pixels change from one frame to the next.

b. Describe a way of sending data to the frame buffer that allows selective updating of the pixels or small windows within the display area.

c. Discuss the overhead due to the selective transmission of part b, both in terms of extra bits sent (besides the actual pixel data) and additional processing time needed to extract the pixel data.

21.6 Scoreboard displays

Some monochrome scoreboard displays are built from 2D arrays of bright lightbulbs that can be turned on or off under programmed control.

a. Describe how a 100×250 scoreboard of this type might be controlled by means of 16 data signals coming from a microcontroller.

b. Discuss the pros and cons of two ways of arranging the lightbulbs on the scoreboard: the jth light bulb in row $2i + 1$ vertically aligned with the jth lightbulb in row $2i$ versus aligning it with the midpoint between the jth and $(j + 1)$th lightbulb in row $2i$.

c. Is it feasible to build a color scoreboard of this type?

21.7 Adjustable resolution in monitors

The designs and methods described for CRT and flat-panel monitors in Section 21.3 suggest fixed pixel spacings. Yet, on a typical personal computer, the user can set the resolution (number of pixels on the screen) via a system utility program. How are these variations actually implemented? In other words, the shadow-mask openings in Figure 21.6b or the row and column lines in Figure 21.7 do not change. So, what does change when one varies the resolution?

21.8 Scanner

Specifications for a scanner indicate that it has a resolution of 600 dpi in the *x* direction and 1200 dpi in the *y* direction.

a. Why do you think that the resolutions are different in the two directions?
b. What type of software processing would allow us to print an image captured by this scanner on a 1200 dpi printer?
c. Repeat part b for a 600 dpi printer.

21.9 Data throughput in a copier

A typical office memo, book page, or other document that is copied contains mostly white space.

a. Discuss how this information can be used to reduce the required data rate for a copier, as derived in Example 21.1.
b. Can similar savings in data rate or storage space be achieved when a page (e.g., a magazine page with black background and white font) includes no white space at all?

21.10 Printer technologies

Based on research that you do on ink-jet and laser printers, compare and contrast the two technologies with respect to the following attributes.

a. Output quality in terms of resolution and contrast
b. Output quality in terms of durability (lack of fading with time)
c. Printing latency and throughput
d. Cost of ink or toner per printed page

e. Total cost of ownership per printed page
f. Ease of use, including physical dimensions, noise, and heat generation

21.11 Drum printers

One particular type of line printer used many years ago was the drum printer. A large metal drum rotated at high speed next to a paper path. The drum had as many stripes as there were characters on a line; say, 132. On each stripe, letters and symbols of interest appeared in a raised form. There were also 132 hammers aligned along the length of the drum. Each hammer was individually controlled and would strike on a ribbon just as the desired character for that position was passing underneath.

a. Why would such a printer tend to smear the characters?
b. How does the printing speed of a drum printer relate to disk memory access latency? In particular, make comparisons with head-per-track and multiple-head disks.
c. Analyze the worst-case and average-case latencies for printing one line.

21.12 Detection and measurement via photocells

One application of photocells in factories is in the classification of objects moving on a conveyor belt. Assuming that objects are not stacked, and do not overlap in length, on the conveyor belt:

a. Specify how a single photocell might be used to classify objects by length. State all your assumptions clearly.
b. Propose a scheme for classifying fixed-height objects by their heights.
c. Repeat part b, but this time assume that the height may vary along the object.
d. Propose a scheme for classifying objects into cubes, spheres, and pyramids.

21.13 Stepper motors

A stepper motor rotates 15° for each control pulse received. Specify the types of mechanism that would be needed if we were to use this stepper motor to control the lateral movement of the print head for a 600 dpi ink-jet printer. Note that the required mechanisms must convert the rotational movement of the stepper motor to linear motion with a much finer granularity.

21.14 Primitive input devices

Toggle switches and jumpers constitute primitive input mechanisms for devices that do not have a keyboard or other input device. A toggle switch can set one input bit to 0 or 1. A jumper does the same by connecting the input to a constant voltage representing 0 or 1. They are typically used when a few bits of input data are needed and the input changes very infrequently.

a. Identify two applications in which such input devices might be used.
b. Compare toggle switches and jumpers with regard to ease of use and flexibility.
c. Describe how 8 toggle switches and a pushbutton might provide a way of inputting more than 8 bits of data.

21.15 Special input devices

Research the following issues regarding special input devices and write a two-page report on each one.

a. Why the numbers printed at the bottom of most bank checks (including bank ID number and account number) have rather unusual shapes.

b. How the universal product code (UPC), found on most products, encodes data and how it is read by a scanner at the checkout counter.
c. How 80-column punched cards (also known as Hollerith cards) encoded data and how their storage density, in bits per cubic centimeter, compared with today's disk and other types of memory.
d. How credit-card readers, found in many retail stores and also on bank ATMs and many fuel pumps in gas stations, work.
e. How handwritten text, entered via a stylus, is sensed and accepted in PDAs or tablet PCs.
f. How wireless keyboards, mice, and remote control pads (for changing slides in a presentation) communicate with the computer.

21.16 Special output devices

Research the following issues regarding special output devices and write a two-page report on each one.

a. How Braille output is produced for blind users
b. How small printers, typically attached to printing calculators, are different from ordinary ink-jet or laser printers
c. How a rear-projection display device works
d. How line-segment displays (e.g., the seven-segment LED displays for numerals) work and why they are no longer in widespread use

REFERENCES AND FURTHER READINGS

[BarC01]   Bar-Cohen, Y., *Electroactive Polymer (EAP) Actuators as Artificial Muscles: Reality, Potential, and Challenges,* SPIE Monograph, Vol. PM98, 2001.

[Clem00]   Clements, A., *The Principles of Computer Hardware,* Oxford University Press, 2000.

[Howa92]   Howard, W. E., "Thin-Film-Transistor/Liquid Crystal Display Technology: An Introduction," *IBM J. Research and Development,* Vol. 36, No. 1, pp. 3–10, January 1992.

[Mint98]   Mintchell, G. A., "Networked I/O Strategies Connect," *Control Engineering International,* November 1988.
             www.manufacturing.net/ctl/index.asp

[Myer02]   Myers, R. L., *Display Interfaces: Fundamentals and Standards,* Wiley, 2002.

CHAPTER 22

INPUT/OUTPUT PROGRAMMING

"What we anticipate seldom occurs; what we least expect generally happens."
Benjamin Disraeli

"I was provided with additional input that was radically different from the truth. I assisted in furthering that version."
Colonel Oliver North, from his Iran-Contra testimony

Input and output, like any other activity within a computer, are controlled by the execution of certain instructions within a program. Whereas early computers had special I/O instructions, modern machines treat I/O devices as occupying part of the memory address space (memory-mapped I/O). Hence, data input is done by reading agreed-upon memory locations that are assigned to specific input devices. Similarly, output is accomplished by writing into agreed-upon memory locations. In this chapter, after showing pertinent details of I/O addressing thorough examples, we review the complementary schemes of polling and interrupts for synchronizing I/O with the rest of a program's actions. We also discuss I/O performance and how it can be improved.

■ 22.1 I/O Performance and Benchmarks

In addition to the obvious reasons of loading program text and data in memory and recording of computation results in hard-copy or other formats, input/output may be performed for a variety of other reasons. Examples include the following:

Data gathering from sensor networks

Actuating robotic arms or other assemblies in plants

Querying or updating databases

Backing up data sets or documents

Checkpointing to avoid restart in the event of a crash

With CPU performance improving rapidly over the past couple of decades, and projected to continue at the same pace in the near future, I/O performance has taken center stage. As with the "memory wall," discussed in Section 17.3, modern computers are experiencing an "I/O wall" that reduces, and at time completely nullifies, the benefits of improved CPU performance.

> **Example 22.1: The input/output wall**   An industrial control application spent 90% of its time on CPU operations and 10% on I/O when it was originally developed in the early 1980s. Since then, the CPU component of the system has been replaced with a newer model every 5 years, but the I/O components have remained the same. Assuming that the CPU performance increased by a factor of 10 with each upgrade, derive the fraction of time spent on I/O over the life of the system.
>
> **Solution:** This requires the application of Amdahl's law, with 90% of the task speeded up by factors of 10, 100, 1000, and 10,000 over a 20-year period. The CPU upgrades have successively reduced the original running time of 1 to $0.1 + 0.9/10 = 0.19$, 0.109, 0.1009, and 0.10009, making the fraction of time spent on input/output operations $100 \times (0.1/0.19) =$ 52.6, 91.7, 99.1, and 99.9%, respectively. We note that the last couple of CPU upgrades did not accomplish much in terms of improved performance.

Unlike CPU performance, which can be modeled or estimated based on application and system characteristics (e.g., instruction mix, cache miss rate, etc.), I/O performance is fairly hard to predict. This is in no small part due to the many different elements involved in I/O operations: from the operating system and device drivers through various buses and I/O controllers to the I/O devices themselves. Interactions of all these elements, and their contention in using shared resources such as memory, add to the difficulty in modeling, even when each individual element (bus, memory, disk) can be modeled fairly accurately.

Input/output performance is variously measured, depending on application requirements. *I/O access latency* is the time overhead for a single I/O operation, which is important for small I/O transactions of the type found in banking or e-commerce. *I/O data rate,* often expressed in megabytes per second, is relevant to the large data transfers typically of interest in supercomputing applications. *I/O data transfer time* is related to the transfer block size and data rate. *Response time* is the sum of access latency and data transfer time; its inverse yields the number of I/O operations per unit time (*I/O throughput*). I/O response time and throughput can often be traded against each other. For example, out-of-order processing of disk accesses makes the latency quite variable, increasing it in many cases, but may improve throughput significantly.

Commensurate with the varying characteristics of I/O in different application areas, there are three types of I/O benchmark:

1. Supercomputer I/O benchmarks focus on reading large volumes of input data, writing many snapshots for checkpointing of lengthy computations, and saving a relatively small set of output results at the end. The key parameter here is I/O data throughput,

expressed in megabytes per second. I/O latency is less important, as long as high throughput can be maintained.

2. Transaction processing I/O benchmarks typically deal with a huge database, but each transaction is fairly small, involving a handful of disk accesses (say, 2–10), with a few thousand instructions executed per disk access. Accordingly, the important parameter in such benchmarks is the I/O rate, expressed in number of disk accesses per second.

3. File system I/O benchmarks focus on file accesses (read and write operations), file creation, directory management, indexing, and restructuring. Given the varying characteristics of files and file accesses in different applications, such benchmarks are often specialized to a particular application domain (say, scientific computation).

Each of these categories can be further refined. For example, transaction processing encompasses a spectrum of application domains, from simple Web interactions to complex queries involving a great deal of processing. As with CPU benchmarks, discussed in Section 4.4, a mixture of characteristics can be incorporated into a synthetic or real I/O benchmark to assess a system for multidomain or general-purpose use.

22.2 Input/Output Addressing

In memory-mapped I/O, each input or output device has one or more hardware registers that can be read from, or written into, as if they were memory locations. Thus, special I/O instructions are not needed and one can use load and store instructions to effect I/O. We consider keyboard input and display output in MiniMIPS as examples.

As shown in Figure 22.1, the keyboard unit in MiniMIPS has a pair of memory locations associated with a 32-bit control register (address 0xffff0000) and a 32-bit data register (0xffff0004). The control register holds various status bits conveying information about device status and data transmission modes. Two bits in the control register that are relevant to our discussion here are the "device ready" indicator R and the "interrupt enable" flag IE in bit positions 0 and 1, respectively (the use of R will be discussed shortly; IE will be needed in Chapter 24). The data register can hold an ASCII symbol in its rightmost byte.

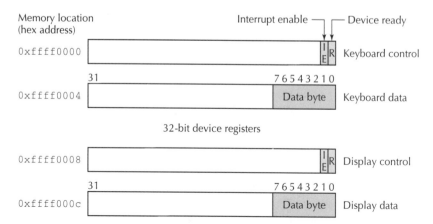

Figure 22.1 Control and data registers for keyboard and display unit in MiniMIPS.

When a key is depressed on the keyboard, the internal keyboard logic determines which symbol is to be sent to the computer and places this symbol in the lowest byte of the keyboard data register, asserting the R bit to indicate that a symbol is ready for transmission. If our program loads the keyboard control word from memory location 0xffff0000 into some register, it will learn, by examining bit 0, that the keyboard has a symbol to transmit. The program can then load the content of location 0xffff0004 into a register to find out which symbol is held in the keyboard data register. Reading out the keyboard data register causes R to be automatically deasserted. Note that R is a read-only bit in the sense that if the processor writes something into the keyboard control register, the state of R will not change.

Example 22.2: Data input from keyboard   Write a sequence of MiniMIPS assembly language instructions to make the program wait until the keyboard has a symbol to transmit and then read the symbol into register $v0.

Solution: The program must continually examine the keyboard control register to find out if the R bit has been asserted. Eventually, when the R bit is found to be asserted, program idling (also knows as busy wait) ends and the symbol in keyboard data register is loaded into $v0.

```
        lui   $t0, 0xffff        # put 0xffff0000 in $t0
idle:   lw    $t1, 0($t0)        # get keyboard's control word
        andi  $t1, $t1, 0x0001   # isolate the LSB (R bit)
        beq   $t1, $zero, idle   # if not ready (R = 0), wait
        lw    $v0, 4($t0)        # retrieve data word from keyboard
```

This type of input is appropriate only if the computer is waiting for some critical input and cannot do anything useful in the absence of this input.

Similarly, the display unit in MiniMIPS has a pair of memory locations associated with its 32-bit control register (location 0xffff0008) and data register (0xffff000c), as shown in Figure 22.1. The display control register is quite similar to that of the keyboard, except that the R bit indicates that the display unit is ready to accept a new symbol in its data register. When a symbol is copied into this data register, R is automatically deasserted. If our program loads the display control word from memory location 0xffff0008 into some register, it will learn, by examining bit 0, that the display unit is ready to accept a symbol. The program can then store the content of a register into location 0xffff000c, thereby sending a symbol to the display unit.

Example 22.3: Data output to display unit   Write a sequence of MiniMIPS assembly language instructions to make the program wait until the display unit is ready to accept a new symbol and then write the symbol from register $a0 to the display unit's data register.

Solution: The program must continually examine the display unit's control register to find out if the R bit has been asserted. Eventually, when the R bit is found to be asserted, the symbol in register $a0 is copied into the display unit's data register.

```
        lui   $t0, 0xffff      # put 0xffff0000 in $t0
idle:   lw    $t1, 8($t0)      # get display's control word
        andi  $t1, $t1, 0x0001 # isolate the LSB (R bit)
        beq   $t1, $zero, idle # if not ready (R = 0), wait
        sw    $a0, 12($t0)     # supply data word to display unit
```

This type of output is appropriate only if we can afford to have the CPU dedicated to data transmission to the display unit.

The hardware provided within each I/O device controller to allow this type of addressing is quite simple. As shown in Figure 22.2, the device controller is connected to the memory bus. The memory address observed on the bus is continually compared against the device's own address stored in an internal register. If this device address is in a read-only register, the device has a *hard* (unchangeable) *address;* otherwise, the device has a *soft* (modifiable) *address*. When a matching address is detected, the content of the status or data register is placed on (read), or loaded from (write), the bus data lines.

Note that the notions discussed in this section are required only if it becomes necessary to write device drivers for general-purpose computers or to perform I/O operations in an application-specific embedded system environment. Most users are shielded from such details because their I/O operations are performed at a fairly high level via calls to the operating system. For example, in the SPIM simulator for MiniMIPS, the user or compiler simply places an appropriate code in register $v0 (and perhaps one or more other parameters in certain agreed-upon registers) and then executes a system call (syscall) instruction. For details, refer to Section 7.6, particularly Table 7.2.

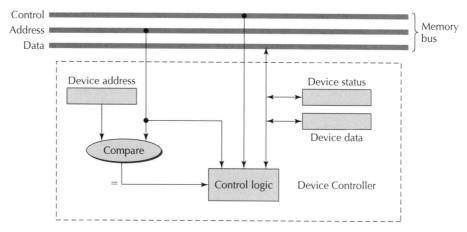

Figure 22.2 Addressing logic for an I/O device controller.

◼ 22.3 Scheduled I/O: Polling

Examples 22.2 and 22.3 represent instances of polled I/O: the processor initiates the I/O by asking the device if it is ready to send/receive data. With each interaction, a single unit of data is transferred. If the device is not ready, the processor need not wait in a busy loop; rather, it might perform other tasks and check back later with the device. No problem arises as long as the processor checks the I/O device frequently enough to ensure that no data is lost.

Example 22.4: Input via polling a keyboard   A keyboard must be interrogated at least 10 times per second to make sure that no keystroke by the user is missed. Assume that each such interrogation and associated data transfer takes 800 clock cycles in a processor with a 1 GHz clock. What fraction of the CPU time is spent on polling the keyboard?

Solution: The fraction of CPU time spent polling the keyboard is obtained by dividing the number of cycles needed for 10 interrogations by the total number of cycles available in a second:

$$(10 \times 800)/10^9 \cong 0.001\%$$

Note that the polling rate of 10 times per second, or 600 times per minute, has been chosen to be higher than the speed of even the fastest typist, so there is no chance of missing a character that is entered, and then overwritten, in the keyboard data buffer.

We see from Example 22.4 that the keyboard is such a slow input device that the processor can easily keep up with it. After each polling of the keyboard, the processor has some $10^9/10 - 800 \cong 10^8$ clock cycles (0.1 s) to attend to other tasks before it has to poll the keyboard again. The next two examples show that other I/O devices are more demanding in this respect.

Example 22.5: Input via polling a floppy disk drive   A floppy disk drive sends or receives data 4 bytes at a time and has a data rate of 50 KB/s. To make sure old data is not overwritten by new data in the device buffer during an input operation, the processor must sample the buffer at the rate of $50K/4 = 12.5K$ times per second. Assume that each such interrogation and associated data transfer takes 800 clock cycles in a processor with a 1 GHz clock. What fraction of the CPU time is spent on polling the floppy disk drive?

Solution: The fraction of CPU time spent polling the floppy disk drive is obtained by dividing the number of cycles needed for 12.5K interrogations by the total number of cycles available in a second:

$$(12.5K \times 800)/10^9 = 1\%$$

Note that the overhead in CPU time for polling the floppy disk drive is 1000 times that of polling the keyboard in Example 22.4.

Example 22.6: Input via polling a hard disk drive   A hard disk drive transfers data 4 bytes at a time and has a peak data rate of 3 MB/s. To make sure old data is not overwritten by new data in the device buffer during an input operation, the processor must sample the buffer at the rate of 3M/4 = 750K times per second. Assume that each such interrogation and associated data transfer takes 800 clock cycles in a processor with a 1 GHz clock. What fraction of the CPU time is spent on polling the hard disk drive?

Solution: The fraction of CPU time spent polling the hard disk drive is obtained by dividing the number of cycles needed for 750K interrogations by the total number of cycles available in a second:

$$(750\text{K} \times 800)/10^9 = 60\%$$

A single I/O device occupying 60% of CPU's time is clearly unacceptable.

Note that the hard disk of Example 22.6 keeps the CPU almost fully occupied: between two consecutive interrogations, the CPU only has $10^9/750{,}000 - 800 \cong 533$ clock cycles (0.5 μs) to attend to other tasks. This may not be enough to perform much useful work. The floppy drive of Example 22.4 is intermediate between the very slow keyboard and the very fast hard disk drive. It leaves the CPU with $10^9/12{,}500 - 800 = 79{,}200$ clock cycles (79 μs) of available time between consecutive interrogations.

22.4 Demand-Based I/O: Interrupts

A great deal of CPU time is wasted in polling when the device is completely inactive or is not yet ready to send or receive data. Even slow devices may cause unacceptable overhead when there are many such devices that must be continually polled. Clearly, polling hundreds or thousands of sensors and actuators in an industrial control setting can be quite wasteful. A temperature sensor, for example, need not send data to the computer unless there is a change that exceeds a predefined threshold or unless some critical temperature is reached. In interrupt-driven I/O, it is the device that initiates the I/O by sending an interrupt signal to the CPU. When an interrupt signal is received by the CPU, it transfers control to a special interrupt routine that determines the cause of the interrupt and initiates appropriate action.

Example 22.7: Interrupt-based input from a hard disk drive   Consider the same disk as in Example 22.6 (transferring 4 B chunks of data at 3 MB/s when it is active) and assume that the disk is active about 5% of the time. The overhead of interrupting the CPU and performing the transfer is about 1200 clock cycles of a 1 GHz processor. What fraction of the CPU time is spent on attending to the hard disk drive?

Solution: We know from Example 22.6 that 750K interrupts will occur in each second when the disk drive is active, given the disk's data rate and transmission of data in 4 B chunks. The fraction of CPU time spent on interrupts from the hard disk is obtained by dividing the number of cycles needed for servicing the expected number of interrupts per second by the total number of cycles available in a second:

$$0.05 \times (750\text{K} \times 1200)/10^9 = 4.5\%$$

So even though the overhead for interrupt-driven I/O is higher when the disk is active, since in fact the disk is usually inactive, the overall CPU time spent on I/O is much less.

Interrupts are controlled by status bits on the device (requester) side and on the CPU (service provider) side. The "interrupt enable" (IE) bit in the control registers of Figure 22.1 tells the device that it should send an interrupt signal to the CPU when the "device ready" bit R is asserted. The CPU side has a corresponding flag that indicates whether interrupts from the keyboard, display unit, or other devices are to be accepted. If interrupts are enabled, the interrupt signal is acknowledged and a protocol is entered that eventually leads to data being accepted from, or sent to, the requesting device. Interrupts that are not enabled are said to be *masked*. Interrupts are usually masked or disabled only for short periods of time when the CPU must attend to critical functions without being interrupted.

Upon detecting an interrupt signal, provided the particular interrupt or interrupt class is not masked, the CPU acknowledges the interrupt (so that the device can deassert its request signal) and begins executing an interrupt service routine. The following steps are followed to service an interrupt request.

1. Save the CPU state and call the interrupt service routine.
2. Disable all interrupts.
3. Save minimal information about the interrupt on the stack.
4. Enable interrupts (or at least higher-priority ones).
5. Identify cause of interrupt and attend to the underlying request.
6. Restore CPU state to what existed before the last interrupt.
7. Return from interrupt service routine.

The overhead of each interrupt request is greater than that of polling because the steps required for the latter correspond to a part of step 5; the other steps, or identifying the cause of interrupt in step 5, are not needed with polling. Note that interrupts are enabled in step 5 before the handling of the current interrupt is completed. This is because disabling interrupts for extended periods of time may lead to loss of data or inefficiencies in input/output. For example, a disk read/write head may pass the desired sector while interrupts are disabled, forcing at least one extra revolution, with its attendant latency. The capability to handle *nested interrupts* is important in dealing with multiple high-speed I/O devices or time-sensitive control applications. Interrupts will be discussed in greater detail in Chapter 24.

22.5 I/O Data Transfer and DMA

Note that if data were transferred between main memory and the I/O device in larger chunks, instead of units of 1–4 bytes assumed in Examples 22.4 to 22.7, the overhead of interrupts would be reduced and less of CPU time would be wasted. The ultimate in this direction is to let the CPU start an I/O operation (on its own initiative or upon receiving an interrupt) and let

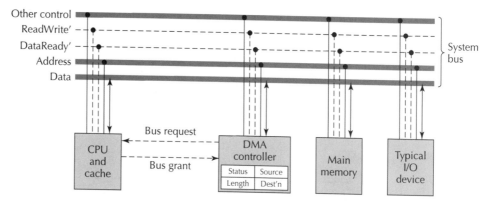

Figure 22.3 DMA controller shares the system or memory bus with the CPU.

an intelligent I/O controller do the work of copying the data from an input device to memory or from memory to an output device. This approach is known as DMA (direct memory access) input/output.

A DMA controller is essentially a simple processor that can acquire the control of the memory bus from the CPU and then act just as the CPU would in controlling data transfers between I/O devices and memory. The CPU interacts with the DMA controller much as it does with an I/O device, except that only control information is exchanged. Like the device controller of Figure 22.2, the DMA controller has a status register that is used to communicate control information with the CPU. Three other registers replace the device data register of Figure 22.2:

1. Source-address register, where the CPU places an address for the data source
2. Destination-address register, which holds the destination for the data transfer
3. Length register, where the CPU places the number of data words to be transferred

Figure 22.3 depicts the relationship of the DMA controller with the CPU, memory, and device controllers, assuming the use of a single system bus for memory accesses and I/O. In practice, most I/O devices are connected to separate buses that are linked to the memory bus through adapters or bridges (see Figure 21.2). However, in our discussion of DMA, we proceed with the assumption of a single system bus, as in Figure 21.1.

Based on information placed by the CPU in various registers of a DMA controller, the latter can take over and perform the steps of a prescribed data transfer from an input device to memory or from memory to an output device in much the same way that the CPU would do. Note that the use of DMA is compatible with both memory-mapped I/O and special I/O instructions. In fact, the memory and I/O devices cannot tell whether the CPU or the DMA controller is controlling the bus transactions, given that in either case, exactly the same bus protocol is followed.

Normally, the CPU is in charge of the memory bus and assumes that the bus is available for its use at any time. Therefore, before the DMA controller can use the bus, it asserts a *bus request* signal that informs the CPU of its intention. The bus control circuitry in the CPU notice this request, and when convenient for the CPU, assert a *bus grant* signal. The DMA controller can now take charge of the bus and perform the required data transfer. When the data transfer has been completed, the DMA controller deasserts the bus request signal and the CPU, in turn, deasserts the bus grant signal, bringing the bus back under its control (Figure 22.4a). Hence, both the bus request and bus grant signals remain asserted during the DMA controller's use of the bus.

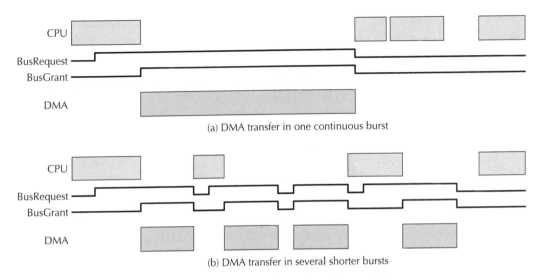

(a) DMA transfer in one continuous burst

(b) DMA transfer in several shorter bursts

Figure 22.4 DMA operation and the associated transfers of bus control.

During a DMA transfer, the CPU can continue to execute instructions as long as doing so does not involve data transfer over the memory bus. This is quite feasible with modern CPUs, given the high hit rate in the cache (or combined L1 and L2 caches) typically integrated on the same chip as the CPU. If, because of cache miss or some other event, the CPU needs to use the memory bus before DMA transfer has been completed, it must wait until the DMA controller releases the bus (Figure 22.4a).

To prevent the CPU from idling for too long, thus leading to significant performance degradation, most DMA controllers are designed to be capable of breaking up a long I/O data transfer into several shorter transfers involving a few words. Once such a DMA controller has acquired the bus, it transfers a preset number of words before relinquishing the bus. After a short delay, the DMA controller requests the bus again for the next stage of its data transfer. In the meantime, the CPU regains control of the bus and can use it to fetch memory words that would allow it to continue its operation. This type of block or cyclic DMA data transfer is depicted in Figure 22.4b.

Example 22.8: DMA-based input from a hard disk drive Consider the hard disk drive of Examples 22.6 and 22.7 (with peak data rate of 3 MB/s during 5% of the time when it is active). The disk has 512 B sectors and rotates at 3600 rpm. Ignore gaps and other overhead in storing data on disk tracks. How does DMA transfer compare, in terms of time overhead for the 1 GHz CPU, with polling and interrupt-based I/O of Examples 22.6 and 22.7? Assume that 800 clock cycles are needed for setting up a DMA data transfer and 1200 clock cycles for handling the interrupt generated at completion and that each data transfer involves (a) one sector, or (b) an entire track.

Solution: The disk track capacity can be obtained from the disk data rate and its rotation speed: $(3 \text{ MB/s})/(60 \text{ revolutions/s}) = 0.05 \text{ MB/revolution}$, or a track capacity of 50 KB = 100 sectors.

The CPU spends $800 + 1200 = 2000$ clock cycles, or 2 μs, to set up and process the termination of each data transfer. Let us first consider sector data transfers. If the disk actively transfers data 5% of the time, it must be reading 0.05×3 MB/s $= 150$ KB/s $= 300$ sectors/s. The time overhead for the CPU is therefore 2 μs $\times 300 = 0.6$ ms (0.06%). This compares quite favorably with the overheads of polling (60%) and CPU-controlled word-by-word transfers (4.5%) derived in Examples 22.6 and 22.7. If entire tracks are transferred, and the disk activity remains at 5%, there must be a factor of 100 fewer data transfers, leading to a reduction by the same factor in CPU overhead. Note that the repeated passing of control of the bus between CPU and DMA controller involves some overhead that we have ignored in this example. This latter overhead is more significant when each data transfer is performed in the cyclic fashion shown in Figure 22.4b. However, this overhead is not enough to seriously detract from the benefits of DMA-based I/O.

Note that it is quite possible to have more than one DMA controller share the memory bus with the CPU. In such a case, as well as when there are multiple CPUs, a bus arbitration mechanism takes the place of the request-grant signaling between one DMA controller and a single CPU. Bus arbitration will be discussed in Section 23.4.

Despite the clear performance advantage of DMA-based I/O, this method is not free of problems and pitfalls. For example, certain implementation problems arise when the interactions of DMA with cache and virtual memories are considered. Because data transfers via DMA involve locations in the memory address space, the problems relate to the use of physical or virtual addresses to specify the source and/or destination of the transfers and the part of the memory hierarchy from (into) which data is taken (copied). Here is a list of problems that need to be considered.

1. *DMA using physical addresses:* Because consecutive virtual pages are not necessarily contiguous in main memory, a multipage transfer of this type cannot be specified with a base address and length; thus, longer data transfers must be broken down into a number of same-page transfers.
2. *DMA using virtual addresses:* DMA controller needs address translation.
3. *DMA writing into, or reading from, main memory:* CPU may access stale data in cache, or the DMA controller may output data that is not up to date.
4. *DMA operating via the cache:* I/O data may displace active CPU data, leading to performance degradation.

In any case, cooperation from the operating system is needed to make sure that once an address has been provided to the DMA controller, it remains valid throughout the data transfer (i.e., pages are not displaced in main memory).

It is worth repeating at this point that all these details of I/O are typically not visible to user programs because they initiate I/O through system calls.

22.6 Improving I/O Performance

As with most books on computer architecture, the bulk of this book is devoted to methods of designing faster CPUs and of overcoming the CPU-memory speed gap. However, improving CPU and memory speed without also dealing with bottlenecks in I/O processing would be of limited value or even futile. It is not uncommon for an application to spend much more time on I/O than on computation. Even when I/O does not dominate the running time of a particular application, Amdahl's law reminds us that the improvement in performance to be expected from tweaking other parts of the system, while ignoring I/O, is rather limited. It is thus important to recognize the bottlenecks in input and output and to be aware of methods for dealing with them. As discussed in Section 22.1, input/output performance is measured by various parameters that are not completely independent of one another and can often be traded off against each other. They are as follows:

Access latency (time overhead of one I/O operation)

Data transfer rate (measured in megabytes per second)

Response time (elapsed time from request to completion)

Throughput (number of I/O operations per second)

Hence, in this section we discuss some methods for improving each of these facets of I/O performance. The methods span a wide array of options, from tuning application programs for reduced I/O activity to providing architectural enhancements and/or hardware aids for low-overhead I/O handling.

Access latency is the total time overhead for one I/O operation. It includes obvious and well-understood delays, such as disk seek time or rotational latency, as well as other overheads that are less obvious but may be quite significant. Such overheads do add up. A striking example of how all the overhead from many layers of hardware and software could bring I/O to the forefront is found in a remote login session in which characters typed on a local site must be transmitted to a remote system. The number of events and layers involved in transmitting one character or command from the local site to the remote computer is mind-boggling [Silb02]:

Sending (local) side	Receiving (remote) side
Typing of character	Packet reception
Interrupt generation	Network adapter
Context switch	Interrupt generation
Interrupt handler	Context switch
Keyboard device driver	Device driver
Operating system kernel	Character extraction
Context switch	Operating system kernel
User process	Context switch
System call for output	Network daemon
Context switch	Context switch
Operating system kernel	Operating system kernel
Network device driver	Context switch
Network adapter	Network subdaemon
Interrupt generation	
Context switch	
Interrupt handler	
Context switch	
System call completion	

On the receiving side, there is a system program called a network daemon that handles the identification and assignment of incoming network data and another program, the subdaemon, dedicated to handling the network I/O for a specific login session. Now, if the receiver has to echo the character back to the sender, the entire process is repeated in the reverse direction! Improvement in each of the steps or agents just listed can lead to better I/O performance. For example, hardware aids for low-overhead context switching (to be discussed in Section 24.5) may have a significant effect, given that "Context switch" appears eight times in the list.

Clearly, even when access latency itself cannot be lowered, an equivalent effect can be achieved by reducing the number of I/O operations via increasing the size of each operation. Reading the same amount of data via a smaller number of I/O requests has the effect of reducing the effective access latency per megabyte of data read.

Example 22.9: Effective I/O bandwidth from disk   Consider a hard disk drive with 512 B sectors, an average access latency of 10 ms (including software overhead), and a peak throughput of 10 MB/s. Plot the variations in the effective I/O bandwidth as the unit of data transfer (block) varies in size from 1 sector (0.5 KB) to 1024 sectors (500 KB). Ignore all data recording overheads and intersector gaps.

Solution: When one sector is transferred per disk access, the data transfer time of $0.5/10 = 0.05$ (transfer amount in kilobytes divided by transfer rate in kilobytes per millisecond) added to the access latency of 10 ms yields a total I/O time of 10.05 ms. This translates to an effective bandwidth of $0.5/10.05 = 0.05$ MB/s. Similar computations for block sizes of 10, 20, 50, 100, 200, 300, 400, and 500 KB produce the trend depicted in Figure 22.5. We note that the effective bandwidth improves rather quickly as the block size increases, reaching half the theoretical peak value at a block size of 100 MB. Afterward, improvement is not as significant, suggesting that it may not be worthwhile to increase the block size further, given the possibility of bringing in less useful data.

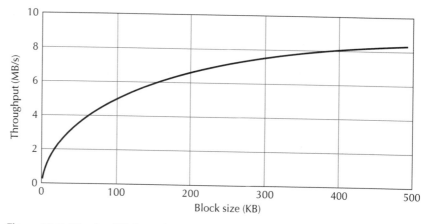

Figure 22.5 Effective I/O throughput versus the amount of data transferred with each I/O request.

I/O data transfer rate is the amount of data that can be transferred between a device and memory in unit time. The peak transfer rates quoted for various I/O devices are usually not achieved in practice. This is in part because the devices themselves may have variable rates;

for example, the transfer rates from a disk's innermost and outermost tracks may differ. More importantly, however, the real transfer rate is a function of not only the device's ability to receive or send the data but also of the capacity of a host of intermediate resources (controllers, buses, bus bridges or adapters, etc.) to relay the data. Note that even though a bus may be fast enough to handle the peak data rate from a disk when disk-to-memory traffic is the only kind present, sharing of the bus by other ongoing activities may reduce its ability to deal with the disk I/O.

Response time is defined as the time elapsed from the issuance of an I/O request to its completion. In the simplest case, when an I/O device is dedicated to a single application or user, response time is simply the sum of I/O access latency and data transfer time (amount of data transferred divided by transfer rate); in such a case, response time is not an independent measure but is derivable from the previous two parameters. More generally, however, a nonnegligible *queuing delay* may be added whose value depends on the current mix of pending I/O operations at various points in the I/O transfer path. Queuing delays are hard to assess but form the focus of an area of study known as *queuing theory,* whose discussion is beyond the scope of this book. Suffice it to say that queues can cause unexpected, and at times counterintuitive, I/O behavior. A good analogy is provided by the queue of customers at a bank. If a queue of 10 customers builds up during lunch hour, even if the bank's service throughput is comparable to the arrival rate of new customers, the long queue may remain in place throughout the afternoon. In other words, even though throughput is not a problem in this case, response time is quite poor. This type of queuing effect may be experienced, for example, in network communication during peak traffic periods.

Another factor that has an adverse effect on I/O latency is the repeated copying of I/O data from one area of memory to another as a result of the multiple layers of software that are involved in the handling of an I/O request. For example, operating systems typically copy output data from the user space into kernel space before sending it out to the device. Among other things, this approach allows the user to continue modifying the data while the output operation is in progress. For example, this is what happens when you issue a print command from a word processor and then continue to make further modifications to the page being printed even before the printing request is completed. The same occurs in the input direction for other reasons such as data integrity verification. In systems or applications where I/O performance is highly critical, some of this copying can be avoided. In the foregoing word processor example, the operating system may accept the output data directly from the user area while giving the user read-only access to the data being printed. Only if the user wants to make changes to the data before printing is complete will the operating system make a copy for printing.

I/O throughput, or the number of I/O operations performed per unit time, is of interest when each I/O operation is fairly simple but many such operations must be performed in rapid succession. In most such applications, latency is also of concern (e.g., in a network of bank ATMs linked to a central computing facility), leading to challenging scheduling problems. This is because high throughput dictates the use of queues for optimal use of resources, while low latency dictates that each request be serviced as early as possible.

Note that many of the problems and challenges described here arise from the desires to hide the complexities of I/O from the user and to make application and system programs to a large extent independent of I/O device technology. These goals have been accomplished by introducing software layers that shield users from hardware device characteristics. Removing some of these layers of complexity is one way for improving I/O latency and throughput. This is routinely done, for example, in game consoles, where the high throughput required for sophisticated graphics output necessitates direct interaction between the graphics hardware and

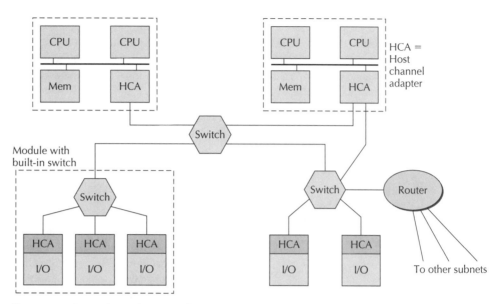

Figure 22.6 Example configuration for the Infiniband distributed I/O.

the display unit with minimal overhead. In fact, the designers of such game consoles have been so successful in tuning their graphics processing for maximum performance that the idea of using a large number of such consoles to build a supercomputer is being pursued by more than one research team.

To achieve the same low-overhead I/O for general-purpose systems, both the number of layers involved performing I/O and the latency at each layer must be reduced. The ultimate in reducing the number of layers is to provide users direct control of I/O devices for certain critical I/O activities. To reduce the latency at each layer, both specialization of the routines to avoid operations that are not applicable to a particular I/O device and reduction in the amount of data copying to the extent possible can be pursued. At the hardware level, providing devices with more intelligent interfaces and the ability to communicate via a switch-based network, as opposed to several layers of buses and the associated adapters, is the thrust of the new Infiniband I/O standard. As shown in Figure 22.6, this scheme allows I/O devices to communicate with each other directly without placing a load on the CPU or even its buses.

PROBLEMS

22.1 Input/output through busy waiting

a. Will the program fragment in Example 22.2 work correctly when beq is a delayed branch with one delay slot? If not, modify the instruction sequence to work. If yes, explain why.
b. Repeat part a for Example 22.3.

22.2 Command-line data entry and echo

Convert the instruction sequences of Examples 22.2 and 22.3 into MiniMIPS procedures. Then write a sequence of MiniMIPS instructions that causes characters entered on the keyboard to be saved in memory and also displayed on the screen, until the

"Enter" key has been depressed. At this point, the null symbol is appended to the end of the stored string and the null-terminated string is passed to a procedure for analysis and appropriate action.

22.3 Repetition on a keyboard

In most computers, if you press a key on the keyboard and hold it down, the character will be repeated. Thus, holding down the hyphen or underscore key will create a dashed or solid line, respectively. The rate of repetition is determined by a user-defined parameter. Discuss how this aspect of keyboard data entry might be handled in the context of Example 22.2.

22.4 Device status registers

In the device control (status) registers of Figure 22.1:

a. Suggest possible uses for at least 2 other bits in the keyboard control register (besides R and IE).
b. Repeat part a for the display control register.
c. Repeat part a for a third I/O device that you choose and describe.

22.5 Addressing logic for I/O devices

In the I/O scheme depicted in Figure 22.2:

a. What happens if two different input devices are assigned the same device address?
b. Repeat part a for output devices.
c. Is it possible to connect two or more different keyboards to the bus? Can you think of a situation in which this capability might be useful?
d. Repeat part c for display units.

22.6 Polling a buffered keyboard

Given the assumption that two successive key depressions on a keyboard can never be less than 0.1 s apart, a polling rate of 10/s, as in Example 22.4, is adequate. Suppose that, in addition, we know that no more than 10 key depressions can occur in any 2 s time interval. By providing a buffer in the keyboard, we can reduce the polling rate while still capturing all keystrokes.

a. Determine the appropriate keyboard buffer size and organization.
b. Propose a hardware realization for the keyboard buffer.
c. What is the appropriate polling rate with the buffer of part a?

d. How can the CPU ensure that the polling rate of part c is honored?
e. Under what condition would a larger buffer help reduce the polling rate even further?

22.7 Polling a hard disk drive

Consider the polling of a disk drive, with disk and CPU characteristics given in Example 22.6.

a. Determine the minimum clock frequency for the CPU if it is to keep up with the hard disk.
b. Would providing a buffer for the disk drive, as done for the keyboard of Problem 22.6, allow the CPU to poll less frequently? Justify your answer.
c. What changes to the assumptions would allow us to accomplish the polling with a 500 MHz CPU? Change only one of the assumptions at a time.
d. Would a 2 GHz CPU be able to poll two hard disks? What about four disks?

22.8 Disk I/O via interrupts

In accordance with Example 22.7, and with the assumptions therein, one disk drive ties up less than 5% of the CPU time if interrupts are used for input and output.

a. Explain why this result does not imply that one CPU can handle I/O from or to 20 disks.
b. Explain why even two hard disks may not be properly handled unless some special provisions that you outline are implemented.

22.9 DMA data transfers

In Section 22.5, we noted that DMA controllers with the ability to transfer data in shorter bursts while returning the bus control to the CPU after each partial transfer offer the benefit that the CPU never has to wait long for using the bus.

a. Can you think of any disadvantage for this scheme?
b. What factors influence the choice of the burst length for partial transfer? What are the trade-offs?
c. Repeat part b for the case when two DMA controllers are attached to the same bus.

22.10 Effects of DMA on CPU performance

a. The operation of a DMA channel, and its effects on CPU performance, may be modeled in the following way. Time is measured in terms of bus cycles and all overheads, including arbitration delay, are ignored. When the DMA channel is not using the bus during a certain bus cycle, it may become active with probability 0.1 in the subsequent bus cycle. Upon activation, it obtains and uses the bus for 12 cycles before relinquishing it. What is the long-term probability that the CPU can use the bus in any given cycle? What is the expected wait time for the CPU?

b. Repeat part a, this time assuming that the DMA releases the bus for one cycle after every 4 cycles of use; hence, the 12 cycles of use occur in three installments, separated by 2 free cycles.

22.11 Effective I/O bandwidth

This problem is a continuation of Example 22.9.

a. Plot the throughput variation versus block size (Figure 22.5), using a logarithmic scale for the block size on the horizontal axis.
b. Repeat part a, this time using logarithmic scales for both axes.
c. Do the plots of parts a and b provide any additional insight on choosing a block size? Discuss.

22.12 Effective I/O bandwidth

Example 22.9 is somewhat unrealistic in that it associates the average access latency of 10 ms with every disk access. In reality, if reading larger blocks of data is to make sense, accesses to smaller blocks must involve a great deal of locality. On the other hand, a truly random access will likely have a higher latency than the average of 10 ms measured over all accesses. Discuss how these considerations can be accounted for in a more realistic analysis. State all your assumptions clearly, and quantify the effect of block size on the effective I/O throughput as in Figure 22.5.

22.13 Infiniband distributed I/O

Prepare a five-page report on the Infiniband distributed I/O scheme, focusing in particular on the structure of the host channel adapter and switch elements (shown in Figure 22.6). Pay special attention to how the two elements differ in structure and function.

22.14 I/O performance

A banking application is an example of a transaction processing workload. Let us focus only on ATM

transactions performed by bank customers and ignore all other transactions that are initiated by bank staff (e.g., check processing, account setup, various updates). Taking a simplified view, each ATM transaction involves three disk accesses (for authentication, account data readout, and account updating).

a. For each of the disk memories listed in Table 19.1, estimate the maximum number of transactions that can be supported per second (ignore the unsuitability of very small disks for this type of application).
b. Allowing 50% spare throughput for future expansion, and 40% waste of disk bandwidth due to administrative overhead, how many of each disk units considered in part a would be needed to support a throughput of 200 transactions per second?
c. What are some of the reasons for an actual ATM bank transaction requiring more than three disk accesses?
d. How do the additional accesses in part c affect transaction processing throughput?

22.15 I/O performance

A computer uses a 1 GB/s I/O bus that can accommodate up to 10 disk controllers, each capable of being connected to 10 disk units. Assume that the interleaved main memory is not a bottleneck, in the sense that it can supply or accept data at the peak rate of the I/O bus. Each disk controller adds a latency of 0.5 ms to an I/O operation and has a maximum data rate of 200 MB/s. Consider the use of the disk memories listed in Table 19.1 and ignore the unlikelihood that very small disks would be used for large storage capacities. Compute the maximum I/O rate that can be achieved in this system with each disk type. Assume that each I/O operation involves a single randomly chosen sector. State all your assumptions clearly.

22.16 Queuing theory

A disk controller receiving disk access requests can be modeled by a queue that holds the requests and a server that satisfies the requests in FIFO order. Each arriving request spends some time in the queue and requires some service time for the actual access. Suppose the disk can perform an average of one access every 10 ms. For simplicity, we assume that the service time is always $T_{serve} = 10$ ms. Let u be the disk utilization; for example, $u = 0.5$ if the disk performs 50 accesses per second (50×10 ms $= 500$ ms). Then, assuming random request arrivals with a Poisson distribution, queuing theory tells us that the time an access request spends waiting in the queue is $T_{queue} = 10u/(1 - u)$ ms, where the factor 10 is the service time in milliseconds. For example, if $u = 0.5$, each request spends an average of 10 ms in the queue and 10 ms for the actual access, for a total average latency of 20 ms.

a. What is the disk utilization if, on average, 80 disk I/O requests are issued per second?
b. Based on the answer to part a, compute the average total latency for each disk access request.
c. Repeat part a, assuming that the disk is replaced with a faster disk of average latency of 5 ms.
d. Repeat part b based on the answer to part c.
e. Compute the speedup of part d over part b (i.e., the performance impact of the faster disk).

22.17 Queuing theory

Little's law in queuing theory states that under equilibrium conditions, the average number of tasks in a system is the product of their arrival rate and the average response time. For example, if bank customers arrive at the rate of one every 2 minutes (arrival rate of 0.5/min) and a customer spends an average of 10 minutes in the bank, then on average there will be $0.5 \times 10 = 5$ customers inside the bank. Based on the explanation in Problem 22.16, assuming a single teller in the bank, a service time of s for each customer implies $T_{queue} = su/(1 - u)$, where u, the teller utilization, is $0.5s$ (i.e., the product of arrival rate and customer service time).

a. Based on the information given, what is the service time for each customer?
b. What is the expected length of the queue (number of customers waiting) at the bank?
c. Relate this bank example to disk input/output.
d. Discuss the impact of having a teller who works twice as fast as the original single teller versus having two tellers of the same speed. Note that exact calculation of the impacts of the second option is rather complicated; so, present an intuitive argument for the relative merits of each option.
e. What would be the disk I/O counterpart of having more than one teller at the bank?

REFERENCES AND FURTHER READINGS

[Brya03]   Bryant, R. E., and D. O'Hallaron, *Computer Systems: A Programmer's Perspective,* Prentice Hall, 2003.

[Henn03]   Hennessy, J. L., and D. A. Patterson, *Computer Architecture: A Quantitative Approach,* Morgan Kaufmann, 3rd ed., 2003.

[Patt98]   Patterson, D. A., and J. L. Hennessy, *Computer Organization and Design: The Hardware/Software Interface,* Morgan Kaufmann, 2nd ed., 1998.

[Rash88]   Rashid, R., A. Tevanian Jr, M. Young, D. Golub, R. Baron, D. Black, W. J. Bolosky, and J. Chew, "Machine-Independent Virtual Memory Management for Paged Uniprocessor and Multiprocessor Architectures," *IEEE Trans. Computers,* Vol. 37, No. 8, pp. 896–908, August 1988.

[Sanc03]   Sanchez, J., and M. P. Canton, *The PC Graphics Handbook,* CRC Press, 2003. Chap. 18, "Keyboard and Mouse Programming," pp. 509–532.

[Scha01]   Schaelicke, L., *Architectural Support for User-Level Input/Output,* PhD dissertation, University of Utah, December 2001. http://www.cse.nd.edu/~lambert/pdf/dissertation.pdf

[Silb02]   Silberschatz, A., P. B. Galvin, and G. Gagne, *Operating Systems Concepts,* Wiley, 6th ed., 2002.

[Wolf01]   Wolf, W., *Computers as Components,* Morgan Kaufmann, 2001.

23

BUSES, LINKS, AND INTERFACING

"Never underestimate the bandwidth of a station wagon full of tapes hurtling down the highway."
—Andrew Tannenbaum

"Digital computers: People who count on their fingers."
—From The Book of Phrases in "B.C." comic strip by Hart

It is common to use shared links or buses to interconnect several subsystems together. This not only leads to fewer wires and pins, thus improving both cost-effectiveness and reliability, but also contributes to flexibility and expandability. In this chapter, we review such shared connections and two key issues in their design and use: arbitration, to ensure that only one sender places data on the bus at any given time, and synchronization, to help ascertain that the receiver sees the same data values that were transmitted by the sender. Interfacing of peripheral devices to computers involves complex issues in signal detection and reconstruction. For this reason, many standard interfaces have been developed that completely define signal parameters and exchange protocols. A peripheral device that produces or receives signals in accordance with one of many standard bus/link protocols can be plugged into a computer and used with minimal effort.

■ 23.1 Intra- and Intersystem Links

Intrasystem connectivity is established for the most part via thin metal layers deposited on, and separated by, insulator layers on microchips or printed-circuit boards. Such links are either point-to-point, connecting one terminal of a particular subsystem to a terminal of

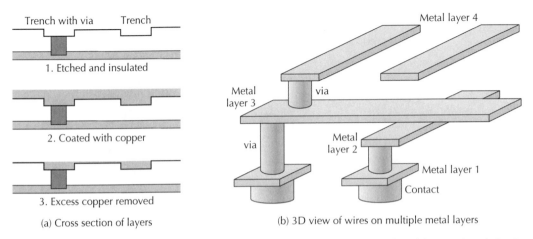

Figure 23.1 Multiple metal layers provide intrasystem connectivity on microchips or printed-circuit boards.

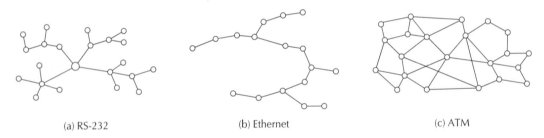

Figure 23.2 Example intersystem connectivity schemes.

another, or shared buses, allowing multiple units to communicate through them. Because of the importance of buses in system implementation and performance, they are dealt with separately in Sections 23.2–23.4. Today's electronic manufacturing processes allow multiple metal layers at the chip and board level, thus affording fairly complex connectivity (Figure 23.1). Wires are "deposited" layer by layer, just like the rest of the processing steps. For example, to deposit two parallel wires on a layer, two trenches are etched where the wires must appear (Figure 23.1a). After the surface has been coated with a thin layer of insulator, a layer of copper is deposited that fills the trenches and also covers the rest of the surface. Polishing the surface removes excess copper, except in the trenches where the wires have been formed.

When components must be removable or interchangeable, they are linked to the rest of the system by means of sockets into which they can be plugged or special cables with standard connectors at either end. Some of the relevant standards in this regard are discussed in Section 23.6.

Beyond the boundary of a circuit board, wires, cables, and optical fibers are used for communication, depending on cost and bandwidth requirements. Figure 23.2 depicts some of these options. Intersystem connectivity takes a variety of forms, ranging from short wires linking

■ TABLE 23.1 Summary of three interconnection schemes

Interconnection properties	RS-232	Ethernet	ATM
Maximum segment length, m	Tens	Hundreds	1000s
Maximum network span, m	Tens	Hundreds	Unlimited
Bit rate, Mb/s	Up to 0.02	10/100/1000	155–2500
Unit of transmission, B	1	Hundreds	53
Typical end-to-end latency, ms	<1	Tens–Hundreds	Hundreds
Typical application domain	Input/Output	LAN	Backbone
Transceiver complexity or cost	Low	Low	High

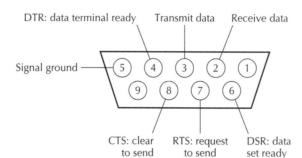

Figure 23.3 RS-232 serial interface 9-pin connector.

nearby units to local- and wide-area networks. The requisite interconnecting structures are characterized by their:

Distance/span:	a few meters to thousands of kilometers
Data rate:	a few kilobits per second to several gigabits per second
Topology:	bus, star, ring, tree, and so on
Line sharing:	point-to-point (dedicated) or multidrop (shared)

To get some idea about the characteristics of interconnections for different distances and data rates, three example intersystem connectivity standards are described in the remainder of this section (Figure 23.2). Table 23.1 contains a summary of the most important characteristics.

Since its inception in the early 1960s as an EIA (Electronics Industries Association) standard, RS-232 has been a widely used scheme for connecting external equipment such as terminals to computers. It is a serial method in which transmission occurs bit by bit over a single data line, which is supported by a number of other lines for various control functions, including handshaking. There are actually three wires to support full-duplex serial data transmission: one data wire for each direction, plus a shared ground. The full RS-232 connector has 25 pins, but most PCs use a reduced 9-pin version depicted in Figure 23.3. The four control signals (CTS, RTS, DTR, DSR) allow handshaking between the transmitter and receiver of data (see Section 23.3). With RS-232, 8-bit plain or parity-encoded symbols are transmitted along with 3 extra bits as the string `0dddddddp11`, where the leftmost 0 is the start bit, `d` represents data, `p` is the parity bit or an eighth data bit, and the two 1s on the right are stop bits. Transmitted symbols may be separated by idle 1 bits following the two stop bits. In view of its short range (tens of meters) and relatively low data rate (0.3–19.6 Kb/s), RS-232 has assumed the status of a legacy standard in recent years, meaning that it is supported for the sake of compatibility with older devices and systems.

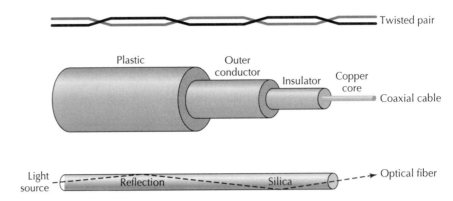

Figure 23.4 Commonly used communication media for intersystem connections.

Ethernet is the most commonly used LAN (local-area network) standard. In its various forms, Ethernet supports transmission rates of 10 Mb/s, 100 Mb/s, and recently, 1 Gb/s. The medium used for transmission can be a twisted pair of wires, coaxial cable, or optical fiber (Figure 23.4). Multiple devices or nodes may be connected to Ethernet that can support one transmission by a single sender at any time with a latency of the order of 1 ms, using packets or frames whose size is hundreds of bytes. Each node connected to Ethernet has a transceiver (transmitter/receiver) capable of sending messages and of monitoring the network traffic. When no node is transmitting over the shared "ether," there is a fixed voltage of +0.7 V on the line. This is known as the *carrier sense* signal or *heartbeat,* which indicates that the network is active and available for use. To transmit over the Ethernet, a node "listens" for a quiet period before it starts. If two nodes begin transmitting at the same time, a collision results. When a collision is detected, the participating nodes produce a "jam" signal and wait randomly for tens of milliseconds before trying again. This type of distributed bus arbitration based on collision detection will be further discussed in Section 23.4. A node starts its transmission by sending a string of 0s and 1s known as the preamble, causing the line voltage to fluctuate between +0.7 and −0.7 V. If no collision has been detected by the end of the preamble, then the node sends the rest of the frame. A common means of tapping into Ethernet is the RJ-45 connector with 8 pins that constitute 4 pairs of lines.

ATM (asynchronous transfer mode) is an interconnection technology used in building long-haul networks of the type shown in Figure 23.2c. Formed of switches connected in an arbitrary topology, an ATM network can transmit data at the rate of 155 Mb/s to 2.5 Gb/s. The transmission does not occur in a continuous bit stream but is rather based on store-and-forward routing of 53 B packets (5 B header followed by 48 B data). The difference with packet routing in the Internet is that a specific route, or virtual connection, is set up and all the packets comprising a particular transmission are forwarded through that route. This allows certain quality-of-service parameters (such as guaranteed data rate and packet loss probability) to be negotiated at the virtual connection setup time. The 48 B data content of a packet was chosen as a compromise to balance the control overhead in each packet against latency requirements in voice communication, where each millisecond of speech is typically represented in 8 bytes, leading to 6 ms intervals per ATM packet; longer intervals would have led to audible delays as well as unpleasant pauses in the case of packet loss. The development of ATM is managed by the ATM Forum [WWW], which has many telecommunications companies and several universities among its members.

Intra- and intersystem links have assumed a central role in the design of digital systems. One reason is that the rapidly increasing density and performance of electronic components has made the provision of the required connectivity at reasonable speeds a very challenging problem. Signal propagation over wires takes place at a third to half the speed of light. This means that electronic signals travel:

Across a memory bus (10 cm)	in	1 ns
Across a large computer (10 m)	in	100 ns
Across a college campus (1 km)	in	10 μs
Across a metropolis (100 km)	in	1 ms
Across a country (2000 km)	in	20 ms
Across the globe (20,000 km)	in	200 ms

Even on-chip signal propagation delay has become nonnegligible and must be accounted for in designing high-performance digital circuits.

23.2 Buses and Their Appeal

A bus is a connector that links together multiple data sources and sinks. The main advantage of bus-based connectivity is that, theoretically, it allows any number of units to communicate among themselves, with each unit requiring only one input and one output port. This minimizes wiring or cabling and allows the flexibility of adding new units with minimal change or disruption. Practically, however, there is an upper limit to the number of units that can share a single bus, with the limit depending on bus technology and speed. Many low-end computers benefit from the simplicity and economy of a single shared bus that connects all system components (see Figure 21.1). Higher-performance systems may include multiple buses or use point-to-point connectivity for greater speed and bandwidth.

A bus typically consists of a bundle of control lines, a set of address lines, and several data lines, as depicted in Figure 23.5. Control lines carry various signals needed for controlling the bus transfers, the devices connected to the bus, and the associated handshaking protocols. Address lines carry information about data source or destination (memory location or I/O device). The most common address width in use today is 32 bits, but both narrower and wider addresses exist in various systems. Data lines carry data values to be sent from one unit to another. Serial buses have a single data line, whereas parallel buses carry 1–16 bytes (8–128 bits) of data simultaneously. Address and data lines can be shared (multiplexed), but this leads to lower performance.

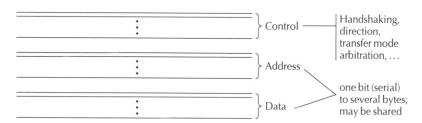

Figure 23.5 The three sets of lines found in a bus.

A typical computer may use a dozen or so different types of buses. There are three main reasons for this multiplicity:

1. *Legacy buses* are buses that have existed in the past and must be supported for the time being so that users can continue to use their older peripheral devices. Examples of legacy buses include PC Bus, ISA, RS-232, and parallel port.

2. *Standard buses* follow popular international standards and are required for connecting most current peripheral devices to the computer. Examples of such common standard buses, discussed further in Section 23.6, include PCI, SCSI, USB, and Ethernet.

3. *Proprietary buses* are custom-designed to maximize the data transfer rate among critical system components, and thus overall system performance. These buses are designed for specific devices known at design time and are not expected to be compatible with other devices or standards.

In what follows, we review certain characteristics of buses that are common among the three categories above. The most important bus specs include the following:

Data rate: Excluding slow, older buses, the data rate ranges from several megabytes per second, through tens or hundreds of megabytes per second (e.g., on Ethernet) to several gigabytes per second on fast memory buses that typically use a 100–500 MHz clock with an 8 B wide data channel.

Maximum number of devices: More devices increase the bus loading as well as the arbitration overhead, making the bus slower. This parameter ranges from a few (e.g., 7 for standard SCSI) to many thousands (e.g., for Ethernet).

Connection method: This characteristic has to do with the connector and cable types that can be used for linking to the bus as well as ease of adding or removing devices. For example, USB is *hot-pluggable,* meaning that devices can be added or removed even when the bus is in operation.

Robustness and reliability: It is important to know how well a bus tolerates malfunctioning devices that are connected to it, or various electrical irregularities such a short-circuit, which may occur before or during data transmission.

Electrical parameters: These include voltage levels, current ranges, surge and short-circuit protection, cross talk, and power requirements.

Communication overhead: Control and error-checking bits added to transmitted data for control, coordination, or improved reliability. This overhead tends to be low for short, fast buses and quite significant for long-haul transmission.

Buses can also be classified according the control or arbitration scheme. In the simplest control scheme, there is a single bus master that initiates all bus transfers (the master sends or receives data). For example, the CPU might be the master that can send data to or receive data from any unit connected to the bus. This is quite simple to implement but has the double drawbacks of wasting CPU time and using two bus transfers for sending one word of data from disk to memory, say.

Slightly more flexible is a scheme in which the bus master may relinquish control of the bus to other devices for a specific number of cycles or until completion of transfer is signaled. The DMA scheme of Section 22.5 is a prime example of this method.

Buses with multiple masters may have an arbiter that decides which master gets to use the bus. Alternatively, a distributed control scheme may be used whereby "collisions" are detected and dealt with through retransmission at a later time (e.g., in Ethernet). The method used for bus arbitration has a profound effect on performance. Arbitration methods and bus performance are discussed in Section 23.4.

Example 23.1: Accounting for bus arbitration overhead   A 100 MHz bus is 8 B wide. Assume that 40% of the bus's bandwidth is wasted owing to arbitration and other control overhead. What is the net bus bandwidth available to other I/O devices and the CPU after the needs of a 1024×768 pixel video display unit with 4 B/pixel and a refresh rate of 70 Hz are accounted for?

Solution: The display unit's data rate is $1024 \times 768 \times 4 \times 70 \cong 220$ MB/s. The effective total bus bandwidth is $100 \times 8 \times 0.6 = 480$ MB/s. The net bandwidth is thus $480 - 220 = 260$ MB/s, which will serve the CPU and the remaining I/O devices. Note that we have assumed that the memory can supply data at the effective bus rate of 480 MB/s. This is not unreasonable: it amounts to 48 bytes every 100 ns.

◼ 23.3 Bus Communication Protocols

Buses are divided into two broad classes of synchronous and asynchronous. Within each class, buses can be custom-designed or based on a prevailing industry standard. In a *synchronous bus,* a clock signal is part of the bus and events occur on specific clock cycles according to an agreed-upon schedule (*bus protocol*). For example, a memory address may be placed on the bus in one cycle, with the memory required to respond with the data on the fifth clock cycle. Figure 23.6 contains a graphic representation of the preceding protocol. Synchronous buses are suitable for a small number of devices of equal or comparable speeds communicating over short distances (otherwise bus loading and clock skew become problematic).

Asynchronous buses can accommodate devices of varying speeds communicating over longer distances, given that the fixed timing of the synchronous bus is replaced by a handshaking protocol. Typical sequence of events on an asynchronous bus in the case of data input or read access to memory (Figure 23.7) is described in the following. The input requesting unit asserts the Request signal, while at the same time putting address information on an address bus. This request is noted ① by the addressee, which acknowledges the request (asserts the Ack signal) and reads the address information from the bus. The requester

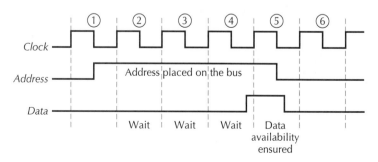

Figure 23.6 Synchronous bus with fixed-latency devices.

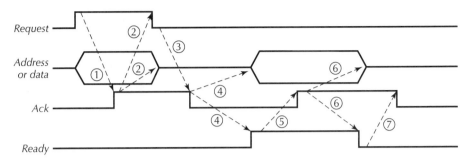

Figure 23.7 Handshaking on an asynchronous bus for an input operation (e.g., reading from memory).

in turn notes ② the acknowledgment, deasserting the Request signal and removing the address information from the bus. The addressee next notes ③ the deassertion of the Request signal and deasserts its acknowledgment. When the requested data is available ④, the Ready signal is asserted and the data is placed on the bus. The requester now notes ⑤ the Ready signal, asserts the Ack signal, and reads the data from the bus. The latter acknowledgment ⑥ leads the sender to deassert the Ready signal and remove the data from the bus. Finally, the requester, noting ⑦ the deassertion of the Ready signal, deasserts the Ack signal to terminate the bus transaction.

To interface asynchronous signals with synchronous (clocked) circuits, we need to use synchronizers; these are circuits that enforce certain timing constraints relating to signal transitions needed for correct operation of synchronous circuits (see Section 2.6). Synchronizers not only add complexity to digital circuits but also introduce delays that nullify some of the advantages of asynchronous operation.

Within a computer system, the processor-memory bus is usually custom-designed and synchronous. The backplane bus may be standard or custom. Finally, the I/O bus is usually standard and asynchronous. The PCI bus is reviewed as an example in the rest of this section. Some of the other commonly used standard interfaces are described in Section 23.6.

The PCI (peripheral component interconnect) standard bus was developed by Intel in the early 1990s and is now managed by PCI-SIG [WWW], a special-interest group with hundreds of member companies. Even though PCI was developed as an I/O bus, it shares some of the characteristics of a high-performance bus, thus allowing it to be used as a focal point for all intersystem communications. For example, PCI combines synchronous (clocked) operation with the provision of wait-cycle insertion by slower devices that cannot keep up with the bus speed. The following description is based on the widely adopted original standard, which has now been augmented in various forms, including PCI-X, mini-PCI, and PCI hot-pluggable for improved performance, greater convenience, and extended application domains. The description also reflects the minimum requirements in terms of data width (32 bits) and control signals. The data width is doubled, and the number of control signals increased, in the optional 64-bit version.

To reduce the number of pins, PCI has 32 *AD* lines that carry address or data. There are four active-low command lines, *C/BE'*, that specify the function to be performed and also double as byte-enable signals during the actual data transmission. Typical commands include memory

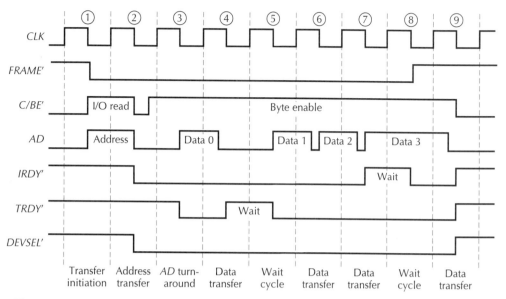

Figure 23.8 I/O read operation via PCI bus.

read, memory write, I/O read, I/O write, and interrupt acknowledge. The byte-enable function simply indicates which of the four bytes carry valid data. There are six basic interface control signals which include:

FRAME'   Stays active for the duration of a transaction, thus delimiting it
IRDY'   Signals that the initiator is ready
TRDY'   Signals that the target is ready
STOP'   Requests that the master stop the current transaction

Additionally, 3 pins are devoted to *CLK* (clock), *RST'* (reset), and *PAR* (parity), 2 bits are used for error reporting, and 2 bits are devoted to arbitration (*REQ'* and *GNT'*, applicable to the master unit only).

Figure 23.8 shows a typical data transfer over PCI. The bus transaction begins in clock cycle ① when the bus master places an address and a command (I/O read) on the bus; it also asserts *FRAME'* to signal the beginning of the transaction. The actual address transfer from the initiator unit to the target unit occurs in clock cycle ② when all units attached to the bus examine the address and command lines to determine whether a transaction is addressed to them; the unit thus selected then prepares to participate in the rest of the bus transaction. The next clock cycle ③ is a "turnaround" cycle during which the master relinquishes the *AD* lines and places a "byte-enable" command on the *C/BE'* lines in preparation for data transmission in each successive cycle. Beginning in clock cycle ④, a 32-bit data word can be transmitted on every clock tick, with the actual transfer rate dictated by the sender and receiver via the *IRDY'* and *TRDY'* lines. For example, Figure 23.8 shows two wait cycles inserted into the data stream: in cycle ⑤, the sender (target) is not ready to transmit, while in cycle ⑧, the wait cycle is inserted by the initiator because, for whatever reason, it is unprepared to receive.

Example 23.2: Effective PCI bus bandwidth   If the bus transaction depicted in Figure 23.7 is typical, what can you say about the effective bandwidth of a PCI bus operating at 66 MHz?

Solution: Accounting for another turnaround cycle (from data to address) at the end of the transaction shown in Figure 23.7, 10 clock cycles are taken for 4 data transfers (16 B). This translates to an effective data rate of $66 \times 16/10 = 105.6$ MB/s. The theoretically maximum transfer rate is $66 \times 4 = 264$ MB/s. Thus, the expected overhead due to handshaking and wait cycles is 60%.

23.4 Bus Arbitration and Performance

Any shared resource requires a protocol that governs fair access to the resource by the entities that need to use it; buses are no exception. Deciding which device gets to use a shared bus, and when, is known as *bus arbitration*. One approach is to use a centralized arbiter that receives bus request signals from a number of devices and responds by asserting a grant signal to the single device that can use the bus. If the requesting devices are not synchronized with a common clock signal, the inputs to the arbiter must pass through synchronizers (Figure 23.9). The bus grant may apply to a fixed number of cycles (after which the bus is assumed to be free), or it may be for an indefinite period of time, in which case the device must explicitly release the bus before another grant can be issued.

For devices with *fixed priority* assignments, the bus arbiter is simply a priority encoder that asserts the grant signal associated with the highest-priority requester if the bus is available. With fixed priorities, the bus arbiter quickly grants the bus to a high-priority requesting unit but has the disadvantage of potentially starving the lowest-priority units when high-priority units happen to use the bus heavily. A *rotating priority* scheme, on the other hand, provides uniform treatment for all devices. A number of intermediate schemes can be envisaged that do allow higher priority for some devices that need quicker attention while preventing starvation for lower-priority devices. Some such alternatives are explored in the end-of-chapter problems.

A central arbiter may become very complex when a large number of units are involved; it also limits expandability. A simple arbitration scheme that can be used alone or in combination with a priority-based arbiter (albeit one with fewer inputs and outputs) is *daisy chaining*. A daisy chain is simply an ordered set of devices that share a single request and grant signal. The request signals of all devices in the chain are tied together and form a single request input to a centralized arbiter (Figure 23.10). The chain as a whole may then be granted permission to use the bus. The grant signal goes to the first device in the chain, which may use the bus or

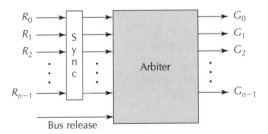

Figure 23.9 General structure of a centralized bus arbiter.

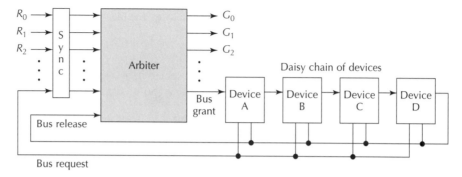

Figure 23.10 Daisy chaining allows a small centralized arbiter to service a large number of devices that use a shared resource.

forward the grant signal to the next device in the chain. In this way, units located near the end of the chain are less likely to get permission to use the bus and thus should not be fast or high-throughput devices.

Distributed arbitration schemes are more desirable because they avoid a centralized arbiter that can become a performance bottleneck. Distributed arbitration may be implemented through *self-selection* or *collision detection*. In one self-selection scheme, each device requesting the bus places a code representing its identity on the bus and immediately examines the bus to figure out if it is has the highest priority among all units requesting the bus. Of course, the codes assigned to various units must be such that the composite of all codes (logical OR) is adequate for telling whether a requesting unit has the highest priority. This tends to limit the number of units that can participate in arbitration. For example, with an 8-bit bus, the codes 00000001, 00000011, 00000111, . . . , 11111111 can be assigned to eight devices connected to an 8-bit bus. When several of these codes are ORed together, the code with the largest number of 1s results; the device putting that particular code on the bus then selects itself for using the bus.

Collision detection, as the name implies, is based on all requesting units simply using the bus, but monitoring the bus to see whether multiple transmissions have been mixed up, or have collided, with each other. If a collision has occurred, the senders simply consider their transmissions to be unsuccessful and try again later, perhaps waiting by a random length of time to minimize the chances of further collisions. The intended receivers will also be able to detect a collision, which causes them to ignore the garbled transmission. To ensure a garbled transmission in the event of collision, the colliding devices may jam the bus, as done in Ethernet. The randomly chosen wait period makes it very unlikely that the same devices will collide many times, thereby wasting the bus bandwidth owing to repeated collisions. As long as the bus is not loaded to near saturation and data is transmitted in large chunks, the added latency due to collisions remains acceptable.

Bus performance is often measured in terms of the peak transmission rate over the bus. For a given bus width, and assuming that no bus cycle is lost to arbitration and other overheads, bus data transmission rate is proportional to its clock frequency. Hence, we hear about 166 or 500 MHz buses. Bus performance (bandwidth) can be increased through one or more of the following:

Greater clock frequency

Wider data transfer path (e.g., 64 data bits instead of 32)

Separate address and data lines (nonmultiplexed)

Block transfers for fewer arbitration overheads

Finer-grain bus control; for example, releasing the bus while waiting for something to happen (split-transaction protocol)

Faster bus arbitration

Note that a 1 GB/s bus, say, can be implemented in a variety of ways. Options range from a very fast serial bus to much slower bus with a 256-bit data width.

Example 23.3: Bus performance   A particular bus is to support transactions that require anywhere from 5 to 55 ns for completion. Assuming a bus data width of 8 B and uniform distribution of bus service times within the range of 5–55 ns (making the average 30 ns), compare the following bus design options with regard to performance.

a. Synchronous bus with a cycle time of 60 ns, which includes allowance for arbitration overhead.

b. Synchronous bus with a cycle time of 15 ns, with 1–4 cycles used for transfers, as needed. Assume that completion signaling and arbitration overheads use up one bus cycle.

c. Asynchronous bus requiring an overhead of 25 ns for arbitration and handshaking.

Solution: The following calculations show that the option in part b offers the best performance.

a. Transferring 8 B every 60 ns leads to the data transfer rate of $8/(60 \times 10^{-9})$ B/s = 133.3 MB/s.

b. In the range of 5–55 ns, 20% of cases need one bus cycle, 30% need two bus cycles, 30% need three bus cycles, and the remaining 20% require four bus cycles. When the one-cycle overhead is factored in, on average 3.5 bus cycles are used for one transaction, leading to the transfer rate of $8/(3.5 \times 15 \times 10^{-9})$ B/s = 152.4 MB/s.

c. The average transfer rate in this case is 8 B every $30 + 25 = 55$ ns, leading to the data transfer rate of $8/(55 \times 10^{-9})$ B/s = 145.5 MB/s.

Performance is not the only design criterion for buses. Robustness of a bus is also important for system reliability and availability. Factors that influence robustness are as follows:

Parity or other type of encoding for error detection

Ability to reject or isolate malfunctioning units

Hot-plug capability for continued operation during unit (dis)connection

For systems in which reliability or availability is very important, multiple buses are often used to allow for continued operation in the event of a bus failure.

■ 23.5 Basics of Interfacing

Interfacing means connecting an external device to a computer. Besides performing input and output from more or less standard devices such as keyboard, visual display unit, and printer, other reasons for such a connection might be:

Sensing and data gathering (temperature, motion, robot vision)

Control by computer (robotics, lighting, voice synthesis)

Adding to computer's capabilities (storage, coprocessors, networking)

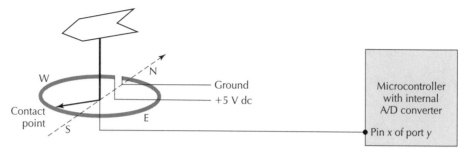

Figure 23.11 Wind vane supplying an output voltage in the range of 0–5 V depending on wind direction.

Interfacing can be as simple as plugging a compatible device into one of the sockets provided on a standard bus and configuring the system software to allow the computer to communicate with the device via that bus. Sometimes, although rather infrequently nowadays, interfacing might involve doing something a bit more elaborate to adapt a particular port of a computer to specific characteristics of a peripheral device.

Microcontrollers (processors that are specifically designed for control applications involving everything from appliances to automobiles) come with special interfacing capabilities such as analog-to-digital (A/D) and digital-to-analog (D/A) converters, communication ports, and built-in timers. Ordinary processors are usually interfaced by tapping into their I/O buses and writing special programs to handle the added device, often via adapting the interrupt handling routine. These device-specific programs are known as *device handlers*.

Consider, as an example, sensing and recording the wind direction via a wind vane that provides a voltage in the range of 0–5 V depending on the direction. The vane may have a built-in potentiometer with its sliding point moving with the wind direction (Figure 23.11). An output voltage close to zero may indicate northward wind, with the voltage increasing to a quarter of its maximum for east, half for south, and three quarters for west. A microcontroller that has a built-in analog-to-digital converter may accept the wind vane's output voltage on a specific pin of one of its ports. The rest is up to the software run on the microcontroller. For example, the software may read the content of a built-in timer that is incremented every millisecond, ascertain that the timer value indicates a predetermined time period since the last reading of the vane direction, sample the corresponding pin if appropriate, and record the data in memory.

If we wish to record the wind direction using MiniMIPS or another processor that does not have a built-in A/D conversion capability, we need to acquire a suitable component to perform the required analog-to-digital conversion with the desired accuracy, storing the result in an 8-bit register, say. Specific addresses are assigned to the converter's status and data registers, and a decoder is designed to recognize these addresses. The A/D converter can then be treated as an I/O device in the manner discussed in Section 22.2.

■ 23.6 Interfacing Standards

Many interfacing standards exist that allow devices of varying speeds and capabilities from different vendors to be connected to computers or to each other. The PCI bus was discussed in Section 23.3, where it provided an example of a bus communication protocol. A number of other commonly used standard interfaces are given in this section. A summary of the characteristics for three of these standards, along with those of PCI, are given in Table 23.2 for comparison.

■ **TABLE 23.2** Summary of four standard interface buses.

Attributes ↓ Name →	PCI	SCSI	FireWire	USB
Type of bus	Backplane	Parallel I/O	Serial I/O	Serial I/O
Standard designation	PCI	ANSI X3.131	IEEE 1394	USB 2.0
Typical application domain	System	Fast I/O	Fast I/O	Low-cost I/O
Bus width, data bits	32–64	8–32	2	1
Peak bandwidth, MB/s	133–512	5–40	12.5–50	0.2–15
Maximum number of devices	1024[*]	7–31[#]	63	127[$]
Maximum span, m	<1	3–25	4.5–72[$]	5–30[$]
Arbitration method	Centralized	Self-select	Distributed	Daisy chain
Transceiver complexity or cost	High	Medium	Medium	Low

[*]32 per bus segment
[#]One less than bus width
[$]With hubs (repeaters)

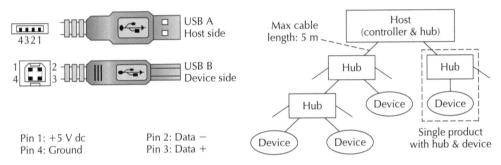

Pin 1: +5 V dc   Pin 2: Data −
Pin 4: Ground   Pin 3: Data +

Figure 23.12 USB connectors and connectivity structure.

SCSI (small computer system interface; pronounced "skuzzy") is a standard bus primarily intended for high-speed I/O devices such as magnetic and optical disk memories. It grew out of the Shugart Associates system interface (SASI) in the mid-1980s. Various versions of SCSI have been introduced over the years. The description that follows is based on SCSI-2, introduced as ANSI Standard X3.131 in 1994, with some improvements and extensions appearing later. The more recent SCSI-3 isn't one standard but rather a family of standards. In most PCs, the IDE/ATA bus, discussed at the end of this section, is used as an interface to magnetic and optical disk memories. The main reason is the lower cost for the latter, which overrides SCSI's greater capabilities and higher performance.

Devices on a SCSI bus communicate with the computer through one of the units connected to the bus. This unit, known as the controller, has access to a primary bus of the computer, such as PCI, and through it, to memory. SCSI can work both in synchronous and asynchronous modes, with the data rate being much higher in synchronous operation. SCSI uses 50- or 68-pin connectors. Address and data are multiplexed and bus control is via self-selection (see Section 23.4). This is why the number of devices connectable to a SCSI bus is one less than its width. More information on this bus can be found through the Web site of SCSI Trade Association, scsita.org.

USB (universal serial bus) is a standard serial bus intended for use with low- to medium-bandwidth I/O devices. USB connectors use small 4-contact plugs attached to a 4-wire cable (Figure 23.12). These connectors carry both data signals, in half-duplex mode, and 5 V power.

Certain low-power peripherals can receive power via the connector, thus obviating the need for a separate power source. One USB port can accommodate up to 127 devices through the use of hubs or repeaters. Up to six tiers, or hub levels, are allowed, which form a daisy chain. The host computer manages the bus using a complex protocol. As a device is plugged into a USB bus (which can be done even during operation), the presence of the device and its properties are detected by the host, which then proceeds to notify the operating system to activate the required device driver. Device disconnection is similarly detected and handled. This hot-plug capability and the ability to support many devices via a single port form the main appeals of USB. For example, a computer with two USB ports may be linked to its keyboard and mouse through one port and a variety of other devices via a hub connected to the second port (a five-port hub, e.g., can accommodate a printer, a joystick, a camera, and a scanner).

USB 2.0 has three data rates: 1.5, 12, and 480 Mb/s (0.2, 1.5, and 60 MB/s, respectively). The highest of these is specific to "Hi-Speed USB," a relatively new standard. The other two rates are intended to provide backward compatibility with previous versions of the standard, including USB 1.1, which operated at 12 Mb/s, and lower-cost implementations for devices that do not need high data rates. Today, virtually every desktop and laptop computer has one or more USB ports. On older products, one finds USB 1.1 ports; however, Hi-Speed USB is quickly gaining ground. More information on USB can be obtained from the literature [Ande97] or via the usb.org Web site.

The IEEE 1394 serial I/O interface is based on Apple Computer's FireWire specification introduced in the mid-1980s. Sony uses the name i.Link for this interface. IEEE 1394 is a general I/O standard interface, although its relatively high cost in comparison to USB has limited its use to applications requiring greater bandwidth to deal with high-quality audio and video I/O. There are some similarities with USB in the shape and size of the connector, maximum cable length, and hot-plug capability. A key difference is the use of peer-to-peer bus arbitration that obviates the need for a single master but also complicates each device interface. Both synchronous and asynchronous transmissions are supported. Any single device can request up to 65% of the available bus capacity, and up to 85% of the capacity can be allocated to such devices. The remaining 15% of capacity guarantees that no device will be completely shut out from using the bus.

Physically, the IEEE 1394 connector has six contacts for power plus two twisted pairs. The latter are transposed at the two ends of the cable to allow the use of the same connector at both ends (Figure 23.13). Each twisted pair is separately shielded within the cable, and the entire cable is also shielded on the outside. A smaller 4-pin connector, with no power lines, has also been used in some products. More information on IEEE 1394 can be obtained via the Web site of the 1394 Trade Association (1394ta.org).

Some of the other standards that one often encounters are UART, AGP, and IDE/ATA. These are described briefly in the following paragraphs for completeness.

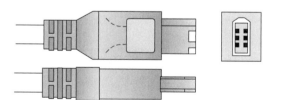

Pin 1: 8-40 V dc, 1.5 A
Pin 2: Ground
Pin 3: Twisted pair B −
Pin 4: Twisted pair B +
Pin 5: Twisted pair A −
Pin 6: Twisted pair A +
Shell: Outer shield

Figure 23.13 IEEE 1394 (FireWire) connector. The same connector is used at both ends.

UART (universal asynchronous receiver/transmitter), an early serial interface standard, is another name often heard in connection with interfacing. Virtually every computer has a UART unit to manage its serial port(s). Characters are transmitted in much the same way as in RS-232 standard, briefly discussed in Section 23.1. However, the bit rate, the character width (5–8 bits), the type of parity (none, odd, even), and the stop sequence (1, 1.5, or 2 bits) are programmable and can be selected at setup time. The 1-to-0 transition that begins the start bit is detected and forms the reference point for the timing of events. If the transmission rate is 19,200 b/s, then a new bit must be sampled every $1/19,200$ s $\cong 52.08$ μs. At a clock rate of several megahertz, this can be accomplished fairly accurately. For example, with a 20 MHz clock, the input is sampled every $20 \times 52.08 = 1041$ clock ticks, with the first sample taken after 520 ticks (middle of the first bit time). Some inaccuracy in the clock frequency or in the sampling rate is tolerable as long as the cumulative effect by the time the stop bit appears is less than half the bit time. For example, if a sample is taken every 1024 ticks rather than every 1040 ticks, the cumulative effect after $9^1/_2$ bit times is $9.5 \times 17 = 161.5$ ticks $= 0.155$ bit time. This still leaves ample room for variations in the clock frequency without leading to sampling errors. Note that the start bit has a synchronizing function in that it limits the aforementioned inaccuracies from accumulating beyond the time frame of a single character transmission. The original UART had a single-character buffer that would fill in about 1 ms at 9600 b/s; so as long as the CPU honored an interrupt within 1 ms, no problem could arise. At today's higher transmission rates, a one-byte buffer is inadequate, so UART is typically provided with a FIFO buffer of up to 128 B to accumulate data and to interact with the CPU via fewer interrupts.

AGP (accelerated graphic port) was developed by Intel to prevent the high data rate needed for graphic rendering from overloading the PCI bus. AGP is a dedicated port rather than a shared bus. As shown in Figure 21.2, it has a separate connection to the memory bus that affords it rapid access to memory, where certain large data sets associated with graphic rendering may be kept. AGP is typically assigned a block of contiguous addresses in the part of address space that lies beyond the available physical memory. A graphics address remapping table (GART) translates AGP virtual addresses to physical memory addresses. In this way, the graphics controller can use a part of main memory as an extension of its dedicated video memory when needed. The alternative of using a larger video memory is both more expensive and wasteful because the dedicated memory might go unused in some applications.

AGP connectors have 124 or 132 pins, for single-voltage (1.5 or 3.3 V) and universal varieties, respectively. Peak bandwidth ranges from 0.25 to 1 GB/s. The high bandwidth is achieved, in part, with help from 8 extra "sideband" address bits that allow AGP to issue new addresses and requests while data is being transferred on the main 32-bit address/data lines. Of course, the high AGP bandwidth is useful only if the main system bus and memory can support a somewhat higher bandwidth, to allow both AGP and CPU to access the memory.

ATA, or AT attachment, is so named because it was developed as an attachment to the first IBM personal computer, PC-AT. ATA, and its descendants such as Fast ATA and Ultra ATA, are commonly used to interface storage units to PCs. IDE (integrated device electronics) is a trade name for the ATA products of Western Digital and is thus virtually equivalent to ATA. ATA uses a 40-pin connector, which is typically attached to a 40-wire flexible flat cable with two connectors. As previously mentioned, this rather limited interface has been superseded in bandwidth and other capabilities by other standards. However, ATA has survived and is still in use primarily because of its simplicity and low implementation cost.

PROBLEMS

23.1 RS-232 serial interface

Answer the following questions about the RS-232 serial interface based on research in books and on the Internet.

a. How are the various control signals, depicted in Figure 23.3, used in the handshaking protocol?
b. How is a device addressed or selected in Figure 23.2a?
c. What types of input and output devices can be supported by this interface?

23.2 Collisions in Ethernet

Consider the following highly simplified analysis of collisions in Ethernet. An Ethernet cable interconnects n computers. Time is divided into 1 ms slices. Within a 0.5 s time interval, every one of the n computers attempts to transmit a message, with the timing of transmission selected randomly from among the 500 time slices available. Regardless of whether the transmission is successful, the transmitter gives up and makes no other transmission attempt in the current 0.5 s interval.

a. What is the probability of having one or more conflicts in a 0.5 s interval with $n = 60$?
b. How is the result of part a related to the "birthday problem," described in Section 17.4 in connection with interleaved memories?
c. On average, within each 0.5 s interval, what fraction of the attempted transmissions of part a will be successful?
d. Repeat part a, this time assuming $n = 150$.
e. Repeat part c with the assumption of part d.

23.3 Asynchronous transfer mode

Answer the following questions about the ATM interconnection technology based on research in books and on the Internet.

a. How is a virtual connection set up via the exchange of messages and acknowledgments?
b. What quality-of-service categories are supported?
c. How many audio or video channels can be supported within the ATM data rates cited near the end of Section 23.1?
d. Under what conditions are ATM cells dropped?

23.4 Bus protocols

In a bus, address and data lines can be separate or shared (multiplexed). Which of these two options is likely assumed in the following buses and why?

a. The synchronous bus whose operation is depicted in Figure 23.6
b. The asynchronous bus whose operation is depicted in Figure 23.7
c. The bus of Example 23.1

23.5 Synchronous buses

Consider the synchronous bus whose operation is depicted in Figure 23.6. Assume that all bus transactions are of the same type and ignore the arbitration overhead.

a. What fraction of the peak bandwidth of the bus is actually used for data transfers?
b. How is the available bandwidth improved if we use a split-transaction protocol?

23.6 Ethernet bridges

Large Ethernet networks are typically formed from smaller segments connected via bridges. A *transparent bridge* (also known as *spanning-tree bridge*) can be used to expand a network without any modification to the hardware or software of existing users. Study how these transparent bridges operate and how they use a backward learning algorithm to build their routing tables, which are blank at start-up time. Describe your findings in a five-page report.

23.7 I/O write operation on PCI bus

a. Draw a diagram similar to that in Figure 23.8 to show an I/O write operation via PCI bus.
b. Explain the elements of your diagram in a manner similar to that of the I/O read operation appearing at the end of Section 23.3.

23.8 Fixed-priority arbiters

A fixed-priority arbiter can be designed much like a ripple-carry adder, with a "permission" signal propagating from the highest-priority to the lowest-priority side and stopping at the first request, if any.

a. Present the complete design of a ripple-type priority arbiter with 4 request signals and 4 grant signals.
b. Show how the arbiter can be made faster by means of lookahead techniques.
c. How can one build an 8-input priority arbiter using two arbiters of the type defined in part a or b?

23.9 Priority schemes without starvation

One problem with a fixed-priority arbitration scheme is that low-priority devices may never get a chance to use the bus if higher-priority units place a heavy demand on it. We refer to this condition as starvation.

a. Design a rotating priority arbiter with 4 request signals and 4 grant signals. The highest-priority device changes every time the bus is granted to a device, so each device gets a chance to become the highest-priority device, which guarantees nonstarvation.
b. The rotating priority scheme of part a is not a genuine priority scheme in that all devices are treated equally. Implement a 4-input priority arbiter in which higher-priority devices are more likely to get the bus, yet low-priority devices are not starved. *Hint:* What if we allow each device at least one chance at using the bus after the next higher-priority device has been granted use of the bus x times, where x is an adjustable parameter of the design?
c. Suggest and implement a different arbiter with the property suggested in part b, but with the number of times a device's bus request has been denied applied as a criterion in the grant decision.

23.10 Distributed bus arbitration

Consider the following distributed bus arbitration scheme. Each device X has an input control signal X_in and an output control signal X_out and it can assert and observe the bus busy signal. The control input to the leftmost device is always asserted, giving it the highest priority. At the beginning of each clock cycle, a device can deassert its control output signal, which serves as a bus request indicator. If X_in is asserted, device X must assert X_out if it does not intend to use the bus. When signal propagation is complete, the only device with its control input

asserted and its control output deasserted has priority for using the bus at the beginning of the next bus cycle. Discuss design considerations for this distributed priority scheme, including the relationship between the clock cycle and signal propagation time in the chain of devices.

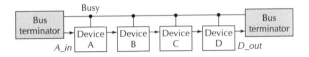

23.11 Distributed bus arbitration

The VAX series of computers used a bus with distributed arbitration and 16 bus request lines R_i, $0 \le i \le 15$, with lower-indexed lines having higher priorities. When device i wanted to use the bus, it made a reservation for a future slot by asserting R_i during the current time slot. At the end of the current time slot, all requesting devices examined the request lines to determine if a higher-priority device had requested the bus; if not, then the device could use the bus during the requested slot.

a. Show how 17 devices can share the bus even though there are only 16 request lines. *Hint:* The additional device would have the lowest priority.
b. Argue that usually, and paradoxically, the lowest-priority device of part a has the shortest average wait time for using the bus. Thus, in VAX, this lowest-priority spot was assigned to the CPU.
c. Discuss conditions under which the assertion of part b would not hold.

23.12 Bus performance

a. Redo Example 23.3, but this time assume that the bus transactions take 5 ns (10% of cases), 25 ns (20%), 35 ns (25%), and 55 ns (45%). Provide intuitive justification for any difference between your results and those obtained in Example 23.3.
b. Repeat part a with these transaction times and percentages: 5 ns (30%), 30 ns (50%), 55 ns (20%).

23.13 Buses for sensing and instrumentation

Buses that are used for communicating data between sensors, instruments, and a control computer are known as *fieldbuses*. A commonly used fieldbus standard is the Foundation fieldbus. Answer the following questions about the Foundation fieldbus standard based on research in books and on the Internet.

a. What are the main design criteria that make a fieldbus different from other buses?
b. How are devices connected to the bus and what is the arbitration method, if any?
c. What is the bus data width and how is data transmitted over the bus?
d. What are the most important application domains for the bus?

23.14 A/D and D/A conversion

a. One way to convert a 4-bit digital signal to an analog voltage level in the range of 0–3 V, say, is to connect a ladder network of resistors to the 4 outputs of a register holding the digital sample. Present a diagram of such a D/A converter and explain why it produces the desired output.
b. Conceptually, the simplest way to convert an analog input voltage in the range of 0–3 V, say, is to use the so-called flash circuit, which consists of resistors, voltage comparators, and a priority encoder. Study the design of flash A/D converters and prepare a two-page report on how they work.
c. When the input to the A/D converter of part b is a rapidly varying voltage, sampling must also capture the signal's frequency besides its amplitude. Briefly discuss how a proper sampling frequency is determined. Consult a digital signal processing text or handbook for this part.

23.15 Interfacing basics

Suppose that the A/D converter used in the wind vane application of Figure 23.11 is rather inaccurate but does not have a systematic error or bias. In other words, the error is truly random and may be in either direction. Outline a procedure that allows the microcontroller to compensate for the conversion error to permit us to obtain more accurate results for the wind direction.

23.16 Other interfacing standards

Many older, lesser known, or domain-specific, interfacing standards, as well as much detail of widely used standards, were not discussed in Section 23.6. Some of these are listed. Prepare a two-page report on the characteristics and application domains of one of the following standard interfaces.

a. ISA (industry standard architecture) bus
b. VESA VL-local bus (an extension of ISA)
c. Plug-and-play technology for PCI
d. Parallel port
e. PCMCIA for notebook computers

23.17 Universal bay on notebook computers

Some notebook computers have a universal bay (sometimes called a multibay) into which a variety of I/O devices, or even a second battery, can be inserted. Speculate on how the inserted device might be connected to the computer (pins, connectors, etc.), how the computer might recognize what type of device is present in the bay, and why such a change of device does not affect the I/O programming.

REFERENCES AND FURTHER READINGS

[Alex93]   Alexandridis, N., *Design of Microprocessor-Based Systems,* Prentice Hall, 1993.

[Ande97]   Anderson, D., *Universal Serial Bus System Architecture,* Addison-Wesley (Mindshare), 1997.

[Bate02]   Bateman, A., and I. Paterson-Stephens, *The DSP Handbook: Algorithms, Applications, and Design Techniques,* Prentice Hall, 2002.

[Buch00]   Buchanan, W., *Computer Busses,* Arnold, 2000.

[Dudr96]   Dudra, F., "Serial and UART Tutorial." See http://freebsd.unixtech.be/doc/en_US.ISO8859-1/articles/serial-uart/

[Lobu02]   LoBue, M. T., "Surveying Today's Most Popular Storage Interfaces," *IEEE Computer,* Vol. 35, No. 12, pp. 48–55, December 2002.

[Myer02]   Myers, R. L., *Display Interfaces: Fundamentals and Standards,* Wiley, 2002.

[Ston82]   Stone, H. S., *Microcomputer Interfacing,* Addison-Wesley, 1982.

[Wolf01]   Wolf, W., *Computers as Components: Principles of Embedded Computing System Design,* Morgan Kaufmann, 2001.

[WWW]   The following organizations present up-to-date information about the various buses and standards covered in this chapter: ansi.org, atmforum.com, pcisig.com, scsita.org, standards.ieee.org, usb.org.

CHAPTER 24

CONTEXT SWITCHING AND INTERRUPTS

"When your work speaks for itself, don't interrupt."
Henry J. Kaiser

"As I was saying the other day, . . ."
Luis Ponce de Léon, on resuming a lecture interrupted by five years' imprisonment

Ordinary users and programmers usually do not need to concern themselves with details of I/O device operation and how to control them. These tasks are relegated to the operating system, which is called by user programs whenever I/O is needed. The operating system in turn activates device drivers, which spawn asynchronous I/O processes that perform their tasks and report back to the CPU via interrupts. When an interrupt is detected, the CPU might switch context, setting aside the then-active program and beginning to execute an interrupt service routine instead. This type of context switching can also be allowed between different user programs, or between threads of the same program, as a mechanism for avoiding long waits due to the unavailability of data or system resources.

■ 24.1 System Calls for I/O

As mentioned in Section 7.6, and again at the end of Section 22.2, most users do not get involved in details of I/O transfers between devices and memory but rather use system calls to accomplish I/O data transfers. One reason for this indirect I/O via the operating system is the need for protecting data and programs against accidental or deliberate damage. Another is that it is more convenient for the user, as well as the system, to rely on operating system routines to provide a clean, uniform interface to such devices in a way that is, to the extent possible, device-independent. A system routine initiates the I/O, which is typically performed through DMA, and then relinquishes the control of the CPU. Later, the CPU will receive an interrupt signifying I/O completion and will let the I/O routine perform its cleanup stage.

For example, in reading data from a disk, an ordinary user should be prevented from accessing or modifying system data or files belonging to another user. Additionally, a dozen or more error types might be encountered during a read operation. Typically, each such error has an associated flag bit in the device status register. Examples include invalid cylinder (track, sector) number, checksum violation, timing anomaly, and invalid memory address. These status bits must be checked on each I/O operation and appropriate action initiated to deal with any anomaly. It makes perfect sense to relieve the user from such complexities by providing I/O service routines whose user interfaces focus on the required data transfer rather then the mechanics of the transfer itself.

Convenience and device-independence are achieved by providing various layers of control between the user program and hardware I/O devices. Typical layers include:

$$\text{OS kernel} \to \text{I/O subsystem} \to \text{Device driver} \to \text{Device controller} \to \text{Device}$$

The device driver is a software link between the two hardware components on the right and the operating system and its I/O subsystem on the left. As such, it is both OS- and device-dependent. A new I/O device that does not follow an already established hardware/software interface must be introduced into the market with device drivers for various popular operating systems. The idea is to capture as much as possible of the specific characteristics of an I/O device in its associated driver so that the I/O subsystem needs to deal only with certain general categories, each encompassing many different I/O devices.

The operating system (OS) is the system software that controls everything on a computer. Its functions include resource management, scheduling of tasks, protection, and exception handling. The I/O subsystem within the operating system handles interactions with I/O devices and manages the actual data transfers. It often consists of a basic layer that is intimately involved with hardware features and other supporting modules that may not be required for all systems. The basic I/O subsystem in the case of the Windows operating system is BIOS (basic input/output system), which, in addition to basic I/O, takes care of booting the system at the initial power-up. BIOS routines are typically stored in ROM or flash memory to prevent loss in the event of power interruption.

The aforementioned grouping of I/O devices into a small number of generic types is referred to as I/O abstraction. In what follows, we review four of the most useful I/O abstractions commonly found in modern operating systems:

Character-stream I/O

Block I/O

Network sockets

Clocks or timers

The character-stream I/O abstraction deals with input or output as a stream of characters. A new input character is simply appended to the end of the input stream, while a new output character is forwarded to output device after the previous character. This type of behavior is captured by the system function calls `get(•)` and `put(•)`, where "get" obtains an input character and "put" sends a character to output. Using these primitives, it is relatively easy to build up I/O routines that input or output strings of several characters. In fact, examining the first 8 lines in Table 7.2, we note that character-oriented I/O is the only type provided in MiniMIPS (and its simulator) at the assembly language level. Character-stream I/O is particularly suited to devices such as keyboards, mice, modems, printers, and audio cards.

The block I/O abstraction is suitable for disks and other block-oriented devices. As few as three basic system calls can capture the essence of block I/O: seek(•), read(•), and write(•). The first of these, "seek," is needed to specify which block is to be transferred, while "read" and "write" perform the actual I/O data transfer to and from memory, respectively. It is possible to build a memory-mapped file system on top of such block-oriented I/O primitives. The idea is for the system call for I/O to return the virtual address of the required data rather than initiate the data transfer. The data is then loaded automatically into memory upon the first access to it via the virtual address provided. In this way, file system access becomes quite efficient because its data transfers are handled by the virtual memory system.

Network sockets are special I/O devices that support data communication via computer networks. An I/O system call in this regard can create a socket, cause a local socket to be connected to a remote address (a socket created by another application), detect remote applications that request to be plugged in to a local socket, or send/receive packets. Servers, which typically support many sockets, may additionally require facilities for more efficient detection of which sockets have packets waiting to be received and which ones have room to accept a new packet for transmission.

Clocks and timers, which are essential components in implementing real-time control applications with microcontrollers, are also found in general-purpose processors in view of their usefulness for determining current time of day, measuring elapsed time, and triggering events at preset times. A *programmable interval timer* is a hardware mechanism that can be preset to a desired time interval and generates an interrupt when that amount of time has elapsed. The operating system uses interval timers for scheduling periodic tasks or to allot a *time slice* to a task in a multitasking environment. It can also allow user processes to make use of this facility. In the latter case, the user's request for interval timers beyond the number available in hardware may be honored by setting up virtual timers. The overhead of maintaining these virtual timers is small compared to time intervals that are measured in typical applications. For example, a time interval of 1 ms corresponds to 10^6 clock ticks with a 1 GHz clock.

24.2 Interrupts, Exceptions, and Traps

We have already discussed (see Sections 22.4 and 22.5) how interrupts are used to relieve the CPU from micromanaging the I/O data transfer process. In this, and the following two sections, we deal with how interrupts are implemented and handled.

Interrupts in a computer are much like telephone and e-mail interruptions during a person's workday or study time (Figure 24.1). When a telephone rings, we set aside what we are doing (bookmark a page we are reading in a book, hit the save button on our computer, press the mute button on the TV) and engage in conversation with the caller. After we hang up, we may scribble some notes about what needs to be done as a result of the telephone call and return to our main work. Studies show that it takes 1–2 minutes for us to "recover" from the interruption and continue working at the same rate as before the telephone rang. The same applies when we get an e-mail alert, although for unknown reasons, perhaps having to do with the relative difficulty of reading and writing versus talking, the recovery time is somewhat longer in this case. We may completely disallow, or selectively disable, such interrupts by unplugging the telephone

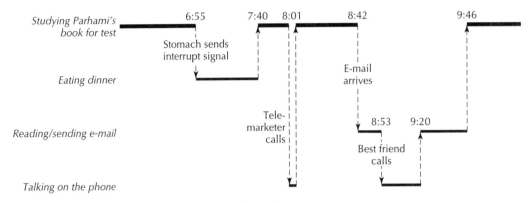

Figure 24.1 The notions of interrupts and nested interrupts.

cord or checking for new e-mail every two hours, instead of continuously. This is akin to what a CPU does when it disables interrupts or restricts them to high-priority ones only.

Interrupt is both the general term used for a CPU diverting its attention from the current task being executed to some unusual or unpredictable event that demands its involvement (for whatever reason) and the specific type of interrupt caused by input/output and other hardware units. In the latter context, we sometimes talk of *hardware interrupts*. The CPU can be diverted from the current task by causes in two other categories:

Exceptions that are caused by illegal operations such as divide-by-0, trying to access a nonexistent memory location, or executing a privileged instructions in user mode. Exceptions are by nature unpredictable and rather infrequent.

Traps, or software interrupts, which are deliberate operating-system calls when particular services are needed. Unlike hardware interrupts and exceptions, traps are preplanned in a program's design and not at all rare.

Much of our discussion in this chapter deals with ways of handling hardware interrupts. However, exceptions and traps are handled similarly in that they require setting aside the program being executed and calling a special software routine to deal with the cause.

In the simplest scheme, there is only one interrupt request line into the CPU. Multiple devices that need to interrupt the CPU share this line. Interrupt handling in this minimal configuration is discussed in Section 24.3. More generally, there may be multiple interrupt request lines of varying priorities. The following example shows why having multiple priority levels for interrupts may be useful. Nested interrupts, and issues in their handling, are discussed in Section 24.4.

Example 24.1: Interrupt priority levels in an automobile on-board computer   Suppose that a microcontroller used in an automobile has four priority levels for interrupts. The units interrupting the controller include an impact sensor subsystem, which needs attention within 0.1 ms, along with four other subsystems as follows:

Subsystem	Interrupt rate	Max service time (ms)
Fuel/ignition	500/s	1
Engine temperature	1/s	100
Dashboard display	800/s	0.2
Air conditioner	1/s	100

Discuss how priorities could be assigned to guarantee the response time of 0.1 ms for the impact sensor and to handle each of the other critical units before the next interrupt is produced.

Solution: The impact sensor must be given the highest priority because its required response time is less than the service time for each of the other interrupt types; no other subsystem can share this highest priority level. The air conditioner can be given the lowest priority level because its function is not safety-critical. We have two priority levels left and three subsystems. Because the engine temperature monitor has a maximum service time of 100 ms, it must have a lower priority than the display and fuel/ignition subsystems, which need several hundreds of service periods per second. Finally, the latter two can share the same priority level, given that each can be served after the other without exceeding the time available before the next interrupt. For example, if the fuel/ignition subsystem service starts right before the display interrupt, a total of 1.2 ms will elapse before both interrupts service routines are completed, whereas there is $1/800$ s $= 1.25$ ms available before the next dashboard display interrupt arrives. Note that we have ignored the service time for impact sensor subsystem interrupts that have the highest priority because they occur very infrequently, and when they do, all else becomes unimportant.

24.3 Simple Interrupt Handling

In this section, we assume a single interrupt line going into, and one interrupt acknowledge signal produced by, the CPU. Multiple interrupt lines with hierarchical priority levels, and the associated nesting of interrupt service activities, will be discussed in Section 24.4.

The interrupt request signals of all participating units are connected to the single IntReq line into the CPU (Figure 24.2). There is an "interrupt mask" flip-flop that the CPU can set to disable interrupts. If IntReq is asserted and interrupts are not masked, a flip-flop within the CPU is set to record the presence of an interrupt request and to:

Acknowledge the interrupt by asserting the IntAck signal

Notify the CPU's next-address logic that an interrupt is pending

Set the interrupt mask so that no new interrupt is accepted

Once devices have noted the assertion of the IntAck signal, they deassert their request signals, thus leading to the resetting of the interrupt acknowledge flip-flop. This sequence of events is

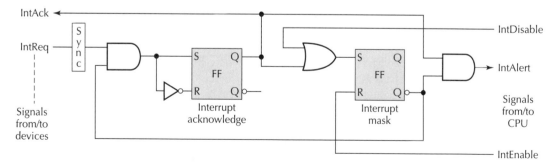

Figure 24.2 Simple interrupt logic for the single-cycle MicroMIPS.

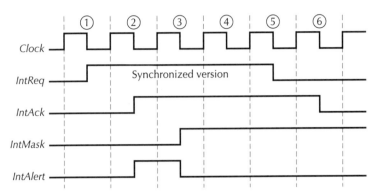

Figure 24.3 Timing of interrupt request and acknowledge signals.

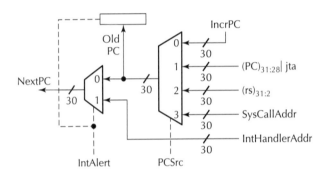

Figure 24.4 Part of the next-address logic for single-cycle MicroMIPS, with an interrupt capability added (compare the lower left part of Figure 13.4).

depicted in Figure 24.3. Meanwhile, immediately following interrupt acknowledgment and before the interrupt mask is set, an interrupt alert (IntAlert) signal is produced that directs the CPU to start executing an interrupt routine. This is done by loading the start address of the interrupt handler into the PC and saving the previous content of PC to be used as the return address once the interrupt has been serviced.

Consider, for example, how such a simple interrupt capability might be added to the single-cycle MicroMIPS implementation of Chapter 13. Figure 24.4 shows the modified part in the next-address logic of Figure 13.4 to allow the address of an interrupt handling routine to be loaded into PC whenever the IntAlert signal is asserted. Of course, the present content of PC must be saved and used as the return address once the interrupt has been serviced. We can assume the inclusion of a special register that is loaded with the old (original) PC content whenever IntAlert is asserted. It is then necessary to provide a "return from interrupt" instruction that places the saved PC content into the PC and asserts the IntEnable signal so that new interrupts can again be accepted. Note that we cannot use register $ra for saving the interrupt return address as we do for procedures. The reason is that an interrupt can occur at any time, including within a procedure that has not yet saved (or has no need to save) its return address on the stack.

Because there is only one interrupt signal into the CPU, the first order of business for the interrupt handler is determining the cause of the interrupt so that appropriate actions can be taken. One way to do this is for the interrupt handler to poll all I/O devices to see which one(s) requested service. The procedure for this is similar to polling for I/O as discussed in

Section 22.3. Polling can occur, and service can be provided, in the order of device priorities. An alternative to polling is to provide the interrupt acknowledge signal only to the highest-priority device and use a daisy chain for passing the signal to other devices in descending order of priorities. This is similar to the forwarding of the bus grant signal in the arrangement of Figure 23.10. A device that requested service may send its identity over the address or data bus upon receiving the acknowledge signal from the CPU. Any lower priority device will not see the interrupt acknowledge signal and thus will continue to assert its interrupt request signal until an acknowledgment is received. Note that polling is more flexible than daisy chaining in that it allows priorities to be easily modified. The disadvantage of polling is that it wastes a lot of time interrogating many I/O devices whenever any one of them generates an interrupt.

Once the CPU has learned the identity of the (highest-priority) device that requested the interrupt, it jumps to the appropriate segment of the interrupt service routine that handles the particular request type. This process can be made more efficient by allowing the device to supply the starting address for its desired interrupt handler; in this way, transition to that handler can occur immediately. One benefit of this method, which is known as *vectored interrupt,* is that a device may supply different addresses depending on its request type, thus avoiding additional interrogations or levels of indirection. In any case, the interrupt service routine must save and, upon termination, restore any register that it needs to use in the course of its execution. This is much like what happens in a procedure, except that here all registers have the same status with regard to saving and restoring (an ordinary procedure is allowed to use some registers without saving them; see the MiniMIPS register usage conventions in Figure 5.2).

The previous arrangement can be extended to multiple levels of interrupts with different priorities by using a priority encoder as shown in Figure 24.5. Each interrupt request line on the left represents a set of devices with identical priorities. If one or more interrupt requests are received, the IntReq signal is asserted to notify the CPU. Additionally, the identity of the highest-priority request line that has been asserted is provided to the CPU. In this way, either the CPU can uniquely identify the interrupting device (when a request line represents a single device), or else it will poll a subset of all devices. This is more efficient than having to poll all devices with each interrupt. If the CPU is to be able to enable or disable each type of interrupt separately, the scheme shown in Figure 24.5 must be modified by moving the interrupt mask capability to the input side of the priority encoder. Supplying the details of the required modification is left to the readers.

The single-cycle MicroMIPS implementation considered thus far continuously monitors the interrupt condition and begins executing the interrupt service routine in the clock cycle following the assertion of IntAlert. Adding interrupt capability to the multicycle MicroMIPS implementation of Chapter 14 is straightforward and does not require any insight beyond

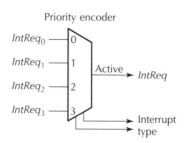

Figure 24.5 Using a priority encoder to produce a single interrupt request signal and an interrupt type from multiple requests.

recognizing the appropriate control state at which interrupt requests must be checked. Supplying the details is left as an exercise.

Adding an interrupt capability to the pipelined MicroMIPS designs of Chapters 15 and 16, however, requires more care. The issues involved are virtually identical to those for exceptions, as discussed in Section 16.6. In the case of a simple linear pipeline, similar to those in Figures 15.9 and 15.11, the pipeline may be flushed by allowing all instructions currently in various stages of the pipeline to run to completion; this might require more than just inserting $q - 1$ bubbles in a q-stage pipeline. For example, if one of the instructions within the pipeline encounters a data cache miss, a lengthy pipeline stall occurs while main memory is accessed. In the case of virtual memory, there is the possibility of a page fault with its even greater latency, which may not be admissible for interrupts requiring a short response time. An alternative is to simply annul all partially completed instructions that have not yet affected the data memory or register contents, while taking care that no inconsistency is introduced as a result. For example, in the pipelined data path of Figure 15.11, various instructions affect the data cache and register contents in different stages of the pipeline. If an instruction has already had an irreversible effect, that instruction, and all instructions ahead of it in the pipeline, must run to completion for the sake of avoiding inconsistencies.

With a branching pipeline or out-of-order instruction issue (Figure 16.8), one can either flush the pipeline by allowing all instructions to run to completion or simply discard all partially executed instructions whose results have not yet been committed. This requires that the next PC value associated with the last committed instruction be maintained in the retirement and commit part of the pipeline. The latter approach wastes some work that was performed on the uncommitted instructions but allows a quicker reaction to interrupts. Note that in a modern processor, dozens of instructions may be in various stages of completion, and some of these may encounter significant delays for reasons outlined in the preceding paragraph. Therefore, given that the retirement and commit logic already ensures the consistency of all completed instructions, discarding all uncommitted instructions is the preferred alternative.

■ 24.4 Nested Interrupts

An obvious idea for handling multiple high-speed I/O devices or time-sensitive control applications is to allow nesting of interrupts so that a high-priority interrupt request can preempt the program that handles a lower-priority interrupt. Execution of the latter would then resume once the high-priority interrupt has been serviced. However, nested interrupts are more difficult to orchestrate than nested procedure calls; the latter are correctly handled with the help of a stack for local variable storage and saving of the return address. Difficulties in dealing with nested interrupts arise from their unpredictable timing. A programmer writing a procedure that calls another procedure can ensure that the second call is not made until after all required preparatory steps have been completed (see Figure 6.2). The same does not hold for interrupts: a high-priority interrupt can occur immediately after a lower priority one, perhaps after only a single instruction has been executed. It is thus important that further interrupts be disabled until the interrupt handler has had a chance to save enough information to enable the handling of the lower priority interrupt to resume once the high-priority one has been serviced.

The need for nested interrupts is evident from Example 24.1 and has to do with required CPU response-time guarantees for certain types of interrupt. If the four-level interrupt scheme depicted in Figure 24.5 were used for the control application of Example 24.1, an interrupt with any priority level would have a worst-case response time of 100 ms, given that the servicing of an air-conditioner interrupt may have just begun when the higher priority interrupt request arrives. This is clearly unacceptable. As another example, a disk drive that reads at 3 MB/s and transfers data to the CPU in 4 B chunks (see Example 22.7) requires that its interrupt request be serviced within 0.75 μs. If there is any type of interrupt whose servicing takes more than 0.75 μs, and if no interrupt is accepted during the servicing of another interrupt, then just giving the disk controller the highest priority would not solve the problem; some type of preemption capability is required.

Consider now the steps pursued by the CPU in servicing of an interrupt, as enumerated in Section 22.4. Assuming a nonpipelined implementation, the following actions occur en route to, and during, servicing the interrupt.

1. Disable (mask) all interrupts.
2. Call the interrupt service routine; save the PC as in a procedure call.
3. Save the CPU state.
4. Save minimal information about the interrupt on the stack.
5. Enable interrupts (or at least higher priority ones).
6. Identify cause of interrupt and attend to the underlying request.
7. Restore CPU state to what existed before the last interrupt.
8. Return from the interrupt service routine.

A new interrupt can be accepted after step 5. Therefore, the faster the first five steps are executed, the lower the worst-case latency before a higher priority interrupt can be accepted. For example, the highest priority interrupt has to wait for the execution of these five steps in the worst case. Any lower priority interrupt will have to wait for the worst-case service time of all possible interrupts of higher priority, including new ones that may occur in the course of servicing of some such interrupts.

Figure 24.6 depicts the relationship of an application program with two nested interrupts. The first (lower priority) interrupt is detected after the completion of instruction (a) and

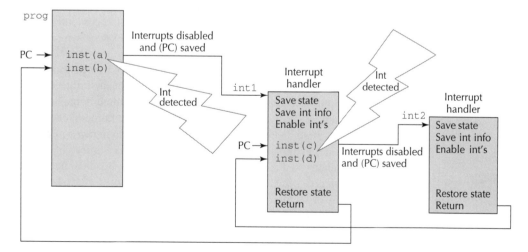

Figure 24.6 Example of nested interrupts.

before instruction (b) starts its execution within the application program. At this point, PC contains the address of instruction (b), so saving its content will allow the hardware to return to the point of interruption and continue running the application as if nothing happened between instructions (a) and (b). All interrupts are immediately disabled (masked), and control is automatically transferred to an interrupt handler. Once the interrupt handler has saved the CPU state and some minimal information about the interrupt, it enables all higher priority interrupts before proceeding to handle the existing interrupt. If shortly after this point, a second (higher-priority) interrupt is detected between instructions (c) and (d), the same process is repeated, with servicing of the lower priority interrupt abandoned in favor of the newly arriving one.

■ 24.5 Types of Context Switching

The transfer of control from a running program to an interrupt handler, or from the handler for a low-priority interrupt to that of a higher priority interrupt, is referred to as *context switching*. The context of an executing process consists of the CPU state, including contents of all registers, along with certain memory management information items that allow the process to access its address space. Note that calling a procedure is not considered to be a context switch because the procedure generally operates within the same context as the calling program; for example, it can access the calling program's global variables and the parameters passed to it via the register file or stack. Besides mandatory context switches due to interrupts, the operating system may perform voluntary context switching for reasons that have to do with improving the overall system performance. This type of context switching is performed within the framework of *multiprogramming* or *multitasking,* concepts that are explained in this section. A related term, *multithreading,* will be explained in Section 24.6.

Execution of instruction sequences within a program can be delayed for various reasons. These include both short stalls for events such as cache miss or TLB miss (see Chapters 18 and 20) and much longer waits for page faults and I/O requests. Thus far in this book, we have viewed such stalls and waits as contributors to reduced performance. This is clearly the correct viewpoint as far as the execution of a single sequential task is concerned. However, just as a person's time does not really go to waste if she or he browses the newspaper or reads e-mail messages while placed on hold on the telephone, the computer's or CPU's resources are also not wasted if there is another program or task to execute while one task encounters a lengthy delay.

The use of multiprogramming, to overlap one program's wait periods with the execution of other programs, began with the time-sharing computer systems of the early 1960s. In a time-sharing system, multiple user programs reside in the computer's main memory, allowing the CPU to switch among them with relative ease. To ensure fairness, each program may be allotted a fixed *time slice* on the CPU, with the task set aside in favor of another one at the end of its allotted time, even if it encounters no waiting. The number of simultaneously active tasks in main memory is the *degree of multiprogramming*. It is beneficial to have a large multiprogramming degree because it makes it more likely for the CPU to find useful work even in the event of many tasks encountering lengthy waits. On the other hand, putting too many tasks in main memory means that each one gets a smaller memory allocation, which is detrimental to performance. Multitasking is essentially the same idea as multiprogramming except that the concurrently active tasks may belong to the same user or may even represent different parts (subcomputations) of a single program.

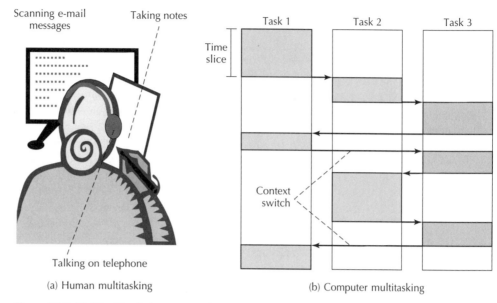

Figure 24.7 depicts multitasking in humans and computers. As seen in Figure 24.7b, one CPU can execute several tasks by shifting attention from one to another through context switching. The CPU switching back and forth among different tasks at a rapid pace creates the illusion of parallel processing even though at any given time, only a single task is being executed. To switch context, the state of the executing process is saved in a process control block and a new process is activated from its beginning or from a previously saved point. Saving and restoring dozens of registers and other control information with each context switch take several microseconds which, in a way, is wasted time. However, the hundreds or even thousands of clock cycles spent on a context switch is still significantly less than many millions of clock cycles required to handle a page fault or an I/O operation.

In the foregoing context, a specific invocation of a program or a task is often referred to as a *process*. Note that two distinct processes may be different invocations of the same program or task. In this sense, *multiprocessing* could be used as a catchall term for multiprogramming or multitasking. However, in the literature on computer architecture, multiprocessing has a specific technical meaning having to do with truly concurrent execution of several processes, as opposed to the apparent concurrency just discussed.

Given that the overhead of context switching is nontrivial, simple context switching is practical only to make use of long wait periods and cannot be used to recover shorter waits due to cache misses and the like. In addition to the tangible overhead for saving and restoring of process states, context switching involves other types of overhead that are much harder to quantify. For example, sharing of instruction and data caches by several processes may lead to conflicts and their attendant cache misses for each process. Similarly, when the processes are not completely independent of one another, synchronization (to ensure that data dependencies are honored) wastes some time and other resources. The following example captures the effects of tangible overhead in context switching.

Example 24.2: Overhead of nested interrupts   Suppose that each time a higher-priority interrupt preempts a low-priority one, an overhead of 20 μs is incurred for saving and restoring the CPU state and other pertinent information. Is this overhead acceptable for the control system application presented in Example 24.1?

Solution: Ignoring the top priority given to the impact sensor, because it does not generate an interrupt during normal system operation, there are three interrupt levels. These are listed, with their associated repetition rates and service times: fuel/ignition (500/s, 1 ms) and dashboard display (800/s, 0.2 ms) have the highest priority, engine temperature (1/s, 100 ms) is in the middle level, and air conditioning (1/s, 100 ms) has the lowest priority. Even assuming that executions of the interrupt handlers for engine temperature and air conditioning are stretched over a full second owing to repeated preemptions, each is preempted no more than about 1300 times, for a total overhead of $2 \times 1300 \times 20 \ \mu$s $= 52$ ms. Considering this preemption overhead along with the total interrupt service time of $500 \times 1 + 1 \times 100 + 800 \times 0.2 + 1 \times 100 = 860$ ms, we note that there will still be a margin of safety equal to $1000 - 860 - 52 = 88$ ms in every second of real time. So, the context switching overhead is acceptable in this application example.

Because of the importance of context switching in efficient handling of interrupts and multi-tasking, some architectures provide hardware resources or aids for this purpose. For example, suppose that a CPU contains four identical register files each of which can be chosen as the active register file by setting a 2-bit control tag. Then, context switching among up to four active processes could be done without any saving or restoring of register contents, by merely adjusting the 2-bit control tag. This is a good example of *low-overhead context switching*. A less drastic alternative is to provide special machine instructions that save or restore the entire register file in one operation. Such instructions are likely to be faster than a sequence of instructions that deal with saving or restoring the registers one at a time.

■ 24.6 Threads and Multithreading

As represented in Figure 24.8, *threads* are streams of instructions (small program segments) within the same task or program that can be executed concurrently with, and for the most part independently of, other threads. As such, they provide an ideal source of independent instructions to fill the CPU execution pipeline and make good use of multiple function units, such as the ones depicted in Figure 16.8. Threads are sometimes called *lightweight processes* because they share a great deal and thus switching between them does not involve as much overhead as conventional (or heavyweight) processes.

Architectures that can handle many threads are referred to as *superthreaded,* where "super" characterizes the width of threading in much the same way that superpipelining is so named because of the pipeline depth. The term *hyperthreading* has also been used for a more flexible form of (simultaneous) multithreading, but we will not dwell on the subtle differences of the two schemes here. Multithreading effectively divides the resources of a single processor into two or more *logical processors,* with each logical processor executing instructions from a

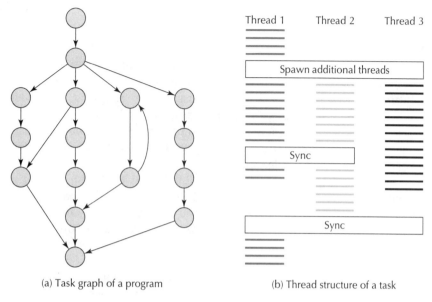

Thread 1   Thread 2   Thread 3

Spawn additional threads

Sync

Sync

(a) Task graph of a program   (b) Thread structure of a task

Figure 24.8 A program divided into tasks (subcomputations) or threads.

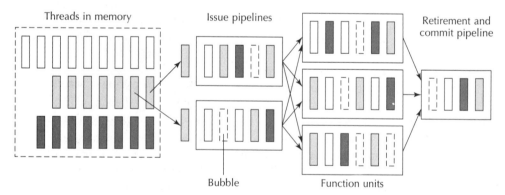

Threads in memory   Issue pipelines   Retirement and commit pipeline

Bubble   Function units

Figure 24.9 Instructions from multiple threads as they make their way through a processor's execution pipeline.

single thread. Figure 24.9 shows how instructions from three different threads may be mixed in the various stages of the execution pipeline in a double-issue processor.

Note that even with multithreading, some pipeline bubbles may appear. However, the number of bubbles is likely to be much smaller when a large number of threads are available for execution. Building a program in multithreaded form is akin to relieving the CPU to a great extent from the burden of discovering instruction-level parallelism and allowing multiple instructions to be issued from disparate parts of a program rather than being confined to nearby instructions in the program's control flow.

PROBLEMS

24.1 Using interval timers

A computer has an interval timer that can be set to a desired length of time (say, 0.1 s), at the end of which it generates an interrupt.

a. Describe how you would use such a timer to build an analog clock, using a stepper motor for output. The stepper motor needs to control only the second hand of the clock, with the minute and hour hands moving appropriately as a result.
b. What are the sources of inaccuracy in the time shown by the clock of part a?

24.2 Interrupt handling notions

Consider the hunger, telephone call, and e-mail alert interrupts depicted in Figure 24.1.

a. Write (in plain English) an interrupt handling routine for these events. Pay special attention to the possibility of interrupt nesting. State all your assumptions clearly.
b. Add two more interrupt levels to the two already present in the figure. Describe the new interrupts in detail and state why they are of higher priority than the existing ones.
c. Briefly discuss how these interrupts and their handling are different from those in a computer.

24.3 Procedure calls versus interrupts

Explain the differences between a procedure call and transfer of control to an interrupt handler. For example, why is it that in the case of a procedure call, changing of the PC content is adequate (i.e., instructions ahead of the procedure call in the pipeline are allowed to complete in the normal way), whereas for an interrupt the pipeline must be flushed?

24.4 Multiple interrupt request lines

a. Show how in Figure 24.5 each type of interrupt can be masked separately.
b. Add interrupt acknowledgment logic to Figure 24.5. Make sure that once the highest-priority interrupt has been acknowledged, continued assertion of a lower-priority interrupt request signal does not lead to spurious or false acknowledgment.

24.5 Interrupts in the multicycle MicroMIPS

Adding interrupt capability to the single-cycle MicroMIPS implementation of Chapter 13 was discussed in Section 24.3. Discuss how the same capability can be added to the multicycle MicroMIPS of Chapter 14. *Hint:* Think in terms of the control state machine in Figure 14.4.

24.6 Nested interrupts

Three devices D_1, D_2, and D_3 are connected to a bus and use interrupt-based I/O. Discuss each of the following scenarios in two ways, once assuming the use of a single interrupt request line and again assuming the use of two interrupt request lines with high and low priorities. In each case, specify when and how interrupts are enabled and disabled.

a. Interrupts are not to be nested.
b. Interrupts for D_1 and D_2 are not to be nested relative to each other, but interrupts from D_3 must be accepted at any time.
c. Three levels of nesting are to be allowed, with D_1 at the low end and D_3 at the high end of the priority spectrum.

24.7 Multitasking concepts

Humans do a great deal of multitasking in everyday life. An example is depicted in Figure 24.7a.

a. What characteristics are required of tasks to make them amenable to multitasking by humans?
b. What types of task are unsuitable for human multitasking?
c. Relate your answers to parts a and b to multitasking in a computer.
d. Construct a realistic scenario in which a human performs five or more tasks concurrently.
e. Is there a limit on the maximum number of concurrent tasks that can be performed by a human?
f. Relate your answer to parts d and e to multitasking in a computer.

24.8 Time-slice granularity in multiprogramming

Consider the following simplifying assumptions in a multiprogramming system. Task running times are uniformly distributed in the range $[0, T_{max}]$. When a time slice of duration τ is assigned to a task, it is used completely and with no waste (this implies that computation and I/O are overlapped), except in the last time slice when the task completes; on average, half of this last time slice is wasted. Context switching time overhead is a constant c and there is no other overhead.

a. Determine the optimal value for τ to minimize waste, assuming that T_{max} is much larger than τ.
b. How does the answer to part a change if task running times are uniformly distributed in $[T_{min}, T_{max}]$? State all your assumptions.

24.9 Multiple interrupt priority levels

Following the lead of Example 24.1, define a real-time system with multiple interrupt priority levels, where response time requirements can be met without a need for nested interrupts. Then, characterize such systems in general.

24.10 Hardware aids for context switching

a. Which of the "complex" instructions listed in Table 8.1 facilitate the implementation of nested interrupts and why?
b. Consider an instruction-set architecture of your choice and list all its machine instructions that have been provided for making context switching more efficient.

24.11 Context switching overhead

In Example 24.2, what is the maximum preemption overhead that would be acceptable?

24.12 Controlling the polling frequency

In Example 22.4, it was stated that a keyboard must be interrogated at least 10 times per second to make sure that no keystroke by the user is missed. Based on what you have learned in this chapter, how can we ensure that the polling is done often enough, but not too often to waste time?

24.13 Interrupt mechanisms in real processors

For a microprocessor of your choosing, describe the interrupt handling mechanism and its impact on instruction execution. Pay special attention to the following aspects of interrupts:

a. Signaling and acknowledgment
b. Enabling and disabling (masking)
c. Priority and nesting
d. Special instructions
e. Hardware versus software

24.14 Interrupt priority levels

There are many similarities between the handling of multiple interrupt priority levels and bus arbitration, as discussed in Section 23.4. For each of the following concepts in interrupts or bus arbitration, indicate whether or not there is a counterpart in the other area. Justify your answer in each case.

a. Rotating priority
b. Daisy chaining
c. Distributed arbitration
d. Interrupt masking
e. Interrupt nesting

24.15 Software interrupt

The `syscall` instruction of MiniMIPS (see Section 7.6) allows a running program to interrupt itself and to pass the control to the operating system. The ARM microprocessor has a similar `SWI` (software interrupt) instruction, where the service being requested is specified in the low-order 8 bits of the instruction itself rather than via the content of a register as in MiniMIPS. Each of the services provided by the operating system has an associated routine in ARM and the starting addresses of these routines are stored in a table.

a. Describe the interrupt mechanism of ARM and indicate how `SWI` fits in it.
b. Provide an overview of ARM's instruction set, focusing on any unusual or unique feature.
c. Identify ARM instructions that the operating system can use to perform the task of transferring control to the appropriate system routine.

24.16 Multilevel interrupt circuit

In this problem, we consider the design of a multilevel priority interrupt circuit external to the processor. The processor has a single interrupt request and one interrupt acknowledge line. The circuit to be designed has a 3-bit internal register that holds the current priority level: a number from 0 to 7. Eight interrupt request lines R_0–R_7 enter the circuit, with R_0 having the highest priority. When a request signal of higher priority than the 3-bit stored level is asserted, an interrupt request signal is sent to the processor. When the interrupt is acknowledged by the processor, the interrupt level is immediately updated and a corresponding acknowledge signal is sent (the acknowledge signal A_i corresponds to the request signal R_i).

a. Present the design of the external priority interrupt circuit as described.

b. Explain the functioning of your circuit, paying special attention to the manner in which the 3-bit level register is updated to hold a smaller or larger value.

REFERENCES AND FURTHER READINGS

[Egge97]   Eggers, S. J., J. S. Emer, H. M. Levy, J. L. Lo, R. L. Stamm, and D. M. Tullsen, "Simultaneous Multithreading: A Platform for Next Generation Processors," *IEEE Micro,* Vol. 17, No. 5, pp. 12–18, September/October 1997.

[Heur04]   Heuring, V. P., and H. F. Jordan, *Computer System Design and Architecture,* Prentice Hall, 2nd ed., 2004.

[Marr02]   Marr, D. T., et al., "Hyper-Threading Technology Architecture and Microarchitecture," *Intel Technology J.,* Vol. 6, No. 1, February 14, 2002. Available at: http://www.intel.com/technology/itj/

[Silb02]   Silberschatz, A., P. B. Galvin, and G. Gagne, *Operating System Concepts,* Wiley, 6th ed., 2002.

[Ward90]   Ward, S. A., and R. H. Halstead Jr, *Computation Structures,* MIT Press, 1990.

PART SEVEN

ADVANCED ARCHITECTURES

"For over a decade, prophets have voiced the contention that the organization of a single computer has reached its limit and that truly significant advances can be made only by interconnection of a multiplicity of computers. . . . [We aim to demonstrate] the continued vitality of the single processor approach."
—*Gene Amdahl, 1967*

"Machines with interchangeable parts can now be constructed with great economy of effort. . . . The world has arrived at an age of cheap complex devices of great reliability; and something is bound to come of it."
—*Vannevar Bush, As We May Think, 1945*

TOPICS IN THIS PART

25. Road to Higher Performance

26. Vector and Array Processing

27. Shared-Memory Multiprocessing

28. Distributed Multicomputing

Having covered basics of computer system architecture and some widely used methods for performance enhancement, we are now ready to look at more advanced design techniques that are in use today or are likely to find their way from supercomputer centers and research laboratories into commodity machines in the near future. Many forms of concurrent processing are already used even in low-end computers. Any systems with peripherals and/or a network interface already has multiple cooperating processors. Workstations with two or more CPUs have been on the market for some time and multiple-CPU personal computers are emerging. Parallel processing is widely viewed as the key to overcoming performance and reliability limits dictated by physical laws and constraints in the manufacturing processes for integrated circuits.

We begin this part with a discussion of methods used in advanced uniprocessors, culminating with an overview of vector and concurrent processing, in Chapter 25. This chapter may be viewed as the concluding chapter of the book for readers who are not interested in a more detailed study of vector and parallel/distributed processing. Rounding up our coverage are three chapters on vector and array processors, which form the oldest categories of high-performance computers, multiprocessor systems with tightly coupled processors sharing a common address space, and multicomputer systems with loosely coupled nodes that typically communicate via message-passing.

■ CHAPTER 25

ROAD TO HIGHER PERFORMANCE

"The most constant difficulty in contriving the engine has arisen from the desire to reduce the time in which the calculations were executed to the shortest which is possible."
—*Charles Babbage, On the Mathematical Powers of the Calculating Engine*

"Rule 8: The development of fast algorithms is slow."
—*Arnold Schönhage, 1994*

TOPICS IN THIS CHAPTER
25.1 Past and Current Performance Trends
25.2 Performance-Driven ISA Extensions
25.3 Instruction-Level Parallelism
25.4 Speculation and Value Prediction
25.5 Special-Purpose Hardware Accelerators
25.6 Vector, Array, and Parallel Processing

Alongside extensive efforts to design instruction sets and hardware organizations that can run at higher clock rates, designers have devised other strategies for improving computer performance. In this chapter, we review four classes of such methods: instruction-set extensions, instruction-level parallelism, speculative execution, and use of special-purpose hardware accelerators. We then show how hardware realization of program loops in vector supercomputers and concurrent processing in parallel and distributed systems allow us to go beyond the performance that is possible with a single-instruction-stream, single-data-stream (SISD) processor, which has been our focus up to now. Vector and parallel processing are covered in greater detail in Chapters 26–28.

■ 25.1 Past and Current Performance Trends

Computer performance grew by a factor of about 10^4 over the last two decades of the twentieth century, to the extent that the level of performance expected of a bulky and expensive top-of-the-line supercomputer in 1980 is now available in desktop or even laptop computers. In approximate terms, the state of available computing power at the outset of the twenty-first century can be summarized thus:

GFLOPS on desktop

TFLOPS in supercomputer center

PFLOPS on drawing board

The factor of 10^4 in improved performance, depicted in accordance with Moore's law in Figure 3.10, came from two complementary sources. A factor of 10^2, or about 25% per year, is attributable to technological advances that continually allowed denser and faster circuits. In other words, if we were to build an early 1980s vintage personal computer using today's technology, with no substantial architectural change, it would likely run the same applications about 100 times as fast. The remaining factor of 100 is due to one-time architectural improvements. We refer to these as "one-time" because it is highly unlikely that the similar performance improvements can be sustained by simply refining and extending these methods. The key ideas are as follows:

Established architectural method	Improvement factor
1. Pipelining (and superpipelining)	3–8
2. Cache memory, 2–3 levels	2–5
3. RISC and related ideas	2–3
4. Multiple instruction issue (superscalar)	2–3
5. ISA extensions (e.g., for multimedia)	1–3

Looking ahead to the year 2020, comparable or even greater improvements relative to the last two decades can be expected. Combined with another factor-of-100 performance increase due to technology advances, the following architectural trends can contribute to matching the aforementioned performance gain over the next two decades. Most of these methods are in fact not that new; what is new is their use in widely available low-cost production machines rather than in one-of-a-kind laboratory prototypes, expensive mainframes, and low-volume supercomputers.

Newer architectural trend	Improvement factor
6. Multithreading (super-, hyper-)	2–5?
7. Speculation and value prediction	2–3?
8. Hardware acceleration	2–10?
9. Vector and array processing	2–10?
10. Parallel/distributed computing	2–1000s?

Note, however, that most of these are methods with limited scopes and may not contribute to performance improvement in all application domains. Despite this cautionary note, it is not too optimistic to predict the availability of EFLOPS (exa $= 10^{18}$) supercomputers and TFLOPS desktop machines by the year 2020. We will discuss architectural methods 5–8 in our list and provide a brief introduction to items 9 and 10 in the rest of this chapter. Vector and array processing are covered in greater detail in Chapter 26. Chapters 27 and 28 are devoted to multiprocessing and multicomputing, respectively, as different approaches to parallel and distributed computing.

Increasingly, performance per unit chip area or unit energy, rather than absolute performance, is becoming important. This is in fact the domain in which most future architectural challenges lie. Modern high-performance processors are quite area-intensive and consume tens of watts of power. Figure 25.1 shows the trend of power consumption in high-end

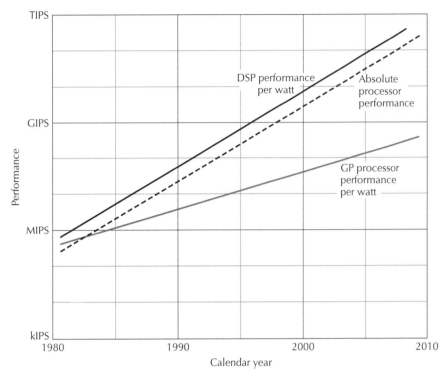

Figure 25.1 Trend in energy consumption for each MIPS of computational power in general-purpose processors and DSPs.

general-purpose processors and digital signal processors (DSPs) that are optimized for use in embedded systems and are thus designed with special attention to energy requirements. Already, many general-purpose processors are implemented in special mobile versions that operate at lower voltage and consume far less power than their standard counterparts. This trend toward lower-power implementations will continue as a result of both increasing reliance on battery-operated devices and the desirability of doing away with bulky power supplies and cooling equipment.

Numerous methods are available, or are being studied, for energy reduction in processors, memory, and I/O devices. These are often categorized as low-power design methods, although low-energy design is a more appropriate designation [Mudg01]. Some of the methods that have been applied at the circuit and logic levels include the following:

Clock gating: turning off the clock signals that go to unused parts of a chip

Asynchronous design: doing away with clocking and the attendant energy waste

Voltage reduction: low-voltage operation is slower, but uses much less energy

Additionally, much can be done at the architectural level, and even in programming and compilation schemes, to achieve energy economy. Architecturally, memory and buses are major consumers of energy. Thus, low-energy memory organizations (with parts of memory deactivated or put to sleep when not in use) and special transfer protocols that reduce the number of signal transitions on system buses are being adopted. In some special mobile designs, the operating system is allowed to dynamically scale the voltage and/or clock frequency based on application requirements. For example, the Intel XScale processor can run at 100 MHz to 1 GHz, consuming less than 30–40 mW of power at the low end of the clock frequency.

Reduction in chip area requirements is motivated, in part, by our desire to fit more functionality on a single VLSI chip. In the early 1980s, even putting a complete processor on a single chip was a challenging task that often necessitated compromising performance. Now, a full CPU (including floating-point hardware) occupies but a small fraction of one chip, with the remaining chip area devoted to cache memories and a number of ancillary units. Eventually, we would like to incorporate all the required processing, storage, and interface units on the same chip, building what is known as a *system on a chip*. Combined with advances in input (e.g., voice recognition) and output (e.g., microdisplays embedded in eyeglasses), such single-chip computers will allow the construction of tiny, nearly invisible, wearable computers.

An interesting trade-off exists between energy and chip area requirements. Given that power is proportional to the square of voltage, it is possible to reduce energy consumption through parallel processing: two low-voltage processors may offer the same performance as a single higher-voltage processor at lower energy cost. This is one of the driving forces behind the development of *chip multiprocessors*. Another embodiment of this trade-off is in advanced cellular phones that use two processors: a low-power, but computationally weak, general-purpose processor and a digital signal processor. One processor would have probably used less area but would not be as energy-efficient. A natural extension of this approach is to place multiple processors (or "cores"), from low-power, low-performance to the other extreme on the same chip and activating the appropriate unit depending on performance requirements [Kuma03]. If these cores could be based on the same instruction-set architecture (ISA), significant simplification in software and applications would result relative to using diverse, specialized processors.

25.2 Performance-Driven ISA Extensions

As mentioned at the beginning of Section 8.4, the instruction-set architectures of modern processors have evolved over many years in the context of engineering and economic considerations. Over time, expanded application domains have led to the introduction of new instructions in ISAs. Examples of instructions that have been introduced to improve performance include the following:

Multiply-add: combining two operations in one instruction

Multiply-accumulate: to compute sum of products with minimal round-off error

Conditional copying: to avoid some branches and their performance penalties

As a rule, functionalities needed only in specific application contexts are incorporated in special-purpose processors and are less attractive for inclusion in general-purpose processors, given possible adverse effect on the complexity of the device, and thus its performance.

Beginning in the 1990s, and especially after the introduction of the World Wide Web, a notable shift in computer applications occurred. As a result, audio, interactive video, graphics, and animation (collectively referred to as *multimedia*) overshadowed traditional number crunching and data manipulation as the dominant workload for general-purpose computers. Hence, various architectural extensions and instruction-set augmentations were introduced for more efficient handling of the new workload. Unfortunately, the desire to preserve backward compatibility and to reduce the cost of modifications led to compromises that prevented the full benefits of such extensions from materializing. Nevertheless, the idea of introducing special instructions to speed up certain frequently used operations is important enough to warrant a brief review in the rest of this section.

The multimedia applications just alluded to are characterized by repetitive operations on subword operands. By "subword" we mean operands that are less than 32 bits wide. Examples include 8-bit pixel attributes and 16-bit audio samples. Even though a word-oriented ALU can perform arithmetic and logic operations on shorter operands, doing so appears to waste both hardware and time. One of the better-known early attempts at taking advantage of this application characteristic to boost performance was Intel's MMX (multimedia extension), devised for the Pentium processor. MMX consisted of adding 57 new instructions to the 80x86 ISA to handle several subword arithmetic operations in a single instruction. MMX-like instructions that allow subword parallelism are now more or less standard on many processors.

To understand Intel's MMX instructions, consider a register file with a number of 64-bit registers. MMX actually uses 8 floating-point registers that double as the MMX integer register file, but this is just a cost-saving design choice. More registers would have increased the performance impact of MMX. A 64-bit MMX register can be viewed as holding a single 64-bit integer or a vector of 2, 4, or 8 progressively narrower integer operands. Various arithmetic, logic, comparison, and rearrangement instructions are provided for each of these vector lengths. Table 25.1 lists the instruction classes and their effects. The column labeled "Vector" indicates the number of independent vector elements that can be specified in the 64-bit operand.

■ **TABLE 25.1** Intel MMX instructions.

Class	Instruction	Vector	Op type	Function or results
Copy	Register copy		32 bits	Integer register ↔ MMX register
	Parallel pack	4, 2	Saturate	Convert to narrower elements
	Parallel unpack low	8, 4, 2		Merge lower halves of 2 vectors
	Parallel unpack high	8, 4, 2		Merge upper halves of 2 vectors
Arithmetic	Parallel add	8, 4, 2	Wrap/Saturate[1]	Add; inhibit carry at boundaries
	Parallel subtract	8, 4, 2	Wrap/Saturate[1]	Subtract with carry inhibition
	Parallel multiply low	4		Multiply, keep the 4 low halves
	Parallel multiply high	4		Multiply, keep the 4 high halves
	Parallel multiply-add	4		Multiply, add adjacent products[2]
	Parallel compare equal	8, 4, 2		All 1s where equal, else all 0s
	Parallel compare greater	8, 4, 2		All 1s where greater, else all 0s
Shift	Parallel left shift logical	4, 2, 1		Shift left, respect boundaries
	Parallel right shift logical	4, 2, 1		Shift right, respect boundaries
	Parallel right shift arith	4, 2		Arith shift within each (half)word
Logic	Parallel AND	1	Bitwise	dest ← (src1) ∧ (src2)
	Parallel ANDNOT	1	Bitwise	dest ← (src1) ∧ (src2)′
	Parallel OR	1	Bitwise	dest ← (src1) ∨ (src2)
	Parallel XOR	1	Bitwise	dest ← (src1) ⊕ (src2)
Memory access	Parallel load MMX reg		32 or 64 bits	Address given in integer register
	Parallel store MMX reg		32 or 64 bit	Address given in integer register
Control	Empty FP tag bits			Required for compatibility[3]

[1]Wrap simply means dropping the carry-out; saturation may be unsigned or signed.

[2]Four 16-bit multiplications, four 32-bit intermediate results, two 32-bit final results.

[3]Floating-point tag bits help with faster context switching, among other functions.

The parallel pack and unpack instructions are quite interesting and useful. Unpacking allows vector elements to be extended to the next larger width (byte to halfword, halfword to word, word to doubleword) to allow computation of intermediate results with greater precision. The unpacking operations can be specified thus,

8-vectors, low:	xxxxabcd, xxxxefgh → aebfcgdh
8-vectors, high:	abcdxxxx, efghxxxx → aebfcgdh
4-vectors, low:	xxab, xxcd → acbd
4-vectors, high:	abxx, cdxx → acbd
2-vectors, low:	xa, xb → ab
2-vectors, high:	ax, bx → ab

where i-vector means a vector of length i and letters stand for vector elements in the operands (on the left of the arrow) and results (on the right). As an example, when the first vector is all 0s, this operation effectively doubles the width of the lower or upper elements of the second operand through 0-extension (e.g., 0000, xxcd → 0c0d). Packing performs the reverse conversion in that it allows returning the results to the original width:

4-vector:	$a_1 a_0 b_1 b_0 c_1 c_0 d_1 d_0$ → 0000abcd
2-vector:	$a_1 a_0 b_1 b_0$ → 00ab

In filtering, for example, pixel values may have to be multiplied by the corresponding filter coefficients; this usually leads to overflow if elements are not first unpacked.

A key feature of MMX is the capability for *saturating arithmetic*. With ordinary unsigned arithmetic, overflow causes the apparent result (after dropping the carry-out bit) to become smaller then either operand. This is known as *wrapped arithmetic*. When applied to arithmetic on pixel attributes, this type of wraparound may lead to anomalies such as bright pixels within regions that are supposed to be fairly dark. With saturating arithmetic, results that exceed the maximum representable value are forced to that maximum value. A saturating unsigned adder, for example, can be built from an ordinary adder and a multiplexer at the output that chooses between the adder result and a constant, depending on the carry-out bit. For signed results, saturating arithmetic can be defined in an analogous way, with the most positive or negative value used depending on the direction of overflow.

Arithmetic with subword parallelism requires modifying the ALU to treat 64-bit words in a variety of ways, depending on the vector length. For wrapped addition, this capability is easy to provide and essentially comes for free (simply disable carries at subword boundaries). Saturating addition requires detection of overflow within subwords and choosing either the adder output or a constant as the operation result within that subword. Multiplication is slightly harder, but still quite cost-effective in terms of circuit implementation (supplying the details is left as an exercise). The effects of parallel multiplication and parallel multiply-add MMX instructions are depicted in Figure 25.2. Parallel comparison instructions are illustrated in Figure 25.3.

Note that MMX deals exclusively with integer values. A similar capability was added in a subsequent extension to the Intel processors to provide similar speedups with 32- or 64-bit floating-point operands, packed within 128-bit quadwords in registers [Thak99]. This latter capability is known as the *streaming SIMD extension* (SSE); the meaning of SIMD will be explained in Section 25.6.

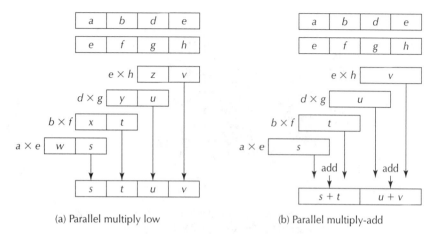

(a) Parallel multiply low   (b) Parallel multiply-add

Figure 25.2 Parallel multiplication and multiply-add in MMX.

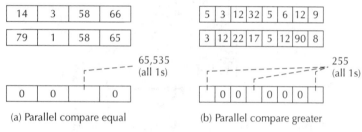

(a) Parallel compare equal   (b) Parallel compare greater

Figure 25.3 Parallel comparisons in MMX.

■ 25.3 Instruction-Level Parallelism

Instruction-level parallelism (ILP) refers to the collection of techniques that allow more than one instruction to be in execution at one time. There is no modern processor that does not have some form of instruction-level parallelism. Pipelining is the most widely used ILP method. We studied pipelining and its impact on performance in Chapters 15 and 16. Multiple instruction issue, or superscalar processing, was discussed briefly in Section 16.5. Both methods are inherently limited in the performance improvement that they offer. The limitations of pipelining were discussed in Section 15.3 with regard to the impact of overhead on speedup (see Figure 15.8), and in Chapter 16 with regard to data and control dependencies.

The limited performance benefit of multiple instruction issue arises from difficulties in identifying independent instructions and then executing them in the face of resource contentions. Identification of independently executable instructions typically occurs within a fairly narrow window of instructions in a preprocessing stage. Widening this window can potentially increase the number of independent instructions for parallel execution, but it may lead to diminishing returns because it produces inefficiencies of the following types:

1. Slowing down the instruction issue logic due to extreme circuit complexity
2. Wasting resources on instructions that will not be executed owing to branching

Figure 25.4a depicts the available instruction-level parallelism under the ideal conditions of no resource limitation, perfect branch prediction, and so on. Even with these optimistic

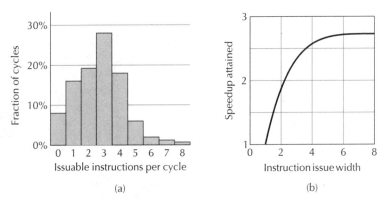

Figure 25.4 Available instruction-level parallelism and the speedup due to multiple instruction issue in superscalar processors [John91].

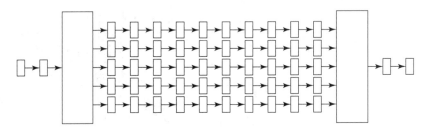

Figure 25.5 A computation with inherent instruction-level parallelism.

assumptions, 5 or more instructions can be issued in no more than 10% of the cases. It is, therefore, not surprising that the attained speedup from multiple instruction issue flattens out beyond the issue width of 4 (Figure 25.4b).

For both pipelining and multiple instruction issue, the programming model is sequential, one-at-a-time instruction execution. This underlying model is enforced by the hardware, despite concurrency and out-of-order execution. This model of computation has served us well in the past but is running out of steam as a tool for supporting high-performance computing. To see why, consider the abstract computation depicted in Figure 25.5, viewing each of the small boxes as an instruction and the arrows as denoting the execution order. Such computations, which begin with an initial setup phase, continue with a number of independent subcomputations, and end with a combining phase, are not at all uncommon. The program representing the computation of Figure 25.5 is likely to have the following general structure: initialize; perform subcomputation 1; perform subcomputation 2; . . . ; perform subcomputation 5; clean up and close. In the resulting machine language program, the available instruction-level parallelism, so clearly visible in Figure 25.5, is completely lost and is unlikely to be recovered by the hardware, which looks for parallelism within a small window of consecutive instructions.

One way around the problem is to use explicit parallelism in instruction specification. The resulting architectural philosophy has come to be known by two different, but more or less equivalent, names:

Very long instruction word (VLIW) architecture

Explicitly parallel instruction computing (EPIC)

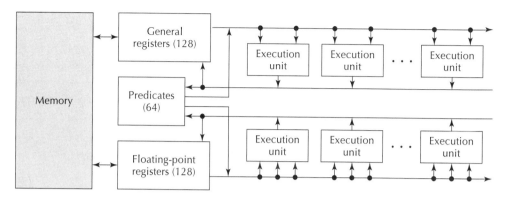

Figure 25.6 Hardware organization for IA-64: general and floating-point registers are 64-bit wide; predicates are single-bit registers.

The idea is to have fairly long instruction words that contain multiple basic operations for concurrent execution, allowing the programmer, or more often the compiler, to specify which operations are capable of being executed at the same time. This is a much more reasonable approach than hiding the concurrency in the sequential program code and then requiring that the hardware rediscover it for us. Because both dependencies and resource limitations can be taken into account during the packing of these operations within the long instruction words, the hardware to execute the operations is considerably simplified. Relieving the hardware from the difficult task of extracting parallelism and ensuring that dependencies are honored leads to circuit economy, reduced energy requirements, and added speed. Besides these advantages, greater parallelism may be possible because the compiler has a global view of the program, whereas the instruction issue logic of a superscalar processor looks through a narrow window.

Intel's 64-bit architecture, dubbed IA-64 and first implemented in the Itanium processor, is an example of the VLIW/EPIC approach. As shown in Figure 25.6, IA-64 has 128 general (64 bits wide), 128 floating-point (82 bits wide), and 64 predicate (1 bit wide) registers. There are also 8 branch registers (64 bits wide), not shown in Figure 25.6, that are used for indirect branching. IA-64's long instruction word ("bundle") contains three somewhat conventional RISC-type instructions ("syllables"), each occupying 41 bits, plus a 5-bit "template" holding scheduling information, for a total of 128 bits. The template specifies the instruction types contained in the bundle and indicates which instructions can be executed concurrently; the specified concurrency may span a part of a bundle to several bundles. As shown in Figure 25.6, there are many execution units of various kinds (integer, multimedia, floating-point, load/store, and branch).

Each 41-bit instruction has a 4-bit major opcode, a 6-bit predicate specification, and 31 bits for operands and modifiers. For example, three registers can be specified in this part, with 10 bits left for other information. Specifying a predicate in every instruction allows for conditional execution that obviates the need for many conditional branches. The results of an instruction are committed only if the specified predicate is 1; otherwise, they are discarded. In this way, instructions along both the "then" and "else" parts of a conditional statement can be executed, but only one set of results committed depending on the condition outcome. This is known as *predicated instruction execution*. Predicate register 0 holds the constant 1, thus allowing unconditional execution as a special case.

Besides predicated execution, IA-64 uses at least three other methods for performance enhancement. The first two, control speculation and data speculation, will be discussed in Section 25.4. Both these speculative methods have to do with performing a register load operation ahead of time, to overlap the memory access latency with other useful work. The third method is *software pipelining,* which allows concurrency among instructions belonging to different loop iterations. For example, in a loop that reads successive elements of one vector, updates each, and stores them in the corresponding elements of another vector, software pipelining allows a new iteration to be executed in each clock cycle, with the compiler assigning different registers to hold the elements of the first vector as they are brought in from memory. Ordinary execution of the loop would require several clock cycles per iteration.

In lieu of VLIW or EPIC, or perhaps in addition to them, one can use the idea of multithreading (see Section 24.6) to expose the available instruction-level parallelism to the hardware. In a multithreaded architecture, each thread may have its own program counter and perhaps a separate register file. The superscalar instruction issue logic now has a choice of issuing multiple instructions from the same thread or mixing instructions from multiple threads. The three main multithreading approaches are as follows:

Interleaved multithreading
Blocked multithreading
Simultaneous multithreading

With *interleaved multithreading,* the instruction issue logic picks instructions from the different threads that are available for execution in a round-robin fashion. This approach essentially spaces out the instructions from the same thread, making it much less likely to need a pipeline bubble for reasons of data or control dependencies or to waste time on speculative execution (see Section 25.4). *Blocked multithreading* essentially deals with only one thread until the execution of that thread encounters a snag (such as a cache miss). It then switches to a different thread. The idea is to fill the long stalls of one thread with useful instructions from another thread. *Simultaneous multithreading* is the most flexible strategy; it allows mixing and matching of instructions from different threads in each cycle to make the best use of available resources.

▪ 25.4 Speculation and Value Prediction

In Section 16.4, we discussed techniques for branch prediction and their importance in reducing the performance penalty of control dependencies. Given the relatively frequent occurrence of branch instructions within typical programs, it is not uncommon to encounter a branch instruction every 1–2 clock cycles in a high-performance multiple-issue or VLIW processor. Simple branch prediction is inadequate in this context. *Speculation* encompasses a collection of techniques for partial execution of instructions before we know for sure that they will be visited in the program's control flow or have obtained all their required operands. This is done without committing the results of such speculative instruction execution. Speculation can be done in hardware or software, with both approaches used in modern high-performance processors.

Software speculation is done by the compiler with help from hardware. Two examples are the control speculation and data speculation mechanisms of IA-64. *Control speculation,* loading data from memory before the program needs it, is an effort to hide the memory latency. In simple terms, this is done by replacing each load by two instructions: a speculative load performed earlier in the program and a checking instruction where the load instruction was

Figure 25.7 Examples of software speculation in IA-64.

originally located (Figure 25.7a). By moving a load instruction to an earlier point, there is a chance that we may execute a load instruction that will not actually be encountered in the normal program flow owing to branching or because the predicate used turns out to be false. To avoid any problems, speculative load keeps a record of any exception (such as protection violation, page fault, etc.) without actually signaling the exception. The checking instruction that replaces the original load performs the function of signaling an exception if appropriate.

Data speculation in IA-64 allows a load instruction to be moved to a point before an earlier store instruction (Figure 25.7b). This is speculative if the instructions use addresses in registers so that it is not known at compile time whether the two instructions refer to the same memory address. Ordinary, nonspeculative processors respect the ordering of memory write versus read accesses, to avoid fetching incorrect data. This must be done even if there is only a slight chance that a write and a read access will have the same memory address. With speculative execution, we again have a speculative load that is moved to an earlier spot and a checking instruction replacing the original load. When the speculative load is performed, the address is recorded and checked against subsequent addresses for memory write operations. In case of a match, the checking instruction annuls the result of the speculative load and any subsequent instruction that has used the loaded value.

Other forms of speculation include issuing instructions from both paths of a branch instructions, with each group predicated on the corresponding condition. When the outcome of the branch condition becomes known, one or the other group of instructions is discarded without committing their results. Note that it is not immediately obvious that this approach would lead to performance gain. Executing instructions that are subsequently discarded uses instruction memory bandwidth as well as processing resources. For branches whose outcomes are easily predicted, either statically by the compiler or dynamically at run time, this type of speculation may not be worthwhile. However, for the types of branch that result from if-then-else statements and are thus quite hard to predict, this approach may lead to performance gain. The context of speculation is also important: in a part of a program where too little instruction-level parallelism is available, speculation offers greater advantage because it uses resources that would otherwise remain idle.

Hardware-based speculation has similar objectives. To see how speculative execution can be added to a processor with out-of-order instruction completion, let us first see how non-speculative out-of-order execution might be implemented in hardware. We alluded to such a capability in Section 16.5 without specifying the hardware implementation details. One way to realize out-of-order execution in a 32-register machine such as MiniMIPS is to provide a much larger number of registers, say 128, in hardware. The latter physical or *microarchitectural registers,* thus called to distinguish them from logical or *architectural registers* that are visible to a program, can accommodate temporary values not yet committed to architectural registers, and can also be used to remove certain types of data hazard. Consider, for example, an add instruction $8 ← ($8) + ($9). As part of the instruction issue process, registers are renamed, so that in terms of physical registers, this add instruction might become #52 ← (#34) + (#12), where #34 and #12 are the physical registers currently designated as architectural registers $8 and $9, respectively, and #52 is chosen to hold the result. Eventually, when the instruction retires, #52 becomes $8, with #34 holding the previous value that appeared in $8. Note that this previous value might still be in use by another instruction whose completion has been delayed due to the unavailability of a second operand. Once this old value of $8 is no longer needed, #34 is returned to the pool of free registers and can be reused.

Adding speculative execution to this scheme is now straightforward. For example, when instructions are fetched and issued based on a predicted branch outcome, they are executed but their results are not committed to registers or memory until it has been determined that the prediction was correct. Any exceptional condition is also recorded alongside the result, with the exception taking effect when the instruction is committed. If a speculatively computed value is used in a subsequent instruction, the result of the latter is also designated as speculative. So, at any given time, multiple versions of a particular architectural register may exist among the physical registers, with each one properly tagged to designate its status and the conditions under which it will be committed. As with software speculation, the extent of speculative execution in hardware is determined by balancing the need to remove pipeline stalls against the cost in memory bandwidth and processing resources of executing instructions whose results are subsequently discarded.

Value prediction is a method that can be used in both nonspeculative and speculative manner and, as such, complements the techniques covered so far in this section. The idea is to predict the value returned by an instruction without, or before, executing it. Even though it may appear that the likelihood of correctly predicting one of 2^{32} possible results of an instruction in a 32-bit machine is quite small, it is not uncommon to achieve a 50% prediction accuracy in certain applications. For example, one might store the operands and result of recent division instructions in a small cache memory known as a *memo table*. This table, which may be organized using direct mapping based on a few bits of each operand, returns the correct division result when repetitive operations (of the type found in image processing, for example) are performed on data elements that tend to have clustered values. This method is useful for high-latency instructions such as division, which typically takes tens of clock cycles in the execution unit and is not beneficial for faster operations such as addition and multiplication. The same approach can be used to predict the results of a sequence of instructions performing a complicated computation. The benefits of successful prediction are much greater here, but the hardware cost in terms of storage needs can become prohibitive.

Note that in the foregoing examples, also known as *instruction reuse*, no speculation is involved: either the required results are in the memo table and are returned or else a miss indication (much like the ones for instruction and data access) is provided, which causes the instruction or instruction sequence to be executed in the normal fashion. However, the full benefits of value prediction materialize when prediction is used in combination with speculation or *superspeculation* (another name for aggressive speculation).

For example, when an operand value is needed to execute an instruction, the value may be predicted and computation performed speculatively. The speculative result is then turned into a normal result when the correctness of the prediction is verified. Prediction strategies range from the very simple *last-value predictor* to methods that take the pattern of previous results and/or control-flow history into account. Given that speculative execution costs us in terms of wasted computation resources and power, the approach is well worth the cost if the

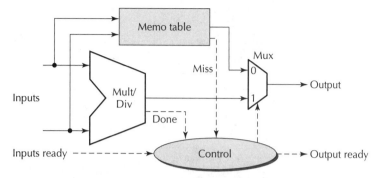

Figure 25.8 Value prediction for multiplication or division via a memo table.

misprediction rate is kept low (a few percent). Note that the statement in the preceding paragraph about up to 50% of results being predictable is not at odds with a prediction accuracy of 98%, say; the processor simply does not speculate in cases that are known to be hard to predict.

Prediction can be applied to computed addresses as well as data. For example, based on a pattern of previous addresses used by a load instruction, it may be possible to predict the next address that will be generated and initiate the load, even though the address computation is still waiting for a needed register value to be supplied. Such a prediction can be quite accurate when the memory is accessed with a fixed stride to read elements of an array or subarray (say a column within a matrix). In fact, if it can be determined with near certainty that a load and a previous store have different addresses, the load can be moved ahead of the store (as in IA-64, discussed earlier) to reduce stalling for data. On the other hand, if it can be established that a store and a subsequent load do use the same address, then the data needed by the load instruction can be forwarded to it from the production source, obviating the need for a memory access.

25.5 Special-Purpose Hardware Accelerators

An alternative to implementing an overly complex processor that performs well for any instruction stream with or without compiler support is to delegate specialized operations to units that are designed or tuned for them. The overall result may be executing the required operations at higher speed (owing to both specialization and concurrency), lower circuit cost, and greater energy economy. The term *hardware accelerator* is used for any hardware resource that helps a general-purpose processor execute specific types of operation faster. In this sense, a digital signal processor that augments the simple processor of a cell phone may be considered to be a hardware accelerator. Other commonly found accelerators are used for the following functions:

3D graphics rendering

Image compression and decompression

Network protocol processing

The continued increase in the number of transistors that can be put on a chip makes the integration of such special-purpose or application-specific resources on the same chip as the main processor feasible.

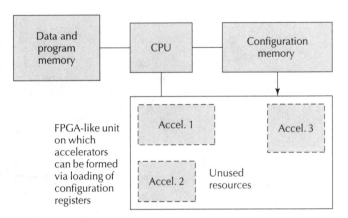

Figure 25.9 General structure of a processor with configurable hardware accelerators.

There are two trends that allow such integration of application-specific features to be economically viable. The first trend is the marketing of such facilities as intellectual property (design) rather than as finished products. The designer of a new system takes various existing designs, perhaps having common or standard interfaces, and combines them on a chip. The designs typically come with software and compiler support, making the integration much less labor-intensive. The second trend is the provision of configurable hardware alongside the processor that can be turned into desired special-purpose units via special setup procedures (Figure 25.9). The configuration can then be chosen at the factory during manufacturing, or it can be dynamically modifiable at run time under software control. Since the latter approach requires the setting of configuration registers, it is a rather slow process and cannot be performed at the level of individual instructions; instead, reconfiguration is often done at the time of task switching.

In the remainder of this section, we consider graphic and network processors as two specific examples of acceleration of processing via the provision of application-specific hardware resources.

A graphic processor has an architecture and the requisite function units that allow graphics-oriented tasks to be completed much faster than in a general-purpose processor. In the case of such tasks, it is not uncommon for a graphics processor to have a peak gigaflops rating that is greater than that of a top-of-the-line microprocessor by a factor of 10 or more. Therefore, given that a graphics processor is comparable in circuit complexity and cost to a general-purpose processor, it offers 10-fold or greater cost-effectiveness for graphics-intensive applications. This improved cost-effectiveness benefits systems of many types, from low-cost game machines to high-end animation and visualization systems used by motion picture studios. Unlike their predecessors, which were hard-wired and architecturally closed, newer graphics processors both are programmable and follow open standards for connectivity. Hence, many more uses for modern high-performance graphic processors are being explored

Graphics applications deal with geometric entities such as points and shapes. Both the location and graphic attributes of a point (pixel) can be expressed as numerical vectors. Transformations (shifting, rotation, and the like) on graphic objects can be formulated as matrix operations. These data-intensive operations contain many independent suboperations that can be performed in parallel. Adding texture to a rendered image also requires the retrieval of large volumes of data from a special texture memory and many independent calculations. Currently popular graphics processors are offered by Nvidia (www.nvidia.com) and ATI (www.ati.com).

A network processor sits between an incoming network "line" and a host processor. It has the responsibility for real-time reception and processing of incoming packets at the line speed. If one considers short 64 B packets arriving at the data rate of 10 Gb/s, one packet time is about 51 ns. A 2 GHz processor executing an average of one instruction per clock cycle has time to execute about 100 instructions to process such a packet in real time, to make sure that critical packets are not dropped and that various quality-of-service requirements can be satisfied. Not much can be accomplished with 100 instructions of a common RISC processor; hence the need for a network processor with a specialized instruction set and other capabilities. The challenge in designing a network processor lies in the simultaneous need for extremely high performance and flexibility to adapt to the needs of future data rates and network protocols.

To achieve the high performance needed for keeping up with the high incoming data rate, network processors are equipped with one or more of the following features:

• Instructions for common communication-related operations such as bit-matching, tree search, and cyclic redundancy check calculations
• Instruction-level parallelism or multithreading to allow the hiding of memory access and other latencies that lead to degraded performance
• Parallel/pipelined packet processing, with each pipeline stage performing a small task and multiple pipelines used for improved throughput

Network processors have been designed and marketed by Cisco Systems, Intel, IBM, and other companies [Crow03]. Figure 25.10 depicts a simplified block diagram of Cisco's network processor, Toaster2, which is intended to provide fast packet forwarding based on packet header processing. As seen in Figure 25.10, this processor is composed of a 4 × 4 matrix of simple processing elements forming four parallel data-flow pipelines. The processing elements in each column share a hierarchical memory system. For each packet, a 128 B context is formed that contains the packet's header and other control information. The context enters one of the four identical processing pipelines and may be sent from the output buffer back to

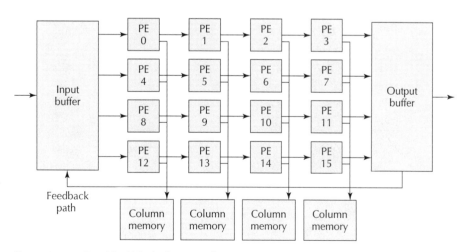

Figure 25.10 Simplified block diagram of Toaster2, Cisco's network processor.

the input buffer if the work of some stage is not finished within the fixed time allotted to it. Each processing element is a VLIW processor with its own private cache memory.

■ 25.6 Vector, Array, and Parallel Processing

In 1966, M. J. Flynn proposed a four-way classification of computer systems based on the notions of instruction streams and data streams. Flynn's classification has become standard and is widely used. Flynn coined the abbreviations SISD, SIMD, MISD, and MIMD (pronounced "sis-dee," "sim-dee," etc.) for the four classes of computers shown in Figure 25.11, based on the number of instruction streams (single or multiple) and data streams (single or multiple). The SISD class represents ordinary "uniprocessor" systems. Computers in the SIMD class, with several processors directed by instructions issued from a central control unit, are sometimes characterized as "array processors." Machines in the MISD category have not found widespread application, but one can view them as generalized pipelines in which each stage performs a relatively complex operation (as opposed to ordinary pipelines found in modern processors, where each stage does a very simple subinstruction-level operation).

The MIMD category increased in popularity over the years so that it encompassed a wide class of computers. For this reason, in 1988, E. E. Johnson proposed a further classification of such machines based on their memory structure (global or distributed) and the mechanism used for communication/synchronization (shared variables or message passing). Again, one of the four categories (GMMP) is not widely used. The GMSV class is what is loosely referred to as "(shared-memory) multiprocessing." At the other extreme, the DMMP class is known as "(distributed-memory) multicomputing." Finally, the DMSV class, which is becoming popular in view of combining the scalability of distributed memory with the programming ease of the shared-variable scheme, is sometimes called "distributed shared memory." When all processors in a MIMD-type machine execute the same program, the result is sometimes referred to as "single-program, multiple-data" or SPMD (spim-dee).

In the SIMD category, parallelism results from executing the same instruction stream on multiple data streams. We discuss SIMD parallel computing and its advantages in the context of a specific example: multiplying a coefficient or weight vector by a data vector on an

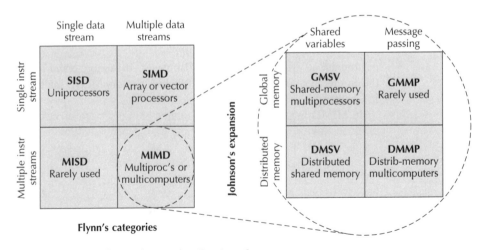

Figure 25.11 The Flynn-Johnson classification of computer systems.

element-by-element basis. In terms of hardware, the concurrency can occur in time or in space. Concurrency in time leads to *vector processing,* where a single deeply pipelined multiplier is fed with the pairs of numbers in turn, producing the products at the output in rapid succession. To keep up with the high throughput of the multiplier, special vector registers are made available to hold the operands and the produced results. Additionally, a high-throughput interleaved memory is used to supply the registers with data or to store results back into memory. Vector processing differs from simply issuing a long sequence of identical add instructions in a pipelined scalar architecture in the following ways, which contribute to the greater performance of a vector processor.

Only one instruction is fetched and decoded for the entire operation.

The multiplications are known to be independent (no checking or interlocks).

Pipelining is applied to memory access as well as to the arithmetic.

Additional performance-enhancing methods include pipeline chaining and conditional execution, to be discussed in the first half of Chapter 26.

SIMD concurrency in space leads to *array processing.* Taking up the same element-by-element multiplication example as in the preceding paragraph, the coefficient and data vectors may be divided among p processing elements, each having its own memory and multiplier. If these vectors are of length n, then each of the p processing elements will be responsible for n/p multiplications. Array processor implementation and performance will be discussed in some detail in the second half of Chapter 26.

MIMD architectures with a shared global memory are implemented by providing a processor-to-memory interconnection network that allows every processor to access any part of a large physical memory. The simplest form of such a network is a common bus to which every processor and memory module is connected. *Chip multiprocessors* (multiple CPUs on one chip) usually follow this approach. Shared memory provides a simple and clean programming model and allows processors to pass operands and results to each other by simply writing into and reading from the shared memory. To ease congestion on the bus and to reduce the memory access latency, which is already a serious problem with a single processor, each of the processors is typically provided with a private cache where it keeps its most frequently used values. If data must be shared among the processors to allow their cooperation in solving problems, multiple copies of the shared data items may exist in the various caches, leading to the challenging problem of cache coherence. Point-to-point interconnection schemes and multistage switching networks provide greater aggregate bandwidth and ease the problem of congestion due to using a common bus. However, these more elaborate schemes also complicate the enforcement of cache coherence. Shared-memory MIMD multiprocessing will be covered in Chapter 27.

In MIMD architectures with distributed memory, each processor and its private memory unit constitute a node. Such nodes, which might range in number from a few to many thousands, communicate among themselves via explicit message passing. Processors can be interconnected by a simple bus, a point-to-point scheme, or a multistage switching network. Distributed-memory MIMD machines offer excellent speedup for applications that can be partitioned into large, more or less independent, chunks capable of running on different nodes with minimal interaction. Applications that are more communication-intensive can suffer from excessive latency of acquiring data from *remote memories* (memory modules at other nodes, as opposed to local memory). Strategies for hiding such remote access latencies through overlapping with local computation are thus essential to the success of this approach.

A currently popular implementation of distributed-memory MIMD systems is based on inter-connecting off-the-shelf processing and communication resources, each with its local appli-cation and system software, under the control of a higher-level coordination mechanism. Use of commercially available PCs or workstation with Ethernet connectivity is one example. The resulting systems are known by names such as *clusters* or *networks of workstations* (COW, NOW). The distributed multicomputing approach to MIMD parallelism is the topic of Chapter 28.

Although Figure 25.11 lumps all SIMD machines together, there are in fact variations sim-ilar to those suggested for MIMD parallel computers. In other words, there can be shared-memory and distributed-memory SIMD machines in which the processors communicate by means of shared variables or explicit message passing.

In terms of development activities and applications, SIMD and MIMD parallel processing have experienced ups and downs with what appears to be a 20-year cycle. Intense interest in parallel processing began in the 1960s with the development of the ILLIAC IV, a research ma-chine built at the University of Illinois. Limited applications, difficulties in software develop-ment, and high cost of hardware tempered this initial phase of enthusiasm. The 1980s brought increased defense spending in the United States. The resulting boom in research funding, combined with vastly improved compiler technology, led to interesting applications of paral-lel processing and the emergence of numerous developers and vendors of parallel computers. Subsequent funding cuts, followed by company bankruptcies, led to renewed skepticism about the applicability of parallel processing techniques beyond certain niche areas. In the 2000s, the needs of Internet portals and large e-commerce companies led to renewed activity in parallel processing. But this time, interest focused on using off-the-shelf processors, rather than custom-designed units, along with buses or routing switches to build a distributed system from interconnected components of fairly low cost.

Ideally, it should be possible to configure large parallel systems from smaller ones just as children build structures from connecting toy blocks, with performance improving linearly as each piece is added. However, owing to a combination of inadequate software support and the curse of Amdahl's law, this ideal of linear speedup is still an illusive goal. Recall from Section 4.3 that if f represents the fraction of a program's running time due to unparallelizable computa-tions, even assuming that the remainder of the program enjoys the perfect speedup of p when run on p processors, the overall speedup would be:

$$s = \frac{1}{f + (1 - f)/p} \leq min\left(p, \frac{1}{f}\right) \qquad \text{[Amdahl's speedup formula]}$$

Whereas Amdahl's sequential fraction f may appear to doom any attempt at parallel process-ing for certain applications, it is quite possible to overlap the sequential parts of one program or task with highly parallel parts of other programs or tasks. This leads to cost-effective par-allel processing; even though each application's speedup may remain suboptimal, the overall system operates at high efficiency and near-peak computational throughput.

To complete the big picture, we briefly discuss the rarely used MISD organization in the context of a special-purpose processor. One reason for MISD's lack of popularity is that most application problems do not map easily onto a MISD architecture, making it hard to develop a general-purpose MISD machine. In special-purpose systems, however, MISD may be quite viable. Figure 25.12 shows an example of a single data stream entering a 5-processor MISD machine. The data stream undergoes various transformations, emerging at the other end as a sequence of results. The transformations may be different for each data item, either owing to data-dependent conditional operations in the instruction streams (control-driven) or based on

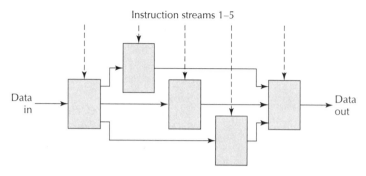

Figure 25.12 Multiple instruction streams operating on a single data stream (MISD).

special control tags carried by the data (data-driven). The MISD organization can thus be viewed as a flexible pipeline with multiple branching paths and programmable stages. A simpler form of MISD processing can be found within each row of PEs in the network processor depicted in Figure 25.10.

PROBLEMS

25.1 Power consumption in processors

Note that the lower growth rate for performance per watt (10 every 10 years) versus absolute performance (100 every 10 years) in Figure 25.1 suggests that the absolute energy consumption of high-performance processors has been growing. Determine the rate of power dissipation growth and verify this by obtaining the power consumption of Pentium processors (regular, not mobile versions) from the literature.

25.2 Using MMX instructions

Use MMX instructions from Table 25.1, as well as ordinary instructions such as those defined for MiniMIPS in Part 2 of the book, to perform the following as efficiently as possible.

a. Obtain from the operand 8-vector `0000000a` the result 8-vector `aaaaaaaa`.
b. Obtain from the operand 4-vectors `abcd` and `efgh` the result 4-vecotr `afch`. *Hint:* Use a mask that has all 1s and all 0s in alternating 16-bit fields [Pele97, p. 31].
c. Compute the sum of the 4 elements in the 4-vector stored in an MMX register.

d. Compute the inner product of two 4-vectors stored in MMX registers.
e. Transpose a 4×4 matrix stored in MMX registers 0 to 3, with each row appearing in one register [Pele97, p. 33].

25.3 MiniMIPS-2D

An extended MiniMIPS is to be implemented that has instructions operating on 2D vectors with halfword-size elements, stored in the upper and lower halves of 32-bit registers.

a. Present the design of a 32-bit adder that can perform ordinary 32-bit additions as well as parallel vector additions with wrapped, unsigned saturating, and signed saturating results. *Hint:* Think in terms of a carry-select adder.
b. Discuss the implementation of a parallel version of the `slt` instruction.
c. How can we modify the hardware multiplier of Figure 11.4 to provide parallel multiplication capability (low and high, as in MMX) in addition to ordinary 32×32 multiplication?
d. Repeat part c for the array multiplier of Figure 11.7.

e. Discuss the implementation of a parallel multiply-add instruction, yielding a 32-bit result.

25.4 Other media ISA extensions

Other processors also have ISA extensions for efficient handling of multimedia applications. Study the following extensions and write a report resembling our discussion of MMX in Section 25.2 for each. Reference [Micr96] contains articles describing the first three of these.

a. Visual instruction set (VIS) of UltraSparc
b. MicroUnity's MediaProcessor architecture
c. Hewlett-Packard's PA-RISC MAX-2 extension
d. Power PC's AltiVec architecture
e. Intel's SSE-2 streaming SIMD extension
f. Intel's extension to the IA-64 architecture

25.5 Multiple instruction issue

Show how the speedup curve in Figure 25.4b can be derived from the bar graph in Figure 25.4a. *Hint:* For an instruction issue width of i, you need to figure out the fraction of cycles in which i or more instructions are available to be issued.

25.6 Example VLIW architecture

The Trimedia TM32 is a VLIW processor that is completely statically scheduled. Each instruction word contains 5 operation fields, with the compiler filling the unusable slots with no-ops. The compiler also ensures that data dependencies are honored through appropriate scheduling, given that the processor has no hazard detection facility. Study the Trimedia TM32 instruction set in enough detail to be able to construct an instruction sequence to add two vectors of length n using MiniMIPS-like instructions in each of the 5 operation fields. Then compare the result with that of a MiniMIPs instruction sequence for the same vector addition, with and without loop unrolling.

25.7 Intel's Itanium architecture

Intel's Itanium architecture allows 5 operations to be specified in each EPIC instruction. However, there are restrictions on what types of operation can appear in each of the 5 slots within an instruction.

a. Study Intel's Itanium architecture and present your findings about the types of operation that can be specified in each slot in the form of a table.
b. Discuss why these restrictions might have been introduced.
c. If any slot in an instruction can hold an arithmetic, shift, or logic operation of the types found in the MiniMIPS instruction set of Table 6.2, discuss the relationship of Itanium's performance to that of MiniMIPS in running computation-intensive applications, when comparable technologies and circuits are used in their implementations.
d. Compare the basic design philosophy of Intel's Itanium architecture with that of AMD's next-generation architecture [Webe01].

25.8 Multiple instruction issue

Consider the following two instruction sequences and assume that all instructions in each sequence fall in the issue window. Ignore all resource limitations, unless explicitly specified.

Sequence 1		Sequence 2	
lw	$5,0($4)	lw	$11,0($10)
sub	$6,$8,$9	lw	$6,4($9)
add	$10,$7,$7	add	$13,$11,$6
sw	$6,4($15)	lw	$12,8($15)
sw	$10,0($14)	and	$14,$16,$17
add	$19,$16,$17	sub	$4,$7,$5
sub	$12,$12,$19	sw	$19,0($4)
sw	$12,8($13)	add	$25,$11,$6
		sw	$25,4($26)
		sw	$27,0($24)

a. For each sequence, determine the minimum number of issue cycles if instructions must be issued in order.
b. Repeat part a, but assume that only one load or store instruction can be issued in each cycle.
c. Repeat part a, but assume out-of-order issue.
d. Repeat part c, but assume that only one load or store instruction can be issued in each cycle.

25.9 Register aliasing

Because of the limited number of registers in most machines, programs tend to reuse the same register to hold several different temporary values. When out-of-order instruction execution is allowed, it is quite possible for one or more instructions that use a temporary value in $t1 to be in various stages of execution when an instruction writing a different temporary value in $t1 is issued. This situation is referred to as *register aliasing*. Discuss how this situation might create problems in correct instruction execution and how register renaming can solve the problem.

25.10 Hardware for value prediction

Last-value prediction is useful when an instruction repeatedly produces the same result value. Stride-value prediction is useful when an instruction produces the values $v, v + s, v + 2s, \ldots$ in succession.

a. Show how last-value prediction can be implemented with a cachelike mechanism.
b. Discuss the implementation of stride-value prediction. *Hint:* Think in terms of a state diagram similar to that used in history-based branch prediction.

25.11 Memo table implementation

The implementation of memo table in Figure 25.8 assumes an asynchronous mode of operation, where the time saved by finding a result value in the memo table translates directly to reduced execution time.

a. How would this scheme work in a synchronous system?
b. Design the control circuit in Figure 25.8.
c. Would a memo table be helpful for multiplication or division in MiniMIPS? Discuss.

25.12 Memo table performance

A memo table functions much like a cache memory. Considering division for example, when the required quotient is present in the memo table, the operation takes one clock cycle. Otherwise, the processor performs radix-2 or radix-4 division in 20 clock cycles, say. This "miss penalty" is also comparable to that caused by accessing main memory when a required word is not in the cache memory. Yet there is a key difference between memoing and caching: whereas cache memory requires a fairly high hit rate (say, 80% or more) to be effective, memoing can be quite beneficial even with a hit rate of 50% or less.

a. Explain the reasons for the difference between memoing and caching.
b. Quantify the performance benefits of memoing in terms of the hit rate h in the memo table.

25.13 Soft hardware

It has been suggested that FPGA-like devices can be used to solve the problem of hardware obsolescence; hardware is bought in the form of an amorphous collection of computation cells that are configured into a particular processor by loading its configuration registers with a specific pattern of 0s and 1s. Hardware can then be upgraded much like software, namely, by purchasing, or downloading for free, extensions and patches from the manufacturer's Web site. Argue that while this approach might be useful for fixing bugs and adding certain capabilities that were not foreseen at design time, it does not completely solve the obsolescence problem.

25.14 Graphic processors

Answer the following questions for a graphic processor of your choosing.

a. What types of fixed-point and/or floating-point operands are supported?
b. What hardware resources, beyond what is available in a general-purpose processor, are used to speed up numeric calculations?
c. What specific instructions and resources are provided to facilitate image scaling and rotation?
d. How are shading, hidden line removal, and display of textured surfaces facilitated?
e. How does the graphic processor interact with the rest of the computer system?

25.15 Network processors

a. The Cisco Systems Toaster2 network processor was briefly described in Section 25.5. Study this network processor and describe, in two to three pages, the internal structure of the PEs and their interactions with column memories and input/output buffers.
b. For another network processor of your choosing, describe the hardware architecture and contrast its operation with that of Cisco's Toaster2.
c. Whereas graphics processors first appeared as inflexible, dedicated hardware units and developed

into programmable devices only recently, network processors were programmable from the beginning. Can you explain the reason for this difference?

25.16 SIMD versus MIMD

The computer architecture community has been debating the relative merits of SIMD versus MIMD parallel computers for a long time. Early parallel computers were predominantly SIMD machines, whereas modern systems are almost exclusively MIMD. Only the vector-processor implementation of the SIMD concept is still in widespread use in general-purpose machines. Study this debate and prepare a five-page report on it, devoting about one page to each of the following questions.

a. Why did SIMD architectures fall out of favor for general-purpose machines?

b. In what application domains are SIMD architectures still used?

c. Why are SIMD architectures used, and are likely to become even more popular, in hardware accelerators?

25.17 Amdahl's speedup formula

a. Show that the sequential fraction f of Amdahl's speedup formula is approximately $1/s - 1/p$ when p is large.

b. What value does the formula of part a yield for f when the speedup is $s = 80$ with $p = 100$ processors? What is the error in this case?

c. Derive an error expression when $1/s - 1/p$ is used to approximate f. Write your expression to make it quite obvious that the relative error is small for large p.

REFERENCES AND FURTHER READINGS

[Bour03]   Bourianoff, G., "The Future of Nanocomputing," *IEEE Computer,* Vol. 36, No. 8, pp. 44–53, August 2003.

[Cho01]   Cho, S., P.-C. Yew, and G. Lee, "A High-Bandwidth Memory Pipeline for Wide Issue Processors," *IEEE Trans. Computers,* Vol. 50, No. 7, pp. 709–723, July 2001.

[Crow03]   Crowley, P., M. A. Franklin, H. Hadimioglu, and P. Z. Onufryk, *Network Processor Design: Issues and Practices,* Vol. 1, Morgan Kaufmann, 2003.

[Flyn96]   Flynn, M. J., and K. W. Rudd, "Parallel Architectures," *ACM Computing Surveys,* Vol. 28, No. 1, pp. 67–70, March 1996.

[Fran03]   Franklin, M., *Multiscalar Processors,* Kluwer, 2003.

[John91]   Johnson, M., *Superscalar Microprocessor Design,* Prentice Hall, 1991.

[Kuma03]   Kumar, R., K. Farkas, N. P. Jouppi, P. Ranganathan, and D. M. Tullsen, "Processor Power Reduction via Single-ISA Heterogeneous Multi-Core Architectures," *Computer Architecture Letters,* Vol. 2, No. 1, pp. 2–5, July 2003.

[Lee02]   Lee, R., "Media Signal Processing," Section 39.1 in *The Computer Engineering Handbook,* V. G. Oklobdzija, ed., pp. 39-1 to 39-38, CRC Press, 2002.

[Lo97]   Lo, J. L., S. J. Eggers, J. S. Emer, H. M. Levy, R. L. Stamm, and D. M. Tullsen, "Converting Thread-Level Parallelism to Instruction-Level Parallelism via Simultaneous Multithreading," *ACM Trans. Computer Systems,* Vol. 15, No. 3, pp. 322–354, August 1997.

[Marr02]   Marr, D. T., et al., "Hyper-Threading Technology Architecture and Microarchitecture," *Intel Technology J.,* Vol. 6, No. 1, February 14, 2002. Available at: http://www.intel.com/technology/itj/

[Micr96]   *IEEE Micro* (Special Issue on Media Processing), Vol. 16, No. 4, August 1996.

[Mudg01]   Mudge, T., "Power: A First-Class Architectural Design Constraint," *IEEE Computer,* Vol. 34, No. 4, pp. 52–58, April 2001.

[Pele97]   Peleg, A., S. Wilkie, and U. Weiser, "Intel MMX for Multimedia PCs," *Communications of the ACM,* Vol. 40, No. 1, pp. 25–38, January 1997.

[Rone01]   Ronen, R., A. Mendelson, K. Lai, S.-L. Lu, F. Pollack, and J. P. Shen, "Coming Challenges in Microarchitecture and Architecture," *Proceedings of the IEEE,* Vol. 89, No. 3, pp. 325–340, March 2001.

[Thak99]   Thakkar, S. T., and T. Huff, "Internet Streaming SIMD Extensions," *IEEE Computer,* Vol. 32, No. 12, pp. 26–34, December 1999.

[Unge02]   Ungerer, T., B. Robic, and J. Silc, "Multithreaded Processors," *Computer J.,* Vol. 45, No. 3, pp. 320–348, 2002.

[Webe01]   Weber, F., "AMD's Next Generation Microprocessor Architecture," available from: http://www.x86-64.org/documentation_folder/

[WWW]   Information about current highest-performance computers is available at: www.top500.org

[Zyub01]   Zyuban, V. V., and P. M. Kogge, "Inherently Lower-Power High-Performance Superscalar Architectures," *IEEE Trans. Computers,* Vol. 50, No. 3, pp. 268–285, March 2001.

26

VECTOR AND ARRAY PROCESSING

"Any mathematical task could, in principle, be solved by direct counting. However, there are counting problems that can presently be solved in a few minutes, but for which without mathematical method a lifetime would not be sufficient."
—*Ernst Mach, 1896*

"Imagine a large hall like a theatre. . . . The walls of this chamber are painted to form a map of the globe. . . . A myriad of computers are at work upon the weather of the part of the map where each sits, but each computer attends only to one equation or part of an equation."
—*L. F. Richardson, British meteorologist, fantasizing about what later became known as SIMD or array processing*

One way to improve computer performance is to let a single instruction stream operate on multiple data streams. This SIMD mode of computation can be orchestrated in two ways. First, repetitive operations on vector elements can be exploited for filling a pipeline continuously and with no danger of data or control hazards. This method, along with a high-bandwidth memory and a provision for pipeline chaining (doing multiple operations without ever storing intermediate values in registers) allows vector supercomputers to achieve their high performance. Second, multiple independent ALUs can be controlled by a single control unit that broadcasts control signals and effects the completion of many operations in the same amount of time that one ALU would complete a single operation. This is the strategy followed in array processors.

26.1 Operations on Vectors

As discussed in Section 25.6, pipelined operations on vectors can lead to significantly higher performance than is achievable in ordinary pipelining. In ordinary high-level programming languages, vector operations are defined via loops and loop indices. For example, multiplying a coefficient or weight vector by a data vector on an element-by-element basis may be expressed by the high-level language loop:

```
for i = 0 to 63 do
    P[i] := W[i] × D[i]
endfor
```

This operation, expressed in vector form as P := W × D, is translated to an assembly language loop that performs two loads, one multiplication, one incrementation of the index, and a conditional branch instruction that checks to determine whether enough iterations have been performed to exit the loop. Within each iteration, there is very limited instruction-level parallelism. Even with loop unrolling, a large number of instructions must still be fetched, decoded, and individually executed.

In a vector processor, the foregoing operation would consist of two vector register loads (given 64-element vector registers), a vector multiplication, and a vector store. Assuming two memory access channels, whose implementation will be discussed in Section 26.2, the operation will consist of three phases (loading, multiplying, and storing):

```
load W
load D
P := W × D
store P
```

Each of these four vector operations is pipelined, so that one new value or operation is handled in every clock cycle. There are of course pipeline start-up and drainage latencies at the beginning and end of each vector operation, but we will ignore them for now. Beyond the straight pipelining advantage of vector processing, a number of other methods can be used to further improve the performance. For example, the load and store phases may be overlapped with the execution of other vector operations, provided there is a sufficient supply of vector registers. Similarly, instead of waiting to start the multiplication pipeline until both the C and D vectors have been completely loaded, it may be started after a few elements of each have become available in registers. The latter method, known as *pipeline chaining,* can obviously be extended to the store pipeline, so that result storage can begin long before the multiplication or even the register loads have been completed.

Vector operations are either written directly into programs, using parallel programming constructs, or are deduced by compilers from loops within ordinary programs. In the latter case, the reformulation of a sequential computation as a vector computation is not always as straightforward as for P := W × D. Consider, for example, the following loop in which there is data dependency from one iteration to the next:

```
for i = 0 to 63 do
    A[i] := A[i] + B[i]
    B[i+1] := C[i] + D[i]
endfor
```

For now, assume distinct 64-element vectors with no overlap in memory; also do not worry about exceeding the boundaries of A and B in the final loop iteration because of the index expression i+1. Note that B[i+1], computed in the second statement of the loop, is used at the start of the next iteration when the loop index has been advanced to i+1. Such a *loop-carried* dependency does not automatically imply that the loop cannot be parallelized. In this case, the loop can indeed be parallelized, because once A[i] has been updated in one iteration based on the value of B[i+1] of the previous iteration, the resulting new value of A[i] is not used again. Supplying the details of this parallelization is left as an exercise.

Consider, in contrast, the following loop in which there are data dependencies both within an iteration and from one iteration to the next:

```
for i = 0 to 63 do
    X[i+1] := X[i] + Z[i]
    Y[i+1] := X[i+1] + Y[i]
endfor
```

Note that X[i+1], computed in the first statement of the loop, is used later in the same iteration as well as at the start of the next iteration when the loop index has been advanced to i+1. In this case, because of circular loop-carried dependencies for X and Y, the loop cannot be parallelized.

It is often the case that such unvectorizable iterative computations can be written in alternate forms that do allow efficient vector processing. However, finding these forms is not always easy.

Besides vector operations with two vector operands and a vector result, a variety of other vector operations have been found useful in practice. These include:

Vector combined with a scalar value, yielding a vector result $(A := c \times B)$
One-operand vector operation with a vector result $(A := \sqrt{B})$
Reduction operation on a vector, yielding a scalar result $(s := \sum A)$

For example, the inner product of two vectors X and Y can be synthesized from a vector operation $Z := X \times Y$ followed by a sum-reduction operation $s := \sum Z$.

Computations on 2D and higher-dimensional arrays can be expressed in terms of vector operations on subarrays (e.g., rows and columns in the case of matrices). A vector that represents a subarray is usually specified by a *base address* (starting point) and a *stride* (separation of two consecutive vector elements in memory). Hence, a vector processor can handle not only vector operations but also operations on matrices and other arrays.

Example 26.1: Access to matrix subarrays   Consider an $n \times n$ matrix A stored in memory in row-major order, meaning that all elements of row i appear in their natural order before those of row $i + 1$. Memory is word-addressed, and each matrix element occupies one word. Thus, the stride for accessing the elements of a given row is 1. If element $A[0, 0]$ is located at the base address b:

   a. Determine the address for element $A[i, j]$.
   b. Find the stride for accessing the elements of column j.

c. Determine whether elements of the main diagonal of the matrix can be accessed with a fixed stride.

d. Do the same for the main antidiagonal.

Solution: Elements of A are stored in the n^2 consecutive memory locations from b to $b + n^2 - 1$.

a. There are i rows, with ni elements, before row i. Accounting for the j elements in row i that precede element $A[i, j]$, the address of the latter element is $b + ni + j$.

b. Elements of column j are stored in addresses $b + j, b + n + j, b + 2n + j, \ldots$, giving a stride of n.

c. Elements $A[i, i]$ of the main diagonal, located at addresses $b, b + n + 1, b + 2n + 2, \ldots$, can be accessed with a stride of $n + 1$.

d. Elements $A[i, n - 1 - i]$ of the antidiagonal can be accessed with a stride of $n - 1$.

Based on the foregoing discussion, the term "vector" can be used to refer to an ordinary vector, stored in memory with a stride of 1, as well as a subarray having an arbitrary stride s. In generating memory addresses to access elements of a vector with base address b and stride s, an address register within the processor is initialized to b and incremented by s after each access. By using these addresses, elements of the vector are fetched into consecutive places of a vector register for use as an operand in a subsequent vector operation. When the vector fits in a vector register in its entirety, the length of the vector operation is controlled by initializing a vector length register, which is decremented by 1 after each vector element is sent to the function unit. Longer vectors are processed in pieces that fit in vector registers. For example, a vector of length 100 may be loaded into two vector registers of length 64, with the vector length specified as 64 and 36 in the processing of the two subvectors, respectively. This type of partitioning is carried out by the compiler; the high-level language programmer need not be concerned with the details, but must be aware of the performance penalty of using a 65-element vector, say, versus one of length 64.

26.2 Vector Processor Implementation

Based on our discussion in Section 26.1, there are three key features of a vector processor:

Deeply pipelined function units for high throughput (very short clock cycle)

Plenty of long vector registers to feed the function units and to receive the results

High-bandwidth data transfer paths between memory and vector registers

Pipeline chaining, or forwarding of computed result values from one function unit pipeline to another, though not absolutely necessary, is a very helpful feature. Any vector processor must also have a high-performance scalar unit, because otherwise a small fraction of scalar operations mixed with vector operations would severely reduce the overall performance (Amdahl's law).

Example 26.2: Vector processor performance   A given application run on a superscalar microprocessor spends 20% of its running time on housekeeping and scalar operations and 80% on vector operations. A vector processor offers an average speedup of 4 for the vector operations but slows down the nonvector parts by a factor of 2 owing to its simpler scalar unit.

What is the expected speedup of the vector processor over the superscalar processor? What mix of scalar and vector operation times would lead to no performance improvement on the vector processor?

Solution: The superscalar running time of $0.2 + 0.8$ becomes $0.2 \times 2 + 0.8/4 = 0.6$ on the vector processor. Hence the speedup is $1.0/0.6 = 1.67$. There will be no speedup if the fraction x of running time due to nonvector operations satisfies $2x + (1 - x)/4 = 1$, leading to $x = 0.43$.

In our study of pipelining, we dealt with design parameters and trade-offs that influence the choice of the number of pipeline stages in the context of scalar or superscalar processor implementation (Section 15.6). In pipelined function units of vector processors, the trade-offs are different. Stalling is not an issue because vectorized operations are by definition free of data dependencies. However, pipeline start-up and drainage overheads would favor shorter pipelines, unless vectors on average were fairly long. This is the case in many scientific and engineering computations, which form the main application domains for vector processors. Having half a dozen to 20 stages in each function unit is not at all unusual. Addition and multiplication typically have pipelines with smaller number of stages, while division and load/store tend to have longer pipelines. Given that memory bandwidth is generally the limiting factor in a pipeline processor, deeper pipelines can be helpful only if vector registers can be filled and emptied at a correspondingly high rate.

Figure 26.1 depicts some of the key components of a simplified vector processor. There are three function units, which may perform various arithmetic operations. The function units are fed from a vector register file. Part of the pipeline setup process consists of specifying the vector register to be used for each operand, starting entries in the registers, and vector length. Then, in each clock cycle, the contents of the indicated vector registers are sent to one of the function units and the register entry numbers are updated. This process continues until the

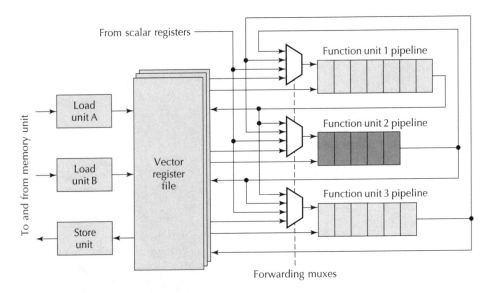

Figure 26.1 Simplified generic structure of a vector processor.

specified number of elements have been processed. Figure 26.1 also shows three multiplexers that allow the outputs of one pipeline to be forwarded to either of the other two pipelines for pipeline chaining. It is also possible to supply a scalar value as one of the two operands in a vector computation. Again the pipeline chain is set up at the outset. For example, if the output of function unit 1 is to be sent to function unit 2, the second operand of the latter, which comes from a vector register, must be appropriately delayed so that the first result from function unit 1 and the first entry from the specified vector register arrive in the same clock cycle. This is relatively easy to ascertain, given the depths of each of the pipelines and their start-up overheads.

The vector register file can be viewed as a 2D array of registers. If there are eight vector registers of length 64 in the register file, then each register is specified by a 3-bit field in vector machine instructions, while each element of a register requires a 6-bit index for access within a particular clock cycle in the course of executing the vector instruction. Typically, at least three different types of vector operation take place simultaneously in a vector processor (to hide the memory access latency):

A function-unit operation on vector operands, returning a vector result

Loading of vector registers in preparation for future vector operations

Storing results of a previous operation from a vector register to memory

A vector processor thus contains a minimum of eight vector registers. More vector registers can, of course, be helpful for keeping a larger number of function units busy, but they also complicate the routing logic between the register file and the function units.

To see why, consider that in Figure 26.1, any vector register must be able to serve as the upper or lower operand for each of the three function units or to receive its results. Counting the load and store units shown, the register file must collectively have seven read ports and five write ports. If each vector register is viewed as a scalar register file of size 64, implemented as in Figure 2.9a, then with eight vector registers, a 16×7 crossbar switch is needed to route the 16 possible register outputs to the seven output ports. Similarly, an 8×5 crossbar switch is needed on the input side of the register file.

Providing adequate memory bandwidth to keep up with the high processing rates of several deeply pipelined function units is perhaps the most challenging part of a vector processor's design. Usually, no data cache memory is used for vector operands and main memory is accessed directly by the processor. To begin with, memory is highly interleaved, 64–256 memory banks being not at all unusual. Recall from our discussion of interleaving in Section 17.4 that a 64-way interleaved memory can supply data at a peak rate that is 64 times that of a simple memory module. Maintaining this peak rate requires that a memory bank not be accessed again before all other banks have also been accessed. This requirement is clearly satisfied in sequential or stride-1 accesses. Similarly, any stride that is relatively prime with respect to the interleaving width leads to the maximum memory bandwidth. Unfortunately, this condition does not occur naturally in applications, given that the interleaving width is usually a power of 2 and the most commonly used strides are also powers of 2 or, at least, even.

A wide array of data arrangement strategies have been devised to deal with the memory bandwidth problem. For example, if we store a 64×64 matrix in row-major order (Figure 26.2a), the stride for accessing columns will be 64, which is the worst possible value for a 64-way interleaved memory: all accesses for reading out a column of the matrix will be directed to the same memory bank, which obviously cannot supply a new element in each clock cycle. On the other hand, if we use the skewed storage scheme of Figure 26.2b, where elements of row i are

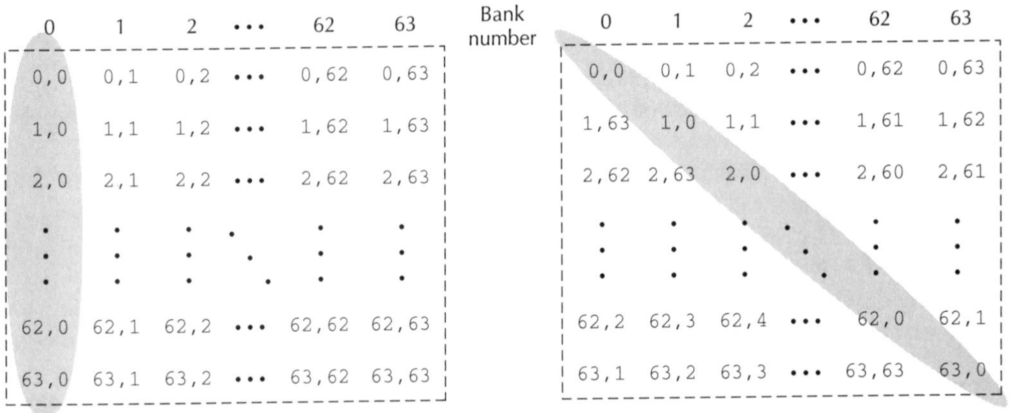

	0	1	2	$\cdots$	62	63	Bank number	0	1	2	$\cdots$	62	63

Figure 26.2 Skewed storage of the elements of a 64×64 matrix for conflict-free memory access in a 64-way interleaved memory. Elements of column 0 are highlighted in both diagrams.

rotated to the right by i positions, then the stride for column access becomes 65. This leads to accessing different memory banks in reading out the 64 elements of one column. Of course, some overhead will be added because a more complex translation between row/column indices and memory addresses is necessary, but the overhead is generally small relative to the gains.

Vector machine instructions are very similar in spirit to those of Intel MMX listed in Table 25.1. A key difference is that the vectors in MMX are rather short and fixed in length, whereas in a vector machine, they are typically long and of variable length. Hence, vector length is often specified as a parameter either explicitly within the instruction or implicitly via initial data definitions. Other than arithmetic on vector operands, or one vector and one scalar operand, typical instructions include the following:

Vector load and store, with implicit or explicitly specified stride

Vector load and store, with memory addresses specified in an index vector

Vector comparisons (several types) on an element-by-element basis

Data copying among registers, including vector-length and mask registers

The vector mask register allows operations on vector elements to be done selectively, based on the associated bit in a mask register. With this masking capability, the execution of an operation on specific vector elements can be predicated on a previously evaluated data-dependent condition (e.g., to avoid division by zero).

We conclude this section by tracing the steps in the execution of a vector instruction such as $Z := X + Y$, where the vector length is not necessarily an integer multiple of the vector register length, which we assume to be 64. The hardware segments the vectors into 64-element subvectors, with the first segments possibly containing fewer than 64 elements. It then loads vector registers with segments of the two vectors X and Y, in turn, beginning with the initial, possibly irregular, segments. The same segmentation is applied to the result vector Z, which is stored in memory as each of its segments is computed in a vector register. Figure 26.3 shows how register load and store operations are overlapped with addition by using the vector registers in a *double-buffering* scheme.

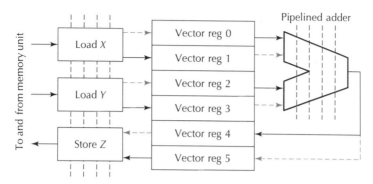

Figure 26.3 Vector processing via segmented load/store of vectors in registers in a double-buffering scheme. Solid (dashed) lines show data flow in the current (next) segment.

26.3 Vector Processor Performance

As with most supercomputers, the performance of vector processors is often specified in terms of peak FLOPS, obtained when a specially tailored program that exercises all computing resources optimally and avoids any bottleneck is executed. More realistic performance figures on benchmarks or real applications can be lower than the advertised peak performance by one or more orders of magnitude. If the clock frequency of a vector processor is x GHz, then each of its function units can execute x GFLOPS, provided it is continuously fed with data (infinitely long vectors). Real performance is significantly lower for a variety of reasons.

First, each vector operation has a start-up time that is spent even for very short vectors. The effect of start-up time on performance becomes negligible only when vectors are extremely long. In fact, for very short vectors, better performance often is obtained by using the scalar unit of a vector processor instead of the vector unit. The start-up time incorporates the pipeline latency before the first result is produced as well as setup time for vector-length and other control registers. Some or all of the setup time may be overlapped with the execution of other vector operations, but the pipeline latency overhead is unavoidable. The start-up time for each type of operation is often specified in terms of clock cycles and ranges from a few to many tens of cycles.

A useful way to characterize the impact of start-up overhead on performance is via the notion of *half-performance vector length,* defined as a vector length that causes the performance to be half that achieved with infinitely long vectors. Typical half-performance vector lengths range from tens to about 100 in real vector machines, with larger values corresponding to greater start-up overhead.

The second factor that limits the performance of a vector processor in comparison to its peak potential is resource idle time and contention. As the timing diagram in Figure 26.4 indicates, both multiply and add function unit pipelines can be busy at the same time for the chained version of the computation $S := X \times Y + Z$. However, if the computation of interest is $S := V \times W + X \times Y$ and there is only one multiply function unit, the adder will go unused during the first multiplication (as well as in the start-up phase of the second multiplication). Memory bank contention is perhaps a more important source of performance degradation. With no memory bank contention, and assuming adequate memory bandwidth, vector register load and store operations are overlapped with computations on previously loaded

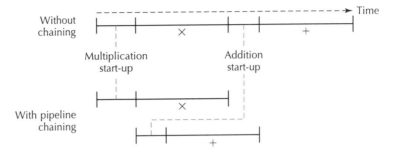

Figure 26.4 Total latency of the vector computation $S := X \times Y + Z$, without and with pipeline chaining.

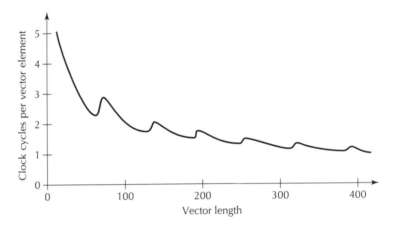

Figure 26.5 The per-element execution time in a vector processor as a function of the vector length.

vectors or vector segments (Figure 26.3). However, this desirable mode of operation cannot always be maintained, particularly when vector elements are to be accessed in irregular positions specified by means of index vectors.

The third factor results from the overhead of vector segmentation when the entire vector does not fit in a vector register. Generally, we expect the performance of a vector processor to improve for longer vectors. However, this improvement is not uniform and smooth (see Figure 26.5). For example, with 64-element vector registers, processing of vectors of length 65 involves a great deal of overhead to take care of the one extra element.

In any comparison of the peak MFLOPS of a vector processor to that of a scalar processor, we must take into account the impact of conditional computations. Consider, for example, a loop in which two different computations are performed depending on whether the condition $A[i] > 0$ holds. To perform such an "if-then-else" computation on a vector processor, first a mask vector is formed that defines the vector elements satisfying the condition. Next, the "then" part of the computation is performed, using the mask to disable the operations for elements not satisfying the condition. Finally, the "else" part is performed for the remaining vector elements. Assuming that the computations for the "then" and "else" parts take the same amount of time and ignoring the time needed to form the mask vector, the computation time roughly doubles and the performance advantage of vector processing is halved. Put another way, the half-performance vector length grows as a result of the overhead for conditional computations. The performance penalty of a multiway "case" statement is correspondingly greater than a two-way "if-then-else" statement.

Various architectural methods have been used to further improve the performance of vector processors and to mitigate the effects of inhibiting factors outlined thus far in this section. One such method, *multilane vector processor* design, allows parallelism in vector operations. For example, a four-lane design might split each vector among four lanes, with elements whose indices are congruent modulo 4 assigned to the same lane. So, for instance, lane 0 will contain elements 0, 4, 8, . . . , 56, 60 of a 64-element vector that is split among four 16-element subregisters (one per lane). To perform a vector add instruction, four pipelined adders are employed to operate on the subregisters in parallel. This type of parallelism is above and beyond the parallelism in having multiple vector processors interconnected using the methods to be discussed in Chapters 27 and 28. To use an analogy, multiple interconnected vector processors can be likened to multiple highways that allow more traffic to flow from point A to point B; multilane design is akin to increasing the number of lanes in a single highway; automobiles following one another in one lane represent simple pipelining. One side benefit of multilane design is that the smaller subregister files for each lane are faster than one large register file.

Another architectural method is to eliminate most or all of the start-up overhead in some vector operations by allowing the reuse of function unit pipelines without draining them at the end of each vector instruction. In practice, it is necessary to allow one or two cycles of separation or *dead time* between consecutive uses of the same function unit pipeline, to ensure that the control circuitry does not become overly complicated. The performance impact of this method is particularly pronounced when computations involve relatively short vectors.

◼ 26.4 Shared-Control Systems

The vector operation $Z := X + Y$ is an abstract specification for m independent additions, where m is the vector length. This abstraction is known as *data-parallel computation*. As far as the semantics of the program encompassing this vector operation is concerned, it does not matter whether the m independent additions are performed in a scalar processor one at a time, by a single deeply pipelined adder in a conventional vector processor, by four adders in a multilane vector processor, or by m adders within m simple processors. The latter approach of using a fairly large number of processors that are centrally directed to execute common operations is an example of *shared-control* architecture. The notion of shared control actually spans a wide spectrum of options, from complete sharing of control in a pure SIMD arrangement (Figure 26.6a) up to, but not including, total separation of control, or MIMD (Figure 26.6c). Intermediate schemes, in which fewer than p control units are shared by p processors, are known as multiple SIMD, or MSIMD (Figure 26.6b). The association of one control unit with a subset of the p processors can be static, or it can be dynamically changed depending on workload. In the rest of this chapter, we focus on simple shared-control (SIMD) architectures also known as *array processors*.

In an array processor, the centralized memory and processor of a vector processor are distributed in space, while its control remains centralized. An immediate advantage is that memory

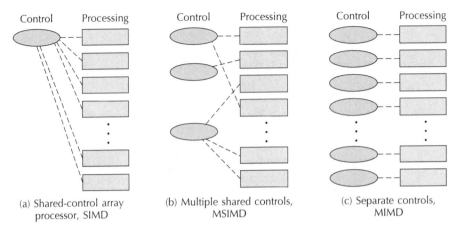

(a) Shared-control array
processor, SIMD

(b) Multiple shared controls,
MSIMD

(c) Separate controls,
MIMD

Figure 26.6 From completely shared control to totally separate controls.

bandwidth ceases to be a major bottleneck. A vector of length m can be distributed to the local memories of the p processors, each one receiving approximately m/p vector elements. A vector operation such as $Z := X + Y$ is then executed rapidly in the time required for m/p additions. The larger the number of processors, the less critical the speed of addition in each one. Actual implementations of array processors span a wide range in the processor multiplicity-versus-performance trade-off: from a relatively small number of high-performance processors to many thousands of bit-serial processors. A good example of the former type is the ILLIAC IV, a 1960s vintage supercomputer, that used 64–256 very fast (for its time) 64-bit processors. The latter extreme is exemplified by the Connection Machine computers of the mid- to late 1980s which had up to 64K single-bit processors, 16 to a VLSI chip. With today's technology, multimillion-processor systems of the latter type are feasible (256 boards × 64 chips per board × 64–256 processors per chip).

The downside of the aforementioned distribution of memory and processing units in space is that it necessitates some form of interprocessor communication for vector operations that involve combining (e.g., $s := \sum X$) or for vectors that are processed in an order other than the one used for spatial distribution. An example of the latter category is performing m multiplications of the form $X[i] \times Y[m - 1 - i]$ for vectors X and Y of length m that are distributed according to the index i. In this case, the processor holding $X[i]$ may require access to nonlocal data to get $Y[m - 1 - i]$.

The pattern of connectivity for interprocessor communication can range from the very simple linear array (or ring), where each processor is connected to two neighboring processors, to highly sophisticated networks to be discussed in Section 28.2 in connection with multicomputer systems. A fairly natural interconnection scheme for array processors is a square or rectangular 2D mesh, which fits quite well to matrix-type operations commonly executed on such systems. For example, 256 × 256 matrices can be processed efficiently by the 4 × 4 mesh-connected array processor of Figure 26.7 if the matrices are divided into 64 × 64 blocks, with each block assigned to a processor in the obvious way. Two-dimensional torus interconnection, which is the same as 2D mesh but with the two processors at the end of each row or column connected to each other, is often more suitable (see Figure 26.7, which also shows a possible way to handle I/O).

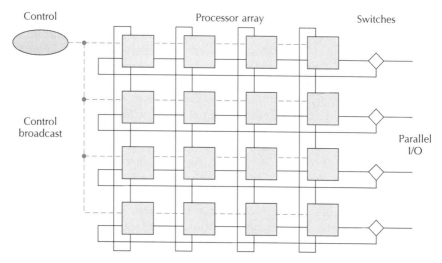

Figure 26.7 Array processor with 2D torus interprocessor communication network.

■ 26.5 Array Processor Implementation

We discuss implementation issues for an array processor in terms of the example system depicted in Figure 26.7. In other words, we assume that the 2D torus processor interconnection scheme has been chosen based on the application characteristics and that I/O is to be done through 3×3 switches that allow the processor array to be connected as an ordinary torus or to operate in one of two I/O modes: data flowing within the row loops in clockwise or counterclockwise direction.

The control unit of an array processor resembles an ordinary scalar processor. It fetches and decodes instructions and broadcasts the appropriate control signals to the identical data paths within all processors. When the number of processors is large, directly connecting the control signals to all processors may be impractical owing to the large fan-out; in such a case, the signals may have to go through repeaters. The control unit also has a register file, an ALU, and a data memory (see, e.g., Figure 13.3) to perform certain control-related computations and maintain scalar values that must be broadcast to processors. The only new element required for the control unit, beyond those of a conventional processor, is a capability to perform branching based on the state of the processor array. This requires the control unit to have some global knowledge about the current state of each processor. A single bit of information from each processor is often adequate for this purpose.

For example, after the array has been instructed to perform a test (such as arithmetic comparison), it may be of interest to determine whether any of the processors in the array had a positive outcome. The cleanest way to provide this capability is to include an *array state register* in the control unit whose width equals the number of processors in the array: bit i in the array state register is associated with processor i. Then, whenever a conditional test operation is issued to the processors, they may record the outcome locally as well as in this state register. If after a test, the array state register contains 0, then the control unit would know that no processor had a successful test outcome. The number of successful outcomes can also be determined by the control unit, if desired, by simply counting the number of 1s in the array state register. A special *population count* instruction may be provided for this purpose. This capability comes handy in conditional "if-then-else" computations. If after testing the condition, locally in each processor, the control unit finds out that none of the local tests was successful, execution of the "then" part can be skipped. Normally, processors that had a successful outcome would be enabled for the duration of the "then" path of the program, with all others participating in executing the "else" path.

The processors within the array are sometimes referred to as bare-bone processors or *processing elements* (PEs) to convey the lack of some of the blocks shown near the left end of Figure 13.3 for fetching and interpreting instructions. They do, however, contain a register file, an ALU, and a data memory, interconnected much like the ones shown on the right side of Figure 13.3. One difference is that the processing elements can be selectively turned off so that they ignore the control signals broadcast to the array. This is necessary for conditional operations. Note that even though all active processors follow the same instruction, they do not necessarily perform identical operations on the contents of the same register or memory locations. Some local autonomy is allowed. For example, when memory is accessed using the address in register $\$12$, the content of register $\$12$ may be different in each processor, leading to different locations of memory to be accessed. This facilitates vector accesses of the form $A[X[i]]$ in processor i, where X is an index vector.

Figure 26.8 shows the main components of a processing element, focusing in particular on the interprocessor communication method. The output of the ALU in each PE is stored in a communication buffer that is visible to the four neighboring PEs in the north, east, west, and south (abbreviated NEWS) directions. In each cycle, when interprocessor communication is enabled (CommunEn signal is asserted), the lower operand to the ALU is taken from a neighboring PE, depending on the communication direction indicated by the CommunDir control signals.

The switches shown near the right edge of Figure 26.7 must be designed to allow three types of connectivity, as seen in Figure 26.9. Each bidirectional connection in Figure 26.7 corresponds to two unidirectional links in Figure 26.9. In the normal array processor mode of operation, the I/O connections are ignored and the array works as a torus (Figure 26.9a). The two I/O modes in Figures 26.9b and 26.9c differ in the direction of data input and output from the row of processing elements. Both these modes allow for new data to be shifted in and results to be shifted out from the processing elements. The mechanism used in the torus operation mode to handle interprocessor communication also handles I/O data transfers that are performed as shifting operations within array rows. Design of the required switch is straightforward and is left as an exercise.

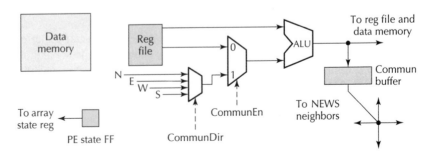

Figure 26.8 Handling of interprocessor communication via a mechanism similar to data forwarding.

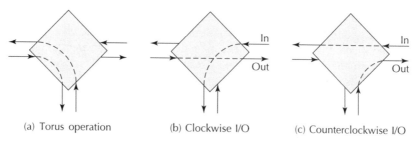

(a) Torus operation   (b) Clockwise I/O   (c) Counterclockwise I/O

Figure 26.9 I/O switch states in the array processor of Figure 26.7.

26.6 Array Processor Performance

Much of what was said in Section 26.3 about vector processor performance applies, with very little change, to array processors as well. The difference between the two architectures is that in a vector processor, one powerful processor handles all vector elements, whereas in an array processor each of a large set of processing elements handles a portion of the work. A multilane vector processor can in fact be viewed as combining vector and array processing techniques. For certain applications, an array processor may offer substantially the same performance as a vector processor with much lower design cost and perhaps even greater energy economy. The lower design cost is attributable to simpler processors with less extensive performance optimization and associated design problems. Reduced energy consumption may be due to the use of lower-voltage circuits to implement the low-performance PEs. Array processors may also be more robust and less prone to transient and timing faults resulting from very high clock frequencies.

A downside of array processing is control broadcasting and synchronization overheads. Typically, the processors run in lock step, so that they execute each instruction, and report their states to the control unit, at the same time. Clock distribution and clock skew are thus issues that must be dealt with. Typically, clock cycle time must be increased to accommodate signal travel time as well as clock skew (see Section 2.6). Communication overhead also contributes to reduced performance, especially if the interconnection scheme calls for long wires between circuit boards or cabinets. Thus, if the same processing element is used in building array processors of varying sizes, it is likely that each processor will have to run slower for larger arrays. Hence, even if data parallelism is unlimited, performance of an array processor does not scale linearly with the number of processors.

Applications that contain a great deal of data parallelism, and can thus run efficiently on an array processor with little interprocessor communication, are sometimes referred to as *embarrassingly parallel* (the author prefers to use more positive characterizations such as *pleasantly parallel*). Examples of such applications abound in domains such as:

Signal and image processing

Database management and data mining

Data fusion in command and control

As was the case for vector processors, conditional operations in array processors are performed by executing the two paths one after the other, using selective activation. What was a pipeline bubble in the case of a vector processor becomes an idle processing element within the array that ignores a particular instruction. This waste or inefficiency due to idle resources is one of the criticisms often voiced about array processing. One can understand the irrelevance of this point by considering the analogy of a bus versus private automobiles. A bus must follow a predetermined, often longer, route to ensure that all areas of interest to passengers are served. It may also have many empty seats on some trips. These points, however, do not imply that buses are less efficient modes of transportation; in fact, by most measures, they are significantly more efficient than the alternative of private autos.

It is feasible for the control unit to broadcast instructions from both paths of a two-way conditional computation, with each PE following the instruction from the appropriate path depending on its local state. This doubles the number of wires used for broadcasting and complicates the PEs because a multiplexer is needed for each control signal. Performance may be improved because the execution time of a two-way conditional computation is dictated by the running time for the longer path rather than the sum of the two paths. Taking this approach a step further, leads to the SPMD (single program, multiple data) architecture in which each processor has its own control unit but all processors execute the same program. In this way, each processor can take the appropriate path within two-way or multiway conditional computations without being slowed down by the other processors. This approach also eases the synchronization burden because the processors need to be synchronized only when they exchange data. This benefit comes at the expense of more complex processors.

One factor that has a significant impact on the performance of an array processor is the way in which data is distributed among the memory modules associated with the processing elements. An intelligent compiler can often distribute the data in a way that ensures good performance. However, the problem is inherently difficult and not always solvable. For example, if a large matrix is distributed one row to each processor, then local row elements are easily accessible by a processor, whereas reading elements of a particular column requires extensive interprocessor communication. Moreover, an array may be accessed differently in various parts of a program. Sometimes, it pays to rearrange the data in preparation for a change in access mode. The communication penalty paid during rearrangement may prevent even more communication activities in the course of subsequent computations.

PROBLEMS

26.1 Loop parallelization

Show how the following loop, discussed in Section 26.1, can be parallelized despite the obvious loop-carried dependency:

```
for i = 0 to 63 do
    A[i] := A[i] + B[i]
    B[i+1] := C[i] + D[i]
endfor
```

Hint: Reverse the order of statements.

26.2 Access to matrix subarrays

Redo Example 26.1, but now assume that matrix elements are indexed from $A[1, 1]$ to $A[n, n]$; that is, use 1-origin instead of 0-origin indexing.

26.3 Recursive doubling

Consider the following loop for computing the sum of elements in a vector X of length 64:

```
for i = 0 to 62 do s := s + X[i] endfor
```

The obvious loop-carried dependency prevents straightforward vectorization of this loop.

a. Show how a vectorizing compiler can produce vector code for this loop by adding pairs of consecutive elements, then adding results from the first stage, and so on. *Hint:* Use an auxiliary vector Y and form pairwise sums of X elements in $Y[1]$, $Y[3]$, ..., $Y[63]$, the next set of sums in $X[3]$, $X[7]$, ..., $X[63]$, and so on, switching back and forth between X and Y; this method is known as *recursive doubling*.

b. Modify your solution to part a so that *prefix sums* of vector X are computed in vector Y, meaning that at the end, $Y[i]$ holds the sum of elements of X, from $X[0]$ up to, and including, $X[i]$.

26.4 Interleaved memory

Assume that the memory unit of a vector processor has a latency of 16 clock cycles and that it is 16-way interleaved. Consider loading a 64-element vector, with the following strides, into a vector register. In each case, compute the fraction of the total memory bandwidth used and the fraction of bandwidth relative to that of the ideal stride of part a. Compare the results and discuss.

a. $s = 1$
b. $s = 2$
c. $s = 4$
d. $s = 5$
e. $s = 18$
f. $s = 20$

26.5 Interleaved memory

Derive conditions to be satisfied by the number b of memory banks, the memory access delay d expressed in clock cycles, and the vector access stride s if bank conflicts are to be avoided during a vector load or store operation.

26.6 Loops with conditional operations

Consider the following loop

```
for i = 0 to 63 do if Y[i] ≠ 0 then
   X[i] := X[i]/Y[i] endfor
```

which cannot be vectorized directly because of the conditional operation within the loop.

a. Show how this loop can be converted to vectorizable form by using masked operations. A masked vector divide, for example, is performed for element i of the vector only if the corresponding bit in the mask vector M is 0; that is, the element is not masked out.

b. Show how results similar to part a can be achieved without masking capability. *Hint:* Divide $X[i]$ by $Y[i] + M[i]$, where $M[i]$ is in $\{0, 1\}$.

26.7 Vector processor performance

Consider in Example 26.2 that the vector operations fall into two categories: operations on relatively short vectors are not speeded up on the vector processor owing to pipeline start-up and drainage overheads, whereas operations on long vectors enjoy a speedup factor of 8 on average.

a. What is the expected speedup of the vector processor over the superscalar processor if short-vector operations account for 30% of the total running time on the superscalar processor?

b. Assuming that the fractions of running time for scalar and short-vector operations are not known, under what conditions is an overall speedup of 2 achievable?

c. What do you think about the cost-effectiveness of the vector processing approach under the conditions of parts a and b? Discuss.

26.8 Vector processor performance

Another useful performance metric for a vector processor is the vector length that is needed to make the vector mode faster than operating on individual vector elements in scalar mode. Discuss how this metric is related to the half-performance vector length and the start-up time. State all your assumptions clearly.

26.9 Vector register load scheduling

Suppose a vector processor has a large set of vector registers. There are two load units sharing a queue of pending load requests that have been issued in anticipation of future vector operations. Each load operation is characterized by a starting address and a stride. Show that it might be helpful to perform the load operations out of order and discuss the criteria to be used for choosing the order of load operations.

26.10 Processing element design

Complete the design of the processing element depicted in Figure 26.8, assuming an instruction set similar to that of MicroMIPS given in Table 13.1 (except that there are no control transfer instructions). Assume that each of the instructions can be conditionalized on the PE state, and add a small number of instructions (no more than five, say) that would allow the setting and resetting of the PE state flip-flop and use of the interprocessor communication capabilities.

26.11 Array processor I/O

a. Design the three-state 3×3 switch of Figure 26.9 so that the appropriate state is assumed based on two control signals supplied by the shared control unit.
b. Show how the switch is simplified if one of the two I/O directions (say, clockwise) is removed.
c. How is I/O different with the switches of parts a and b? In other words, is the additional flexibility offered by the more complex switches of part a worth the added cost? Discuss.

26.12 Associative processors

An associative processor is an array processor in which the processing elements are extremely simple. Each PE has a single word of memory (say 256 bits wide) and can execute the following operations: set or reset the PE state flip-flop or load it with the content of a specified bit in the memory word; perform various logic operations (say, AND, NAND, OR, NOR, XOR, XNOR) on two specified bits of the memory word, placing the result in another specified bit. Typically, most of the stored word contains data in various fields, with a few bits reserved for holding scratch results as the computation proceeds. For example, the stored word in one PE may contain data about one aircraft flying in a monitored airspace, with data fields corresponding to aircraft ID, its coordinates, and speed. Recall that the control unit has access to the PE state bits and can treat these bits as the content of a register. Devise associative processor algorithms for the following computations,

in each case storing the single-bit results in PE state flip-flops. Assume that the field F of interest holds an unsigned integer and extends from bit i to bit j, where $j > i$.

a. Determine which PEs hold a nonzero value in field F.
b. Determine whether any PE holds the value 23 in field F.
c. Determine whether any PE holds a value greater than or equal to 18 in field F.
d. Determine which PEs hold a value between 18 and 25 in field F.
e. Determine which PEs hold the largest value in field F.

26.13 Membership searches

In Problem 26.12, you were asked to show how some simple searches are performed on a generic associative processor. This problem deals with *membership searches* on associative processors using the same assumptions as in Problem 26.12.

a. Show how we can identify all processing elements that hold one of the bit patterns 0101, 0110, 0111, 1101, 1110, or 1111 in a particular 4-bit field with the fewest instructions possible.
b. Formulate a general procedure for performing membership searches of the type given in part a with a minimum number of instructions.

26.14 Conway's game of life

Design a simple SIMD machine to play John Conway's Game of Life. In this game, the world of microorganisms is modeled by a Boolean matrix, where 1 represents the presence and 0 the absence of a living organism. Discrete time is assumed, and the new state of each matrix cell at time $t + 1$ is determined by three rules based on the number of living organisms in its eight nearest neighbors at time t: (1) Any living organism with two or three neighbors survives. (2) Any living organism with four or more neighbors dies of overcrowding. (3) Any living organism with zero or one neighbor dies of solitude. (4) An organism is born in any empty cell with exactly three neighbors. Your machine should be able to simulate the Game of Life on a 256×256 matrix for many millions of time steps (generations).

26.15 Vector versus array processing

a. Does the ripple effect shown in Figure 26.5 in connection with vector processors apply to array processor as well? In what way, or why not?

b. What characteristics of an application or its input/output data dictate whether vector or array processing will be appropriate or more cost-effective for it?

26.16 SIMD accelerator for image processing

Two types of operation are commonly used in image processing. Assume that an image is represented by a 2D matrix of 0s and 1s corresponding to dark and light pixels, respectively. Noise removal has the goal of removing isolated 0s and 1s (say those that have at most one pixel of the same type among their 8 horizontally, vertically, or diagonally adjacent neighbors). Smoothing is done by replacing each pixel value with the median of 9 values consisting of the pixel itself and its 8 neighbors.

a. Discuss the design of a SIMD unit composed of a 2D array of simple cells to accelerate noise removal or smoothing.

b. Propose suitable generalizations for noise removal and smoothing if each pixel value is a binary integer (say 4 bits wide) representing a gray level.

c. Sketch the modifications required to the cells of part a if part b is to be implemented.

REFERENCES AND FURTHER READINGS

[Asan03]   Asanovic, K., "Vector Processors," Appendix G of *Computer Architecture: A Quantitative Approach,* by J. L. Hennessy and D. A. Patterson, Morgan Kaufmann, 3rd ed., 2003 (available on line at www.mkp.com/CA3/).

[Crag96]   Cragon, H. G., *Memory Systems and Pipelined Processors,* Jones and Bartlett, 1996.

[Hord90]   Hord, R. M., *Parallel Supercomputing in SIMD Architectures,* CRC Press, 1990.

[Parh95]   Parhami, B., "SIMD Machines: Do They Have a Significant Future?" *ACM Computer Architecture News,* Vol. 23, No. 4, pp. 19–22, September 1995 (shorter version in *IEEE Computer,* Vol. 28, No. 6, pp. 89–91, June 1995).

[Thom93]   Thomborson, C. D., "Does Your Workstation Computation Belong on a Vector Supercomputer?" *Communications of the ACM,* Vol. 36, No. 11, pp. 41–49, 94, November 1993.

27

SHARED-MEMORY MULTIPROCESSING

"One friend in a lifetime is much; two are many; three are hardly possible. Friendship needs a certain parallelism of life, a community of thought, a rivalry of aim."
—*Henry Brooks Adams*

"Technology advances in both hardware and software have rendered most Instruction Set Architecture conflicts moot.... Computer design is focusing more on the memory bandwidth and multiprocessing interconnection problems."
—*Robert Tomasulo, looking forward, circa 1998*

The idea of using multiple processors to cooperate on a computationally intensive problem by accessing common data structures in a shared memory, each contributing its share to an overall solution, may seem naïve at first. Did we not come to the conclusion that it is in fact the speed of memory, not that of the processor, that often limits performance? How, then, does it make sense to expect a single memory unit to keep up with several processors? Answering this question is the goal of this chapter. We note, for example, that by providing a private cache for each processor, the frequency of accesses to the common shared memory can be reduced. This provision, however, leads to the challenging problem of ensuring consistency between the data in multiple caches. We will see how this and other problems are solved in various classes of multiprocessors.

■ 27.1 Centralized Shared Memory

Memory modules that are shared by a number of processors can be centrally located or distributed and packaged with the processors. In the former case, the entire address space in memory is equally accessible to all processors, leading to *symmetric multiprocessors* or

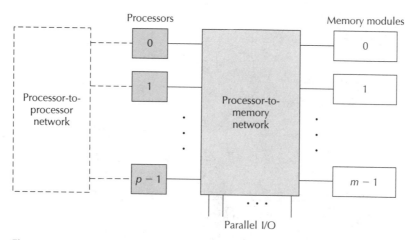

Figure 27.1 Structure of a multiprocessor with centralized shared memory.

uniform memory access (UMA) architectures. In the latter case, *local memory* is more readily accessible to a processor than *remote memory* located with other processors. Distributed shared memory leads to *asymmetric multiprocessors* or *nonuniform memory access* (NUMA) architectures. We discuss centralized shared memory in this section, leaving consideration of distributed shared memory to Section 27.4.

Figure 27.1 depicts the general structure of a multiprocessor with centralized shared memory. Processors can access the shared memory via a processor-to-memory interconnection network that allows any processor to read or write data from/to any memory module. The simplest such network is a shared bus to which all the processors and memory modules are connected. Using a shared bus as the interconnection network is not viable in the structure shown in Figure 27.1, although it may be once caches have been added (see Section 27.2). At the other extreme, one may use a permutation network that allows all processors to simultaneously access distinct memory modules. Most practical processor-to-memory interconnection networks fall between these two extremes. There may also be a separate interprocessor interconnection network typically devoted to passing of data and control information for coordination and synchronization (such as interrupt signals) between the processors.

The processor-to-memory interconnection network is the most critical component in the shared-memory multiprocessor of Figure 27.1. It must be able to support conflict-free and high-speed access to memory by several processors at once. Even though the memory access latency via the interconnection network is quite important, the communication bandwidth that can be supported is even more important, given that multithreading and other methods can be used to allow processors to continue to do useful work while waiting for requested data to arrive from memory. Collectively, these methods are said to provide *latency tolerance* or *latency hiding*.

To provide an interconnection network with multiple paths and adequate bandwidth to support simultaneous memory accesses from many processors, a large number of switches arranged in layers are often used. The resulting *multistage interconnection network* may follow many different design strategies, leading to varying complexities and throughputs. Available designs offer a wide spectrum of choices in terms of cost/performance trade-offs. The theory of

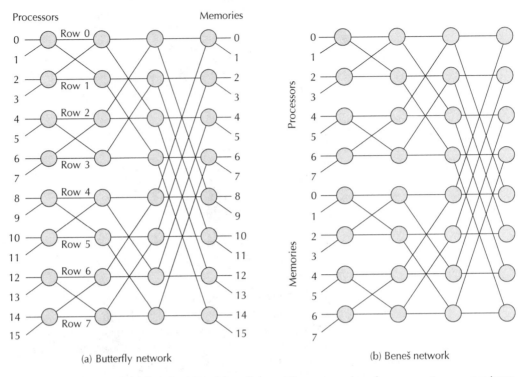

Figure 27.2 Butterfly and the related Beneš networks as examples of processor-to-memory inter-connection networks in multiprocessors.

interconnection networks is quite rich, and new structures are still being discovered that offer certain advantages in terms of implementation ease and/or performance [Parh99].

One of the oldest, and most versatile, multilevel interconnection structures is the *butterfly network,* which consists of switches arranged in 2^q rows and $q + 1$ columns. Proceeding from left to right, each switch in row r has a straight connection to a switch in the same row and a cross connection to a switch in row $r \pm 2^c$, where c is the column number. Figure 27.2a shows how an 8-row butterfly network can be used to connect 16 processors to 16 memory modules. Any processor i can be connected to any memory module j. Furthermore, there is a unique path for this connection, which can be determined easily from the binary representations of i and j. For example, the path from processor 5 to memory module 9 is determined by first noting that the path leads from row $2 = (010)_{two}$ of the butterfly to row $4 = (100)_{two}$. XORing 010 and 100 yields the *routing tag* 110, which can be used to trace a path from the butterfly network's row 2 to row 4. A message entering a switch can leave it by taking the straight path or the cross path. Reading the routing tag backward yields the path. In our example, we get the path 0 (straight), 1 (cross), 1 (cross), which is easily verified to lead from row 2 to row 4. A message carrying the routing tag can find its way through the network without a need for external control. For this reason, the butterfly network is an example of a *self-routing network.*

The butterfly network is capable of connecting several processors on one side to memory modules on the other side; however it cannot establish connections according to an arbitrary

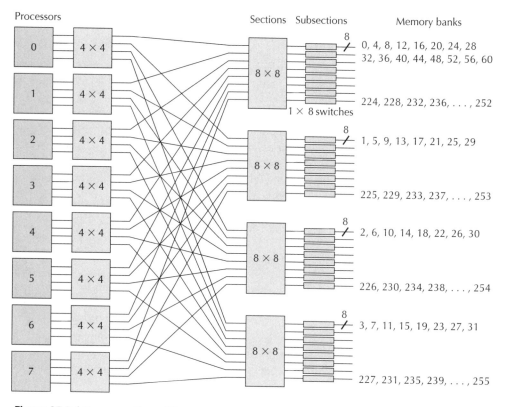

Figure 27.3 Interconnection of 8 processors to 256 memory banks in Cray Y-MP, a supercomputer with multiple vector processors.

permutation. In other words, it is not a permutation network. A particular type of $p \times p$ permutation network, known as a Beneš network, can be derived from a p-row butterfly as shown in Figure 27.2b. The network depicted in Figure 27.2b has some redundancies in that switches in its rightmost column do not perform any useful function. It is easily seen that the network can be simplified to two back-to-back 4-row butterfly networks. Supplying the details is left as an exercise.

The networks shown in Figure 27.2 both use 2×2 switches. Switches of other types can be employed to build more sophisticated networks, to reduce the memory access latency, and/or to accommodate different numbers of processors and memory modules. For example, Figure 27.3 shows the Cray Y-MP network used to connect 8 vector processors to 256 memory banks. It is composed of 4×4, 8×8, and 1×8 switches in three layers.

The shared-memory programming model is quite intuitive, and this constitutes one of the advantages of shared-memory multiprocessing. An abstraction of a shared-memory computer, known as parallel random-access machine (PRAM), allows a computation and memory read and write accesses to be specified for each of the p processors in each operation cycle. For example, assuming a p-element vector B in the shared memory, the following program copies the value in $B[0]$ into all other vector elements; this is a form of broadcasting in that it subsequently allows all p processors to gain access to the common value via conflict-free memory accesses, provided the elements of B are distributed among different memory modules.

```
for k = 0 to [log₂p] - 1 processor j, 0 ≤ j < p, do
    B[j + 2ᵏ] := B[j]
endfor
```

Note that in each step, the p processors read from and write into different memory locations. A similar algorithm can be used to determine the sum of all elements in a vector X. Even though the following algorithm looks different from the preceding one, it follows fundamentally the same logic. Determining the differences in the appearance of the two algorithms, and specifying reasons for them, are left as an exercise.

```
processor j, 0 ≤ j < p, do Z[j] := X[j]
s := 1
while s < p processor j, 0 ≤ j < p - s, do
    Z[j + s] := X[j] + X[j + s]
    s := 2 × s
endfor
```

The point of these examples is to show that other than having multiple processors for which a computation must be specified in each step, the programming of shared-memory multiprocessors is quite intuitive and conceptually similar to ordinary programming.

■ 27.2 Multiple Caches and Cache Coherence

The multiprocessor organization of Figure 27.1 suffers from two main problems. First, the high volume of data traffic between processors and memory modules makes the processor-to-memory interconnection network quite critical and likely to become a performance bottleneck unless it is designed for an extremely high bandwidth; this makes the network quite complex, and thus, costly. Second, even if the interconnection network latency and bandwidth are not limiting factors, contention among processors for access to memory modules may slow down the accesses significantly and reduce the effective speedup due to parallel processing. For example, if there exist pieces of shared data that are continually accessed by many processors, the effective memory bandwidth will be much lower than the maximum offered by m memory modules. Such pieces of shared data are referred to as hot spots and the corresponding access conflicts as *hot-spot contention*. Memory access contention creates a serious barrier to performance, particularly considering that memory is a limiting resource even with a single processor (see "hitting the memory wall" in Section 17.3).

A possible solution to both the foregoing problems is to reduce the frequency of accesses to main memory by equipping each processor with a private cache memory. This would work perfectly were it not for the requirement for sharing of data among processors to allow them to solve problems cooperatively. A hit rate of 95% in the caches would reduce the traffic through the processor-to-memory network to 5% of that without caches, thus mitigating the impact of network and memory access latencies as well as the possibility and impact of memory access conflicts. To understand some of the complexities created by shared data in the face of multiple caches, consider the situations in Figure 27.4, where four cache lines w, x, y, and

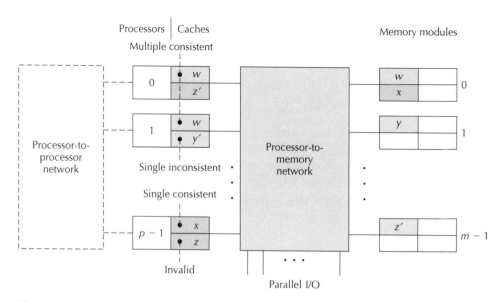

Figure 27.4 Cached data blocks in a parallel processor with centralized main memory and private processor caches.

z are shown. Line w has been copied into two caches, with the two copies being consistent with each other and with that in main memory. As long as the two copies of w are accessed in read-only mode, the line's status remains "multiple consistent." Hence, multiple copies of read-only data in the various caches presents no problem. Similarly, a single cached copy of a particular line, whether the copy is unmodified (clean) or modified (dirty) is not problematic as long as the modified line is written back to main memory when it is replaced.

However, if processors are allowed to write into their cached data lines, inconsistencies may develop among the multiple copies. Strategies for ensuring data consistency are known as *cache coherence algorithms*. A possible strategy for ensuring cache coherence is as follows. Designate each cache line as exclusive or shared. An exclusive line is a line that is in only one cache; we say that such a line is owned by the cache or the associated processor. A processor can freely read from a shared or exclusive cache line, but it can modify only an exclusive cache line. Modifying a shared line requires that its status be changed to exclusive via invalidating all copies of that line in other caches. In other words, the intention to modify the line must be broadcast to all other caches so that each cache can invalidate the copy that it holds, if any. This approach is an instance of a *write-invalidate* cache coherence algorithm. Many other algorithms are possible, however.

Figure 27.5 represents the *snoopy protocol,* a particular implementation of the preceding write-invalidate cache coherence algorithm assuming writeback caches. The snoopy protocol relies on a shared bus to which all cache units are connected. Snoop control units, associated with each of the cache units, continuously monitor the bus. Each cache line can be in one of three states: shared, exclusive, or invalid. Alternate names for the shared and exclusive states are "valid clean" and "valid dirty," respectively. Transitions between states occur in response to local events (CPU read hit, CPU read miss, CPU write hit, CPU write miss) and events in other caches, as observed on the bus (bus read miss, bus write miss). CPU read hits are never problematic and do not lead to a state change. A CPU write hit for a line in exclusive state similarly causes no problem or change of state. A write hit for a line in shared state, however,

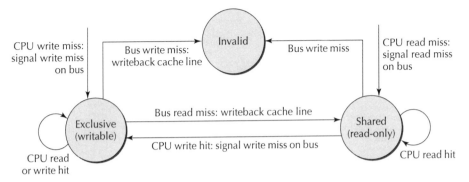

Figure 27.5 Finite-state control mechanism for a bus-based snoopy cache coherence protocol with writeback caches.

causes the state to change to exclusive and a write miss to be signaled to other caches, causing them to invalidate their copies. If a bus write miss is observed for a line that is in exclusive state, the line is written back to memory and the state changed to invalid. A bus read miss in exclusive state similarly causes a writeback operation, but the state is changed to shared. Finally, CPU read or write miss causes the event to be signaled on the bus and the missing line to be brought into the cache in shared or exclusive state, respectively.

Note that whenever a request for access to an exclusive cache line appears on the bus, the use of writeback policy forces the owner of that line to intervene to make sure that stale data from main memory is not used. Thus, in addition to writing back the line to main memory, transitions from exclusive to shared and invalid states require that any memory access initiated as a result of the read or write miss be inhibited (or the memory access, which may be in progress, to be aborted).

The state diagram in Figure 27.5 is sometime drawn with additional transitions between the three states. For example, there may be a transition from exclusive to shared state labeled "CPU read miss: write back cache line, signal read miss on bus." It is somewhat puzzling to encounter a miss transition for a state that indicates the availability of cached data! The implication here is that a read miss is encountered for some desired line that must be placed where we currently have another line in exclusive state. Obviously, in this case, the exclusive line (which is dirty) must be written back to memory before it can be replaced with the desired line. This new line assumes the shared state because the miss occurred for a read operation. We have chosen to draw the diagram in the simpler form shown in Figure 27.5 to avoid clutter and confusion. Proper handling of any block that is replaced by another one is always implied.

■ 27.3 Implementing Symmetric Multiprocessors

The most common implementation of a *symmetric multiprocessor* (SMP) uses a shared bus to interconnect a small to moderate number (4-64) of processors, each with its own private cache; large-scale parallel processing, involving hundreds to many thousands of processors, is impractical with this method. In this section, we focus on bus-based implementations so as to provide a reasonably complete picture of the implementation issues and tradeoffs. We will make a number of simplifying assumptions in order to reduce our presentation to an appropriate

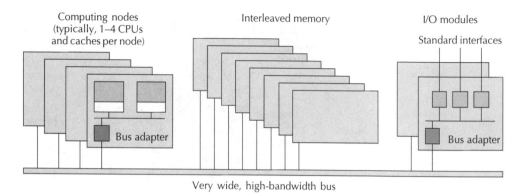

Figure 27.6 Structure of a generic bus-based symmetric multiprocessor.

length for this book. Chapter 6 in [Cull99] contains a much more extensive discussion of implementation issues for snoop-based multiprocessors, including the effects of many parameters that we do not deal with here.

Figure 27.6 shows the structure of a generic bus-based symmetric multiprocessor. Three main types of component are connected to a high-bandwidth, and typically very wide, bus. The bus performance is absolutely critical in such a system, given that even in a single-bus uniprocessor, it is not unusual for the bus bandwidth to dictate the overall performance.

Example 27.1: Bus bandwidth limits performance   Consider a shared-memory multiprocessor built around a single bus with a data bandwidth of x GB/s. Instructions and data words are typically 4 B wide, each instruction executed requires access to an average of 1.4 memory words (including the instruction itself), and the combined hit rate for caches is 98%. Compute an upper bound on the multiprocessor performance in GIPS. Assume that addresses are transmitted over separate bus lines and thus do not affect the data bandwidth of the bus.

Solution: Given the collective miss rate of 0.02, execution of one instruction implies a bus data transfer of $1.4 \times 0.02 \times 4 = 0.112$ B. Thus, an absolute upper bound on performance is $x/0.112 = 8.93x$ GIPS. Assuming a bus width of 32 B, no bus cycle or data going to waste, and a bus clock rate of y GHz, the performance upper bound becomes $286y$ GIPS. Note that the upper bound thus derived is highly optimistic, and actual performance may be a small fraction of this bound. This, combined with the fact that high-performance buses presently operate in the range of 0.1–1 GHz, implies that a performance level approaching 1 TIPS (perhaps even 0.25 TIPS) is beyond reach with this type of architecture, regardless of the number of processors used.

As shown in Figure 27.6, other than the bus, one typically finds three types of component in a shared-bus symmetric multiprocessor. There are a number of computing nodes, each containing 1–4 processors plus the associated cache memories. Multiple processors in a computing node are linked together by an internal node bus and share a bus bridge for connection to the main system bus. Interleaved memory modules allow high-bandwidth access to memory.

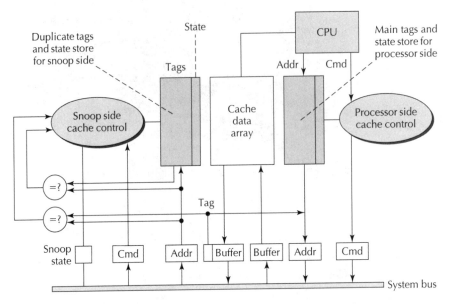

Figure 27.7 Main structure for a snoop-based cache coherence algorithm.

There may be 4–16 independently accessible memory modules. Because the bus cycle is much shorter than the memory access latency, the bus may use a *split-transaction protocol* whereby the bus is released between the transmission of memory address and the return of data. There may thus be several outstanding memory access request in progress at any one time. Rounding up the components are several I/O modules, each organized around an I/O bus that is linked to the main system bus via a bridge. Various standard interfaces are provided for I/O devices via controllers connected to each module's I/O bus.

Because enforcing cache coherence is one of the key aspects of such a multiprocessor, we next discuss, in highly simplified form, the design of a snoop-based coherence unit assuming a single level of cache for each processor. To further simplify the design, we assume an atomic bus rather than a split-transaction bus. This last decision is strictly to limit the complexity of the design and is not a good choice for a practical system. Figure 27.7 depicts the main components in the cache control system. Because snooping must take place continuously, the tags and state bits for the cache are duplicated to allow the processor access to the cache concurrent with snooping. Any update to the tags and state information must, of course, be performed in both copies. On the processor side, a cache miss causes an address and command to be placed on the bus, with the returned data later placed in a read buffer. A writeback event causes data and the associated tag to be placed in a writeback buffer for subsequent transmission on the bus. On the snoop side, the command and address on the bus are examined and tag comparisons performed with both the cache data and the content of the writeback buffer.

Because the single atomic system bus can carry one transaction at a time, a total order is imposed on these transactions, meaning that all caches will "see" them in the same order. Despite these simplifying circumstances, some complications arise owing to simultaneous events in multiple processors and associated caches. For example, if two processors issue requests for writing into a shared cache line (change its state from shared to exclusive) at the same time, the bus arbiter will allow one of these to go through first. The other processor must then invalidate the line and issue a different request corresponding to a cache write miss. A convenient way to handle this and similar cases is to include intermediate states in the state diagram of Figure 27.5. For example, the transition from shared to exclusive state does not occur instantaneously but rather via a shared/exclusive intermediate state. The processor's request in this scenario will change the state from shared to shared/exclusive. Subsequently, transition from shared/exclusive state to exclusive or invalid state will occur, depending on the outcome of the request. Implementation details, as well as more subtle issues of deadlock and starvation due to repeated requests by multiple processors for the same cache line, are beyond the scope of our discussion; they can be found elsewhere [Cull99].

A shared-memory multiprocessor design must also provide two useful mechanisms. The first mechanism allows locking of shared resources for exclusive use of one processor. Such *mutual exclusion* can be ensured via special hardware mechanisms or through software if certain atomic instructions are supported by the hardware. An atomic instruction is one that is performed as a whole, without the possibility of memory content changing before it is completed. To see why such an instruction is needed, consider using a software lock in memory, with 0 (1) representing the open (locked) state. A processor wishing to lock a resource for exclusive use might read out the lock content, observe that it is 0, and then write a 1 to acquire the resource. After reading the lock and before changing its value with another instruction, however, a second processor may read the lock and presume that the resource is available for use. Both processors then write 1 into the lock and continue with the presumption that they have exclusive use of the resource. The availability of an atomic *test-and-set instruction,* which reads the lock into a register and sets its value in shared memory to 1, all in one uninterruptible process, solves this problem.

The second useful mechanism is one that allows *barrier synchronization*. Suppose that p processors must be synchronized. For example, we may want to prevent processors from advancing beyond predetermined points in their computations until all p processors have signaled some event. This can be viewed as a barrier to further progress, hence the name barrier synchronization. The problem is solved by using a counter that is initialized to 0, incremented by each process as it reaches the required point, and tested by all processes to see whether it has reached p. The counter must be accessed by means of the locking process outlined in the preceding paragraph. The problem with this approach is that it requires many accesses to the same lock and counter variables. Each of these accesses is a write access with associated state changes and invalidation in the cache memories. Given that barrier synchronization for p processors is essentially a logical AND function on p bits, it is fairly simple to provide a special hardware mechanism for performing it at much higher performance than is possible with the software-based method.

27.4 Distributed Shared Memory

The scalability problems of multiprocessors with centralized memory give rise to a natural question: Does sharing of a global address space require that the memory be centralized? The answer is that it does not. Memory can be distributed, with a portion of the address space packaged with each processor. When a processor generates an address for memory access and the address refers to a memory location that is not local, a remote access is initiated and after some latency that is fairly large in comparison to the latency of local memory access, the requested data is returned to the processor. The resulting multiprocessor is thus known as NUMA (nonuniform memory access), as noted in Section 27.1. The time penalty for remote memory access can be reduced by a combination of caching and data management (moving data to the physical location where it is needed most often).

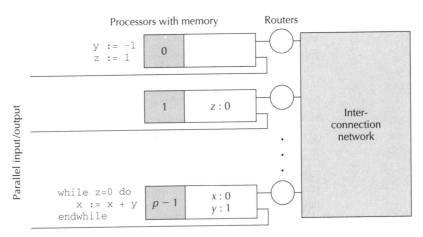

Figure 27.8 Structure of a distributed shared-memory multiprocessor.

Figure 27.8 shows the general structure of a distributed shared-memory multiprocessor. The interconnection network can again range from a shared bus to a variety of direct and indirect networks (see Section 28.2). The reason that even a shared bus may not severely limit scalability is that data transfer through the interconnection mechanism is needed only when a nonlocal memory access is initiated. With proper data distribution, and typical applications that have a great deal of access locality, the volume of data traffic through the interconnection network of Figure 27.8 can be a very small fraction of that in Figure 27.1 and less than that in Figure 27.4. Another advantage of distributed memory over centralized memory is that high-bandwidth parallel I/O is significantly simplified because transfers can occur to/from the separate memory modules using conventional DMA controllers without the data having to go through the interconnection networks.

To see some of the problems that nonuniform memory access may produce, consider the three data items x, y, and z, with their locations and initial values shown in Figure 27.8, along with simple program fragments executed in two of the processors. Suppose the processors begin executing the two program fragments at the same time. The final value for x is a function of the relative ordering of memory accesses, which in turn depends on latencies between various nodes in the interconnection network. For example, it is quite possible for the "while" loop to be executed several times before the value of y is changed to -1 and several more times before z is changed to 1. On the other hand, z may be set to 1 by processor 0 before access to the value of z is completed by processor $p - 1$, leading to no execution of the loop at all.

Note that the two program fragments in the preceding example are parts of a parallel program being executed on the distributed-memory multiprocessor of Figure 27.8. The intended function of this parallel program cannot be deduced from the small parts shown. However, one may legitimately ask whether a program whose computed values depend on nondeterministic ordering of events in hardware can ever be useful. Such nondeterminism is a key source of difficulty in designing efficient parallel programs. In our example, all the programmer can reasonably expect is that $y := -1$ will be completed before $z := 1$, that the while-loop iterations will be executed in the natural order and that in each iteration, the value of z will be tested before x is modified. In the absence of explicit synchronization between events in different processors, nothing should be assumed about the timing of instruction executions on different processors (e.g., ordering of the assignment $z := 1$ vs the test $z = 0$ cannot be predicted). In other words, instructions from different processors can be interleaved in any way, as long as instructions for any particular processor appear in their specified order. The following are some of the possible orderings of events for the example shown in Figure 27.8:

assign y, assign z, test z, assign x, test z, assign x, . . .

test z, assign y, assign x, test z, assign y, assign x, . . .

test z, assign x, test z, assign y, assign x, assign z, . . .

A consequence of the expectation for maintaining instruction ordering in each processor is that if any processor "sees" that z has assumed the value 1, it must also be aware of the new value -1 for y. This property is known as *sequential consistency,* and it is quite intuitive and reasonable to expect. Referring to the example in Figure 27.8, no processor should ever deduce that the condition $y = z$ is satisfied, because this would be inconsistent with $y := -1$ preceding $z := 1$. Unfortunately, however, ensuring sequential consistency is not easily accomplished and comes with a performance penalty. Note that for sequential consistency, it is insufficient to ensure that the change in the value of y precedes the change for z, because a processor that has widely differing latencies for accessing the memory units where y and z are stored can still "see" them in reverse order. This is akin to an astronomer seeing events in distant stars in reverse chronological order owing to different distances and, hence, travel times for light coming from each star.

Note that the problem of sequential consistency is not unique to distributed-memory multi-processors and must be tackled in many systems with centralized memory as well; it is discussed here, however, because it has more serious effects, and is harder to enforce, when memory is distributed. More relaxed consistency models can be defined in the interest of better performance; but then parallel programs must be written so that they make sense, and produce correct results, with the particular model assumed. A discussion of various models of memory consistency and their properties and implementation issues is beyond the scope of this book.

◼ 27.5 Directories to Guide Data Access

Static distribution of data in the various memory modules in Figure 27.8 may be adequate for some applications. In most cases, however, while access locality still exists, the focus of attention within the address space changes dynamically for each processor. This requires either that data elements be physically moved between the memory modules or that local (cached) copies be made available at other locations to maximize the fraction of accesses that are local. Of course, data relocation involves some waste in transfer time as well as management overhead and should not be used indiscriminately. The management overhead is incurred because in abandoning static data distribution, we must keep track of the where-abouts of various data elements, to be able to find them when needed. Caching also involves an overhead for ensuring coherence of multiple copies. In either case, a directory facility is required to indicate where particular data items can be found or where cached copies are located (in case invalidation becomes necessary).

We will continue our discussion in this section by assuming that each data line has a stati-cally assigned home location within one of the memory modules but may have multiple cached copies at various locations. Figure 27.9 shows one system organization that allows this type of data sharing. Assume that a cache line is taken as the unit of data transfers. Associated with each such data element is a directory entry that specifies which caches currently hold a copy of the data. The set of caches holding copies is the *sharing set* for the line. The sharing set can be

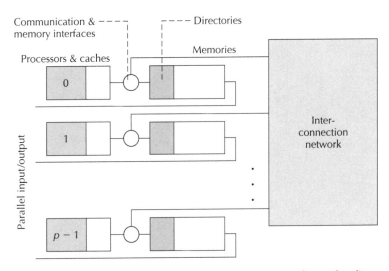

Figure 27.9 Distributed shared-memory multiprocessor with a cache, directory, and memory module associated with each processor.

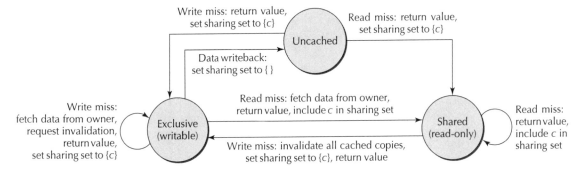

Figure 27.10 States and transitions for a directory entry in a directory-based cache coherence protocol (*c* is the requesting cache).

specified in different forms. If the number of processors is fairly small, then a bit vector is quite efficient. For example, with 32 processors, a 32-bit word can be used to show which of the 32 cache memories holds a copy. An alternative is to provide a listing of the caches; this is quite efficient when sharing sets are typically very small. Neither of these two methods is scalable. A scalable method, which is used in the *Scalable Coherent Interface* (SCI) standard, is for the directory entry to specify one of the caches holding a copy, with each copy containing a pointer to the next cache copy. This is in effect a distributed directory scheme.

As in the snoop-based protocol discussed in Section 27.2, each cache line is associated with a finite-state control mechanism that is quite similar to that in Figure 27.5, except that interaction with other caches is accomplished via messages sent to, and received from, the directory rather than by monitoring a bus. Another finite-state control mechanism is associated with each directory entry for a line-size section of the shared address space. The directory receives messages from various cache units regarding particular data lines, updates its state in the directory, and (if required) sends messages to other caches holding copies of the data line. Figure 27.10

shows the states and associated transitions for a directory entry. The shared and exclusive states are quite similar to their counterparts in Figure 27.5. A directory entry that is in the uncached state implies that the data line does not exist in any of the caches. When a directory entry is in the exclusive state, the corresponding data line exists in a single cache and is said to be owned by it. When a copy of that line is required by another cache, the owner either sends a copy of the updated line (read miss in the requesting cache), with the state becoming shared, or writes back the line and invalidates its copy (write miss in the requesting cache).

The triggering events for the state transitions in Figure 27.10 are messages sent by cache memories to the directory holding the requested line. When cache c indicates a read miss, one of the following occurs, after which the data line becomes (remains) shared:

Line is shared: data value is sent to c and c is added to the sharing set.

Line is exclusive: a fetch message is sent to the owner, returned data is sent to c, and c is added to the sharing set.

Line is uncached: data value is sent to c and the sharing set is set to $\{c\}$.

If the cache message indicates a write miss, one of the following occurs, after which the data line becomes (remains) exclusive:

Line is shared: an invalidation message is sent to caches belonging to the sharing set, the sharing set is set to $\{c\}$, and data value is sent to c.

Line is exclusive: a fetch/invalidate message is sent to the owner, returned data is sent to c, and the sharing set is set to $\{c\}$.

Line is uncached: data value is sent to c and the sharing set is set to $\{c\}$.

If a writeback message is received from a cache (occurring when the cache needs to replace a dirty line with another line), the state of the line is changed to uncached and the sharing set becomes empty.

In an extreme variation of distributed shared memory known as *cache-only memory architecture* (COMA), data lines have no fixed homes. Rather, the entire memory associated with each processor is organized as a cache, with each line having one or more temporary copies in these cachelike memories, which are known as *attraction memories* because they attract data lines that their associated processors access.

An approach to data sharing and coherence that requires little or no hardware support is *shared virtual memory*. Because virtual memory support is already provided in many systems, building a coherence scheme on top of it is rather straightforward. When a page fault occurs in a particular node, the page fault handler obtains the page from a remote memory, if required, using standard message passing. However, given that both the CPU and the operating system get involved in this process and a large amount of data must be transferred, the time overhead is quite large.

■ 27.6 Implementing Asymmetric Multiprocessors

Even though it is possible to use a shared bus as the interconnection mechanism in the multiprocessor of Figure 27.8, the scalability benefits of distributed shared memory will be somewhat muted with a bus. Distributed shared-memory multiprocessors have been implemented by means of a variety of interconnection networks, including ring, mesh, and hypercube (see Section 28.2). In this section, we take the simplest of these options, the ring network, to provide a reasonably complete picture of the implementation issues and trade-offs. To reduce our

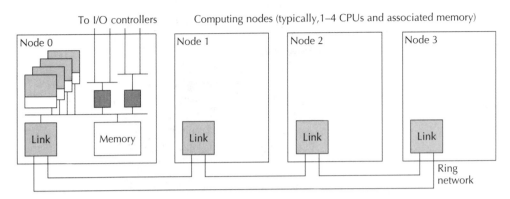

Figure 27.11 Structure of a ring-based, distributed-memory multiprocessor.

presentation to an appropriate length for this book, we will make a number of simplifying assumptions. Chapter 8 in [Cull99] contains a much more extensive discussion of implementation issues for directory-based multiprocessors, including the effects of many design decisions that we do not deal with here.

Figure 27.11 shows the structure of a generic ring-based, distributed-memory multiprocessor. The system is structured around a ring network that connects a number of computing nodes. Each computing node contains one or more processors with cache memory, a local main memory, and I/O bridges connected to I/O controllers via I/O buses, all linked via a node bus. The key component is the box labeled "Link," which allows one computing node to communicate with the other nodes via the ring network and also enforces the coherence protocol between nodes. It contains a cache memory to hold data from other nodes (remote cache), a local directory, and interface controllers for the bus side and network side. When remote data is needed and is not found in the remote cache within the link box, a request is sent via the ring network. Coherence is enforced in two levels. Within each computing node, snooping is used to ensure coherence among processor caches, the remote cache embedded in the link box, and main memory. Internode coherence is enforced by a directory-based protocol, to be described shortly.

The multiprocessor depicted in Figure 27.11 is an instance of two-level hierarchical architectures that are quite popular because they reduce the structural complexity at each level and allow local communications within nodes (or clusters) to be performed at higher speed. The advent of chip multiprocessors, accommodating a number of processors, cache memories, and perhaps controllers and interfaces on a single chip, makes such multilevel architectures even more desirable.

The coherence protocol depicted in part in Figure 27.10 and described in Section 27.5, can be used with any representation of the sharing set. Figure 27.12 depicts a linked-list method for representing the sharing set that is scalable to an arbitrary number of processors. This method is used in the SCI standard. In what follows, we describe the SCI coherence protocol assuming single-processor nodes. Interaction of this protocol with the snoop-based protocol used to enforce coherence within each node will be described later. In SCI, data lines in memory are of two types: coherent and noncoherent. Coherence is not enforced for the latter type of data to avoid paying the enforcement overhead for data that is not intended for sharing or is shared in read-only mode. The directory entry and associated data line reside in the memory module of a particular processor. The directory entry points to one of the caches that holds

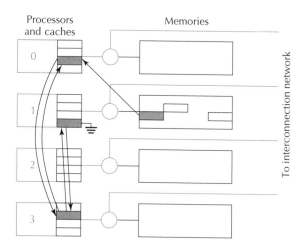

Processors and caches

Memories

To interconnection network

Figure 27.12 Structure of the sharing set in the Scalable Coherent Interface. Shaded blocks are coherent and constitute the sharing set {0, 3, 1}.

a copy of the data line. If the line is uncached, then a null link appears in the directory. Each cache in turn hold a pointer to the next cache and one to the previous cache within a doubly linked chain. The last cache in this chain holds a null forward link.

When a cache is to be added to the sharing set, it is included in the linked list between the directory entry and the cache to which it points. Thus, only a handful of pointer modifications need to occur for this change in the sharing set. When the sharing set is a singleton, as in the case of an exclusive data line, the data is readily available, when needed, from the cache pointed to by the directory entry. When a cache overwrites a line and must thus be removed from the sharing set, it simply notifies the two caches in the forward and backward directions so that they point to each other rather than to the removed cache. Only the cache at the beginning of the linked list can invalidate data lines in all member caches of the sharing set; this is done by relaying a message along the chain until it reaches the last cache. For this reason, the invalidation latency is a function of system size. Thus, even though this protocol is scalable from the viewpoint of representing the sharing set, it is not fully scalable from the performance standpoint. If a cache that wants to gain exclusive status for a data line is not at the beginning of the list, it removes itself from the sharing set, then regains membership, this time as the head element of the list, and finally proceeds to send the invalidation request.

Note that in the organization of Figure 27.11, each computing node is a symmetric multiprocessor that uses a bus-based, snoopy cache coherence protocol. This protocol enforces coherence within the node's processor caches, main memory, and remote cache embedded in the link box. Interactions between this node-level coherence protocol and the internode coherence protocol of the preceding paragraphs is discussed next. Consider first a read miss in a processor's cache that is signaled on the node bus. The link box finds out about this miss by snooping the bus. It checks the remote cache as well as the directory for locally allocated lines to see whether the request can be satisfied within the node. Otherwise, the link box invokes the directory protocol to obtain the required line from another node. If the node bus uses a split-transaction protocol, this event simply corresponds to a late response and needs no special handling. Meanwhile, other accesses within the node can proceed to use the bus with no performance degradation. A write miss is handled similarly. Writing to local blocks is straightforward. If invalidation in other nodes is needed, this is done by the link box before writing actually takes place, and an acknowledgment is issued. For nonlocal lines, the directory protocol ensures correct handling of the write request.

Like its centralized-memory counterpart, a distributed-memory multiprocessor must also provide mechanisms for mutual exclusion and synchronization. Consider, for example, the problem of providing an atomic *test-and-set instruction,* discussed near the end of Section 27.3. Because executing this instruction involves a write operation, the processor must acquire an exclusive copy of the line containing the lock variable. Then, the instruction is executed in an atomic fashion on the symmetric multiprocessor node, as discussed in Section 27.3. Another processor performing test-and-set must acquire its exclusive copy after causing invalidation for the existing exclusive copy. These repeated invalidations induce a great deal of overhead. It would be more efficient to simply declare such shared control variables as permanently un-cached. Test-and-set is sent as a transaction over the network to the home location of the lock variable, the lock is set, and its previous value returned to the initiating processor. Note that even though multiple test-and-set transactions may overlap during transmission over the network, they are serialized by the memory module holding the lock variable, and a correct response corresponding to this serialization is sent back to each initiator.

PROBLEMS

27.1 Cost-effectiveness of multiprocessing

The cost of a p-processor shared-memory multiprocessor, within its scaling limit in terms of the number of processors, can be expressed in the form $a + bp$, where a is the fixed base cost and b is the per-processor cost. The cost of a uniprocessor with comparable power to one of the processors of the multiprocessor is c, where $c > b$. What computation speedup must be achieved by the p-processor system for it to be considered more cost-effective that the uniprocessor solution? Discuss.

27.2 Butterfly and Beneš networks

Consider the butterfly and Beneš interconnection networks depicted in Figure 27.2.

a. Present a permutation that cannot be routed by the 8-row (16-input) network of Figure 27.2a.
b. Does the network of Figure 27.2a become a permutation network if we use it to connect 8 processors to 8 memory modules (i.e., if the switches in the leftmost and rightmost columns are 1 × 2 and 2 × 1, respectively)?
c. Redraw the Beneš network of Figure 27.2b so that the memory modules appear on the right.

That is, draw the lower half of the network to the right of the upper half, with column order reversed.

d. Remove the redundancies from the network of part c by observing that the middle three columns of switches do not lead to a change in row number for transmitted messages. The resulting simplified network is a true Beneš network.

27.3 Processor-to-memory networks

Consider the interconnection network depicted in Figure 27.3.

a. Explain why the memory banks are numbered as shown on the right side of the figure. *Hint:* Stride of 1 is the most common stride used in memory accesses.
b. What access stride would cause the most difficulty with this network?
c. Is the network a permutation network? Why?

27.4 Parallel random access machine

Consider the two PRAM algorithms for broadcasting and summation of vector elements presented at the end of Section 27.1.

a. Rewrite the broadcasting algorithm so that no processor attempts to read or write elements that do not belong to the vector B.

b. Apply the doubling method of the summation algorithm to the broadcasting algorithm so as to avoid computing a power of 2 in each execution of the loop.

c. Combine the algorithms of parts a and b into a single algorithm that fills all elements of the result vector Z with the computed sum.

d. Suppose we are interested in computing all the partial sums $Z[i] := X[0] + X[1] + \cdots + X[i]$ rather than only the overall sum $X[0] + X[1] + \cdots + X[p-1]$. Modify the summation algorithm to yield all the required partial sums.

27.5 Coherence of register values

Strictly speaking, registers are part of the memory hierarchy. We load variable values into registers, modify them via one or more computation steps, and store them back. Why isn't coherence a problem with registers, as it is with cache memory?

27.6 Snoop-based coherence protocols

Consider the snoop-based cache coherence protocol depicted in Figure 27.5.

a. Is there any benefit in adding a fourth "private" (nonsharable) state to the protocol's finite-state control mechanism? Justify your answer.

b. Modify the finite-state control mechanism to correspond to a multiprocessor system with write-through caches. Discuss the changes and their cost/performance impacts.

27.7 Implementing a snoop-based protocol

Consider the write buffer that holds a cache line to be written to main memory in Figure 27.7. Why is the write-buffer tag connected to the address buffer for memory access on the lower right of the diagram?

27.8 Scalability limit with write-through caches

A bus-based multiprocessor has limited scalability to begin with, but scalability may become even more limited if write-through caches are used. Consider using 1 GHz processors with an average CPI of 0.8 to build a bus-based multiprocessor with centralized shared memory. Assume that 10% of all instructions are stores with 8-byte data width.

a. What is an upper bound on the number of processors that a 4 GB/s bus can support?

b. What is a lower bound on the bus width needed to support 32 processors?

27.9 Optimal line width for caches

We discussed in Section 18.6 the benefits and drawbacks of wider cache lines and stated that an optimal cache line width can often be determined. Discuss whether in a bus-based shared-memory multiprocessor, such as the one in Figure 27.6, a narrower or wider cache line is likely to be optimal compared to that of a uniprocessor. *Hint:* It is possible for two processors to repeatedly invalidate each other's data even though they do not share any variable. This is known as *false sharing*.

27.10 Cache coherence with updating

Some cache coherence protocols update (rather than invalidate) the other copies of a cache line when one shared copy is modified. The obvious advantage of updating is that it prevents some future cache misses. The downside is that updates produce additional bus or network traffic. Discuss which approach, invalidation or updating, is likely to lead to better performance with each of the following access patterns to a single shared variable. State all your assumptions clearly.

a. Repeat many times: one processor writes a new value into the shared variable and all other $p-1$ processors read the new value.

b. Repeat many times: one processor writes m times into a shared variable; this is followed by one other processor reading the value of the shared variable.

27.11 Sequential consistency

A shared-memory parallel machine presents the illusion of a single memory unit to all its processors. Such a multiprocessor is said to provide *sequential consistency* (also known as *strong consistency*) if its memory system behaves as if there were a single memory unit that different processors take turns using. Thus, data written by one processor into a particular memory location becomes immediately "visible" to all processors. The effect of this behavior on the part of the memory system is that the processors produce results that would have been produced if accesses to each memory location were serialized in some order.

a. Explain why sequential consistency may not be provided naturally in a distributed-memory multiprocessor and needs additional effort to enforce.

b. Because enforcing sequential consistency entails performance penalties, *relaxed consistency* models are often used in an effort to allow greater concurrency in memory accesses [Adve96]. Identify two relaxed consistency models and compare them with each other and with sequential consistency for programming ease, implementation cost, and performance impact.

27.12 Remote memory in a memory hierarchy

Read access latencies for a distributed shared-memory multiprocessor are as follows: 5 cycles for a primary cache miss that hits in the on-chip secondary cache; 15 cycles for a secondary cache miss that hits in the tertiary (board-level) cache; 50 cycles for a miss that is served by the memory; 100 cycles for a miss that has to be served from another processor's memory. Determine the average read access time in terms of the hit rates in the various caches and in local memory.

27.13 Directory entries for various data

Consider Figure 27.4, which shows various types of cached data. Add similar notations to Figure 27.9 and, in each case, define the corresponding directory entry.

27.14 Directory-based cache coherence

Figure 27.10 shows the finite-state control mechanism associated with each directory entry in a directory-based cache coherence protocol. Supply the finite-state control that must be associated with the cache lines. *Hint:* The required diagram is quite similar to that in Figure 27.5.

27.15 Directory-based coherence protocols

Our discussion of directory-based cache coherence protocols in Section 27.5 was based on *flat directories,* so named because directory information for each block is found in a fixed location uniquely determined by its address. When a miss occurs, a single request is sent to the unique home node for directory lookup, whose result then guides the actual data access. Hierarchical directories, by contrast, are organized as logical trees that are embedded in the particular interconnection scheme being used by the system. Each block is associated with a particular logical tree and requests for that block are always forwarded by a node to its parent within that logical tree. Study such hierarchical directories [Cull99] and write a brief report that includes the following information.

a. Implementation cost in comparison to flat directories

b. Performance benefits, if any, relative to flat directories

c. Methods for defining and maintaining the logical trees

d. Scalability, reliability, and robustness aspects

27.16 Real symmetric multiprocessors

Select an actual symmetric multiprocessor and prepare a report on its design, devoting at least one page to describing each of the following aspects. Sequent, SGI, and Sun are some of the companies that market such systems.

a. Basic hardware components (processors, caches, memory)

b. Processor-to-memory interconnection

c. Cache coherence protocol

27.17 Real asymmetric multiprocessors

Select an actual asymmetric multiprocessor and prepare a report on its design, devoting at least one page to describing each of the following aspects. IBM, Sequent, and SGI are some of the companies that market such systems.

a. Node structure in terms of processors and cache memories

b. Interconnection network

c. Cache coherence protocol

REFERENCES AND FURTHER READINGS

[Adve96]   Adve, S. V., and K. Gharachorloo, "Shared Memory Consistency Models: A Tutorial," *IEEE Computer,* Vol. 29, No. 12, pp. 66–76, December 1996.

[Cull99]   Culler, D. E., and J. P. Singh, *Parallel Computer Architecture: A Hardware/Software Approach,* Morgan Kaufmann, 1999.

[Henn03]   Hennessy, J. L., and D. A. Patterson, *Computer Architecture: A Quantitative Approach,* Morgan Kaufmann, 3rd ed., 2003.

[Hord93]   Hord, R. M., *Parallel Supercomputing in MIMD Architectures,* CRC Press, 1993.

[Leno95]   Lenoski, D. E., and W.-D. Weber, *Scalable Shared-Memory Multiprocessing,* Morgan Kaufmann, 1995.

[Parh99]   Parhami, B., *Introduction to Parallel Processing: Algorithms and Architectures,* Plenum Press, 1999.

[Unge02]   Ungerer, T., B. Robic, and J. Silc, "Multithreaded Processors," *Computer J.,* Vol. 45, No. 3, pp. 320–348, 2002.

[WWW]   Web names of some of the manufacturers of shared-memory multiprocessors: fujitsu.com, hp.com, ibm.com, sgi.com, sun.com.

CHAPTER 28

DISTRIBUTED MULTICOMPUTING

"A distributed system is one in which the failure of a computer you didn't even know existed can render your own computer unusable."
—*Leslie Lamport, 1992*

"A person with one watch knows what time it is; a person with two watches is never sure."
—*Proverb*

Computer architects have long dreamed of a day when it will be possible to connect an arbitrary number of processors and requisite memory modules to build a machine with desired computational power and storage capacity, much as one connects toy blocks to build complex structures. As our storage and computational needs grew, we would simply tack on a few more blocks to bring the system's capabilities in line with our needs. While this dream is still unrealized, recent advances in processor, memory, and communication technologies have brought us quite close in some important ways. In this chapter, we review strategies for building multicomputers from loosely connected nodes that communicate by exchanging messages. This is an exciting and active area of research and development, and many alternative schemes are being tried.

■ 28.1 Communication by Message Passing

Loosely coupled distributed multicomputers, or *multicomputers* for short, are formed by interconnecting a collection of independent computers by means of an interconnection network that allows them to communicate via message passing. Figure 28.1 shows the structure of

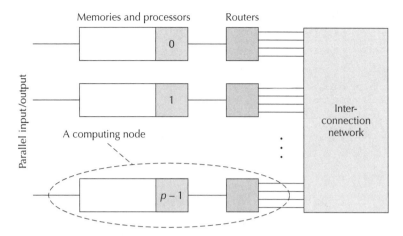

Figure 28.1 Structure of a distributed multicomputer.

such a multicomputer. At first glance, Figure 28.1 appears quite similar to the distributed shared-memory multiprocessor depicted in Figure 27.8. Closer inspection, however, reveals a number of subtle differences in the structure. These in turn lead to different programming models and application domains. The first key difference is that data transmission through the network of Figure 28.1 occurs not as a result of memory access requests that refer to remote memories but because of execution of message-passing commands in the program being executed. Hence, unlike the norm in Figure 27.8, here it is the processor, not the memory controller, that activates the node's router.

The interconnection network can be a simple shared transmission medium (such as bus or Ethernet), a collection of wires with no logic or decision-making capability (direct network), or a system of routers and/or switches that direct a message from a source node to its intended destination(s) in several steps (indirect network). The second key difference of Figure 28.1 from Figure 27.8 is that, in a multicomputer, there is usually more than one connection from each node to the interconnection network. The multiple connections are necessary in the case of direct interconnection networks and enable routing via a small number of switches for indirect networks (see Section 28.2). For now, we view the interconnection network as a mechanism that can accept injected messages from source nodes, guide them through properly chosen paths, and deliver them at the intended destination node(s).

With a shared-medium interconnection network, the routing phase is eliminated and communication degenerates into bus acquisition followed by data placement on the bus at the source node, and address detection followed by offloading of data from the bus at the destination, all according to the shared medium's protocol (see Chapter 23).

Direct, or point-to-point, communication is similarly simple because it entails physically connecting an output port of the sending node's router to an input port of the receiver. With this method, only a small subset of nodes are directly accessible from a source node (e.g., 4 in Figure 28.1). For a message to get to other nodes, it must be relayed or forwarded by one or more intermediate nodes. The protocol for performing this is hardwired or programmed into the router's control unit. In other words, upon receiving an incoming message, the router examines its destination node address. If this address matches the current node's address, then the message is ejected to the local node's input buffer (or input queue). Otherwise, one of the

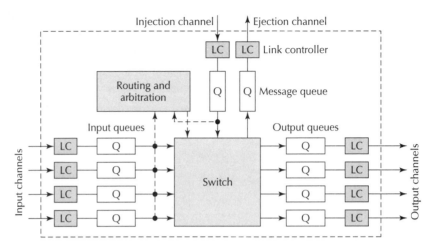

Figure 28.2 The structure of a generic router.

outgoing links is chosen for forwarding the message to a different node. The selection is a function of the routing algorithm used, the status of various channels in the network, and information embedded in the message itself. The latter might include tags specifying message priority, size, and latency already experienced in the network.

Figure 28.2 shows the structure of a generic router. The local node connected to the router sends messages into the network through the *injection channel* and removes incoming messages addressed to it through the *ejection channel*. Locally injected messages compete with messages that are passing through the router for use of the available output channels, with any message that cannot be forwarded kept in the associated queue until the next arbitration cycle. Routing decisions (choice of output channel) can be made in different ways, including the use of routing tables within the router and/or reliance on routing tags carried with messages. Routing strategies include *packet routing,* in which an entire message or a sizable part of it is stored in the router before it is forwarded to the next node, and *wormhole routing,* where a small portion of a message (a *flit*) is forwarded, with the expectation that the remaining flits will follow in rapid succession, much like a worm moving through an apple.

In addition to being communication endpoints, as in Figure 28.1, routers can be interconnected to form the interconnection network, using structures quite similar to the local- and wide-area networks in Figure 23.2. In practice, it is possible to combine these two functions of routers by using a subset of the router channels for injection and ejection and the rest for receiving and forwarding. This approach blurs the distinction between direct and indirect networks by allowing many intermediate organizations.

Switches can likewise be used to build interconnection networks. In practice, switches may contain queues and routing logic that make them quite similar to routers. However, very simple switches, which establish connections only between their inputs and outputs, may also be used in a *circuit-switched* interconnection network. In this case, a path is established through the network and data is then sent over that path from a source to a destination. Crossbar switches, with p^2 crosspoint switches between p horizontal and p vertical lines, allow connection between p inputs and p outputs in an arbitrary pattern. A simple 2×2 switch, which is capable of point-to-point connection or broadcasting, is depicted in Figure 28.3. A 3×3 switch, with limited permutation capability, was presented in Figure 26.9 in connection with I/O in an array processor.

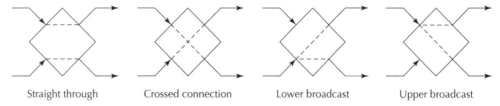

| Straight through | Crossed connection | Lower broadcast | Upper broadcast |

Figure 28.3 Example 2 × 2 switch with point-to-point and broadcast connection capabilities.

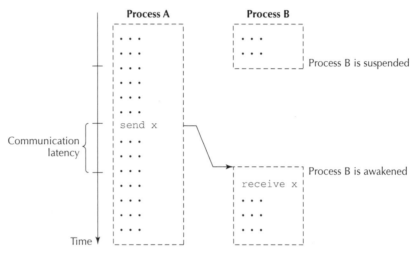

Figure 28.4 Use of send and receive message-passing primitives to synchronize two processes.

Regardless of how messages find their way from their sources to destinations, there are application-level primitives for message transmission and reception that can be used to build parallel programs. These primitives provide an abstract, hardware-independent method for specifying desired program behavior in a message-passing environment. As an example, consider processes A and B running on different nodes of a multicomputer, with A required to send a data value to B before B can complete its computation. So, process B is data-dependent on process A. In such a simple, one-way dependence, we can allow process A to complete execution, store its results in memory, and then start process B whose required data is now available. A better approach, which allows concurrency between processes as well as more complicated mutual dependencies, is to use message passing as depicted in Figure 28.4.

One way to allow send-receive and other types of interprocess communication is to incorporate the required primitives as a library of functions within standard high-level programming languages. The *Message-Passing Interface* (MPI) standard is one such library that is intended to provide application portability among parallel computers. MPI includes functions for point-to-point communication (as in send-receive) as well as various types of collective communication:

Broadcasting: one node sending a message to all nodes

Scattering: one node sending distinct messages to every node

Gathering: one node receiving a message from all nodes

Complete exchange: all nodes performing scattering and gathering

Because communication activities, like memory references, exhibit locality (in the sense that a process sending a message to another one is likely to do it again in the near future), MPI includes features for *persistent communication* that allow some of the overhead of sending and receiving messages to be shared across multiple transmissions. Additionally, there are facilities for barrier synchronization (as defined at the end of Section 27.3) and global reduction operations. For more detail on MPI, consult [Snir96].

28.2 Interconnection Networks

The structure and function of interconnection networks is best understood through the power grid analogy. The power grid consists of nodes (stations and substations) and links (transmission lines) connecting the nodes. Some nodes are associated with local power generation, which are analogs of message generation sources. Other nodes, not necessarily distinct from the previous set, represent local power consumption within communities. The latter are analogs of message destinations. Finally, some nodes are merely relays or voltage converters, without having any local power generation or consumption. These are analogs of switches or routers. In interconnection networks, message sources and destinations are generally the same set: the computing nodes. When every node in the system is a computing node, the network is known as a *direct network,* since all links lead directly from a computing node to another. When computing nodes are separated by at least one noncomputing node, we have an *indirect network.* As mentioned in Section 28.1, intermediate designs are possible that blur the distinction between direct and indirect networks. Figure 28.5 shows examples of direct and indirect networks with similar topologies.

A large variety of direct interconnection networks have been proposed or implemented. Direct interconnection networks can be represented by graphs that show the connectivity of their routers. Because each router is associated with a computing node, the nodes themselves need not be shown and circles representing routers can be referred to as nodes. Figure 28.6 depicts some such networks, all of size $p = 16$. The *2D torus* network is obtained from a 2D mesh by connecting the nodes at the two ends of a row or column to each other via a wraparound link. Each node is numbered by a pair of integers denoting the row and column numbers. This structure can be generalized to nonsquare variants and to more than two dimensions in a straightforward manner. The qD *hypercube* network is defined recursively as follows.

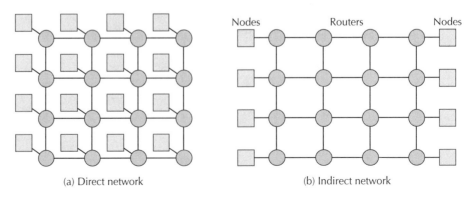

(a) Direct network (b) Indirect network

Figure 28.5 Examples of direct and indirect interconnection networks.

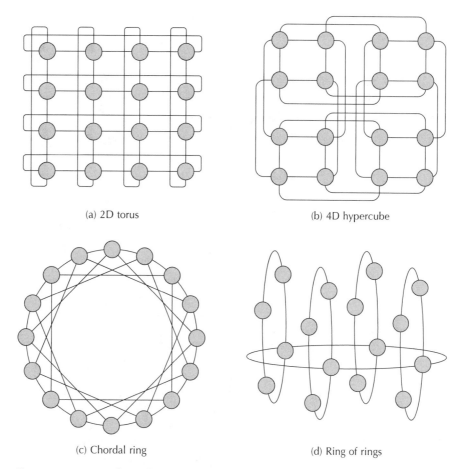

(a) 2D torus

(b) 4D hypercube

(c) Chordal ring

(d) Ring of rings

Figure 28.6 A sampling of common direct interconnection networks. Only routers are shown; a computing node is implicit for each router.

A 1D hypercube is simply a pair of nodes, labeled 0 and 1, that are linked to each other. A qD hypercube is obtained from two $(q - 1)$D hypercubes by connecting their corresponding nodes to each other using a total of 2^{q-1} new links. Furthermore, the labels in one of the $(q - 1)$D subcubes are preceded with 0 and those in the other by 1. A *chordal ring* is a ring to which some bypass connections, or chords, have been added. The nodes are numbered 0 through $p - 1$ in their natural order around the ring. In the example of Figure 28.6c, the chords connects each node i to node $i + 4$ mod 16. More than one chord per node can be provided, or the chords can have different bypass distances, leading to many variations. Our final example of a direct interconnection network, depicted in Figure 28.6d, is known as ring of rings. It is simply a collection of rings connected to each other by including one node from each ring within a second-level ring. Generalization to more than one second-level ring, or to more than two levels of rings, is straightforward.

Indirect interconnection networks can similarly be represented by graphs that specify the connectivity of the switches or routers. However, because not every switch or router is connected to a computing node, the latter must also be shown or their locations specified.

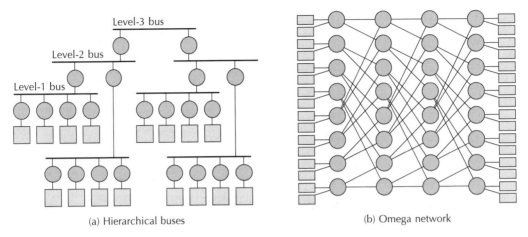

(a) Hierarchical buses   (b) Omega network

Figure 28.7 Two commonly used indirect interconnection networks.

Figure 28.7 depicts two examples of indirect interconnection networks. *Multilevel or hierar-chical bus structures* are quite popular because they allow the construction of large multi-computers while overcoming the limitations of buses in terms of scalability and communica-tion bandwidth. Local communications are performed through level-1 buses, whereas global data transfers are done via higher-level buses with greater latency. As long as local communi-cations dominate in terms of frequency, acceptable overall performance results. Note that in this case the single-input, single-output routers are often referred to as bus interfaces (next to computing nodes) or bus bridges (elsewhere). Note also that, strictly speaking, the diagram in Figure 28.7a is not a graph but a hypergraph because it contains edges that connect more than two nodes. Another example of an indirect network is the multistage *omega network,* depicted in Figure 28.7b. Here, the computing nodes shown on the left and right of the switch network are usually the same set of nodes (the figure wraps around). In each column of this 8-row omega network, the switch located on row i is connected to the switches on rows $2i$ mod 8 and $2i + 1$ mod 8 in the next column to the right.

Interconnection networks are assessed based on a number of properties that affect their im-plementation cost and performance. Cost is related to the node complexity as well as the den-sity and regularity of wiring between nodes. More wires generally mean higher cost. This is because at the VLSI chip level, denser wiring implies greater chip area; moreover, at the higher levels of the packaging hierarchy, limitations in pins and other off-module connectors may force the use of more modules (chips, boards, etc.) to accommodate all the required connec-tions. Short, regularly connected wires, as found in 2D mesh networks, allow greater perfor-mance owing to faster signal propagation and simpler drivers. Long, nonlocal wires impose the double penalty of greater complexity and lower performance.

Besides the indirect effect of wiring pattern and density on communication speed, inter-connection network performance is directly affected by two key network parameters. The first is network *diameter,* defined at the number of hops (router-to-router transfers) needed in the longest of the shortest paths between any pair of nodes. For example, the diameter of the torus network in Figure 28.6a is 4. A larger diameter generally means higher worst-case latency in message transmission between nodes. The second is network *bisection width,* defined as the minimum number of channels that must be cut if the p-node network is to be divided into two parts containing $\lfloor p/2 \rfloor$ and $\lceil p/2 \rceil$ nodes. For example, the bisection width of the torus network in Figure 28.6a is 8. The greater a network's bisection width, the higher the available communication bandwidth for transmitting messages from one side to the other side of the network. This is important when communication traffic between nodes is random. When communication is predominantly local, even the hierarchical bus network of Figure 28.7a with its small bisection width of 1 can offer high performance. Note that this narrow bisecting channel can become a bottleneck if a great deal of message traffic must flow through the level-3 bus.

28.3 Message Composition and Routing

Messages can be viewed at different levels of abstraction. At the application level, a message is a byte string of fixed or variable length. From the viewpoint of the application programs sending or receiving messages, specific meanings are associated with these byte strings (e.g., a sequence of integer or floating-point numbers). However, the mechanism that implements message passing need not be concerned with the meaning of a message, only with the correct delivery of the byte string to its intended destination(s). Long or variable-length messages may be divided into fixed-size *packets* for efficient transmission, as depicted in Figure 28.8. A packet, or the entire message in case packets are not used, is appended with a *header,* and possibly a *trailer,* containing control and error-checking information. The header, for example, may contain a packet sequence number and the identity of sending and receiving nodes, as well as certain control fields that identify the length and type of the message or the route to be taken by it through the network. These components of a message are quite similar to their counterparts used in computer networks, except that because of the limited number of possible sources and destinations, the amount of control information is typically less. For example, in a 256-processor parallel computer, the source and destination node identifiers are 8-bit numbers. A packet may in turn be divided into *flow control digits* (*flits,* for short) whose size is typically a few to several tens of bits.

The network's switching strategy determines how messages are routed. *Circuit switching,* which requires the establishment of a physical circuit between the source and destination before a message is transmitted, and for the entire duration of transmission, is seldom used in modern computers because it is so wasteful. With *packet switching,* packets are routed separately from the source to the destination, where they are reassembled into the original message using sequencing information within the packets. This is analogous to a large group of people traveling to their common destination in several buses, with each bus taking an independent

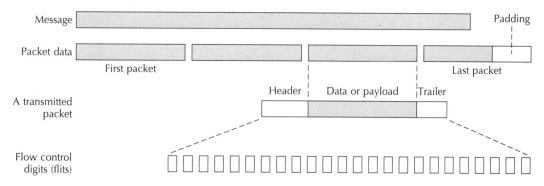

Figure 28.8 Messages and their parts for message passing.

route and arriving at a different time. If a packet must go through intermediate nodes or routers, the entire packet is stored in the intermediate node before being forwarded to the next point en route to its destination. For this reason, the name "*store-and-forward* switching" is also used. The choice of packet size is an important design decision. Smaller packets tend to use the network bandwidth more efficiently but imply greater overhead for packet headers and trailers.

Wormhole switching is another option that has been used widely because it combines the best features of circuit and store-and-forward switching. To continue with the bus analogy, a large group of people headed to a common destination can ride a tram with many cars instead of a number of independent buses. The lead car of the tram wends its way through the city streets, choosing an open route and avoiding busy streets to reduce travel time. The remaining cars simply follow the lead car. If the lead car comes to a stop, all others also stop. If other travelers cross paths with the tram, they may have to wait until the tram passes through. This type of blocking is a negative attribute that needs careful analysis and handling. However, in return, we get lower overhead, smaller buffer size (each intermediate node needs to store only one flit), and shorter transmission delays. The name "wormhole switching" reflects the similarity of data movement in the network with this method to the movement of a worm inside an apple. A message spread across multiple nodes as it travels through the network is referred to as a *worm* (not to be confused with Internet worms). Figure 28.9 shows two worms as they move through the network and how worms might block each other, causing deadlocks. Note that the tram analogy is imperfect in the sense that worms can actually cross each other if they enter and leave a node through different links but cannot travel along the same link in the same direction (as in single-lane streets).

With either packet switching or wormhole switching, a procedure is required to decide which of several existing paths from the source node to the destination node will be taken by the packet or worm. Even when the path is unique, the source and destination information must somehow be translated to the choice of an outgoing link at each step along the way. This is the function of the *routing algorithm*. Routing algorithms range from very simple to extremely complex. Simpler algorithms generally allow faster local decision making and can thus offer high node-level throughput; however, they often do not provide adaptivity to changing conditions (such as traffic levels in links) or ability to tolerate resource failures. So, the

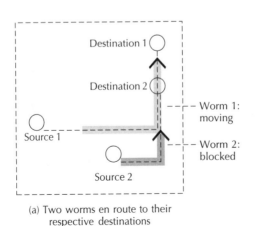

(a) Two worms en route to their respective destinations

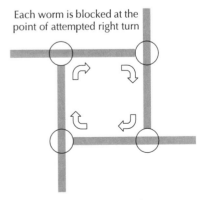

(b) Deadlock due to circular waiting of four blocked worms

Figure 28.9 Concepts of wormhole switching.

choice of a suitable routing algorithm entails the classical engineering trade-off: simplicity and low implementation cost versus greater adaptivity and better worst-case latency and throughput guarantees. Wormhole switching is often implemented with simple routing because complex routing can in part nullify its advantages. For example, it is not uncommon to simply drop any blocked worm, to avoid the overhead of buffering and control. Lack of acknowledgment from the destination node is then interpreted by the sender as a signal to resend the message. If this type of dropping and the subsequent retransmission is rare, the speed gained due to the simplification may be worth its cost in wasted bandwidth.

The best routing algorithm is both topology- and application-dependent. When the path taken by a message depends only on the source and destination nodes, the routing algorithm is *deterministic* or *oblivious*. *Nondeterministic* routing algorithms, in which one of several available routing options is chosen, come in two flavors. In *adaptive* routing algorithms, the choice may be based on criteria such as link availability or traffic load (to avoid failed or congested paths and thereby achieve lower latency). *Probabilistic* or *randomized* algorithms are used to engender fairer or more uniform traffic distribution across the available communication channels. With oblivious routing, the unique path to be followed by the message can be determined at the source node and information about it included in the message. Such a *source-based routing* scheme obviates the need for decision logic in the intermediate nodes, which leads to hardware simplification and routing speedup. At the other extreme, each node or intermediate switch may only be allowed to decide the next node or switch (connected to one of its outgoing channels) en route to the destination. An example of such a scheme is *row-first routing* on 2D mesh or torus networks (Figures 28.5a and 28.6a), whereby a message is first sent along a row to the appropriate column and is then routed up or down the column until it reaches the destination node. The decision may be based on a simple algorithm that is executed on the fly. Alternatively, the outgoing link option(s) to reach each destination node may be precomputed and stored in *routing tables* for quick access.

Once the type of message-passing mechanism and an associated routing algorithm has been chosen, the issue of message handling at the software (operating system) level must be dealt with. A user process initiates messages by calling relevant operating system routines, much as in performing input/output. For each message sent, the operating system assigns buffer space, does the required checks, and sets up the relevant message parameters before injecting it into the network. At the receiving end, the same process occurs in reverse. Message parts are received, assembled into a buffer, and checked. At this point the message has arrived but has not yet been delivered to the destination user process. The arrival of a message may then generate an interrupt that leads to the appropriate user process being notified or awakened. This involvement by the operating system software causes message initiation and reception to be relatively slow processes. It is not uncommon for the overhead to approach, or even exceed, 1 ms. For this reason, the actual message latency at the hardware level is much less critical than was the case for distributed-memory multiprocessors. Network throughput, however, remains important because it reflects the overall communication capacity.

28.4 Building and Using Multicomputers

As is the case with asymmetric (distributed memory) multiprocessors, it is possible to implement a multicomputer using a shared bus as the interconnection network. Multiple parallel buses may be used to ease the bandwidth bottleneck and also to ensure continued operation in the face of bus malfunctions. For example, one can envisage 16 processors connected to four different buses, so that there are four alternate communication paths from every processor to every other processor. As the number of processors grows, hierarchical buses, such as those in Figure 28.7a (again with more than one bus at each level, for performance and reliability reasons), may be used. Note that there is no shared address space here and no communication for enforcing data coherence. So, traffic over the buses consists entirely of explicit messages sent between processes. The volume of such messages is application-dependent but in general tends to be lower than the data communication required in a shared-memory multiprocessor.

Multicomputers are used in two distinct modes. First, the multiple computers may execute independent tasks. In this independent mode, the multicomputer acts as a collection of simple machines that share I/O, storage, and other resources. For example, thousands of PC-type computers may be employed at an Internet search engine site, with each query assigned to one of the available computers for processing. Such queries are completely independent and do not interact with each other except when they access shared data files and indices; the latter are typically replicated to ease conflicts. Second, the nodes of a multicomputer may be required to cooperate in solving a problem that has high computational requirements. In this cooperative mode, the problem of interest must be divided into a set of *communicating processes*. Mechanisms for communication were discussed earlier in this chapter. What remains for the proper implementation of a multicomputer is a facility, at the level of the operating system, to allow task assignment to the nodes, monitoring of the progress of each task, preventing deadlocks (circular waiting), and generally ensuring that the overall computation is completed swiftly and efficiently in terms or resource utilization.

Task scheduling is extremely difficult. An example of a set of communicating tasks, or a *task system,* is depicted in Figure 28.10a. Each block in the diagram represents an indivisible task, with its execution time *t*. Arrows indicate communication, with the assumption that communication occurs after the task at the tail of the arrow has been completed and before the task at the head of the arrow can begin execution (we ignore the communication latency for simplicity). This type of dependency is akin to relationships of courses at a university in terms of prerequisites. Figure 28.10b shows how the task system of Figure 28.10a might be scheduled on 1, 2, or 3 computing nodes to honor the prerequisite dependencies (e.g., both B and C completed before F starts) and to complete the task system in the minimum possible time. Note that it is impossible to execute the task system of Figure 28.10 in less than 7 time units, so

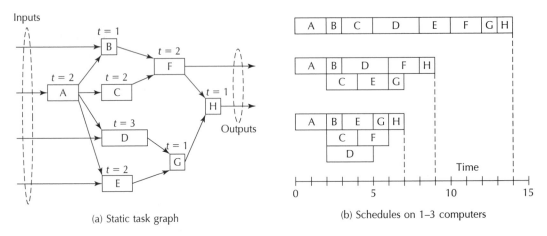

(a) Static task graph

(b) Schedules on 1–3 computers

Figure 28.10 A task system and schedules on 1, 2, and 3 computers.

using more than 3 nodes would not help reduce the total execution time. This is a manifestation of Amdahl's law, as discussed in the following example.

Example 28.1: Task scheduling and Amdahl's law   Consider the task system of Figure 28.10a. Tasks A and H cannot be executed in parallel with any other task, thus implying that the task system has an inherently sequential fraction of $f = 3/14$ (3 time units out of 14 total). Amdahl's law suggests that the achievable speedup is upper bounded by $14/3 = 4.67$. Show that in this case, owing to the assumption of indivisible tasks, the speedup is actually upper-bounded by 2. Then, formulate an alternative to Amdahl's law that actually yields this tighter bound.

Solution: Examining the scheduling charts in Figure 28.10b, we observe that tasks A and H "stick out" at the two ends, with parallelism being limited to the tasks in between. Amdahl's law suggests that with infinite speedup in this parallelizable part, bringing its execution time to 0, the total execution time will be reduced from 14 to 3, for a speedup of $14/3$. This would require that tasks be chopped into tiny pieces that can be executed in parallel. However, given that task D is indivisible, its execution requires 3 time units, no matter how many computers we use. In fact, because D and G must be executed in sequence (requiring 4 time units), no amount of parallelism can reduce the execution time of the tasks between A and H to less than 4 time units. Thus, the best possible running time is $3 + 4 = 7$, for a speedup of $14/7 = 2$, which is already achievable with three computers. More generally, each task graph has one or more *critical paths,* defined as the longest execution path for a chain of nodes between the inputs and the outputs. In the task graph of Figure 28.10a, the critical path consists of A, D, G, and H, with a total execution time of 7 units. Hence, an upper bound on speedup is the sum of running times for all tasks, divided by the length of the critical path ($14/7 = 2$ in our example).

Our discussion of task systems and scheduling was highly simplified. The following is a partial list of factors that make it even more difficult to find an optimal schedule for a task system on a multicomputer.

Task running times are not constants (they are data-dependent).

All tasks are not known a priori (tasks may be spawned or killed dynamically).

Communication time overhead must be factored in.

Message passing does not occur at task boundaries.

It may be that not every node in the multicomputer is capable of executing all tasks.

A two-tiered approach to this dynamic problem is often taken. An assignment of tasks to computing nodes is made at the outset, and the progress of each task and its communication behavior are monitored. If some nodes are much more overloaded than others, or if the distribution of tasks is such that excessive communication slows the system down, tasks may be reassigned as part of a *load balancing* process.

A common strategy for building multicomputers is via stacking self-contained modular computers in racks and interconnecting them via commodity network technology (see Figure 28.11a). The resulting systems are often referred to as *clusters*. With appropriate front-end hardware and software for work distribution and load balancing, such an organization can be scaled up to very large sizes for certain types of workload commonly encountered in

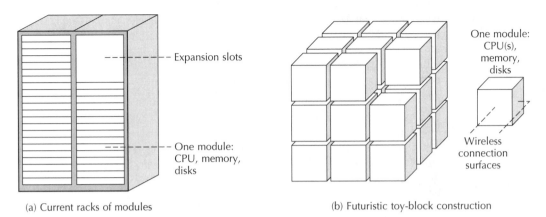

(a) Current racks of modules   (b) Futuristic toy-block construction

Figure 28.11 Growing clusters using modular nodes.

e-commerce and database applications. Compact hardware, along with advances in wireless connectivity, will allow a toy-block composition approach to building large multicomputers in the near future (Figure 28.11b).

28.5 Network-Based Distributed Computing

The multicomputers considered thus far in this chapter tend to have identical or similar computing nodes and to be connected by fairly regular interconnections of the types shown in Figures 28.6 and 28.7. Such uniformity and regularity simplifies replacement of a failed node (few spare components are needed), scheduling of tasks on computing nodes (since each node is capable of executing every task), and numerous other operations. Such a structure, however, impedes simple scalability and does not allow the use of a mix of general-purpose and special-purpose resources to solve large problems cooperatively. The area of network-based distributed computing has therefore received considerable attention in the past two decades.

Besides simple expansion via adding more computing nodes and network bandwidth, an important side benefit of this approach is the ability to pool idle computational, storage, and communication resources for use as a virtual supercomputer. To see this, recall that virtually all personal computers sit idle most of the time, disk units are on average less than half full, and data traffic over most network links consumes a small fraction of their peak bandwidths. In fact, for some limited application domains, these idle resources are already being utilized to form multiteraflops virtual supercomputers. SETI@home, an organization devoted to search for extraterrestrial intelligence, has successfully exploited this approach, providing the required programs and data to volunteer participants and using their idle computing capability in analyzing data from radio telescopes for signs of intelligent life outside the earth.

Network-based distributed computing is used in many forms. When the network is a local-area network with limited span and the computing nodes are workstations or personal computers, the resulting distributed systems are sometimes referred to as *networks* or *clusters of workstations* (NOW, COW). Usually, "cluster" is used for a collection of nodes that are intended to work together and do not have externally distinct identities, whereas nodes in a network of workstations can be used and externally addressed separately. When a wide-area network (at the extreme, the Internet) is used for communication among computing nodes, the resulting system is a *metacomputer*. The computational nodes in distributed computing are complete computers, each with its own input/output capability and operating system. These are often referred to as *end systems* or *platforms*. It is common to characterize a platform (albeit incompletely) by naming its processor architecture and operating system. The most commonly used platform today is Intel-x86/Windows. Sun-SPARC/SunOS, Intel-x86/Linux, and PowerPC/MacOS are other common examples of platforms or end systems.

To pool computational resources connected to a local- or wide-area network for solving large problems or many instances of smaller problems, a coordination strategy is required. The strategy differs according to the computational model being used. In a *client-server* architecture, service requests from client processes are sent to specialized servers that perform the required service or arrange for it to be performed elsewhere. In this architecture, there may be multiple servers for a particular type of service and some servers may have *proxies* that reduce the load on the original servers and on the network by caching recently accessed data objects (as is common for Web servers). Variations of the client-server architecture include *mobile code* and *mobile agents,* which transfer the computation to sites closer to the required data and other services in an attempt to reduce the communication load and delay. In a *peer-to-peer* architecture, on the other hand, processes running on different nodes interact as peers. This is the appropriate model for many computational nodes solving a large problem cooperatively. Such processes need system routines, commonly referred to as *middleware,* to help coordinate their actions. For example, a *group communication* facility may be used to notify all participating processes of changes in the computational environment.

Use of commodity computing nodes and communication facilities with the peer-to-peer interaction model is a natural choice from the cost, implementation ease, and maintenance viewpoints. Sterling has argued [Ster01] that for each MFLOPS of computing power, a custom-made supercomputer may cost 10 times as much to procure as a standard PC. And this is before usage and maintenance costs are taken into account. Figure 28.12 shows the structure of a network of workstations. The network interface contains a dedicated processor and a fairly large (SRAM) memory, to be able to feed messages into, or receive them from, the high-speed network. For example, multiple DMA channels may be employed in the network interface unit for message injection, message ejection, and message transfer to/from the host PC.

Besides the message handling software running in the network interface, a higher-level coordination system is also needed. This system is essentially a distributed operating system

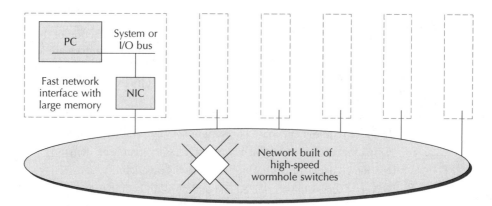

Figure 28.12 Network of workstations.

that most often is not built from scratch but rather formed by adding another layer of capabilities to a standard operating system. Among the capabilities that might be provided by the extensions are the following:

Maintenance of system status information for efficient use and recovery

Task partitioning and scheduling

Initial task assignment to nodes (and, perhaps, dynamic load balancing)

Distributed file system management

Compilation of system usage data for planning and accounting purposes

Enforcement of intersystem privacy and security policies

As the use of network-based distributed computing becomes more widespread, some or all of these functions will be incorporated into standard operating systems, making it easier to set up and use networks of workstations.

28.6 Grid Computing and Beyond

The current mode of using computing resources, that is, having a computer at each location at which there is a need for computing, is akin to installing an electric power generator in each home or office. Just as an electric power grid allows a decoupling between where power is generated and where it is used, a *computing grid* allows the distribution of computational capability to users without regard to where the processing power originates. Grid computing, in its ideal form, allows users to plug simple devices, consisting merely of suitable user interfaces, into wall plugs that make computing power readily available at a nominal cost. Just as electric power is sold at a certain price per kilowatt-hour, computing energy may be charged in GFLOPS-hours, say. Other computing-related resources, such as archival storage space, application software, and remote troubleshooting service, can be offered similarly to users, who will then get a monthly bill for all computing services used.

The idealized scenario in the preceding paragraph has not yet materialized, but grid computing researchers are working on various tools needed to integrate heterogeneous computing resources into a seamless system with many diverse users. The collection of hardware and software resources thus provided appears to each user as a *metacomputer* with vast computational capabilities. The multiple logical metacomputers seen by different users may overlap in their use of resources.

Grid computing is significantly different from time-shared computing, which was quite common in the 1960s and 1970s. Time-sharing was motivated primarily by the scarcity and high cost of computers and allowed many users to share in the acquisition and maintenance cost of computing resources. Grid computing, on the other hand, seeks to provide reliable and ubiquitous computing services to virtually anyone. Advantages of grid computing are similar, but not limited, to those for power grids:

Near continuous availability of computational and related resources

Resource requirements based on sum of averages, rather than sum of peaks

Paying for services based on actual usage rather than peak demand

Distributed data storage for higher reliability, availability, and security

Universal access to specialized and one-of-a-kind computing resources

A computing grid encompasses a hierarchy of systems, from end systems or platforms, through clusters of nodes, to intranets and internets. Each of these levels currently exists in highly evolved form as a result of many years of research and development and extensive use. However, successful integration of these levels into a computing grid requires greater emphasis on the interaction requirements for typical grid applications which are quite different from the way in which systems interact today.

The foregoing considerations affect all levels of the grid hierarchy, from the end systems to the internets.

1. At the end-system or platform level, more emphasis should be placed on communication capabilities and interfaces, to improve the communication performance and allow easier integration of nodes into clusters.

2. At the cluster level, improvements are needed in both the hardware capabilities and the operating system software to support cluster coordination and communication with the outside world. In particular, convergence between the end-system software and cluster-level software is a welcome trend.

3. Intranets encompass independent computing resources with limited, though practically significant, centralized (organizational) control. Current focus in intranets is flexibility and ease of expansion. Improving the communication performance by using lighter-weight interaction, much as in clusters, is needed.

4. Internets typically have no centralized control whatsoever. Other complicating factors include wide geographical distribution leading to nonnegligible signal propagation time, security enforcement, and interorganizational as well as international issues in data exchange.

Three complementary approaches are being pursued [Fost99]. The first approach relies on commodity components and uses the so-called three-tiered architecture in which the midtier application servers mediate between sophisticated back-end services (such as vast databases) and relatively simple front ends. The second approach is based on an object-oriented design strategy where computing resources are host objects, storage resources are data-vault objects, and so on, each with its specific properties and access methods. This is exemplified by the Legion system. The third approach, followed by the Globus system, takes the view that the current commodity technology is inadequate and that grid architecture should provide basic services without restricting the programming model. Accordingly, this approach favors the development of a toolkit of low-level services for security, communication, resource location, resource allocation, process management, data access, and the like.

If successfully deployed, a computing grid will allow distributed supercomputing (pooling the computing powers of many nodes to serve one application), high-throughput computing, on-demand computing, data-intensive computing (analyzing and assimilating vast amounts of data that are geographically distributed), and collaborative computing.

PROBLEMS

28.1 Message passing

In a 64-processor multicomputer interconnected as an 8×8 mesh, the following 2D finite difference computation is to be performed. The computation progresses in phases, where in each phase, every element $A_{i,j}$ of a 1024×1024 matrix must be updated according to the values of its four neighbors $A_{i,j-1}$, $A_{i,j+1}$, $A_{i-1,j}$, and $A_{i+1,j}$ at the end of the preceding phase, where these elements exist. Thus, updating each element requires access to four 8-byte values that may be available locally or from a neighboring node. Consider dividing the matrix into 32×32 submatrices that are stored in the nodes of the 8×8 mesh in the natural order.

a. Compute the total amount of data exchange among nodes if the computation proceeds for 1000 phases.
b. What is the total number of communication steps if a processor can send a message to all four of its neighbors in one step?
c. Repeat part b, but assume that messages to four neighbors must be sent one at a time.
d. Show that the suggested partitioning of the matrix is the best possible as far as the amount of data exchange among nodes is concerned.

28.2 Mailbox memory

A *mailbox memory* is a RAM that has a full/empty flag bit associated with each of its words. Consider a "put" instruction that specifies a register, a memory location, and a branch target address. The instruction is executed atomically and causes one of two actions: if the addressed memory location is empty, the content of the register is stored in it and its flag is changed to "full"; otherwise, no memory write takes place and control is transferred to the specified branch address.

a. Provide an appropriate description for the complementary "get" instruction.
b. Discuss how two processes can communicate via the mailbox memory using one-word or multiword messages.
c. Show how the effect of mailbox memory can be achieved with an ordinary shared memory using the test-and-set instruction discussed in Section 27.3.

28.3 Direct interconnection networks

a. Show that 4×4 torus and 16-node hypercube of Figure 28.6 are really the same network.
b. Show that the 16-node chordal ring in Figure 28.6 is similar to the 4×4 torus, except for a different connectivity for the end-around links.

28.4 Direct interconnection networks

a. Derive the diameter of each of the networks depicted in Figure 28.6.

b. Derive the bisection width of each of the networks depicted in Figure 28.6.
c. Generalize the results of part a to similar networks with 2^{2q} nodes, where q is an integer. Assume that the skip distance of the chordal ring is 2^q.
d. Repeat part c in connection with the results of part b.
e. How are the diameters and bisection widths of a 2^{2q}-node 2D mesh and torus different?

28.5 Direct interconnection networks

An interconnection network is robust if its nodes remain connected (can communicate with each other) despite node and/or link failures. One measure of robustness for a network is its *node connectivity,* defined as the minimum number of nodes whose removal from the graph representation of the network disconnects some nodes from the others. A second measure of robustness is *edge connectivity,* defined as the minimum number of edges whose removal leads to disconnection.

a. What are node connectivities of the networks depicted in Figure 28.6?
b. What are edge connectivities of the networks depicted in Figure 28.6?
c. Compare node and edge connectivities of a 2D square mesh with those of the corresponding torus.
d. Generalize the comparison of part c to qD mesh and torus networks.
e. Are the node and edge connectivities of a network related in any way?

28.6 Indirect interconnection networks

a. Show that in the omega network of Figure 28.7b, every node is connected to each other node via a unique path through 4 switches.
b. Show that the butterfly network of Figure 27.2a can be redrawn as the omega network of Figure 28.7b via renumbering of the nodes on its left and right sides.

28.7 Waksman permutation network

A $2^q \times 2^q$ Waksman permutation network with 2^q inputs and 2^q outputs is constructed recursively from 2×2 switches as follows. First, 2^{q-1} switches are used in column 0 to switch inputs 0 and 1, 2 and 3, and so on. The upper and lower outputs of the switches in column 0 are separately permuted by using two $2^{q-1} \times 2^{q-1}$ networks constructed in the same way. The switches of these networks will form columns 1 to $2q - 3$ in the eventual $(2q - 1)$-stage network. Finally, the corresponding outputs of the two half-size permutation networks, except for their lowermost ones, are switched using $2^{q-1} - 1$ switches in column $2q - 2$.

a. Show that in all, $2^q q - 2^q + 1$ switches are used in the construction of the network.
b. Draw a complete 4×4 Waksman permutation network and demonstrate that it can actually route all permutations.
c. Show that an arbitrary $n \times n$ permutation network, where n is not a power of 2, can be obtained by pruning the next larger power-of-2 Waksman permutation network.
d. Apply the result of part c to the construction of a 6×6 permutation network.

28.8 Routing in multicomputers

Ignoring contention by multiple messages for using the same link (i.e., assuming a very lightly loaded network), it takes $hk/b + (h - 1)d$ time units to send a message of size k along a path of h links (h hops) using store-and-forward routing, where b is the link bandwidth and d is the routing delay per hop. The corresponding formula for wormhole switching is $k/b + (h - 1)d$. Ignore the fact that the per-hop routing delay d may be different depending on interconnection network and the routing algorithm used. In your calculations, assume $b = 100$ MB/s and $d = 200$ ns.

a. Justify the routing delay equations given.
b. For each network in Figure 28.6, calculate the maximum routing delay separately for short and long messages of size 256 and 1024 B, respectively, assuming store-and-forward routing.
c. Repeat part b for wormhole switching.
d. Compute the per-byte latencies of short and long messages in parts b and c and comment on the results.

28.9 Wormhole switching

Consider wormhole switching with very short messages consisting of one header flit (holding the destination address) and a single information flit.

a. Does wormhole switching still have advantages over packet switching in this case?
b. Is deadlock possible with such short messages?
c. Suppose that the single information flit holds the identity of the sending node. Can a message that holds only the identities of source and destination nodes serve any useful purpose?
d. Going a step further, does it make sense for a message to hold only the destination address and no information flit?

28.10 Broadcasting in multicomputers

Consider a $2^q \times 2^q$ mesh-connected multicomputer and the following recursive broadcasting algorithm based on sending point-to-point messages. At the outset, the source node sends four messages to the four nodes located at the lower left corner of each of the four quadrants of the mesh. Each of these four nodes then uses the same method to broadcast the message within its own quadrant.

a. If message transmission to a neighbor takes unit time and a node can send a message to only one neighbor in each step, what is the total broadcasting time?
b. What is the total number of messages sent between nodes during broadcasting?
c. Discuss the behavior of the algorithm, including conflicts in routing, when wormhole switching is used instead of store-and-forward routing.

28.11 Task scheduling

Consider the task graph in Figure 28.10a and its associated schedules in Figure 28.10b. Without changing the existing elements of the task graph, add a single new task I to the graph such that the conditions given in parts a–e are satisfied, or show that satisfying the conditions is impossible. Compute the new speedup figures for each case that is feasible.

a. The lengths of the 2- and 3-processor schedules (9 and 7) are not increased.
b. Use of 4 processors yields a greater speedup than 3 processors.
c. Use of 3 processors does not yield a greater speedup than 2 processors.
d. A speedup of at least 2.5 is achieved with 3 processors.

e. Executing an infinite series of instances of the task graph on 3 processors keeps all processors completely and continuously busy.

28.12 Task scheduling

Consider a task graph with a single input task and one output task (like Figure 28.10a, but with task F not supplying an output), both of which are unit-time. Between these input and output tasks, there are k parallel tasks with identical running time t, where t is not necessarily an integer.

a. Show how this task graph is scheduled to run on p processors and find its total running time. Assume that k is divisible by p.
b. Determine the speedup resulting from the schedule of part a. What is the minimum value of k for which a speedup of s or more can be achieved?
c. Relate the speedup formula of part b to Amdahl's speedup formula. In particular, find the sequential fraction f of Amdahl's formula in terms of the parameters k and t.

28.13 Brent's scheduling theorem

Let T_p be the minimum time needed to execute a particular task graph with p processors. Brent's scheduling theorem asserts that $T_p < T_\infty + T_1/p$, where T_∞, the execution time with an unlimited number of processors, is the depth (or critical path length) of the graph.

a. Prove Brent's scheduling theorem for the special case of unit-time tasks. *Hint:* Consider the earliest time slot in which each task can be initiated and let there be n_i tasks whose earliest possible start time is i; these tasks can be executed in $\lceil n_i/p \rceil$ time units using p processors.
b. Show that for $p \geq T_1/T_\infty$, we have $1 \leq T_p/T_\infty < 2$.
c. Show that for $p \leq T_1/T_\infty$, we have $p/2 < T_1/T_p \leq p$.
d. Based on the results of parts b and c, argue that $p = T_1/T_\infty$ is, in a sense, a suitable number of processors to use for executing a task graph.

28.14 Workstation clusters and networks

A network of workstations consists of personal computers in a number of adjacent offices linked together by optical cables 10 m long, in which light travels at two-thirds the free-space speed of light.

a. If each workstation executes instructions at the rate of 2 GIPS, how many instructions will be executed during signal travel time between adjacent offices?
b. What type of limit does the observation in part a impose on the granularity of parallel computation on such a distributed computing system?

28.15 Shared variables versus message passing

Consider the problem of converting a parallel program written for a shared-memory multiprocessor so that it can be executed on a message-passing multicomputer, and vice versa. Which of the two conversions would you say is simpler and why?

28.16 IBM's Deep Gene Project

In late 1999, IBM announced a research and development project, code named "Deep Gene," designed to lead to the first PFLOPS-class supercomputer for tackling the protein-folding grand-challenge computational problem, which is of interest to the medical and pharmaceutical research communities. According to preliminary reports, the design is to use one million "simple" cacheless GFLOPS processors, integrated with memory, 32 per chip, 8 threads per processor, 64 chips on each 60×60 cm^2 board (2 TFLOPS), 8 boards in a 1.8 m high rack (16 TFLOPS), 64 racks, occupying approximately a 200 m^2 area. Study this project and write a five-page report focusing on its architectural features.

28.17 Grid computing

One issue that must be resolved before computing services can be sold (in the same way as electricity, natural gas, and telephone service) is reaching consensus on an appropriate unit for charging the service (similar to kilowatt-hours, cubic feet, and minutes of connectivity for common utilities). Study this problem and write a five-page report that outlines and compares the various proposals in this regard.

REFERENCES AND FURTHER READINGS

[Coul01]   Coulouris, G., J. Dollimore, and T. Kindberg, *Distributed Systems: Concepts and Design,* Addison-Wesley, 3rd ed., 2001.

[Cull99]   Culler, D. E., and J. P. Singh, *Parallel Computer Architecture: A Hardware/Software Approach,* Morgan Kaufmann, 1999.

[Duat97]   Duato, J., S. Yalmanchili, and L. Ni, *Interconnection Networks: An Engineering Approach,* IEEE Computer Society, 1997.

[Fost99]   Foster, I., and C. Kesselman, *The Grid: Blueprint for a New Computing Infrastructure,* Morgan Kaufmann, 1999.

[Harg01]   Hargrove, W. W., F. M. Hoffman, and T. Sterling, "The Do-It-Yourself Supercomputer," *Scientific American,* Vol. 285, No. 2, pp. 72–79, August 2001.

[Hord93]   Hord, R. M., *Parallel Supercomputing in MIMD Architectures,* CRC Press, 1993.

[Mile03]   Milenkovic, M., et al., "Toward Internet Distributed Computing," *IEEE Computer,* Vol. 36, No. 5, pp. 38–46, May 2003.

[Parh99]   Parhami, B., *Introduction to Parallel Processing: Algorithms and Architectures,* Plenum Press, 1999.

[Snir96]   Snir, M., et al., *MPI: The Complete Reference,* MIT Press, 1996.

[Ster01]   Sterling, T., "How to Build a Hypercomputer," *Scientific American,* Vol. 285, No. 1, pp. 38–45, July 2001.

[WWW]   Web names of some of the manufacturers of distributed multicomputers: fujitsu.com, hp.com, ibm.com, sgi.com, sun.com.

INDEX

End-of-chapter problems have not been indexed unless they introduce new concepts or point to references for further study. Names of people are included only if they pertain to key concepts (e.g., Amdahl's law) or designs (e.g., Brent-Kung carry network).